Legislation, Statutory Interpretation, and Election Law

Legislation, Statutory Interpretation, and Election Law

Richard L. Hasen

Chancellor's Professor of Law and Political Science
University of California
Irvine School of Law
rhasen@law.uci.edu

Wolters Kluwer
Law & Business

Published by Wolters Kluwer Law & Business in New York.

Wolters Kluwer Law & Business serves customers worldwide with CCH, Aspen Publishers, and Kluwer Law International products. (www.wolterskluwerlb.com)

To contact Customer Service, e-mail customer.service@wolterskluwer.com, call 1-800-234-1660, fax 1-800-901-9075, or mail correspondence to:

Wolters Kluwer Law & Business
Attn: Order Department
PO Box 990
Frederick, MD 21705

Printed in the United States of America.

2 3 4 5 6 7 8 9 0

ISBN 978-1-4548-4541-6

Library of Congress Cataloging-in-Publication Data

Hasen, Richard L. author.
Legislation, statutory interpretation, and election law: examples and explanations / Richard L. Hasen, Chancellor's Professor of Law and Political Science, University of California, Irvine School of Law.
      p. cm.
ISBN 978-1-4548-4541-6 (alk. paper)
1. Legislation — United States. 2. Law — United States — Interpretation and construction. 3. Election law — United States. I. Title.

KF4930.H37 2014
342.73'07 — dc23
                                                                2014018421

About Wolters Kluwer Law & Business

Wolters Kluwer Law & Business is a leading global provider of intelligent information and digital solutions for legal and business professionals in key specialty areas, and respected educational resources for professors and law students. Wolters Kluwer Law & Business connects legal and business professionals as well as those in the education market with timely, specialized authoritative content and information-enabled solutions to support success through productivity, accuracy and mobility.

Serving customers worldwide, Wolters Kluwer Law & Business products include those under the Aspen Publishers, CCH, Kluwer Law International, Loislaw, ftwilliam.com and MediRegs family of products.

CCH products have been a trusted resource since 1913, and are highly regarded resources for legal, securities, antitrust and trade regulation, government contracting, banking, pension, payroll, employment and labor, and healthcare reimbursement and compliance professionals.

Aspen Publishers products provide essential information to attorneys, business professionals and law students. Written by preeminent authorities, the product line offers analytical and practical information in a range of specialty practice areas from securities law and intellectual property to mergers and acquisitions and pension/benefits. Aspen's trusted legal education resources provide professors and students with high-quality, up-to-date and effective resources for successful instruction and study in all areas of the law.

Kluwer Law International products provide the global business community with reliable international legal information in English. Legal practitioners, corporate counsel and business executives around the world rely on Kluwer Law journals, looseleafs, books, and electronic products for comprehensive information in many areas of international legal practice.

Loislaw is a comprehensive online legal research product providing legal content to law firm practitioners of various specializations. Loislaw provides attorneys with the ability to quickly and efficiently find the necessary legal information they need, when and where they need it, by facilitating access to primary law as well as state-specific law, records, forms and treatises.

ftwilliam.com offers employee benefits professionals the highest quality plan documents (retirement, welfare and non-qualified) and government forms (5500/PBGC, 1099 and IRS) software at highly competitive prices.

MediRegs products provide integrated health care compliance content and software solutions for professionals in healthcare, higher education and life sciences, including professionals in accounting, law and consulting.

Wolters Kluwer Law & Business, a division of Wolters Kluwer, is headquartered in New York. Wolters Kluwer is a market-leading global information services company focused on professionals.

To
Dan Lowenstein
Scholar, Teacher, Mentor, Friend

Summary of Contents

Table of Contents   xi
How to Use This Book   xvii
Acknowledgments   xix

PART I. THE LEGISLATIVE PROCESS

Chapter 1   How a Bill Becomes a Law: From *Schoolhouse*
                Rock to Vetogates and Unorthodox Lawmaking   3
Chapter 2   Regulating Legislators   35
Chapter 3   Lobbying, Bribery, and External Legislative
                Influence   59
Chapter 4   Direct Democracy   91

PART II. STATUTORY INTERPRETATION

Chapter 5   Theories and Practice of Statutory Interpretation   113
Chapter 6   Canons of Statutory Interpretation   133
Chapter 7   Legislative History   163
Chapter 8   Agency Interpretation: Statutory Interpretation
                in the Administrative State   183

PART III. VOTING RIGHTS AND REPRESENTATION

Chapter 9   The Right to Vote, Representation,
                and Redistricting   209
Chapter 10 Political Parties, Partisan Gerrymandering,
                and Political Competition   241
Chapter 11 The Voting Rights Act, Race, and Redistricting   265
Chapter 12 Election Administration   297

PART IV. CAMPAIGN FINANCE

Chapter 13 Introduction to Campaign Finance: Spending
Limits from Buckley to Citizens United   319

Chapter 14 Campaign Contribution Limits from Buckley
to Citizens United and Beyond   347

Chapter 15 Campaign Finance Disclosure   367

Chapter 16 Public Financing   385

Correlation Table   401
Table of Books and Articles Cited   405
Table of Cases   413
Index   419

Table of Contents

How to Use This Book   *xvii*
Acknowledgments   *xix*

PART I. THE LEGISLATIVE PROCESS

**Chapter 1   How a Bill Becomes a Law: From
               Schoolhouse Rock to Vetogates
               and Unorthodox Lawmaking**   **3**

1.1   Introduction: How a Bill Becomes a Law   3
1.2   Formal Requirements for Federal Legislation   6
       1.2.1   Bicameralism and Presentment
                (including the Enrolled Bill Rule
                and Origination Clause)   6
       1.2.2   The Veto Power (including the Line-Item Veto)   14
1.3   Details of the Formal Federal Legislative Process   19
       1.3.1   Rules for Consideration of Bills in the House of
                Representatives   19
       1.3.2   Rules for Consideration of Bills in the Senate,
                Including Filibuster Rules   22
1.4   Theories of the Legislative Process   25
       1.4.1   Positive Theories   25
       1.4.2   Normative Theories   27
1.5   The Modern Federal Legislative Process: Majority
       Power, Political Polarization, and the Decline of
       Regular Order   29

Chapter 2   Regulating Legislators   **35**

2.1   Qualifications for Office, Term Limits, and Punishment   35
2.2   Legislative Deliberation   46
       2.2.1   Speech or Debate Clause Issues   46
       2.2.2   Single Subject Rules and Logrolling   52
       2.2.3   Due Process of Lawmaking   55

**Chapter 3   Lobbying, Bribery, and External
Legislative Influence   59**

    3.1 Lobbying   59
        3.1.1 How Lobbying Works   59
        3.1.2 Lobbying Disclosure Rules   64
        3.1.3 Other Lobbying Regulations   71
    3.2 Bribery and Related Offenses   76
        3.2.1 The Elements of Bribery   76
        3.2.2 More on Intent to Influence: Campaign
              Contributions as Bribes   79
        3.2.3 Related Offenses   86
    3.3 Ethics and Gift Rules   88

Chapter 4   Direct Democracy   91

    4.1 Direct Democracy as "Hybrid Democracy"   91
    4.2 The Single Subject Rule and Other Content
        Restrictions on Initiatives   97
    4.3 Petitioning Rules and Financing Ballot Qualification
        Drives   105

PART II. STATUTORY INTERPRETATION

**Chapter 5   Theories and Practice of Statutory
Interpretation   113**

    5.1 Introduction: The *Holy Trinity Church* Problem . . . or
        "The Food Stays in the Kitchen"   113
    5.2 Theories of Interpretation: Intentionalism, Purposivism,
        Textualism, and Dynamic Interpretation   119
    5.3 The Great Debate over Legislative History and
        the New Textualism   122
    5.4 *Stare Decisis* and Statutory Interpretation   129

Chapter 6   Canons of Statutory Interpretation   133

    6.1 Why Canons?   133
    6.2 Textual Canons   140
    6.3 Substantive Canons   153

Chapter 7   Legislative History   163

7.1   Committee Reports, Floor Statements, and Other Types of Legislative History   163

7.2   Legislative Silence or Failure as Legislative History   173

7.3   Other Statutes   179

Chapter 8   Agency Interpretation: Statutory Interpretation in the Administrative State   183

8.1   Why Is Agency Interpretation Different?   183

8.2   *Chevron* Deference   189

8.3   Other Types of Agency Deference   198

PART III. VOTING RIGHTS AND REPRESENTATION

Chapter 9   The Right to Vote, Representation, and Redistricting   209

9.1   Who (Decides Who) Votes?   209

     9.1.1   Introduction: Three Questions About Literacy Tests   209

     9.1.2   Voting as a Fundamental Right for Citizen, Adult, Non-felon Residents   213

9.2   Vote Dilution and the One Person, One Vote Rule   220

     9.2.1   *Baker, Reynolds,* and the Emergence of the One Person, One Vote Rule   220

     9.2.2   One Person, One Vote: Extensions and Complications   228

9.3   Special Purpose Election Districts   232

9.4   Introduction to Redistricting   237

Chapter 10   Political Parties, Partisan Gerrymandering, and Political Competition   241

10.1   Why Parties? Political Competition in Political Science and Law   241

10.2   Partisan Gerrymandering   247

10.3   Obligations and Associational Rights of Political Parties   254

10.4   Minor Parties and Independent Candidates   260

Chapter 11 The Voting Rights Act, Race, and Redistricting   **265**

11.1 Origins of the Voting Rights Act and the Workings of Section 5 Preclearance   265

11.2 *Shelby County* and the End of Section 5 Preclearance   273

11.3 Section 2 of the Voting Rights Act: Redistricting and Beyond   280

    11.3.1 Section 2 and Redistricting   280

    11.3.2 Section 2 Beyond Redistricting   288

11.4 Racial Gerrymandering Claims and the Future of the Voting Rights Act   292

Chapter 12 Election Administration   **297**

12.1 Introduction: Florida 2000 as the Modern Start of the Voting Wars   297

12.2 The Fight over Voter Identification Laws, and Broader Disputes over Election Administration Laws Since 2000   303

12.3 NVRA, HAVA, UOCAVA, and Limits on the Federal Power to Regulate Elections   312

PART IV. CAMPAIGN FINANCE

Chapter 13 Introduction to Campaign Finance: Spending Limits from *Buckley* to *Citizens United*   **319**

13.1 Introduction   319

13.2 The *Buckley v. Valeo* Framework   322

    13.2.1 Before *Buckley*: The History of U.S. Campaign Finance Law   322

    13.2.2 *Buckley*'s Major Holdings on Contributions and Expenditures   329

13.3 Spending Limits After *Buckley*   333

    13.3.1 Before *Citizens United*   333

    13.3.2 *Citizens United* and Beyond   337

Chapter 14 Campaign Contribution Limits from *Buckley* to *Citizens United* and Beyond   **347**

14.1 The Path from *Buckley* to Deference   347

14.2 New Skepticism About Contribution Limits   351

14.3 The Rise of Super PACs and Other Outside Groups   361

Chapter 15.   Campaign Finance Disclosure   367

15.1 The Path from *Buckley* to *McIntyre*   367
15.2 After *McIntyre*: Broad Disclosure Laws
and a Narrow Harassment Exemption   372
15.3 The Rise of 501(c) Organizations and the Failures
of Federal Disclosure Law   381

Chapter 16.   Public Financing   385

16.1 Why Public Financing?   385
16.2 Constitutional Issues with Public Financing Plans   388
16.2.1 Discrimination Against Minor Parties and
Voluntariness   388
16.2.2 Impermissibility of Matching Funds Tied
to Others' Campaign Spending   394

Correlation Table   401
Table of Books and Articles Cited   405
Table of Cases   413
Index   419

How to Use This Book

This book covers a number of related issues at the intersection of law and politics. Among them: Does the means by which Congress passes a statute affect how courts interpret the statute? When can a campaign contribution to a member of Congress be a bribe? Can senators be sued for defaming someone in a speech on the Senate floor? Should courts use different rules in interpreting legislation passed by a legislature, in contrast to legislation passed through an initiative or other vote of the people? What are the rules for drawing legislative districts? How does the law assure or limit minority representation in legislatures? How may or should money in politics be limited?

Every Legislation, Statutory Interpretation, and Election Law course covers at least some of these questions. Yet each course considers somewhat different material, and the order of discussing this material varies. For this reason, you can start this book from any one of its four parts: I. Legislation and Representation; II. Statutory Interpretation; III. Voting Rights and Representation; and IV. Campaign Finance.

The easiest way to figure out which parts of this book track your course's casebook is to use the Correlation Table, which tracks each of the major casebooks and shows which parts of each casebook match up to the material in this book. You can find the Correlation Table in the back of this book, just before the Table of Authorities, Table of Cases, and Index.

For the most part, this book follows standard Bluebook citation format. However, I usually avoid putting in pin cites and *ids* in an effort not to clutter the text, and I don't always note when I've deleted internal citations or footnotes. Before quoting any material in this book, be sure to check the original source.

I welcome your questions, corrections, and suggestions to improve this book. Please send me an e-mail to rhasen@law.uci.edu. I hope you enjoy this material as much as I do, but even if you don't, I hope this book makes the material clearer and easier for you to understand. Gluttons for further punishment can keep up with the field through my Election Law Blog (http://electionlawblog.org). Thanks for reading!

Acknowledgments

This book would not be possible without the support of the University of California Irvine School of Law, Dean Erwin Chemerinsky, and the top-notch librarians and staff of the law school. Special thanks to my excellent research assistant, Justin O'Neill, and my faculty assistants, Sara Galloway and Robert Medeiros. Emily Cross provided careful proofreading assistance.

Thanks also to current and past staff at Wolters Kluwer Law, including Lynn Churchill, Sue McClung, Carol McGeehan, Roberta O'Meara, and Peter Skagestad. They took a chance on this book and I am grateful that they did. Kenny Chumbley ably shepherded this book through production.

Thanks to Dan Lowenstein and the election law community on the election law listserv. It is fair to say that without Dan's guidance, wisdom, and exemplary role as a scholar, teacher, and mentor, I would not have been able to write this book. Over the years, I have learned so much from my exchanges with some of the smartest people around. They are very generous with their time.

Thanks to my election law and legislation students over the years. In helping teach them, they have taught me much.

Thanks to my wife, Lori, and children, Deborah, Shana, and Jared, who support me in all I do, both in work and in life.

In the course of writing this book, I relied upon some of my earlier law review articles on related topics. I reprint with permission, in somewhat altered form, material appearing originally in the following publications:

Buckley Is Dead, Long Live Buckley: The New Campaign Finance Incoherence of McConnell v. Federal Election Commission, 152 University of Pennsylvania Law Review 31 (2004). © 2004 University of Pennsylvania Law Review.

Chill Out: A Qualified Defense of Campaign Finance Disclosure Laws in the Internet Age, 27 Journal of Law and Politics 557 (2012). Used with permission.

Citizens United and the Illusion of Coherence, 109 Michigan Law Review 581 (2011). Used with permission.

Clipping Coupons for Democracy: An Egalitarian/Public Choice Defense of Campaign Finance Vouchers, 84 California Law Review 1 (1996). © 1996 by the California Law Review, Inc. Citation: 84 Calif. L. Rev. 1 (1996) by permission of the California Law Review, Inc.

Acknowledgments

Constitutional Avoidance and Anti-Avoidance at the Roberts Court, 2009 SUPREME COURT REVIEW 181 (2010). © 2010 by the University of Chicago. All rights reserved.

The Democracy Canon, 62 STANFORD LAW REVIEW 69 (2009). A version of this work previously appeared at 62 STANFORD LAW REVIEW 69 (2009). When possible and appropriate, please cite to that version. For more information, visit http://stanfordlawreview.org.

Entrenching the Duopoly: Why the Supreme Court Should Not Allow the States to Protect the Democrats and Republicans from Political Competition, 1997 SUPREME COURT REVIEW 331. © 1998 by the University of Chicago. All rights reserved.

Lobbying, Rent Seeking, and the Constitution, 64 STANFORD LAW REVIEW 191 (2012). A version of this work previously appeared at 64 STANFORD LAW REVIEW 191 (2009). When possible and appropriate, please cite to that version. For more information, visit http://stanfordlawreview.org.

The Newer Incoherence: Competition, Social Science, and Balancing in Campaign Finance Law After Randall v. Sorrell, 68 OHIO STATE LAW JOURNAL 849 (2007).

The Nine Lives of Buckley v. Valeo (in FIRST AMENDMENT STORIES, Richard Garnett and Andrew Koppelman, eds., 2011). Reprinted with the permission of West Academic.

Rethinking the Unconstitutionality of Contribution and Expenditure Limits in Ballot Measure Campaigns, SOUTHERN CALIFORNIA LAW REVIEW 885 (2005), reprinted with permission of the Southern California Law Review.

Shelby County and the Illusion of Minimalism, 22 WILLIAM AND MARY BILL OF RIGHTS JOURNAL 713 (2014). Used with permission.

The Surprisingly Complex Case for Disclosure of Contributions and Expenditures Funding Sham Issue Advocacy, 48 UCLA L. REV. 265 (2000). Used with permission.

Legislation, Statutory Interpretation, and Election Law

PART I

The Legislative Process

How a Bill Becomes a Law: From *Schoolhouse Rock* to Vetogates and Unorthodox Lawmaking

1.1. INTRODUCTION: HOW A BILL BECOMES A LAW

When I was a kid, one of my favorite parts of watching Saturday morning cartoons was ABC's *Schoolhouse Rock*, which taught points of grammar, math, and civics through catchy songs and cartoons. One the most famous of these cartoons, still watched today, is a *Schoolhouse Rock* cartoon, "I'm Just a Bill," which tells the story of how a bill becomes a law.[1]

In the cartoon, some "folks back home" come up with a good idea for legislation: "School bus must stop at railroad crossing."[2] They bring the idea to their member of Congress, who writes the idea up as proposed legislation (a bill). "Bill" tells the rest of the story to a young boy. Bill gets referred to a committee where "a few key Congressmen discuss and debate" whether he should become a law.[3]

Unlike most bills, which "die" in committee, Bill gets voted favorably out of committee, and the House of Representatives then also votes in favor (from all the "Yes" votes above the Capitol Dome in the cartoon, it looks to

---

1. Although these things change, as of the time I wrote this you can watch the video at: http://www.youtube.com/watch?v=tyeJ55o3El0.
2. The cartoon inexplicably did not pause to consider whether Congress would have the power to enact such health and safety legislation under its Commerce Clause powers.
3. The cartoon premiered in 1976, and the use of "Congressman" instead of "Member of Congress" shows the cartoon's age.

be a unanimous vote). Bill now has to start all over again, on the Senate side. ("Oh no!" the boy who hears Bill's story laments. "Oh yes!" responds Bill, recognizing this as progress.) Bill passes the Senate and then goes to the president, who has the choice to sign or veto. (Bill alludes to the possibility of Congress overriding the veto without giving any details.) The president signs Bill, and he becomes a law, to the cheers of everyone. "Oh yes!" exclaims Bill.

In recent years "I'm Just a Bill" has been mercilessly but lovingly mocked by *The Simpsons, Family Guy, The Daily Show,* and many others.[4] *Schoolhouse Rock* presents an idealized view of the legislative process and is familiar to many viewers, making it exceptionally suitable for mockery. The 1976 cartoon aimed as a rudimentary civics lesson for children obviously does not cover any of the most salient features of the current legislative process in Congress: political polarization, grandstanding at committee hearings, gridlock, filibusters, extensive influence of professional lobbyists, bills thousands of pages long that legislators don't read, and Congress's increasing need to resort to emergency temporary legislation to get through a series of governmental crises as Democrats and Republicans appear locked in a never-ending legislative deathmatch.

The *Daily Show* send-up[5] of "I'm Just a Bill" featured a beat-up Dodd-Frank Bill (played by comedian John Oliver) explaining to host Jon Stewart why many of the features of a financial reform bill passed by Congress in the wake of the 2008 financial crisis had not yet been put into place. After singing and pretending to be upbeat despite his black eye, the new Bill confesses: "This whole financial reform thing is a sham. The only way that Congress would pass me was if the details of my rules and regulations were left unspecified, giving K Street lobbyists all the time they would need to water me down post-passage. . . . If any actual tough rule managed to squeak through, Congresspeople cut the budget of the agency responsible for enforcing it. The whole thing is a giant punt. I'm no law— I'm no law, Jon. I'm just an undefined, impotent 2,300-page piece of legislative #@#! You see this [pointing to a button on his body reading "Law"]? You see this here, Jon? I stole this off the Voting Rights Act of 1965!"

The aim of this chapter is to explain the legislative process, from the formal requirements of bicameralism and presentment à la *Schoolhouse Rock* to the legislative roadblocks built into the process that may stall legislation to current thinking about how political polarization and other factors have led to profound changes in the federal legislative process.

---

4. I have collected links to video satires of "I'm Just a Bill" at http://electionlawblog.org/ ?s=%22I%27m+just+a+bill%22.

5. "Dodd-Frank Update," *The Daily Show,* July 28, 2011, http://www.thedailyshow.com/ watch/thu-july-28-2011/dodd-frank-update.

Nineteenth-century European politician Otto von Bismarck is famous for remarking that "[i]f you like laws and sausages, you should never watch either one being made," a statement that *New York Times* health care law reporter Robert Pear recently described as an insult to sausage makers.[6] But seeing how legislation gets made is an occupational requirement for today's lawyers. Understanding the formal and informal hurdles for creating legislation is important to everyone in order to have a clear understanding of the inner workings of our democracy. But they are especially important to lawyers for two reasons.

First, lawyers handling statutory interpretation issues (discussed in Part II of this book) must have a clear understanding of the legislative process in order to explain to courts the origins and meaning of particular statutory language. Statutory interpretation issues pervade modern legal practice for both litigators and transactional lawyers. Most lawyers have to deal with statutes every day in their practice, especially when they interact with administrative agencies, which must apply statutes and often issue regulations and decisions interpreting statutes. Second, understanding the legislative process can help lawyers identify those points in the legislative process when it will be most important to shepherd through, alter, or block legislation affecting their clients' interests.

Example 1

Aaron tells Betty she's a fool to take a course in legislation: "All I need to know about how a bill becomes a law I learned on *Schoolhouse Rock*," he says. Betty tells Aaron that he's the fool. Is Betty right?

Explanation

In my view, Betty is right. Modern legal practice requires lawyers to interact with statutes (and regulations based on statutes) all the time. Whether interpreting statutes, helping clients pass or block legislation, or determining the validity of legislation, lawyers today need to appreciate not only the formal means by which bills become law, but also current political practice. The *Schoolhouse Rock* approach to legislation presents the legislative process in an uplifting, ideal way that will catch naive lawyers off guard: The current actual legislative process deviates sharply from this reality. Good lawyers

---

6. Robert Pear, *If Only Laws Were Like Sausages*, N.Y. TIMES, Dec. 4, 2010, http://www.nytimes.com/2010/12/05/weekinreview/05pear.html.

need to understand reality to be able to interpret and apply statutes; guide or block legislative actions at the federal, state, or local level; and help clients navigate legislative, administrative, and judicial proceedings. We can still celebrate the federal legislative process, but we should not pretend that it is simple or straightforward.

1.2. FORMAL REQUIREMENTS FOR FEDERAL LEGISLATION

1.2.1. Bicameralism and Presentment (including the Enrolled Bill Rule and Origination Clause)

The U.S. Constitution provides the basic rules for how a bill becomes a federal law.[7] According to Article I, section 7,

> All bills for raising revenue shall originate in the House of Representatives; but the Senate may propose or concur with amendments as on other Bills.
>
> Every bill which shall have passed the House of Representatives and the Senate, shall, before it become a law, be presented to the President of the United States; if he approve he shall sign it, but if not he shall return it, with his objections to that House in which it shall have originated, who shall enter the objections at large on their journal, and proceed to reconsider it. If after such reconsideration two thirds of that House shall agree to pass the bill, it shall be sent, together with the objections, to the other House, by which it shall likewise be reconsidered, and if approved by two thirds of that House, it shall become a law. But in all such cases the votes of both Houses shall be determined by yeas and nays, and the names of the persons voting for and against the bill shall be entered on the journal of each House respectively. If any bill shall not be returned by the President within ten days (Sundays excepted) after it shall have been presented to him, the same shall be a law, in like manner as if he had signed it, unless the Congress by their adjournment prevent its return, in which case it shall not be a law.
>
> Every order, resolution, or vote to which the concurrence of the Senate and House of Representatives may be necessary (except on a question of adjournment) shall be presented to the President of the United States; and before the same shall take effect, shall be approved by him, or being

---

7. This section focuses, as indeed do Parts I and II of this book, mostly on federal legislation and action (a notable exception is Chapter 4, which focuses on state and local initiatives and ballot measures). This chapter focuses on federal legislative processes; state and local legislative processes will differ in some respects from federal legislative processes, and you cannot rely upon the description here to understand how a particular state or locality's processes will work.

disapproved by him, shall be repassed by two thirds of the Senate and House of Representatives, according to the rules and limitations prescribed in the case of a bill.

We will get to vetoes and the special rules for raising revenue later in this chapter. For now, we focus on the basic constitutional requirements for passing a law. As the Supreme Court has explained the rules, "(1) a bill containing its exact text [must be] approved by a majority of the Members of the House of Representatives; (2) the Senate [must] approve [] precisely the same text; and (3) that text [must be] signed into law by the President." *Clinton v. City of New York*.[8] The requirement that both chambers pass the exact same bill is known as the *bicameralism* requirement. The bill must pass both the 435-member House and the 100-member Senate, worded identically in both cases, and then be signed by the president (or subject to a veto override).

Bicameralism sounds pretty straightforward, as when one chamber passes a bill, the other picks up the bill and passes it without amendment, and the president signs it; but sometimes it is not. To begin with, legislation may start out with the same text when a bill is introduced in the House and Senate, but thanks to amendments in each chamber, bills that pass out of each house may differ in small or large ways. Bills can also start in each chamber with different language and different provisions. When that happens, the path to such a bill becoming law usually happens in one of two ways:

(1) Leaders in each chamber appoint members to a House–Senate conference committee to hash out differences. The members of the conference ("conferees") may produce compromise legislation and a conference report explaining the compromises. Each chamber then votes on the exact conference version of the bill, which becomes law if passed in both chambers and signed by the president (or subject to a veto override).

(2) One chamber gives up on its own version of the legislation and simply passes the exact bill passed by the other chamber. This can happen when there is a rush on the legislation or when there may be procedural or other impediments to a conference or delay of legislation. (As we will see later this chapter, this is part of the story of how Democrats were able to get the controversial 2010 health care law through the Congress.)

---

8. 524 U.S. 417, 448 (1998) (quoted in *Public Citizen v. United States District Court*, 486 F.3d 1342 (D.C. Cir. 2007)).

Example 2

The House of Representatives unanimously passes a bill declaring November 15 to be National Canned Food Awareness Day. Around the same time, the Senate passes a bill declaring November 16 to be National Canned Food Awareness Day. The president expresses strong support for the Senate bill. Is National Canned Food Awareness Day on November 15 or November 16?

Explanation

This is a trick question, but an exceptionally easy one to get us started. It is on neither day. There is no law related to National Canned Food Awareness Day, because the bill fails both the test of *bicameralism* (the identical bill was not passed in the House and Senate chambers) and *presentment* (the president did not sign any bill). If the supporters of this piece of legislation want it to become law, they will have to convince one of the chambers to acquiesce in the other chamber's version of the bill and have that signed by the president, or have a conference to iron out the differences (perhaps National Canned Food Awareness *Week* is on the way?) and present an identical bill to be passed again by each chamber and signed by the president.

The Enrolled Bill Rule. No one would seriously claim that Congress passed a law when both chambers passed bills that members thought were different. But occasionally, each chamber passes its own version of a bill that its members believe to be identical to that passed by the other chamber, the president signs such a bill, and it then turns out there is at least one discrepancy in the versions of the bill passed by the House and Senate. That discrepancy is possible because modern bills in the House and the Senate can be long and quite complex, with provisions changed all along the way. Mistakes happen, even (especially?) in Congress. A lawyer who discovers the discrepancy might argue that his or her client is not bound by a "law" passed with such a flaw, because such a "law" could not really be a law under the rules set forth in Article I of the Constitution.

The Supreme Court long ago foreclosed such an argument in *Marshall Field & Co. v. Clark*.[9] *Marshall Field* establishes what has come to be known as the *Enrolled Bill Rule*. Under this rule, courts will not consider extrinsic (or outside) evidence showing that the chambers of Congress passed bills that were not identical so long as Congress followed its own procedures and attested that identical bills were passed by having its presiding officers

---

9. 143 U.S. 649 (1892).

sign what Congress calls the "enrolled bill."[10] The Supreme Court would not consider a challenge by importers to the Tariff Act of 1890 even though "it [was] shown by the congressional records of proceedings, reports of committees of each house, reports of committees of conference, and other papers printed by authority of Congress" that the bill that was passed in each chamber differed from the enrolled bill.

The Supreme Court offered two reasons for the Enrolled Bill Rule. First, the rule eliminated the potential for great uncertainty in the law: "Better, far better, that a provision should occasionally find its way into the statute through mistake, or even fraud, than that every act . . . should, at any and all times, be liable to be put in issue and impeached. . . . Such a state of uncertainty in the statute laws of the land would lead to mischiefs absolutely intolerable." Second, the Court cited separation of powers concerns, reasoning that allowing in outside evidence to contradict the attestation on an enrolled bill would "subordinate" Congress to the judiciary.[11]

The Enrolled Bill Rule is a rule barring only challenges to the *validity* of a federal law. The rule does not prevent a party in court from pointing to information in the legislative history, even to conflicts in versions of the bill passed by each chamber of Congress, in an argument about the law's *meaning*.[12] In other words, the Enrolled Bill Rule is not a limitation on *statutory interpretation rules* available to litigants or courts.

Example 3

On February 8, 2006, President Bush signed a budget bill known as the Deficit Reduction Act of 2005. In ten titles, the DRA amends a variety of familiar statutes, including the Federal Deposit Insurance Act, the Communications Act of 1934, and the Social Security Act. The provisions of the DRA are sweeping: the Act, *inter alia*, effects extensive changes to Medicare and Medicaid

---

10. Congress established those procedures in a federal statute, 1 U.S.C. § 106:

> [1] Every bill . . . in each House of Congress shall, when such bill . . . passes either House, be printed, and such printed copy shall be called the engrossed bill. . . .
>
> [2] Said engrossed bill . . . shall be signed by the Clerk of the House or the Secretary of the Senate, and shall be sent to the other House, and in that form shall be dealt with by that House and its officers, and, if passed, returned signed by said Clerk or Secretary.
>
> [3] When such bill . . . shall have passed both Houses, it shall be printed and shall then be called the enrolled bill, . . . signed by the presiding officers of both Houses and sent to the President of the United States.

11. For a criticism of the Enrolled Bill Rule, *see* Ittai Bar-Siman-Tov, *Legislative Supremacy in the United States? Rethinking the "Enrolled Bill" Doctrine*, 97 Geo. L.J. 323 (2009) (arguing that the Enrolled Bill Rule is an impermissible delegation of judicial and legislative power to legislative leaders and "that it amounts, in effect, to a view of the legislative process as a sphere of unfettered legislative supremacy, immune from judicial review").

12. U.S. Nat. Bank of Oregon v. Indep. Ins. Agents of Am., Inc., 508 U.S. 439, 455 n.7 (1993).

laws, provides relief for victims of Hurricane Katrina, creates a program through which households may obtain coupons to defray the cost of digital-to-analog converter boxes for their televisions, and, significantly, for purposes of this lawsuit, amends the U.S. Code to increase the filing fee for civil actions in federal district courts from $250 to $350.

Approximately six weeks after the President signed the DRA, Public Citizen filed a complaint against the Clerk of the U.S. District Court for the District of Columbia . . . , arguing that as an organization that routinely files civil suits, it anticipated having to pay the $100 fee increase on a regular basis. Public Citizen asked the District Court to declare the Act unconstitutional and compel the Clerk to maintain the $250 filing fee. . . .

According to the complaint, in the Fall of 2005, the House and Senate passed different versions of a budget bill referred to as S. 1932. To iron out the differences, the legislation was sent to a conference committee. The committee produced a conference report which failed to pass the Senate. Shortly thereafter the Senate passed an amended version of S. 1932 wherein §5101 specified a 13-month duration of Medicare payments for certain durable medical equipment. However, when the Senate clerk transmitted the engrossed S. 1932 to the House, he mistakenly changed §5101 of the bill to reflect a 36-month duration of payments for durable medical equipment rather than the 13-month duration actually approved by the Senate. The House voted on this engrossed bill, including the erroneous duration figure. Because the legislation originated in the Senate, the House returned it to the Senate for enrollment. The Senate clerk, recognizing the transcription error in the engrossed bill, altered the text of the enrolled bill so that it included a 13-month rather than a 36-month duration. The version of the DRA signed by the presiding officers contains the 13-month figure. Thus, since the 13-month duration term in the enrolled bill passed the Senate but not the House, the President signed legislation that did not actually pass both houses of Congress in precisely the same form."

The record contains a copy of the DRA bearing the signatures of then Speaker of the House of Representatives Dennis Hastert and President pro tempore of the Senate Ted Stevens.

Can Public Citizens successfully change the DRA's increase in filing fees?

Explanation

The facts of this case come from *Public Citizen v. United States District Court.*[13] The United States Court of Appeals for the D.C. Circuit rejected Public Citizens' argument, relying squarely on *Marshall Field* and the Enrolled Bill Rule. The court wrote that Public Citizens was trying to do exactly what the importers were trying to do in the *Marshall Field* case: rely on outside materials to prove that the House and Senate did not pass identical versions of the same bill and

---

13. 486 F.3d 1342 (D.C. Cir. 2007).

that therefore the DCA never became law. Public Citizen tried to argue that the type of legislative material it relied upon was different than the type of legislative materials the importers relied upon in *Marshall Field*. Public Citizen's evidence that the House and the Senate passed slightly different versions of the DCA was quite strong. Nonetheless, the court was unconvinced that the difference in the type of legislative materials mattered, and it strongly endorsed the policy arguments behind the Enrolled Bill Rule. The rule appears to be safe from attack for the foreseeable future.

The Origination Clause.   Turn back a few pages to take a look at the first part of Article I, section 2 of the Constitution: "All bills for raising revenue shall originate in the House of Representatives; but the Senate may propose or concur with amendments as on other Bills." According to the Supreme Court, the Framers of the Constitution gave this power to raise revenue to the House, whose members were elected every two years, rather than to the Senate, whose members were chosen by state legislatures (until the later passage of the Seventeenth Amendment):

> [T]he Framers' purpose [in including the Origination Clause in the Constitution] was to protect individual rights. As James Madison said in defense of that Clause: "This power over the purse may, in fact, be regarded as the most complete and effectual weapon with which any constitution can arm the immediate representatives of the people, for obtaining a redress of every grievance, and for carrying into effect every just and salutary measure." The Federalist No. 58, p. 359 (C. Rossiter ed. 1961).

United States v. Munoz-Flores.[14]

The Origination Clause raises a few questions: What counts as a "bill[] for raising revenue?" And what happens if such a bill starts in the Senate rather than the House — is it a "law" and if so is it constitutional? As it turns out, the answer to the first question is easier than the answer to the second.

The Supreme Court's most important recent pronouncement on these questions occurred in the *Munoz-Flores* case. On the first question, the Court reaffirmed earlier precedent that "revenue bills are those that levy taxes in the strict sense of the word, and are not bills for other purposes which may incidentally create revenue. The Court has interpreted this general rule to mean that a statute that creates a particular governmental program and that raises revenue to support that program, as opposed to a statute that raises revenue to support Government generally, is not a 'Bil[l] for raising Revenue' within the meaning of the Origination Clause."

In *Munoz-Flores*, the Court rejected an Origination Clause challenge to the Victims of Crime Act of 1984, which required the person challenging the

---

14. 495 U.S. 385, 395 (1990).

law to pay a "special assessment" established under the act to a victim of a crime he or she perpetrated. The Court held that the act was not a revenue bill: "the special assessment provision was passed as part of a particular program to provide money for that program — the Crime Victims Fund. Although any excess was to go to the Treasury, there is no evidence that Congress contemplated the possibility of a substantial excess, nor did such an excess in fact materialize."

The Court never reached the second question under the Origination Clause: What would be the *consequences* of a holding that a bill raising revenue originated in the Senate rather than the House? ("We therefore need not consider whether the Origination Clause would require its invalidation if it *were* a revenue bill.") However, in a lengthy portion of the opinion on the justiciability of the Origination Clause claims, the Court suggested that such a law would be unconstitutional (with the remedy for a constitutional violation being unclear).

Justice Stevens in his concurrence argued that the House could always protect itself from Origination Clause violations by never passing bills raising revenue that began in the Senate; he saw no need for judicial intervention when the House did not object.

Justice Scalia, separately concurring, argued for application of the rule, or at least the principle, from the *Marshall Field* Enrolled Bill Rule case: The Victims of Crime Act came to the president as a bill from the House — "The enrolled bill which, when signed by the President, became the Victims of Crime Act of 1984, 98 Stat. 2170, bore the indication 'H.J. Res. 648.' The designation 'H.J. Res.' (a standard abbreviation for 'House Joint Resolution') attests that the legislation originated in the House." Justice Scalia would look no further in an Origination Clause challenge.[15]

---

15. In response to Justice Scalia's argument, the majority wrote a footnote whose meaning is unclear:

> Justice SCALIA . . . contends that Congress' resolution of the constitutional question in passing the bill bars this Court from independently considering that question. The only case he cites for his argument is *Marshall Field*. But *Field* does not support his argument. That case concerned "the nature of the evidence" the Court would consider in determining whether a bill had actually passed Congress. Appellants had argued that the constitutional Clause providing that "[e]ach House shall keep a Journal of its Proceedings" implied that whether a bill had passed must be determined by an examination of the journals. The Court rejected that interpretation of the Journal Clause, holding that the Constitution left it to Congress to determine how a bill is to be authenticated as having passed. In the absence of any constitutional requirement binding Congress, we stated that "[t]he respect due to coequal and independent departments" demands that the courts accept as passed all bills authenticated in the manner provided by Congress. Where, as here, a constitutional provision is implicated, *Field* does not apply.

The D.C. Circuit in the *Public Citizen* case wrote that the footnote, and especially the last two sentences of the footnote, are a "puzzle" and "defy easy comprehension." It offered a few possible explanations of the footnote, and it definitively rejected the idea that the Supreme Court in the footnote was silently overruling *Marshall Field* and the Enrolled Bill Rule.

Example 4

In 2009, Congress passed the Patient Protection and Affordable Care Act (the major health care law more commonly known now as "Obamacare"). The very long bill made a huge number of changes related to the provision of health care in the United States. A number of courts considered constitutional challenges to the law, including Congress's power to mandate that individuals purchase or obtain health insurance or pay a penalty. The cases reached the Supreme Court, with Chief Justice Roberts agreeing with the four other conservatives on the Court that this "individual mandate" exceeded Congress's power under the Commerce Clause. *Fed'n of Indep. Bus. v. Sebelius*.[16] But the chief justice held (contrary to the position of the four other conservatives on the Court) that the individual mandate was a constitutional exercise of Congress's taxing power.

In response, a conservative legal group filed a lawsuit contending that Obamacare violated the Origination Clause. The bill that became the health care bill started as H.R. 3590, providing a tax credit for certain homeowners. After the bill passed the House, the Senate amended it by gutting the entire measure and inserting what became the health care bill, including the individual mandate provision. The Senate passed its version of H.R. 3590, and then the House passed the Senate's amended version, which President Obama signed.

If you were a lawyer for the government defending the health care law from an attack under the Origination Clause, what arguments would you raise?

Explanation

The facts of this case come from *Sissel v. U.S. Dep't of Health & Human Services*,[17] currently on appeal. The district court rejected the challenge for three reasons:

(1) The bill is not one for raising revenue under the Supreme Court's standard in *Munoz-Flores*. Its primary purpose was to revamp health care law; its purpose is not to raise revenue for the government generally. Thus, it is not subject to Origination Clause limits.

(2) Even if the bill is one that raises revenue, it does not violate the Origination Clause. Under Justice Scalia's concurrence, the bill begins "H.R.," which Justice Scalia would accept as conclusive evidence that the bill began in the House. Even looking deeper at the history, it appears that H.R. 3590 did originate in the House, even if its provisions were gutted

---

16. 132 S.Ct. 2566, 2600 (2012).
17. 951 F. Supp. 2d 159 (D.D.C. 2013).

and replaced with another bill. To reach the conclusion that this bill originated in the Senate would require courts to delve deeply into the legislative process to figure out whether a bill *really can* fairly be said to have originated in the House. The court rejected such a "germaneness" requirement.

(3) Even if the bill is one that raises revenue and it does violate the Origination Clause, there is no judicial remedy. The House had the choice not to vote in favor of the amended H.R. 3590; but a majority did so and therefore there is no remedy (at least under Justice Stevens's understanding of the Origination Clause).

We shall see how these arguments fare on appeal.

1.2.2. The Veto Power (including the Line-Item Veto)

The veto procedures in the Constitution's Article I are pretty straightforward, with one key exception. Let's walk through the different permutations of what can happen after an enrolled bill is sent to the president, as well as the effect that each permutation has on whether an enrolled bill becomes law.

Scenario 1 — *President signs the bill.* When the president signs an enrolled bill, that bill becomes law.

Scenario 2 — *President vetoes the bill.* When the president vetoes an enrolled bill, that bill does not become law. However, if the same bill passes with a two-thirds vote in each chamber after it is returned to Congress, then the bill comes law.

Scenario 3 — *President neither signs nor vetoes the bill, while Congress remains in session.* When the president receives an enrolled bill and does nothing, and Congress remains in session for 10 days (not counting Sundays) after receipt, the bill becomes law without the president's signature.

Scenario 4 — *President nether signs nor vetoes the bill, and Congress is in "adjournment"* within 10 days of the president's receipt of the bill. The Constitution provides that in Scenario 4, the president's choice to do nothing acts as a veto of the law, a scenario sometimes known as a *pocket veto.* This is a stronger veto, because the bill is not returned to Congress (which is not in session) for a possible override. But there is a dispute about which kind of adjournments count for purposes of a pocket veto.

The Pocket Veto Controversy. This discussion is about as arcane as this book is going to get, so please bear with me. There are three possible times when Congress "adjourns." (1) A *sine die* adjournment when the two-year terms of the current members of the House end before the newly elected

House takes office; (2) an adjournment between the first and second sessions of the same Congress (an *intersession* adjournment); and (3) an adjournment within a single session of Congress, as when Congress takes a summer recess (an *intrasession* adjournment).

There seems to be no controversy that the president's pocket veto is effective when occurring at the end of a Congress (*sine die* adjournment). But there is considerable controversy over whether a pocket veto occurs during an intrasession or intersession adjournment. Unsurprisingly, modern presidents have taken the view that they can issue intrasession or intersession vetoes, and congressional leaders have disagreed.

The details, court cases, and machinations surrounding the pocket veto are spelled out beautifully in an article by Professor Robert J. Spitzer.[18] Without going into all the details, in the modern era, some courts have reached the conclusion that a president could not issue a pocket veto during any time aside from *sine die* adjournments. But the Supreme Court has ducked the issue. In the meantime, both Republican and Democratic presidents from Reagan to Obama have not only issued pocket vetoes during intrasession or intersession adjournments — they have also done so with a "protective return," which is a statement seeming to veto and return a bill to Congress for possible override in the event a court rules that the pocket veto during one of these adjournments is unconstitutional. As Spitzer explained:

> Obama's first veto was of a defense appropriations spending bill that duplicated another he had signed into law earlier that month. The vetoed bill was a stop-gap spending bill that became unnecessary when the regular annual Pentagon appropriations bill was passed in time. On December 30, 2009, during Congress's Christmas recess, the president announced that he was pocket vetoing H.J. Res 64. Yet in pocket vetoing the bill, he also did something that, under the terms of the pocket veto power described in the Constitution, is impossible: he returned the pocket vetoed bill to the clerk of the House of Representatives. Obama . . . explained his action in his veto message this way:
>
>> To leave no doubt that the bill is being vetoed as unnecessary legislation, in addition to withholding my signature, I am also returning H.J. Res. 64 to the Clerk of the House of Representatives, along with this Memorandum of Disapproval.

At some point it is possible that the question of the validity of the pocket veto might end up back in court with a definitive resolution.[19] Until then, we will just have to live with this uncertainty and go about our normal routines.

---

18. Rober J. Spitzer, *The Historical Presidency: Growing Executive Power: The Strange Case of the "Protective Return" Pocket Veto*, 42:3 Pres. Stud. Q. 637 (2012).
19. The Supreme Court is considering a case about whether the president may use intrasession and intersession recesses to make "recess appointments" to the judiciary and to other

Example 5

In rejecting H.J. Res. 64, why did President Obama not simply veto the measure and return it to Congress? Why did he prefer to assert that he had done a pocket veto, and then he only "protectively" vetoed and returned the measure to Congress? Why did both Democratic and Republican House leaders oppose his use of the protective return?

Explanation

This example is a bit different from the others in that it asks you to assess political strategy rather than apply legal principle. Simply put, presidents prefer pocket vetoes because when such vetoes occur, Congress cannot override by a two-thirds vote. Instead, Congress has to start over, passing legislation in each house and sending it to the president for signature once again. That makes it much less likely that legislation that the president does not like will not become law.

The battle here is not between the political parties; it is between the branches of government. The pocket veto with protective return is an attempt to expand presidential power over Congress. Both Democratic and Republican members of Congress want to protect Congress's powers from an encroaching president.

The Line-Item Veto. Before we leave the rules on vetoes, we consider one other issue. In many states, governors have the ability to exercise a line-item veto, at least on appropriations items. This power lets governors strike out portions of bills (such as an appropriation for a particular governmental program) while letting the rest of the bill stand.

Supporters of the line-item veto see it as a way to curb government waste and special interest legislation that legislators sometimes put in legislation as a cost for support of a larger bill. The theory is that the governor might be less beholden to special interests and thus be more willing to cut wasteful spending from the budget. Opponents believe that the line-item veto gives too much power to the executive and that it can make legislators unlikely to enter into beneficial compromises if the governor can unravel deals to pick and choose only the parts the governor likes.

Whatever the merits of the line-item veto concept, it is clear that the U.S. Constitution does not give the president the line-item veto power. Article I, section 7 gives the president the power to sign legislation, veto legislation, or let the legislation become law without the president's signature. Of course, we could amend the Constitution to give the president such power, but

---

positions. NLRB v. Canning, cert. granted, 133 S.Ct. 2861 (2013). Any decision on that issue could be relevant to this question as well.

amendments are very tough to pass, requiring a vote of two-thirds of Congress and three-quarters of state legislatures. U.S. Const. Art. V.

In the 1990s, supporters of the line-item veto came up with an ingenious way to give the president such power without amending the Constitution. Congress passed the Line-Item Veto Act of 1996, which gave the president new powers. The Supreme Court later described how the act worked:

> The Line Item Veto Act gives the President the power to "cancel in whole" three types of provisions that have been signed into law: "(1) any dollar amount of discretionary budget authority; (2) any item of new direct spending; or (3) any limited tax benefit." 2 U. S. C. §691(a). . . .
>
> The Act requires the President to adhere to precise procedures whenever he exercises his cancellation authority. In identifying items for cancellation he must consider the legislative history, the purposes, and other relevant information about the items. He must determine, with respect to each cancellation, that it will "(i) reduce the Federal budget deficit; (ii) not impair any essential Government functions; and (iii) not harm the national interest." Moreover, he must transmit a special message to Congress notifying it of each cancellation within five calendar days (excluding Sundays) after the enactment of the canceled provision. . . .
>
> A cancellation takes effect upon receipt by Congress of the special message from the President. If, however, a "disapproval bill" pertaining to a special message is enacted into law, the cancellations set forth in that message become "null and void." The Act sets forth a detailed expedited procedure for the consideration of a "disapproval bill". . . . A majority vote of both Houses is sufficient to enact a disapproval bill. The Act does not grant the President the authority to cancel a disapproval bill, but he does, of course, retain his constitutional authority to veto such a bill.
>
> The effect of a cancellation is plainly stated in [the Act]. With respect to both an item of new direct spending and a limited tax benefit, the cancellation prevents the item "from having legal force or effect."

Clinton v. New York.[20]

In Clinton, the Supreme Court in a 6-3 vote held that the provisions of the Line Item Veto Act were unconstitutional. The majority, in an opinion by Justice Stevens, viewed the act as an impermissible end run around Article I, section 7. Considering a challenge to two cancellations of spending by President Clinton, Justice Stevens explained: "In both legal and practical effect, the President has amended two Acts of Congress by repealing a portion of each. '[R]epeal of statutes, no less than enactment, must conform

---

20. 524 U.S. 417, 436-437 (1998).

with Art. I.' There is no provision in the Constitution that authorizes the President to enact, to amend, or to repeal statutes."[21]

Proponents of the Line Item Veto Act also argued that the act's cancellation power was no different from the power of the president to not spend funds appropriated by Congress when Congress has specifically authorized presidential discretion if certain conditions are met. The Court rejected this argument as well. Justice Kennedy, concurring, focused on the separation of powers problems inherent in giving the president this cancellation power. He added: "The Constitution is not bereft of controls over improvident spending. Federalism is one safeguard, for political accountability is easier to enforce within the States than nationwide. The other principal mechanism, of course, is control of the political branches by an informed and responsible electorate."

Justice Breyer, speaking for the three dissenters, did not agree that the president in canceling items of spending had unconstitutionally amended any laws: "When the President 'canceled' the two appropriation measures now before us, he did not *repeal* any law nor did he *amend* any law. He simply *followed* the law, leaving the statutes, as they are literally written, intact." Congress, rather than putting the right to cancel items of spending within each particular bill (something that the majority thought was acceptable) passed a separate statute giving the president that power: "Literally speaking, the President has not 'repealed' or 'amended' anything. He has simply *executed* a power conferred upon him by Congress, which power is contained in laws that were enacted in compliance with the exclusive method set forth in the Constitution." The dissenters then rejected the argument that the act violated separation of powers principles.

Example 6

Congress passes a bill providing, among other things, financial aid for a foreign country, but it includes a proviso that the president may withhold the aid if the president determines that the country has not taken "significant steps" toward establishing "free and fair elections." The president signs the bill. The president then issues a proclamation withholding the aid, finding that the country "has not taken significant steps toward establishing free and fair elections."

---

21. Further, the majority explained: "There are important differences between the President's 'return' of a bill pursuant to Article I, § 7, and the exercise of the President's cancellation authority pursuant to the Line Item Veto Act. The constitutional return takes place *before* the bill becomes law; the statutory cancellation occurs *after* the bill becomes law. The constitutional return is of the entire bill; the statutory cancellation is of only a part. Although the Constitution expressly authorizes the President to play a role in the process of enacting statutes, it is silent on the subject of unilateral Presidential action that either repeals or amends parts of duly enacted statutes."

Does the president's determination amount to an unconstitutional partial veto or amendment to the law providing for foreign aid in violation of Article I, section 7?

Explanation

No. Both the majority and dissenters in *Clinton v. New York* agree that it is constitutional for a law to include a provision that allows the president to withhold certain appropriated funds upon a finding that certain conditions specified in the law were not met. (In *Clinton*, the majority said such a provision may be particularly appropriate in foreign affairs, where the president has broader powers.) The ability of Congress to include such a provision constitutionally *within* a particular law but its inability for Congress to do so with a *separate law* granting the president this power was a particularly strong argument for the dissent as to why the Line Item Veto Act should have been held constitutional. The majority distinguished the two circumstances in its opinion.

1.3. DETAILS OF THE FORMAL FEDERAL LEGISLATIVE PROCESS

1.3.1. Rules for Consideration of Bills in the House of Representatives

The website of the House of Representatives makes passing a federal law seem straightforward, even easy, much as depicted by *Schoolhouse Rock*:[22]

> Laws begin as ideas. First, a representative sponsors a bill. The bill is then assigned to a committee for study. If released by the committee, the bill is put on a calendar to be voted on, debated or amended. If the bill passes by simple majority (218 of 435), the bill moves to the Senate. In the Senate, the bill is assigned to another committee and, if released, debated and voted on. Again, a simple majority (51 of 100) passes the bill. Finally, a conference

---

22. The quotations here and below come from this portion of the House of Representatives' website on the legislative process (as of May 2013): http://www.house.gov/content/learn/legislative_process/. The current version of the House's rules is posted at http://clerk.house.gov/legislative/house-rules.pdf. The House parliamentarian has also prepared a helpful pamphlet, *How Our Laws Are Made*, available at http://www.gpo.gov/fdsys/pkg/CDOC-110hdoc49/pdf/CDOC-110hdoc49.pdf, which provides additional details on House procedures. It should go without saying, but anyone who wants to understand the full intricacies of House procedure should check these sources and not rely simply on the brief summary in this chapter.

committee made of House and Senate members works out any differences between the House and Senate versions of the bill. The resulting bill returns to the House and Senate for final approval. The Government Printing Office prints the revised bill in a process called enrolling. The President has 10 days to sign or veto the enrolled bill.

Although nothing in this description is false, it is nevertheless incomplete (note, for example, the simplified discussion of the president's veto power), and parts are pretty misleading considering that few pieces of significant legislation follow this regular order. Furthermore, in both the House and the Senate there are additional substantial barriers to passing legislation. Some scholars refer to these barriers, such as a committee chair, as a "vetogate" that can stop legislation from proceeding further.[23] Legislation must pass through each of these gates in order to become law, unless legislative leaders can use exceptions to the rules to work around the barriers.

The technical rules of consideration of bills in the House and Senate are so complicated that we will only scratch their surface here. There are legislators, staffers, lobbyists, and others who become masters of the detailed rules of legislative process, as well as of the personalities and interests of committee chairs and other key members who often hold the fate of legislation in their hands. Having one of these masters working with you is key to getting legislation to the president for signature.

A member of the House will submit a bill as a sponsor by putting it in the "hopper" with the Clerk of the House. The member himself or herself is unlikely to have drafted any of the legislation. Instead the member's and Congress's staff likely played a significant role in its drafting. Outside groups, including lobbyists, sometimes propose language or even entire bills for the member to introduce.[24]

The House website explains that after a member places a bill in the hopper, "[t]he bill is assigned its legislative number by the Clerk and referred to the appropriate committee by the Speaker, with the assistance of the Parliamentarian." This *referral* process puts a lot of power in the

---

23. "Vetogates" are the "choke points in the [legislative] process," such as the ability to kill a bill in committee or subject it to a Senate filibuster. WILLIAM N. ESKRIDGE JR., PHILIP P. FRICKEY, & ELIZABETH GARRETT, CASES AND MATERIALS ON LEGISLATION: STATUTES AND THE CREATION OF PUBLIC POLICY 66 (4th ed. 2007). In the rest of this book, I cite this source simply as ESKRIDGE, FRICKEY, & GARRETT.

24. Eric Lipton & Ben Protess, *Banks' Lobbyists Help in Drafting Bills on Finance*, N.Y. TIMES, May 23, 2013, http://dealbook.nytimes.com/2013/05/23/banks-lobbyists-help-in-drafting-financial-bills. ("Bank lobbyists are not leaving it to lawmakers to draft legislation that softens financial regulations. Instead, the lobbyists are helping to write it themselves. One bill that sailed through the House Financial Services Committee this month — over the objections of the Treasury Department — was essentially Citigroup's, according to e-mails reviewed by *The New York Times*. The bill would exempt broad swathes of trades from new regulation.")

speaker's hands. The speaker often can put the bill into the hands of a committee chair who is likely to kill the legislation or who is likely to get it to the floor. House Rule XII provides detailed procedures about how the speaker must make decisions about which committees should have jurisdiction over a particular piece of legislation; the rule gives great flexibility to the speaker about referrals.

After legislation gets referred to a committee, that often is the end. Only a smaller percentage of bills get a committee hearing, and only a subset of those are voted favorably out of committee. When a committee chair refuses to move a bill out of committee, there are a few procedural steps that other members can take, but they are hard to achieve. For example, House Rule XV allows for a majority of members (218) to sign a "discharge petition" to get to the floor a bill that has been in committee for at least 30 days.

Before a bill gets voted out of committee, the committee will often hold hearings, take evidence, and hear from witnesses, among other things. The bill will be subject to a mark-up session wherein committee members will offer amendments to the bill under a set of additional rules and procedures. If the bill as marked up gets a majority vote, it then goes to the Rules Committee.

The Rules Committee is not only an important vetogate itself, where a bill can be stopped and go no further, but the Rules Committee also proposes to the House *the rule* for consideration of the bill on the House floor. The rule might specify how many amendments supporters and opponents may offer, as well as the timing for consideration of a bill. Sometimes members want to use amendments strategically to kill a bill (by including a provision that would make other members vote against it, sometimes known as a "poison pill"); the Rules Committee can facilitate or block such a process.

If a bill passes out of the Rules Committee, it can go to the floor of the House. Even then, the House leadership, including the speaker, has control of the calendar and thus of when items come up. When a bill first makes it to the floor, the House first votes on *the rule* for debating the measure itself. If the rule passes, then the bill itself gets debated under the procedures established by the rule, including the possibility of offering amendments. The House votes on the amendments, first without a tally of recorded votes, and then again there may be recorded votes on accepted amendments. Following additional procedural steps, the House votes on the bill as amended.

All of this is the "regular order" for consideration of legislation in the House. It turns out, however, that more and more legislation doesn't follow this regular order and goes through a different path set by the House leadership. We will take that up later in this chapter.

Imagine if *Schoolhouse Rock* had tried to explain all of these complications!

Example 7

Representative Donogood has just put a new bill in the hopper that would put your client out of business. Your client is very worried about the bill and thinks that it could get the support of a majority of the House. What can you say to put your client at ease, and what would you advise your client to do?

Explanation

To begin with, most bills don't get farther than being assigned to a committee. The road from bill to law is a very tough one, and many things can happen along the way to derail the progress of a bill. If your client is really worried that the bill could gain some traction, you might advise your client to hire lobbyists or others who could try to influence those members who act as vetogates and who can strategize about the best ways to defeat the bill. (Much more about lobbyists in Chapter 3.) It may be enough to get the relevant committee chair, or Rules Committee chair, or someone in the leadership willing to intercede on your client's behalf to kill the bill. If not, it might be possible to come up with an amendment strategy to include a "poison pill" or other provision in the legislation that would make it less likely to pass the House.

Finally, even if the bill passes the House, it will have to get through the Senate, where many House bills go to die. And of course then the president will get to decide whether to sign any bill that passes Congress.

1.3.2. Rules for Consideration of Bills in the Senate, Including Filibuster Rules

As with House rules, I present here just a bare bones sketch of Senate procedures.[25] The byzantine details of Senate procedures are beyond the ken of mere mortals. The 1992 version of *Riddick's Senate Procedure*, named after a former Senate parliamentarian, incorporates over 10,000 different Senate legislative precedents.[26]

There are many differences between the House and Senate: Senate terms are six years, not two, meaning that only one-third of the Senate comes up for a vote at each federal election; there are only 100 senators (two from

---

25. Links to the standing rules of the Senate, as well as other documents describing various Senate procedures, are available at http://www.senate.gov/pagelayout/legislative/d_three_sections_with_teasers/process.htm. A helpful legislative flow chart appears at http://www.senate.gov/reference/resources/pdf/legprocessflowchart.pdf. Some of the material below comes from this flowchart.
26. It is available in searchable form at http://www.riddick.gpo.gov.

each state, regardless of size), compared to 435 House members (divided among the states by relative population, with each state guaranteed at least one House member); only senators get to vote on executive nominations and treaties. There are also differences in how the Senate considers legislation, the issue on which this section focuses.

As slow as legislative consideration is in the House, things can go much slower in the Senate, a body designed by the Framers to allow extensive (and sometimes) unlimited deliberation — a tool that can be used to end consideration of a measure without a final vote. As a 2002 Congressional Research Service report explained,

> All senators have two traditional freedoms that, so far as is known, no other legislators worldwide possess. These two freedoms are unlimited debate and an unlimited opportunity to offer amendments, relevant or not, to legislation under consideration. The small size of the Senate permitted these traditional freedoms to emerge and flourish, subject to very few restrictions. Not until 1917 did the Senate adopt its first cloture rule (Rule XXII). Thus, from 1789 until 1917, there was no way for the Senate to terminate extended debates (called "filibusters" if employed for dilatory purposes) except by unanimous consent, compromise, or exhaustion.[27]

A senator introduces a new bill through the Senate parliamentarian, and the bill is considered having been read twice (to comply with Senate rules) unless a senator objects. (As we shall see, the Senate process provides ample opportunities for a senator to object, and usually the objection may be overcome only through a vote of "cloture" to end debate, a vote that typically takes a supermajority of 60 senators.)

If there is no objection, the majority leader will then refer the bill to an appropriate committee; the Senate, however, has fewer committees and thus the majority leader has fewer options to avoid particular committees. As in the House, committee chairs have great discretion about taking up a matter, scheduling a hearing, and marking up the bill with potential amendments. Members of the minority party on the committee can take a number of steps under the Senate rules to delay the consideration of a bill in committee.

If the bill is voted out of committee, it is put on the legislative calendar, and the majority leader may ask unanimous consent to bring the measure for consideration before the full Senate. If there is an objection, then there can be debate upon whether to bring the bill for consideration to the floor. The Senate's consideration of whether to bring the measure to the floor for debate and a vote is subject to various delaying tactics that again can be overcome only through a 60-Senator vote. The senators may fight over

---

27. The report is posted at http://www.senate.gov/legislative/common/briefing/Senate_legislative_process.htm.

whether and what amendments may be considered on the floor, and these fights, too, are subject to this type of delay. Complicated rules dictate the type and number of amendments that the Senate may consider.

For many of these delaying tactics, a single senator could decide to keep talking on the Senate floor to block consideration of a bill — a so-called "talking filibuster." Although such filibusters used to be common, today they are rare; most senators who seek to block consideration of legislation do so by requiring a cloture vote. Indeed, it has become exceedingly common for bills to be subject to one or more cloture votes.

Measures of one important class are not subject to 60-member cloture votes: certain budget-related members contained in "reconciliation" bills. What might count as a bill subject to this special reconciliation process has become of increasing importance in recent years as the Senate has become more strongly divided between Democrats and Republicans. Democrats passed some important clean-up provisions of their health care bill under the reconciliation process; during the 2012 elections, Republicans said they would use the process to repeal the health care bill if they captured the Senate and Presidency in the election. If they had tried to do so, there would have been a parliamentary dispute in the Senate over whether that was an acceptable use of the reconciliation process.[28]

Example 8

Representative Donogood's bill (*see* Example 7) has passed in the House, and your client is worried about the bill and thinks that it could get the support of a majority of the Senate. What can you say to put your client at ease, and what would you advise your client to do?

Explanation

As with the answer to Example 7, many roadblocks stand in the way of bills becoming law. The good news for your client is that Senate consideration of a bill is less likely than House consideration, even if a majority in both chambers favor the measure. This disparity exists because of the cloture rule, which requires a 60-vote supermajority to get almost any bill out of the Senate. Furthermore, a single senator has a number of additional procedural tools with which to slow down or block consideration of a bill that the senator opposes.

As with the House, the Senate, too, has its share of lobbyists and others who can work the Senate to seek to block the legislation. Indeed, many

---

28. Matthew Yglesias, *The Filibuster Won't Save Obamacare from Mitt Romney*, SLATE, Jun. 29, 2012, http://www.slate.com/blogs/moneybox/2012/06/29/the_filibuster_won_t_save_obamacare_from_president_romney_.html.

retired senators today have become lobbyists (or provide "strategic advice" without registering as lobbyists). A client with means has ample ways to try to influence just a few senators, which may be enough to scuttle most pieces of legislation.

Finally, even if the bill makes it through the House, the Senate, a conference committee, and additional votes on an identical version of the conference committee bill, your client can always seek to try to influence the president to veto the bill.

1.4. THEORIES OF THE LEGISLATIVE PROCESS

With all the complexity built into the federal legislative process, there is much disagreement over both *how* legislative procedures affect which laws make it through Congress (these are *positive* questions about how Congress works) and *whether* the complex federal legislative process is well designed (these are *normative* questions about whether Congress and our legislative process works well). One can take an entire course just on these theories. Here I just give a brief introduction to them.

1.4.1. Positive Theories

Pluralism and Public Choice Theory. Considering positive theories first, various *pluralist* theories conceive of Congress as an arena in which interest groups fight over their desired programs; interest group strength helps determine political outcomes, and such strength depends upon the resources that groups bring into battle, including the number of supporters and the money they have available, as well as the group members' intensity of preference for a particular governmental action. The more resources, the greater the ability of the group to gets its preferences enacted into law.[29] Classic pluralism described a relatively benign marketplace with competing groups with different ideological agendas and visions of the public good. Intensity of belief drives group strength; sweat and forthrightness determine political outcomes.

---

29. Some of the classic works in this field include Arthur F. Bentley, The Process of Government: A Study of Social Pressures (1908) and David B. Truman: The Governmental Process: Political Interests and Public Opinion (1951). The next few paragraphs draw from my article, Richard L. Hasen, *Clipping Coupons for Democracy: An Egalitarian/Public Choice Defense of Campaign Finance Vouchers*, 84 Cal. L. Rev. 1 (1996).

Economists then formalized the pluralist model and, in the process, eliminated its rosy, democracy-affirming undertones.[30] Public choice theory applies economic insights about rational behavior to a self-interested, group-oriented model of politics. These theorists understand political outcomes as depending on groups' political capital rather than on their ideological commitment. For example, small, cohesive groups have an advantage organizing for political activity over large, diffuse groups, because they more easily overcome collective action problems.[31] Thus small, cohesive groups control political capital disproportionate to the interests they represent in society. Similarly, wealthy and well-organized groups also enjoy disproportionate influence: Campaign contributions are an important source of political capital, and the wealthy have more wealth to contribute.

Proceduralism, Positive Political Theory, and Other Institutionalist Theories.
Proceduralists accept much of what pluralism and public choice theory have to say about how interest groups seek to influence the legislative process. But they see these theories as not sufficiently emphasizing the role that institutions and institutional structures play in affecting legislative outcomes. Bargaining, negotiation, and game theory may all be relevant.

In other words, a theory that seeks to predict whether new banking bills are likely to become law cannot focus solely on how strong the banking and consumer lobbies are. It must consider the vetogates: Is the measure supported by the chair of the Senate Finance Committee? Is passing such a bill a legislative priority of the House leadership? Do opponents of the banking bill have a means to amend the bill with a poison pill to make its passage unlikely? Is there a legislative leader in the House who can attach this bill to a larger, desirable piece of legislation to make its passage more likely?

Positive political theory uses formal models based in game theory and negotiation theory to predict whether laws are likely to pass and whose preferences among members of Congress, the president, the Supreme Court, and government agencies are likely to be reflected in how the law is passed, interpreted, and implemented.[32] Vetogates are key to predicting whether legislation passes through Congress; the preferences of the "median"

---

30. Richard A. Posner, *Theories of Economic Regulation*, 5 Bell J. Econ. & Mgmt. Sci. 335, 337 (1974) (contrasting economic analysis of politics with political scientists' pluralism).

31. Mancur Olson, The Logic of Collective Action: Public Goods and the Theory of Groups (2d ed. 1971).

32. For some of the important scholarship in this area, *see* William N. Eskridge Jr. & John Ferejohn, *The Article I, Section 7 Game*, 80 Geo. L.J. 523 (1992); Jonathan R. Macey, *Separated Powers and Positive Political Theory: The Tug of War over Administrative Agencies*, 80 Geo. L.J. 671 (1992); Mathew McCubbins, Roger Noll, & Barry Weingast, *Legislative Intent: The Use of Positive Political Theory in Statutory Interpretation*, 57 Law & Contemp. Probs. 3 (1994); Daniel B. Rodriguez & Barry R. Weingast, *The Positive Political Theory of Legislative History: New Perspectives on the 1964 Civil Rights Act and Its Interpretation*, 151 U. Pa. L Rev. 1417 (2003).

Supreme Court justice — the middle justice, who is likely to be the swing voter on a question of statutory interpretation — have an outsized role in determining how courts will interpret the meaning of the statute.

Of course, any positive theory of the legislative process today needs to account for one of its most important features: intense partisan competition between Democrats and Republicans. We return to this issue in the next section of this chapter.

1.4.2. Normative Theories

People who study how Congress works likely would not dispute some of the central findings of these positive theories: that Congress does not always act in line with a vague notion of the "public interest"; that interest groups matter, especially to parts of legislation that are not well known to the public; and that institutions and vetogates matter significantly in assessing a bill's chances of legislative success. (Chapter 3's discussion of lobbying returns to consider how much interest groups matter to the outcome of legislative struggles.) But although the positive descriptions of the legislative process are pretty similar, normative analyses vary widely. Here is a basic sampling of normative views of an idealized legislative process.

Facilitate Interest Group Bargaining. Some pluralists celebrate no-holds-barred interest group legislative battles as democracy working. Others see pathologies and inequities in a system wherein groups with the most resources are better able than others to induce the legislature to follow their preferences. They may seek to limit certain outside influences (such as through campaign finance regulation or lobbying regulation) to ensure a fairer fight among groups.

Stop Inefficient Rent-Seeking. Some public choice theorists criticize the legislative process not for any democracy deficit but for its potential effect on the nation's economy. They worry that interest groups will expend resources fighting over redistribution of resources rather than putting their resources to productive use. This rent-seeking behavior could damage the national economy. For this reason, some public choice theorists, such as Mancur Olson, have argued for shrinking the size of government, so that it has fewer rents to distribute. Others, such as Jonathan Macey, have argued that courts should interpret legislation in a public-regarding way so as to scuttle inefficient deals embodied in legislation.

Foster Legislative Deals. Some positive political theorists, such as Rodriguez and Weingast, believe that courts should interpret statutes so that the interpretations line up with the interests of the pivotal legislators (or vetogates) whose votes and actions were essential to the passage of legislation. They argue for doing so in order to encourage more legislation, as the pivotal legislators can count on courts to enforce legislatively brokered deals. Note how this view is quite the opposite of the view of some public choice theorists that courts should *not* seek to enforce special interest deals.

Encourage Deliberation. Finally, civic republicans and others take the position that more emphasis should be put on deliberation and consensus building among legislators than on the final product of legislation.[33] For example, the Framers designed the Senate to facilitate deliberation, through rules such as that giving senators a right to unlimited debate. Civic republicans evaluating the current Congress would ask whether the current cloture system encourages or discourages meaningful dialogue — and indeed whether dialogue is likely to be fruitful in legislative bodies highly divided by partisanship, the issue to which we now turn.

Example 9

Consider the following statement from Rodriguez and Weingast, *supra*:

> [C]ourts engaged in statutory interpretation of contentious statutes should use available legislative history to appreciate the bargaining process between ardent supporters and moderates that precipitated the statute. By honoring this bargain when construing such laws, courts may create incentives for future legislators to be accommodating and to behave in more moderate ways. At the same time, by decreasing incentives among moderates to become polarized, courts interpreting statutes can facilitate legislative agreement and therefore fulfill the objective of getting controversial social legislation enacted.

How would a pluralist, a public choice theorist, and a civic republican react to this statement? How do you react to this statement?

---

33. Cass R. Sunstein, *Interest Groups in American Public Law*, 38 STAN. L. REV. 29, 31 (1985) ("To the republicans, the role of politics was above all deliberative. . . . The ideal model for governance was the town meeting, a metaphor that played an explicit role in the republican understanding of politics."). As Frank Michelman explains his critique of pluralist and other interest group theories:

> Legislative intercourse is not public-spirited but self-interested. Legislators do not deliberate toward goals, they dicker towards terms. There is no right answer, there are only struck bargains. There is no public or general or social interest, there are only concatenations of particular interests or private preferences. There is no reason, only strategy; no persuasion, only temptation and threat. There are no good legislators, only shrewd ones; no statesmen, only messengers; no entrusted representatives, only tethered agents.

Frank I. Michelman, *Political Markets and Community Self-Determination: Competing Judicial Models of Local Government Legitimacy*, 53 IND. L.J. 145, 148 (1977-1978).

Explanation

A pluralist who favors uninhibited interest group competition for legislation likely would agree with Rodriguez and Weingast. They provide a way of enforcing legislative bargains — by having courts interpret statutes so as to further the views of those legislators whose votes were instrumental in passing the law. Such an approach could have the effect of encouraging more legislative dealmaking. Pluralists more concerned about inequality in interest group resources might question whether median legislators are more or less likely to follow the lead of interest groups with the most wealth or material resources.

A public choice theorist concerned with economic efficiency might not like the Rodriguez and Weingast approach. If the public choice theorist believes that many deals struck by Congress are economically inefficient, then having courts interpret inefficient laws in a way that will encourage more dealmaking is the wrong way to go. Instead, it might make more sense for courts to interpret laws in a publicly interested way to scuttle interest group deals. Some public choice theorists concerned about inefficiency of legislation call on courts to more broadly protect economic rights of individuals against the government as a means of limiting government redistributions.

It is less clear how a civic republican would react to the Rodriguez and Weingast proposal. One the one hand, civic republicans don't want "bargaining" or an interest group bazaar; they want careful deliberation. A rule that helps to encourage legislative "deals" will cause legislators to think less about the public interest and more about narrower interests or their own interests. On the other hand, to the extent that a judicial focus on pivotal legislators helps courts understand the scope of consensus or agreement reached by carefully deliberating legislators, then this approach could have merit. The approach could be a way for courts to ensure that they were faithful to the reasoned deliberation of Congress.

As for your own opinion, I leave that one for you to develop as you work your way through the material in this book.

1.5. THE MODERN FEDERAL LEGISLATIVE PROCESS: MAJORITY POWER, POLITICAL POLARIZATION, AND THE DECLINE OF REGULAR ORDER

A course in a law school (as opposed to a political science department) can only touch briefly on the profound changes to the federal legislative process that have taken place over the last few decades. Students interested in the details of these changes, as well as the complex reasons for these changes, should read the very important Barbara Sinclair, Unorthodox Lawmaking: New Legislative Processes in the U.S. Congress (4th ed. 2011). The latest edition includes a chapter giving the fascinating story of the enactment of the 2010 health care law. This section describe some of Sinclair's findings, but readers interested in the details should read Sinclair's book in its entirety.

In the House, under both Democratic and Republican leadership, power has shifted from committee chairs to the general House leadership. House leaders maintain more control through multiple committee referrals, post-committee adjustments to legislation, bypassing of committees altogether, and more closed rules for consideration of legislation. Republicans also instituted term limits for committee chairs. Furthermore, the House majority leadership has made it harder for the minority party to exercise much power, and the rules give the majority party great control over the legislative agenda and the passage of legislation.

Things have changed in the Senate as well, under both Democratic and Republican leadership. As in the House, multiple committee referrals, post-committee adjustments, and bypassing of committees have become more common in the Senate. The greatest change in the Senate is that virtually all major legislation now requires the support of 60 senators to become law. It is not just that the number of 60-member "cloture" votes to cut off debate has dramatically increased. Many measures never make it to the cloture vote stage, because Senate leaders know that the bill will not survive such a vote, and bringing a measure up for a vote allows the minority to waste time debating it.

Members in the Senate minority use cloture votes, "holds" on legislation or nomination, and other procedural devices to slow down Senate business — thereby making it harder for the majority to enact the laws it favors. Furthermore, minority (or sometimes majority) senators use these devices to extract changes to laws, or concessions or changes from the executive branch (which may be only tangentially related to the issue before the Senate) when the president favors legislation being held up by the Senate. One response by the majority has been for the majority leader to "fill the amendment tree" when a measure is brought up for consideration on the Senate floor to prevent the minority from seeking amendments to majority-supported legislation.

Things have gotten so bad in the Senate, not only in terms of delayed legislation but also delays in the confirmation of judges, cabinet members, and executive officials, that members of the Democratic majority recently eliminated the 60-vote requirement for executive and judicial nominations (except for Supreme Court nominations). Eliminating the filibuster and cloture requirements, even for just a subset of Senate votes, seemed to be a very tall order: The Senate considers itself a "continuing body" (because only one-third of all senators are elected at each two-year federal election), and it has standing rules. These rules can ordinarily be changed only through a two-thirds (or 67-senator) vote. So how did we get this rule change?

Democrats used the so-called "nuclear option" to make this change. The details are complicated, but the basic idea is this: The Senate majority leader eliminated the 60-vote requirement through a simple majority vote of 51 senators. The majority leader asked the president of the Senate, who is the U.S. vice president, to accept a "point of order" that the rule change could be made with a simple majority vote. (Some said this could only be done at the beginning of the new two-year session; others say the power is broader.) The president of the Senate so ruled, the majority voted for such a change, and the rules changed.[34] Quickly the Senate confirmed a number of judicial nominees that had been bottled up in the Senate.[35]

Democrats did not eliminate the other procedural tools that the minority has to slow down or change Senate business. Republicans have said that this the change will slow down the Senate more and that the Senate could become even further divided. Some have also said that when Republicans retake the Senate and there is a Republican president, Republicans will eliminate the filibuster entirely — making the Senate more like the House as a majoritarian institution.

Overlaying the battles in the House and Senate is a dramatic rise in the amount of political polarization. Although polarization was not a cause in the rise of unorthodox lawmaking, polarization has accelerated both its use and its importance. "Regular order," that is, following the textbook way that a bill becomes a law, is out the window, and unorthodox lawmaking is in fact now the new normal. Many pieces of legislation roll a number of different issues into mammoth (multi–thousand-page) bills, sometimes referred to as omnibus legislation. Rather than beginning (or even going through) a committee process, important legislation is more likely to be negotiated by party leaders in the House and Senate, along with the White House, sometimes at a "summit" and sometimes in small negotiations between just a few of these leaders.

The reasons for tremendous rise in political polarization are also beyond the scope of this book and a law school legislation course. But it is worth flagging a major factor (which will be explored in Part III of this book): the increased ideological homogeneity of our two major political parties. Before the civil rights movement and the Voting Rights Act's passage in the 1960s, there were far more conservative Democrats (especially from the South) and

---

34. Jeremy W. Peters, *In Landmark Vote, Senate Limits Use of Filibuster*, N.Y. TIMES, Nov. 21, 2013, http://www.nytimes.com/2013/11/22/us/politics/reid-sets-in-motion-steps-to-limit-use-of-filibuster.html.
35. Jeremy W. Peters, *With Filibuster Threat Gone, Senate Confirms Two Presidential Nominees*, N.Y. TIMES, Dec. 8, 2013, http://www.nytimes.com/2013/12/11/us/politics/senate-democrats-filibuster-threat-gone-approve-appeals-court-nominee.html.

liberal Republicans (especially from the Northeast). Since then, Democratic conservatives have left the party, retired, or been voted out of office; the same has happened with most liberal Republicans. The number of moderate Democrats and Republicans has fallen off a cliff. As the political parties have become more internally the same ideologically, they also have become stronger political parties in the legislature, becoming more likely to vote together as a party even on issues that do not have a strong ideological cast. The result is more party-line votes, more trampling of the majority by the minority, more attempts by the minority to obstruct or delay the majority's legislative program, greater acrimony, more unorthodox lawmaking wherein party leaders have to intervene to pass larger bills ("omnibus" pieces of legislation), and less legislation overall. In the last congressional term, as the amount of total legislation fell, a full 20% of the passed bills were those naming post offices.[36] That may be about the only kind of legislation these days that follows the *Schoolhouse Rock* model.

Professor Sinclair concludes: "Unorthodox lawmaking tends to empower House majorities and Senate minorities, but so far it has made it possible for our most representative branch to continue to perform it essential function of lawmaking in a time of popular division and ambiguity." SINCLAIR, at 276.

Example 10

The Affordable Care Act, the 2010 health care reform bill, was one of the most controversial pieces of legislation of the last few decades. Given the intense partisan divide on the wisdom of health care legislation, it only had a chance of passage because not only did Democrats control the presidency, Senate, and House, but they also, briefly, had a 60-vote majority in the Senate. There were many twists and turns in the legislation, in both the House and Senate, all of them covered by Professor Sinclair in her book.

One of the most dramatic moments in the passage of the legislation came near the end of the process. Both the House and Senate had passed their own versions of the health care law. The ordinary process at that point would have been a conference between House and Senate members, producing a piece of compromise legislation that then would have been subject to votes in both chambers. However, after the Senate passed its bill, Democratic Senator Edward Kennedy from Massachusetts, who was one of the longest-serving and strongest supporters of this type of health care legislation, died. At a special elections to fill the Senate vacancy, Massachusetts voters chose a Republican, Scott Brown, to replace Kennedy. Democrats at

---

36. Jeremy W. Peters, *One Area in Which Congress Excels: Naming Post Offices*, N.Y. TIMES, The Caucus Blog, May 28, 2013, 12:38 pm, http://thecaucus.blogs.nytimes.com/2013/05/28/one-area-in-which-congress-excels-naming-post-offices/.

that point lost their filibuster-proof majority, and the chances of the Senate passing a conference bill seemed unlikely in light of strong and united Republican opposition to the legislation.

To get around the problem, Democrats in the House passed the Senate's version of the law, thereby satisfying the bicameralism requirement. President Obama signed the legislation. Democratic House members then passed another bill that fixed some of the problems that House members had with the Senate bill. The bill then came to the Senate as a budget reconciliation bill, which cannot be filibustered. In order for the bill to count as a valid budget reconciliation bill, the bill had to satisfy the "Byrd rule," named after long-serving West Virginia Senator Robert Byrd. The Byrd rule is complicated, but it generally requires that reconciliation bills contain only items related to budgetary issues, and not extraneous items. Democrats in the House and Senate, along with members of the Obama administration, worked hard to make sure that the second House bill would satisfy the Senate parliamentarian that it complied with the Byrd rule. Republicans tried to convince the Senate parliamentarian that it did not. The parliamentarian generally sided with the Democrats, but during Senate deliberations the parliamentarian agreed that two minor provisions of the bill violated the Byrd rule, and the Senate took those provisions out and passed the bill in a 56-43 vote. Because of slight changes in bill, the House had to meet again to satisfy the bicameralism requirements. The House approved the revised bill in a 220-207 vote.

Does the story of the passage of the health care law indicate that the legislative process works or that it is broken? Did Democrats abuse the legislative process? Did Republicans? To what extent does your view on this question depend upon whether you are a Democrat or a Republican? Does the health care story suggest that changes to the federal legislative process are desirable?

Explanation

On this last question, the answer is up to you. Having read this chapter, you could craft a thoughtful response going in one of many directions on these questions. The question about your political affiliations is meant to get you to think about how much your thinking about these issues may depend, even subconsciously, on which party you think benefits from the current rules or from rule changes and your views about the merits of each party's ideological program.

Regulating Legislators

2.1. QUALIFICATIONS FOR OFFICE, TERM LIMITS, AND PUNISHMENT

Legislators are human beings like everyone else and subject to the same pressures and issues many face in life: mortgages, spouses, kids, and waiting for the cable guy. Things are even more complicated when legislators need to maintain one home near legislative offices and another in their home district or state and often are not paid enough to comfortably maintain two homes. Legislators also seem to have more than their share of sex scandals (think of Representative Anthony Weiner sending sexually inappropriate images via Twitter to a college woman he met online[1] or Senator Larry Craig being charged with soliciting sex in an airport bathroom[2]) and bribery scandals (think of Representative William J. Jefferson, caught keeping $90,000 of bribe money in his freezer — talk about cold cash![3]). Recently Representative Jesse Jackson Jr. pled guilty to using about $750,000 in campaign donations

---

1. Raymond Hernandez, *Weiner Resigns in Final Chaotic Scene*, N.Y. TIMES, Jun. 16, 2011, http://www.nytimes.com/2011/06/17/nyregion/anthony-d-weiner-tells-friends-he-will-resign.html.
2. Christina Capecchi, *Senator Seeks Withdrawal of Guilty Plea in Sex Sting*, N.Y. TIMES, Sep. 10, 2008, http://www.nytimes.com/2008/09/11/washington/11craig.html.
3. Jerry Markon, *Ex-Rep. Jefferson Gets 13 Years in Freezer Cash Case*, WASH. POST, Nov. 14, 2009, http://articles.washingtonpost.com/2009-11-14/news/36786791_1_william-j-jefferson-prison-term-robert-p-trout.

for personal use, including buying a $43,000 Rolex watch and $8,000 in Michael Jackson memorabilia.[4]

In the next chapter (on lobbying and bribery) and in Part IV (on campaign finance) we consider rules that regulate politicians and money. Those rules are important to ensure that legislators make decisions in the public interest, but they are not the only way society regulates legislators. The U.S. Constitution, federal statutes, and internal legislative ethics rules provide additional requirements, limitations, and immunities. In this chapter we consider some of these rules, beginning with qualifications for running for the U.S. House or Senate and the potential for legislative term limits. We then turn to two rules affecting legislative deliberation: the Speech or Debate Clause (applicable to Congress, with similar rules on the state level) and legislative single subject rules (not applicable to Congress, but applicable to many state legislatures). Finally we consider the concept of "due process of lawmaking." None of these laws and rules will turn legislators into angels, but in this chapter we consider whether the rules are more likely to make them better legislators — or at least capable of making better legislative decisions.

Qualifications. The United States Constitution provides in Article I, section 2 that "No person shall be a Representative who shall not have attained to the age of twenty five years, and been seven years a citizen of the United States, and who shall not, when elected, be an inhabitant of that state in which he shall be chosen." Similarly, Article 1, section 3 provides that "No person shall be a Senator who shall not have attained to the age of thirty years, and been nine years a citizen of the United States and who shall not, when elected, be an inhabitant of that state for which he shall be chosen."

Let's begin with the requirements that appear in the Qualification Clauses before turning to what is absent. Age and citizenship requirements seem aimed at ensuring that legislators are mature enough to hold office (apparently it takes more maturity to be a senator than a representative![5]) and have enough allegiance to the United States as judged by the number of years of citizenship (again, the Constitution seems to demand more proof of allegiance of senators than of representatives). In Part III of this book, we will consider age and citizenship requirements applied to *voters*. At this point, ask yourself whether such requirements are likely to produce better legislators. Would voters vote for a very young person for Congress?

---

4. Carol Cratty & Tom Cohen, *Jesse Jackson Jr., Wife Plead Guilty to Charges Involving Campaign Funds*, CNN, Feb. 21, 2013, http://www.cnn.com/2013/02/20/politics/jackson-plea-deal.

5. And still more maturity to be president. *See* U.S. Const. Art. II, §1 (requiring president to be at least 35 years of age, 14 years a resident of the United States, and a "natural born" citizen).

2. Regulating Legislators

For someone who is not a citizen or who has been a citizen for just a short time?

The "inhabitant" requirement[6] contained in the Qualifications Clauses actually is no impediment to running for the House or Senate, at least as the clauses have been interpreted by the courts. The Qualifications Clauses require only that the representative or senator be an "inhabitant" of the state "when elected." The Founders specifically debated and rejected a stronger residency requirement, and courts have rejected state laws that purport to impose residency requirements on candidates. Thus, a resident of Nevada can run to be U.S. Representative for a district in California—and need only become a California resident if elected.[7] Note that even in-state residents

---

6. Why "inhabitant" and not "resident"?

The records of the federal convention reveal the framers' deliberate selection of the word "inhabitant." The original term was "resident." 2 RECORDS OF THE FEDERAL CONVENTION 216 (M. Farrand Ed.) (1911), reprinted in 2 THE FOUNDERS' CONSTITUTION at 71 (Philip B. Kurland & Ralph Lerner Eds.) (1987)). Roger Sherman (Connecticut) moved to strike "resident" replacing it with "inhabitant." He reasoned that latter term was "less liable to misconstruction." James Madison (Virginia) seconded the motion agreeing that "both were vague, but the latter is least so in common acceptation, and would not exclude persons absent occasionally for a considerable time on public or private business." He wished to avoid the abuses in construing the term "resident" that had occurred in Virginia. Gouverneur Morris (Pennsylvania) and John Francis Mercer (Maryland) agreed reporting disputes that erupted in New York and Maryland over the term "resident." No issue regarding the possible distinction between the Framers' use of the word "inhabitant" and the California residence requirement is raised by this case, and for present purposes we view them as interchangeable.

Schaefer v. Townsend, 215 F.3d 1031 (9th Cir. 2000), cert. denied sub nom. *Jones v. Schaefer*, 532 U.S. 904 (2001).

7. *See id.* ("California's requirement that candidates to the House of Representatives reside within the state *before* election, violates the Constitution by handicapping the class of nonresident candidates who otherwise satisfy the Qualifications Clause.") As the Ninth Circuit explained:

The Framers discussed and explicitly rejected any requirement of in-state residency before the election. The Records of the Federal Convention show that the Framers intended to preclude any further requirement of residency prior to the date of election. Debate on the matter of an in-state residency requirement was touched off when John Rutledge (South Carolina) proposed a seven-year requirement. Others thought a one-year or three-year period sufficient. George Read (Delaware), opposing any period of previous residence, "reminded [Mr. Rutledge] that we were now forming a Natil. Govt. and such a regulation would correspond little with the idea that we were one people." James Wilson (Pennsylvania) concurred. Mercer suggested that "such a regulation would present a greater alienship among the States than existed under the old federal system. It would interweave local prejudices & State distinctions in the very Constitution which is meant to cure them." Hugh Williamson (North Carolina) opined that "[n]ew residents if elected will be most zealous to Conform to the will of their constituents, as their conduct will be watched with a more jealous eye." Still others argued against the in-state residency requirement for other reasons. Madison suggested that the newly formed States in the West could not have representation if the Constitution included a residency requirement. Wilson was concerned that legislators residing at the seat of Congress would be disqualified for not residing in their state. Those favoring the

may run for any congressional office they choose, and the Constitution does not demand that representatives live in the district that they represent even when elected.

The U.S. Constitution's approach to residency trusts the voters to decide whether a candidate has enough ties to a congressional district or state to deserve election. To be sure, a candidate without ties to a district or state will have a harder time getting elected because voters will rightly think that the candidate is less likely to understand the needs of the area and the views of the voters: Candidates from outside the area sometimes are referred to derogatorily as "carpetbaggers."[8] Yet there have been prominent outsiders who have been successful candidates, such as former First Lady Hillary Clinton, who successfully ran for U.S. Senator from New York despite having not lived in the state for a number of years.

For state and local elections, however, residency requirements are much more common[9] and are also often the subject of considerable controversy. Candidates sometimes try to get their opponents disqualified from appearing on the ballot on grounds they are not residents, and doing so sometimes requires election boards or courts to look at indicia of residency (such as how many nights someone slept at a particular location and where the candidate kept his or her clothes) to decide whether someone qualifies as a resident. Former White House chief of staff and member of Congress from

---

restriction expressed concern that a nonresident would not have adequate familiarity with the affairs of the state represented. The delegates voted down in turn three-year and one-year requirements of in-state residence. The Framers thus drafted the Constitution having explicitly rejected any residency requirement. It would appear then that California law imposes the very requirement that the Framers purposefully excluded from the Constitution.

8. *Taegan Goddard's Political Dictionary* explains the meaning of the term:

The name Southerners used to describe Northerners who moved to the South during the Reconstruction era, between 1865 and 1877.

The term comes from the Carpetbags — luggage literally made from the pieces of old carpet — that were used by travelers during this period. Anyone with a Carpetbag was easily identified as an outsider. However, it was very much a derogatory term that suggested both political opportunism and exploitation by the outsiders. In the South, Northern carpetbaggers usually allied themselves with the newly-freed slaves to win political office.

[Its] modern usage refers to any outsider who moves into an area to seek political power at the expense of the locals.

See http://politicaldictionary.com/words/carpetbagger/.

9. For example, the California Constitution provides in part:

A person is ineligible to be a member of the Legislature unless the person is an elector and has been a resident of the legislative district for one year, and a citizen of the United States and a resident of California for 3 years, immediately preceding the election . . .

CAL. CONST. Art. IV, §2(c).

Chicago Rahm Emanuel originally was kept off the ballot for Chicago's mayor on grounds that he was a resident of D.C. rather than Chicago while serving the president. The Illinois Supreme Court later reversed the ruling, allowing Emanuel to run,[10] which he did successfully. Other residency challenges have led to criminal charges and convictions against state or local legislators who may have lied about their residency.

Example 1

You have been assigned the task to draft provisions of your city's charter dealing with the qualifications to run for city council. Should you include a residency requirement? Why, or why not?

Explanation

There is no right or wrong answer to this question, and the U.S. Constitution takes a different position from many state constitution and local charters. You could reasonably take either position. Candidate residency requirements can help assure that a candidate has sufficient ties to the community and understanding of the preferences of local voters. Yet there are two significant arguments against imposing residency requirements. First, voters always have the final say over whether someone should be elected: A candidate with insufficient ties to a community is likely to be rejected by voters. The U.S. Constitution leaves residency issues in the hands of the voters. Second, a residency requirement will require election boards or courts to adjudicate whether someone qualifies as a resident of a particular area. Judging residency can require evaluation of a candidate's motives and intent, and this can lead to conscious or subconscious bias in favor of or against candidates on a political basis. As we shall see throughout this book, when there are not clear lines governing the rules for regulating the political process, the danger of partisan manipulation or bias is always present.

Legislative Term Limits. We began the discussion of qualifications with a look at what the United States Constitution *requires* for candidates to run for House or Senate; we now turn to what is *absent* from the list of qualifications. One notable omission is *felon status*. Nothing in the Qualifications Clause bars felons from running for office, even though many states would bar a felon candidate from voting in his or her own election (an issue we shall return to in Part III of this book).

---

10. Monica Davey, *Court Allows Emanuel on Ballot for Chicago Mayor*, N.Y. Times, Jan. 27, 2011, http://www.nytimes.com/2011/01/28/us/politics/28chicago.html.

Another omission is congressional term limits. The Constitution did not limit presidential terms until passage of the Twenty-second Amendment (ratified in 1951), limiting the president to two terms. For a long time supporters of congressional term limits have sought a constitutional amendment, but amendments are difficult to pass, and so far Congress has not approved such term limits.

As with residency requirements, which are absent on the congressional level but exist in many state constitutions and local charters, term limits are more common on the state and local level. They are controversial. Supporters of term limits argue that they prevent politicians from making a career out of serving, creating the conditions for more "citizen legislators" who, supporters claim, are more likely to represent the interests of the people. Opponents claim that term limits do not lead to more citizen legislators and that they prevent legislators from developing expertise in legislative areas, giving more power to outsiders such as lobbyists and staffers.[11]

Term limits are also odd in that nothing prevents voters from voting legislators out of office after two (or however many) terms on grounds that legislators have served too long. But close watchers of Congress are not surprised: While approval ratings for Congress as a whole are dismally low, voters tend to approve of their own member of Congress.[12] The term limits movement seems more concerned about representatives from *other* districts and the broader problem of entrenched legislative representation than about dissatisfaction with one's own member of Congress.

Although it is clear from the residency cases that states cannot impose term limits on U.S. Representatives or U.S. Senators through a state law or state constitutional provision, a few states tried to impose substantially the same thing through a ballot access restriction: laws purporting to bar federal candidates who had served more than a certain number of terms from appearing on the ballot. The argument was that these laws were not an additional (unconstitutional) qualification because they were not an absolute bar to serving. The candidates could still run and win as a "write-in" candidate whose name was not on the ballot.

In *U.S. Term Limits v. Thornton*,[13] the Supreme Court held that Arkansas's rules keeping congressional candidate who had served at least three terms in Congress off the ballot violated the Qualifications Clause. In a lengthy discussion of constitutional history, the Court first concluded, in a 5-4 vote, that states lacked the power to add additional qualifications for U.S. Representatives. The Court then held that the Arkansas ballot access rule violated the Clause:

---

11. *See* THAD KOUSSER, TERM LIMITS AND THE DISMANTLING OF STATE LEGISLATIVE PROFESSIONALISM (2005).
12. Richard L. Hasen, *Political Dysfunction and Constitutional Change*, 61 DRAKE L. REV. 989 (2013).
13. 514 U.S. 779 (1995).

Petitioners . . . contest the Arkansas Supreme Court's conclusion that the amendment has the same practical effect as an absolute bar. They argue that the possibility of a write-in campaign creates a real possibility for victory, especially for an entrenched incumbent. One may reasonably question the merits of that contention. Indeed, we are advised by the state court that there is nothing more than a faint glimmer of possibility that the excluded candidate will win. Our prior cases, too, have suggested that write-in candidates have only a slight chance of victory. But even if petitioners are correct that incumbents may occasionally win reelection as write-in candidates, there is no denying that the ballot restrictions will make it significantly more difficult for the barred candidate to win the election. In our view, an amendment with the avowed purpose and obvious effect of evading the requirements of the Qualifications Clauses by handicapping a class of candidates cannot stand. To argue otherwise is to suggest that the Framers spent significant time and energy in debating and crafting Clauses that could be easily evaded. More importantly, allowing States to evade the Qualifications Clauses by "dress[ing] eligibility to stand for Congress in ballot access clothing" trivializes the basic principles of our democracy that underlie those Clauses. Petitioners' argument treats the Qualifications Clauses not as the embodiment of a grand principle, but rather as empty formalism. "It is inconceivable that guaranties embedded in the Constitution of the United States may thus be manipulated out of existence."

In a lengthy dissent, also long on constitutional history, for four justices, Justice Thomas wrote: "Nothing in the Constitution deprives the people of each State of the power to prescribe eligibility requirements for the candidates who seek to represent them in Congress. The Constitution is simply silent on this question. And where the Constitution is silent, it raises no bar to action by the States or the people."

Example 2

In 1996, the voters of Missouri adopted a state constitutional amendment that, among other things, instructed U.S. Representatives and U.S. Senators from Missouri to support a U.S. constitutional amendment to impose term limits on Congress. One provision of the state constitutional amendment prescribes that the statement "DISREGARDED VOTERS' INSTRUCTION ON TERM LIMITS" be printed on all primary and general ballots adjacent to the name of a senator or representative who fails to take any one of eight legislative acts in support of the proposed amendment. Another provision requires that the statement "DECLINED TO PLEDGE TO SUPPORT TERM LIMITS" be printed on all primary and general election ballots next to the name of every nonincumbent congressional candidate who refuses to take a "Term Limit" pledge that commits the candidate, if elected, to support a constitutional amendment.

Does the Missouri state constitutional amendment violate the Qualifications Clause?

Explanation

The facts of this Example come from *Cook v. Gralike*.[14] In *Gralike*, the Supreme Court first held that states cannot give binding (as opposed to advisory) instructions to U.S. representatives or senators. It then held under *U.S. Term Limits* that the ballot designation violated the Qualifications Clause:

> [The requirement] is plainly designed to favor candidates who are willing to support the particular form of a term limits amendment set forth in its text and to disfavor those who either oppose term limits entirely or would prefer a different proposal. [T]he state provision does not just "instruct" each member of Missouri's congressional delegation to promote in certain ways the passage of the specified term limits amendment. It also attaches a concrete consequence to noncompliance — the printing of the statement "DISREGARDED VOTERS' INSTRUCTIONS ON TERM LIMITS" by the candidate's name on all primary and general election ballots. Likewise, a nonincumbent candidate who does not pledge to follow the instruction receives the ballot designation "DECLINED TO PLEDGE TO SUPPORT TERM LIMITS."
>
> In describing the two labels, the courts below have employed terms such as "pejorative," "negative," "derogatory," "intentionally intimidating," "particularly harmful," "politically damaging," "a serious sanction," "a penalty," and "official denunciation." The general counsel to petitioner's office, no less, has denominated the labels as "the Scarlet Letter." We agree with the sense of these descriptions. They convey the substantial political risk the ballot labels impose on current and prospective congressional members who, for one reason or another, fail to comply with the conditions set forth in [the provision] for passing its term limits amendment. Although petitioner now claims that the labels "merely" inform Missouri voters about a candidate's compliance with [the provision], she has acknowledged under oath that the ballot designations would handicap candidates for the United States Congress. To us, that is exactly the intended effect of [the provision].
>
> Indeed, it seems clear that the adverse labels handicap candidates "at the most crucial stage in the election process — the instant before the vote is cast." At the same time, "by directing the citizen's attention to the single consideration" of the candidates' fidelity to term limits, the labels imply that the issue "is an important — perhaps paramount — consideration in the citizen's choice, which may decisively influence the citizen to cast his ballot" against candidates branded as unfaithful. While the precise damage the labels may exact on candidates is disputed between the parties, the labels surely place their targets at a political disadvantage to unmarked candidates for congressional office. Thus, far from regulating the procedural mechanisms of elections, [the provision]

---

14. 531 U.S. 510 (2001).

attempts to "dictate electoral outcomes." *U.S. Term Limits*. Such "regulation" of congressional elections simply is not authorized by the Elections Clause.

Justice Thomas concurred despite his disagreement with the majority in *U.S. Term Limits*, because the challengers to the law had conceded that states could not impose additional qualifications on members of Congress. Chief Justice Rehnquist, joined by Justice O'Connor, concurred in the judgment, believing that the provision "violates the First Amendment right of a political candidate, once lawfully on the ballot, to have his name appear unaccompanied by pejorative language required by the State."

Who Judges Legislators' Qualifications?

Who Judges Legislators' Qualifications? What if voters elect a member of Congress who has not been a citizen for long enough, or who is too young? What if voters elect a state legislator who is not a resident of the legislative district, in violation of the state Constitution? Is the appropriate remedy a judicial action that the elected official be declared ineligible to serve? A common law writ of *quo warranto* was (and still is) available in some jurisdictions to challenge a legislator's eligibility for office. However, some states hold, pursuant to constitutional language, that only the legislators in the same house have the right to judge the qualifications of its members. In *Fuller v. Bowen*,[15] for example, a California appellate court refused to decide whether a one-year residency requirement for state legislative candidates violated the U.S. Constitution's Equal Protection Clause. "The California Constitution vests in each house of the Legislature the sole authority to judge the qualifications and elections of a candidate for membership in that house, even when the challenge to the candidate's qualifications is brought prior to a primary election. Under the facts presented in this case, California courts lack jurisdiction to judge Tom Berryhill's qualifications to serve as a Senator for the 14th Senate district."

The U.S. Constitution contains similar provisions about judging qualifications. Article I, section 5 provides that "Each House shall be the judge of the elections, returns and qualifications of its own members. . . ." That section further states that "Each House may determine the rules of its proceedings, punish its members for disorderly behavior, and, with the concurrence of two thirds, expel a member." Do these provisions allow for judicial review of disputes over qualifications?

The issue came before the Supreme Court in *Powell v. McCormack*.[16] As the Supreme Court described *Powell* in the *U.S. Term Limits* case:

> In November 1966, Adam Clayton Powell, Jr., was elected from a District in New York to serve in the United States House of Representatives for the 90th

---

15. 203 Cal. App. 4th 1476 (2012).
16. 395 U.S. 486 (1969).

Congress. Allegations that he had engaged in serious misconduct while serving as a committee chairman during the 89th Congress led to the appointment of a Select Committee to determine his eligibility to take his seat. That committee found that Powell met the age, citizenship, and residency requirements set forth in Art. I, 2, cl. 2. The committee also found, however, that Powell had wrongfully diverted House funds for the use of others and himself and had made false reports on expenditures of foreign currency. Based on those findings, the House after debate adopted House Resolution 278, excluding Powell from membership in the House, and declared his seat vacant.

Powell and several voters of the District from which he had been elected filed suit seeking a declaratory judgment that the House Resolution was invalid because Article I, 2, cl. 2, sets forth the exclusive qualifications for House membership. We ultimately accepted that contention, concluding that the House of Representatives has no "authority to *exclude* any person, duly elected by his constituents, who meets all the requirements for membership expressly prescribed in the Constitution." In reaching that conclusion, we undertook a detailed historical review to determine the intent of the Framers. Though recognizing that the Constitutional Convention debates themselves were inconclusive, we determined that the "relevant historical materials" reveal that Congress has no power to alter the qualifications in the text of the Constitution.

Powell is significant for two reasons.

First, it shows that the Supreme Court was willing to engage in judicial review of a decision by the House to exclude a member on the grounds that he was not qualified to serve; the Court did not hold that this issue was a political question that could be resolved only by Congress. It is not clear, however, whether the Court would review a finding by the House that a member did not meet the age, citizenship, or residency requirements.

Second, *Powell* nicely illustrates the difference between *excluding* a member who lacks the constitutionally mandated power to serve and *expelling* a member for "disorderly behavior." Congress could have voted to expel Powell for his alleged bad deeds under a two-thirds vote, not a mere majority as in the case of exclusion for a failure to meet constitutionally required qualifications. Ironically, the vote in *Powell* to exclude Representative Powell exceeded two-thirds, and the House argued unsuccessfully to the Supreme Court that this vote should count as equivalent to expulsion. The Court responded: "The [House] Speaker ruled that the House was voting to exclude Powell, and we will not speculate what the result might have been if Powell had been seated and expulsion proceedings subsequently instituted." Furthermore, the Court suggested that the way House leaders strategically put the exclusion issue up for a vote with an "all-or-nothing" choice indicated that two-third might not have voted for expulsion if given that opportunity. The politics of race also infused the controversy; Powell was an African-American member of Congress representing Harlem, and Justice Douglas in a separate opinion opined on the "racist overtones" of the vote.[17]

Even after *Powell*, many questions about the justiciability of qualifications disputes and expulsion disputes remain.

Example 3

In 2006, House Democrats asked U.S. Representative William J. Jefferson of Louisiana, who was then under investigation for multiple bribery claims, to resign from his assignment to the powerful House Ways & Means Committee. Jefferson refused to do so, and the Congressional Black Caucus, which counted Jefferson as a member, argued that it was wrong to punish Jefferson before he was convicted of any crime or even indicted. On a voice vote, the House of Representatives then voted to remove Jefferson from the committee.

Did Congress have the power to remove Representative Jefferson from the committee? Should it have exercised this power? Could Representative Jefferson have challenged the punishment in court?

(Jefferson was later indicted and convicted on a number of charges. He lost his congressional race before conviction and is now in federal prison.)

Explanation

Recall that the Constitution gives each house the power to "punish its members for disorderly behavior, and, with the concurrence of two thirds, expel a member." The Constitution does not further define "disorderly behavior," and it may be that this is a political question within the power of the House to determine. It is possible that Representative Jefferson could have challenged the punishment in court, but it is not clear from *Powell* whether courts would view such a challenge as justiciable in court (or instead left to the House itself to determine). Jefferson did not request a recorded vote, which would have showed how many members voted for the punishment.[18] Because this was a lesser punishment and not an expulsion, it appears a two-thirds vote would not be necessary.

---

17. On the strategic choices facing the legislators, *see* ESKRIDGE, FRICKEY, & GARRETT, *supra* at 206. On the racial undertones of the case, *see id.* at 207.

18. The Associated Press reported

> Under House rules, any lawmaker could have sought a roll call vote that would have required all members of the House to make their positions known publicly.
> None did.
> [Rep.] Clyburn told reporters afterward that most members of the Congressional Black Caucus did not want a vote, despite their accusation that Pelosi was subjecting Jefferson to a sanction without a rule or precedent to justify it.

House Lawmakers Strip Jefferson of Panel Seat, ASSOCIATED PRESS, Jun. 16, 2006, http://www.nbcnews.com/id/13348896/.

Once again, I leave the normative question to you. Should the presumption of innocence prevail for serving on important congressional committees when there is strong evidence a member of Congress could soon be indicted for serious crimes?

2.2. LEGISLATIVE DELIBERATION

2.2.1. Speech or Debate Clause Issues

Theorists offer varying normative assessments of how legislators should decide upon legislative action. Edmund Burke, a famous 18th-century Irish politician, gave a famous speech to the Electors of Bristol in which he argued against voters giving legislators "instructions" regarding how to vote.[19] Burke's position was that a legislator's job was to exercise independent judgment on the issues of the day, and vote according to conscience. Other theories of legislative action stressed independence less and accountability more; indeed, the entire purpose of periodic elections is to ensure that legislators are at least somewhat responsive to majority preferences.

Many theories of legislation stress the need for legislators to deliberate, or compromise, to decide which legislation is in the public interest. Even more pluralist theories that view the legislature as an arena for interest group competition, or proceduralists who focus on vetogates and others whose cooperation is necessary for legislation to succeed, recognize that the passage of legislation requires compromises between competing views and interests. Can legislative rules be fashioned to encourage legislative deliberation or compromise? Should they be?

A few provisions we have already considered seem aimed, at least in part, at facilitating deliberation and compromise. *Bicameralism* requires the agreement of the House and Senate, and the *presentment* requires the agreement of the president (except in cases in which supermajorities of the House and Senate each agree). The *longer terms and smaller size* of the Senate, as well as internal Senate rules on debate, may be seen as ways of raising the prospects for deliberation by increasing the length of time in which it is advantageous for senators to cooperate.

Other rules we have might be seen as promoting greater accountability of legislators to the people. Think of the frequent election of members of the House or the requirement that bills raising revenue originate in the more populous House.

---

19. Edmund Burke, *Speech to the Electors of Bristol*, 1 Burke's Works (1854).

2. Regulating Legislators

In this section we consider rules that might be seen as facilitating legislative deliberation, beginning with the Speech or Debate Clause.

Article I, section 6 of the United States Constitution provides that "for any speech or debate in either House, [senators and representatives] shall not be questioned in any other place." With this language, the Constitution gives legislators immunity from criminal prosecution or any legal action for activities falling within the scope of this Clause. Its purpose is aimed a facilitating deliberation without fear of interference from anyone, including from the judicial or executive branches[20] — for example, a senator making a disparaging but important statement about another person need not worry about a later lawsuit for libel.

The Speech or Debate Clause immunity raises a number of questions, most importantly: What conduct by legislators is protected by the Clause? The question is important because very little deliberation actually takes place on the floor of the House and Senate. Legislative deliberation, when it

---

20. The Supreme Court explained the origins of the clause:

> The Speech or Debate Clause of the Constitution was approved at the Constitutional Convention without discussion and without opposition. *See* V. Elliot's Debates 406 (1836 ed.); II Records of the Federal Convention 246 (Farrand ed. 1911). The present version of the clause was formulated by the Convention's Committee on Style, but the original vote of approval was of a slightly different formulation which repeated almost verbatim the language of Article V of the Articles of Confederation: "Freedom of speech and debate in Congress shall not be impeached or questioned in any court, or place out of Congress * * *." The language of that Article, of which the present clause is only a slight modification, is in turn almost identical to the English Bill of Rights of 1689: "That the Freedom of Speech, and Debates or Proceedings in Parliament, ought not to be impeached or questioned in any Court or Place out of Parliament.' 1 W. & M., Sess. 2, c. 2.
>
> This formulation of 1689 was the culmination of a long struggle for parliamentary supremacy. Behind these simple phrases lies a history of conflict between the Commons and the Tudor and Stuart monarchs during which successive monarchs utilized the criminal and civil law to suppress and intimidate critical legislators. Since the Glorious Revolution in Britain, and throughout United States history, the privilege has been recognized as an important protection of the independence and integrity of the legislature. *See, e.g.,* Story, Commentaries on the Constitution s 866; II The Works of James Wilson 37-38 (Andrews ed. 1896). In the American governmental structure the clause serves the additional function of reinforcing the separation of powers so deliberately established by the Founders. As Madison noted in Federalist No. 48:
>
> "It is agreed on all sides, that the powers properly belonging to one of the departments, ought not to be directly and compleatly administered by either of the other departments. It is equally evident, that neither of them ought to possess directly or indirectly, an overruling influence over the others in the administration of their respective powers. It will not be denied, that power is of an encroaching nature, and that it ought to be effectually restrained from passing the limits assigned to it. After discriminating therefore in theory, the several classes of power, as they may in their nature be legislative, executive, or judiciary; the next and most difficult task, is to provide some practical security for each against the invasion of the others. What this security ought to be, is the great problem to be solved." (Cooke ed.)

U.S. v. Johnson, 383 U.S. 169, 177-179 (1966).

occurs, is more likely to take place in a committee hearing or behind closed doors.[21]

The question of the Clause's scope has become even more important today, because when courts read the Clause broadly, it may impede the government's ability to investigate and prosecute bribery and other wrongdoing by legislators.

To begin with, the Clause protects not just literal speeches and debates in Congress, but also *legislative acts*. As the Supreme Court explained in *United States v. Brewster*.[22]

> A legislative act has consistently been defined as an act generally done in Congress in relation to the business before it. In sum, the Speech or Debate Clause prohibits inquiry only into those things generally said or done in the House or the Senate in the performance of official duties and into the motivation for those acts.
>
> It is well known, of course, that Members of the Congress engage in many activities other than the purely legislative activities protected by the Speech or Debate Clause. These include a wide range of legitimate "errands" performed for constituents, the making of appointments with Government agencies, assistance in securing Government contracts, preparing so-called "news letters" to constituents, news releases, and speeches delivered outside the Congress. The range of these related activities has grown over the years. They are performed in part because they have come to be expected by constituents, and because they are a means of developing continuing support for future elections. Although these are entirely legitimate activities, they are political in nature rather than legislative, in the sense that term has been used by the Court in prior cases. But it has never been seriously contended that these political matters, however appropriate, have the protection afforded by the Speech or Debate Clause.

It is a difficult balance. As the Supreme Court wrote in *Brewster*, the "Clause's "purpose [is not] to make Members of Congress super-citizens, immune from criminal responsibility."

"Legislative acts" include not just floor speeches, but also writing committee reports, speaking at committee hearings, and other core *legislative* action. But "legislative acts" do not include all core *legislator* action.

---

21. As Professor Sinclair explains:

> It is unrealistic, I would argue, to expect deliberation, as a great many people use the term, to take place on the floor of either chamber and certainly not in the House. If *deliberation* is defined as the process by which a group of people gets together and talks through a complex problem, maps the problem's contours, defines the alternatives, and figures out where its members stand, it is unrealistic to expect all of that to occur on the chambers floors. Deliberation is a nonlinear, free-form process that depends upon strict limits on the size of the group; subcommittees, other small groups, and possibly, committees are the forums in which it might be fostered.

Sinclair, *supra*, at 269-270.
22. 408 U.S. 501, 512 (1972).

Furthermore, while legislative acts are protected, *republication* does not count as a legislative act. In *Gravel v. United States*,[23] Senator Mike Gravel obtained a copy of a classified Defense Department report on Viet Nam known as "The Pentagon Papers." He read portions of the report into the public record. He and his aides also arranged for the papers to be republished as part of a book by Beacon Press. The Supreme Court held that while anything Gravel read into the record or included in a committee report was absolutely protected as a legislative act by Speech or Debate Clause immunity, the republication with the private press was not.[24] This is in line with the Court's reference in *Johnson* to newsletters prepared for constituents.

The Court in *Gravel* also held that the privilege applies not only to legislators themselves but also to legislative aides who may serve as the *alter ego* of the legislator: "Rather than giving the clause a cramped construction, the Court has sought to implement its fundamental purpose of freeing the legislator from executive and judicial oversight that realistically threatens to control his conduct as a legislator. We have little doubt that we are neither exceeding our judicial powers nor mistakenly construing the Constitution by holding that the Speech or Debate Clause applies not only to a Member but also to his aides insofar as the conduct of the latter would be a protected legislative act if performed by the Member himself."

One of the big questions dividing courts these days in the Speech or Debate Clause arena is whether federal officials investigating bribery or other federal crimes may examine evidence related to legislative acts in determining whether or not the senator or representative has committed a crime. (The legislative acts themselves would not be used to prove the crime, but examination of legislative act evidence could lead to admissible evidence of a crime.)

---

23. 408 U.S. 606 (1972).

24. The Court wrote:

> That Senators generally perform certain acts in their official capacity as Senators does not necessarily make all such acts legislative in nature. Members of Congress are constantly in touch with the Executive Branch of the Government and with administrative agencies — they may cajole, and exhort with respect to the administration of a federal statute — but such conduct, though generally done, is not protected legislative activity. *United States v. Johnson* decided at least this much. "No argument is made, nor do we think that it could be successfully contended, that the Speech or Debate Clause reaches conduct, such as was involved in the attempt to influence the Department of Justice, that is in no wise related to the due functioning of the legislative process."
>
> Legislative acts are not all-encompassing. The heart of the Clause is speech or debate in either House. Insofar as the Clause is construed to reach other matters, they must be an integral part of the deliberative and communicative processes by which Members participate in committee and House proceedings with respect to the consideration and passage or rejection of proposed legislation or with respect to other matters which the Constitution places within the jurisdiction of either House. As the Court of Appeals put it, the courts have extended the privilege to matters beyond pure speech or debate in either House, but "only when necessary to prevent indirect impairment of such deliberations."

A case decided by the United States Court of Appeals for the D.C. Circuit arising out of an investigation of Representative Jefferson's activities held that the executive may not examine such evidence. After Representative Jefferson refused to comply with various discovery requests, the FBI went into Jefferson's offices and confiscated both computer files and paper documents. The FBI set up a separate team to go through materials to determine which materials were not legislative acts covered by the privilege. The D.C. Circuit held that this was an improper procedure, and that these materials may not be examined even by a separate team from the legislative branch; a judge would have to decide which materials were not covered and might be examined by the FBI or other executive officials.[25] Both Democratic and Republican legislators sided with Jefferson on the privilege question. Since this case, law enforcement officers have complained that the ruling has made it much harder to investigate and prosecute legislators for bribery and other improper conduct.[26]

The U.S. Court of Appeals for the Ninth Circuit expressly disagreed with the D.C. Circuit on this point in *United States v. Renzi*.[27] It held that executive agents such as the FBI may examine evidence of legislative acts to ferret out criminal wrongdoing. That the legislative acts themselves were inadmissible in a prosecution did not make them immune from discovery and examination by either the executive or the judiciary.

Bipartisan House members disagreed with this decision, arguing that *Renzi* encroaches too far on legislative immunity. The Supreme Court declined to hear either the D.C. Circuit or the Ninth Circuit case, leaving the law in a condition of uncertainty.

When the *Renzi* case went to trial, the government took the position that if former Representative Renzi introduces evidence of legislative acts as part of his defense in his criminal prosecution, he would waive his Speech or Debate Clause immunity, and the government could then use legislative act evidence against him as well.[28]

Example 4

Consider the following facts from the allegations in the indictment in the *Renzi* case:

---

25. *United States v. Rayburn House Office Bldg.*, 497 F.3d 654 (D.C. Cir. 2007).

26. Jerry Markon & R. Jeffrey Smith, *Hill Probes Deflected by Clause in Constitution*, Wash. Post, Jan. 16, 2011, http://www.washingtonpost.com/politics/speech_or_debate_clause_invoked_in_investigations_of_house_members/2011/01/03/ABz0NfD_story.html.

27. 651 F.3d 1012 (2011).

28. Billy House, *The Curious Case of Rick Renzi*, Nat'l J., May 30, 2013, http://www.nationaljournal.com/daily/the-curious-case-of-rick-renzi-20130528.

Renzi was elected to the United States House of Representatives in November 2002 as the representative for Arizona's First Congressional District. He was sworn in the following January and, as a freshman congressman ("Member"), obtained a seat on the House Natural Resources Committee ("NRC") — the committee responsible for, among other things, approving of any land exchange legislation before it can reach the floor of the House.

In 2004 and 2005, Resolution Copper Mining LLC ("RCC") owned the mineral rights to a large copper deposit located near Superior, Arizona, an area east of Phoenix. RCC was planning to extract the copper, but wanted first to secure ownership of the surface rights from the United States Government. To obtain these rights, RCC hired Western Land Group, a consulting firm, to assist it in acquiring private property that it could offer to the Government in exchange for the desired surface rights.

In 2005, Western Land Group approached Renzi about developing and sponsoring the necessary land exchange legislation. According to the allegations, Congressman Renzi met with RCC representatives in his congressional office in February 2005 and instructed them to purchase property owned by James Sandlin ("the Sandlin property") if RCC desired Renzi's support. Renzi never disclosed to RCC that Sandlin was a former business partner who, at that time, owed Renzi some $700,000 plus accruing interest.

RCC's negotiations with Sandlin were not fruitful. In March 2005, an RCC representative called Renzi to tell him that RCC had been unable to reach an agreement with Sandlin because Sandlin was insisting on unreasonable terms. Renzi reassured the representative that Sandlin would be more cooperative in the future. Later that day, RCC received a fax from Sandlin stating, "I just received a phone call from Congressman Renzi's office. They have the impression that I haven't been cooperating concerning this water issue. I feel I have been very cooperative. . . . I still want to cooperate." Nevertheless, no deal could be struck. In April, RCC informed Renzi that it would not acquire the Sandlin property. Renzi responded simply, "[N]o Sandlin property, no bill."

Within the week following the collapse of "negotiations" with RCC, Renzi began meeting with an investment group led by Philip Aries ("Aries"), which desired the same surface rights. According to the Government, Renzi again insisted that the Sandlin property be purchased and included as part of any land exchange that took place. Again, he failed to disclose his creditor relationship with Sandlin. Upping the ante, Renzi told Aries that if the property was purchased and included, he would ensure that the legislation received a "free pass" through the NRC. Within a week, Aries agreed to purchase the property for a sum of $4.6 million and wired a $1 million deposit to Sandlin shortly thereafter.

Upon receiving that $1 million deposit, Sandlin wrote a $200,000 check payable to Renzi Vino, Inc., an Arizona company owned by Renzi. Renzi deposited the check into a bank account of Patriot Insurance — an insurance company he also owned — and used $164,590.68 to pay an outstanding Patriot Insurance debt. Later, when Aries appeared to grow nervous about the deal prior to closing on the Sandlin property, Renzi personally assured the group that he would introduce its land exchange proposal once the sale was complete. The day Aries closed, Sandlin paid into a Patriot Insurance account the remaining $533,000 he owed Renzi. Ultimately, Renzi never introduced any land exchange bill involving Aries and the Sandlin property.[29]

If the prosecution could prove these facts, would the Speech or Debate Clause bar prosecution of former Representative Renzi for bribery or related claims? If not, how would the prosecution going about proving allegations against Representative Renzi without violating the Clause? (Note that the next chapter will consider the elements of bribery and related claims; for now consider what evidence might be introduced to show that Representative Renzi agreed to take official action in exchange for something of value.)

Explanation

If these facts are proven, Renzi would not be immune from prosecution. (In fact, Renzi was later convicted of 17 corruption charges.[30])

The Speech or Debate Clause does not make legislators into a class of "super-citizens" immune from liability for ordinary crimes. Nor is it a license for legislators to commit bribery or other crimes. However, prosecutors need to prove the elements of any crimes without relying on evidence of Renzi's "legislative acts," such as statements made at committee hearings or legislation actually introduced by Renzi. This can make prosecution of Renzi a challenge. (The courts are split on whether prosecutors may look at evidence of legislative act evidence as part of their investigation — even though all agree that the evidence is not admissible to prove the crime.)

The prosecution could rely on communications that Renzi and his staff had with RCC, Sandlin, or anyone else with knowledge of the negotiations. These negotiations, while arguably part of Renzi's job as a legislator, do not count as "legislative acts" under governing Supreme Court precedent. As we will see in the next chapter, it is not necessary to prove that Renzi actually introduced legislation in exchange for a personal benefit in order to be guilty of a crime, and therefore proof of such an act, had it occurred, would not be necessary for a bribery conviction.

2.2.2. Single Subject Rules and Logrolling

We have seen various tools, such as the Speech or Debate Clause, that free up lawmakers to deliberate and speak without fear of outside litigation or

---

29. United States v. Renzi, 651 F.3d 1012, 1016-1017 (2011).

30. John Bresnahan, Former Rep. Rick Renzi Convicted in Corruption Trial, POLITICO, Jun. 11, 2013, http://www.politico.com/story/2013/06/rick-renzi-guilty-on-17-counts-92619.html.

interference. We also have seen one instance of a *content* restriction on the type or form of legislation that Congress may consider: The Origination Clause requires certain revenue bills to originate in the House of Representatives rather than the Senate.

Another type of content restriction that appears in certain state constitutions but that is lacking in the U.S. constitution is a *single subject rule*. Roughly speaking, such a rule requires that any particular piece of legislation include only a single subject. Such rules go back as far as ancient Rome.[31]

Given the rise of omnibus legislation and other unorthodox lawmaking in Congress, which sometimes leads to federal bills running into the thousands of pages, imposing a single subject rule in Congress would lead to profound changes in federal lawmaking. Certainly if Congress kept the same procedures for passing (and delaying) legislation, but required that legislation involving different subjects be unbundled, there would likely be much less federal legislation. First, Congress would not have time to consider all the legislation it now passes unbundled as separate bills. Second, without the bundles, legislators might be less likely to come to agreement on many of these bills.

This last point is worth some careful thought. A very common legislative process is *logrolling*, whereby legislators agree to a package deal on a piece of legislation in a bundle. There will be times when Bill A could not pass alone, and Bill B could not pass alone, but a Bill A + B would have enough support to pass. As Professor Gilbert explains, one of the key justifications offered for legislative single subject rules is that they prevent such logrolling.[32]

Putting aside for the moment whether a single subject rule could effectively stop the practice of bundling Bill A and B together, it is not clear that doing so is a social good. Economists have demonstrated that sometimes logrolling provides social benefits, while sometimes it is socially harmful; a single subject rule cannot distinguish between "good" and "bad" logrolls.[33]

Furthermore, it is not clear that a single subject rule could be fairly and consistently enforced. We will return to this issue in detail Chapter 4, where the single subject rule plays a major role in many states in regulating the initiative and referendum process. Determining whether Bill A and Bill B

---

31. Michael D. Gilbert, *Single Subject Rules and the Legislative Process*, 67 U. PITT. L. REV. 803, 811 (2006).

32. The other justifications Professor Gilbert mentions are: "(2) eliminat[ing] 'riders,'" unpopular provisions that are attached to otherwise popular bills; and (3) improv[ing] political transparency, both for citizens and politicians." *Id.* at 809. Gilbert would distinguish between logrolls and riders, and have courts do more to ensure against the inclusion of such riders. Can we trust courts to distinguish between the two?

33. John G. Matsusaka & Richard L. Hasen, *Aggressive Enforcement of the Single Subject Rule*, 9 ELECTION L.J. 399 (2010).

embrace one or more "subjects" depends entirely upon how one defines "subject," and whether the definition is clear enough that it reins in judges from rejecting or accepting single subject arguments about legislation the judges may like or dislike. Furthermore, in a legislature where legislators constantly interact with each other over the long term, they may develop bonds of trust on voting that would allow them to continue to logroll through votes on separate pieces of legislation.

For good or for bad, courts do not aggressively police the single subject rule in legislative races, meaning that much logrolling goes on in jurisdictions that require legislatures to abide by the rule.[34] (In contrast, as we will see, the rule has been aggressively, although unevenly, enforced in the state ballot measure context.)

Example 5

Do you favor amending the U.S. Constitution to include a single subject requirement for legislation? Why, or why not?

Explanation

There is no right answer to this question. As noted in the text, including a single subject requirement in the Constitution would likely decrease the amount of legislation passed by Congress. So your answer to this question may depend in part on your normative view as to whether decreasing federal legislation is a good thing or bad thing.

The single subject rule also may inhibit some logrolling (although whether the rule is effective at doing so is uncertain). Limiting logrolling might be seen as a way of encouraging more deliberation by having each piece of legislation considered on its own merits. (This is not necessarily the case — even civic republicans might agree that some social issues are best resolved through legislation that covers multiple subjects, such as a health care bill that makes changes to the tax code). Pluralists could well dislike limits on logrolling, because they prevent the creation of legislative deals that are the product of interest group dealmaking. Public choice theorists, however, may like the rule to the extent that it makes it harder to make inefficient deals facilitating rent-seeking.

---

34. Philip P. Frickey & Steven S. Smith, *Judicial Review and the Legislative Process: Some Empirical and Normative Aspects of Due Process of Lawmaking*, UC Berkeley School of Law, Public Law and Legal Theory Working Paper No. 63 4 (2001), http://papers.ssrn.com/paper.taf?abstract_id=279433.

2.2.3. Due Process of Lawmaking

Professor and later Oregon Supreme Court Justice Hans Linde coined the term "due process of lawmaking" to discuss judicial review of the rationality of legislation.[35] Justice Linde questioned the legitimacy of having courts examine whether a legislature had a rational reason—or under rational basis review whether lawyers for the government could conjure up a rational reason the legislature might have relied upon—in determining whether legislation is constitutional. Rational basis review, and certainly tougher forms of review such as strict scrutiny, asks courts to examine the reasons why a legislative body passed a law and the fit between those reasons and the law the legislature chose. Justice Linde believes that judicial review of legislative motivation violates separation of powers principles and that courts should review only legislative outcomes for possible unconstitutionality.

Professor Phil Frickey, one of the giants of the legislation field, who recently passed away, used the term "due process of lawmaking" more broadly to refer to a series of rules and procedures, such as the legislative single subject rule, whereby courts examine the process by which legislatures pass laws or administrative agencies make rules and decisions in passing on a decision's legality or constitutionality. Frickey believed it was appropriate for courts to ensure that legislative and administrative bodies followed procedural regularities in passing legislation. Doing so ensures that legislative and administrative bodies have the opportunity to deliberate. The procedural rules (such as the Origination Clause) may promote the constitutional values embedded in the rules (such as the idea that revenue bills should start with the part of government closest to the people). Frickey pointed to the Supreme Court case of *Hampton v. Mow Sun Wong,*[36] which struck down a rule from the federal Civil Service Commission barring noncitizens from federal government employment. Justice Stevens's opinion for the Court struck down the rule but said the same rule could be constitutional if readopted by Congress or the president.[37] The president then reinstated the rule by executive order, and the Supreme Court declined to review the case. Having the right body consider the issue could promote the right kind of deliberation.

---

35. Hans A. Linde, *Due Process of Lawmaking*, 55 NEB. L. REV. 197 (1976).
36. 426 U.S. 88 (1976).
37. "[I]n *Mow Sun Wong* the federal government contended that its prohibition on alien federal employment could serve as a bargaining chip in foreign relations or to encourage noncitizens to become citizens. But none of the proffered reasons why the federal government might legitimately consider alienage were the business of the Civil Service Commission, as opposed to the Congress or the President, which had never considered the question." Frickey & Smith, *supra*, at 8.

Frickey was more critical of having courts review evidence considered by a legislature in determining the constitutionality of legislation. One prominent example Frickey and Smith discuss in an important unpublished paper is the U.S. Supreme Court's federalism line of cases requiring Congress to amass a sufficient evidentiary record of constitutional violations by states in order to justify laws punishing states for unconstitutional conduct.[38] Frickey and Smith, echoing Linde, are skeptical that judicial review of a congressional evidentiary record will actually facilitate deliberation or an appropriate procedure for lawmaking:

> Review of the details of the *legislative deliberation* is unviable. Staying on this path will require further specification of the legislative actors and the kind of record that must be found for each of them. Consistency will require that the justifying record be closely tied to outcomes, which involve compromised means and ends. Eventually, we are persuaded, the courts will find this to be impractical, if they do not first find it a breach of separation of powers.

Example 6

An adult business took over some existing commercial property and wanted to have zoning conditions at the property changed so it could keep its nude dancing adult cabaret open longer hours. A zoning commissioner approved the zoning chambers and neighbors appealed, putting the issue before the local city council, where it came up for a hearing.

"A picture is worth a thousand words, and here the picture was a videotape. [The business] recorded the city council hearing, slowly moving the camera's gaze back and forth from one end of the council table to the other, at times lingering on particular council members, capturing their behavior at that moment. The tape shows that when the council president summoned [the business] to the speaker's lectern to present its case, eight council members—three of whom were absent—were not in their seats. Only two council members were visibly paying attention. Four others might have been paying attention, although they engaged themselves with other activities, including talking with aides, eating, and reviewing paperwork.

"One minute into [the] presentation, a council member began talking on his cell phone and two council members, one of whom had been paying attention when the hearing opened, started talking to each other. A minute later, two other council members struck up their own private conversation. Three minutes into his presentation, [the business's] counsel complained 'it doesn't appear that too many people are paying attention,' an observation

---

38. *See, e.g.,* Board of Trustees v. Garrett, 531 U.S. 356 (2001).

the videotape verifies, as only a few council members were sitting in their seats not talking to others.

"Despite [the business's] public reproach of council members, their private conversations and pursuit of other activities continued. For example, the council member with the cell phone started another conversation on it and four council members talked among themselves or with others. One council member was especially peripatetic, walking from one side of the council chamber to the other to talk to different colleagues. Only five council members and the council president sat at their desks spending most of their time not talking to anyone — but even some of them turned their attention to other things from time to time.

"After 10 minutes, [the business's] presentation ended and those opposed to the zoning modifications began. Although the speakers changed, the council's behavior did not. Some members paid attention, but even some of them divided their attention among things such as reviewing paperwork and getting up from their seats to talk to others. At one point, the camera zoomed out for a wide angle shot of the entire council table. At that moment, only five members were at their seats, and only one member appeared to be focusing on what the speakers were saying."

The city council voted to reverse the zoning commissioner and to keep the old restrictions on the business. The business sued. Should the court hold that the city council needs to redo the hearing and pay attention this time?

Explanation

Once again, this is a normative question for which there is no right answer. You should see how it implicates due process of lawmaking issues. Do you think deliberation requires paying attention to speakers? To what extent should legislators be able to decide that other legislative priorities take precedence over an issue about which they likely already decided how they were going to vote?

The facts of this case come from a California Court of Appeal decision, (which was later ordered not published — making it not citable as precedent — by the California Supreme Court), *Lacy St. Hospitality Service, Inc. v. City of Los Angeles*.[39] The court concluded

> We do not presume to tell the city council how it must conduct itself as a legislative body. Here, however, the city council was sitting in a quasi-judicial role, adjudicating the administrative appeal of constituents. A fundamental principle of due process is "he who decides must hear." The inattentiveness of council members during the hearing prevented the council from satisfying that principle. . . . The council's distraction with a multitude of other things

---

39. 22 Cal. Rptr. 3d 805 (Ct. App. 2004), *ordered not published*, 2005.

during the hearing is especially troubling because it was reversing its own zoning administrator who took great care to reach his decision. It is not our province to insist that the council members consider every word of every witness. Good judgment and common sense are entitled to prevail. Here, however, the tape shows the council cannot be said to have made a reasoned decision based upon hearing all the evidence and argument, which is the essence of sound decision making and to which [the business] was entitled as a matter of due process. Accordingly, we reverse and remand. . . . We reverse and remand to the city council for a hearing that satisfies [the business's] due process right to be heard.

After winning the ruling, the lawyer for the business returned to criticize the council.[40] A few months later, on rehearing, the Los Angeles City Council unanimously voted against the business.[41] Presumably no councilmembers were on their cell phones during the deliberations.

---

40. Jessica Garrison, *Lawyer Finally Gets Council's Attention*, L.A. TIMES, Jan. 8, 2005, http://articles.latimes.com/2005/jan/08/local/me-porn8.

> Councilman Jack Weiss, who appears in Diamond's videotape engaged in a long cellphone conversation, also dismissed Diamond as "the porn industry's lawyer" and accused him of "bellyaching."
>
> Diamond objected to those comments, saying, "I was shocked to hear that a number of you were defiant." Diamond said that his case was about much more than whether the Blue Zebra could allow its dancers to keep gyrating until 4 a.m. "It's a broader issue of respect," he said.
>
> Diamond singled out Weiss, saying that the Westside councilman and former prosecutor had personally attacked him and that "for a lawyer to criticize another lawyer for the client he represents is outrageous."
>
> Diamond has asked city officials for Weiss' cellphone records, to learn who he was talking to during the hearing that day, and has also asked that Weiss recuse himself from any further decisions on strip clubs that Diamond represents.
>
> Weiss appeared unmoved by Diamond's visit.
>
> "Mr. Diamond's presentation reminds me of that great line from 'Macbeth,' about a tale of sound and fury signifying nothing," he said.
>
> As to whether he would recuse himself from matters involving Diamond's clients, Weiss did not answer, saying that he had "responded more than enough on this issue."

41. http://cityclerk.lacity.org/lacityclerkconnect/index.cfm?fa=ccfi.viewrecord&cfnumber=05-0065.

Lobbying, Bribery, and External Legislative Influence

3.1. LOBBYING

3.1.1. How Lobbying Works

In the last chapter, we looked at how various rules and procedures may influence legislative deliberation as well as influence who may serve, and how they may serve, as legislators. These legislative influences are all *internal*, built into the constitutional or governmental structure.

We turn in this chapter to *external* means of influence: How do individuals outside the legislature seek to influence the actions legislators take, and when do those attempts at external influence cross the line from legal to illegal or unethical? We begin with laws regulating lobbying, the process by which individuals seek to influence legislative action. We then turn to consideration of bribery and related issues, where certain exchanges of benefits between elected officials and others are illegal. The line between acceptable political deals and criminality can be fuzzy in both theory and practice. The issue is especially tricky when it comes to campaign contributions and political benefits. We conclude with a brief description of ethics and gift laws that interact with both lobbying activity and the law of bribery. If that's not enough material for you to consider about external legislative influences, Part IV of this book returns to the issue with a detailed discussion of campaign finance laws.

3. Lobbying, Bribery, and External Legislative Influence

We begin with lobbying.[1] *Lobbying* is the activity of seeking to influence government action, usually through contact with legislators and their staff or through contact with those in the executive branch or administrative agencies.[2] The First Amendment of the U.S. Constitution recognizes the right to lobby, not only in granting freedom of *speech* and *association*, but also the right to *petition* the government for the redress of grievances. Any laws or regulations of lobbying must comply with the First Amendment.

Clients employ lobbyists to try to influence public policy on a particular issue in a certain direction. Lobbyists use a variety of tools to achieve such influence, including mobilizing individual citizens to contact legislators (grassroots lobbying), testifying at hearings, submitting written comments to an agency or committee, issuing press releases, and engaging in other activities. But a lobbyist's most important tool is personal contact with legislators and staff members. A lobbyist with access to a legislator is in the best position to influence public policy. After a lobbyist secures access, he or she influences policy primarily by providing credible information to a legislator or staffer to argue for a particular legislative action.[3]

Lobbyists are not magicians. Though a common misunderstanding of lobbying is that lobbyists commonly *change legislators' positions* on a particular legislative issue through favors or threats, such change appears to be relatively rare. Instead, the lobbyist's most common role is to provide support and useful information for a position a legislator already holds. At other times, the issue of interest to the lobbyist (and his or her client) is one about which the legislator has no firm position or even knowledge, and one about which the public is not paying any attention. In such circumstances the legislator is often willing to help a friendly lobbyist achieve his or her client's interests, especially when the client is a constituent or has business affecting the legislator's district.

---

1. This discussion draws from Richard L. Hasen, *Lobbying, Rent Seeking and Democracy*, 64 STAN. L. REV. 191 (2012). That article cites the relevant social science literature on lobbying that forms the basis for the description below. Some of the leading studies are FRANK R. BAUMGARTNER ET AL., LOBBYING AND POLICY CHANGE: WHO WINS, WHO LOSES, AND WHY (2009); KAY LEHMAN SCHLOZMAN & JOHN T. TIERNEY, ORGANIZED INTERESTS AND AMERICAN DEMOCRACY (1986); and ANTHONY J. NOWNES, TOTAL LOBBYING: WHAT LOBBYISTS WANT (AND HOW THEY TRY TO GET IT) (2006).

2. The focus in this chapter is on lobbying of legislators and staffers. Executive and administrative agency lobbying is more properly the focus of a course on administrative law.

3. The lobbyists have a number of incentives to provide credible information. First, lobbyists are involved in repeated interactions with elected officials and staffers. A lobbyist who is not credible will not be listened to in the future. Second, even if clients wish for lobbyists to provide information that is not credible to elected officials and staffers, it is in the lobbyist's own long-term interest in securing future clients to maintain good relationships with elected officials and staffers by providing credible information. For a general discussion of principal-agent problems between clients and lobbyists, *see* Matthew C. Stephenson & Howell E. Jackson, *Lobbyists as Imperfect Agents: Implications for Public Policy in a Pluralist System*, 47 HARV. J. ON LEGIS. 1 (2010).

Lobbyists rarely can sway resistant legislators on high-salience issues about which the public appears to be paying a great deal of attention. Even the most highly paid professional lobbyists were unable to derail a large corporate tax increase that became part of the political popular Tax Reform Act of 1986, a major tax bill passed during the Reagan administration with bipartisan support.

Rather than working primarily to change legislative minds on issues of high public salience, lobbyists, like mushrooms, thrive in areas of low light. After it became apparent that the 1986 tax bill was going to pass, lobbyists were much more successful in working to get favorable treatment for their clients in the details of the bill and its implementation. The more general lesson appears to be that lobbyists are most likely to be successful when (1) they have direct access to legislative officials and their staff, (2) they are working on issues of lower salience, and (3) the legislators being lobbied are either already in agreement with the position of the lobbyist or are indifferent about the policy proposals of the lobbyists.

Securing access. Lobbyists gain access through the cultivation of relationships with legislators and staffers using a variety of tools permissible under the law, especially the raising of campaign contributions for legislators. Campaign contributions are a key part of a culture of reciprocity. Feelings of reciprocity are formed easily and without the outlay of considerable resources, but those who help out the most are likely to get the greatest access. It is a natural instinct to help someone out who has helped you. In this context, why *shouldn't* a legislator help a lobbyist supporter by favoring his or her client's interests on an issue about which the legislator has no personal preference?

Lobbyists typically do not raise campaign contributions for any and all legislators. Republican lobbyists raise funds for Republicans, and Democratic lobbyists raise funds for Democrats — though often such lobbyists are in the same firm as a means of hedging against future political change and having the ability to work both sides of the aisle in Congress. Lobbying and fundraising patterns follow the fortunes of the parties in Congress. Following the "K Street Project" period in which the House Republican leadership built close relationships with lobbyists who engaged in major fundraising for the party, many Republican lobbyists lost their jobs in 2006 and 2008 as Democrats took control of the House, Senate, and executive branch and Democratic lobbyists had greater career opportunities. (K Street is the street in Washington, D.C., where many lobbying firms have their offices.) When it became clear in 2010 that Republicans were poised to retake control of the House, Republican lobbyists again grew in demand.

Lobbyists often do much more than simply contribute money themselves to these pivotal legislators; they have become prolific fundraisers and bundlers of campaign contributions for key legislators and party leaders. For example, during the 2010 period when Republicans appeared poised to retake control of the House of Representatives, House Minority Leader John Boehner provided special access to lobbyists who contributed the maximum $37,800 contribution to various committees supporting him or who raised at least $100,000 from other contributors.

Another key means of securing legislative access is for clients to hire former legislators and staffers as lobbyists (through the so-called "revolving door"). Many prominent former senators and members of Congress have become lobbyists, as have dozens of former staffers of sitting senators and members of Congress. Indeed, half the senators who left office between 1998 and 2004 became lobbyists. These revolving door lobbyists have preexisting reciprocal relationships with current legislators and staffers that they can then use to secure access to help clients. Though it is no longer permissible for a former senator to use the Senate gym as a place for lobbying, and there is a waiting period for senators after leaving the Senate to engage in certain lobbying activities, there is no question that a former senator or major House staffer who is lobbying for a client is likely to get a phone call returned and a chance to make the case for the lobbyist's clients. In fact, as evidence that who you know is more important than what you know, one study found that revolving door lobbyists tend to follow their former legislative bosses from committee to committee, switching from lobbying on an issue such as health care to one such as defense. Expertise is secondary to personal contacts.

Moving from legislator/staffer to lobbyist can be quite lucrative. Former staffers can expect their salaries to increase significantly, and former senators and members of Congress can earn seven-figure salaries. Another study found that lobbyists with past working experience in the office of a U.S. senator suffer an average sharp 24% drop in revenue when that senator leaves office.[4] That is, when the main connection to the elected official disappears, the revolving door lobbyist's value on the market drops.

After the access. After lobbyists gain access to elected officials, lobbyists solidify relationships of trust and influence by providing credible information (on both policy and politics) to elected officials and staffers in order to help the legislative office make informed policy choices and succeed in achieving legislative goals. Today is an era of information overload; the best lobbyists recognize that their long-term reputations depend upon their credibility and the usefulness of the information they provide. Access certainly does not guarantee lobbyist success. Indeed, lobbyists often have a difficult time getting elected officials to take action on their proposed policy changes. Moreover, it is easier for lobbyists to react to a changing policy environment than to facilitate major legislative change. It is more accurate to

---

4. Jordi Blanes i Vidal, Mirko Draca, & Christain Fons-Rosen, *Revolving Door Lobbyists*, 102 Am. Econ. Rev. 3731 (2012).

think of access as a necessary but insufficient condition for a lobbyist to achieve a client's goals.

Example 1

Before the passage of the Affordable Care Act, a study of health care lobbying by the *Chicago Tribune*, Northwestern University, and the Center for Responsive Politics found that

> [a]t least 166 former aides from the nine congressional leadership offices and five committees involved in shaping health overhaul legislation — along with at least 13 former lawmakers — registered to represent at least 338 health care clients since the beginning of last year. . . . Their health care clients spent $635 million on lobbying over the past two years. . . . The total of insider lobbyists jumps to 278 when non-health-care firms that reported lobbying on health issues are added in. . . .[5]

The article describes how a former congressional staffer who became a lobbyist for a medical device trade association was able to successfully lobby to change a $40 billion proposed tax on the industry to a $20 billion tax in the bill, saving his clients $20 billion.

How would a pluralist, a civic republican, and a public choice theorist react to this story? (If you are unfamiliar with these terms, they are described in Chapter 1.) How do *you* react to this story?

Explanation

A pluralist would not be surprised by this story. Pluralists believe that legislatures are arenas in which various interest groups compete for influence. The mammoth health care law meant that there were many opportunities for interest groups to compete over varying provisions. Interest groups frequently use lobbyists to influence legislator action. From a normative perspective, many pluralists would see this outlay on lobbying as simply democracy in action, and something, if not to be celebrated, at least inevitable with a government as large as the current federal government and with stakes so high. Other normative pluralists, who might be concerned about political inequality, could find aspects of the story troubling, because those who have special connections are better able to get their deals through.

Civic republicans likely would find this story quite troubling. While not necessarily disagreeing with the pluralist picture of a legislature as a

---

5. Andrew Zajac, *Congressional Staffers Turn Lobbyists: Health Care Lobby Drafts Army of Insiders to Help Fight Overhaul*, Chi. Trib., Dec. 20, 2009, http://articles.chicagotribune.com/2009-12-20/news/0912190289_1_health-care-lobbyists-insiders.

bazaar from a positive perspective, they would find such bargaining and influence troubling from a normative perspective. Civic republicans want legislators to make decisions that reflect their considered judgment in line with the public interest. To the extent lobbyists use personal connections and campaign fundraising to grease the wheels for special interest deals, legislation is likely to diverge from that which is in the public's interest.

Public choice theorists could be concerned about the normative implications of this story for a different reason: It suggests that interest groups may be seeking inefficient deals as part of the health care legislation. Interest groups engage in rent seeking that is economically inefficient, and the large health care law poses many opportunities for rent-seeking activities.

As to your own normative view of this process, I leave that to you.

3.1.2. Lobbying Disclosure Rules

The details of federal, state, and local lobbying disclosure and tax rules are byzantine and keep many lawyers in business. My purpose here is not to provide practical details for lobbying compliance.[6] Rather, I aim to give you enough detail to understand roughly both the nature of (especially federal) lobbying regulation and the courts' responses to constitutional challenges to such regulation.

Concerns about the role of lobbyists in influencing legislative bodies are not new. Georgia, for example, outlawed lobbying of state legislators in its 1877 constitution,[7] and in 1890 Massachusetts imposed a requirement that lobbyists register and disclose their expenses incurred in state lobbying activity. Federal legislation took much longer to enact, and even after being enacted it was hardly effective.

Political activists, members of the public, and reform-minded elected officials raised concerns about federal lobbying activity and the growth of government beginning with the *Crédit Mobilier* scandal during the Ulysses S. Grant administration. Periodic congressional investigations revealed unsavory lobbying practices. For example, a 1913 investigation into the activities of the

---

6. An excellent resource to get started with practical registration and other requirements is THE LOBBYING MANUAL (William V. Luneburg et al. eds., 4th ed. 2009). Updates to the book chapters, along with additional materials, appear at the book's web page, http://www .americanbar.org/groups/administrative_law/publications/lobbyingmanual2011supplement .html. Another very useful source is TREVOR POTTER & JOSEPH M. BIRKENSTOCK, POLITICAL ACTIVITY, LOBBYING LAWS AND GIFT RULES GUIDE (3d ed. 2008).

7. William N. Eskridge, *Federal Lobbying Regulation: History Through 1954*, in THE LOBBYING MANUAL, *supra*, at 1, 7 n.7 (noting that criminal prohibitions on lobbying survived under Georgia law until 1992). As Eskridge notes, such a requirement today would "very probably be held to violate the First Amendment's right to petition." The next two paragraphs draw from and quote from Eskridge's excellent historical essay.

National Association of Manufacturers revealed how "NAM controlled some committee appointments, paid the chief page of the House to report conversations by House Members on the floor and the cloakroom, and enjoyed its own office in the Capitol. Less surprising, though still disturbing were the large sums of money the lobbyists had at their disposal to influence legislation." A 1935 congressional investigation uncovered what we would now term an "astroturf" campaign,[8] whereby utility companies paid for the sending of over 250,000 telegrams to Washington, written by utility company employees, and often forging the signature of senders.

Despite periodic scandal, investigation, and legislative proposals, Congress passed no generally applicable federal lobbying bills until 1946, aside from a short-lived lobbyist registration requirement that lasted only as long as the 44th Congress. In 1946, Congress passed the Federal Regulation of Lobbying Act "almost by accident" as part of a larger bill and without any legislative hearings. The law imposed registration requirements for those who lobbied Congress, as well as a requirement of quarterly reports of money spent and received for lobbying activities. But the law lacked "a workable enforcement mechanism," and it suffered from drafting problems that "resulted in a statute of remarkable opaqueness," leading to "very uneven" compliance.

The statute's drafting problems proved its downfall. Responding to a constitutional challenge to the statute (on grounds it was both fatally vague under the Due Process Clause and a violation of the First Amendment), the Supreme Court in *United States v. Harriss*[9] significantly rewrote and narrowed the statute to avoid the vagueness problem, holding the rewritten statute acceptable under the First Amendment. In rewriting the statute, the Court "crippled an already frail statute" through an interpretation that "all but ended" federal prosecutions under the statute.

Though it was clear by the mid-1950s that the 1946 act was ineffective as a disclosure mechanism,[10] it took another 40 years before Congress imposed new lobbying disclosure requirements. Although Congress passed the Lobbying Disclosure Act of 1995[11] ("LDA") in unanimous votes of 421-0 in the House and 98-0 in the Senate, the bill earlier faced serious Republican opposition. It passed subsequent to assurances that the bill did not seek to require disclosure by those engaged in "grassroots lobbying."

---

8. "Astroturfing" is "[a]n artificially-manufactured political movement designed to give the appearance of grass roots activism." *Astroturfing*, TAAGEN GODDARD'S POLITICAL DICTIONARY, http://politicaldictionary.com/words/astroturf/.
9. 347 U.S. 612 (1954).
10. Susman and Luneburg identified five perceived weaknesses in the 1946 disclosure regime, as rewritten by the Supreme Court in *Harriss*. Thomas M. Susman & William V. Luneburg, *History of Lobbying Disclosure Reform Proposals Since 1955*, in THE LOBBYING MANUAL, *supra*, at 23, 23-24. The authors trace the history of lobbying reform proposals over the 40-year period.
11. Pub. L. 104-65.

The LDA improved on the 1946 act in a number of ways. It applies to lobbying of congressional staffs, and not just members of Congress; it covers executive branch lobbying; and it expands the scope of who needed to register as a lobbyist and what information needed to be included in filed reports. The LDA's complex registration requirement is keyed to new definitions of "lobbyist," "client," "lobbying contact," "lobbying activities," and "communication." Along with other federal laws,[12] it provides the current framework for federal lobbying regulation.

Without covering all the intricate details, it is worth briefly describing who must register as a lobbyist and file reports.[13] Under the rules a lobbyist is any individual (1) who is either employed or retained by a client for financial or other compensation; (2) whose services include more than one lobbying contact; and (3) whose lobbying activities constitute 20 percent or more of his or her services' time on behalf of that client during any three-month period. A firm employing a lobbyist is exempt from registering for a client if its income for that client is not expected to exceed $3,000 in a quarter. For firms that use in-house lobbyists, no registration is required if lobbying expenses do not exceed $12,500 in a quarter. A lobbying contact is an oral, written, or electronic communication with a covered legislative or executive official[14] (except for certain communications, such as that in response to a government subpoena). Lobbying activities are lobbying contacts and any efforts in support of such contacts, including preparation or planning activities, research, and other background work that is intended, at the time of its preparation, for use in contacts, and coordination with the lobbying activities of others.

In response to these technical definitions, many people seek to influence government action without having to register as lobbyists. Registering as a lobbyist not only triggers reporting requirements but has other consequences as well, as we will see in the next section of this chapter. Some individuals, such as former senators, may provide "strategic advice" to companies or groups about how to achieve legislative goals in Congress, making sure their activities do not trigger a lobbyist registration requirement. In response, the lobbying community has argued that the definition

---

12. Other significant federal lobbying laws include the Foreign Agents Registration Act and the "Byrd Amendment," which "prohibits the use of funds appropriated by Congress to lobby for any type of federal award—a federal contract, grant, loan, or cooperative agreement." Thomas M. Susman, *The Byrd Amendment*, in The Lobbying Manual, *supra*, at 349.

13. A clear description of the complex rules appears at the House of Representatives' website section on lobbying at http://lobbyingdisclosure.house.gov/amended_lda_guide.html, from which I have drawn some of the language and examples below.

14. This category includes members of Congress, their staffs and the staffs of committees and leadership, and certain executive branch officials and employees.

of lobbyist should be expanded so that these individuals competing with lobbyists would have to register as lobbyists as well.

Example 2

"Corporation 'C' does not employ an individual who meets the definition of 'lobbyist.' Employee 'X' is told by her supervisor to contact the Congressman representing the district in which Corporation 'C' is headquartered. 'X' makes a lobbying contact on June 1, 2008. 'X' does not anticipate making any further lobbying contacts, but spends 25% of her time on this legislative issue. In August 2008, 'X' is instructed to follow up with the Congressman again."

Was Corporation "C" required to file a lobbying report in June 2008? In August 2008?

Explanation

This example comes from the House of Representatives' website explaining lobbying disclosure requirements. It states that there was no requirement for Corporation "C" to register in June 2008 (presumably because there was only a single lobbying contact, by its employee "X"). However, Corporation "C" must register and disclose in August 2008 "as the effective date of registration (the date that 'X' contacted the Congressman for the second time and thereby met the definition of a lobbyist)."

Consider these additional examples from the House website that show how the lobbying registration rules depend upon detailed technical requirements:

> Example 1: A law firm has two lawyers who perform services for a particular client. Lawyer "A" spends 15 percent of the time she works for that client on lobbying activities, including some lobbying contacts. Lawyer "B" spends 25 percent of the time he works for the client on lobbying activities, but makes no lobbying contacts. Neither lawyer falls within the definition of "lobbyist," and therefore the law firm is not required to register for that client, even if the income it receives for lobbying activities on behalf of the client exceeds $3,000.
>
> Example 2: Employee "A" of a trade association is a "lobbyist" who spends 25 percent of his time on lobbying activities on behalf of the association. There are $6,500 of expenses related to Employee "A's" lobbying activities. Employee "B" is not a "lobbyist" but engages in lobbying activities in support of lobbying contacts made by Employee "A." There are $6,500 of additional expenses related to the lobbying activities of Employee "B." The trade association is required to register because it employs a "lobbyist" and its total expenses in connection with lobbying activities on its own behalf exceed $12,500.

Example 3: Same as Example 2, except the expenses related to the lobbying activities of Employees "A" and "B" total only $9,000, but the trade association also pays $5,000 to an outside firm for lobbying activities. Registration is still required because payments to outside contractors (including lobbying firms that may be separately registered under the LDA) must be included in the total expenses of an organization employing lobbyists on its own behalf.

Although the LDA certainly required more disclosure than the 1946 act, it is still a weak enforcement regime. "[T]he disclosures required by the act are minimal and made in a format that is neither easily accessible nor decipherable by average citizens."[15] "[L]obbyists need only state generally that they contacted the House of Representatives or the Senate or a particular federal agency, such as the Department of Energy at large, rather than specify individual legislators, committees, or federal employees with whom they corresponded."[16]

Here is part of a page from a recent lobbying disclosure report filed by the Microsoft Corporation related to its own lobbying in connection with a particular bill:

Registrant	MICROSOFT CORPORATION	Client Name	MICROSOFT CORPORATION

LOBBYING ACTIVITY. Select as many codes as necessary to reflect the general issue areas in which the registrant engaged in lobbying on behalf of the client during the reporting period. Using a separate page for each code, provide information as requested. Attach additional page(s) as needed.

15. General issue area code	SCI	Science/Technology	(one per page)

16. Specific lobbying issues

HR 28, High-Performance Computing Revitalization Act of 2005.
HR 2862, Science, State, Justice, Commerce, and Related Agencies Appropriations Act of 2006.
American Competitiveness Initiative

17. House(s) of Congress and Federal agencies   Check if None   ✓ House ✓ Senate ✓ Other

Department of Commerce, Executive Office of the President, National Science Foundation, Department of Energy

Note what is absent from the reporting requirements. We do not know whether Microsoft supported or opposed the listed legislation or wanted particular additions to or removals from the bill; who in the House, Senate, Executive Office of the President, Department of Commerce, Department of Energy, or National Science Foundation was lobbied; how much Microsoft spent on this aspect of its lobbying (although the year-end report from which this excerpt came indicates that Microsoft spent $4 million that year on its own lobbying—not counting what it paid to hire lobbyists

---

15. Anita S. Krishnakumar, *Toward a Madisonian, Interest-Group Based, Approach to Lobbying Regulation*, 58 Ala. L. Rev. 513, 520 (2007).
16. *Id.* at 521.

outside the company); or how much contact Microsoft had with legislators, staffers, or executive officials on this question (or any other question). In the end, the disclosure reports tell us very little.

In 2007, Congress again revisited lobbying regulation, prompted in large part by a scandal involving lobbyist Jack Abramoff. "Among other exploits, Abramoff arranged lavish trips to the United Kingdom and South Pacific for [former House Majority Leader Tom] Delay; one such outing involved an outlay of $70,000 to pay for DeLay, his wife, and two aides to visit Scotland and play golf at the famous St. Andrews Links. He also allegedly enriched himself at the expense of various Native American tribes he represented; at one point he worked both for and against a tribe with regard to approval of a casino."[17] Abramoff eventually pleaded guilty to charges of fraud, tax evasion, and conspiracy to bribe public officials.

Congress passed the Honest Leadership and Open Government Act of 2007 ("HLOGA")[18] in the wake of the Jack Abramoff scandal. HLOGA strengthened the 1995 LDA through "expanded disclosure of lobbying coalitions; a new reporting system for lobbyist contributions and disbursements to or on behalf of legislative and executive branch officials and candidates for federal office; [and] improved public access to information disclosed under the LDA and the Foreign Agents Registration Act."[19] The HLOGA made reporting more frequent and reports easier for the public to search, but it did not do anything to require more detailed information about the specific members of Congress, staff, or federal agency officials who were lobbied on particular bills or issues. It also made some other changes, discussed in the next section of this chapter.

The Supreme Court has only once ruled on constitutional issues related to disclosure of lobbying activities, and it has not yet considered any HLOGA issues.[20] In *U.S. v. Harriss*,[21] the Court held that government-compelled disclosure of lobbying information is generally constitutional. The Court, after

---

17. Susman & Luneburg, *supra*, at 32.
18. Pub. L. No. 110-81, 121 Stat. 735 (2007).
19. Susman & Luneburg, *supra*, at 37.
20. The Supreme Court thus far has not viewed the Petition Clause as providing any greater or different protection than the Free Speech Clause of the amendment. *McDonald v. Smith*, 472 U.S. 479 (1985). However, the Court recently clarified that

> [t]his Court's opinion in *McDonald* has sometimes been interpreted to mean that the right to petition can extend no further than the right to speak; but *McDonald* held only that speech contained within a petition is subject to the same standards for defamation and libel as speech outside a petition. . . . There may arise cases where the special concerns of the Petition Clause would provide a sound basis for a distinct analysis; and if that is so, the rules and principles that define the two rights might differ in emphasis and formulation.

Borough of Duryea v. Guarnieri, 131 S.Ct. 2488, 2495 (2011).
21. 347 U.S. 612 (1954).

narrowly construing the 1946 Lobbying Act, held that the state's interest in providing information to legislators justified the disclosure requirements. While *Harriss* relied on the state's interest in providing information *to lawmakers* about lobbying activities as a rationale for disclosure law, today that rationale "is at best a secondary consideration."[22] Indeed, the 1995 LDA "findings" do not mention this interest, focusing instead on public awareness of lobbyist activities and public confidence. Practically speaking, challenges to lobbying disclosure laws today are unlikely to rely on the *Harriss* discussion and more likely to be decided under campaign finance law jurisprudence about disclosure, discussed in the last chapter of this book. Recently, the Supreme Court in *Citizens United v. FEC*, a campaign finance case, cited approvingly *Harriss*'s upholding of lobbying disclosure rules.[23]

Example 3

One provision of HLOGA, section 4(b)(3), requires disclosure by any organization that contributes more than $5,000, and actively participates in, another organization's lobbying efforts. The purpose of the rule appears to be to ensure that organizations do not try to hide their lobbying activities by sending their money through another organization. The National Association of Manufacturers challenged the rule, claiming it interfered with the organization's First Amendment rights.

In *National Association of Manufacturers v. Taylor*,[24] the United States Court of Appeals for the D.C. Circuit rejected the constitutional challenge. The court held that the government had a compelling interest in revealing to the public those who were behind the funding of lobbying activities. Following campaign finance law, the appeals court held that a group could be entitled to an as-applied exemption from disclosure requirements if it could demonstrate that it would be subject to government or other harassment for revealing its lobbying activities.

In order to fully assess NAM's constitutional arguments, you first need to become familiar with the campaign finance disclosure cases, described in Chapter 15. Putting aside the constitutional question, do you think this part of HLOGA is good policy? Would you support more disclosure or less disclosure than that required by current federal disclosure law?

---

22. Elizabeth Garrett, Ronald M. Levin & Theodore Ruger, *Constitutional Issues Raised by the Lobbying Disclosure Act*, in The Lobbying Manual, *supra*, at 197, 198.

23. 558 U.S. 310, 369 (2010) ("the Court has upheld registration and disclosure requirements on lobbyists, even though Congress has no power to ban lobbying itself"); *see also McIntyre v. Ohio Elections Comm'n*, 514 U.S. 334, 356 n.20 (1995) ("[t]he activities of lobbyists who have direct access to elected representatives, if undisclosed, may well present the appearance of corruption.").

24. 582 F.3d 1 (D.C. Cir. 2009).

Explanation

Again this is a normative question with no right answer. You should consider what value disclosure might serve in informing the public about which groups and interests are behind or opposing proposed legislation, especially less obvious changes to legislation that could be very valuable to particular individuals, companies, groups, or industries.

On the other hand, disclosure could chill some groups' willingness to engage in lobbying activities, activities protected by the First Amendment freedoms of speech, association, and the right to petition the government for the redress of grievances. The courts have recognized that the Constitution requires that groups especially likely to face harassment for taking unpopular positions are entitled to an exemption from generally applicable disclosure laws, but that exemption certainly would not apply to a mainstream industry group such as NAM. Is the harassment exception enough?

To take a third perspective, one might argue that current disclosure rules provide *too little* information to the public. The public needs to know not only the general issue about which a group lobbies and the governmental body it lobbies: It should know the specific policy positions taken by the group and the specific individuals in government contacted. Such detailed disclosure would provide the public with much more information, but it also could deter more people from exercising their First Amendment rights.

3.1.3. Other Lobbying Regulations

HLOGA. In addition to making some changes to the lobbyist disclosure rules, HLOGA also (1) extended the waiting period from one year to two years for senators (though not their staffers) to work as lobbyists, (2) required reports on lobbyists' "bundling" of campaign contributions for federal candidates, and (3) banned gifts from lobbyists to members of Congress and staffers. The first requirement arguably caused Senator Trent Lott to retire from the Senate earlier than planned, so that he could begin a major lobbyist venture with former Senator John Breaux under a one-year, rather than two-year, waiting period. Representative van Hollen explained that the basis for the bundling disclosure provision was to guard against the use of bundling by a lobbyist to enhance the lobbyist's stature and thereby "exert an undue influence over public policy."[25]

Tax Laws. Federal tax laws have long touched lobbying activities. From 1915 to 1962, the Treasury Department denied business income tax deductions

---

25. 153 Cong. Rec. H9209 (daily ed. July 31, 2007).

for "lobbying expenses."[26] An amendment to the Internal Revenue Code allowed for the deduction beginning in 1962,[27] but in 1993, Congress repealed the deduction for certain lobbying expenses, including for "influencing legislation." In addition, the Internal Revenue Code bars or limits certain 501(c) organizations in their lobbying activities. Section 501(c)(3) organizations are very limited in the amount of lobbying that they do without jeopardizing their tax-exempt status.[28] Such organizations that engage in prohibited lobbying lose their tax exemption; moreover, donations to the organization are no longer deductible and the organization (along with its managers) faces additional excise taxes.[29] Social welfare organizations organized as Section 501(c)(4) organizations may operate as "action" organizations and under that organization "may have, as a primary purpose, an aim that can be only accomplished by legislation, and they may lobby without limit to accomplish such a purpose."[30] However, candidate-related activity may not become the "primary purpose" of the action organization,[31] and since the 1995 LDA, 501(c)(4) entities that engage in lobbying are ineligible for federal awards, grants and loans. Though (c)(4) organizations are tax exempt, contributions to such organizations are not deductible. Section 501(c)(3) organizations often form (c)(4) affiliates to engage in lobbying activities.[32] Given these complex rules, tax scholars have devoted considerable attention to the question of what constitutes "lobbying" for purposes of tax laws.

The Supreme Court has issued three major opinions at the intersection of tax law and lobbying law. In *Textile Mills Securities Corporation v. Commissioner of Internal Revenue*,[33] the Court upheld a Treasury Department regulation barring the deduction of lobbying costs as a business expense. It found that the regulation did not "contravene[] any congressional policy. Contracts to spread such invidious influences through legislative halls have long been condemned." Eighteen years later, in *Cammarano v.*

---

26. *See* Timothy W. Jenkins & A.L. (Lorry) Spitzer, *Internal Revenue Code Limitations on Deductibility of Lobbying Expenses by Business and Trade Associations*, in The Lobbying Manual, *supra*, at 377, 378.

27. *Id.*

28. Under that section "no substantial part of the activities of [the organization may] include carrying on propaganda, or otherwise attempting to influence legislation (except as otherwise provided in subsection (h)." Subsection (h), in turn, gives certain 501(c)(3) organizations the option of using an "expenditure test" to allow the organization to make certain lobbying expenditures within dollar or formula limits.

29. Timothy W. Jenkins & A.L. (Lorry) Spitzer, *Internal Revenue Code Limitations on Lobbying by Tax-Exempt Organizations*, in The Lobbying Manual, *supra*, at 393, 394.

30. *Id.* at 397.

31. *See* Ellen P. Aprill, *Regulating the Political Speech of Noncharitable Exempt Organizations After Citizens United*, 10 Election L.J. 363 (2011).

32. "However, it is very important that the two entities be created and maintained as separate and that the Section 501(c)(3) organization not subsidize the Section 501(c)(4) organization's lobbying activities." Jenkins & Spitzer, *supra*, at 397.

33. 314 U.S. 326 (1941).

United States,[34] the Court rejected, among other arguments, a First Amendment challenge to non-deductibility rules for business lobbying expenses. "Petitioners are not being denied a tax deduction because they engage in constitutionally protected activities, but are simply being required to pay for those activities entirely out of their own pockets." The Court explained that the tax treatment was valid based upon Congress's determination that "since purchased publicity can influence the fate of legislation that will affect, directly or indirectly, all in the community, everyone in the community should stand on the same footing as regards its purchase so far as the Treasury of the United States is concerned." In *Regan v. Taxation with Representation of Washington,*[35] a nonprofit ideological group that wished to engage in lobbying activities but keep its 501(c)(3) tax-exempt status argued that the lobbying prohibition on such groups violated its First Amendment rights. Explaining that both tax exemptions and tax deductions are a form of government subsidy, the Supreme Court held that there was no First Amendment violation. Relying on its earlier opinion in *Cammarano,* the Court held that Congress's failure to subsidize lobbying through its tax laws did not amount to a First Amendment violation. "It appears that Congress was concerned that exempt organizations might use tax-deductible contributions to lobby to promote the private interests of their members. It is not irrational for Congress to decide that tax-exempt charities . . . should not further benefit at the expense of taxpayers at large by obtaining a further subsidy for lobbying."[36]

State Laws.   States vary widely in their approach to lobbying. Many states have long imposed various limitations or bans on campaign contributions, at least during some time periods, by lobbyists to elected officials. A few states bar lobbyists from serving fundraising roles in campaigns. Forty-three states ban contingent fee lobbying, whereby lobbyists receive a percentage of any contracts a lobbyist helps procure for a client.[37] Many states also impose some kind of anti–revolving door provision. These vary along three dimensions: temporally (typically one or two years following government service), the nature of the lobbying restriction (sometimes the restrictions are limited only to matters in which the elected official or staff member was involved in while in government), and whether it applies only to lobbying for compensation.

---

34. 358 U.S. 498 (1959).
35. 461 U.S. 540 (1983).
36. *Id.* at 550. Justice Blackmun, for himself and Justices Brennan and Marshall, stated his belief that lobbying is an activity protected by the First Amendment, and that the only reason the tax provision did not impose an unconstitutional condition upon 501(c)(3) organizations is the ease with which they could create a 501(c)(4) affiliate. *Id.* at 551-553 (Blackmun, J., concurring).
37. *See Ethics: Contingency Fees for Lobbyists,* NATIONAL CONFERENCE OF STATE LEGISLATURES, http://www.ncsl.org/default.aspx?tabid=15351.

Obama Administration Rules. After taking office in 2009, President Obama rolled out a series of new lobbying regulations that, among other things, provided that (1) lobbyists could not communicate orally with the administration regarding the economic stimulus package;[38] (2) absent a waiver, lobbyists could not serve as a presidential appointee;[39] (3) no one working for the administration could lobby the Obama administration for the remainder of the administration's term in office;[40] and (4) lobbyists could not be appointed to federal advisory panels.[41] These new rules provoked controversy among lobbyists and others in Washington. Facing some criticism of these lobbying rules, the administration changed some aspects of the presidential directive on communications over the stimulus package, applying it beyond registered lobbyists but narrowing the time frame to which it applied. Its ban on lobbyists serving on advisory panels is currently in litigation before the United States Court of Appeals for the D.C. Circuit.[42] The government defended the ban on grounds of reducing the influence of "special interests," preserving voter confidence in government, and ensuring that the government gets advice from those other than people routinely giving the government input.

New Proposals to Limit Lobbyist Fundraising. An American Bar Association task force on lobbying, of which I was a member, advocated that limits be placed on the fundraising activities of Congress.[43] So far Congress has not acted on the recommendation.

Constitutionality of These Other Lobbying Laws. Though the Supreme Court has not considered the constitutionality of other types of lobbying laws, lower courts have ruled upon a number of challenges. In the past, most courts have tended to uphold lobbying regulations. Courts have upheld bans on lobbyist contributions to legislators,[44] bans on lobbyist contingency

---

38. President Barack Obama, Memorandum of March 20, 2009: *Ensuring Responsible Spending of Recovery Act Funds*, 74 Fed. Reg. 12,531 (Mar. 25, 2009).

39. Executive Order No. 13490, 74 Fed. Reg. 4,673 (Jan. 26, 2009) sets forth the rules, as well as the provisions for obtaining a waiver.

40. Id. For an overview of the Obama initiatives, *see* James A. Thurber, *Changing the Way Washington Works? Assessing President Obama's Battle with Lobbyists*, 41 PRESIDENTIAL STUD. Q. 358 (2011).

41. President Barack Obama, *Presidential Memorandum: Lobbyists on Agency Boards and Commissions*, June 18, 2010, http://www.whitehouse.gov/the-press-office/presidential-memorandum-lobbyists-agency-boards-and-commissions.

42. The district court rejected the lobbyists' challenge. *Autor v. Blank*, 892 F. Supp. 2d 264 (D.D.C. 2012).

43. *See* Task Force on Federal Lobbying Laws, *Lobbying Law in the Spotlight: Challenges and Proposed Improvements*, AMERICAN BAR ASSOCIATION (2011), http://www.americanbar.org/content/dam/aba/migrated/2011_build/administrative_law/lobbying_task_force_report_010311.authcheckdam.pdf.

44. *Kimbell v. Hooper*, 164 A.2d 44 (Vt. 1995); *N.C. Right to Life v. Bartlett*, 168 F.3d 705 (4th Cir. 1999); *State v. Alaska Civil Liberties Union*, 978 P.2d 597 (Alaska 1999); *Inst. of Governmental Advocates v. Fair Political Practices Comm'n*, 164 F. Supp. 2d 1183 (E.D. Cal. 2001); *Preston v. Leake*, 660 F.3d 726 (4th Cir. 2011).

fees,[45] anti–revolving door statutes,[46] and restrictions on lobbyists' serving on campaign committees[47] or bundling campaign contributions.[48]

However, constitutional questions related to limits on lobbying activities may have begun to shift since the Supreme Court's important campaign finance decision in *Citizens United v. FEC*, discussed in detail in Chapter 13. *Citizens United* rejected equality or leveling the playing field arguments to limit campaign spending, and offered a narrow definition of "corruption" to justify campaign finance laws.

In *Green Party of Connecticut v. Garfield*,[49] the United States Court of Appeals for the Second Circuit struck down two provisions of Connecticut law related to lobbyists. First, the court struck down as a First Amendment violation a ban on campaign contributions to state elected officials imposed on state-registered lobbyists and their families. The court similarly rejected a law banning lobbyists from collecting campaign contributions for elected officials. In *Brinkman v. Budish*,[50] a federal district court struck down on First Amendment grounds a law barring former members of the state assembly and their staff from lobbying the state assembly for a year after leaving the assembly. It remains to be seen whether these cases are the start of a new trend.

Example 4

What purposes, aside from disclosure, might lobbying laws serve? How should courts balance those purposes against First Amendment rights of speech, association, and petition?

Explanation

These lobbying laws may serve different purposes. The tax laws seem geared to deny government benefits (such as deductibility) for groups' political activities. Limits on lobbyist involvement in executive branch decision making seem aimed at preventing lobbyists from having too much influence and in preserving public confidence in government. Limits on lobbyist fundraising and anti–revolving door laws may be

---

45. *Associated Indus. of Ky. v. Commonwealth*, 912 S.W.2d 947, 951 (Ky. 1995); *Fla. League of Prof'l Lobbyists v. Meggs*, 87 F.3d 457, 462 (11th Cir. 1996); *but see Mont. Auto. Ass'n v. Greely*, 632 P.2d 300 (Mont. 1981).

46. *United States v. Nasser*, 476 F.2d 1111, 1115 (7th Cir. 1973).

47. *Md. Right to Life State Political Action Comm. v. Wathersbee*, 975 F.Supp. 791, 797-798 (D. Md. 1997).

48. *Preston, supra*.

49. 616 F.3d 189 (2d Cir. 2010).

50. 692 F.Supp.2d 855 (S.D. Ohio 2010).

justified on similar grounds. A public choice theorist might also argue in favor of these limits to minimize the power of lobbyists to assist their clients in pursuing economically inefficient (or rent-seeking) activities.

Which rationales along these lines would survive scrutiny before the Supreme Court that decided *Citizens United* is unclear. Reducing the power of special interests sounds as though it may be offering an impermissible political equality rationale for some of these laws, and it is not clear whether the laws may be justified on the narrow anti-corruption rationale recognized in *Citizens United*. Laws that merely seek to deny a government subsidy for lobbying, such as the tax laws, appear to stand on stronger constitutional footing.

3.2. BRIBERY AND RELATED OFFENSES

3.2.1. The Elements of Bribery

A bribe occurs when someone corruptly gives or offers to give a government official or employee or when a government official or employee takes or agrees to take anything of value with the intent of allowing the receipt of that thing to influence official action.[51] Federal law bars bribery

---

51. The relevant portion of the federal bribery statute, 18 U.S.C. §201(b), reads

Whoever—

(1) directly or indirectly, corruptly gives, offers or promises anything of value to any public official or person who has been selected to be a public official, or offers or promises any public official or any person who has been selected to be a public official to give anything of value to any other person or entity, with intent—

(A) to influence any official act; or

(B) to influence such public official or person who has been selected to be a public official to commit or aid in committing, or collude in, or allow, any fraud, or make opportunity for the commission of any fraud, on the United States; or

(C) to induce such public official or such person who has been selected to be a public official to do or omit to do any act in violation of the lawful duty of such official or person;

(2) being a public official or person selected to be a public official, directly or indirectly, corruptly demands, seeks, receives, accepts, or agrees to receive or accept anything of value personally or for any other person or entity, in return for:

(A) being influenced in the performance of any official act;

(B) being influenced to commit or aid in committing, or to collude in, or allow, any fraud, or make opportunity for the commission of any fraud, on the United States; or

(C) being induced to do or omit to do any act in violation of the official duty of such official or person. . .

shall be fined under this title or not more than three times the monetary equivalent of the thing of value, whichever is greater, or imprisoned for not more than fifteen years, or both, and may be disqualified from holding any office of honor, trust, or profit under the United States.

concerning federal officials and employees, and various state laws bar it concerning state and local officials and employees. Furthermore, as we will see in section 3.2.3, other federal statutes sometimes allow the federal government to prosecute state and local officials for bribery and related crimes.

Consider the facts of the prosecution of former Representative Renzi, described in Chapter 2, Example 4. A jury convicted Renzi of agreeing to support (and later to "fast track") land use legislation in Congress if the supporters of the legislation agreed to purchase separate land owned by someone who owed Renzi money. The prosecution proved that the supporters of the legislation made the purchase of land from Renzi's debtor, who then turned around and paid a corporation owned by Renzi money owed to him.

Does this conduct count as a bribe under the federal statute?

There is no question that Representative Renzi at the time was a *public official*.[52] Agreeing to propose or to "fast track" land use legislation is an *official act*.[53] Promising or purchasing the land owned by Renzi's debtor should count as *anything of value* under the statute; Renzi personally stood to gain from his debtor getting a land deal. The facts may also indicate (more below) an *intent to influence* Renzi in doing an official act: If the facts as alleged are proven, Renzi required the purchase of his debtor's land in order to push the legislation through Congress; those desiring the legislation agreed to purchase the debtor's land in order to get Renzi to push the legislation through Congress. Note that none of these factors required proof that Renzi actually introduced the legislation (or even that money changed hands). Such proof could violate the Speech or Debate Clause (discussed in Chapter 2).

Now consider the fact that for this set of actions to count as a bribe, the intent to offer or accept the thing of value must be done "corruptly." What

---

52. 18 U.S.C. §201(a):

> For the purpose of this section —
> (1) the term "public official" means Member of Congress, Delegate, or Resident Commissioner, either before or after such official has qualified, or an officer or employee or person acting for or on behalf of the United States, or any department, agency or branch of Government thereof, including the District of Columbia, in any official function, under or by authority of any such department, agency, or branch of Government, or a juror. . . .

53. 18 U.S.C. §201(a):

> For the purpose of this section — . . .
> (3) the term "official act" means any decision or action on any question, matter, cause, suit, proceeding or controversy, which may at any time be pending, or which may by law be brought before any public official, in such official's official capacity, or in such official's place of trust or profit.

does the "corrupt" element add to all of this? Daniel Lowenstein, one of the leading writers in election law (and especially on the law of bribery) has argued that corrupt intent is not a factual element of the crime of bribery (like the other elements), but it instead requires jurors to make a normative judgment about the wrongfulness of the conduct:[54] "'[C]orruptly' need not be regarded as a redundancy but . . . it functions differently from the other elements, which describe 'factual' aspects of actions constituting bribes. The element of corrupt intent requires that the facts described by the other elements be subject to characterization as wrongful and thus requires the application, implicitly or explicitly, of normative political standards." To understand what Lowenstein means, try the next example and read the explanation.

Example 5

A city councilmember sends a note to the commissioner of street cleaning complaining about the firing of Mr. Covino as a driver. In response, the commissioner sends a letter stating that the department is short on funds for equipment and drivers. If the city council provided more money for the department, "this would give more employment to more drivers, and as the heavy season comes on, having made a note of your favorable recommendation, the case of Covino will be reconsidered." In reply, the councilmember wrote: "If you will reinstate Antonio Covino, who I think was too severely punished by being dismissed from your department, I will vote and otherwise help you to obtain the money needed for a new plant."

The city's bribery law is similar to federal law. Is the councilmember guilty of bribery?

Explanation

The facts come from a famous bribery case, *People ex rel. Dickinson v. Van de Carr*.[55] Let's begin by clearing away the easy questions. The councilmember is a *public official*, and the councilmember's intent to vote for and support more money for the Department of Street Cleaning would be an *official act*. Furthermore, it appears that the commissioner offered and the councilmember agreed to consider an official act in order to get Mr. Covino reinstated, such reinstatement thus being offered with the *intent to influence* the councilmember's official act, and it appears the councilmember *intended* to act in exchange for Mr. Covino being rehired.

---

54. Daniel H. Lowenstein, *Political Bribery and the Intermediate Theory of Politics*, 32 UCLA L. Rev. 784 (1985).
55. 84 N.Y.S. 461 (N.Y. App. Div. 1903).

Was this a promise to reconsider or to rehire Mr. Covino *anything of value* redounding to the benefit of the councilmember? We probably need more facts to answer this question. Suppose, for example, that Mr. Covino was a constituent of the councilmember, who complained to the councilmember that he was unfairly fired from his job. In that case, at best the councilmember would be seeking a political benefit rather than a personal benefit. (In contrast, imagine if Mr. Covino promised money to the councilmember if he got his job back. That would look more like a personal benefit.)

It is not clear whether political benefits should count as *anything of value* for purpose of bribery statutes. If it did, imagine the number of prosecutions that could be brought for legislative logrolls. (Some states even have laws against logrolls, which are "rarely enforced."[56])

But even if such political benefits count as *anything of value* for purpose of the bribery statutes, the *corrupt* intent element ensures that juries have the ability to not convict in a bribery prosecution allowing for the exchange of political benefits. If Mr. Covino was a constituent who believed he was fired unfairly, then a jury could well determine there was nothing wrong with the councilmember's conduct; a jury hearing about money going from Mr. Covino into the councilmember's pocket would have less trouble finding the councilmember's conduct to be wrongful.

3.2.2. More on Intent to Influence: Campaign Contributions as Bribes

One recurring and knotty question in the law of bribery is when can campaign contributions count as bribes?[57] Consider the following scenario: John gives Senator X a campaign contribution of $2,500 (the maximum allowed by law) and gives $1 million to an independent "Super PAC" supporting Senator X.[58] John then says to Senator X, I hope you'll take a very close look at the new farm bill, which I am supporting. John gives the money hoping it will induce Senator X to vote for the farm bill. Senator X expresses gratitude for the support. Senator X tells his or her legislative aide that he or she plans to vote for the farm bill because of John's support (testimony that could well be barred by the

---

56. DANIEL H. LOWENSTEIN, RICHARD L. HASEN, & DANIEL P. TOKAJI, ELECTION LAW — CASES AND MATERIALS 613 (5th ed. 2012). (citing Cal. Penal Code §86); *see also People v. Montgomery*, 61 Cal. App. 3d 718 (Cal. Ct. App. 1976).This casebook will be cited in the rest of this book as LOWENSTEIN, HASEN, & TOKAJI.
57. This section draws heavily on Daniel H. Lowenstein, *When Is a Campaign Contribution a Bribe?* in PUBLIC AND PRIVATE CORRUPTION 127 (William C. Heffernan & John Kleinig eds., 2004).
58. More on these Super PACs in Chapter 14.

Speech or Debate Clause). Has John bribed Senator X, and has Senator X accepted a bribe?

If this behavior counts as a bribe, there may be a whole lot of bribery going on in Washington, D.C.! This looks like business as usual and the kind of thing that is inevitable in a system of private campaign financing wherein many of those donating money are doing so in pursuit of a legislative strategy (giving money to advance a particular legislative program). Senator X is a *public official* and voting on the farm bill is an *official act*. A campaign contribution appears to be *anything of value* under the statute. John gave the money with the *intent to influence* Senator X's vote on the farm bill, and perhaps a jury would say that Senator X accepted John's money *intending to be influenced* by the contributions to himself or herself and to the independent super PAC.

It is possible we might try to resolve this question by stating that John did not give his contribution *corruptly* in that exchanges of campaign contributions for legislative positions is a political benefit or otherwise not normatively objectionable. But on this question of corruption, juries may differ. Some juries may view the John–Senator X exchange as corrupt, and other juries may not. With such uncertainty and the vagaries of juries, it is possible that there could be many prosecutions under bribery laws of elected officials, and some of those prosecutions could be politically motivated by prosecutors who want to go after political enemies.

One possible solution to this problem is to require prosecutors to prove an explicit *quid pro quo* between John and Senator X to meet the *intent to influence* requirement for bribery prosecutions when campaign contributions are involved. Thus, the example treated above could not count as a bribe (even if jurors believed it "corrupt"), because there was never any explicit statement from John and Senator X agreeing to a deal (as in: "I will give these contributions if you vote for the farm bill." "Okay, I'll do it."). This possible solution raises three issues.

First, not all *quids pro quo* will be bribes. An express agreement to give serious consideration to John's position on the farm bill likely would not count as a bribe, either on grounds that it is *not corrupt* or perhaps that giving careful consideration to John's position is not an *official act*.

Second, limiting bribery prosecutions to explicit *quids pro quo* might leave out prosecutions in which the parties appear to have acted corruptly but there is no express agreement. What if there are just "winks and nods" about the agreement, as when John hands over the checks and says, "I hope you'll do the *right thing*," and Senator X replies, "You know I will"?

Third, and most significant, the federal bribery statute (reprinted in footnote 51) speaks only of an "intent to influence" and does not include a requirement of an explicit *quid pro quo*. It is not clear that reading in a *quid pro quo* requirement — especially if done only for campaign contributions — is a fair act of statutory interpretation. In a confused opinion in *United States v.*

Brewster,[59] the United States Court of Appeals for the D.C. Circuit wrote that the federal bribery statute (unlike the illegal gratuity statute, which we discuss in the next section) requires a *quid pro quo*. The Supreme Court has not addressed the issue under the bribery statute, but in a prosecution under the Hobbs Act for extortion, the Court did require an explicit quid pro quo. Justice White wrote for the Court

> Serving constituents and supporting legislation that will benefit the district and individuals and groups therein is the everyday business of a legislator. It is also true that campaigns must be run and financed. Money is constantly being solicited on behalf of candidates, who run on platforms and who claim support on the basis of their views and what they intend to do or have done. Whatever ethical considerations and appearances may indicate, to hold that legislators commit the federal crime of extortion when they act for the benefit of constituents or support legislation furthering the interests of some of their constituents, shortly before or after campaign contributions are solicited and received from those beneficiaries, is an unrealistic assessment of what Congress could have meant by making it a crime to obtain property from another, with his consent, "under color of official right." To hold otherwise would open to prosecution not only conduct that has long been thought to be well within the law but also conduct that in a very real sense is unavoidable so long as election campaigns are financed by private contributions or expenditures, as they have been from the beginning of the Nation. It would require statutory language more explicit than the Hobbs Act contains to justify a contrary conclusion.[60]

Following this *McCormick* case, the Supreme Court in *Evans v. United States*[61] somewhat confused the issue, at least in Hobbs Act cases. The Court seemed to back off the explicit *quid pro quo* requirement, endorsing instead an "in return for" standard (at least outside the context of campaign contributions). Furthermore, Justice Kennedy in a separate concurring and dissenting opinion wrote, "The official and the payor need not state the *quid pro quo* in express terms, for otherwise the law's effect could be frustrated by knowing winks and nods. The inducement from the official is criminal if it is express or if it is implied from his words and actions, so long as he intends it to be so and the payor so interprets it."

Whether or not an explicit *quid pro quo* remains required in Hobbs Act cases, and whether or not an *explicit* quid pro quo can be *implicit* (!), as Justice Kennedy implies, it is not clear that these Hobbs Act ruling would apply in the context of a federal bribery prosecution. The Supreme Court recently declined the opportunity to consider the question in a high-profile prosecution of

---

59. 506 F.2d 62 (D.C. Cir. 1974).
60. *McCormick v. United States*, 500 U.S. 257, 272-273 (1991).
61. 504 U.S. 255 (1992).

Alabama Governor Donald Siegelman.[62] A federal district court in U.S. v. McGregor[63] recently set forth a very helpful clarification of the debate in the lower courts on these issues. Judge Myron Thompson, who wrote the opinion, concluded

> It is often true that "unexamined assumptions have a way of becoming, by force of usage, unsound law." *McCormick* (Scalia, J., concurring). In the public-corruption context, courts have been particularly lax in the use of certain words — explicit, express, agreement, promise, and quid pro quo — that should have clear legal meanings. Imprecise diction has caused considerable confusion over the scope of federal corruption laws as applied to campaign contributions. Uncertainty in this area of law breeds corruption and chills legitimate political speech.
>
> Much ink has been spilled over the contours of campaign finance law. Far less attention has been paid to what actually constitutes a "bribe." A precise definition of "bribery" could bring coherence to campaign finance jurisprudence, as the government's interest in curbing corruption is now the sole basis for placing limits on campaign contributions. *See Citizens United v.* FEC (rejecting the anti-distortion rationale for campaign finance restrictions).
>
> The court hopes that its jury instructions and this opinion have helped clarify the case law. Ultimately, the Supreme Court needs to address this issue and provide guidance to lower courts, prosecutors, politicians, donors, and the general public.

In the *McGregor* case, following Judge Thompson's instructions, all the defendants were acquitted on all counts.

Example 6

Consider the following facts from the *Siegelman* case, which will give you a sense of the types of prosecutions for bribery that have become increasingly common:

> Don Siegelman was elected Governor of Alabama in 1998 on a campaign platform that advocated the establishment of a state lottery to help fund education in Alabama. After his election, he established the Alabama Education Lottery Foundation to raise money to campaign for voter approval of a ballot initiative to establish a state lottery. Darren Cline, the Foundation's fundraising director, testified that Siegelman "called the shots" on the lottery campaign. The lottery initiative was eventually defeated in a referendum held in October of 1999. On March 9, 2000, the Foundation borrowed $730,789.29 from an Alabama bank in order to pay down debt incurred by the Alabama Democratic

---

62. U.S. v. *Siegelman*, 640 F.3d 1159 (11th Cir. 2011), *cert. denied*, 132 S.Ct. 2711 and 132 S.Ct. 2712 (2012).
63. 879 F. Supp. 2d 1308 (M.D. Ala. 2012).

Party for get-out-the-vote expenses during the lottery campaign. This note was personally and unconditionally guaranteed by Siegelman.

Richard Scrushy, the CEO of HealthSouth had served on the CON Board under three previous governors of Alabama. The CON Board is an arm of the State Health Planning and Development Agency and exists to prevent unnecessary duplication of healthcare services in Alabama. The Board determines the number of healthcare facilities in Alabama through a process that requires healthcare providers to apply for and obtain a certificate of a healthcare need before opening a new facility or offering a special healthcare service. The CON Board decides which healthcare applications will be approved for an announced healthcare need, choosing between competing applications and ruling on objections filed by an applicant's competitor. The Governor of Alabama has sole discretion to appoint the members of the CON Board, who serve at his pleasure. Scrushy had supported Siegelman's opponent in the just prior election.

Nick Bailey was one of Siegelman's closest associates and had worked on Siegelman's campaign for governor. Cline testified that "whatever [Bailey] told me that the Governor wanted was what the Governor said." Cline also testified that "if the Governor wanted to get something done, then [Bailey] went ahead — blindly went ahead and did it."

Bailey testified that, after Siegelman's election in 1998, Siegelman met with Eric Hanson, an outside lobbyist for HealthSouth, and told Hanson that because Scrushy had contributed at least $350,000 to Siegelman's opponent in the election, Scrushy needed to "do" at least $500,000 in order to "make it right" with the Siegelman campaign. Bailey testified that Siegelman was referring to the campaign for the lottery initiative, and that Hanson was to relay this conversation to Scrushy. Bailey also testified that, in another conversation, Hanson told Bailey that Scrushy wanted control of the CON Board.

Mike Martin is the former Chief Financial Officer of HealthSouth. He testified that having influence over the CON Board was important to Scrushy and Health-South because it determined the number of healthcare facilities in the state, thereby affecting HealthSouth's ability to grow. He testified that Scrushy told him that to "have some influence or a spot on the CON Board," they had to help Siegelman raise money for the lottery campaign. Scrushy said that if they did so, "[they] would be assured a seat on the CON Board." Martin testified, "[W]e were making a contribution . . . in exchange for a spot on the CON Board."

Bailey testified that lobbyist Hanson "made it clear to him that if Mr. Scrushy gave the $500,000 to the lottery campaign that we could not let him down" with respect to the CON Board seat. Bailey also testified that he "reminded the Governor periodically of the conversations that [Bailey] had with Eric Hanson and the conversations that the Governor had with Eric Hanson about what Mr. Scrushy wanted for his contributions, and that was the CON Board."

Martin also testified that Scrushy told him that HealthSouth could not make the payment to the lottery campaign, nor could he do it personally because "we [HealthSouth] had not supported that and that his wife, Leslie, was against the lottery, and it would just look bad if HealthSouth made a direct contribution to the lottery, so we needed to ask — he instructed me in particular to ask our investment banker, Bill McGahan, from [the Swiss bank] UBS, to make the contribution."

Bill McGahan did not want to make such an "out of the norm" donation and hoped the matter would "go away." Over the next two weeks, Martin called McGahan at least once a day to ask him about the status of the UBS donation, and told McGahan that Scrushy was going to fire UBS if it did not make the contribution. Finally, Martin testified, Scrushy himself called McGahan to "put more pressure" on him to make the contribution.

McGahan testified that he did not want UBS to make such a large contribution directly, so he told Martin that he would get Integrated Health Services ("IHS") of Maryland to make the donation to the lottery campaign in exchange for UBS reducing an outstanding fee that IHS owed UBS. IHS agreed to this arrangement and donated $250,000 to the Foundation in exchange for a reduction of $267,000 in the fee it owed UBS.

The IHS "donation" was in the form of a check dated July 19, 1999, made payable from itself to the Foundation. Martin testified that Scrushy told him it was important that he, Scrushy, hand deliver the IHS check to Siegelman, so Martin delivered the check to Scrushy so that he could do so.

Some time later, Siegelman and Scrushy met in Siegelman's office. Bailey testified that after Scrushy left, Siegelman showed the IHS check to Bailey and told him that Scrushy was "halfway there." Bailey asked, "what in the world is he [Scrushy] going to want for that?" Siegelman replied, "the CON Board." Bailey then asked, "I wouldn't think that would be a problem, would it?" Siegelman responded, "I wouldn't think so."

Siegelman appointed Scrushy to the CON Board on July 26, 1999 — one week after the date on the IHS check. . . .

The district court in this case instructed the jury that they could not convict the defendants of bribery in this case unless "the defendant and the official *agree* that the official will take specific action in exchange for the thing of value." (emphasis added). [The jury convicted the defendants]. Defendants, however, assert that this instruction was inadequate under *McCormick*. Defendants assert [on appeal] that the instruction failed to tell the jury that not only must they find that Siegelman and Scrushy agreed to a *quid pro quo*, the CON Board seat for the donation, but that this agreement had to be *express*.

How should the appeals court rule on the defendants' arguments?

Explanation

The Eleventh Circuit rejected the defendants' arguments about *McCormick* and the applicable standard:

We disagree that *McCormick* requires such an instruction.

McCormick uses the word "explicit" when describing the sort of agreement that is required to convict a defendant for extorting campaign contributions. Explicit, however, does not mean *express*. Defendants argue that only "proof of actual conversations by defendants," will do, suggesting in their brief that only *express* words of promise overheard by third parties or by means of electronic surveillance will do.

But *McCormick* does not impose such a stringent standard. One year after *McCormick* the Supreme Court approved the following jury instruction:

> However, if a public official demands or accepts money in exchange for [a] specific requested exercise of his or her official power, such a demand or acceptance does constitute a violation of the [federal extortion statute] regardless of whether the payment is made in the form of a campaign contribution.

Evans. The Court held that the instruction "satisfies the *quid pro quo* requirement of *McCormick*." The Court said that the "Government need only show that a public official has obtained a payment to which he was not entitled, knowing that the payment was made in return for official acts."

The instruction approved in *Evans* required that the acceptance of the campaign donation be in return for a *specific* official action — a *quid pro quo.* No generalized expectation of some future favorable action will do. The official must agree to take or forego some specific action in order for the doing of it to be criminal under [the applicable bribery statute]. In the absence of such an agreement on a specific action, even a close-in-time relationship between the donation and the act will not suffice.

But there is no requirement that this agreement be memorialized in a writing, or even, as defendants suggest, be overheard by a third party. Since the agreement is for some specific action or inaction, the agreement must be *explicit*, but there is no requirement that it be *express*. To hold otherwise, as Justice Kennedy noted in *Evans* would allow defendants to escape criminal liability through "knowing winks and nods." Furthermore, an explicit agreement may be "implied from [the official's] words and actions." *Evans* (Kennedy, J., concurring). . . .

In this case, the jury was instructed that they could not convict the defendants of bribery unless they found that "the Defendant and official agree[d] that the official will take *specific* action in *exchange* for the thing of value." This instruction required the jury to find an agreement to exchange a specific official action for a campaign contribution. Finding this fact would satisfy *McCormick*'s requirement for an explicit agreement involving a *quid pro quo.* Therefore, even assuming a *quid pro quo* instruction is required to convict the defendants under [the statute], we find no reversible error in the bribery instructions given by the district court. Furthermore, the evidence of a corrupt agreement between Siegelman and Scrushy to exchange the CON Board seat for a campaign donation was sufficient to permit a reasonable juror to find such a *quid pro quo.*

Despite strong certiorari petitions supported by amicus briefs from a large group of former attorneys general, the Supreme Court declined to hear the *Siegelman* case.

3.2.3. Related Offenses

Bribery prosecutions are not the only way that the government prosecutes those who seek to improperly influence governmental action. This section considers a few other types of prosecutions.

Illegal Gratuities.   We have already examined the main federal bribery statute, contained in 18 U.S.C. 201(b). The same statute, in subsection (c) makes it a crime to give or accept an illegal gratuity.[64] The language is similar to the bribery statute, but it does not require proof of corrupt intent, may be brought against a former official, and requires proof of something of value being given "for or because of any illegal act."

As written, the section would seem to criminalize routine behavior. Lowenstein gives the example of someone who writes to members of Congress urging them to vote a certain way on a bill, and then sends each a $25 donation after they vote in that way, to show his or her appreciation for how the member of Congress voted. He notes that the conduct would appear to be criminal under the illegal gratuities statute, but that's a result that cannot be right. Lowenstein suggests that campaign contributions be expressly exempt from these statutes, or that the statutes be interpreted so that campaign contributions are not considered "anything of value."

In *United States v. Sun-Diamond Growers of California*,[65] the Supreme Court considered an illegal gratuities prosecution based upon gifts that an agricultural trade association gave to former Secretary of Agriculture Mike Espy, including $2,300 in tickets to the U.S. Open tennis tournament and $2,400 in luggage. The group apparently gave the gifts to curry favor with Espy generally, not because of any particular action he took. (On other limits on gifts, *see* section 3.3.)

The Court held that it was not enough to prove that someone gave the gifts (or an elected official accepted the gifts) as a way of building goodwill. Instead,

---

64. It provides in part:

(c) Whoever —
   (1) otherwise than as provided by law for the proper discharge of official duty —
   (A) directly or indirectly gives, offers, or promises anything of value to any public official, former public official, or person selected to be a public official, for or because of any official act performed or to be performed by such public official, former public official, or person selected to be a public official; or
   (B) being a public official, former public official, or person selected to be a public official, otherwise than as provided by law for the proper discharge of official duty, directly or indirectly demands, seeks, receives, accepts, or agrees to receive or accept anything of value personally for or because of any official act performed or to be performed by such official or person . . .
shall be fined under this title or imprisoned for not more than two years, or both.

65. 526 U.S. 398 (1999).

there must be some connection between the gifts and an official act: "the government must prove a link between a thing of value conferred upon a public official and a specific 'official act' for or because of which it is given."

Other Federal Statutes.   We have already seen in our discussion of the *McCormick* and *Evans* cases that the federal government sometimes prosecutes state and local individuals under the Hobbs Act for extortion under color of state right. The Hobbs Act is one of a number of statutes under which the federal government prosecutes state and local corruption; the normal federal bribery statute, 18 U.S.C. §201, applies only to federal officials. Federal prosecutors use the Hobbs Act and other statutes to go after state and local corruption. Other statutes also include mail fraud, wire fraud, and RICO claims. The details of these prosecutions are beyond the scope of this book.[66] One of the most controversial aspects of the mail and wire fraud statutes is application of 18 U.S.C. §1341, which allows the federal government to prosecute someone engaged in a "scheme to defraud [which includes a scheme or artifice to deprive another of the intangible rights to honest services]." This term is hardly clear, and Justice Scalia and others have taken the position that it is unconstitutionally vague. In *Skilling v. United States*,[67] the Supreme Court, to avoid vagueness problems with the statute, interpreted it to apply only to claims of bribery and kickbacks. There remain questions about whether and what kind of quid pro quo might be required under these statutes as well.

Example 7

Thought question: Bribery-like statutes such as those allowing for prosecution of honest services fraud give the federal government great power to go after state and local officials for corruption. What are the costs and benefits of federal prosecution in this area?

Explanation

The benefits are pretty clear. State and local prosecutors may not be willing or able to prosecute local corruption. The federal government is not involved in the same way in local politics, and has considerable resources to go after corrupt politicians. Some of the most important corruption scandals in the modern era have been uncovered by federal investigations and prosecuted by federal prosecutors.

---

66. State and local prosecutors may also use state and local law to prosecute bribery directly.
67. 561 U.S. 358 (2010).

But there are costs to federal prosecutions as well. To begin with, there are federalism costs. Particularly in light of the uncertainties surrounding corruption and bribery standards, federal prosecutors will be imposing their own standard on what might properly be a decision left to state and local government.

More ominously, federal prosecutions may be motivated either by federal prosecutors either with a partisan axe to grind or who want to make a name by going after a prominent local politician. Recent corruption cases involving former U.S. Senators Ted Stevens and John Edwards, as well as the prosecution of former Alabama governor Don Siegelman, have led to charges of selective prosecution and unfair charges brought for political gain. Although such charges may or may not have merit in the particular prosecutions, the danger of unfairness is real, especially given the murkiness of some of the legal standards, and the line separating normal politics from corruption and illegality.

3.3. ETHICS AND GIFT RULES

As with the lobbying disclosure rules discussed earlier in this chapter, the rules limiting gifts and travel for senators, representatives, staffers, and executive branch officials are technical and complex. I do not cover the details here.[68] Instead, I sketch only the basic points.

Gifts. The House and Senate have long limited the amounts that individuals may spend on gifts to members of the House and Senate and their staffers. An individual can give a gift of no more than $50 and a total of gifts aggregating to no more than $100 per year. HLOGA tightened up the rules and completely barred gifts from lobbyists. The gift rules are subject to some tricky exemptions (for personal friends, for example) and modifications (for gifts to family members). The rules can be funny. One exemption to the gift rule is for food of nominal value, which includes stand-up food and continental breakfasts but not hot food. The Bauer and Gordon article explains how the Senate Ethics Committee has opined on whether the doughnut exemption includes croissants and bagels. (The answer is yes.) Importantly, these rules do not stop members and candidates from attending $2,500 per plate (or more) campaign fundraising events that raise funds

---

68. For the congressional rules, *see* Robert F. Bauer & Rebecca H. Gordon, *Congressional Ethics: Gifts, Travel, Income, and Post-Employment Restrictions*, in THE LOBBYING MANUAL, *supra*, at 477. Chapter 24 of the manual covers executive rules: Kathleen Clark & Beth Nolan, *Restrictions on Gifts and Outside Compensation for Executive Branch Employees*, in THE LOBBYING MANUAL, *supra*, at 513. This section draws from these two articles.

from lobbyists and others for their own reelections or the election of other candidates.

Executive officials and employees cannot receive gifts from certain people and entities, including anyone with business before the official's agency, who conducts business with the agency, or who is regulated by the agency. (These rules are subject to an exception for gifts under $20 [with a $50 annual cap] and snack foods not part of a meal, among other exemptions.) President Obama signed an executive order banning gifts from lobbyists and lobbying organizations.

Travel.   HLOGA also tightened up the rules for congressional travel. It cannot be paid for by lobbyists, and trips by those who employ lobbyists are limited. Trips must be necessary for official duties and not just recreational. The House does not allow representatives to accept corporate jet travel, but the senate allows it under limited circumstances and subject to strict rules. High-level executive employees may not accept even reimbursement for travel expenses. Lately, to get around some of these rules, members of Congress have funded some travel from their leadership PACs, PACs that take donations from lobbyists and their clients.[69]

Outside Income and Post-Employment Restrictions.   House members and senators are generally banned from receiving honoraria for speaking about their official duties. There are many limitations on outside income, especially for members, senators, and senior staff. Members of the House may not lobby the House for one year after leaving the House; members of the Senate face a two-year post-employment ban. As noted above, a federal district court in Ohio struck the post-employment ban down as a violation of the First Amendment. The federal limits do not seem to have been challenged.

The honorarium ban for executive branch employees was found to be unconstitutional concerning lower-level employees, and the White House's Office of Legal Counsel found it unenforceable concerning all executive employees. President Obama put in place a ban on White House employees' lobbying the White House for the remainder of the Obama administration.

Example 8

A lobbyist wants to cozy up to his or her former boss, a senator. The lobbyist arranges a $10,000 per plate dinner with the senator, with $2,500 going to the senator's reelection campaign (an amount permitted by federal law) and the remaining $7,500 going to the senator's national party (again,

---

69. Eric Lipton, *A Loophole Allows Lawmakers to Reel in Trips and Donations*, N.Y. TIMES, Jan. 19, 2014, http://www.nytimes.com/2014/01/20/us/politics/a-loophole-allows-lawmakers-to-reel-in-trips-and-donations.html.

permitted by federal law). Many people sign up for the dinner thanks to the lobbyists' persistence, and the event brings in more than $1 million dollars.

The lobbyist files reports required by HLOGA about this "bundling activity." Which gift prohibition or other prohibitions does the lobbyist-organized dinner violate?

Explanation

This is a trick question meant to show you how limited the gift rules and other rules are at limiting influence over members of Congress and senators. While the gift rules are quite stingy (allowing only "finger food" for example, and not full meals, at events with members or senators), fundraising activities are exempt. Even though lobbyists may not give any gifts, they may give campaign contributions and can use their connections to organize fundraisers for members or senators. These fundraisers can be very valuable and build up goodwill, but so long as the activities are disclosed pursuant to HLOGA, they violate no law.

Direct Democracy

4.1. DIRECT DEMOCRACY AS "HYBRID DEMOCRACY"

The first three chapters of this book examined the federal legislative process, with a few references to how state legislatures or local legislative bodies sometimes differ from Congress in legislative procedures, rules, powers, and immunities. Congress, state legislatures, and city and county councils and boards are all systems of *representative government*: Voters choose legislators in elections to represent their interests in a legislative body. Legislators then make the laws, subject to approval of the executive (or override of a veto). Voters' role is indirect.

On the federal level, representative government is the entire picture. It is true that additional lawmaking happens in courts and in administrative agencies, but there is no direct federal voter governance. However, in many states and many localities — especially in the American West — *direct democracy* is available as a supplement to representative government.[1] Under direct

---

1. *See* Nathaniel A. Persily, *The Peculiar Geography of Direct Democracy: Why the Initiative, Referendum and Recall Developed in the American West*, 2 MICH. L. & POL'Y REV. 11 (1997). "About 82 percent of cities across the country allow citizens to propose and approve laws directly. Direct democracy is sometimes seen as primarily a Western phenomenon, with 97 percent of cities in the West allowing the initiative; but the process is also available in 82 percent of cities in the Northeast and the South, and 59 percent of cities in the Midwest. Fifteen of the country's 20 largest cities also allow initiatives." John Matsusaka, *A Time-Tested Part of Our Democracy*, "Room for Debate," N.Y. TIMES, Jun. 18, 2013, http://www.nytimes.com/roomfordebate/2013/06/18/ballot-initiatives-at-the-local-level/voter-initiatives-are-a-time-tested-part-of-our-democracy.

democracy, the people play a more direct role in lawmaking by collecting enough signatures to place proposed laws and other matters directly before the voters.

Jurisdictions using direct democracy give voters one or more of the following three tools. First, under the *initiative power*, voters may pass new laws directly. Second, under the *referendum power*, voters may put a legislatively passed law on hold until voters can approve or reject it. Third, under the *recall power*, voters may kick an elected official out of office (and choose a replacement) before the official's term expires. A total of 24 states allow initiatives and popular referendums; 18 states allow for the recall of state officials.[2]

In addition, sometimes state legislatures put *ballot measures* before voters, on topics such as taxes or for a vote on state constitutional amendments, which must be approved by voters before they may go into effect according to that state's constitution. In California, for example, an election may feature as many legislative ballot measures as initiatives included on the list of ballot propositions voted upon by voters. The California legislature occasionally puts measures on the ballot that *compete* with voter initiatives by presenting the legislature's proposal on the same subject.

Eight states offer the *indirect initiative*. "In the indirect initiative process, a proposed initiative is referred to the legislature after proponents have gathered the required number of signatures. The legislature has the option to enact, defeat or amend the measure. Depending on the legislature's action, the proponents may continue to pursue placement on the ballot for a popular vote."[3]

No state or large locality uses the initiative as the sole way to make laws; it is hard to imagine even a small city trying to do so in our complex society. Instead, direct democracy serves as a *supplement* to representative government. Why have such a supplement?

To begin with, the initiative process provides a way to *bypass the legislature* on matters about which the legislature will not or cannot act. Legislative inaction can happen for many reasons:

- The subject matter might be about something in which legislators' self-interest could conflict with voters' preferences. Think of laws limiting legislators' term limits, or imposing rules for redistricting or campaign financing that might hurt incumbents.
- A law might be supported by a majority of legislators and voters but blocked by a committee chair in one house or face some other vetogate

---

2. *Initiative, Referendum, and Recall*, NATIONAL CONFERENCE OF STATE LEGISLATURES, http://www.ncsl.org/legislatures-elections/elections/initiative-referendum-and-recall-overview.aspx.
3. *The Indirect Initiative*, NATIONAL CONFERENCE OF STATE LEGISLATURES, http://www.ncsl.org/legislatures-elections/elections/the-indirect-initiative.aspx.

or procedural hurdle. Or there could be a divide in the legislature or branches between Democrats and Republicans that makes it hard generally for legislation to pass.

- A law might be supported by a majority of legislators and voters but face intense opposition from a minority of legislators who feel passionately about an issue and who might threaten to withhold cooperation on other issues if the law is enacted.

In all three of these situations, the legislature for one reason or another fails to pass a law supported by a *majority of voters*. Unsurprisingly, the main rationale for the initiative process (and, to a similar extent, for the other devices of direct democracy[4]) is this idea of *majoritarianism*: The initiative process makes it more likely that the laws of a jurisdiction reflect majority preferences. Importantly, this may happen both directly (as when voters pass initiative) or indirectly, when the legislators act preemptively to pass a law knowing that if the legislature doesn't act, then voters will bypass the legislature (perhaps passing a worse law from legislators' perspective). An important study by Professor John Matsusaka found that states that have the initiative process are more likely to have budgeting and financial policies favored by a majority of voters than states that do not.[5]

Just about everyone agrees that direct democracy can promote majoritarianism (or at least the preferences of a majority of voters[6]); the big debate is over whether such majoritarianism is a good thing. The strongest case for the initiative process is in the first instance, where the subject matter of the initiative directly affects legislators' self interest.

Consider the following criticisms of initiatives:[7]

- Voting majorities may be more likely than legislatures to pass laws hurting minorities.[8]

---

4. A referendum ensures that a majority of voters supports a legislatively enacted law. The recall ensures that a majority of voters continue to support an elected official.

5. JOHN G. MATSUSAKA, FOR THE MANY OR THE FEW: THE INITIATIVE, PUBLIC POLICY AND AMERICAN DEMOCRACY (2004).

6. When ballot measures appear at "off year" elections (where there is no federal election or major state election on the ballot), voter turnout may be low and could be less representative of the full voting population than at major elections. *See* LOWENSTEIN, HASEN, & TOKAJI, at 357.

7. For a history of the initiative process, *see* RICHARD J. ELLIS, DEMOCRATIC DELUSIONS: THE INITIATIVE PROCESS IN AMERICA (2002). For criticisms, *see* DAVID S. BRODER, DEMOCRACY DERAILED: INITIATIVE CAMPAIGNS AND THE POWER OF MONEY (2000); PETER SCHRAG, PARADISE LOST: CALIFORNIA'S EXPERIENCE, AMERICA'S FUTURE (1998).

8. *See* Derrick A. Bell Jr., *The Referendum: Democracy's Barrier to Racial Equality*, 54 WASH. L. REV. 1 (1978) for an early statement of the argument. For a response, *see* Richard Briffault, *Distrust of Democracy*, 63 TEX. L. REV. 1347 (1985) ("it is difficult to argue that historically minorities — in particular, blacks and other racial minorities — did all that well in state legislatures.").

- Voting majorities cannot engage in compromise and logrolling to pass more acceptable legislation; initiatives are offered to voters on a take-it-or-leave it basis without room for deliberation and negotiation.
- Voting majorities consider issues piecemeal and may make decisions (for example on budgeting) that may seem desirable when considered in isolation but that are problematic or nonsensical when considering the budgeting process as a whole.
- Voters may be swayed by slick advertising campaigns and cannot understand the complexities of legislation they consider. They also might be swayed by temporary passions (while in the legislature the slow moving of the normal legislative process can temper such passions).

Many of these points are contested.[9] Proponents of initiatives disagree with the claims that initiated laws are more likely to harm minorities than laws passed by legislatures, that the budgeting process is worse in states that have the initiative process, and that voters make decisions ignorantly or inconsistent with their interests. Some opponents of the initiative process argue that initiatives are so much more likely than legislation passed by

---

9. Lowenstein, Hasen & Tokaji at p. 350-351 summarize the pros and cons of the initiative process that Thomas Cronin evaluates in his book Direct Democracy 224-232 (1989):
   Supportive arguments that [Cronin] assesses include:

   a. Direct democracy enhances government responsiveness and accountability.
   b. It provides a safety valve "when legislators prove timid, corrupt, or dominated by special interests."
   c. It protects against bossism.
   d. It brings about rule by the common people.
   e. It reduces the influence of special interests.
   f. It permits less well-represented groups to bring their ideas before the public.
   g. It stimulates educational debate on important policy issues.
   h. It stimulates voter interest in public issues and stimulates turnout.
   i. It promotes trust in government.

   Cronin also evaluates arguments raised by opponents:

   a. Direct democracy undermines representative democracy.
   b. It produces unsound legislation.
   c. It endangers minority rights.
   d. It depends on voters who are not capable of competent policy judgments.
   e. It amplifies special interest influence.
   f. It lacks accountability because it is not subject to the usual checks and balances.

   Cronin finds some merit in a couple of the supportive arguments, that direct democracy provides a safety valve and that it helps some less-represented groups find a forum. The opponents, he concludes, raise a serious objection with respect to the lack of checks and balances. Mostly, though, he finds that empirical support for the arguments on both sides ranges from none to mixed. "Both proponents and opponents have too often overstated their positions," he concludes. "The existing direct democracy processes have both virtues and liabilities."

legislatures to infringe on minority rights that courts should take a "hard look" at laws passed by initiative alleged to infringe on such rights.[10]

Proponents of the initiative process sometimes point out that opponents compare the real initiative process to an idealized legislative process in which legislators act as faithful agents of the common good, deliberating carefully after poring over legislative texts. The earlier chapters should have already convinced you that this idealized legislative process has never existed, not even during the time of *Schoolhouse Rock*.

There is also fierce disagreement over whether campaign spending on ballot measures has great influence over public opinion. Early studies showed that "no" spending tended to be more important than "yes" spending in influencing voter choices on ballot measures.[11] An important later study by Elisabeth Gerber found that citizen groups tend to have an easier time than economic groups (such as business groups) getting voters to pass initiatives, but that economic groups were often successful spending money to block initiatives and to get their way in state legislatures.[12] (Chapter 13 of this book returns to the issue of campaign spending's influence on voters.)

For good or for ill, the importance of direct democracy seems only to be increasing. Public support for direct democracy is high, and although voters see problems with the process in those states that use it, support is usually higher for direct democracy than the state legislature.

In recent years, direct democracy has become an important supplement to direct democracy in states such as California, which recalled its governor in 2003. Professor Elizabeth Garrett has termed the increasing use of direct democracy in California and elsewhere a type of "hybrid democracy" in which governance depends upon the actions of both representatives and the voters acting using the devices of direct democracy.[13] In a state such as California, where Democrats far outnumber Republicans in the state legislature, direct democracy has especially become an important tool for Republicans. The notable ouster of Democratic governor Gray Davis in 2003 through a recall ushered in the governorship of actor Arnold Schwarzenegger, who, facing a Democratic legislature, tried to use the initiative process to further his policy agenda. Parties and candidates in California long tied their campaigns to ballot measure elections, but the trend accelerated in the 2000s.

---

10. Julian N. Eule, *Judicial Review of Direct Democracy*, 99 YALE L.J. 1503 (1990). For a critique, *see* Robin Charlow, *Judicial Review, Equal Protection and the Problem with Plebiscites*, 79 CORNELL L. REV. 527 (1994).

11. Daniel H. Lowenstein, *Campaign Spending and Ballot Propositions: Recent Experience, Public Choice Theory and the First Amendment*, 29 UCLA L. REV. 505 (1982).

12. ELISABETH R. GERBER, THE POPULIST PARADOX: INTEREST GROUP INFLUENCE AND THE PROMISE OF DIRECT LEGISLATION (1999).

13. Elizabeth Garrett, *Hybrid Democracy*, 73 GEO. WASH. L. REV. 1096 (2005).

As Garrett explains it,

First, candidate elections can be influenced by the presence of initiatives on the ballot. . . . Second, democratic structures and the laws regulating elections are likely to be different in a Hybrid Democracy than in a wholly representative democracy. . . . Third, Hybrid Democracy affects the policies that lawmakers adopt because they are aware that the political game includes the possibility of initiative and referendum. Strategic politicians, notably, Arnold Schwarzenegger, take advantage of Hybrid Democracy as they govern using the threat of initiative as a bargaining tool.

To put it another way, it is wrong to think of representative democracy and direct democracy as separate paths to governance. Instead, in states with vibrant direct democracy tools, legislative and voter-initiated laws are intertwined and representative government and direct democracy influence each other.

Example 1

The federal system has no devices of direct democracy. Should it have any? If so, which ones, and why?

Explanation

You can of course answer this normative question however you like; here are some things to think about (and my own personal skepticism about such a proposal will be clear).

Proposals for a national initiative are not new,[14] but there has never been great support for such a proposal (even apparently among those who support the initiative on the state and local level). One reason might be the sheer size of the United States. The size and complexity of running a national plebiscite is daunting. It would also be quite expensive. Think of how expensive presidential campaigns are, and recognize that those campaigns focus upon only those states that are likely to be competitive for the outcome of the electoral college vote; in a national ballot measure election, it would be important to get votes from everywhere. The large amounts of money that would need to be raised might be a concern.

Another issue to consider is polarization. Imagine national initiatives on issues such as abortion, gun control, taxes, or gay marriage. It is possible that voting on such divisive issues could increase polarization and tensions

---

14. See Ronald J. Allen, *The National Initiative Proposal: A Preliminary Analysis*, 58 Neb. L. Rev. 965 (1979).

between (and within) "red" and "blue" states. The question is whether majoritarianism makes sense in a country that is closely, but deeply, divided, and what "hybrid democracy" would look like on a national scale in the divided United States.

Finally is the issue of competence and interests: Do we trust voters to make decisions about complex issues with a national priority? Do we trust them more than Congress? Do we believe voters are better able than Congress to deal with issues that Congress is afraid to touch? Is the national voter initiative a solution to congressional gridlock and polarization?

4.2. THE SINGLE SUBJECT RULE AND OTHER CONTENT RESTRICTIONS ON INITIATIVES

In those states and localities allowing voters to use devices of direct democracy, state or local law often imposes limits on the content, timing, or subject matter of ballot measures. Recall laws, for example, may prevent circulating recall petitions too close to the last or next election. Referendum petitions often must be filed soon after a legislative body passes a law and cannot be brought to reverse a legislatively enacted law at a later time. Initiatives may be limited in subject matter; for example, initiatives generally cannot change the way that the legislature conducts its business.[15] And as we will see a bit later in this section, most states block initiatives that include more than a single subject.

In some states, such as California, voter initiatives may propose both statutory law and constitutional amendments. Proposed constitutional amendments require collecting more signatures (8 percent, rather than 5 percent of the number of voters who voted in the last gubernatorial election), but still need only a majority vote to pass.[16] As a consequence, California's constitution can be amended much more easily and frequently than the U.S. Constitution.

Although California and some other states allow initiated constitutional amendments, an initiative purporting to amend the constitution may not "revise" it. A constitutional revision, which is a more fundamental change to governance structure, requires a more elaborate process for passage: Two-thirds of the legislature must approve the calling of a constitutional convention, which then may propose revisions to the constitution that must then be approved by a majority of California voters.[17]

---

15. In Illinois, however, that is the only purpose for the initiative. *See* LOWENSTEIN, HASEN & TOKAJI, *supra*, at 369 (explaining ILL. CONST. Art. XIV, §3).
16. *See* CAL. CONST. Art. II, §8.
17. *Id.*, Art. XVIII.

States impose limits on direct democracy tools for structural and separation-of-powers reasons. Elected officials who could be subject to consecutive recall attempts could never focus on governing. Giving voters the power to put laws on hold at any time would create great uncertainty in the law, making it hard for anyone to rely on the law as written. The rule barring constitutional revisions through a simple majority vote seems especially important. Imagine, for example, that someone wants to propose a state constitutional amendment to take away the legislature's power to pass laws or to greatly curtail judicial review. Such a change would be dramatic and it could have far-reaching consequences. By making the constitutional revision process more onerous, it makes revisions both harder to pass and more likely to be blocked by groups with intense preferences against such revisions.

As with many content restrictions or limits on direct democracy, courts must police the borders, in this case between permissible constitutional amendments and impermissible constitutional revisions. That gives courts great power to decide which important matters may go before the voters for decision and which may not. The California Supreme Court explained that it must look at both "qualitative and quantitative" factors in deciding what counts as an impermissible revision. It has held that the famous "Proposition 13," which fundamentally changed the taxing power in California, did not count as a revision.[18] It also rejected a revision challenge to a law imposing term limits on state legislators and other elected officials.[19] But the court barred as an impermissible revision another initiative that would have required California courts to interpret the California Constitution to provide no greater procedural protection to criminal defendants than those offered under the U.S. Constitution.[20] The decisions are hard to reconcile with one another if measured against a standard of which laws would have brought about the most drastic changes to California governance. Imposing term limits and limiting the taxing authority of state and local officials seems at least as qualitatively important as a measure limiting how courts are to interpret constitutional protections for criminal defendants.

Example 2

California voters passed Proposition 8, an initiated constitutional amendment adding a single sentence to the California Constitution reading: "Only marriage between a man and a woman is valid or recognized in California."

---

18. *Amador Valley Joint Junior High Sch. Dist. v. State Bd. of Equalization*, 583 P.2d 1281 (Cal. 1978).
19. *Legislature v. Eu*, 816 P.2d 1309 (Cal. 1991), *cert. denied* 503 U.S. 919 (1992).
20. *Raven v. Deukmejian*, 801 P.2d 1077 (Cal. 1990).

Proponents of Proposition 8 passed the law after the California Supreme Court had held that the state's ban on same sex marriage violated other provisions of the state constitution. Is Proposition 8 an impermissible revision to the California Constitution?

Explanation

Considering the three authorities cited above, it is quite difficult to know whether the court would find Proposition 8 to be such a qualitative change as to count as an impermissible revision. As in *Raven*, Proposition 8 appears to interfere with the judiciary, although in *Raven* the initiative told judges how to do their jobs, whereas in the Proposition 8 case the voters overturned a single constitutional ruling from the court through a constitutional amendment.

In *Strauss v. Horton*,[21] the California Supreme Court rejected the revision argument against Proposition 8:

> As we have seen, the numerous past decisions of this court that have addressed this issue all have indicated that the type of measure that may constitute a revision of the California Constitution is one that makes "far reaching changes in the nature of our *basic governmental plan*" (*Amador*), or, stated in slightly different terms, that "substantially alter[s] *the basic governmental framework set forth in our Constitution.*" *Legislature v. Eu*, italics added. Thus, for example, our decision in *Amador*, in providing an example of the type of "relatively simple enactment" that may constitute a revision, posed a hypothetical enactment "which purported to vest *all judicial power in the Legislature.*" (*Amador*, italics added.) Similarly, in *Raven* — the only case to find that a measure constituted a revision of the California Constitution because of the qualitative nature of the proposed change — the court relied upon the circumstance that the provision there at issue "would substantially alter the substance and integrity of the state Constitution as a document of independent force and effect" (*Raven*) by implementing "a broad attack on state court authority to exercise independent judgment in construing a wide spectrum of important rights under the state Constitution." (*Id.*) . . .
>
> Proposition 8 works no such fundamental change in the *basic governmental plan or framework* established by the preexisting provisions of the California Constitution — that is, "in [the government's] fundamental structure or the foundational powers of its branches." (*Legislature v. Eu.*) Instead, Proposition 8 simply changes the substantive content of a state constitutional rule in one specific subject area — the rule relating to access to the designation of "marriage." Contrary to petitioners' contention, the measure does not transform or

---

21. 207 P.3d 48 (Cal. 2009).

undermine the judicial function: California courts will continue to exercise their basic and historic responsibility to enforce *all* of the provisions of the California Constitution, which now include the new section added by the voters' approval of Proposition 8.

Petitioners contend, however, that even if Proposition 8 does not make a fundamental change in the basic *governmental plan* or *framework* established by the Constitution, the measure nonetheless should be found to constitute a revision because it allegedly "strike[s] directly at the foundational constitutional principle of equal protection . . . by establishing that an unpopular group may be selectively stripped of fundamental rights by a simple majority of voters." Petitioners' argument rests, initially, on the premise that a measure that abrogates a so-called *foundational constitutional principle of law*, no less than a measure that makes a fundamental change in the basic governmental structure or in the foundational power of its branches as established by the state Constitution, should be viewed as a constitutional revision rather than as a constitutional amendment. Petitioners suggest that their position is not inconsistent with our past amendment/revision decisions, on the theory that none of those decisions *explicitly* held that *only* a measure that makes a fundamental change in the state's governmental plan or framework can constitute a constitutional revision. . . .

In our view, a fair and full reading of this court's past amendment/ revision decisions demonstrates that those cases stand for the proposition that in deciding whether or not a constitutional change constitutes a qualitative revision, a court must determine whether the change effects a substantial change in the governmental plan or structure established by the Constitution. As we have seen, a number of our past amendment/ revision decisions have involved initiative measures that made very important substantive changes in fundamental state constitutional principles such as the right not to be subjected to cruel or unusual punishment and the right to be protected against unlawful searches and seizures — initiative measures that, like the current Proposition 8, cut back on the greater level of protection afforded by preceding court decisions and were challenged as constitutional revisions on the ground that the constitutional changes they effected deprived individuals of important state constitutional protections they previously enjoyed and left courts unable to fully protect such rights. Nonetheless, in each case this court did not undertake an evaluation of the relative importance of the constitutional right at issue or the degree to which the protection of that right had been diminished, but instead held that the measure did not amount to a qualitative revision *because it did not make a fundamental change in the nature of the governmental plan or framework established by the Constitution.* . . .

Is the court's effort to distinguish the other cases convincing? Does your answer depend upon what you think of Proposition 8 on the merits? The concern is that judges may subconsciously let their views of the merits of the initiatives seep into analysis of content restrictions such as the amendment/revision line.

The Single Subject Rule.   Perhaps no content limitation over the devices of direct democracy gets litigated more than the single subject rule.[22] California's statement of the rule is typical: "An initiative measure embracing more than one subject may not be submitted to the electors or have any effect."[23] As with the amendment/revision line, the rule can give judges great discretion to keep measures off the ballot (or strike them down after voters approve them). Note how the California single subject rule is written, both preventing such measures from being submitted to the voters and holding that such measures are entitled to "no effect." In California, this means that measures that may have a single subject violation can be submitted for pre-election review to be taken off the ballot. Those that make it through the voting with a single subject violation will be declared unconstitutional by the courts.

It is easy to see why the single subject rule may lead reasonable judges to different results. Imagine a single initiative that imposes taxes on sugared candy and provides subsidies for low income state residents for dental care. Is this an initiative on one or two subjects? Supporters of the measure would argue that it is about a single subject: good dental health. Opponents would argue that it is about two topics: taxes on candy and dental subsidies.

Who's right?

There's no way to answer that question without having a more fine-tuned definition of "subject." The term "subject" is not self-defining.[24] One can define the concept of "subject" broadly so that everything is in the same subject ("policy") or narrowly so that nothing is the same subject. "There has to be a limit on how broad the subject can be, if the rule is to have any meaning at all. The difficulty is that the rule gives no guidance as to what that limit should be."[25]

Courts have used different tests to determine when a measure violates the single subject rule. Florida courts, for example, look for a Zen-like "logical and natural oneness of purpose" within the initiative. Under that muscular test, Florida courts have blocked from the ballot many measures that many people could regard as having a single subject, such as a state measure that would have prevented cities from passing anti-gay discrimination ordinances. Rather than saying straightforwardly that anti-discrimination measures protecting LGBT people are banned, the measure tried to hide its obvious purpose from voters by stating ten classifications of people (age, sex, religion, national origin, etc.) that were the only ones permitted to be the subject of local anti-discrimination laws. This did not satisfy the Florida Supreme Court. "The proposed amendment . . . violates

---

22. Chapter 2 discusses the single subject rule as applied to legislatively enacted measures.
23. Cal. Const. Art. II, §8(d).
24. *See* Daniel Hays Lowenstein, *California Initiatives and the Single-Subject Rule*, 30 UCLA L. Rev. 936 (1983).
25. Lowenstein, Hasen & Tokaji, *supra*, at 384.

the single-subject requirement because it enumerates ten classifications of people that would be entitled to protection from discrimination if the amendment were passed."[26] The Florida Supreme Court also held it violated the single-subject rule for other reasons, including the fact that it "encroaches on municipal home rule powers and on the rulemaking authority of executive agencies and the judiciary."

In contrast to Florida's test, which has doomed many initiatives from appearing on the ballot, California uses a much more permissive "reasonably germane" test, rejecting the idea that different parts of an initiative must be "functionally related" to one another.[27] Under the reasonably germane standard, a California court would likely uphold the candy tax/dental subsidy initiative on grounds that the two measures are reasonably germane to the topic of dental health. But note that the term "reasonably germane" is not infinitely elastic. In *Senate of the State of California v. Jones*,[28] the California Supreme Court barred from the ballot a measure that would have changed the method by which state legislative salaries are calculated; limited legislators' travel and living expenses; imposed penalties on legislators who were late with the budget; and took away the legislators' power to redistrict. The California Supreme Court held that the redistricting portion was not reasonably germane to the rest of the initiative, and it rejected the argument that all four parts were reasonably germane to the topic of "legislative self-interest." Some view the Court's decision in *Jones* as perhaps tightening up California's reasonably germane standard, a result that may have been driven in *Jones* by the state supreme court's dislike of the substance of the challenged initiative.[29]

A recent empirical study found that states using tough single subject standards, such as Florida, have much more variation in judicial votes than states that have easier standards, such as California. In states such as Florida that see aggressive enforcement of the single subject rule, judges are more likely to uphold a challenged initiative if it is in line with the judge's partisan preferences than if it is not. Judges in aggressive states voted to uphold a measure against single-subject challenge an average of 41% of the time for measures with which the judge likely disagreed ideologically but did so a whopping 83% of the time for measures with which the judge likely agreed ideologically.[30]

Why have the single subject rule? The two rationales usually offered to support it are to prevent logrolling and to prevent voter confusion. The first point recognizes that voters must vote on initiatives as a package and cannot

---

26. In re *Advisory Opinion of the Attorney General*, 632 So.2d 1018 (Fla. 1994).
27. *Fair Political Practices Comm'n v. Superior Court*, 599 P.2d 46 (Cal. 1979).
28. 988 P.2d 1089 (Cal. 1999).
29. Daniel H. Lowenstein, *Initiatives and the New Single Subject Rule*, 1 ELECTION L.J. 35 (2002).
30. *See* John G. Matsusaka & Richard L. Hasen, *Aggressive Enforcement of the Single Subject Rule*, 9 ELECTION L.J. 399 (2010).

vote on the parts separately, and some parts of the measure may carry others. Imagine an initiative that cuts everyone's taxes by $100 but gives a huge tax break to the oil industry. Standing alone, voters likely wouldn't support the huge oil industry tax break, but the $100 individual tax cut could carry the measure along.

The anti-logrolling argument for the single subject rule seems pretty weak, though. To begin with, it is not clear that the tax measure I just described would violate the single subject rule; after all, it is possible to classify the measure as on the subject of "taxes" or "tax breaks." Why not say that the measures have that "oneness of purpose" or are "reasonably germane" to one another? For another thing, there may be logrolls or packages that would not pass alone but that increase overall social welfare; sometimes such packaging is the only way to get things done (as is true in the legislature as well).[31] The other argument offered for the single-subject rule is prevention of voter confusion. But one can easily imagine a very complex measure reforming the state's income tax code that would not violate the single-subject rule but that could be very confusing. Similarly, many measures that may violate the single-subject rule may be simple, as with the dental health or tax initiatives described above.

Professors Robert Cooter and Michael Gilbert have proposed changing the single subject rule to apply a "separable preferences" test.[32] Under this test, if a voter could decide whether to favor one part of an initiative without knowing if the other part passes, then the measure violates the single subject rule. But if the different parts create contingent preferences (the voter cannot decide whether she favors the candy tax without knowing whether dental subsidies to the poor would be available) then the measure would not violate the single subject rule. Critics (like me!) worry that this single subject test would give too much discretion to judges, leading judges to subconsciously rely upon their views of the underlying merits of the initiative.[33]

Example 3

In addition to a single subject requirement for initiatives, some state constitutions include a "separate vote" requirement for initiated constitutional amendments, requiring that "each amendment" be subject to a separate

---

31. For a mathematical demonstration that logrolling may be socially beneficial or socially harmful, *see* Matsusaka & Hasen, *supra.*

32. Robert D. Cooter & Michael D. Gilbert, *A Theory of Direct Democracy and the Single Subject Rule,* 110 COLUM. L. REV. 687 (2010).

33. Richard L. Hasen & John G. Matsusaka, *Some Skepticism About the "Separable Preferences" Approach to the Single Subject Rule: A Comment on Cooter & Gilbert,* 110 COLUM. L. REV. SIDEBAR 35 (2010). For a response, *see* Robert D. Cooter & Michael D. Gilbert, *Reply to Hasen and Matsusaka,* 110 COLUM. L. REV. SIDEBAR 59 (2010).

vote. In recent years, some states that had a rather lax single subject requirement have aggressively enforced the separate vote requirement to knock off the ballot or reject initiated constitutional amendments.

Voters in Oregon, which has a separate vote requirement, adopt a state constitutional amendment that imposes term limits on executive and legislative state officials as well as on members of Congress elected from Oregon.[34]

Does the measure violate the single subject rule? The separate vote requirement?

Explanation

It is impossible to answer this question in the abstract without more knowledge about how Oregon enforces both requirements. Provisions imposing term limits on various Oregon elected officials seem "reasonably germane" to one another. Less certain would be whether the measure would have a "oneness of purpose" as used in Florida: A court otherwise hostile to term limits could say that term limits for the executive function differently than those for legislators or members of Congress.

As to whether each of these are separate amendments requiring "separate votes," it is not clear how this analysis would or should differ from a single subject requirement. As Lowenstein explains, the two seem to ask the same questions,[35] and the separate vote requirement seems to give courts yet another way to strike down (or keep off the ballots) initiatives that they do not like. In *Armatta v. Kitzhaber*, 959 P.2d 49 (Or. 1998), the Oregon Supreme Court breathed new life into the separate vote requirement, and other courts

---

34. This aspect of the initiative is unconstitutional, for reasons explained in Chapter 2.
35. Lowenstein, *Initiatives and the New Single Subject Rule, supra*:

> The only discernible "purpose" behind [the Oregon Supreme Court's] construal of the separate vote requirement as more restrictive than the single subject rule was that doing so enabled the Oregon Supreme Court to strike down an initiative constitutional amendment that its members did not like while pretending not to reverse its long string of precedents liberally interpreting both the legislative and initiative single subject rules. In addition, the court's conjuring up of the separate vote doctrine permitted it to throw out a constitutional amendment while avoiding rewriting the single subject rule as applied to initiative and legislatively enacted statutes. But this advantage is paid for at the cost of greatly confusing the law as it applies to constitutional amendments. For what is the difference between saying that provisions belong to the same "subject" and that they are "closely related"? Provisions belong to the same subject *because* they are related. [The two formulations] use different words to describe the same concept. The establishment of two rules applicable to constitutional amendments, purporting to be distinct but delineated with words having the same meaning, can only muddy the waters considerably. And on top of this problem, the court's new rule requires it to decide the obscure questions whether provisions in a constitutional amendment make one change or several, and whether such changes as are made are "substantive."

followed suit. In *Lehman v. Bradbury*, 37 P.3d 989 (Or. 2002) the court struck down the term limits measure described in the Example as violating Oregon's separate vote requirement. Here is a small excerpt from that decision:

> When the people were asked in Measure 3 to add section 20 to Article II of the Oregon Constitution, they were asked to change the eligibility of members of Congress, a topic found nowhere else in the Oregon Constitution. The problem was not necessarily that the provision was new. Newness, in and of itself, may be a neutral factor. But the specific addition made by section 20, affecting eligibility for federal public office, had little or nothing to do with term limits for the Oregon State Treasurer, for example, as those limits were established in section 19. Nonetheless, the voters were asked to vote for or against both sections in a single measure. In terms of Article XVII, section 1, Measure 3 submitted two or more amendments to the voters in a manner that prevented the voters from voting on each amendment separately. That was impermissible.

More recently, Oregon may have pulled back a bit on the stringency of the separate vote requirement. *See Meyer v. Bradbury*, 142 P.3d 1031 (Or. 2006). Too much discretion for judges?

4.3. PETITIONING RULES AND FINANCING BALLOT QUALIFICATION DRIVES

After a state or local government decides to allow one or more of the devices of direct democracy, it has to decide how measures may qualify for the ballot. Make qualification too easy, and voters will be overwhelmed with ballot measures to vote on; make qualification too hard, and the power will be illusory.

Most states require that ballot measure proponents collect a certain number of signatures from registered voters to qualify a measure for the ballot. The number of signatures often is tied to earlier turnout; for example, initiative proponents in California must collect signatures equal to 5 percent of the number of voters who voted in the last gubernatorial election. This threshold has proven to be pretty easy to cross for people with enough money to pay professional signature gatherers but an almost insurmountable threshold for people who would like to rely solely upon volunteers to collect signatures. So enough money gets an issue before the voters — although it is hardly a guarantee that voters will approve the measure.

Some critics want to raise signature thresholds because they do not like the initiative process and anything that makes it harder to qualify initiatives is, to them, a good thing. Others, including those who like direct democracy but who see flaws with the petition rules, tend to worry about two things: fraud in the signature gathering process and the role of money in that process.

On issues of fraud, election officials must verify signatures. In many places, officials verify a representative sample of signatures, and if the verification rate is high enough, the petition is accepted without checking every signature. (Because some signatures will not be verified — a voter may sign twice, or someone not eligible to sign may sign anyway — signature gatherers usually get extra signatures as a cushion to ensure that the petition is accepted). States and localities have passed some laws, purportedly aimed at preventing fraud (although sometimes merely to make the signature gathering process harder), such as those limiting who may circulate petitions.

In *Buckley v. American Constitutional Law Foundation*,[36] the Supreme Court rejected a number of limitations on the circulation of ballot measure petitions in Colorado, including a law that required that petition circulators be registered voters. The Court held that such a law interfered with the First Amendment speech and association rights of ballot proponents and circulators. Colorado argued that the law would prevent fraud (because registered voters would be more likely to be in the jurisdiction and therefore easier to investigate and serve in the case of fraud), but the Court held that Colorado had less burdensome ways to prevent fraud, such as through a residency requirement, which was not challenged in the *ACLF* case. It was not clear what level of scrutiny applies to such challenges.

Since *ACLF*, lower courts have split over the constitutionality of residency requirements. In one of the most recent cases, the Fourth Circuit, applying strict scrutiny, struck down Virginia's residency requirement:[37]

> The Board maintains that the witness residency requirement serves the Commonwealth's interest in policing fraud potentially permeating the electoral process, in that: (1) it is less difficult to confirm the identities of resident witnesses, and thereby ensure they are qualified by age and not disqualified by felon status; (2) witness residents in Virginia are subject to being subpoenaed by the authorities to answer questions under oath concerning the circulation process, or to be prosecuted for criminal activity; and (3) residents are simply easier to locate for investigatory or prosecutorial purposes. The plaintiffs do not seriously dispute that the prevention of election fraud is a compelling state interest. . . .
>
> The more substantial question, and the crux of this appeal, is whether the Commonwealth's enactment banning all nonresidents from witnessing nominating petitions — a measure we presume to be effective in combatting fraud — is, notwithstanding its efficacy, insufficiently tailored to constitutionally justify the burden it inflicts on the free exercise of First Amendment rights. The Board

---

36. 525 U.S. 182 (1999). You should not confuse this case with *Buckley v. Valeo*, 424 U.S. 1 (1976), the most important U.S. case on campaign finance laws challenged on First Amendment grounds. *See* Part IV of this book.

37. *Libertarian Party of Va. v. Judd*, 718 F.3d. 308 (4th Cir. 2013).

insists that the integrity of the petitioning process depends on "state election official access to the one person who can attest to the authenticity of potentially thousands of signatures," access made more difficult, perhaps, if the witness resides beyond the subpoena power of the state.

The plaintiffs counter that the Commonwealth could compel nonresidents, as a condition of witnessing signatures on nominating petitions, to enter into a binding legal agreement with the Commonwealth to comply with any civil or criminal subpoena that may issue. Indeed, "[f]ederal courts have generally looked with favor on requiring petition circulators to agree to submit to jurisdiction for purposes of subpoena enforcement, and the courts have viewed such a system to be a more narrowly tailored means than a residency requirement to achieve the same result." More recently, in [Yes on Term Limits, Inc. v.] Savage, the Tenth Circuit reiterated that "requiring non-residents to sign agreements providing their contact information and swearing to return in the event of a protest is a more narrowly tailored option."

According to the Board, ostensible consent to the extraterritorial reach of the Commonwealth's subpoena power does not guarantee the requisite access, because nonresident witnesses must yet be located and retrieved, perhaps by extradition or rendition. There are few guarantees in life, however, and it is hardly an iron-clad proposition that a similarly situated resident witness will be amenable to service and comply with a lawfully issued subpoena.

Simply stated, the Board has produced no concrete evidence of persuasive force explaining why the plaintiffs' proposed solution, manifestly less restrictive of their First Amendment rights, would be unworkable or impracticable. Surely nonresidents with a stake in having the signatures they have witnessed duly counted and credited — whether that stake be political, financial, or otherwise — will possess the same incentive as their resident counterparts to appear at the Commonwealth's request and answer any questions concerning the petitioning process.

Having fallen short of adducing the quantum of proof necessary to place into issue the relative effectiveness of the plaintiffs' proposed alternative to the patently burdensome witness residency requirement, the Board cannot prevail. Given the facts as developed below and viewed in the proper light, we have scant choice but to conclude, as the district court did, that the requirement fails strict scrutiny and is unconstitutional.

Supporters and opponents of direct democracy also worry about the role of money in the signature gathering process. It may be troubling from the perspective of equality that enough money almost guarantees getting an issue before voters while not enough money almost guarantees that the issue will not get before the voters. Before the ACLF case, Colorado passed a law barring paid circulators from collecting signatures. In Meyer v. Grant,[38] the Supreme Court held that this law violated the First Amendment rights of ballot measure proponents and circulators.

---

38. 486 U.S. 414 (1988).

The Court held the measure infringed on the First Amendment in two ways: "First, it limits the number of voices who will convey appellees' message and the hours they can speak and, therefore, limits the size of the audience they can reach. Second, it makes it less likely that appellees will garner the number of signatures necessary to place the matter on the ballot, thus limiting their ability to make the matter the focus of statewide discussion."

The Court then rejected the state's interest in insuring that measures that appeared before voters got enough "grass roots support" to deserve to be placed on the ballot or in insuring the integrity of the ballot process. On the grassroots point, the Court held that the interest "is adequately protected by the requirement that no initiative proposal may be placed on the ballot unless the required number of signatures has been obtained." On the integrity point, the Court stated that Colorado put forward no evidence showing that paid circulators were more likely to submit false signatures than others and that other Colorado laws served an antifraud purpose (a point the Court later echoed in *ACLF*).

Critics of *Meyer* argue that the Court should not have looked at petition circulation as a restriction on speech (because petition circulators, even if they could not accept signatures, could still say what they wanted and advocate for people to sign the petition) but rather as a means by which the state decides which measures it will let on the ballot.[39]

Since *Meyer*, critics of paid petition circulation have tried other laws only to face constitutional challenge. In *ACLF*, for example, the Court rejected a Colorado law requiring paid petition circulators to wear a badge disclosing whether the petition circulator was a paid circulator or a volunteer.

These questions about payments to petition circulators consider only one aspect of campaign financing surrounding ballot measure elections. Part IV returns to other issues surrounding campaign financing and ballot measure elections, focusing on campaign finance issues surrounding campaigns for and against ballot measures that have qualified for the ballot.

Example 4

The state of Pacifica's legislature passes a law barring the payment of petition circulators on a per signature basis. The state legislature did so based upon evidence from the state's voter registration experience that payments per signature increase the risk of false and fraudulent signatures.[40]

Is Pacifica's law unconstitutional?

---

39. *See* Daniel Hays Lowenstein & Robert M. Stern, *The First Amendment and Paid Initiative Petition Circulators: A Dissenting View and a Proposal*, 17 HASTINGS CONST. L.Q. 175 (1989).

40. Chapter 12, on election administration, discusses issues with voter registration fraud.

Explanation

The answer is uncertain. Neither *Meyer* nor *ACLF* answers the question whether rules on *how* a petition circulator may be paid violate the First Amendment rights of petition circulators and ballot measure proponents. *Meyer* struck down a law banning paid circulators *at all*; *ACLF* struck down a number of limits on petition circulators, including the requirement that circulators wear badges showing their paid or volunteer status.

Lower courts have divided on the constitutionality of per signature payment bans. The Eighth Circuit, crediting the antifraud aspects of the law, upheld North Dakota's law.[41] The Sixth Circuit struck down an Ohio law barring the payment of paid signature gatherers on any basis other than time worked.[42] The Sixth Circuit noted that Ohio's law was stricter than other state laws, and that it precluded even bonuses for productivity or longevity.

There is no question that payments per signature motivate petition circulators to collect more signatures; circulators who are desperate for money might be tempted to falsify signatures to make more money. On the other hand, paying someone to collect signatures by the hour, without being able to reward or punish them for productivity, could lead to some very lazy signature gatherers and a decline in the number of successful petitions. (Critics of these laws believe that is their very purpose.) Unsurprisingly, courts disagree over whether these laws are justified on antifraud grounds or are too much of an infringement on First Amendment speech and association rights in the ballot measure context.

---

41. *Initiative and Referendum Inst. v. Jaeger*, 241 F.3d 614 (8th Cir. 2001).
42. *Citizens for Tax Reform v. Deters*, 518 F.3d 375 (6th Cir. 2008), *cert. denied* 555 U.S. 1031 (2008).

PART II

Statutory Interpretation

Theories and Practice of Statutory Interpretation

5.1. INTRODUCTION: THE *HOLY TRINITY CHURCH* PROBLEM . . . OR "THE FOOD STAYS IN THE KITCHEN"

Many studies of statutory interpretation begin with the Supreme Court's controversial 1892 decision in the *Holy Trinity Church* case,[1] a case in which the United States contended that a church violated a statute prohibiting the importation of foreign workers by hiring a pastor from another country. We will get to *Holy Trinity Church* in a bit, but perhaps there is an easier way to get into the thorny topic of statutory interpretation than to start with the words of a congressional immigration statute more than a century old.

One of my favorite law review articles in the field of legislation is by Professor Hillel Levin of the University of Georgia law school.[2] The article, *The Food Stays in the Kitchen: Everything I Needed to Know About Statutory Interpretation I Learned by the Time I Was Nine*, is only 8 pages long (many law review articles have footnotes that seem that long!) and it appears in the *Green Bag*, which publishes the best academic legal humor around (admittedly a very low bar).

The article begins with an "ordinance" issued by "the Supreme Lawmaker, Mother": "I am tired of finding popcorn kernels, pretzel crumbs, and pieces of cereal all over the family room. From now on, no food may be

---

1. Rector, Etc. of Holy Trinity Church v. United States, 143 U.S. 457 (1892).
2. Hillel Y. Levin, *The Food Stays in the Kitchen: Everything I Needed to Know About Statutory Interpretation I Learned by the Time I Was Nine*, 12 GREEN BAG 2D 337 (2009).

eaten outside the kitchen." The remainder of the article consists of "litigation" over the "ordinance."

First there was a dispute over whether bringing a glass of water into the family room violated the ordinance. Answer: No. Food and water are separate things, a decision "Father" reached using dictionary definitions of "food" and other edicts from the Supreme Lawmaker (recognizing that food and drink are separate things), as well as through reliance on the purpose of the ordinance to prevent messes (water is not messy). Next the dispute moved to orange juice, a dispute resolved relying on the water precedent and the plain language of the ordinance to conclude that beverages are not food. Then followed a dispute over popcorn eaten by a child walking into the family room. Held: The popcorn was not in violation of the ordinance as it was in the child's mouth when the child left the kitchen, meaning it would not be likely to make a mess and thus not within the definition of food being "eaten" outside the kitchen. A new ruling allowed a "double thick mint chocolate shake" into the family room, even though such a holding appeared to violate the purpose of the ordinance, based upon the earlier beverage precedents and the Supreme Leader's failure to clarify or change the law after those beverage precedents issued. Eventually, apple slices, pretzels, popcorn, cereal, birthday cake, a bagel with cream cheese, cottage cheese, and a chocolate bar get eaten in the family room without violating the ordinance. Exasperated, the Supreme Leader issues a new edict: "No food, gum, or drink of any kind, on any occasion or in any form, is permitted in the family room. Ever. Seriously. I mean it."

The Levin article illustrates with good humor the essence of the statutory interpretation problem: Legislative bodies, such as Congress (or "Mom") do not pass abstract "laws." Instead they pass statutes (or, for local governments, often called "ordinances") that the executive branch enforces and that the judiciary interprets. Statutes set forth the rules to apply to future conduct (as in the prohibition on food being eaten outside the kitchen). They are an imperfect way of creating law, both because of the limits and ambiguities of language and because of the inability of legislatures to perfectly draft statutes to deal with all future contingencies. In the real world, intent and purpose are infinitely more complicated than in Levin's example: Though "Mom" may have an intent or purpose in issuing a new law, Congress is a multi-member body without a single intent or purpose in doing anything.[3] Furthermore, statutes do not enforce themselves; they require someone to figure out what they mean. As courts issue precedential decisions about a statute's meaning, those decisions become part of the understanding of the statute's meaning and affect its enforcement, at least

---

3. Kenneth A. Shepsle, *Congress Is a "They," Not an "It:" Legislative Intent as Oxymoron*, 12 INT'L REV. L. & ECON. 239 (1992). As applied to courts, *see* Adrian Vermeule, *The Judiciary Is a They, Not an It: Interpretive Theory and the Fallacy of Division*, 14 J. CONTEMP. LEGAL ISSUES 549 (2005).

until the legislative body comes in and amends the statute. Sometimes judicial or administrative statutory interpretation deviates widely from the text of the statute or initial legislative intent.

The Food Stays in the Kitchen also illustrates some of the common tools of interpretation: looking at the text of the statute, sometimes by using dictionaries or other uses of the same word in other statutes or contexts; considering the intent of the statute's drafters, such as the prevention of messes; analyzing the broader purpose of the statute, sometimes as interpreted by the agency ("Dad") in charge of enforcing the statute; and viewing the statute in light of earlier judicial interpretation and the responses or non-responses of the drafters to those interpretations. Furthermore, these tools sometimes point in conflicting directions: The decision allowing the milkshake in the family room seemed to violate the drafter's intent and broader purpose of the ordinance, but its ruling was supported by a narrow textual reading of the ordinance's prohibition on food being *eaten* in the family room.

Holy Trinity Church illustrates these similar tensions, albeit in a far less entertaining way.[4] In the case, an incorporated church hired a rector from overseas to work for the church. The U.S. government contended that the hiring violated a federal statute, the pertinent part of which read

> Be it enacted by the senate and house of representatives of the United States of America, in congress assembled, that from and after the passage of this act it shall be unlawful for any person, company, partnership, or corporation, in any manner whatsoever, to prepay the transportation, or in any way assist or encourage the importation or migration, of any alien or aliens, any foreigner or foreigners, into the United States, its territories, or the District of Columbia, under contract or agreement, parol or special, express or implied, made previous to the importation or migration of such alien or aliens, foreigner or foreigners, to perform labor or service of any kind in the United States, its territories, or the District of Columbia.

The Supreme Court began by conceding that the church's conduct seemed to violate the statute under a textual reading:

---

4. The lack of entertainment value certainly has not deterred law professors from writing about the case. Just in the last few years, the following articles have discussed the case: Carol Chomsky, *The Story of* Holy Trinity Church v. United States (1892): *Spirit and History in Statutory Interpretation*, in STATUTORY INTERPRETATION STORIES 2 (William N. Eskridge Jr., Philip P. Frickey, & Elizabeth Garrett eds., 2011); John F. Manning, *The New Purposivism*, 2011 SUP. CT. REV. 113; David M. Driesen, *Purposeless Construction*, 48 WAKE FOREST L. REV. 97 (2013); John F. Manning, *Federalism and the Generality Problem in Constitutional Interpretation*, 122 HARV. L. REV. 2003 (2009); William S. Blatt, *Missing the Mark: An Overlooked Statute Redefines the Debate over Statutory Interpretation*, 104 Nw. U. L. REV. COLLOQUY 147 (2009); Anita S. Krishnakumar, *The Hidden Legacy of* Holy Trinity Church: *The Unique National Institution Canon*, 51 WM. & MARY L. REV. 1053 (2009).

It must be conceded that the act of the corporation is within the letter of this section, for the relation of rector to his church is one of service, and implies labor on the one side with compensation on the other. Not only are the general words "labor" and "service" both used, but also, as it were to guard against any narrow interpretation and emphasize a breadth of meaning, to them is added "of any kind;" and, further, as noticed by the circuit judge in his opinion, the fifth section, which makes specific exceptions, among them professional actors, artists, lecturers, singers, and domestic servants, strengthens the idea that every other kind of labor and service was intended to be reached by the first section.

Perhaps the Court conceded the point too easily. For example, one might argue, that the term "labor" refers only to manual labor.[5] Furthermore, it turns out that Congress later passed another statute specifically exempting ministers from its coverage, a fact missed by the Court.[6] On the other hand, the statute did contain a list of exemptions for certain professions, including musicians, but not mentioning members of the clergy. Despite the textual concession, the Court concluded that the church did not violate the statute, because Congress did not intend to bar the hiring of a pastor by a church.

While there is great force to [the textual] reasoning, we cannot think congress intended to denounce with penalties a transaction like that in the present case. It is a familiar rule that a thing may be within the letter of the statute and yet not within the statute, because not within its spirit nor within the intention of its makers. This has been often asserted, and the Reports are full of cases illustrating its application. This is not the substitution of the will of the judge for that of the legislator; for frequently words of general meaning are used in a statute, words broad enough to include an act in question, and yet a consideration of the whole legislation, or of the circumstances surrounding its enactment, or of the absurd results which follow from giving such broad meaning to the words, makes it unreasonable to believe that the legislator intended to include the particular act.

How did the Supreme Court divine Congress's intent, figuring out the "spirit" of the statute in contrast to its "letter"? It began with the title of the statute:

It will be seen that words as general as those used in the first section of this act were by that decision limited, and the intent of congress with respect to the act was gathered partially, at least, from its title. Now, the title of this act is, "An act to prohibit the importation and migration of foreigners and aliens under contract or agreement to perform labor in the United States, its territories, and the District of Columbia." Obviously the thought expressed in this

---

5. "The first definition of the term 'labor' listed in the 1879 and 1886 editions of *Webster's Dictionary* was 'Physical toil or bodily exertion * * * hard muscular effort directed to some useful end, as agriculture, manufactures, and the like.' The second (less authoritative) definition was 'Intellectual exertion, mental effort.'" ESKRIDGE, FRICKEY & GARRETT, at 699-700.
6. Chomsky, *supra*, at 24-25. Blatt, *supra*.

reaches only to the work of the manual laborer, as distinguished from that of the professional man. No one reading such a title would suppose that congress had in its mind any purpose of staying the coming into this country of ministers of the gospel, or, indeed, of any class whose toil is that of the brain. The common understanding of the terms "labor" and "laborers" does not include preaching and preachers, and it is to be assumed that words and phrases are used in their ordinary meaning. So whatever of light is thrown upon the statute by the language of the title indicates an exclusion from its penal provisions of all contracts for the employment of ministers, rectors, and pastors.

The Court next looked to the "evil" the statute was designed to prevent:

Again, another guide to the meaning of a statute is found in the evil which it is designed to remedy; and for this the court properly looks at contemporaneous events, the situation as it existed, and as it was pressed upon the attention of the legislative body. The situation which called for this statute was briefly but fully stated by Mr. Justice Brown when, as district judge, he decided the case of U.S. v. Craig, 28 Fed. Rep. 795, 798: 'The motives and history of the act are matters of common knowledge. It had become the practice for large capitalists in this country to contract with their agents abroad for the shipment of great numbers of an ignorant and servile class of foreign laborers, under contracts by which the employer agreed, upon the one hand, to prepay their passage, while, upon the other hand, the laborers agreed to work after their arrival for a certain time at a low rate of wages. The effect of this was to break down the labor market, and to reduce other laborers engaged in like occupations to the level of the assisted immigrant. The evil finally became so flagrant that an appeal was made to congress for relief by the passage of the act in question, the design of which was to raise the standard of foreign immigrants, and to discountenance the migration of those who had not sufficient means in their own hands, or those of their friends, to pay their passage.'

It appears, also, from the petitions, and in the testimony presented before the committees of congress, that it was this cheap, unskilled labor which was making the trouble, and the influx of which congress sought to prevent. It was never suggested that we had in this country a surplus of brain toilers, and, least of all, that the market for the services of Christian ministers was depressed by foreign competition. Those were matters to which the attention of congress, or of the people, was not directed.

The Court next quoted from a report issued by a Senate committee examining the legislation, which similarly indicated that Congress's concern was with the importation of *manual laborers*.

The last portion of the opinion (and the one that is perhaps the most controversial for present times) pointed to religion, rejecting the idea that Congress would have intended the statute to bar the hiring of clergy from abroad. "But, beyond all these matters, no purpose of action against religion can be imputed to any legislation, state or national, because this is a religious people." The Court continued,

> If we pass beyond these matters to a view of American life, as expressed by its laws, its business, its customs, and its society, we find every where a clear recognition of the same truth. Among other matters note the following: The form of oath universally prevailing, concluding with an appeal to the Almighty; the custom of opening sessions of all deliberative bodies and most conventions with prayer; the prefatory words of all wills, "In the name of God, amen;" the laws respecting the observance of the Sabbath, with the general cessation of all secular business, and the closing of courts, legislatures, and other similar public assemblies on that day; the churches and church organizations which abound in every city, town, and hamlet; the multitude of charitable organizations existing every where under Christian auspices; the gigantic missionary associations, with general support, and aiming to establish Christian missions in every quarter of the globe. These, and many other matters which might be noticed, add a volume of unofficial declarations to the mass of organic utterances that this is a Christian nation. In the face of all these, shall it be believed that a congress of the United States intended to make it a misdemeanor for a church of this country to contract for the services of a Christian minister residing in another nation?

Hard as it may be to believe, but in some of the fiercest disputes on the current Supreme Court over statutory interpretation today, judges and scholars still fight over the result and reasoning in the *Holy Trinity Church* case.

Example 1

If you were on the Supreme Court, how would you have decided the *Holy Trinity Church* case and why? (Bonus question: Should the consuming of the double thick mint chocolate shake have been held to violate the Supreme Lawmaker's ordinance, and why?)

Explanation

I start things off here with a normative question for which there is no right answer. Some of you will be tempted to answer the question the Supreme Court considers in the *Holy Trinity Church* case solely by looking at the text. Others may be persuaded to look at other factors, such as Congress's intent as reflected in the Senate committee report, or based upon the justices' (or your own) supposition about why Congress passed the law at the time.

As you consider your answer to the *Holy Trinity Church* question, try to be self-reflective: To what extent does your answer depend upon your views on the wisdom of the law or the soundness or fairness of congressional intent? To what extent is the exercise into examining purpose one more about the purpose of the interpreter than the drafter? As you try to discern congressional intent, what does that term mean? Is it the intent of all the members of Congress? Those who read the bill? Those who wrote the bill or who led on its passage? How would you know such intent? How does the Court decide the United States is a "Christian nation," and what role can and should such a decision play in interpreting the statute? Are the rules that you choose for this case the same rules you would apply in every statutory interpretation case? There are no Federal Rules of Statutory Interpretation.[7]

If you do not have firm answers on these questions, do not worry. We will continue to explore these issues in the rest of this chapter and in the next few chapters.

On the milkshake problem, this is a nice way to ask whether and to what extent statutory interpreters should rely upon potentially erroneous earlier judicial precedents, and how to resolve (apparent) conflicts between the text of a statute and the statute's purposes. We will take up these issues later on.

5.2. THEORIES OF INTERPRETATION: INTENTIONALISM, PURPOSIVISM, TEXTUALISM, AND DYNAMIC INTERPRETATION

Let's get a little more specific about the main different modes of statutory interpretation and how they differ from one another. In the next section, we consider the debate over these forms of interpretation. Of course many judges use a mix of these theories of interpretation, sometimes inconsistently. But it is useful to start with a typology. Future chapters will explore the tools used to interpret statutes consistent with these theories.

Once again, let's begin with application of Professor Levin's Mom's edict that "no food be eaten out of the kitchen" to the milkshake in the family room.

An *intentionalist* would ask what Mom intended when she issued her initial ordinance in relation to milkshakes. Mom might or might not have had a specific intent on that question, and if she had such intent it might be contained in what we would think of as the "legislative history" if Mom were a legislature. Imagine, for example, if the evidence showed that Mom had issued the ordinance right after she criticized one of her children for spilling a milkshake on the family's sofa. With such evidence, the intentionalist's resolution of the milkshake problem would be easy: The milkshake in the family room violated the ordinance. Without such evidence, however,

---

7. For a proposal to create one, *see* Nicholas Quinn Rosenkranz, *Federal Rules of Statutory Interpretation*, 115 Harv. L. Rev. 2085 (2002).

the intentionalist would have a harder time trying to imagine what Mom at the time she issued the ordinance *would have thought* about the question had she considered it at the time.

A *purposivist* would ask a similar question to the intentionalist, but at a broader level of abstraction, looking at the main purpose of the ordinance: Think of the discussion in *Holy Trinity Church* about the "evil" Congress was trying to avoid in the statute. Rather than asking — as the intentionalist would — what Mom would have thought about milkshakes in the family room, the purposivist would ask about the general purpose of the statute. Perhaps the judge would identify that purpose as preventing hard-to-clean messes on the nice family room furniture. If that is the right purpose, the purposivist likely would decide that a thick mint chip milkshake in the family room violated the ordinance because it could well make a mess.

A *dynamic interpretivist*[8] would consider legislative intent and the purpose of the ordinance, as updated to take into account modern times and the current views of the legislative body and other political actors. Imagine, for example, that the milkshake is brought into the family room ten years after the ordinance issued, when all the children are grown up and much less likely to make a mess with food. Or imagine that ten years later, the family room furniture and carpet are trashed, and Mom doesn't really care any longer about messes in the family room. Or imagine that Mom finally got really nice furniture for the room and was extra-cautious about messes. Or, finally, imagine that Mom just got tired of telling people to stop bringing food into the family room, and people did it all the time without any punishment — until the milkshake spill. The *dynamic interpretivist* could well decide whether bringing a milkshake into the family room violates the ordinance by considering current conditions and contemporary norms, rather than the original intent of the drafters or the text of the statute. Dynamic interpretation trusts judges to be able to update statutes for modern times.

A *textualist* would not look abstractly at legislative intent or purpose, much less consider how to make the ordinance make sense in light of modern needs and preferences. Instead, a textualist would resolve the milkshake issue by examining the words of the ordinance as those words would have been understood by an ordinary reader of the English language at the time Mom issued it. Would an ordinary reader decide that a milkshake is "food" that shall not be "eaten" outside the kitchen? To answer such a question the textualist might consult dictionaries, might apply linguistic or policymaking rules of thumb (or "canons") to decide the question, or

---

8. *See* William M. Eskridge Jr., *Dynamic Statutory Interpretation*, 135 U. Pa. L. Rev. 1479 (1987).

might rely upon the textualist's own understanding of what "food" that is "eaten" is. For example, food is generally not liquid, nor is it consumed with a straw. A textualist could well conclude that the milkshake drinking in the family room does not violate Mom's ordinance.

Example 2

Based upon the information presented in the last section,[9] how would an intentionalist, a purposivist, a dynamic interpretivist, and a textualist resolve the dispute in the *Holy Trinity Church* case?

Explanation

The Supreme Court in *Holy Trinity Church* took the position that a textualist would find that the church's decision to import the pastor violated the congressional statute. However, there are decent textualist arguments against that position. For example, a reasonable reader might read the term "labor" to include only manual labor, and acting as a pastor is not manual labor. On the other hand, the statute references "labor or service of any kind," suggesting a much broader reading of the statute. The inclusion of exceptions to the statute (for musicians and others) without mentioning an exception for ministers suggests that ministers are included (under the *expressio unius* canon discussed in the next chapter).

Purposivists and intentionalists could reach different conclusions, as shown by the Court's opinion itself. The Court focused on the "evil" Congress attacked in the statute — the importation of cheap manual labor that was hurting the country's manual labor market. Furthermore, the Court believed that had Congress thought of it, they would not have banned the importation of "brain toilers." This is especially true because the rule would impede on freedom of religion, and the United States, according to the Court at the time, is a "Christian nation." Of course, it is possible a different set of judges would view Congress's purpose or intent differently and reach a contrary conclusion.

This is a case where dynamic interpretation does not come much into play — the Court was applying a relatively recent statute, and therefore there was no need for the Court to consider "updating" the statute to take into account changes in norms or the preferences of the current Congress.

---

9. There is much more detail about the relevant legislative history, text, and congressional intent in the articles cited in footnote 4. I have given you no more than a brief overview.

5.3. THE GREAT DEBATE OVER LEGISLATIVE HISTORY AND THE NEW TEXTUALISM

Since *Holy Trinity Church*, the Supreme Court and lower courts used a wide variety of tools and interpretive theories to decide on a statute's meaning in the context of a legal dispute. Sometimes text mattered more; sometimes a statute's "spirit" was paramount. In some cases courts parsed the words of a statute, and resorted to dictionaries or textual canons to pull out statutory meaning; in other cases courts relied upon snippets of legislative history from a committee report, a floor speech of a senator, or something else to support a particular interpretation of a statute. In some cases, courts paid close attention to contemporary social circumstances and the evil addressed by statutes; in other cases courts seem more concerned with the original intent of the drafting legislators.

Despite this history of eclecticism in statutory interpretation, the last generation has seen a major shift toward textual interpretation of statutes. The rise of this "New Textualism"[10] has had a profound effect on U.S. statutory interpretation, even though few judges today, even those who regard themselves as textualists, rely solely on textual methods to decide the meaning of statutes in cases, and even though some critics of textualism have declared the methodology dead and the debate over.[11]

The main change caused by the New Textualism debate is that Supreme Court (and lower federal court)[12] statutory interpretation cases these days almost always start with the text of the statute and focus on the statute's syntax and structure before turning to other tools of interpretation. Furthermore, when a court interpretation deviates from apparent statutory text, justices and judges feel the need to justify the deviation. In short, textualism is the 800-pound gorilla in the room when courts consider every statutory interpretation case, even if most justices and judges do not consider themselves textualists and do not confine themselves in statutory interpretation to a strict textual reading of the statute.

The leading proponent of the New Textualism is Supreme Court Justice Antonin Scalia, although there are other important proponents of the textualist approach as well, including Seventh Circuit Court Judge Frank Easterbrook and Harvard Law school professor John F. Manning. I focus here on Justice Scalia's critique and the responses to Justice Scalia from those who oppose textualism.

---

10. William N. Eskridge Jr., *The New Textualism*, 37 UCLA L. Rev. 621 (1990).

11. Jonathan T. Molot, *The Rise and Fall of Textualism*, 106 Colum. L. Rev. 1 (2006).

12. Statutory interpretation in state courts has taken a somewhat different path, with some state courts developing precedents over their methodological approaches to the interpretation of statutes. *See* Abbe R. Gluck, *The States as Laboratories of Statutory Interpretation: Methodological Consensus and the Modified New Textualism*, 119 Yale L.J. 1750 (2010). I focus in this chapter on federal statutory interpretation issues.

Justice Scalia's main argument for textualism and against reliance on legislative history is his belief that the latter is "nothing but an invitation to judicial lawmaking."[13] He believes the use of legislative history is illegitimate because legislative history is not voted upon by Congress and signed by the president (failing the bicameralism and presentment requirements discussed in Chapter 1). Congress passes statutory texts, and it exceeds judicial powers to go beyond those texts.

Justice Scalia further believes that intent is an indeterminate methodology of statutory interpretation. As he explains, "*Holy Trinity* is cited to us whenever counsel wants to ignore the narrow, deadening text of the statute, and pay attention to the life-giving legislative intent."[14] Or, as he explained in a 1993 case, judges can use legislative history to impose their own value judgments on what the statute should mean:

> The greatest defect of legislative history is its illegitimacy. We are governed by laws, not by the intentions of legislators. As the Court said in 1844: "The law as it passed is the will of the majority of both houses, *and the only mode in which that will is spoken is in the act itself.* . . ." *Aldridge v. Williams,* 3 How. 9, 24, 11 L.Ed. 469 (emphasis added). But not the least of the defects of legislative history is its indeterminacy. If one were to search for an interpretive technique that, *on the whole,* was more likely to confuse than to clarify, one could hardly find a more promising candidate than legislative history. And the present case nicely proves that point.
>
> Judge Harold Leventhal used to describe the use of legislative history as the equivalent of entering a crowded cocktail party and looking over the heads of the guests for one's friends. If I may pursue that metaphor: The legislative history of [the statute the Court interprets] contains a variety of diverse personages, a selected few of whom — its "friends" — the Court has introduced to us in support of its result. But there are many other faces in the crowd, most of which, I think, are set against today's result.[15]

Justice Scalia believes that at bottom, legislative history allows for judges to engage in the kind of *dynamic statutory interpretation* advocated by Professor Eskridge, but behind the subterfuge of discerning true legislative "intent." "What I think is needed, however, is not rationalization of this process but abandonment of it. It is simply not compatible with democratic theory that laws mean whatever they ought to mean, and that unelected judges decide what that is."[16]

Justice Scalia turns to legislative history in a few contexts. He will look to legislative history when there is an apparent "scrivener's error" — that is, when a statute appears to have "a mistake of expression (rather than legislative

---

13. ANTONIN SCALIA, A MATTER OF INTERPRETATION: FEDERAL COURTS AND THE LAW 21 (1997).
14. *Id.*
15. *Conroy v. Aniskoff,* 507 U.S. 511, 519 (1993) (Scalia, J., concurring in the judgment).
16. SCALIA, at 22.

wisdom),"[17] or when a statute's interpretation is "absurd" — for the limited purpose of making sure the legislature did not intend the absurd interpretation. Justice Scalia also will sometimes point to contrary legislative history to make a point that other justices' reliance on such history is biased — kind of like having one's cake and eating it, too.

Although Justice Scalia will not rely upon legislative history to interpret statutes, he instead relies upon canons and presumptions.[18] The next chapter delves into these devices. Some of these devices are purely textual. To use a variation on a common example: Suppose a city ordinance says, "No automobiles or other vehicles in the park." If someone gets a ticket for riding a bicycle in the park, a textualist would not look at the ordinance's legislative history in determining whether a bicycle is a vehicle. But the textualist might rely upon the mention of "automobiles" in the statute to figure out whether the statute also covers bicycles. (The mention of the term "automobile" could cut either way in the act of statutory interpretation here.) Other devices are not textual, but policy-oriented. For example, the rule of lenity tells courts to interpret ambiguous criminal law statutes against imposition of criminal liability.

The other area in which Justice Scalia does not rely upon pure textualism is administrative law. There, Justice Scalia favors deference to interpretation of statutes undertaken by the agency charged with enforcing the statute. We explore this issue in Chapter 8.

Plenty of critics have attacked Justice Scalia's textualism. One critique focuses on textualism's indeterminacy. Justice Scalia is a fan of using dictionaries from the time of a statute's drafting to determine the meaning of words to an ordinary reader at the time the statute was written. But dictionaries often have multiple meanings, and it is possible to engage in "dictionary shopping" to find a definition most in line with a judge's own preferred interpretation of the statute.[19]

The use of canons and presumptions as well can lead to indeterminacy, as well as a thumb on the scale for or against particular statutory interpretations. Why should an ambiguous statute be judicially interpreted with a

---

17. *Id.* at 20.

18. Furthermore, Justice Scalia does rely upon drafting history in interpreting the meaning of constitutional provisions. *See* Eskridge, *supra.*

19. Furthermore, dictionary definitions may not always reflect the understanding of ordinary readers. *See* Ellen P. Aprill, *The Law of the Word: Dictionary Shopping in the Supreme Court,* 30 ARIZ. ST. L.J. 275 (1998); Jeffrey L. Kirchmeier and Samuel A. Thumma, *Scaling the Lexicon Fortress: The United States Supreme Court's Use of Dictionaries in the Twenty-First Century,* 94 MARQ. L. REV. 77 (2010); Adam Liptak, *Sidebar: Justices Turning More Frequently to Dictionary, and Not Just for Big Words,* N.Y. TIMES, Jun. 13, 2011, http://www.nytimes.com/2011/06/14/us/14bar.html ("A new study in The Marquette Law Review found that the justices had used dictionaries to define 295 words or phrases in 225 opinions in the 10 years starting in October 2000. That is roughly in line with the previous decade but an explosion by historical standards. In the 1960s, for instance, the court relied on dictionaries to define 23 terms in 16 opinions.").

thumb on the scale against criminal enforcement? The rule of lenity incorporates a value judgment within it. Critics argue these value judgments are no more valid than the value judgments contained in the legislative history, and perhaps less valid, because legislative history can reveal the intent of the drafters of the statute as opposed to the judicially created value judgments of the courts.

Canons also may not reflect true legislative intent. Professors Abbe Gluck and Lisa Schultz Bressman conducted a survey of legislative drafters in Congress — the staffers most responsible for actually drafting legislation. They found mixed support for the use of canons of construction:[20]

> Contrary to the prevailing wisdom, a majority of our respondents were not only aware of some of the interpretive rules that courts employ — including the presumption against preemption and *Chevron* — but told us that these legal rules affect how they draft, although not always in ways that courts expect. We call these rules "feedback canons," as they at least partially substantiate the existence of an interpretive conversation between the Supreme Court and Congress that many have assumed impossible. For other canons, such as many textual canons like *noscitur a sociis* and a surprising number of the administrative delegation doctrines . . . our respondents displayed unfamiliarity with them as legal doctrines but told us that the assumptions underlying those rules accurately reflect how they draft legislation. We call these rules "approximation canons" — rules in which the Court seems to be correctly intuiting how Congress signals its intent even as Congress remains unaware of the rules' existence.
>
> At the same time, however, there were a host of canons that our respondents told us that they do not use, either because they were unaware that the courts relied on them or *despite* known judicial reliance. For example, our respondents were mostly unaware of and do not use "clear statement rules" — an example of a rule that we therefore call a "disconnected canon." And although they were well aware of other rules, including the rule against superfluities, the Court's penchant for dictionary consultation, and some Justices' distaste for legislative history, our respondents told us that they nevertheless do not generally draft in accordance with the rule against superfluities, that they do not consult dictionaries when drafting, and that legislative history remains a critical tool regardless of whether courts use it. Indeed, despite the decades of judicial squabbling over it, legislative history was overwhelmingly viewed by our Democratic and Republican respondents alike as the most important tool of interpretation after statutory text. We call this last set of rules, collectively, "rejected canons," because our drafters knowingly reject judicial preferences relating to their application in favor of institutional or other pragmatic considerations.

---

20. Abbe R. Gluck & Lisa Schultz Bressman, *Statutory Interpretation from the Inside — An Empirical Study of Congressional Drafting, Delegation, and the Canons: Part I*, 65 STAN. L. REV. 901 (2013). Do not worry if you are unfamiliar with some of the terms and canons described in the Gluck & Bressman excerpt. We discuss them in the next few chapters.

Example 3

While in custody at a county prison, Paul Green obtained work-release employment at a car wash. On his sixth day at work, Green reached inside a large dryer to try to stop it. A heavy rotating drum caught and tore off his right arm. Green brought a product liability action against respondent Bock Laundry Co., manufacturer of the machine. At trial Green testified that he had been instructed inadequately concerning the machine's operation and dangerous character. Bock impeached Green's testimony by eliciting admissions that he had been convicted of burglary and conspiracy to commit burglary, both felonies. The jury returned a verdict for Bock. On appeal Green argued that the District Court erred by denying his pretrial motion to exclude the impeaching evidence, arguing that under a balancing test that evidence was prejudicial.

At the time of the dispute, Federal Rule of Evidence 609(a) provided the following:

> General Rule. For the purpose of attacking the credibility of a witness, evidence that the witness has been convicted of a crime shall be admitted if elicited from the witness or established by public record during cross-examination but only if the crime (1) was punishable by death or imprisonment in excess of one year under the law under which the witness was convicted, and the court determines that the probative value of admitting this evidence outweighs its prejudicial effect to the defendant, or (2) involved dishonesty or false statement, regardless of the punishment.

Mr. Green was a civil plaintiff in the suit, and the District Court, examining rule 609(a) found that the rule did not allow for such balancing as to prejudice to the plaintiff.

How would a textualist respond to Mr. Green's argument that rule 609(a) requires balancing of the probative value of evidence of the prior convictions with its possible prejudicial effect?

Explanation

The facts of this case come from *Green v. Bock Laundry Machine Co.*, 490 U.S. 504 (1989). In a majority opinion by Justice Stevens, the Court noted the textual problem:

> The Rule's plain language commands weighing of prejudice to a defendant in a civil trial as well as in a criminal trial. But that literal reading would compel an odd result in a case like this. Assuming that all impeaching evidence has at least minimal probative value, and given that the evidence of plaintiff Green's convictions had some prejudicial effect on his case — but surely none on defendant Bock's — balancing according to the strict language of Rule 609(a)(1) inevitably

leads to the conclusion that the evidence was admissible. In fact, under this construction of the Rule, impeachment detrimental to a civil plaintiff always would have to be admitted.

After a lengthy analysis of the legislative history, Justice Stevens concluded that rule 609(a) provided a balancing benefit only for defendants in criminal cases. The rule "requires a judge to permit impeachment of a civil witness with evidence of prior felony convictions regardless of ensuant unfair prejudice to the witness or the party offering the testimony."

Justice Scalia concurred in the judgment and offered this analysis in a brief concurrence:

> We are confronted here with a statute which, if interpreted literally, produces an absurd, and perhaps unconstitutional, result. Our task is to give some alternative meaning to the word "defendant" in Federal Rule of Evidence 609(a)(1) that avoids this consequence; and then to determine whether Rule 609(a)(1) excludes the operation of Federal Rule of Evidence 403.
>
> I think it entirely appropriate to consult all public materials, including the background of Rule 609(a)(1) and the legislative history of its adoption, to verify that what seems to us an unthinkable disposition (civil defendants but not civil plaintiffs receive the benefit of weighing prejudice) was indeed unthought of, and thus to justify a departure from the ordinary meaning of the word "defendant" in the Rule. For that purpose, however, it would suffice to observe that counsel have not provided, nor have we discovered, a shred of evidence that anyone has ever proposed or assumed such a bizarre disposition. The Court's opinion, however, goes well beyond this. Approximately four-fifths of its substantive analysis is devoted to examining the evolution of Federal Rule of Evidence 609, from the 1942 Model Code of Evidence, to the 1953 Uniform Rules of Evidence, to the 1965 Luck case and the 1970 statute overruling it, to the Subcommittee, Committee, and Conference Committee Reports, and to the so-called floor debates on Rule 609 — all with the evident purpose, not merely of confirming that the word "defendant" cannot have been meant literally, but of determining what, precisely, the Rule does mean.
>
> I find no reason to believe that any more than a handful of the Members of Congress who enacted Rule 609 were aware of its interesting evolution from the 1942 Model Code; or that any more than a handful of them (if any) voted, with respect to their understanding of the word "defendant" and the relationship between Rule 609 and Rule 403, on the basis of the referenced statements in the Subcommittee, Committee, or Conference Committee Reports, or floor debates — statements so marginally relevant, to such minute details, in such relatively inconsequential legislation. The meaning of terms on the statute books ought to be determined, not on the basis of which meaning can be shown to have been understood by a larger handful of the Members of Congress; but rather on the basis of which meaning is (1) most in accord with context and ordinary usage, and thus most likely to have been understood by the *whole* Congress which voted on the words of the statute (not to mention the

citizens subject to it), and (2) most compatible with the surrounding body of law into which the provision must be integrated — a compatibility which, by a benign fiction, we assume Congress always has in mind. I would not permit any of the historical and legislative material discussed by the Court, or all of it combined, to lead me to a result different from the one that these factors suggest.

I would analyze this case, in brief, as follows:

(1) The word "defendant" in Rule 609(a)(1) cannot rationally (or perhaps even constitutionally) mean to provide the benefit of prejudice-weighing to civil defendants and not civil plaintiffs. Since petitioner has not produced, and we have not ourselves discovered, even a snippet of support for this absurd result, we may confidently assume that the word was not used (as it normally would be) to refer to all defendants and only all defendants.

(2) The available alternatives are to interpret "defendant" to mean (a) "civil plaintiff, civil defendant, prosecutor, and criminal defendant," (b) "civil plaintiff and defendant and criminal defendant," or (c) "criminal defendant." Quite obviously, the last does least violence to the text. It adds a qualification that the word "defendant" does not contain but, unlike the others, does not give the word a meaning ("plaintiff" or "prosecutor") it simply will not bear. The qualification it adds, moreover, is one that could understandably have been omitted by inadvertence — and sometimes is omitted in normal conversation ("I believe strongly in defendants' rights"). Finally, this last interpretation is consistent with the policy of the law in general and the Rules of Evidence in particular of providing special protection to defendants in criminal cases.[*]

(3) As well described by the Court, the "structure of the Rules," makes it clear that Rule 403 is not to be applied in addition to Rule 609(a)(1).

I am frankly not sure that, despite its lengthy discussion of ideological evolution and legislative history, the Court's reasons for both aspects of its decision are much different from mine. I respectfully decline to join that discussion, however, because it is natural for the bar to believe that the juridical importance of such material matches its prominence in our opinions — thus producing a legal culture in which, when counsel arguing before us assert that "Congress has said" something, they now frequently mean, by "Congress," a committee report; and in which it was not beyond the pale for a recent brief to say the following: "Unfortunately, the legislative debates are not helpful. Thus, we turn to the other guidepost in this difficult area, statutory language." Brief for Petitioner in *Jett v. Dallas Independent School District*, O.T.1988, No. 87-2084, p. 21.

For the reasons stated, I concur in the judgment of the Court.

---

[*] Acknowledging the statutory ambiguity, the dissent would read "defendant" to mean "any party" because, it says, this interpretation "extend[s] the protection of judicial supervision to a larger class of litigants" than the interpretation the majority and I favor, which "takes protection *away* from litigants." But neither side in this dispute can lay claim to generosity without begging the policy question whether judicial supervision is better than the automatic power to impeach. We could as well say — and with much more support in both prior law, and this Court's own recommendation — that our reading "extend[s] the protection of [the right to impeach with prior felony convictions] to a larger class of litigants" than the dissent's interpretation, which "takes protection *away* from litigants."

Note that Justice Scalia, facing what he calls an absurd construction of the statute, rewrites the statute in such a way, he says, as to do "the least violence to the statutory text." But that point is debatable: "In essence, Justice Blackmun's dissent rewrote Rule 609(a)(1) to permit impeaching convictions only when 'the court determines that the probative value of admitting this evidence outweighs its prejudicial effect to *a party*' (new language italicized). Does this do more 'violence' to the text than Justice Scalia's rewrite[?]"[21]

Justice Scalia's use of the absurdity doctrine also has met with skepticism among other textualists. John Manning, for example, seems to believe that the doctrine, even in Justice Scalia's hands, will give judges too much discretion to decide cases in line with their own understanding of absurdity.[22] One alternative for the Court in *Bock Laundry* was to strike down the statute as unconstitutional in the context of civil trials, leading Congress potentially to clarify its intent through a rewrite of the statute.

I leave you with these questions: Is Justice Scalia's use of the absurdity doctrine inconsistent with his general textualist approach? Should that matter for purposes of statutory interpretation?

You will likely gain a stronger sense of what you think about textualism when you consider the material in the next three chapters, on canons, on legislative history, and on judicial deference to administrative interpretations of statutes.

5.4. *STARE DECISIS* AND STATUTORY INTERPRETATION

Whatever tools courts use to interpret statutes, a judicial act of statutory interpretation is of lower stakes than an act of constitutional interpretation. When a court strikes down an act of Congress as unconstitutional, it takes supermajorities of both Congress and state legislatures to overturn it — something that rarely happens.[23] However, in the case of statutory interpretation, Congress can overturn a judicial act of statutory interpretation by passing a normal piece of legislation.

---

21. ESKRIDGE, FRICKEY, & GARRETT, *supra*, at 776.
22. John F. Manning, *The Absurdity Doctrine*, 116 HARV. L. REV. 2387, 2481-84 (2003).
23. Congress sometimes responds to a constitutional decision by rewriting a statute in a way that may make it less vulnerable to constitutional attack. For example, after the Supreme Court struck down on First Amendment grounds the Stolen Valor Act, a statute making it a crime to lie about having been awarded a military honor, *U.S. v. Alvarez*, 132 S.Ct. 2537 (2012), Congress passed a new Stolen Valor Act of 2013. Lee Ferran, *Obama Signs Stolen Valor Act into Law*, ABC NEWS, June 3, 2013, http://abcnews.go.com/blogs/headlines/2013/06/obama-signs-stolen-valor-act-into-law/.

Given the relatively easier hurdle for Congress to respond to statutory judicial decisions compared to constitutional decisions, courts have adopted different approaches to *stare decisis* (or respect for precedent). In statutory cases, in which Congress can overturn a judicial decision through an ordinary law, courts use a strong version of *stare decisis*. In contrast, in constitutional cases, in which it is rare to overturn the court, courts use a weaker version of *stare decisis*.

The best illustration of the principle of strong *stare decisis* for judicial decisions is the Supreme Court's decision in *Flood v. Kuhn*.[24] *Flood* involved the Supreme Court's failure to overturn earlier precedents that had concluded that professional baseball was exempt from federal antitrust laws. In the years after the Court had initially held that baseball was entitled to an exception, the Court then inconsistently held that professional boxing and professional football were not entitled to such an exemption. In *Flood*, the Court reaffirmed its earlier inconsistent precedent giving baseball the exemption even though "[i]t appears that every member of the Court thought that [the earlier precedent] was wrongly decided."[25] Justice Blackmun, for the Court, wrote that "[i]f there is any inconsistency or illogic in all this, it is an inconsistency and illogic of long standing that is to be remedied by the Congress and not by this Court."

One question is whether the principle of *stare decisis* for statutory decisions deserves rethinking given the sharp rise of political polarization in Congress discussed in Chapter 1. This polarization seems to be contributing to a decline in the number of statutory decisions that Congress overrules. In fact, in the last two decades the rate of congressional overriding of Supreme Court statutory decisions has plummeted dramatically, from an average of 12 overrides of Supreme Court cases in each two-year congressional term during the 1975-1990 period to an average of 5.8 overrides for each term from 1991-2000, and to a mere 2.8 average number of overrides for each term from 2001-2012.[26]

Legislative overrides in the past were often bipartisan. These days, however, we see that the few overrides taking place are *partisan overridings*. In polarized times, these require conditions of near-unified control of both branches of Congress and the presidency. Two recent examples are the Military Commissions Act of 2006, in which Republicans overturned the Court's statutory interpretation decision in *Hamdan v. Rumsfeld*[27] on the habeas corpus rights of enemy combatants, and the Lilly Ledbetter Fair Pay Act

---

24. 407 U.S. 258 (1972).

25. Eskridge, Frickey & Garrett, *supra*, at 640.

26. Richard L. Hasen, *End of the Dialogue? Political Polarization, the Supreme Court, and Congress*, 86 S. Cal. L. Rev. 205 (2013); Adam Liptak, Sidebar: *In Congress's Paralysis, A Mightier Supreme Court*, N.Y. Times, Aug. 20, 2012, http://www.nytimes.com/2012/08/21/us/politics/supreme-court-gains-power-from-paralysis-of-congress.html. The next paragraphs draw from my article.

27. 548 U.S. 557 (2006).

of 2009, in which Democrats overturned the Court's statutory interpretation decision in *Ledbetter v. Goodyear Tire & Rubber Company*[28] on how to measure the statute of limitations period in certain employment discrimination lawsuits. In a highly polarized atmosphere, and with Senate rules usually requiring 60 votes to change the status quo, the Court's word on the meaning of statutes is now final almost as often as is its word on constitutional interpretation.

Example 4

Should the rise in political polarization in Congress cause the Supreme Court to rethink its strong presumption of *stare decisis* in statutory cases?

Explanation

This is a normative question, and a tough one at that. *Flood* indicates that at least implicitly the justices consider congressional dialogue relatively easy and straightforward. Although such dialogue has never been easy, in the last few decades dialogue has almost disappeared.

It is hard to know whether polarization will be an enduring phenomenon or will change in a few years.[29] If polarization decreases, then it is possible that the Court–Congress dialogue could resume once again. It is not clear whether the Supreme Court should make a change in its doctrine now or wait to see whether polarization endures. On the one hand, Court doctrines should not change for ephemeral reasons. On the other hand, to the extent that polarization continues, the Court now ends up being final much more often on statutory cases than the *stare decisis* doctrine supposes, shifting perhaps too much power to the Court from Congress.

Wasn't it simpler when we were simply worrying about whether we could bring a milkshake into the family room?

---

28. 550 US. 618 (2007).
29. Richard L. Hasen, *Political Dysfunction and Constitutional Change*, 61 Drake L. Rev. 989 (2013).

Canons of Statutory Interpretation

6.1. WHY CANONS?

In the last chapter we saw the sharp debate over textualist modes of interpretation. Although most federal courts do not engage in strictly textualist interpretations of statutes, most courts do begin with the text of the statute and turn to legislative history and other tools of interpretation only after first examining the text. As a practice tip, you should always begin an exam, paper, or legal brief's statutory analysis with the text of the relevant statute; hiding the text in the hopes that professors, courts, or administrative agencies will ignore the actual words of the statute is a strategy sure to backfire and likely to anger the person who must interpret the statute. If the plain language of the statute works against you, acknowledge that point and explain why the plain language should not be the sole guide to interpretation in your case. Better yet, see whether you can begin with a plausible argument that the "plain language" is less plain, and more ambiguous, than it first appears to be.

Courts and others almost always begin with text, but what does it mean for a court to begin with a textual reading of a statute? How are judges to know what the words of a statute means, both in general and in the specific context of the dispute before the court? We have already seen that judges sometimes rely upon their own knowledge of the English language to explain what the judges believe to be the plain language of the text. That statute means "X" because I say it means "X," a kind of *ipse dixit* (a bare assertion) or *res ipsa loquitur* (the thing speaks for itself). At other times, courts will turn to dictionaries from the time of the statute's drafting to define a word. As we have also seen, this tends to make dictionary shopping more common among judges and litigants.

Sometimes a court's act of textualist statutory interpretation is an exercise in parsing language, making judicial opinions look more like a lesson in English grammar than an exercise in legal reasoning. This will become clear from some of the extended excerpts below, which are here to give you a flavor of the work judges do in this area. These excerpts can be tough reading, but it is important for you to pay close attention to them so you understand just how detailed and intricate judicial textual interpretations have become.

These textualist judges and others often rely upon "canons of construction," or rules of thumb to interpret a statute. Here's a formal definition: Textual canons "consist of predictive guidelines as to what the legislature likely meant based on its choice of certain words rather than others, or its grammatical configuration of those words in a given sentence, or the relationship between those words and text found in other parts of the same statute or in similar statutes."[1]

Think back to the *Holy Trinity Church* case from the last chapter. The statute forbidding the importation of workers from other countries included a provision exempting some classes of workers from coverage under the statute. Pastors were not included on that list of exemptions. From that omission, a court might conclude that pastors were not exempt, with the theory being that the inclusion of some professions for exemption implied the exclusion of other professions.

There's a Latin name for this concept: *expressio unius est exclusio alterius* (the inclusion of one implies the exclusion of the other), or "the *expressio unius* canon" for short. *Expressio unius* is one of a number of textual or linguistic canons used in textual interpretation of a statute.

Justice Scalia and noted lawyer and writer Byran A. Garner recent wrote a 567-page book that is mostly an exploration and defense of various textual canons of interpretation and rejection of other modes of statutory interpretation.[2] Justice Scalia and Garner defend textual canons as neutral, in line with judicial responsibilities under the Constitution and a fair method of adjudication. To critics however, reliance on textualism and textual canons has an inherent conservative bias.

Consider the views of Judge Richard A. Posner of the United States Court of Appeals for the Seventh Circuit, himself no liberal:[3]

---

1. James J. Brudney & Corey Ditslear, *Canons of Construction and the Elusive Quest for Neutral Reasoning*, 58 Vand. L. Rev. 1, 12 (2005).
2. Antonin Scalia & Bryan A. Garner, Reading Law: The Interpretation of Legal Texts (2012).
3. Richard A. Posner, *The Incoherence of Antonin Scalia*, The New Republic, Aug. 24, 2012, http://www.newrepublic.com/article/magazine/books-and-arts/106441/scalia-garner-reading-the-law-textual-originalism.

Does an ordinance that says that "no person may bring a vehicle into the park" apply to an ambulance that enters the park to save a person's life? For Scalia and Garner, the answer is yes. After all, an ambulance is a vehicle — any dictionary will tell you that. If the authors of the ordinance wanted to make an exception for ambulances, they should have said so. And perverse results are a small price to pay for the objectivity that textual originalism offers (new dictionaries for new texts, old dictionaries for old ones). But Scalia and Garner later retreat in the ambulance case, and their retreat is consistent with a pattern of equivocation exhibited throughout their book.

One senses a certain defensiveness in Justice Scalia's advocacy of a textualism so rigid as to make the ambulance driver a lawbreaker. He is one of the most politically conservative Supreme Court justices of the modern era and the intellectual leader of the conservative justices on the Supreme Court. Yet the book claims that his judicial votes are generated by an "objective" interpretive methodology, and that, since it is objective, ideology plays no role. It is true, as Scalia and Garner say, that statutory text is not inherently liberal or inherently conservative; it can be either, depending on who wrote it. Their premise is correct, but their conclusion does not follow: text as such may be politically neutral, but textualism is conservative.

A legislature is thwarted when a judge refuses to apply its handiwork to an unforeseen situation that is encompassed by the statute's aim but is not a good fit with its text. Ignoring the limitations of foresight, and also the fact that a statute is a collective product that often leaves many questions of interpretation to be answered by the courts because the legislators cannot agree on the answers, the textual originalist demands that the legislature think through myriad hypothetical scenarios and provide for all of them explicitly rather than rely on courts to be sensible. In this way, textualism hobbles legislation — and thereby tilts toward "small government" and away from "big government," which in modern America is a conservative preference.

Garner responded to Posner, calling his review "tendentious" and noting that his and Justice Scalia's approach to textualism is "inimical — if not seriously threatening — to those who promote nontextual means of deciding cases in which a governing legal text is at issue."[4] On the specific question of the ambulance in the park:

> Judge Posner's critiques repeatedly miss the mark. Take, for example, his opening criticism, which deals with the book's treatment of a sign that reads "no person may bring a vehicle into the park." The book considers whether that prohibition would apply to, among other things, an ambulance. Judge Posner would have the reader believe that "[f]or Scalia and Garner, the answer is yes," simply because "[a]fter all, an ambulance is a vehicle — any dictionary will tell you that." That is a gross distortion of our analysis, which explicitly rejects an uncritical acceptance of definitions from just "any dictionary." Our analysis

---

4. Bryan A. Garner, *Response to Richard A. Posner*, LawProse Blog, Sept. 5, 2012, http://www.lawprose.org/blog/?p=570.

declines to apply the available dictionary definitions of "vehicle" — "means of conveyance with wheels," "receptacle in which something is placed in order to be moved," and "self-propelled conveyance that runs on tires" — because these would literally cover "remote-controlled model cars, baby carriages, tricycles, or perhaps even bicycles." The book rejects that meaning since, as we explain, it is common usage that we are looking for, and not all colloquial meanings are to be found in dictionaries.

Adding insult to distortion, Judge Posner claims that we "later retreat in the ambulance case, and their retreat is consistent with a pattern of equivocation exhibited throughout the book." To the contrary, we do not retreat. And nuance is not equivocation. The assertion that we "retreat" is consistent with a pattern of distortion exhibited throughout his review.

My coauthor and I consistently maintain that ambulances *are* covered by the prohibition but also explain that "[s]ome of the imperfections [in a statute] can be cured or mitigated by doctrines and devices other than the mauling of text. . . . For example, it may well be that the undeniable exclusion of ambulances by the text of the ordinance is countermanded by an ordinance or court-made rule exempting emergency vehicles from traffic rules." Posner ignores that and pounces on a statement made 273 pages later as a retreat: "The driver who violates a criminal law against high-speed driving while taking a seriously injured person to the emergency room could be excused by the common-law defense of necessity." This is not a retreat: it's an illustration of a mitigating doctrine. Posner himself distorts his claim by first referring to the ambulance in the third paragraph of his review, unsupported by evidence, then presents his off-point "evidence" only four paragraphs from the end of the essay — thirty paragraphs later.

As controversial as textual canons are, "substantive canons" are even more controversial.[5] Substantive canons "are generally meant to reflect a judicially preferred policy position. [They] reflect judicially-based concerns, grounded in the courts' understanding of how to treat statutory text with reference to judicially perceived constitutional priorities, pre-enactment common law practices, or specific statutorily based policies."[6] Among the most important substantive canons are the rule of lenity (a "rule against applying punitive sanctions if there is ambiguity as to underlying criminal liability or criminal penalty"[7]), the avoidance canon (courts should "avoid interpretations that would render a statute unconstitutional *or* that would raise serious constitutional difficulties"[8]), and a host of "federalism" canons protecting state sovereignty against congressional intrusion.[9] We consider each of these below.

---

5. The next few paragraphs draw from Richard L. Hasen, *The Democracy Canon*, 62 STAN. L. REV. 69 (2009).

6. Brudney & Ditslear, *supra* at 13.

7. ESKRIDGE, FRICKEY, & GARRETT, *supra*, app. B at 32.

8. *Id.* app. B at 29.

9. *Id.* app. B at 30-32.

Eskridge and Frickey have defended substantive canons as part of an "interpretive regime" serving rule of law and coordination functions.[10] That is, substantive canons can act as gap-filling devices that provide clarity for the law and allow courts to signal policy preferences to legislatures, who may draft around such preferences when desired.[11] Eskridge further defends them as "a way for 'public values' drawn from the Constitution, federal statutes, and the common law to play an important role in statutory interpretation."[12] Anglo-American courts have accepted some substantive canons as legitimate for at least 400 years.[13]

Justice Scalia, one of the most prominent critics of substantive canons, nicely states the oft-heard main objections. He argues against substantive canons, which he characterizes as "the use of certain presumptions and rules of construction that load the dice for or against a particular result."[14] Calling substantive canons "a lot of trouble" to "the honest textualist,"[15] Justice Scalia describes them as indeterminate,[16] leading to "unpredictability, if not arbitrariness" of judicial decisions. He also questions "where the courts get the authority to impose them,"[17] doubting whether courts can "really just decree we will interpret the laws that Congress passes to mean more or less than they fairly say."[18]

Justice Scalia surely is right that substantive canons "load the dice" or constitute a "thumb on the scale" as courts engage in statutory interpretation. And if courts were writing on a clean slate, it might be that the best course would be to recognize no substantive canons. But courts have long used substantive rules to color their interpretations of statutes, and few (in Congress or state legislatures) appear to have questioned courts' legitimacy in doing so as a general matter. Indeed, even Justice Scalia recognizes the validity of some traditional substantive canons. Speaking of the avoidance canon, he argues, without elaboration, that "constitutional doubt may validly be used to affect the interpretation of an ambiguous statute."[19] Concerning the rule of lenity, he "suppose[s] it is valid by sheer antiquity" given that the canon "is almost as old as the common

---

10. William N. Eskridge Jr. & Philip P. Frickey, *The Supreme Court, 1993 Term Foreword: Law as Equilibrium*, 108 HARV. L. REV.26, 66 (1994).

11. Id. at 66-69.

12. WILLIAM N. ESKRIDGE JR. & PHILIP P. FRICKEY, CASES AND MATERIALS ON LEGISLATION: STATUTES AND THE CREATION OF PUBLIC POLICY 710 (2d ed. 1995).

13. Brudney & Ditslear, *supra* at 8.

14. ANTONIN SCALIA, A MATTER OF INTERPRETATION: FEDERAL COURTS AND THE LAW 27 (1997).

15. Id. at 28.

16. Id. ("it is virtually impossible to expect uniformity and objectivity when there is added, on one side or the other, a thumb of indeterminate weight").

17. Id. at 29.

18. Id.

19. Id. at 20 n.22.

law itself."[20] He also defends the clear statement rule for finding congressional abrogation of state sovereign immunity and for finding congressional waiver of its own immunity as "merely an exaggerated statement of what a normal, no-thumbs-on-the-scales interpretation would produce anyway."[21] In this context, he appears to view use of the federalism canons as a kind of harmless error. These views might explain why Justice Scalia has chosen to concur in a fair number of Supreme Court cases relying on substantive canons.[22] In his most recent work with Garner, Justice Scalia seems to go further, accepting the rule of lenity and other rules as those that "must be known to both drafter and reader alike so that they may be considered inseparable from the meaning of the text."[23]

In the end, despite his rhetoric Justice Scalia seems less disturbed by the use of substantive canons generally than by the use of *particular* substantive canons. He takes aim at canons that seem to him to be especially indeterminate or unwise, such as the rule that statutes in derogation of the common law should be strictly construed,[24] and that "remedial statutes" should be liberally construed to achieve their purposes.[25]

The indeterminacy objection is a serious objection.[26] In a groundbreaking study, Jim Brudney and Corey Ditslear examined more than 600 Supreme Court cases on workplace law from 1969 to 2003 to see how the Supreme Court used language and substantive canons in opinions. They "discovered little evidence to support legal process scholars' claims that the canons serve

---

20. *Id.* at 29.

21. *Id.*

22. According to the study by Brudney & Ditslear, *supra*, at 50, Justice Scalia did not rely upon substantive canons in any of his written opinions on workplace law from 1989 to 2003. "Justice Scalia, however, does regularly join majority opinions that rely on the substantive canons, and he has not distanced himself from such reasoning in separate concurrence as he has often done with respect to legislative history reliance by the majority." *Id.* at 51 n.180. He also has written opinions outside the context of workplace law relying on the avoidance canon. *See, e.g., Clark v. Martinez,* 543 U.S. 371, 382 (2005).

23. Scalia & Garner, *supra* at 31.

24. Scalia, *supra*, at 29.

25. *Id.* at 28. Justice Scalia laid out his attack on this particular canon in Antonin Scalia, *Assorted Canards of Contemporary Legal Analysis,* 40 Case W. Res. L. Rev. 581, 581-586 (1990). He notes that there is not even general agreement over what a "remedial statute" is.

26. Popkin offers two reasons for the indeterminacy of the application of substantive canons. "First, the interaction of the canons with both the statute's text and purpose varies too widely to provide much certainty. . . . Second, the canons cannot provide sufficient certainty in application because their weight varies over time." William D. Popkin, Statutes in Court: The History and Theory of Statutory Interpretation 201 (1999); *see also* Einer Elhauge, Statutory Default Rules: How to Interpret Unclear Legislation 2 (2008) ("there appear to be no consistently followed rules about which canons to invoke in particular cases"); Jane S. Schacter, *Metademocracy: The Changing Structure of Legitimacy in Statutory Interpretation,* 108 Harv. L. Rev. 593, 653 (1995) ("Under the traditional approach, judges have the 'power' to choose between competing, reasonable interpretations of a statute, and to choose from among a long list of canons of construction that often embody highly contestable normative choices.").

as consistent or predictable guides to statutory meaning."[27] Instead, the authors found that majority opinions relying on language canons were met with dissents similarly relying on language canons, and majority opinions relying on substantive canons were challenged by dissenting opinions similarly relying on substantive canons. "Such results suggest that the Justices themselves are inclined to disagree about the clarity or predictability of the canon-based reasoning."

Even worse, the authors found evidence that the canons were used "in an instrumental if not ideologically conscious manner." Their empirical study found "that canon usage by Justices identified as liberals tends to be linked to liberal outcomes, and canon reliance by conservative Justices tends to be associated with conservative outcomes." Moreover, "[d]octrinal analysis of illustrative [workplace law] decisions indicates that conservative members of the Rehnquist Court are using the canons in such contested cases to ignore—and thereby undermine—the demonstrable legislative preferences of Congress." Other scholars have similarly argued that the canons are "a façade, useful to support decisions that reflect judicial policy preferences notwithstanding a different congressional intent."[28]

Example 1

Are textual canons justified as a means of statutory interpretation? What about substantive canons? Is one set of tools more justified than the other?

Explanation

These are hard questions to answer in the abstract, and you likely will have a stronger opinion about these questions after you read cases in which you see Supreme Court justices and lower court judges applying and arguing about the canons. These are also highly contested questions, ones that go to the heart of the debate over statutory interpretation.

Supporters of textual canons see them as a fair-minded approach to statutory interpretation questions, ones that cabin judicial discretion and encourage legislators to write statutes clearly, with an understanding that the statutes will be interpreted literally. To textualists applying canons, a statute

---

27. Brudney & Ditslear, *supra*, at 6.
28. *Id.* at 10, citing Stephen F. Ross, *Where Have You Gone Karl Llewellyn? Should Congress Turn Its Lonely Eyes to You?*, 45 VAND. L. REV. 561, 562 (1992); Edward L. Rubin, *Modern Statutes, Loose Canons, and the Limits of Practical Reason: A Response to Farber and Ross*, 45 VAND. L. REV. 579, 590 (1992); and David L. Shapiro, *Continuity and Change in Statutory Interpretation*, 67 N.Y.U. L. REV. 921, 958-959 (1992).

is like a linguistic puzzle that often has a right answer that reasonable English speakers, regardless of ideology, would accept.

Opponents of textual interpretation argue that language is more inde-terminate, and more contextual, than judges solely applying textual canons could appreciate. Some of these critics believe that textualism leads to a conservative bias in the law through a narrow interpretation of statutes that does not consider important policy considerations and that does not have the flexibility to deal with surprising or unexpected consequences of textual interpretations.

Substantive canons can allow for consideration of policy, by, for example, putting a thumb on the scale in favor of interpretations that allow courts to avoid deciding difficult constitutional questions. There are two layers of criticism against substantive statutes: First, some textualists argue against the idea of using such canons to put a thumb on the scale, advocating a "fair" reading of the text not considering policy. (Although even textualists such as Justice Scalia seem to accept some substantive canons as background rules that everyone knows will be applied when reviewing a statute.) Second, critics may have problems with *particular* substantive statutes. Why *should* courts avoid deciding constitutional questions, or interpret crim-inal statutes to favor criminal defendants? The third part of this chapter takes up this question.

Between textual and substantive canons, which is more legitimate? It is really hard to say. Some textual canons make a lot of intuitive sense, and some substantive canons advance important policy goals. The biggest problem with both canons is their inconsistent use by judges. It may be an exaggeration to say every canon has a counter-canon, but smart judges (and their hardworking clerks) often can selectively deploy certain canons to reach results that are consistent with the judges' ideological predispositions. In the hard cases, where a lot is on the line, canons may be more of an after-the-fact justification than a set of neutral tools employed by judges to reach fair results.

6.2. TEXTUAL CANONS

The Scalia and Garner book lists dozens of textual canons, and in this book I cannot cover them all. Instead I focus on some of the most important of the textual canons to give a flavor of the issues they present.

Words and their companions (or lack of companions). We begin with the *expressio unius* (also sometimes knows as the *inclusio unius*) canon mentioned briefly above in connection with the *Holy Trinity Church* case: The inclusion of one thing implies the exclusion of others.

Here is a recent example of the canon's use from a Supreme Court case, *Bruesewitz v. Wyeth LLC*.[29] The National Childhood Vaccine Injury Act of 1986, 42 U.S.C. §300aa-22(b)(1), provides that

> No vaccine manufacturer shall be liable in a civil action for damages arising from a vaccine-related injury or death associated with the administration of a vaccine after October 1, 1988, if the injury or death resulted from side effects that were unavoidable even though the vaccine was properly prepared and was accompanied by proper directions and warnings.

Does this statutory provision pre-empt a state tort law claim for design defect?

Justice Scalia, writing for the Court majority, held that it did, relying in part on the *expressio unius* canon:

> The "even though" clause clarifies the word that precedes it. It delineates the preventative measures that a vaccine manufacturer *must* have taken for a side-effect to be considered "unavoidable" under the statute. Provided that there was proper manufacture and warning, any remaining side effects, including those resulting from design defects, are deemed to have been unavoidable. State-law design-defect claims are therefore preempted.
>
> If a manufacturer could be held liable for failure to use a different design, the word "unavoidable" would do no work. A side effect of a vaccine could *always* have been avoidable by use of a differently designed vaccine not containing the harmful element. The language of the provision thus suggests that the *design* of the vaccine is a given, not subject to question in the tort action. What the statute establishes as a complete defense must be unavoidability (given safe manufacture and warning) *with respect to the particular design*. Which plainly implies that the design itself is not open to question.
>
> A further textual indication leads to the same conclusion. Products-liability law establishes a classic and well known triumvirate of grounds for liability: defective manufacture, inadequate directions or warnings, and defective design. If all three were intended to be preserved, it would be strange to mention specifically only two, and leave the third to implication. It would have been much easier (and much more natural) to provide that manufacturers would be liable for "defective manufacture, defective directions or warning, and defective design." It seems that the statute fails to mention design-defect liability "by deliberate choice, not inadvertence." *Barnhart v. Peabody Coal Co.*, 537 U.S. 149 (2003). *Expressio unius, exclusio alterius.*

Justice Sotomayor, joined by Justice Ginsburg, dissented. The dissent offered an extensive analysis of the legislative history as well as an alternative

---

29. 131 S.Ct. 1068 (2011).

textual reading of the statute. On the *expressio unius* point of the majority, Justice Sotomayor wrote

> The majority's only other textual argument is based on the *expressio unius, exclusio alterius* canon. According to the majority, because blackletter products liability law generally recognizes three different types of product defects, "[i]f all three were intended to be preserved, it would be strange [for Congress] to mention specifically only two" — namely, manufacturing and labeling defects in the "even though" clause — "and leave the third to implication." The majority's argument, however, ignores that the default rule under the Vaccine Act is that state law is preserved. As explained above, §22(a) expressly provides that the "[g]eneral rule" is that "State law shall apply to a civil action brought for damages for a vaccine-related injury or death." Because §22(a) already preserves state-law design defect claims (to the extent the exemption in §22(b)(1) does not apply), there was no need for Congress separately and expressly to preserve design defect claims in §22(b)(1). Indeed, Congress' principal aim in enacting §22(b)(1) was not to preserve manufacturing and labeling claims (those, too, were already preserved by §22(a)), but rather, to federalize [Restatement Second of Torts §402A] comment k-type protection for "unavoidably unsafe" vaccines. The "even though" clause simply functions to limit the applicability of that defense. The lack of express language in §22(b)(1) specifically preserving design defect claims thus cannot fairly be understood as impliedly (and categorically) pre-empting such traditional state tort claims, which had already been preserved by §22(a).

Note that Justice Sotomayor did not argue against application of the *expressio unius* canon. Instead she argued that Congress did consider the question, and that a full reading of the entire law (a means of interpretation generally strongly supported by textualists) indicated that Congress did consider the issue and preserved state design-defect claims.

Although Justice Sotomayor did not take the canon on in this case, it does not always make sense. As Eskridge, Frickey, and Garrett explain, "if Mother tells Sally, 'Don't hit, choke, or kick your sister Anne,' and Sally immediately pinches and punches her sister, she cannot legitimately argue that pinching and pushing were implicitly authorized because they were omitted from the prohibition . . ."[30]

Noscitur a sociis (*a word is known by the company it keeps*). In *Green v. New York*,[31] plaintiffs brought suit under a provision of the Americans with Disabilities Act against St. Luke's Hospital, a private hospital. The hospital contended that because it was a private hospital, it could not be held liable under the ADA. The Second Circuit agreed with that position:

---

30. William N. Eskridge Jr., Philip P. Frickey, & Elizabeth Garrett, Legislation and Statutory Interpretation 264 (2d ed. 2006).
31. 465 F.3d 65 (2d Cir. 2006).

[W]e affirm the district court's dismissal of the ADA claim against St. Luke's because it is not a public entity subject to suit under Title II. By statute, a "public entity" is defined as "(A) any State or local government; (B) any department, agency, special purpose district, or other instrumentality of a State or States or local government; and (C) the National Railroad Passenger Corporation, and any commuter authority." 42 U.S.C. §12131(1). Plaintiffs contend that St. Luke's is a public entity because in the actions under review in this lawsuit, it carried out a public function pursuant to a contract with the City, in accord with City rules, and under the direction of City employees. Plaintiffs fail, however, to grapple with the actual words of the statute.

"Statutory analysis begins with the text and its plain meaning, if it has one." *Gottlieb v. Carnival Corp.*, 436 F.3d 335, 337 (2d Cir.2006). Only if an attempt to discern the plain meaning fails because the statute is ambiguous, do we resort to canons of construction. If both the plain language and the canons of construction fail to resolve the ambiguity, we turn to the legislative history.

In parsing the statute, we note that it is clear that St. Luke's, a private hospital, is not (1) a state or local government, (2) a department, agency, or special purpose district of a state or local government, or (3) the National Railroad Passenger Corporation or a commuter authority. Therefore, we are left to determine whether "instrumentality" was meant to include private hospitals that contract with a municipality to provide services

One relevant canon of construction is that in searching for the meaning Congress intended, we consider the context in which a particular word occurs because a statutory term "gathers meaning from the words around it." *Jarecki v. G.D. Searle & Co.*, 367 U.S. 303, 307 (1961). Although "[t]he maxim *noscitur a sociis*, that a word is known by the company it keeps, [is] not an inescapable rule, [it] is often wisely applied where a word is capable of many meanings in order to avoid the giving of unintended breadth to the Acts of Congress." *Id.*

"Instrumentality," like "discovery," the word considered in *Jarecki*, is a word susceptible of more than one meaning and is therefore potentially ambiguous. It may, for instance, mean "something by which an end is achieved." Websters Third New International Dictionary 1172 (Philip Babcock Grove ed., 1993). But, it may also mean "a part, organ, or subsidiary branch, esp. of a governing body." *Id.* The former meaning supports the conclusion that a hospital that contracts with a municipality to provide services is an instrumentality, while the latter suggests that to be an instrumentality, an entity must somehow belong to the government or have been created by it.

Because of the "company ['instrumentality'] keeps," *Jarecki*, we hold that Congress intended the latter meaning. "Instrumentality," is one of a string of words that includes "agency," "department," and "special purpose district." All of the words in this string are qualified by "of a State or States or local government." Agencies and departments are units of a governmental entity while a special purpose district, at least in New York, is understood to mean a district set up by a municipality to serve certain needs such as sewer, drainage, parking, and the like. Each of the entities listed other than "instrumentalities" is thus a creature of the municipality or state whose ends it serves. We therefore conclude that "instrumentality" is likewise best read as referring to a creature of a state or municipality. A private hospital performing services pursuant to a contract with a municipality even if it does so according to the municipality's rules and under its direction, is not a creature of any governmental entity. Instead it is a parallel private entity. Because St. Luke's is a private, and not a public, entity, the district court correctly dismissed the ADA claim against St. Luke's.

Ejusdem generis. In *Green*, the Second Circuit noted that its analysis was supported not just by the *noscitur a sociis* canon but also by *ejusdem generis*. "The same result would be achieved through application of *ejusdem generis*, 'a rule of statutory construction that provides that when general words follow the enumeration of particular classes, the general words should be construed as applying only to things of the same general class as those enumerated.'"

Justice Scalia and Brian Garner say that the justification for *ejusdem generis* is twofold: "When the initial terms all belong to an obvious and readily identifiable genus, one presumes that the speaker or writer has that category in mind for the entire passage. . . . And second, when that tagalong general term is given its broadest application, it renders the prior enumeration superfluous."[32] Scalia and Garner write approvingly of the resolution of a South Dakota case involving a statute providing that "[n]o equine activity, sponsor, equine professional, doctor of veterinary medicine, or any other person is liable for an injury to or the death of a participating resulting from the inherent risk of equine activities." A woman was killed riding a horse when her horse tripped over a cable trench dug by AT&T. AT&T argued it was immune from liability as an "other person" under the statute. The Supreme Court of South Dakota disagreed. Using the *ejusdem generis* canon, it held that only "other persons" involved in equine activities (which AT&T was not) were exempt from liability under the Act.[33]

Example 2

Consider the facts of the *Jarecki* case, which the *Green* court relied upon:

> These cases present problems in the interpretation of § 456(a) of the Internal Revenue Code of 1939, a section of the Excess Profits Tax Act of 1950. The Act, which is intended to tax at high rates unusually high profits earned during the Korean War, imposes a tax on profits in excess of an amount deemed to represent the taxpayer's normal profits. Recognizing, however, that some profits otherwise subject to tax under this scheme might stem from causes other than the inflated wartime economy, Congress enacted § 456. This section

---

32. Scalia & Garner, *supra*, at 199-200.
33. *Nielson v. AT&T Corp.*, 597 N.W.2d 434 (S.D. 1999).

grants relief in certain cases of "abnormal income" as defined in § 456(a)[34] by allocating some of this income to years other than those in which it was received for purposes of computing the tax.

The dispute in these cases is whether income from the sales of certain new products falls within the statutory definition of "abnormal income." Taxpayers claim that the income from the sales of their products is income resulting from "discovery." They claim it is therefore "abnormal income" within the class defined by § 456(a)(2)(B) as

"Income resulting from exploration, discovery, or prospecting, or any combination of the foregoing, extending over a period of more than 12 months."

Taxpayer in No. 151 is a corporation engaged in the manufacture and marketing of drugs. As a result of research extending for more than 12 months, it produced two new drugs, "Banthine," used in the treatment of peptic ulcers, and "Dramamine," for relief from motion sickness. Taxpayer received patents on both drugs, and it asserts that both were new products and not merely improvements on pre-existing compounds. Taxpayer received income from the sale of "Banthine" and "Dramamine" in the years 1950 through 1952. It paid its tax without claiming relief under §456, and then claimed a refund. On denial of its claim, taxpayer filed a complaint in the District Court for the Northern District of Illinois. The District Court dismissed the complaint, but the Court of Appeals for the Seventh Circuit reversed. It held that "discovery" might include the preparation of new products and that the case must be remanded for a trial on the issue of whether taxpayer's drugs "were actually discoveries."

Taxpayer in No. 169 is the inventor and producer of the "Polaroid Land Process," a camera and film which produce a photograph in 60 seconds, and the "Polaroid 3-D Synthetic Polarizer," a device incorporated in the "viewers" through which audiences watched the three dimensional motion pictures in

---

34. Section 456(a) provides in part:'(a) Definitions. — For the purposes of this section — '(1) Abnormal income. — The term 'abnormal income' means income of any class described in paragraph (2) includible in the gross income of the taxpayer for any taxable year under this subchapter if it is abnormal for the taxpayer to derive income of such class, or, if the taxpayer normally derives income of such class but the amount of such income of such class includible in the gross income of the taxable year is in excess of 115 per centum of the average amount of the gross income of the same class for the four previous taxable years, or, if the taxpayer was not in existence for four previous taxable years, the taxable years during which the taxpayer was in existence.'(2) Separate classes of income. — Each of the following subparagraphs shall be held to describe a separate class of income: '(A) Income arising out of a claim, award, judgment, or decree, or interest on any of the foregoing; or '(B) Income resulting from exploration, discovery, or prospecting, or any combination of the foregoing, extending over a period of more than 12 months; or '(C) Income from the sale of patents, formulae, or processes, or any combination of the foregoing developed over a period of more than 12 months; or'(D) Income includible in gross income for the taxable year rather than for a different taxable year by reason of a change in the taxpayer's method of accounting.' All the income which is classifiable in more than one of such subparagraphs shall be classified under the one which the taxpayer irrevocably elects. The classification of income of any class not described in subparagraphs (A) to (D), inclusive, shall be subject to regulations prescribed by the Secretary.'

vogue some years ago. These inventions, each the product of more than 12 months' research, are novel, according to taxpayer, and each has been patented. The Polaroid Land equipment was the subject of 238 patents by the end of 1958, and taxpayer characterizes this invention as "revolutionary." Its production was a new departure in the business of taxpayer, which had hitherto been engaged primarily in manufacturing and selling such optical products as polarizing sunglasses, visors and camera filters. In its returns for 1951 through 1953 taxpayer utilized the provisions of §456 in computing its tax on income from the sales of its photographic equipment and 3-D polarizers. The Commissioner determined that §456 was not applicable, and the Tax Court upheld his determination of a deficiency. The Court of Appeals for the First Circuit affirmed, holding that taxpayer's inventions were not "discoveries" and its income from their sale not "abnormal income."

If you were applying a textual interpretation of §456, would you say that the taxpayers are entitled to the special tax treatment?

Explanation

The Supreme Court in Jarecki rejected the taxpayers' arguments for special tax treatment under §456. Here is the textual portion of their analysis (leaving out the legislative history analysis):

> For present purposes we accept, as did the First Circuit, taxpayers' assertions of the novelty of their products. But we also agree with that court that taxpayers' inventions are not "discoveries" as that word is used in §456(a)(2)(B) and that income from sales of the new products may not receive the special treatment provided by §456.
>
> We look first to the face of the statute. "Discovery" is a word usable in many contexts and with various shades of meaning. Here, however, it does not stand alone, but gathers meaning from the words around it. These words strongly suggest that a precise and narrow application was intended in §456. The three words in conjunction, "exploration," "discovery" and "prospecting," all describe income-producing activity in the oil and gas and mining industries, but it is difficult to conceive of any other industry to which they all apply. Certainly the development and manufacturer of drugs and cameras are not such industries. The maxim noscitur a sociis, that a word is known by the company it keeps, while not an inescapable rule, is often wisely applied where a word is capable of many meanings in order to avoid the giving of unintended breadth to the Acts of Congress. The application of the maxim here leads to the conclusion that "discovery" in §456 means only the discovery of mineral resources.
>
> When we examine further the construction of §456(a)(2) and compare subparagraphs (B) and (C), it becomes unmistakably clear that "discovery" was not meant to include the development of patentable products. If "discovery" were so wide in scope, there would be no need for the provision in subparagraph (C) for "Income from the sale of patents, formulae, or processes."

146

All of this income, under taxpayers' reading of "discovery," would also be income "resulting from * * * discovery" within subparagraph (B). To borrow the homely metaphor of Judge Aldrich in the First Circuit, "If there is a big hole in the fence for the big cat, need there be a small hole for the small one?" The statute admits a reasonable construction which gives effect to all of its provisions. In these circumstances we will not adopt a strained reading which renders one part a mere redundancy.

Taxpayers assert that it is the "ordinary meaning" of "discovery" which must govern. We find ample evidence both on the face of the statute and, as we shall show, in its legislative history that a technical usage was intended. But even if we were without such evidence we should find it difficult to believe that Congress intended to apply the layman's meaning of "discovery" to describe the products of research. To do so would lead to the necessity of drawing a line between things found and things made, for in ordinary present-day usage things revealed are discoveries, but new fabrications are inventions. It would appear senseless for Congress to adopt this usage, to provide relief for income from discoveries and yet make no provision for income from inventions. Perhaps in the patent law "discovery" has the uncommonly wide meaning taxpayers suggest, but the fields of patents and taxation are each lores unto themselves, and the usage in the patent law (which is by no means entirely in taxpayers' favor) is unpersuasive here. All the evidence is to the effect that Congress did not intend to introduce the difficult distinction between inventions and discoveries into the excess profits tax law.

Note how the courts in *Jarecki* and in the other cases quoted above seek to weave a full textual analysis of the provision. Courts look to read an entire statute in harmony (the "whole act" rule), to avoid rendering any part of the statute without meaning (the rule against "surplusage"), and to apply common sense and ordinary meaning in *context* to the statute. Context is so important: The word *discovery* in isolation easily could be interpreted to mean a scientific discovery or invention; but in the context of the tax statute, discovery meant something much narrower.

Grammar and Punctuation.   Grammar and punctuation also matter a great deal in construing statutes. A whole set of canons consider these issues down to the level of the difference between a comma and a semicolon. Consider this discussion from a recent bankruptcy case:[35]

> Because North Dakota has opted out of the Code's exemption scheme, we look to North Dakota law to determine whether Debtor's interest in the Annuity is exempt. The North Dakota exemption statute in question, N.D. CENT. CODE §28–22–03.1(3), provides in relevant part that a resident of North Dakota may exempt:

---

35. *In re Kukowski*, 356 B.R. 712 (B.A.P. 8th Cir. 2006).

"Pensions, annuity policies or plans, and life insurance policies that, upon the death of the insured, would be payable to the spouse, children, or any relative of the insured dependent, or likely to be dependent, upon the insured for support and which have been in effect for a period of at least one year; . . ."

The bankruptcy court held that because the "upon the death of the insured" qualification modifies the three preceding types of assets, pensions, annuities and life insurance policies, the Annuity did not fall within the scope of §28–22–03.1(3). Debtor initially argues that the "upon the death of the insured" language only modifies the immediately preceding noun, life insurance policies. Given the unique context in which the North Dakota Legislature amended the statute in 1991, we find that the bankruptcy court's construction of the statute is correct.

Prior to 1991, the three types of assets listed in the first part of §28–22–03.1(3), pensions, annuities and life insurance policies, were separated by semi-colons. *See* N.D. CENT. CODE §28–22–03.1(3) (1990). Judge Hill, who also issued the opinion *sub judice*, held in 1990 that because the Legislature used semi-colons instead of commas to separate the three nouns, the modifying phrase beginning with "upon the death of the insured" only applied to life insurance policies, which is the immediately preceding noun. *In re Smith*, 113 B.R. 579, 585 (Bankr.D.N.D.1990). Judge Hill expressly stated that if the Legislature had intended for the modifying phrase to apply to all three of the assets listed, it would have separated the three by commas instead of semi-colons. *Id.*

A year after Judge Hill issued the *Smith* opinion, the North Dakota Legislature amended §28–22–03.1(3) by separating the three types of assets listed in the statute with commas instead of semi-colons. 1991 NORTH DAKOTA LAWS CH. 341 (H.B.1335). This is the only change that the Legislature made to the statute during the 1991 session. Because it is clear that the Legislature enacted the 1991 Amendment in response to Judge Hill's opinion in *In re Smith*, the amendment unequivocally demonstrates the Legislature's intent to overrule Judge Hill's interpretation of §28–22–03.1(3) contained in *In re Smith*.

Under North Dakota's rules of statutory construction, a court must give meaning to amendments to statutes. Also, it is presumed that the Legislature is aware of prior judicial constructions of a statute when it amends that same statute. Thus, when the Legislature amends a statute that substantively differs from a prior and recent judicial interpretation of the same statute, a court should infer that the Legislature intended to overrule the judicial construction of the statute announced in that prior case.

Here, Judge Hill expressly stated in *Smith* that because the Legislature separated pensions, annuities and life insurance policies with semi-colons instead of commas, the modifying clause beginning with "upon the death of the insured" only applied to life insurance policies. A year later, the North Dakota Legislature amended §28–22–03.1(3) by replacing the semi-colons with commas. This is the only change that the Legislature made to §28–22–03.1(3) during the 1991 legislative session.

Given this context in which the North Dakota Legislature enacted the 1991 Amendment, it is clear that Legislature intended to overrule Judge Hill's interpretation of §28–22–03.1(3) contained in *Smith*. Thus, the 1991 Amendment demonstrates that Legislature's intent that the modifying phrase beginning with "upon the death of the insured" should modify pensions, annuities and life insurance policies. Thus, the bankruptcy court's finding that the term "upon the death of the insured" modifies the noun "annuities" is not erroneous.

By this point in the book you will not be shocked to learn that this discussion of the deep meaning of the semicolon provoked a sharp dissent. Here is an excerpt:

[The majority opinion] misconstrues the plain language of the statute. From a purely grammatical standpoint, the clause beginning with "upon the death of the insured" does not, as the bankruptcy court held and the majority affirms, modify "pensions, annuity policies or plans, *and* life insurance policies." Rather, it modifies only "life insurance policies." To accomplish the interpretation advanced by the bankruptcy court and the majority, the statute would have to be rewritten with a comma between "life insurance policies" and "that," *i.e.*, "Pensions, annuity policies or plans, and life insurance policies, that, upon the death of the insured, would be payable to the spouse . . . and which have been in effect for a period of at least one year." But that isn't the way it is written. And until the statute is so rewritten, it does not matter whether there is a comm[a] or semicolon at the end of that list.

The statute's grammar isn't the only barrier to the bankruptcy court's interpretation of the statute; there are semantic inconsistencies as well. Why would the phrase "upon the death of the '*insured*'" apply to an annuitant and a pensioner? It is hard to imagine a clearer sign that the phrase only modifies insurance policies. In fact, the word "*insured*" appears three times in the questioned phrase, further reinforcing the conclusion that the phrase applies only to life insurance policies. In contrast, annuitants and pensioners are generally referred to as "*annuitants*" and "*pensioners;*" they are not called "*insureds.*" Moreover, it defies logic and common sense to interpret the statute as applying to pensions and annuities that are only payable upon the death of the "insured" (pensioner or annuitant). Pensions and annuities are usually, if not always, paid to pensioners or annuitants while they are alive, not upon their death, although both pensions and annuities may—like the annuity in this case—contain survivorship provisions as well. Quite simply, the bankruptcy court's (and the majority's) interpretation of §28–22–03.1(3) leads to a grammatically and semantically strained reading of the statute which is at odds with its plain language and unwarranted in light of the policy to construe exemption statutes liberally in favor of a debtor.

Even putting semicolons aside, the placement of commas or lack of commas can lead to great grief among litigants and courts. Lurking in the last case's dissent is the *last antecedent rule*, "[a] pronoun, relative pronoun, or demonstrative adjective generally refers to the nearest reasonable antecedent."[36] Consider *Barnhart v. Thomas*,[37] a unanimous opinion by Justice Scalia:

> Under the Social Security Act, the Social Security Administration (SSA) is authorized to pay disability insurance benefits and Supplemental Security Income to persons who have a "disability." A person qualifies as disabled, and thereby eligible for such benefits, "only if his physical or mental impairment or impairments are of such severity that he is not only unable to do his previous work but cannot, considering his age, education, and work experience, engage in any other kind of substantial gainful work which exists in the national economy." 42 U. S. C. §§423(d)(2)(A), 1382c(a)(3)(B). The issue we must decide is whether the SSA may determine that a claimant is not disabled because she remains physically and mentally able to do her previous work, without investigating whether that previous work exists in significant numbers in the national economy. . . .
>
> [The Third Circuit, "[o]ver the dissent of three of its members . . . held that the statute unambiguously provides that the ability to perform prior work disqualifies from benefits only if it is 'substantial gainful work which exists in the national economy.'"] The Third Circuit's reading disregards — indeed, is precisely contrary to — the grammatical "rule of the last antecedent," according to which a limiting clause or phrase (here, the relative clause "which exists in the national economy") should ordinarily be read as modifying only the noun or phrase that it immediately follows (here, "any other kind of substantial gainful work"). While this rule is not an absolute and can assuredly be overcome by other indicia of meaning, we have said that construing a statute in accord with the rule is "quite sensible as a matter of grammar." In *FTC v. Mandel Brothers, Inc.*, 359 U. S. 385 (1959), this Court employed the rule to interpret a statute strikingly similar in structure to §423(d)(2)(A) — a provision of the Fur Products Labeling Act, 15 U. S. C. §69, which defined "'invoice'" as "'a written account, memorandum, list, or catalog . . . transported or delivered to a purchaser, consignee, factor, bailee, correspondent, or agent, *or any other person who is engaged in dealing commercially in fur products or furs.*'" (emphasis added). Like the Third Circuit here, the Court of Appeals in *Mandel Brothers* had interpreted the phrase "any other" as rendering the relative clause ("who is engaged in dealing commercially") applicable to all the specifically listed categories. This Court unanimously reversed, concluding that the "limiting clause is to be applied only to the last antecedent."
>
> An example will illustrate the error of the Third Circuit's perception that the specifically enumerated "previous work" "must" be treated the same as the more general reference to "any other kind of substantial gainful work." Consider, for example, the case of parents who, before leaving their teenage son alone in the house for the weekend, warn him, "You will be punished if you throw a party or engage in any other activity that damages the house." If

---

36. SCALIA & GARNER, *supra* at 144.
37. 540 U.S. 20 (2003).

the son nevertheless throws a party and is caught, he should hardly be able to avoid punishment by arguing that the house was not damaged. The parents proscribed (1) a party, and (2) any other activity that damages the house. As far as appears from what they said, their reasons for prohibiting the home-alone party may have had nothing to do with damage to the house — for instance, the risk that underage drinking or sexual activity would occur. And even if their only concern was to prevent damage, it does not follow from the fact that the same interest underlay both the specific and the general prohibition that proof of impairment of that interest is required for both. The parents, foreseeing that assessment of whether an activity had in fact "damaged" the house could be disputed by their son, might have wished to preclude all argument by specifying and categorically prohibiting the one activity — hosting a party — that was most likely to cause damage and most likely to occur.

What is the takeaway from this discussion? As a legislative drafter, this discussion should teach you to write with as much precision as possible. As a litigator, this discussion should teach you that when construing a statute textually, you should begin with a focus on grammatical rules and textual canons on the micro level, and consider the structure and logic of the statute as a whole. This kind of deep textual analysis will be more important to some judges than any policy arguments or legislative history you can muster.

Example 3

Alleging that she sustained an on-the-job injury, Maria Guillen–Chavez sued ReadyOne, a federal contractor, for negligence. ReadyOne moved to compel arbitration pursuant to an agreement requiring that claims of on-the-job injuries be submitted to binding arbitration. In response, Guillen–Chavez moved for limited discovery on the issue of arbitrability to develop her case. In particular, she claimed that a federal statutory provisions, the Franken Amendment (named after Senator Al Franken), precluded arbitration of workplace claims based upon an employer's negligent supervision of her while on the job.

The Franken Amendment reads in relevant part

(a) None of the funds appropriated or otherwise made available by this Act may be expended for any Federal contract for an amount in excess of $1,000,000 that is awarded more than 60 days after the effective date of this Act, unless the contractor agrees not to:

. . .

(2) take any action to enforce any provision of an existing agreement with an employee or independent contractor that mandates that the employee or independent contractor resolve through arbitration any claim under title VII of the Civil Rights Act of 1964 or any tort related to or arising out of sexual assault or harassment, including assault and battery, intentional infliction of emotional distress, false imprisonment, or negligent hiring, supervision, or retention. Pub.L. 111–118, §8116, 123 Stat. 3409, 3454–55 (2009).

ReadyOne had agreed to this provision in signing federal contracts. According to a textual analysis, does the statute bar arbitrability of Guillen-Chavez's negligent supervision claim against ReadyOne? Should the court allow discovery into the negligent supervision claim?

Explanation

The facts of this case come from *In Re ReadyOne Industries, Inc.*[38] The court applied a textual analysis to resolve the claim to require arbitration for a case of negligent supervision. Here is the relevant part of the court's analysis:

> The dispute here centers on the meaning of the clause "any claim under title VII of the Civil Rights Act of 1964 or any tort related to or arising out of sexual *assault* or harassment, *including* assault and battery, intentional infliction of emotional distress, false imprisonment, or negligent hiring, supervision, or retention." [Emphasis added]. ReadyOne asserts that "the list of generic torts following 'including' are not additional torts to which the arbitration prohibition would apply," but are "simply a descriptive list of some of the type of torts that could arise out of sexual assault or harassment." Guillen–Chavez, on the other hand, posits that, when read in the disjunctive, the conjunction "or" serves to identify the types of claims to which the Amendment applies and to cast them as claims independent of one another. Thus, according to Guillen–Chavez, the phrase "or negligent hiring, supervision, or retention" is independent of and does not modify the phrase "any tort related to or arising out of sexual assault or harassment, including. . . ." We disagree.
>
> When identifying the types of claims not subject to arbitration, the Amendment begins by listing title VII claims, followed by the clause "or any tort related to or arising out of sexual assault or harassment," which in turn is followed by the adjectival phrase "including assault and battery, intentional infliction of emotional distress, false imprisonment. . . ." The concluding phrase "or negligent hiring, supervision, or retention" immediately follows the beginning of the adjectival phrase identifying torts that fall in the class of claims related to or arising out of sexual assault or harassment. Applying the doctrine of *ejusdem generis* in conjunction with the maxim *noscitur a sociis* and the last antecedent rule, we conclude that the phrase "or negligent hiring, supervision, or retention" refers only to claims "such like" the class of claims immediately preceding the use of the present participle "including," i.e., torts related to or arising out of sexual assault or harassment. This is because negligent hiring, negligent supervision, and negligent retention are torts analogous to those expressly mentioned as the type of torts that could arise out of sexual assault or harassment — assault and battery, intentional infliction of emotional distress, and false imprisonment. Furthermore, because all of these torts are similar in nature, are grouped together, and follow the word "including," which precedes the phrase "any tort related to or arising out of

---

38. 394 S.W.3d 680 (Tx. App. 2012).

sexual assault or harassment," they qualify the phrase and are therefore confined to it. Accordingly, the phrase "or negligent hiring, supervision, or retention" was not intended to define a category of claims separate and apart from title VII claims or torts related to or arising out of sexual assault or harassment.

As noted above, Guillen–Chavez argues that because the various types of claims and torts identified in the disputed clause are separated by the disjunctive "or," they should be construed as alternative claims, separate from and independent of one another. However, the structure and composition of the statutory text belie this argument and compel the conclusion that "negligent hiring, supervision, or retention" are not claims separate from and independent of the other non-arbitrable claims identified in the statute. If Guillen–Chavez is correct that the phrase "or negligent hiring, supervision, or retention" identifies the third element in a list of three items, then a comma would have been placed between the conjunction "or" separating the phrases "any claim under title VII" and "any tort related to or arising out of sexual assault or harassment" to identify each of the three members in the series. The fact that the conjunction "or" between the phrases identifying title VII claims and sexual assault claims is not separated by a comma indicates that there are no more than two elements identified in the list of claims not subject to arbitration. Indeed, the use of the comma before the conjunction "or" to separate the phrase "assault and battery, intentional infliction of emotional distress, false imprisonment" from "negligent hiring, supervision, or retention" denotes that the drafters of the Amendment used it as a serial comma to identify the disputed phrase as the final item in the list of the torts encompassing sexual assault and harassment. According to the Oxford Style Manual, "[t]he [use of a serial comma] serves . . . to resolve ambiguity, particularly when any of the items *are compound terms joined by a conjunction*." Oxford Style Manual, Oxford University Press, 2002, p. 122 [Emphasis added].

Because the Franken Amendment does not apply to personal injury claims related to or arising out of negligent hiring, supervision, or retention, we hold that the trial court abused its discretion by ordering discovery concerning the applicability of the Franken Amendment to the arbitrability of Guillen–Chavez's personal injury claims.

Do you agree the court got the textual analysis right? Should the textual analysis be the end of the analysis? (It was for this particular court.)

6.3. SUBSTANTIVE CANONS

Unlike textual canons, substantive canons are policy choices built into the system of statutory interpretation. As we have seen, some judges and scholars justify substantive canons on a textual basis as a kind of background or default drafting rule that was in the drafters' minds as they drafted legislation. Others justify individual substantive canons based upon the particular policy "thumb on the scale" they represent.

Consider, for example, the *rule of lenity*, which requires ambiguous criminal statutes to be interpreted in favor of the criminal defendant. How realistic is it that legislators, known to be "tough on crime," draft with the idea in mind that unclear criminal laws should be interpreted to the benefit of criminal defendants? The rule does seem more justified on pure policy grounds to give extra due process protections to those accused of crimes.

Note that the rule kicks in only when there is an *ambiguous* statute. Considering all the textual tools that courts now use to construe statutes, there may well be fewer statutes that courts conclude, after textual analysis, remain ambiguous. Indeed, in recent years the Supreme Court has articulated a test that makes it very hard for a court engaged in statutory interpretation to get to the rule of lenity: "[T]he rule of lenity only applies if, after considering text, structure, history, and purpose, there remains a grievous ambiguity or uncertainty in the statute, such that the Court must simply guess as to what Congress intended."[39]

Consider the Supreme Court's decision in *Begay v. U.S.*[40] Here is how the Court described the issue before it:

> Federal law prohibits a previously convicted felon from possessing a firearm. §922(g)(1) (2000 ed.). A related provision provides for a prison term of up to 10 years for an ordinary offender. §924(a)(2). The Armed Career Criminal Act imposes a more stringent 15-year mandatory minimum sentence on an offender who has three prior convictions "for a violent felony or a serious drug offense." §924(e)(1) (2000 ed., Supp. V).
>
> The Act defines a "violent felony" as "any crime punishable by imprisonment for a term exceeding one year" that
>
> "(i) has as an element the use, attempted use, or threatened use of physical force against the person of another; or
>
> "(ii) is burglary, arson, or extortion, involves use of explosives, or otherwise involves conduct that presents a serious potential risk of physical injury to another." §924(e)(2)(B) (2000 ed.).
>
> We here consider whether driving under the influence of alcohol (DUI), as set forth in New Mexico's criminal statutes, falls within the scope of the second clause.

The Court majority began with a textual analysis (you should see the implicit use of *noscitur a sociis* or *ejusdem generis*), but one that did not rely upon the rule of lenity:

> In our view, the provision's listed examples — burglary, arson, extortion, or crimes involving the use of explosives — illustrate the kinds of crimes that fall

---

39. *Barber v. Thomas*, 130 S.Ct. 2499, 2508-2509 (2010).
40. 553 U.S. 137 (2008).

within the statute's scope. Their presence indicates that the statute covers only *similar* crimes, rather than *every* crime that "presents a serious potential risk of physical injury to another." If Congress meant the latter, i.e., if it meant the statute to be all-encompassing, it is hard to see why it would have needed to include the examples at all. Without them, clause (ii) would cover *all* crimes that present a "serious potential risk of physical injury." Additionally, if Congress meant clause (ii) to include *all* risky crimes, why would it have included clause (i)? A crime which has as an element the "use, attempted use, or threatened use of physical force" against the person (as clause (i) specifies) is likely to create "a serious potential risk of physical injury" and would seem to fall within the scope of clause (ii).

Of course, Congress *might* have included the examples solely for quantitative purposes. Congress might have intended them to demonstrate no more than the degree of risk sufficient to bring a crime within the statute's scope. But were that the case, Congress would have likely chosen examples that better illustrated the "degree of risk" it had in mind. . . .

These considerations taken together convince us that, "'to give effect . . . to every clause and word'" of this statute, we should read the examples as limiting the crimes that clause (ii) covers to crimes that are roughly similar, in kind as well as in degree of risk posed, to the examples themselves.

The concurrence complains that our interpretive approach is insufficiently specific. But the concurrence's own approach demands a crime-by-crime analysis, uses a standard of measurement (comparative degree of risk) that even the concurrence admits is often "unclear," requires the concurrence to turn here to the still less clear "rule of lenity," and, as we explain, is less likely to reflect Congress' intent.

In his concurrence, Justice Scalia turned to the rule of lenity:

The Court is correct that the clause "otherwise involves conduct that presents a serious potential risk of physical injury to another" signifies a similarity between the enumerated and unenumerated crimes. It is not, however, *any* old similarity, such as (to take a random example) "purposeful, 'violent,' and 'aggressive' conduct." Rather, it is the *particular* similarity specified after the "otherwise" — i.e., that they all pose a serious potential risk of physical injury to another. They need not be similar in any other way. As the Court correctly notes, the word "otherwise" in this context means "'in a different way or manner.'" [See also] Webster's New International Dictionary 1729 (2d ed.1957) ("in another way or in other ways"). Therefore, by using the word "otherwise" the writer draws a substantive connection between two sets only on one specific dimension — i.e., whatever follows "otherwise." What that means here is that "committing one of the enumerated crimes . . . is *one way* to commit a crime 'involv[ing] a serious potential risk of physical injury to another'; and that *other ways* of committing a crime of that character similarly constitute 'violent felon[ies].'"

The Court rejects this seemingly straightforward statutory analysis, reading the residual clause to mean that the unenumerated offenses must be similar to the enumerated offenses not only in the degree of risk they pose, but also "in kind," despite the fact that "otherwise" means that the common element of risk must be presented "'in a *different* way or manner.'" The Court's explanation for this interpretation seems to be that the enumerated crimes are "so far from clear in respect to the degree of risk each poses that it is difficult to accept clarification in respect to degree of risk as Congress' only reason for including them." While I certainly agree that the degree of risk associated with the enumerated crimes is unclear, I find it unthinkable that the solution to that problem is to write a different statute. The phrase "otherwise involves conduct that presents a serious potential risk of physical injury to another" limits inclusion in the statute only by a crime's degree of risk. The use of the adjective "serious" seems to me to signify a purely quantitative measure of risk. If both an intentional and a negligent crime pose a 50% risk of death, could one be characterized as involving a "serious risk" and the other not? Surely not. . . .

[Justice Scalia rejected the Court's support for "its argument with that ever-ready refuge from the hardships of statutory text, the (judicially) perceived statutory purpose."] Under my interpretation of §924(e), I must answer one question: Does drunk driving pose at least as serious a risk of physical injury to another as burglary? From the evidence presented by the Government, I cannot conclude so. Because of that, the rule of lenity requires that I resolve this case in favor of the defendant.

The Government cites the fact that in 2006, 17,062 persons died from alcohol-related car crashes, and that 15,121 of those deaths involved drivers with blood-alcohol concentrations of 0.08 or higher. Drunk driving is surely a national problem of great concern. But the fact that it kills many people each year tells us very little about whether a single act of drunk driving "involves conduct that presents a serious potential risk of physical injury to another." It may well be that an even greater number of deaths occurs annually to pedestrians crossing the street; but that hardly means that crossing the street presents a serious potential risk of injury. Where the issue is "risk," the annual number of injuries from an activity must be compared with the annual incidents of the activity. Otherwise drunk driving could be said to pose a more serious risk of physical harm than murder. In addition, drunk driving is a combination of two activities: (1) drinking and (2) driving. If driving alone results in injury in a certain percentage of cases, it could hardly be said that the entirety of the risk posed by drunk driving can be attributed to the combination. And finally, injuries to the drunk drivers themselves must be excluded from the calculus, because the statute counts only injuries to other persons.

Needless to say, we do not have these relevant statistics. And even if we did, we would still need to know similar statistics for burglary, which are probably even harder to come by. This does not mean that I will never be able to identify a crime that falls under the residual clause. For some crimes, the severity of the risk will be obvious. Crimes like negligent homicide, see ALI, Model Penal Code §210.4 (1980), conspiracy to commit a violent crime, *id.*, §5.03 (1985), inciting to riot, 18 U.S.C. §2101, and the production of chemical weapons, §229, certainly pose a more serious risk of physical injury to others than burglary. (By contrast, the Court's approach eliminates from the residual clause all negligent crimes, even those that entail a 100% risk of physical injury such as negligent homicide.) But I can do no more than guess as to whether drunk driving poses a more serious risk than burglary, and I will not condemn a man to a minimum of 15 years in prison on the basis of such speculation. Applying the rule of lenity to a statute that demands it, I would reverse the decision of the Court of Appeals.

Three dissenters, led by Justice Alito, rejected both the majority and Justice Scalia's textual analyses:

[The majority's] interpretation cannot be squared with the text of the statute, which simply does not provide that an offense must be "purposeful," "violent," or "aggressive" in order to fall within the residual clause. Rather, after listing burglary, arson, extortion, and explosives offenses, the statute provides (in the residual clause) that an offense qualifies if it "otherwise involves conduct that presents a serious potential risk of physical injury to another." Therefore, offenses falling within the residual clause must be similar to the named offenses in one respect only: They must "otherwise" — which is to say, "in a different manner," 10 OED 984 (def. B(1)); see also Webster's 1598 — "involv[e] conduct that presents a serious potential risk of physical injury to another." Requiring that an offense must also be "purposeful," "violent," or "aggressive" amounts to adding new elements to the statute, but we "ordinarily resist reading words or elements into a statute that do not appear on its face." . . .

Justice SCALIA's concurrence takes a different approach, but his analysis is likewise flawed. Justice SCALIA would hold (1) that an offense does not fall within the residual clause unless it presents a risk that is at least as great as that presented by the least dangerous of the enumerated offenses; (2) that burglary is the least dangerous of the enumerated offenses; (3) that the relevant measure of risk is the risk that the typical burglary, DUI, etc. would result in injury; and (4) that the risk presented by an incident of DUI is less than the risk presented by a burglary.

Justice SCALIA, like the Court, does not follow the statutory language. The statute says that offenses falling within the residual clause must present "a serious potential risk of physical injury to another." The statute does not say that these offenses must present at least as much risk as the enumerated offenses.

The statute also does not say, as Justice SCALIA would hold, that the relevant risk is the risk that each incident of DUI will result in injury. I see no basis for concluding that Congress was not also concerned with the risk faced by potential victims, particularly since the statute explicitly refers to "potential risk." Drunk driving is regarded as a severe societal problem in large measure because of the very large number of victims it produces each year.

Who has the better of the argument here? More to the point, is this an appropriate case for the rule of lenity?

Another very important substantive canon is the *avoidance canon*.[41] Justice
Scalia has approved of and repeatedly applied the avoidance canon, as have
all other current members of the Supreme Court. The avoidance canon
provides that courts in appropriate circumstances should "avoid [statutory]
interpretations that would render a statute unconstitutional or that would
raise serious constitutional difficulties."[42] As with the rule of lenity, the
stated rule of the modern Court is that the avoidance canon only comes into
play only when the statutory interpretation that avoids constitutional doubt
is in fact *reasonable or plausible*:

> The doctrine of constitutional doubt does not require that the problem-
> avoiding construction be the preferable one — the one the Court would
> adopt in any event. Such a standard would deprive the doctrine of all function.
> "Adopt the interpretation that avoids the constitutional doubt if it is the right
> one" produces precisely the same result as "adopt the right interpretation."
> Rather, the doctrine of constitutional doubt comes into play when the statute is
> "susceptible of" the problem-avoiding interpretation — when *that interpretation
> is reasonable, though not necessarily the best.*[43]

Supporters of the canon's use raise three justifications: First, the avoidance canon "may be a rule of thumb for ascertaining legislative intent."[44]
The underlying assumption is that Congress either prefers not to press the
limits of the Constitution in its statutes, or it prefers a narrowed (and
constitutional) version of its statutes to a statute completely stricken by
the Court. This is the rationale often raised by the Supreme Court in applying
the canon.[45] Second, the canon may provide "a low-salience mechanism for
giving effect to what Larry Sager calls 'underenforced constitutional
norms.'"[46] As Eskridge explains: "While a Court that seeks to avoid
constitutional activism will be reluctant to invalidate federal statutes in

---

41. The next few paragraphs draw from Richard L. Hasen, *Constitutional Avoidance and
Anti-Avoidance by the Roberts Court*, 2009 Sup. Ct. Rev. 181 (2010).

42. Eskridge, Frickey, & Garrett, *supra*, app. B at 29.

43. *Almendarez-Torres v. United States*, 523 U.S. 224, 270 (1998) (Scalia, J. dissenting) (emphasis
added and citations omitted). Though Justice Scalia wrote this as part of his dissenting
opinion, on this point, the majority agreed: "[For the canon to apply,] the statute must
be genuinely susceptible to two constructions after, and not before, its complexities are
unraveled. Only then is the statutory construction that avoids the constitutional question a
'fair' one." *Id.* at 238. The majority and dissent disagreed in the *Almendarez-Torres* case over
whether the statutory language at issue pointed "significantly in one direction," id., and over
whether there was "grave[] doubt" about the constitutionality of the statute under one of the
interpretations. *Id.* at 239.

44. Eskridge, Frickey, & Garrett, *supra*, at 918.

45. *Rust v. Sullivan*, 500 U.S. 173, 191 (1991) ("This canon is followed out of respect for
Congress, which we assume legislates in the light of constitutional limitations."); *Clark v.
Martinez*, 543 U.S. 371, 382 (2005) ("The canon is thus a means of giving effect to congres-
sional intent, not of subverting it.").

46. Eskridge, Frickey, & Garrett, *supra* at 918.

close cases, it might seek other ways to protect constitutional norms. One way is through canons of statutory construction."[47] Avoidance in effect remands the statute to Congress. The canon "makes it harder for Congress to enact constitutionally questionable statutes and forces legislators to reflect and deliberate before plunging into constitutionally sensitive issues."[48] Third, the canon may help "courts conserve their institutional capital."[49]

Much other recent scholarship has expressed skepticism about the avoidance canon, at least as traditionally defended. Fred Schauer rejects the assumption that the avoidance canon furthers congressional intent, in the absence of any evidence that Congress would prefer a narrow interpretation of its statute to a court actually confronting whether the statute passes constitutional muster.[50] Judge Friendly worried that the canon would be applied selectively, making it "have almost as many dangers as advantages."[51]

Although modern legislation scholars see the avoidance canon as sometimes playing an important role in Supreme Court adjudication and its relation with Congress, there seems to be consensus that the canon's use signals a Supreme Court that is actively engaged in shaping law and policy, not acting modestly.

One recent example of the selective use of the avoidance canon came in two controversial Supreme Court cases decided in the same term. In *Northwest Austin Municipal Utility District No. One v. Holder*,[52] a case discussed in detail in Chapter 11, the Court engaged in (what I argue) was a disingenuous act of statutory interpretation of the Voting Rights Act and application of the avoidance canon to avoid striking down a portion of the Act as unconstitutional.[53] In the same term, the Court in *Citizens United v. FEC*,[54] a case discussed in detail in Chapter 13, the Court refused to apply the avoidance canon so as to avoid striking down longstanding federal law making it illegal for corporations to spend their treasury funds in federal elections. The Court could have avoided the issue by construing the statute in question so as not to apply to the conduct of the plaintiff in that case. Four years after *Northwest Austin*, as we will see in Chapter 11, the Court struck down a provision of the Voting Rights Act, relying heavily on the *Northwest Austin*'s case discussion of why the provision raised serious constitutional concerns.

---

47. WILLIAM N. ESKRIDGE JR., DYNAMIC STATUTORY INTERPRETATION 286 (1994).
48. Id.
49. ESKRIDGE, FRICKEY, & GARRETT, supra at 919.
50. Frederick Schauer, Ashwander Revisited, 1995 SUP. CT. REV.71, 74 (1996); Ernest A. Young, Constitutional Avoidance, Resistance Norms, and the Preservation of Judicial Review, 78 TEX. L. REV. 1549, 1581 (2000).
51. HENRY FRIENDLY, BENCHMARKS 211 (1967). Judge Friendly remarked that challenging the avoidance canon "is rather like challenging Holy Writ," but he worried that wide use of the rule would become one of "evisceration and tergiversation." Id. at 211-212.
52. 557 U.S. 193 (2009).
53. See Hasen, Constitutional Avoidance and Anti-Avoidance, supra.
54. 558 U.S. 310 (2010).

Finally, we consider the *federalism* canons and its controversial use in a Supreme Court case, *Gregory v. Ashcroft*.[55] Plaintiffs in *Gregory* challenged a provision of the Missouri state constitution imposing a mandatory retirement age of 70 for judges. The state judges argued that the retirement provision violated a federal statute, the Age Discrimination in Employment Act of 1967. Though the ADEA expressly applied to state employees, Missouri argued that the state judges did not constitute "employees" as that term was defined by the statute:

> The term "employee" means an individual employed by any employer except that the term "employee" shall not include any person elected to public office in any State or political subdivision of any State by the qualified voters thereof, or any person chosen by such officer to be on such officer's personal staff, or an *appointee on the policymaking level* or an immediate adviser with respect to the exercise of the constitutional or legal powers of the office.[56]

The state of Missouri argued that judges, appointed in Missouri (but subject to retention elections), were appointees "on the policymaking level" and therefore exempt from the coverage of the ADEA.

A court might apply a number of language canons to decide whether judges should be considered "on the policymaking level" for purposes of the ADEA. The result of such an analysis is not obvious. Indeed, in interpreting the statute, the Supreme Court in *Gregory* conceded that "it is at least ambiguous whether a state judge is an 'appointee on the policymaking level.'" But the Court held that in the circumstances of this case, it was appropriate to put a fat thumb on the scale to protect state sovereignty and federalism values:

> [I]n this case we are not looking for a plain statement that judges are excluded [from coverage under the ADEA]. We will not read the ADEA to cover state judges unless Congress has made it clear that judges are *included*. This does not mean that the Act must mention judges explicitly, though it does not. Rather, it must be plain to anyone reading the Act that it covers judges.

Eskridge, Frickey, and Garrett term the *Gregory* federalism canon a "superstrong clear statement rule:" Unless Congress is very clear in its statutory language showing a contrary intention, the Court will read a statute potentially limiting state power or regulating states in as narrow a way possible to protect the interests of federalism.[57]

---

55. 501 U.S. 452 (1991). The next few paragraphs draw from Hasen, *The Democracy Canon*.
56. 29 U.S.C. §630(f) (emphasis added).
57. Eskridge, Frickey, and Garrett, noting the strength of the federalism canon in *Gregory*, ask: "Why create the canonical equivalent of a nuclear weapon when a fly swatter would have been sufficient?" ESKRIDGE, FRICKEY, & GARRETT, *supra*, at 934. The answer seems to be that the court calibrates the strength of the clear statement rule to its belief in the importance of the policy behind it.

Note how this is a stronger standard than the one applied to the rule of lenity or the avoidance canon, both of which kick in only if the court first finds the statute to be ambiguous under a textual analysis. The ADEA provision at issue in *Gregory* may or may not have been ambiguous, but the standard for the federalism canon set out in *Gregory* reverses the usual presumption: The Court will read the statute in line with federalism goals unless there is unmistakably clear language that Congress intended to use its power against the states.

Example 4

State courts have long applied something I have termed "the Democracy Canon" to the interpretation of statutes related to election law. In 1885, the Supreme Court of Texas declared in *Owens v. State* that "[a]ll statutes tending to limit the citizen in the exercise of [the right of suffrage] should be liberally construed in his favor."[58] The *Owens* court rejected an argument by one of the candidates in an election contest that ballots marked with information such as the name and address of the president and vice president or the counties in which presidential electors resided should not be counted because they violated a state statute barring the counting of ballots containing pictures, signs, vignettes, stamp marks, or devices.[59]

Since *Owens*, the Democracy Canon has been applied primarily in three contexts: *vote counting cases*, in which someone relies upon the canon to argue, following an election, for the counting of ballots that have not been counted because of minor voter error, election official error, or a disputed reading of a relevant statute; *voter eligibility/registration cases*, in which someone relies upon the canon to argue, before an election, that a voter or certain group of voters who have been told they cannot vote should be allowed to cast a ballot that will be counted even through election officials have determined that they cannot register or vote because of minor voter error, election official error, or a disputed reading of a relevant statute; and *candidate/party competitiveness cases*, in which a candidate or political party relies upon the canon (and particularly upon the voters' right to vote in a competitive election) to argue, before an election, that a certain candidate or party should be allowed to run in an election or appear on an election ballot, even though election officials have excluded the candidate or party from the ballot because of minor candidate or party error, election official error, or a disputed reading of a relevant statute. Vote counting cases are the most prevalent type of cases relying on the Democracy Canon, but the canon has been deployed in all three kinds of cases across a number of states over more than a century.

---

58. *Owens v. State*, 64 Tex. 500, 509 (1885).
59. *Id.*

Should federal courts adopt the Democracy Canon for the interpretation of election law statutes? Why, or why not?

Explanation

This is a normative question, and its purpose is to get you to think about (1) whether you like substantive canons generally to aid in interpretation and (2) whether, if you do accept *some* substantive canons, such as the rule of lenity, the avoidance canon, or the federalism canons, you like this particular canon, the Democracy Canon.

My own opinion, set forth in the article *The Democracy Canon*, is that if courts are generally going to accept substantive canons for statutory interpretation, then courts should also embrace the Democracy Canon. The Canon serves two important purposes. First, as with some other substantive canons, the Democracy Canon can help protect *an underenforced constitutional norm*. In this case, the Democracy Canon protects constitutional equal protection rights in voting, rights that courts for various reasons have declined to protect directly through constitutional litigation. Second, the Democracy Canon is a *preference-eliciting* mechanism. A clear statement rule requires the legislature to take affirmative steps to express its intent to limit voter enfranchisement only when justified by other important interests.

On the other hand, in the context of a hot-button election law case, a court's use of a substantive canon such as the Democracy Canon may appear illegitimate and result-oriented. Moreover, because of the political stakes, judges may subconsciously rely on the canon in ways consistent with their political preferences. For this latter reason, I argue that judges should be sensitive to the problem but yet not abandon the Democracy Canon. State legislatures, by passing clear rules, are best positioned to avoid judicial overreaching by writing clearly in advance.

Legislative History

7.1. COMMITTEE REPORTS, FLOOR STATEMENTS, AND OTHER TYPES OF LEGISLATIVE HISTORY

In the last chapter we saw the strong influence of textualist statutory interpretation. Even judges and justices who reject the more strident textualist claims of Justice Scalia and others now usually begin judicial statutory interpretation opinions with a textual analysis. This has been Justice Scalia's triumph and the victory of the new textualism.

But for most judges and justices, liberal or conservative, legislative history provides another relevant tool for the interpretation of statutes. This has been the loss of the new textualism. Justice Samuel Alito may be a strong conservative like Justice Scalia, but he has relied upon legislative history in some of his opinions as one source of statutory meaning.[1] Professors Law and Zaring found that liberal Supreme Court justices were more likely to rely upon legislative history than conservative justices, although conservatives also make use of legislative history and noted conservative Chief Justice William Rehnquist frequently did so.

---

1. *See* Elliott M. Davis, Note, *The Newer Textualism: Justice Alito's Statutory Interpretation*, 30 HARV. J. L. & PUB. POL'Y 983 (2007). An early look at Chief Justice Roberts found it hard to tell how much he would use legislative history in his opinions. David S. Law & David Zaring, *Law Versus Ideology: The Supreme Court and the Use of Legislative History*, 51 WM. & MARY L. REV. 1653, 1729 (2010).

For many judges, textualism is the beginning of the analysis, but it is not the end. Why rely on legislative history in addition to text? A judge who believes in intentionalist or purposivist interpretation is likely to rely upon legislative history to discover the legislature's true intent or purpose. In Justice Alito's hands, legislative history can provide confirmation of a textual analysis or add context or nuance.

Difficult questions arise when the text of the statute and legislative intent (at least as discerned by judges) diverge: Think of the likely divergence between text and intent in *Holy Trinity Church*. Divergences are rare, however. Typically judges issue opinions that reach the conclusion that textual analysis and legislative history line up on the same side: That should not be a surprise. Not only do clerks draft opinions for justices that marshal all the evidence on the side that the clerk's justice is taking, but also in most instances, legislative staff draft statutes using language that is consistent with legislators' intent, leading to a convergence between text and intent.

Reliance on legislative history used to be commonplace but has become more controversial. Recall from earlier chapters some of the key criticisms made of the use of legislative history by textualists:

- Reliance on legislative history violates the bicameralism and presentment requirements of the Constitution, because such history is not voted upon by Congress and approved by the president.
- Legislative history does not reflect the true intent of "Congress," because Congress is a multi-member body. The history may reflect the views of committee leaders, or just one member, or perhaps just staff. (This is the "Congress Is a They, Not an It" objection).
- Legislative history is malleable (as in the quip about being at a party and looking over the heads of the crowd to pick out one's friends) and manipulable, as when members of Congress lard the legislative history with favorable interpretations of a contested statute to try to influence later judicial interpretation.

A colorful example of the second criticism comes in an exchange over a tax bill between Senators Dole and Armstrong on the floor of the Senate, which Justice Scalia quoted in a D.C. Circuit court opinion.[2]

> Mr. ARMSTRONG. . . . My question, which may take [the chairman of the Committee on Finance] by surprise, is this: Is it the intention of the chairman that the Internal Revenue Service and the Tax Court and other courts take guidance as to the intention of Congress from the committee report which accompanies this bill?
> Mr. DOLE. I would certainly hope so. . . .

---

2. *Hirschey v. F.E.R.C.*, 777 F.2d 1, 7 n.1 (D.C. Cir. 1985) (concurring opn.).

Mr. ARMSTRONG. Mr. President, will the Senator tell me whether or not he wrote the committee report?

Mr. DOLE. Did I write the committee report?

Mr. ARMSTRONG. Yes.

Mr. DOLE. No; the Senator from Kansas did not write the committee report.

Mr. ARMSTRONG. Did any Senator write the committee report?

Mr. DOLE. I have to check.

Mr. ARMSTRONG. Does the Senator know of any Senator who wrote the committee report?

Mr. DOLE. I might be able to identify one, but I would have to search. I was here all during the time it was written, I might say, and worked carefully with the staff as they worked. . . .

Mr. ARMSTRONG. Mr. President, has the Senator from Kansas, the chairman of the Finance Committee, read the committee report in its entirety?

Mr. DOLE. I am working on it. It is not a bestseller, but I am working on it.

Mr. ARMSTRONG. Mr. President, did members of the Finance Committee vote on the committee report?

Mr. DOLE. No.

Mr. ARMSTRONG. Mr. President, the reason I raise the issue is not perhaps apparent on the surface, and let me just state it:. . . . The report itself is not considered by the Committee on Finance. It was not subject to amendment by the Committee on Finance. It is not subject to amendment now by the Senate. . . . If there were matter within this report which was disagreed to by the Senator from Colorado or even by a majority of all Senators, there would be no way for us to change the report. I could not offer an amendment tonight to amend the committee report. . . . [F]or any jurist, administrator, bureaucrat, tax practitioner, or others who might chance upon the written record of this proceeding, let me just make the point that this is not the law, it was not voted on, it is not subject to amendment, and we should discipline ourselves to the task of expressing congressional intent in the statute.

128 CONG.REC. S8659 (daily ed. July 19, 1982).

No one relying upon legislative history to interpret a statute believes that legislative history is a perfect window into legislative intent, and all who rely agree that some types of legislative history are more persuasive than others. Committee reports, which often feature section-by-section analyses of bills, are considered the most reliable type of legislative history. Committee reports usually are drafted by committee staff with expertise in the area and often provide important background information and detailed explanation of statutory language. These days, with polarization in Congress and the rise of unorthodox lawmaking, committee reports are issued less frequently and are not always available for use by lawyers in constructing legislative history arguments. When committee reports exist, however, many judges find them quite persuasive.

Sometimes a committee report will dominate interpretation of a statutory provision. We will see in Chapter 11 that the Senate Judiciary

Committee report accompanying the 1982 amendments to the Voting Rights Act has been exceedingly influential, and that the Supreme Court in the 1986 *Thornburg v. Gingles* case[3] relied heavily on the report in construing the meaning of oblique statutory language in Section 2 of the act. The language in Section 2 was deliberately oblique to ensure passage of the bill; part of the bill seemed to require proportional representation for minority voters under some circumstances, but Senator Dole crafted a compromise (known as the "Dole Compromise") according to which Section 2 also states that it does not create a right of proportional representation.

Chapter 11 turns to the substance of Section 2 in some detail. What's important at this point is the *means* by which the Court construed the inherent contradiction over proportional representation in Section 2: A Court majority relied upon the report to definitively resolve the debate over the meaning of the statute, as opposed to resolving the debate (or even starting) with a textual analysis.

Eight years later, after many courts relied upon the *Gingles* standards to construe the meaning of Section 2 in various cases, Justice Thomas criticized *Gingles*'s reliance on the Senate report to set Section 2's meaning:

> From the foregoing, it should be clear that, as far as the text of the Voting Rights Act is concerned, "§2 does not speak in terms of 'vote dilution.'" *Gingles* (O'CONNOR, J., concurring in judgment). One might wonder, then, why we have consistently concluded that "[w]e know that Congress intended to allow vote dilution claims to be brought under §2." The juxtaposition of the two statements surely makes the result in our cases appear extraordinary, since it suggests a sort of statutory construction through divination that has allowed us to determine that Congress "really meant" to enact a statute about vote dilution even though Congress did not do so explicitly. In truth, our method of construing §2 has been only little better than that, for the only source we have relied upon for the expansive meaning we have given §2 has been the legislative history of the Act.
>
> We first considered the amended §2 in *Thornburg v. Gingles*. Although the precise scope of the terms "standard, practice, or procedure" was not specifically addressed in that case, *Gingles* nevertheless established our current interpretation of the amended section as a provision that addresses vote dilution, and in particular it fixed our understanding that the results test in §2(b) is intended to measure vote dilution in terms of electoral outcomes. In reaching its interpretation of §2, the *Gingles* Court rejected the argument advanced by the United States as *amicus curiae* that §2(b)'s test based on an equal "opportunity . . . to participate in the political process and to elect representatives" suggested a focus on nothing more than securing equal *access* to the political process, not a focus on measuring the influence of a minority group's

---

3. 478 U.S. 30 (1986).

votes in terms of electoral outcomes. That understanding of §2 is, of course, compatible with the interpretation I have set out above.

In approaching §2, the *Gingles* Court, based on little more than a bald assertion that "the authoritative source for legislative intent lies in the Committee Reports on the bill," bypassed a consideration of the text of the Act and proceeded to interpret the section based almost exclusively on its legislative history.[28] It was from the legislative history that the Court culled its understanding that §2 is a provision encompassing claims that an electoral system has diluted a minority group's vote and its understanding that claims of dilution are to be evaluated based upon how closely electoral outcomes under a given system approximate the outcomes that would obtain under an alternative, undiluted norm.

Contrary to the remarkable "legislative history first" method of statutory construction pursued in *Gingles*, however, I had thought it firmly established that the "authoritative source" for legislative intent was the text of the statute passed by both Houses of Congress and presented to the President, not a series of partisan statements about purposes and objectives collected by congressional staffers and packaged into a committee report. "We have stated time and again that courts must presume that a legislature says in a statute what it means and means in a statute what it says there." Nevertheless, our analysis in *Gingles* was marked conspicuously by the absence of any attempt to pursue a close reading of the text of the Act. As outlined above, had the Court addressed the text, it would have concluded that the terms of the Act do not address matters of vote "dilution."

Moreover, the legislative history of §2 itself, and the Court's use of it in *Gingles* aptly illustrate that legislative history is often used by this Court as "a forensic rather than an interpretive device," *Wisconsin Public Intervenor v. Mortier,* 501 U.S. 597, 621 (1991) (SCALIA, J., concurring in judgment), and is read selectively to support the result the Court intends to achieve. It is well documented in the history of the 1982 amendments to the Act that §2 was passed only after a compromise was reached through the addition of the provision

---

28. In offering two citations to support the sweeping proposition that committee reports provide the authoritative source for legislative intent, *Gingles* plainly misread the import of our prior decisions. Far from giving an unqualified endorsement of committee reports as a guide to congressional intent, the Court in *Garcia v. United States,* 469 U.S. 70 (1984), merely indicated that, when resort to legislative history is necessary, it is only committee reports, not the various other sources of legislative history, that should be considered. The Court, however, carefully repeated Justice Jackson's admonition that "[r]esort to legislative history is only justified where the face of the [statute] is inescapably ambiguous. Similarly, in *Zuber v. Allen,* 396 U.S. 168 (1969), we considered the reliability of committee reports only as a relative matter in comparing them to statements made by individual Congressmen during floor debates.

Even if I agreed with Justice Jackson that resort to legislative history is permissible when the text of a statute is "inescapably ambiguous," I could not agree with the use the Court has made of legislative history in interpreting §2. I think it is clear, first, that in interpreting §2 the Court has never undertaken any inquiry into the meaning of the plain language of the statute to determine whether it is ambiguous, and second, that the text of §2 is not riddled with such hopeless ambiguity.

in §2(b) disclaiming any right to proportional representation. See S.Rep. No. 97-417, pp. 2-4 (1982); id., at 94-97 (additional views of Sen. Hatch). But the views of the author of that compromise, Senator Dole, hardly coincide with the gloss the Court has placed on §2.

According to Senator Dole, amended §2 would "[a]bsolutely not" provide any redress to a group of voters challenging electoral mechanisms in a jurisdiction "if the process is open, if there is equal access, if there are no barriers, direct or indirect, thrown up to keep someone from voting or having their vote counted, or registering, whatever the process may include." 128 Cong.Rec. 14133 (1982). Contrary to the Court's interpretation of the section in Gingles, Senator Dole viewed §2 as a provision more narrowly focused on access to the processes surrounding the casting of a ballot, not a provision concerned with ensuring electoral outcomes in accordance with some "undiluted" norm. See S.Rep. No. 97-417, supra, at 193-194 (additional views of Sen. Dole). The legislative history thus hardly provided unambiguous support for the Court's interpretation; indeed, it seems that the Court used what was helpful to its interpretation in the legislative history and ignored what was not.[4]

Justice Thomas's aversion to committee reports is atypical; as I noted, most judges accept committee reports as authoritative when on point. But committee reports are not the only type of legislative history. Committees also hold hearings, and witnesses and others submit testimony that goes into the record. Sponsors of legislation also circulate materials, and sometimes explain the meaning of provisions of bills at committee hearings or on the floor of the House and Senate. Sometimes "colloquies" between members are scripted, and are intended to provide assurances to wavering legislators about the meaning of different provisions.

Each of these items in the record are fair game for a lawyer arguing for the particular interpretation of a statute. But these reports are of varying authority as a guide to congressional intent. For example, one should not always expect sponsors (or perhaps one should never expect sponsors) to be candid in their public statements about a bill's meaning. Proponents may say all kinds of things to whip votes or to assuage nervous supporters. Opponents of measures may introduce evidence or statements into the record as well, sometimes to paint the bill in a negative light or to affect how the bill might be viewed by a court in a later battle over the meaning of legislative history.

It is probably safe to say that whereas committee reports are the highest form of legislative history, floor statements are the lowest. As the Supreme Court stated in Zuber, cited by Justice Thomas in the excerpt above, "A committee report represents the considered and collective understanding of those Congressmen involved in drafting and studying proposed legislation. Floor debates reflect at best the understanding of individual

---

4. Holder v. Hall, 512 U.S. 874 (1994).

Congressmen. It would take extensive and thoughtful debate to detract from the plain thrust of a committee report in this instance."[5]

A search through legislative history is a search for legislative "intent." But whose intent? We have already seen that committee reports may represent the intent of committee leaders, or committee staffers. Likely most of the House and Senate have no meaningful intent on many provisions of most passed federal laws.

Professors Daniel Rodriguez and Barry Weingast offer an interesting take on the "whose intent" question.[6] They argue that the passage of legislation requires legislative leaders to secure the votes of "pivotal legislators" who could vote for or against the bill. To secure these votes, leaders need to make credible statements to the pivotal legislators about ambiguous language or gaps in the proposed legislation. After the legislation passes, courts interpret this ambiguous language or fill gaps in the legislation. Rodriguez and Weingast advocate that courts enforce the legislative deal by interpreting the statute in line with the preferences of these pivotal legislators. The authors argue that when courts instead adopt an "expansionist" view of ambiguous language, as the authors claim the Supreme Court did in reading portions of the Civil Rights Act of 1964, they make it less likely that pivotal legislators will pass future legislation. In other words, if pivotal legislators know that the courts will not enforce legislative deals, and will instead interpret the statute in a way consistent with the views of its most ardent supporters, they will be less likely to enter into future deals.

It is not clear that expansionist interpretations of statutes by the judiciary decrease the volume of legislation passed by Congress. Perhaps pivotal legislators will simply demand clearer language in order to secure their votes, assuming they even pay attention at all to the scope of judicial interpretations of statutes. The authors' normative assumption is questionable as well. Assuming that following the preferences of the pivotal legislator will make it easier to enforce legislative "deals," is that a good thing? From a pluralist perspective it might be. A progressivist perspective might say that courts should not enforce legislative deals, but should engage in statutory interpretation that favors the broader public interest (however that is defined and found by judges). And a textualist perspective would reject any judicial focus on legislative dealmaking as improper.

Example 1

Courts look to legislative intent not only to decide the meaning of a statute, but also sometimes to determine whether the legislature has an impermissible,

---

5. *Zuber v. Allen*, 396 U.S. 168, 186 (1969).
6. *See* Daniel B. Rodriguez & Barry R. Weingast, *The Paradox of Expansionist Statutory Interpretations*, 101 Nw. U. L. Rev. 1207 (2007).

unconstitutional purpose in taking legislative action. For example, in Chapter 11 we will see that when legislatures make race the "predominant factor" in redistricting, that redistricting plan may be an "unconstitutional racial gerrymander" in violation of the Equal Protection Clause of the Fourteenth Amendment.

Recently, the Supreme Court in *United States v. Windsor*[7] divided over Congress's intent in passing the Defense of Marriage Act, which, among other things, prevented the federal government from providing federal benefits to same-sex couples who were legally married according to state law. According to Justice Kennedy's opinion for the Court majority, congressional purpose was animus against gays and lesbians:

> The history of DOMA's enactment and its own text demonstrate that interference with the equal dignity of same-sex marriages, a dignity conferred by the States in the exercise of their sovereign power, was more than an incidental effect of the federal statute. It was its essence. The House Report announced its conclusion that "it is both appropriate and necessary for Congress to do what it can to defend the institution of traditional heterosexual marriage. . . . H.R. 3396 is appropriately entitled the 'Defense of Marriage Act.' The effort to redefine 'marriage' to extend to homosexual couples is a truly radical proposal that would fundamentally alter the institution of marriage." The House concluded that DOMA expresses "both moral disapproval of homosexuality, and a moral conviction that heterosexuality better comports with traditional (especially Judeo Christian) morality." The stated purpose of the law was to promote an "interest in protecting the traditional moral teachings reflected in heterosexual-only marriage laws." Were there any doubt of this far-reaching purpose, the title of the Act confirms it: The Defense of Marriage.

Justice Scalia, in dissent, rejected this finding of bad legislative intent:

> The majority concludes that the only motive for this Act was the "bare . . . desire to harm a politically unpopular group." Bear in mind that the object of this condemnation is not the legislature of some once-Confederate Southern state (familiar objects of the Court's scorn), but our respected coordinate branches, the Congress and Presidency of the United States. Laying such a charge against them should require the most extraordinary evidence, and I would have thought that every attempt would be made to indulge a more anodyne explanation for the statute. The majority does the opposite — affirmatively concealing from the reader the arguments that exist in justification. It makes only a passing mention of the "arguments put forward" by the Act's defenders, and does not even trouble to paraphrase or describe them. I imagine that this is because it is harder to maintain the illusion of the Act's

---

7. 133 S.Ct. 2675 (2013).

supporters as unhinged members of a wild-eyed lynch mob when one first describes their views as *they* see them.

To choose just one of these defenders' arguments, DOMA avoids difficult choice-of-law issues that will now arise absent a uniform federal definition of marriage. Imagine a pair of women who marry in Albany and then move to Alabama, which does not "recognize as valid any marriage of parties of the same sex." When the couple files their next federal tax return, may it be a joint one? Which State's law controls, for federal-law purposes: their State of celebration (which recognizes the marriage) or their State of domicile (which does not)? (Does the answer depend on whether they were just visiting in Albany?) Are these questions to be answered as a matter of federal common law, or perhaps by borrowing a State's choice-of-law rules? If so, *which* State's? And what about States where the status of an out-of-state same-sex marriage is an unsettled question under local law? . . .

The Court mentions none of this. Instead, it accuses the Congress that enacted this law and the President who signed it of something much worse than, for example, having acted in excess of enumerated federal powers — or even having drawn distinctions that prove to be irrational. Those legal errors may be made in good faith, errors though they are. But the majority says that the supporters of this Act acted with *malice* — with the *"purpose"* "to disparage and to injure" same-sex couples. It says that the motivation for DOMA was to "demean"; to "impose inequality"; to "impose . . . a stigma"; to deny people "equal dignity"; to brand gay people as "unworthy"; and to "humiliat[e]" their children (emphasis added).

I am sure these accusations are quite untrue. To be sure (as the majority points out), the legislation is called the Defense of Marriage Act. But to defend traditional marriage is not to condemn, demean, or humiliate those who would prefer other arrangements, any more than to defend the Constitution of the United States is to condemn, demean, or humiliate other constitutions. To hurl such accusations so casually demeans *this institution*. In the majority's judgment, any resistance to its holding is beyond the pale of reasoned disagreement. To question its high-handed invalidation of a presumptively valid statute is to act (the majority is sure) with *the purpose* to "disparage," "injure," "degrade," "demean," and "humiliate" our fellow human beings, our fellow citizens, who are homosexual. All that, simply for supporting an Act that did no more than codify an aspect of marriage that had been unquestioned in our society for most of its existence — indeed, had been unquestioned in virtually all societies for virtually all of human history. It is one thing for a society to elect change; it is another for a court of law to impose change by adjudging those who oppose it *hostes humani generis*, enemies of the human race.

For purposes of this question, take the *Windsor* majority's supposition as given that a law motivated by anti-gay animus is unconstitutional. Does the excerpt from Justice Kennedy's opinion citing the legislative history of DOMA convince you that Congress had this animus? If not, what else would you want to look at, and what else would be available, to find such animus?

Explanation

All the quotations on which Justice Kennedy relied come from the House Committee on the Judiciary report discussing DOMA. Readers may have different opinions upon whether the statements from the report show animus towards gays and lesbians. The report itself, however, addresses the issue of animus:

> It would be incomprehensible for any court to conclude that traditional marriage laws are . . . motivated by animus toward homosexuals. Rather, they have been the unbroken rule and tradition in this (and other) countries primarily because they are conducive to the objectives of procreation and responsible child-rearing. By extension, the Defense of Marriage Act is also plainly constitutional under [the Supreme Court's opinion in *Romer v. Evans*]. The Committee briefly described above at least four legitimate government interests that are advanced by this legislation — namely, defending the institution of traditional heterosexual marriage; defending traditional notions of morality; protecting state sovereignty and democratic self-governance; and preserving government resources. The Committee is satisfied that these interests amply justify the enactment of this bill.[8]

The report also mentions choice-of-law questions that would arise without DOMA.

What to make of all of this? To begin with, it is possible that the House report shows a mixed congressional intent: Perhaps some of the motivation was animus, and some of the motivation was legitimate. A constitutional rule predicated upon bad legislative intent will have to figure out how to deal with the mixed case.

More broadly, the House report was likely drafted by congressional staffers. If anything, it shows a mixed staffer animus toward same-sex relationships. Arguably it sheds some light on the views of the committee members or leaders who drafted the report. What about the rest of the House? The Senate? President Bill Clinton, who signed DOMA? The same criticisms Justice Scalia and others have voiced against the reliance on legislative history to discern legislative intent in the statutory interpretation area apply in this constitutional space as well.

On the other hand, what is the alternative to a look at legislative history, if the Court enunciates a test based upon improper motive? Sometimes it is possible, as in the unconstitutional racial gerrymandering cases, to obtain emails or other informal communications that might exhibit unconstitutional intent. The Speech or Debate Clause (Chapter 2) makes getting much of this material from Congress difficult if not impossible. Giving up on

---

8. H.R. Rep. No. 104-664, at 33 (1996).

legislative history to prove bad legislative intent may mean giving up on the search for bad legislative intent.

7.2. LEGISLATIVE SILENCE OR FAILURE AS LEGISLATIVE HISTORY

In Chapter 5, we considered the Supreme Court's view of *stare decisis* (respect for precedent) when it comes to statutory interpretation decisions. The theory is that Congress and the Supreme Court are in a dialogue, and when the Supreme Court gets a statutory interpretation decision wrong, Congress can fix it by passing an amendment to the statute or a new statute to fix it. On this basis, the Court has adopted a strong *stare decisis* rule for statutory decisions, leaving any fixing to Congress. (We also saw that in the modern polarized era, Congress is much less likely than it has been in the past to override Supreme Court congressional interpretations, making the premise of dialogue questionable.)

A corollary of the strong *stare decisis* rule for statutory decisions is that courts can interpret congressional silence or inaction as an approval of earlier judicial interpretation of a statute. Under the "acquiescence rule," "[i]f Congress is aware of an authoritative agency or judicial interpretation of a statute and doesn't amend the statute, the Court has sometimes presumed that Congress has 'acquiesced' in the interpretation's correctness."[9] Under the "reenactment rule," "[i]f Congress reenacts a statute without making any material changes in its wording, the Court will often presume that Congress intended to incorporate authoritative agency and judicial interpretations of that language into the reenacted statute."[10]

Legislative silence or inaction, or the failure of Congress to pass a statutory provision after considering it, is a form of legislative history. When courts rely upon legislative silence, inaction, or failure to determine congressional intent, they are doing the same thing functionally that they do when they examine committee reports and other pieces of history — inferring meaning from history rather than the text of the statute.

This idea is sometimes known as the "Dog That Did Not Bark Canon," or, in Justice Scalia's variation, the "Canon of Canine Silence."[11] The name comes from Chief Justice Rehnquist's reference to a Sherlock Holmes story

---

9. Eskridge, Frickey, & Garrett, *supra*, at 1048.
10. *Id.*
11. *Koons Buick Pontiac GMC, Inc. v. Nigh*, 543 U.S. 50, 73-74 (2004) (Scalia, J., dissenting).

in which the fictional detective solves the crime thanks to a dog that unexpectedly failed to bark.[12]

Inferring congressional intent from silence is problematic for some obvious reasons. To begin with, Congress is busy, and failure of Congress to respond to a Supreme Court decision does not mean that Congress agrees with the decision. In addition, thanks to vetogates such as party leaders and committee chairs, a bill or amendment may be blocked and not voted upon even if a majority of the members of Congress support it. Finally, legislative silence in response to a judicial decision might indicate what the *current* Congress thinks of a judicial decision, but may not indicate what the *enacting* Congress thought of it — and if one is seeking the original legislative intent, then it is the enacting Congress's preferences that matter. For these reasons and others, courts, including the Supreme Court, do not always infer congressional intent from congressional silence.[13]

A stronger case for inferring legislative intent comes when Congress explicitly rejects a proposal (the "rejected proposal rule"). "If Congress (in conference committee) or one chamber (on the floor) considers and rejects specific statutory language, the Court has often been reluctant to interpret the statute along lines of the rejected language."[14] In *FDA v. Brown & Williamson Tobacco Corp.*,[15] the Supreme Court held that the Food and Drug Administration lacked the authority under the Food, Drug, and Cosmetic Act to regulate tobacco as a "drug" or cigarettes as a "device." Justice O'Connor's opinion canvassed Congress's 35 years of passing statutes regulating tobacco. Not only did it act "against the backdrop of the FDA's consistent and repeated statements that it lacked authority under the FDCA to regulate tobacco," Congress on occasion also rejected amendments to bills that would have given the FDA the ability to do so. Justice Scalia, who has been critical of inferring legislative intent from silence, signed onto Justice O'Connor's opinion without comment.

Even the rejected proposal rule is somewhat problematic: Legislators may not believe that clarification is necessary because the statute is already clear. Furthermore, sometimes clarification of legislative language will break up the coalition supporting a bill. An amendment that breaks up a coalition can be a "poison pill" proposed by and supported by a bill's opponents in an effort to scuttle the bill. Indeed, sometimes there might be no discernible "congressional" intent as to the particular amendment that Congress has rejected.

---

12. *Church of Scientology v. IRS*, 484 U.S. 9, 17-18 (1987) ("All in all, we think this is a case where common sense suggests, by analogy to Sir Arthur Conan Doyle's 'dog that didn't bark,' that an amendment having the effect petitioner ascribes to it would have been differently described by its sponsor, and not nearly as readily accepted by the floor manager of the bill.").

13. *See* William N. Eskridge Jr., *Interpreting Legislative Inaction*, 87 Mich. L. Rev. 67 (1988).

14. Eskridge, Frickey & Garrett, *supra*, at 1049.

15. 529 U.S. 120 (2000).

Example 2

Section 2 of the Voting Rights Act (which we will consider in much more depth in Chapter 11) initially provided that "[n]o voting qualification or prerequisite to voting, or standard, practice, or procedure shall be imposed or applied by any State or political subdivision to deny or abridge the right of any citizen of the United States to vote on account of race or color." The terms "vote" and "voting" were defined elsewhere in the act to include "all action necessary to make a vote effective in any primary, special, or general election." The statute further defined vote and voting as "votes cast with respect to candidates for public or party office and propositions for which votes are received in an election."

In 1982, Congress passed a major amendment to the Voting Rights Act, intended to override the Supreme Court's 1980 decision in *City of Mobile v. Bolden*[16] holding that a jurisdiction could violate Section 2 of the act only through an act of intentional discrimination. The relevant portion of the 1982 version of Section 2 reads

> (a) No voting qualification or prerequisite to voting or standard, practice, or procedure shall be imposed or applied by any State or political subdivision in a manner which results in a denial or abridgement of the right of any citizen of the United States to vote on account of race or color, or in contravention of the guarantees set forth in section 4(f)(2), as provided in subsection (b).
>
> (b) A violation of subsection (a) is established if, based on the totality of circumstances, it is shown that the political processes leading to nomination or election in the State or political subdivision are not equally open to participation by members of a class of citizens protected by subsection (a) in that its members have less opportunity than other members of the electorate to participate in the political process and to elect representatives of their choice. The extent to which members of a protected class have been elected to office in the State or political subdivision is one circumstance which may be considered: Provided, That nothing in this section establishes a right to have members of a protected class elected in numbers equal to their proportion in the population."

In *Chisom v. Roemer*,[17] the Supreme Court considered whether Louisiana's judicial elections were subject to Section 2 of the Voting Rights Act. Everyone agreed that judicial elections were covered by the original Section 2, but they disagreed strongly on judicial elections were covered under the updated Section 2.

One of the arguments Louisiana made against application of Section 2 to judicial elections is that judges were not "representatives" within the meaning of the statute.

---

16. 446 U.S. 55 (1980).
17. 501 U.S. 380 (1991).

The legislative history indicates nothing about whether Congress thought judges were "representatives" under the amended Section 2 or more broadly about whether the amended section 2 included judicial elections.

What relevance, if any, should a court considering the statutory interpretation question in *Chisom* give to congressional silence?

Explanation

One could easily reach the conclusion that Congress's silence is relevant or not; I suspect that one's views of the overall question whether judicial elections should be subject to Section 2 of the Voting Rights Act colors one's views on the congressional silence question.

The majority thought that Congress's silence was a good indication that Congress intended Section 2 to continue covering judicial elections while Justice Scalia in dissent (unsurprisingly) did not. The majority wrote:

> Respondents contend . . . that Congress' choice of the word "representatives" in the phrase "have less opportunity than other members of the electorate to participate in the political process and to elect representatives of their choice" in section (b) is evidence of congressional intent to exclude vote dilution claims involving judicial elections from the coverage of §2. We reject that construction because we are convinced that if Congress had such an intent, Congress would have made it explicit in the statute, or at least some of the Members would have identified or mentioned it at some point in the unusually extensive legislative history of the 1982 amendment.

It added the following in a footnote:

> Congress' silence in this regard can be likened to the dog that did not bark. *See* A. Doyle, Silver Blaze, in The Complete Sherlock Holmes 335 (1927). Cf. *Harrison v. PPG Industries, Inc.*, 446 U.S. 578, 602, (1980) (REHNQUIST, J., dissenting) ("In a case where the construction of legislative language such as this makes so sweeping and so relatively unorthodox a change as that made here, I think judges as well as detectives may take into consideration the fact that a watchdog did not bark in the night"). *See also American Hospital Assn. v. NLRB*, 499 U.S. 606 (1991).

Here is Justice Scalia's response:

> As the Court suggests, the 1982 amendments to the Voting Rights Act were adopted in response to our decision in *Mobile v. Bolden*, which had held that the scope of the original Voting Rights Act was coextensive with the Fifteenth Amendment, and thus proscribed intentional discrimination only. I agree with the Court that that original legislation, directed toward intentional discrimination, applied to all elections, for it clearly said so:

"No voting qualification or prerequisite to voting, or standard, practice, or procedure shall be imposed or applied by any State or political subdivision to deny or abridge the right of any citizen of the United States to vote on account of race or color."

The 1982 amendments, however, radically transformed the Act. As currently written, the statute proscribes intentional discrimination only if it has a discriminatory effect, but proscribes practices with discriminatory effect whether or not intentional. This new "results" criterion provides a powerful, albeit sometimes blunt, weapon with which to attack even the most subtle forms of discrimination. The question we confront here is how broadly the new remedy applies. The foundation of the Court's analysis, the itinerary for its journey in the wrong direction, is the following statement: "It is difficult to believe that Congress, in an express effort to broaden the protection afforded by the Voting Rights Act, withdrew, without comment, an important category of elections from that protection." There are two things wrong with this. First is the notion that Congress cannot be credited with having achieved anything of major importance by simply saying it, in ordinary language, in the text of a statute, "without comment" in the legislative history. As the Court colorfully puts it, if the dog of legislative history has not barked nothing of great significance can have transpired. Apart from the questionable wisdom of assuming that dogs will bark when something important is happening, see 1 T. Livius, The History of Rome 411-413 (1892) (D. Spillan transl.), we have forcefully and explicitly rejected the Conan Doyle approach to statutory construction in the past. See *Harrison v. PPG Industries, Inc.*, 446 U.S. 578, 592 (1980) ("In ascertaining the meaning of a statute, a court cannot, in the manner of Sherlock Holmes, pursue the theory of the dog that did not bark"). We are here to apply the statute, not legislative history, and certainly not the absence of legislative history. Statutes are the law though sleeping dogs lie.

The more important error in the Courts starting point, however, is the assumption that the effect of excluding judges from the revised §2 would be to "withdr[aw] . . . an important category of elections from [the] protection [of the Voting Rights Act]." There is absolutely no question here of *withdrawing* protection. Since the pre-1982 content of §2 was coextensive with the Fifteenth Amendment, the entirety of that protection subsisted in the Constitution, and could be enforced through the other provisions of the Voting Rights Act. Nothing was lost from the prior coverage; *all* of the new "results" protection was an add-on. The issue is not, therefore, as the Court would have it, whether Congress has cut back on the coverage of the Voting Rights Act; the issue is how far it has extended it. Thus, even if a court's expectations were a proper basis for interpreting the text of a statute, while there would be reason to expect that Congress was not "withdrawing" protection, there is no particular reason to expect that the supplemental protection it provided was any more extensive than the text of the statute said.

The majority and dissenting opinions in *Chisom* are well worth reading in full, including the interesting textualist discussion of whether elected judges are "representatives." Here is a taste from Justice Scalia's discussion, which also mentions the failure of the Court to apply the clear statement rule applicable to the federalism canon (discussed in the last chapter), which the Court had applied the very same day as it decided *Chisom* in *Gregory v. Ashcroft*:

> There is little doubt that the ordinary meaning of "representatives" does not include judges, see Webster's Second New International Dictionary 2114 (1950). The Court's feeble argument to the contrary is that "representatives" means those who "are chosen by popular election." On that hypothesis, the fan-elected members of the baseball all-star teams are "representatives" — hardly a common, if even a permissible, usage. Surely the word "representative" connotes one who is not only *elected by* the people, but who also, at a minimum, *acts on behalf of* the people. Judges do that in a sense — but not in the ordinary sense. As the captions of the pleadings in some States still display, it is the prosecutor who represents "the People"; the judge represents the Law — which often requires him to rule against the People. It is precisely because we do not *ordinarily* conceive of judges as representatives that we held judges not within the Fourteenth Amendment's requirement of "one person, one vote." *Wells v. Edwards*, 347 F.Supp. 453 (MD La.1972), aff'd, 409 U.S. 1095 (1973). The point is not that a State could not make judges in some senses representative, or that all judges must be conceived of in the Article III mold, but rather, that giving "representatives" its ordinary meaning, the ordinary speaker in 1982 would not have applied the word to judges, see Holmes, The Theory of Legal Interpretation, 12 Harv.L.Rev. 417 (1899). It remains only to ask whether there is good indication that ordinary meaning does not apply.
>
> There is one canon of construction that might be applicable to the present cases which, in some circumstances, would counter ordinary meaning — but here it would only have the effect of *reinforcing* it. We apply that canon to another case today, concerning, curiously enough, the very same issue of whether state judges are covered by the provisions of a federal statute. In *Gregory v. Ashcroft*, we say that unless it is *clear* that the term "appointee[s] on the policymaking level" does not include judges we will construe it to include them, since the contrary construction would cause the statute to intrude upon the structure of state government, establishing a federal qualification for state judicial office. Such intrusion, we say, requires a "plain statement" before we will acknowledge it. If the same principle were applied here, we would have double reason to give "representatives" its ordinary meaning. It is true, however, that in *Gregory* interpreting the statute to include judges would make them the only high-level state officials affected, whereas here the question is whether judges were excluded from a general imposition upon state elections that unquestionably exists; and in *Gregory* it was questionable whether Congress was invoking its powers under the Fourteenth Amendment (rather than merely the Commerce Clause), whereas here it is obvious. Perhaps those factors suffice to distinguish the two cases. Moreover, we tacitly rejected a "plain statement" rule as applied to the unamended §2 in *City of Rome v. United States*, 446 U.S. 156, 178-180 (1980), though arguably that was before the rule had developed the significance it currently has. I am content to dispense with the "plain statement" rule in the present cases, cf. *Pennsylvania v. Union Gas Co.*, 491 U.S. 1, 41-42 (1989)

(opinion of SCALIA, J.) — but it says something about the Court's approach to this decision that the possibility of applying that rule never crossed its mind.

7.3. OTHER STATUTES

We conclude our look at legislative history with a somewhat less controversial tool of statutory interpretation: reliance upon other similar statutes. Imagine that Congress passes a statute banning certain kinds of race discrimination. Courts interpret the meaning of various parts of the statute, on issues such as burdens of proof, the meaning of "discrimination," and so forth. Congress then passes a statute banning certain kinds of age discrimination. Congress explicitly uses the earlier race discrimination statute as a model, and much of the statutory language and framework in the two statutes is the same. Courts are likely to conclude that Congress intended the age discrimination statute's provisions to be interpreted identically to the parallel provisions in the race discrimination statute.[18]

Note that although the whole act rule seeks to interpret a single statute so that it is internally consistent and harmonious, without any provisions rendered meaningless ("surplusage"), the rule to interpret similar statutes similarly (the in pari materia) looks outside the statute at issue for consistency. In this way, the earlier statute and the earlier judicial (or agency) glosses on the statute are types of legislative history.

Although Justice Scalia endorses the in pari materia rule, he does not do so based on legislative intent. "That would assume an implausible legislative knowledge of related legislation in the past, and an impossible legislative knowledge of related legislation yet to be enacted. The canon is, however, based upon a realistic assessment of what the legislature ought to have meant. It rests on two sound principles: (1) that the body of the law should make sense, and (2) that it is the responsibility of the courts, within the permissible meanings of the text, to make it so."[19]

Justice Scalia's argument seems to prove too much. After all, one might rely upon committee reports under the same rationale. Committee reports often aim to give an overall structure and logic to a complex statute. If courts, without going beyond the permissible reading of the text, can use the reports to make the statute more logical and sensical, courts have a responsibility to do so.

One practical issue that arises under in pari materia is how related statutes need to be for the principle to apply. Justice Scalia concedes that on this point the cases show "a good deal of leeway." Part of the task of good lawyering is

---

18. *Lorillard v. Pons*, 434 U.S. 575 (1978).
19. SCALIA & GARNER, *supra*, at 252.

to make arguments regarding the closeness or distance between two statutes, depending on how the results support the position of your client.

Example 3

Consider the issue Justice Ginsburg laid out in *Wachovia Bank v. Schmidt*:[20]

> This case concerns the citizenship, for purposes of federal-court diversity juris- diction, of national banks, i.e., corporate entities chartered not by any State, but by the Comptroller of the Currency of the U.S. Treasury. Congress empowered federal district courts to adjudicate civil actions between "citizens of different States" where the amount in controversy exceeds $75,000. A business organized as a corporation, for diversity jurisdiction purposes, is "deemed to be a citizen of any State by which it has been incorporated" and, since 1958, also "of the State where it has its principal place of business." State banks, usually chartered as corporate bodies by a particular State, ordinarily fit comfortably within this prescription. Federally chartered national banks do not, for they are not incor- porated by "any State." For diversity jurisdiction purposes, therefore, Congress has discretely provided that national banks "shall . . . be deemed citizens of the States in which they are respectively located." 28 U.S.C. §1348.
>
> The question presented turns on the meaning, in §1348's context, of the word "located." Does it signal . . . that the bank's citizenship is determined by the place designated in the bank's articles of association as the location of its main office? Or does it mean . . . that a national bank is a citizen of every State in which it maintains a branch? . . .
>
> The Fourth Circuit panel majority advanced three principal reasons for decid- ing that Wachovia is "located" in, and therefore a "citizen" of, every State in which it maintains a branch office. First, consulting dictionaries, the Court of Appeals observed that "[i]n ordinary parlance" the term "located" refers to "physical presence in a place." Banks have a physical presence, the Fourth Circuit stated, wherever they operate branches. Next, the court noted, "Section 1348 uses two distinct terms to refer to the presence of a banking association: 'established' and 'located.'" "To give independent meaning" to each word, the court said, "it is most reasonable to understand the place where a national bank is 'established' to refer to a bank's charter location, and to understand the place where it is 'located' to refer to the place or places where it has a physical presence." Finally, the Court of Appeals stressed that in *Citizens & Southern Nat. Bank v. Bougas*, 434 U.S. 35, (1977), this Court interpreted the term "located" in the former venue statute for national banks, see 12 U.S.C. §94 (1976 ed.), as encompassing any county in which a bank maintains a branch office. Reasoning that "the jurisdiction and venue statutes pertain to the same subject matter, namely the amenability of national banking associations to suit in federal court," the panel majority concluded that, "under the *in pari materia* canon[,] the two statutes should be interpreted" consistently.

---

20. 546 U.S. 303 (2006).

Was the Fourth Circuit right on the last point regarding use of the venue statute under *in pari materia*? Or should the Supreme Court reach a contrary conclusion?

Explanation

If the venue and subject matter statutes are sufficiently related, then *in pari materia* could well apply: The question of the "location" of a national bank appears to be the same under both the statutes. And to someone unfamiliar with the intricacies of civil procedure, as I am, the subject matter of both statutes appears very related.

Yet the Supreme Court in a unanimous opinion reversed the Fourth Circuit and rejected its application of *in pari materia* to the two statutes:

> *Bougas* does not control the meaning of §1348. In that case, we construed a now-repealed venue provision, which stated that actions against national banking associations could be filed "in any State, county, or municipal court in the county or city in which said association [was] located." We held that, for purposes of this provision, a national bank was located, and venue was therefore proper, in any county or city where the bank maintained a branch office. True, under the *in pari materia* canon of statutory construction, statutes addressing the same subject matter generally should be read "'as if they were one law.'" But venue and subject-matter jurisdiction are not concepts of the same order. Venue is largely a matter of litigational convenience; accordingly, it is waived if not timely raised. Subject-matter jurisdiction, on the other hand, concerns a court's competence to adjudicate a particular category of cases; a matter far weightier than venue, subject-matter jurisdiction must be considered by the court on its own motion, even if no party raises an objection.
>
> Cognizant that venue "is primarily a matter of choosing a convenient forum," the Court in *Bougas* stressed that its "interpretation of [the former] §94 [would] not inconvenience the bank or unfairly burden it with distant litigation." Subject-matter jurisdiction, however, does not entail an assessment of convenience. It poses a "whether," not a "where" question: Has the Legislature empowered the court to hear cases of a certain genre? Thus, the considerations that account for our decision in *Bougas* are inapplicable to §1348, a prescription governing subject-matter jurisdiction, and the Court of Appeals erred in interpreting §1348 *in pari materia* with the former §94.
>
> Significantly, this Court's reading of the venue provision in *Bougas* effectively aligned the treatment of national banks for venue purposes with the treatment of state banks and corporations. For venue in suits against state banks and other state-created corporations typically lies wherever those entities have business establishments. By contrast, the Court of Appeals' decision in the instant case severely constricts national banks' access to diversity jurisdiction as compared to the access available to corporations generally. For purposes of diversity, a corporation surely is not deemed a citizen of every State in which it maintains a business establishment. Rather, under 28 U.S.C. §1332(c)(1), a corporation is

7. Legislative History

"deemed to be a citizen" only of "any State by which it has been incorporated" and "of the State where it has its principal place of business." Accordingly, while corporations ordinarily rank as citizens of at most 2 States, Wachovia, under the Court of Appeals' novel citizenship rule, would be a citizen of 16 States. *Bougas* does not call for this anomalous result.

Agency Interpretation: Statutory Interpretation in the Administrative State

CHAPTER 8

8.1. WHY IS AGENCY INTERPRETATION DIFFERENT?

The federal government is big. Really big. So big that the federal government itself cannot say how many federal agencies there are — the various federal bodies that are responsible for keeping track of other federal agencies cannot agree.[1] Furthermore, "in the last 15 years, Congress has launched more than 50 new agencies. And more are on the way."[2]

Congress creates federal agencies, such as the Federal Aviation Administration, that are part of the executive branch. Congress passes statutes establishing each agency and then passes various statutes administered and followed by one or more agencies. Federal agencies have great autonomy even from the president, as Chief Justice Roberts recently noted:

> Although the Constitution empowers the President to keep federal officers accountable, administrative agencies enjoy in practice a significant degree of independence. As scholars have noted, "no President (or his executive office staff) could, and presumably none would wish to, supervise so broad a swath of regulatory activity." Kagan, Presidential Administration, 114 Harv. L. Rev. 2245, 2250 (2001); see also S. Breyer, Making Our Democracy Work 110 (2010)

---

1. Josh Peterson, *The Government Has No Idea How Many Agencies It Has*, DAILY CALLER, May 3, 2013, http://dailycaller.com/2013/05/03/the-government-has-no-idea-how-many-agencies-it-has/.
2. *City of Arlington v. FCC*, 133 S.Ct. 1863, 1878 (2013) (Roberts, C.J., dissenting).

("the president may not have the time or willingness to review [agency] decisions"). President Truman colorfully described his power over the administrative state by complaining, "I thought I was the president, but when it comes to these bureaucrats, I can't do a damn thing." See R. Nathan, The Administrative Presidency 2 (1986). President Kennedy once told a constituent, "I agree with you, but I don't know if the government will." See id., at 1. The collection of agencies housed outside the traditional executive departments, including the Federal Communications Commission, is routinely described as the "headless fourth branch of government," reflecting not only the scope of their authority but their practical independence. See, e.g., Administrative Conference of United States, D. Lewis & J. Selin, Sourcebook of United States Executive Agencies 11 (2012).[3]

Federal agencies do a lot of things. One of their most important tasks is issuing regulations implementing congressional statutes. Regulations issue after a formal period of "notice and comment" and fill volumes of the *Code of Federal Regulations* ("CFR"). For example, the FAA issues regulations on the permissible use of electronic devices during flight. Some agencies issue licenses. Others process requests for benefits, as when someone applies to the Social Security Administration for disability benefits. Agencies, and sometimes administrative law judges assigned to agency cases, adjudicate disputes, such as when an employee of the Social Security Administration determines that an individual does not qualify as "disabled" in order to receive disability benefits and that person brings an administrative appeal. Some of the powers of federal agencies are spelled out in statutes particular to the agency. Some agencies have greater autonomy from the president than others, such as the Federal Election Commission, which has six members but no more than three from any single political party. Other agencies are under the control and watchful eye of the administration, with agency heads answering to members of the president's cabinet.

The scope of agency action is nuanced and complex; an administrative law course covers key issues in great detail. This book cannot and does not cover all of that complexity. But there is significant overlap between a legislation course and an administrative law course on the question of judicial review of agency action. When an agency makes a decision — for example, it issues a new rule, adjudicates a dispute, denies a license, advances an opinion — someone adversely affected by the agency's action may challenge it as inconsistent with congressional legislation or the agency's own regulations or procedures. Among other things, opponents may claim that the agency exceeded its authority in issuing the regulation, or its dispute

---

3. *Id.* Note that the "scholars" the chief justice references are Justices Kagan and Breyer, who disagreed with the chief justice in this case.

resolution is arbitrary, or the agency's opinion is based upon an unreasonable interpretation of a federal statute or the agency's own regulations.

With the huge growth of the federal government and federal bureaucracy, it is unsurprising that so much of statutory interpretation in the federal courts involves the action of a federal agency. (This is especially true for the U.S. Court of Appeals for the D.C. Circuit, which hears a great many challenges to agency actions.) The key question the courts face is how, if at all, a court's act of statutory interpretation should be influenced by the agency's own interpretation of the statute: Should courts defer greatly to agency action, giving agencies wide space to interpret congressional directives? Or should courts grant little or no deference, considering that it is the province of the courts to say what the law is? Should the rules be the same regardless of the type of agency action, for example whether the interpretation comes after a formal review process or adjudication, in an informal opinion, or even in an amicus brief in litigation?

The rest of this chapter explores the basics of these complex rules on agency deference. But be warned of two things. First, we will only scratch the surface in this exceedingly complex area, leaving greater detail to an administrative law course. Second, even the simplified version is confusing. After nearly 100 pages in a leading legislation casebook devoted to the question of judicial deference to agency review, the authors simply declare: "What a mess."[4]

Before turning to these complex rules, however, it is worth exploring briefly what is at stake. The case for judicial deference to agency interpretations of relevant statutes is twofold. First, agencies have expertise that courts do not. When courts interpret technically complex statutes (for example, on pollution emissions), they cannot always understand the technical limitations and policy implications of their interpretations. Second, agencies can respond to changed factual circumstances and can reflect the views of the current executive branch on statutory interpretation. This means that at least in theory, agency interpretation can be more democratically responsive than judicial interpretation. We should expect, for example, that a Republican administration's Environmental Protection Agency will be more likely to lean toward lighter regulatory solutions to pollution issues than a Democratic administration's Environmental Protection Agency.

Consider this statement of reasons for deference:

Judges are not experts in the field, and are not part of either political branch of the Government. Courts must, in some cases, reconcile competing political interests, but not on the basis of the judges' personal policy preferences. In contrast, an agency to which Congress has delegated policymaking responsibilities may,

---

4. ESKRIDGE, FRICKEY, & GARRETT, *supra*, at 1278.

within the limits of that delegation, properly rely upon the incumbent administration's views of wise policy to inform its judgments. While agencies are not directly accountable to the people, the Chief Executive is, and it is entirely appropriate for this political branch of the Government to make such policy choices — resolving the competing interests which Congress itself either inadvertently did not resolve, or intentionally left to be resolved by the agency charged with the administration of the statute in light of everyday realities.[5]

On the other hand, if we take seriously Chief Justice Roberts's concerns about the unaccountability of federal bureaucracy, then judicial interpretation might be preferable to agency interpretation. The chief justice sees agencies as exercising strong legislative and judicial functions, and he wants to rein in what he believes to be unaccountable agency power:

An agency's interpretive authority, entitling the agency to judicial deference, acquires its legitimacy from a delegation of lawmaking power from Congress to the Executive. Our duty to police the boundary between the Legislature and the Executive is as critical as our duty to respect that between the Judiciary and the Executive. In the present context, that means ensuring that the Legislative Branch has in fact delegated lawmaking power to an agency within the Executive Branch, before the Judiciary defers to the Executive on what the law is. That concern is heightened, not diminished, by the fact that the administrative agencies, as a practical matter, draw upon a potent brew of executive, legislative, and judicial power. And it is heightened, not diminished, by the dramatic shift in power over the last 50 years from Congress to the Executive — a shift effected through the administrative agencies.[6]

The complexity in dealing with judicial deference to agency action that we will see in the rest of this chapter is a response to these conflicting impulses. Courts have tried to balance these competing concerns by calibrating the amount of deference to the nature of the agency's relevant statutory interpretation.

Example 1

In the Clean Air Act Amendments of 1977, Congress enacted certain requirements applicable to States that had not achieved the national air quality standards established by the Environmental Protection Agency (EPA) pursuant to earlier legislation. The amended Clean Air Act required these "nonattainment" states to establish a permit program regulating "new or modified major stationary sources" of air pollution. Generally, a permit may not be issued

---

5. *Chevron v. Nat'l Res. Def. Council*, 467 U.S. 837, 865-866 (1984).
6. *City of Arlington v. FCC*, 133 S.Ct. at 1886 (Roberts, C.J., dissenting).

for a new or modified major stationary source unless several stringent conditions are met. In part the statute (at the time) read

> The plan provisions required by subsection (a) shall — . . . . (6) require permits for the construction and operation of new or modified major stationary sources in accordance with section 173 (relating to permit requirements). (42 U.S.C. §7502(b)(6).)

The EPA issued a regulation to implement this permit requirement that allows a state to adopt a plantwide definition of the term "stationary source":

> "(i) 'Stationary source' means any building, structure, facility, or installation which emits or may emit any air pollutant subject to regulation under the Act. "(ii) 'Building, structure, facility, or installation' means all of the pollutant-emitting activities which belong to the same industrial grouping, are located on one or more contiguous or adjacent properties, and are under the control of the same person (or persons under common control) except the activities of any vessel." (40 CFR §§51.18(j)(1)(i) and (ii).)

Under this definition, which treats the entire plant as a "bubble," an existing plant that contains several pollution-emitting devices may install or modify one piece of equipment without meeting the permit conditions if the alteration will not increase the total emissions from the plant. The EPA administrator who was in charge when EPA issued these regulations was part of the Reagan administration, which opposed high-cost environmental and other regulations.

Environmentalists challenge the regulation as an impermissible reading of the congressional statute that will allow more pollution than Congress allowed under the Clean Air Act Amendment of 1977. If an agency were not involved, how should a court decide the meaning of the "statutory source" permit requirement? How much, if at all, should courts defer to the EPA when considering the EPA's interpretation of the "stationary source" permit requirement?

Explanation

A portion of this fact pattern comes from the Supreme Court's opinion in *Chevron U.S.A., Inc. v. Natural Resources Defense Council*,[7] arguably the Supreme Court's most important modern opinion on the scope of judicial deference to agency interpretations. We will discuss *Chevron*'s approach, and its alternatives, in the next few sections of this chapter. But before we get to what

---

7. 467 U.S. 837 (1984).

the Court has to say, this example asks you to evaluate what *you* think about the question.

Imagine first that you were a judge who had to decide this statutory interpretation issue without any input from the EPA or other federal agency. Does a "stationary source" at a plant emitting pollution mean a building, a "bubble" of buildings, or both? To answer that question, you would begin with the text of the statute. You might look up the definition of "stationary" and "source" in various dictionaries or rely upon the definition or use of the same term elsewhere in the Clean Air Act (whole act rule) or in other similar statutes (*in pari materia*). You might consider whether any textual canons might apply. (Which way does the modifier "major" before "stationary sources" cut?) You also could turn to any substantive canons that might apply. Most judges would also look at legislative purpose and legislative intent, examining committee reports and other reliable parts of the Clean Air Act 1977 Amendment's legislative history to see both whether anyone in Congress (or on staff) wrote anything at the time on this particular issue or more broadly on the purpose behind this aspect of the statute.

Some judges might also consider what makes the most sense today, using dynamic statutory interpretation. For example, if Congress passed the statute in 1977 but climate change is a bigger problem today than it was in 1977, a judge deciding this issue in 2014 rather than 1984 might be inclined to read the "stationary source" permit requirement more narrowly so as to make it more difficult to build and operate older polluting power plants.

Now consider whether and how the question changes with the involvement of an agency. As we saw above, there are arguments for great deference and arguments against deference. Arguments for deference include the technical expertise of the agency as well as the democratic accountability argument: Voters elected a Republican president who ran on a platform of smaller government and less government regulation, and the EPA's regulation furthered that agenda. Furthermore, this was a considered decision of the EPA. The interpretation came in a formal rule, after the opportunity for the public to see the draft rule and to comment. Perhaps this formality or thoughtfulness should give the interpretation extra deference?

On the other hand, the EPA's creative interpretation of the term "stationary source" may have gone much further than Congress intended, beyond a fair textual reading of the statute. Concern about out-of-control agencies in the era of the powerful administrative state would suggest less, rather than more, deference to agency constructions of statutory language.

Now that you have formed your own opinion about the appropriate role of deference to agency interpretations of statutes, we will turn to the courts' treatment of this subject. As we shall see, the Supreme Court has not adopted a single level of deference to agency actions. Instead, the amount of deference depends in some significant degree on the nature and timing of the agency's action.

8.2. *CHEVRON* DEFERENCE

If you are one of those readers who has been skipping over the examples in this book, you need to go back and read and answer Example 1 in this chapter. It is crucial in order for you to be culturally literate in this area. Go ahead. I can wait.

Welcome back.

It is hard to overstate the dominance of the *Chevron* Doctrine in discussions about the appropriate amount of judicial deference to agency interpretations of federal statutes. Although Justice Stevens's opinion for the Court in *Chevron* did not start as a blockbuster case,[8] and there were plenty of Supreme Court cases on the topic of deference before *Chevron* reaching similar conclusions on deference,[9] and the *Chevron* Doctrine as it is understood today is only tangentially related to *Chevron* itself,[10] no case on this topic has commanded more attention and commentary than this one. One recent count found the case cited 8,656 times in the law reviews,[11] and another count found it cited in 11,760 judicial decisions and 2,130 administrative decisions.[12]

The most famous paragraph in *Chevron* is Justice Stevens's enunciation of what came to be considered a two-part test for when courts should defer to agency interpretations of statutes:

> When a court reviews an agency's construction of the statute which it administers, it is confronted with two questions. First, always, is the question whether Congress has directly spoken to the precise question at issue. If the intent of Congress is clear, that is the end of the matter; for the court, as well as the agency, must give effect to the unambiguously expressed intent of Congress. If, however, the court determines Congress has not directly addressed the precise question at issue, the court does not simply impose its own construction on the statute, as would be necessary in the absence of an administrative interpretation. Rather, if the statute is silent or ambiguous with respect to the

---

8. Thomas Merrill, *The Story of* Chevron: *The Making of an Accidental Landmark*, in ADMINISTRATIVE LAW STORIES 398 (Peter Strauss ed. 2006).
9. Peter L. Strauss, *"Deference" Is Too Confusing — Let's Call Them "Chevron Space" and "Skidmore Weight,"* 112 COLUM. L. REV. 1143 (2012).
10. Gary Lawson & Stephen Kam, *Making Law Out of Nothing at All: The Origins of the* Chevron *Doctrine*, 65 ADMIN. L. REV. 1 (2013).
11. *Id.*
12. Thomas W. Merrill, *Justice Stevens and the Chevron Puzzle*, 106 NW. U. L. REV. 551, 552 (2012).

specific issue, the question for the court is whether the agency's answer is based on a permissible construction of the statute.[13]

But despite this apparent enunciation of a two-part test, courts and commentators have puzzled over and argued about how this deference is supposed to work. "Even after almost 30 years and thousands of recitations, unanswered questions about this *Chevron* framework abound. Does this framework involve two distinct analytical steps or just one unitary decision about the reasonableness of an agency's interpretation? When is the intent of Congress 'clear' on a 'precise' question of statutory interpretation? What might make an agency's statutory interpretation something other than a 'permissible construction'? To what class of agency legal interpretations does this framework apply?"[14]

Let's begin to disentangle these questions and see where the disagreements are, beginning with the last question.

To what class of agency interpretations does this framework apply? This has become known as the *Chevron* "Step Zero" question.[15] That is, the *Chevron* framework does not apply to *all* agency interpretations of federal statutes. Instead it applies only to a subset of more formal agency interpretations, such as those coming in a rulemaking (as in the *Chevron* case itself). The reason Professor Merrill and others have called this "Step Zero" is that before we get to the two-part *Chevron* test, we need to decide whether it even applies. The next section of this chapter explores the Step Zero issue and explains what types of deference apply when *Chevron* does not apply.

Does this framework involve two analytical steps or just one unitary decision about the reasonableness of the agency's interpretation? Let's begin with what is considered *Chevron*'s "Step One." As the Supreme Court recently explained in setting forth the *Chevron* test, "First, applying ordinary tools of statutory construction, the court must determine whether Congress has directly spoken to the precise question at issue. If the intent of Congress is clear, that is the end of the matter; for the court, as well as the agency, must give effect to the unambiguously expressed intent of Congress."[16]

There is disagreement over exactly what courts are supposed to do at Step One. In a footnote in *Chevron*, Justice Stevens explained that "[i]f a court, *employing traditional tools of statutory construction*, ascertains that Congress had an intention on the precise question at issue, that intention is the law and must be given effect." (My emphasis.) But what are the "traditional tools of statutory interpretation?" Do they include legislative history, or just

---

13. *Chevron*, 467 U.S. at 842-843.

14. Lawson & Kam, *supra*.

15. Thomas W. Merrill & Kristin E. Hickman, Chevron's *Domain*, 89 GEO. L.J. 833, 836 (2001); *see also* Cass R. Sunstein, Chevron *Step Zero*, 92 VA. L. REV. 187 (2006).

16. *City of Arlington*, 133 S.Ct. at 1868 (quoting *Chevron*).

textualist analysis? And at Step One, can courts consider whether an agency's interpretation deserves deference?[17]

Justice Scalia, who has been one of the leaders on the Supreme Court pushing the *Chevron* formula, also believes that many cases fitting into the *Chevron* framework easily can be resolved through a textual analysis.

> In my experience, there is a fairly close correlation between the degree to which a person is (for want of a better word) a "strict constructionist" of statutes, and the degree to which that person favors *Chevron* and is willing to give it broad scope. The reason is obvious. One who finds more often (as I do) that the meaning of a statute is apparent from its text and from its relationship with other laws, thereby finds less often that the triggering requirement for *Chevron* deference exists. It is thus relatively rare that *Chevron* will require me to accept an interpretation which, though reasonable, I would not personally adopt.[18]

There is a tension here: On the one hand, *Chevron* seems to be a doctrine giving considerable leeway to agencies to craft interpretations of federal statutes within a zone of permissible policymaking. On the other hand, if federal statutes usually have a "right answer" under a textualist analysis, the statute could well be declared "clear" and therefore courts would leave little room for the agency's reasonable interpretation.

Other justices will look at legislative history and use other "traditional tools of statutory interpretation" at *Chevron* Step One.[19] Unsurprisingly, judges and justices differ, after using such tools of statutory interpretation, on whether Congress has spoken to the "precise" question and whether Congress's intent is "unambiguous" and "clear." At least in theory, judges who use these other "traditional tools" are more likely to find ambiguity and get to Step Two than avid textualists such as Justice Scalia. Yet the empirics are unclear. Justice Stevens agreed with agency interpretations in just under 61% of the cases he considered, compared to 64.5% for Justice Scalia, 72% for Justice Breyer (who has been critical of *Chevron* in favor of a more open-ended approach to the question of judicial deference), and 52.6% for Justice Brennan.[20] What does this tell us about whether *Chevron* is actually influencing the bottom line of judicial decisions?

---

17. Ronald M. Levin, Mead *and the Prospective Exercise of Discretion*, 54 Admin. L. Rev. 771, 776-780 (2002); Peter L. Strauss, In Search of Skidmore, Columbia Public Law Research Paper 13-355 (Jun. 30, 2013), http://papers.ssrn.com/sol3/papers.cfm?abstract_id=2287343.
18. Antonin Scalia, *Judicial Deference to Administrative Interpretations of Law*, 1989 Duke L.J. 511, 521.
19. However, traditional deference to persuasive agency arguments no longer seems to be part of Step One. *See* Strauss, *supra*; Levin, *supra*.
20. William N. Eskridge Jr. & Lauren E. Baer, *The Continuum of Deference: Supreme Court Treatment of Agency Statutory Interpretations from* Chevron *to* Hamdan, 96 Geo. L.J. 1083, 1153 Table 20 (2008).

For those cases in which the agency's interpretation gets over the hurdle of *Chevron* Step One, there is *Chevron* "Step Two." Under Step Two, if Congress "is silent or ambiguous with respect to the specific issue, the question for the court is whether the agency's answer is based on a permissible construction of the statute." Lawson and Kam argue that "Step two of *Chevron* remains a mystery, beyond the observation that agencies usually win when they get to it."[21]

It is easy to see why agencies could well win if they get to Step Two in the courts. In siding with the agency in Step One, a court has already found the statute ambiguous or silent on the question the agency is addressing. This leaves space for a range of interpretations from the agency. So long as the agency does not do something wildly deviating from the statutory scheme, a court is likely to consider the interpretation "permissible" or "reasonable." To be sure, sometimes an agency will deviate beyond the space of ambiguity or silence; but if it does so, a court would be more likely to conclude under Step One that the statute was "clear" on the impermissibility of such a deviant interpretation.

For example, imagine that a very anti-regulatory EPA decided that "stationary source" meant all of a company's power plants in the United States. Whatever else "stationary source" might mean, it is clear that Congress would not intend this interpretation, which would exempt virtually all power companies from the new requirement. We would never get beyond Step One.

As should be clear by now, leading administrative law and legislation scholars have questioned just about every aspect of the *Chevron* two-step doctrine, from the number of steps it has, to the meaning of each step, to the empirical question whether *Chevron* even matters as a predictor of how judges and Supreme Court justices will actually decide cases raising the question of agency interpretation of federal statutes.

But as a law student or a litigator, you will be expected to apply the two-step (or is it three-step? or one-step?) *Chevron* test when considering the question of judicial deference to agency discretion. And although you should do your best to argue within the framework, you will want to incorporate the full range of statutory interpretation methods in your answer, beginning with *Chevron* Step One. How much deference the court should or will give to the agency's interpretation remains unclear.

Example 2

Consider these facts taken from the majority and dissenting opinions in from *MCI Communications v. AT&T Co.*[22]

---

21. Lamson & Kam, *supra*.
22. 512 U.S. 218 (1994).

8. Agency Interpretation

In 1934, Congress authorized the Federal Communications Commission to regulate "a field of enterprise the dominant characteristic of which was the rapid pace of its unfolding." *National Broadcasting Co. v. United States,* 319 U. S. 190, 219 (1943). The Communications Act of 1934 gives the FCC broad discretion to meet new and unanticipated problems in order to fulfill its sweeping mandate "to make available, so far as possible, to all the people of the United States, a rapid, efficient, Nation-wide and world-wide wire and radio communication service with adequate facilities at reasonable charges." 47 U.S.C. §151 (1934) (amended 1996). At the time the act was passed, the telephone industry was dominated by the American Telephone & Telegraph Company (AT&T) and its affiliates. Title II of the act, which establishes the framework for FCC regulation of common carriers by wire, was a response to that dominance. The wire communications provisions of the act address problems distinctly associated with monopoly.

Section 203 of the act, modeled upon the filed rate provisions of the Interstate Commerce Act, requires that common carriers other than connecting carriers "file with the Commission and print and keep open for public inspection schedules showing all charges for itself and its connecting carriers." A telephone carrier must allow a 120-day period of lead time before a tariff goes into effect, and, "unless otherwise provided by or under authority of this chapter," may not provide communication services except according to a filed schedule. The tariff-filing section of the act, however, contains a proviso that states

> (b) Changes in schedule; discretion of Commission to modify requirements . . .
> (2) The Commission may, in its discretion and for good cause shown, modify any requirement made by or under the authority of this section either in particular instances or by general order applicable to special circumstances or conditions except that the Commission may not require the notice period specified in paragraph (1) to be more than one hundred and twenty days.

In the 1970s, technological advances reduced the entry costs for competitors of AT&T in the market for long-distance telephone service. The commission, recognizing the feasibility of greater competition, passed regulations to facilitate competitive entry. By 1979, competition in the provision of long-distance service was well established, and some urged that the continuation of extensive tariff filing requirements served only to impose unnecessary costs on new entrants and to facilitate collusive pricing. The commission held hearings on the matter (1979), after which it issued a series of rules that have produced litigation.

The commission tentatively concluded that costly tariff-filing requirements were unnecessary and actually counterproductive as applied to non-dominant carriers such as MCI — that is, those whose lack of market power leaves them unable to extract supracompetitive or discriminatory rates from customers. Relaxing the regulatory burdens upon new entrants would foster competition into the telecommunications markets; at the same time, the forces of competition would ensure that firms without monopoly power would comply with the act's prohibitions on "unreasonable rates" and price discrimination. Accordingly, in a series of rulings in the early 1980s, the commission issued orders progressively exempting specified classes of non-dominant carriers from the obligation to file tariff schedules. The commission's *Fourth Report and Order* extended and reaffirmed its "permissive detariffing" policy, under which dominant long-distance carriers, such as AT&T, must file tariff schedules whereas nondominant carriers such as MCI, although subject to the act's prohibitions on unreasonable rates and price discrimination, may, but need not, file them.

The FCC has now issued a new order following rulemaking adhering to its policy of excusing nondominant providers of long-distance telephone service from the §203 filing requirement and has codified that longstanding forbearance policy. As it had since its initial stages of detariffing, the commission found principal statutory authority for detariffing in the "modify any requirement" language of §203(b)(2). AT&T has complained, and the dispute has reached the Supreme Court.

How should the Court resolve the statutory question raised by this case?

Explanation

Under *Chevron* Step Zero (more on that in the next section), the agency's interpretation of section 203 came in a formal order and rulemaking. This makes the agency's interpretation subject to the *Chevron* two-step framework.

Under Step One, "applying ordinary tools of statutory construction, the Court must determine whether Congress has directly spoken to the precise question at issue. If the intent of Congress is clear, that is the end of the matter; for the court, as well as the agency, must give effect to the unambiguously expressed intent of Congress."

It probably would not surprise you to learn that Justice Scalia, who wrote the majority opinion in the MCI case, applied a textual analysis to the question and concluded that the statute was clear; but Justice Stevens, who wrote the dissent in the MCI case, looked more broadly at legislative history and purpose to conclude that the statute was ambiguous, leading him (under what we — but not Justice Stevens — would call *Chevron* Step Two) to defer to what he viewed as the FCC's reasonable interpretation of the statute.

At issue is the use of the term "modify" in Section 203. Here is a piece of Justice Scalia's textual analysis:

> The dispute between the parties turns on the meaning of the phrase "modify any requirement" in §203(b)(2). Petitioners argue that it gives the Commission

authority to make even basic and fundamental changes in the scheme created by that section. We disagree. The word "modify" — like a number of other English words employing the root "mod-" (deriving from the Latin word for "measure"), such as "moderate," "modulate," "modest," and "modicum" — has a connotation of increment or limitation. Virtually every dictionary we are aware of says that "to modify" means to change moderately or in minor fashion. See, e. g., Random House Dictionary of the English Language 1236 (2d ed. 1987) ("to change somewhat the form or qualities of; alter partially; amend"); Webster's Third New International Dictionary 1452 (1981) ("to make minor changes in the form or structure of: alter without transforming"); 9 Oxford English Dictionary 952 (2d ed. 1989) ("[t]o make partial changes in; to change (an object) in respect of some of its qualities; to alter or vary without radical transformation"); Black's Law Dictionary 1004 (6th ed. 1990) ("[t]o alter; to change in incidental or subordinate features; enlarge; extend; amend; limit; reduce").

In support of their position, petitioners cite dictionary definitions contained in, or derived from, a single source, Webster's Third New International Dictionary 1452 (1981), which includes among the meanings of "modify," "to make a basic or important change in." Petitioners contend that this establishes sufficient ambiguity to entitle the Commission to deference in its acceptance of the broader meaning, which in turn requires approval of its permissive detariffing policy. See *Chevron*. In short, they contend that the courts must defer to the agency's choice among available dictionary definitions. . . .

Most cases of verbal ambiguity in statutes involve . . . a selection between accepted alternative meanings shown as such by many dictionaries. One can envision (though a court case does not immediately come to mind) having to choose between accepted alternative meanings, one of which is so newly accepted that it has only been recorded by a single lexicographer. (Some dictionary must have been the very first to record the widespread use of "projection," for example, to mean "forecast.") But what petitioners demand that we accept as creating an ambiguity here is a rarity even rarer than that: a meaning set forth in a single dictionary (and, as we say, its progeny) which not only *supplements* the meaning contained in all other dictionaries, but *contradicts* one of the meanings contained in virtually all other dictionaries. Indeed, contradicts one of the alternative meanings contained in the out-of-step dictionary itself — for as we have observed, Webster's Third itself defines "modify" to connote *both* (specifically) major change *and* (specifically) minor change. It is hard to see how that can be. When the word "modify" has come to mean *both* "to change in some respects" *and* "to change fundamentally" it will in fact mean *neither* of those things. It will simply mean "to change," and some adverb will have to be called into service to indicate the great or small degree of the change.

If that is what the peculiar Webster's Third definition means to suggest has happened — and what petitioners suggest by appealing to Webster's Third — we simply disagree. "Modify," in our view, connotes moderate change. It might be good English to say that the French Revolution "modified" the status of the French nobility — but only because there is a figure of speech called understatement and a literary device known as sarcasm. And it might be unsurprising to discover a 1972 White House press release saying that "the Administration is modifying its position with regard to prosecution of the war in Vietnam" — but only because press agents tend to impart what is nowadays called "spin." Such intentional distortions, or simply careless or ignorant misuse, must have formed the basis for the usage that Webster's Third, and Webster's Third alone, reported. It is perhaps gilding the lily to add this: In 1934, when the Communications Act became law — the most relevant time for determining a statutory term's meaning — Webster's Third was not yet even contemplated. To our knowledge *all* English dictionaries provided the narrow definition of "modify," including those published by G. & C. Merriam Company. See Webster's New International Dictionary 1577 (2d ed. 1934); Webster's Collegiate Dictionary 628 (4th ed. 1934). We have not the slightest doubt that is the meaning the statute intended.

Beyond the word itself, a further indication that the §203(b)(2) authority to "modify" does not contemplate fundamental changes is the sole exception to that authority which the section provides. One of the requirements of §203 is that changes to filed tariffs can be made only after 120 days' notice to the Commission and the public. §203(b)(1). The only exception to the Commission's §203(b)(2) modification authority is as follows: "except that the Commission may not require the notice period specified in paragraph (1) to be more than one hundred and twenty days." Is it conceivable that the statute is indifferent to the Commission's power to eliminate the tariff-filing requirement entirely for all except one firm in the long-distance sector, and yet strains out the gnat of extending the waiting period for tariff revision beyond 120 days? We think not. The exception is not as ridiculous as a Lilliputian in London only because it is to be found in Lilliput: in the small-scale world of "modifications," it is a big deal.

Since an agency's interpretation of a statute is not entitled to deference when it goes beyond the meaning that the statute can bear, the Commission's permissive detariffing policy can be justified only if it makes a less than radical or fundamental change in the Act's tariff-filing requirement. The Commission's attempt to establish that no more than that is involved greatly understates the extent to which its policy deviates from the filing requirement, and greatly undervalues the importance of the filing requirement itself.

Justice Stevens in his dissent brushed off the deep lesson in grammar and etymology, focusing much more on statutory purpose, and in particular Congress's goals to provide the FCC with the authority to respond to rapidly changing technological and financial changes in the communications field:

In my view, each of the Commission's detariffing orders was squarely within its power to "modify any requirement" of §203. Section 203(b)(2) plainly confers at least some discretion to modify the general rule that carriers file tariffs, for it speaks of "*any* requirement." Section 203(c) of the Act, ignored by the Court, squarely supports the FCCs position; it prohibits carriers from providing service without a tariff "*unless otherwise provided by or under authority of this Act.*" Section 203(b)(2) is plainly one provision that "otherwise provides," and thereby authorizes, service without a filed schedule. The FCC's authority to modify §203's requirements in "particular instances" or by "general order applicable to special circumstances or conditions" emphasizes the expansive character of the Commission's authority: modifications may be narrow or broad, depending upon the Commission's appraisal of current conditions. From the vantage of a Congress seeking to regulate an almost completely monopolized industry, the advent of competition is surely a "special circumstance or condition" that might legitimately call for different regulatory treatment. . . .

According to the Court, the term "modify," as explicated in all but the most unreliable dictionaries, rules out the Commission's claimed authority to relieve nondominant carriers of the basic obligation to file tariffs. Dictionaries can be useful aides in statutory interpretation, but they are no substitute for close analysis of what words mean as used in a particular statutory context. Even if the sole possible meaning of "modify" were to make "minor" changes, further elaboration is needed to show why the detariffing policy should fail. The Commission came to its present policy through a series of rulings that gradually relaxed the filing requirements for nondominant carriers. Whether the current policy should count as a cataclysmic or merely an incremental departure from the §203(a) baseline depends on whether one focuses on particular carriers' obligations to file (in which case the Commission's policy arguably works a major shift) or on the statutory policies behind the tariff-filing requirement (which remain satisfied because market constraints on nondominant carriers obviate the need for rate filing). When §203 is viewed as part of a statute whose aim is to constrain monopoly power, the Commission's decision to exempt nondominant carriers is a rational and "measured" adjustment to novel circumstances — one that remains faithful to the core purpose of the tariff-filing section. See Black's Law Dictionary 1198 (3d ed. 1933) (defining "modification" as "A change; an alteration which introduces new elements into the details, or cancels some of them, but leaves *the general purpose and effect of the subject-matter* intact").

The Court seizes upon a particular sense of the word "modify" at the expense of another, long-established meaning that fully supports the Commission's position. That word is first defined in Webster's Collegiate Dictionary 628 (4th ed. 1934) as meaning "to limit or reduce in extent or degree." The Commission's permissive detariffing policy fits comfortably within this common understanding of the term. The FCC has in effect adopted a general rule stating that "if you are dominant you must file, but if you are nondominant you need not." The Commission's partial detariffing policy — which excuses nondominant carriers from filing *on condition that* they remain nondominant — is simply a relaxation of a costly regulatory requirement that recent developments had rendered pointless and counterproductive in a certain class of cases. . . . Extolling the "enormous importance" of filed rates and resorting to dictionary definitions and colorful metaphors are unsatisfactory substitutes for a reasoned explanation of why the statute requires rate filing even when the practice serves no useful purpose and actually harms consumers.

The filed tariff provisions of the Communications Act are not ends in themselves, but are merely one of several procedural *means* for the Commission to ensure that carriers do not charge unreasonable or discriminatory rates. The Commission has reasonably concluded that this particular means of enforcing the statute's substantive mandates will prove counterproductive in the case of nondominant long-distance carriers. Even if the 1934 Congress did not define the scope of the Commission's modification authority with perfect scholarly precision, this is surely a paradigm case for judicial deference to the agency's interpretation, particularly in a statutory regime so obviously meant to maximize administrative flexibility. Whatever the best reading of §203(b)(2), the Commission's reading cannot in my view be termed unreasonable. It is informed (as ours is not) by a practical understanding of the role (or lack thereof) that filed tariffs play in the modern regulatory climate and in the telecommunications industry. Since 1979, the FCC has sought to adapt measures originally designed to control monopoly power to new market conditions. It has carefully and consistently explained that mandatory tariff-filing rules frustrate the core statutory interest in rate reasonableness. The Commission's use of the "discretion" expressly conferred by §203(b)(2) reflects "a reasonable accommodation of manifestly competing interests and is entitled to deference: the regulatory scheme is technical and complex, the agency considered the matter in a detailed and reasoned fashion, and the decision involves reconciling conflicting policies." *Chevron*. The FCC has permissibly interpreted its §203(b)(2) authority in service of the goals Congress set forth in the Act. We should sustain its eminently sound, experience-tested, and uncommonly well-explained judgment.

8.3. OTHER TYPES OF AGENCY DEFERENCE

In the last section, we saw that before a court considering an agency's interpretation of a federal statute gets subject to the *Chevron* Doctrine's two-step analysis, there is a preliminary question that is referred to as the *Chevron* "Step Zero" question: *When* is an agency's interpretation entitled to deference? Imagine, for instance, that a federal agency advances its interpretation of a statute for the first time in an *amicus* brief filed in the Supreme Court. Does *that* interpretation get *Chevron* deference?

The Supreme Court addressed the Step Zero question most directly in a 2001 case, *United States v. Mead*.[23] If you thought the facts from the MCI case in the last example were dry, just wait for these. *Mead* resolved the question "whether a tariff classification ruling by the United States Customs Service deserves judicial deference."

---

23. 533 U.S. 218 (2001).

8. Agency Interpretation

A federal statute gave the secretary of the treasury the authority to set rules and regulations related to tariffs (or taxes) on imported goods. The secretary of the treasury

> provides for tariff rulings before the entry of goods by regulations authorizing "ruling letters" setting tariff classifications for particular imports. 19 CFR §177.8 (2000). A ruling letter
>
>> "represents the official position of the Customs Service with respect to the particular transaction or issue described therein and is binding on all Customs Service personnel in accordance with the provisions of this section until modified or revoked. In the absence of a change of practice or other modification or revocation which affects the principle of the ruling set forth in the ruling letter, that principle may be cited as authority in the disposition of transactions involving the same circumstances." §177.9(a).
>
> After the transaction that gives it birth, a ruling letter is to "be applied only with respect to transactions involving articles identical to the sample submitted with the ruling request or to articles whose description is identical to the description set forth in the ruling letter." As a general matter, such a letter is "subject to modification or revocation without notice to any person, except the person to whom the letter was addressed," and the regulations consequently provide that "no other person should rely on the ruling letter or assume that the principles of that ruling will be applied in connection with any transaction other than the one described in the letter." Since ruling letters respond to transactions of the moment, they are not subject to notice and comment before being issued, may be published but need only be made "available for public inspection," and, at the time this action arose, could be modified without notice and comment under most circumstances. . . .
>
> Any of the 46 port-of-entry Customs offices may issue ruling letters, and so may the Customs Headquarters Office, in providing "[a]dvice or guidance as to the interpretation or proper application of the Customs and related laws with respect to a specific Customs transaction [which] may be requested by Customs Service field offices . . . at any time, whether the transaction is prospective, current, or completed" (2000). Most ruling letters contain little or no reasoning, but simply describe goods and state the appropriate category and tariff. A few letters . . . set out a rationale in some detail.

Mead concerned a company's disagreement with a Customs Department ruling letter considering its looseleaf "Day Planners" to be "Diaries . . . bound" and subject to a 4 percent tariff. Before that they were classified in an "other" category and not subject to a tariff. The department issued a brief letter not explaining the change, and then after the company protested it issued a longer letter.

> This letter considered two definitions of "diary" from the Oxford English Dictionary, the first covering a daily journal of the past day's events, the second

a book including "'printed dates for daily memoranda and jottings; also . . . calendars. . . .'" (quoting Oxford English Dictionary 321 (Compact ed. 1982)). Customs concluded that "diary" was not confined to the first, in part because the broader definition reflects commercial usage and hence the "commercial identity of these items in the marketplace." As for the definition of "bound," Customs concluded that [the tariff table] was not referring to "book-binding," but to a less exact sort of fastening described in the Harmonized Commodity Description and Coding System Explanatory Notes to Heading 4820, which spoke of binding by "'reinforcements or fittings of metal, plastics, etc.'"

The Supreme Court held that the Customs Department's ruling letter was not entitled to *Chevron* deference but was entitled to what has come to be called *Skidmore* deference thanks to a 1944 case, *Skidmore v. Swift & Co.*[24] Justice Souter, writing for the Court, explained:

> When Congress has "explicitly left a gap for an agency to fill, there is an express delegation of authority to the agency to elucidate a specific provision of the statute by regulation," *Chevron,* and any ensuing regulation is binding in the courts unless procedurally defective, arbitrary or capricious in substance, or manifestly contrary to the statute. But whether or not they enjoy any express delegation of authority on a particular question, agencies charged with applying a statute necessarily make all sorts of interpretive choices, and while not all of those choices bind judges to follow them, they certainly may influence courts facing questions the agencies have already answered. "[T]he well-reasoned views of the agencies implementing a statute constitute a body of experience and informed judgment to which courts and litigants may properly resort for guidance," *Bragdon v. Abbott,* 524 U.S. 624, 642 (1998) (quoting *Skidmore*)), and "[w]e have long recognized that considerable weight should be accorded to an executive department's construction of a statutory scheme it is entrusted to administer. . . ." *Chevron.* The fair measure of deference to an agency administering its own statute has been understood to vary with circumstances, and courts have looked to the degree of the agency's care, its consistency, formality, and relative expertness, and to the persuasiveness of the agency's position, *see Skidmore.* The approach has produced a spectrum of judicial responses, from great respect at one end, see, *e. g., Aluminum Co. of America v. Central Lincoln Peoples' Util. Dist.,* 467 U.S. 380, 389-390 (1984) ("substantial deference" to administrative construction), to near indifference at the other, see, *e.g., Bowen v. Georgetown Univ. Hospital,* 488 U.S. 204, 212-213 (1988) (interpretation advanced for the first time in a litigation brief). Justice Jackson summed things up in *Skidmore:*
>
>> "The weight [accorded to an administrative] judgment in a particular case will depend upon the thoroughness evident in its consideration, the validity of its reasoning, its consistency with earlier and later pronouncements, and all those factors which give it power to persuade, if lacking power to control."

---

24. 323 U.S. 134 (1944).

8. Agency Interpretation

Since 1984, we have identified a category of interpretive choices distinguished by an additional reason for judicial deference. This Court in *Chevron* recognized that Congress not only engages in express delegation of specific interpretive authority, but that "[s]ometimes the legislative delegation to an agency on a particular question is implicit." Congress, that is, may not have expressly delegated authority or responsibility to implement a particular provision or fill a particular gap. Yet it can still be apparent from the agency's generally conferred authority and other statutory circumstances that Congress would expect the agency to be able to speak with the force of law when it addresses ambiguity in the statute or fills a space in the enacted law, even one about which "Congress did not actually have an intent" as to a particular result. When circumstances implying such an expectation exist, a reviewing court has no business rejecting an agency's exercise of its generally conferred authority to resolve a particular statutory ambiguity simply because the agency's chosen resolution seems unwise, see *id.*, at 845-846, but is obliged to accept the agency's position if Congress has not previously spoken to the point at issue and the agency's interpretation is reasonable.

We have recognized a very good indicator of delegation meriting *Chevron* treatment in express congressional authorizations to engage in the process of rulemaking or adjudication that produces regulations or rulings for which deference is claimed. It is fair to assume generally that Congress contemplates administrative action with the effect of law when it provides for a relatively formal administrative procedure tending to foster the fairness and deliberation that should underlie a pronouncement of such force. Thus, the overwhelming number of our cases applying *Chevron* deference have reviewed the fruits of notice-and-comment rulemaking or formal adjudication. That said, and as significant as notice-and-comment is in pointing to *Chevron* authority, the want of that procedure here does not decide the case, for we have sometimes found reasons for *Chevron* deference even when no such administrative formality was required and none was afforded. The fact that the tariff classification here was not a product of such formal process does not alone, therefore, bar the application of *Chevron*.

There are, nonetheless, ample reasons to deny *Chevron* deference here. The authorization for classification rulings, and Custom's practice in making them, present a case far removed not only from notice-and-comment process, but from any other circumstances reasonably suggesting that Congress ever thought of classification rulings as deserving the deference claimed for them here.

The Supreme Court sent the case back to the lower courts to apply *Skidmore* deference in the first instance. Justice Scalia alone dissented, taking a *Chevron*-or-nothing approach to agency determinations. Justice Scalia predicted lots of confusion about when *Skidmore* deference would apply and believed it would create a great deal of litigation policing the boundary between the two. He added

Worst of all, the majority's approach will lead to the ossification of large portions of our statutory law. Where *Chevron* applies, statutory ambiguities remain ambiguities subject to the agency's ongoing clarification. They create a space, so to speak, for the exercise of continuing agency discretion. As *Chevron* itself held, the Environmental Protection Agency can interpret "stationary source" to mean a single smokestack, can later replace that interpretation with the "bubble concept" embracing an entire plant, and if that proves undesirable can return again to the original interpretation. For the indeterminately large number of statutes taken out of *Chevron* by today's decision, however, ambiguity (and hence flexibility) will cease with the first judicial resolution. *Skidmore* deference gives the agency's current position some vague and uncertain amount of respect, but it does not, like *Chevron, leave* the matter within the control of the Executive Branch for the future. Once the court has spoken, it becomes *unlawful* for the agency to take a contradictory position; the statute now *says* what the court has prescribed. It will be bad enough when this ossification occurs as a result of judicial determination (under today's new principles) that there is no affirmative indication of congressional intent to "delegate"; but it will be positively bizarre when it occurs simply because of an agency's failure to act by rulemaking (rather than informal adjudication) before the issue is presented to the courts.

Justice Scalia's worst fears do not appear to have materialized. And Justice Scalia recently seemed to admit the *Skidmore/Mead* framework for informal settings.[25] There have been some cases policing the *Chevron–Skidmore* boundary, and *Skidmore* deference is probably even more ad hoc than *Chevron* deference; after all, there is something circular in a rule that pegs the amount of deference to give to an agency interpretation to how persuasive the argument is.

Justice Scalia continues to argue for strong application of *Chevron* deference. In *City of Arlington v. FCC*,[26] Justice Scalia wrote the opinion for a six-justice majority rejecting the argument that *Chevron* is inapplicable to an agency's determination of its own jurisdiction. "[T]he distinction between 'jurisdictional' and 'nonjurisdictional' interpretations [by an agency] is a mirage. No matter how it is framed, the question a court faces when confronted with an agency's interpretation of a statute it administers is always, simply, *whether the agency has stayed within the bounds of its statutory authority.*" Chief Justice Roberts, for himself and Justices Alito and Kennedy, dissented, viewing the question of agency authority to decide its own jurisdiction as analytically distinct and as a question to be decided by the judiciary in light of the extensive powers of agencies in the administrative state.

---

25. "The dissent is correct that *United States v. Mead Corp.*, 533 U. S. 218 (2001), requires that, for *Chevron* deference to apply, the agency must have received congressional authority to determine the particular matter at issue in the particular manner adopted. No one disputes that. But *Mead* denied *Chevron* deference to action, by an agency with rulemaking authority, that was not rulemaking." *City of Arlington, supra.*
26. 133 S.Ct. 1863 (2013).

City of Arlington will not be the last word on the scope of judicial deference to agency interpretations. Indeed, the picture in the courts is much, much more complicated than simply a choice between *Chevron* and *Skidmore* (or no deference), as Eskridge and Baer's key empirical study of Supreme Court deference in agency cases reveals. There are many other forms of deference that the Court has explicitly or implicitly used in agency cases. Perhaps somewhat surprisingly, the agency win rates between Court application of the two regimes was quite similar, with agencies winning 73.5% of cases applying *Skidmore* deference and 76.2% of cases applying *Chevron* deference.[27] At least during the period studied by Eskridge and Baer, ideological voting by each justice was a better predictor of how a justice would vote in an agency case than the form of deference applied.

And on that moderately depressing and cynical note, we will end our exploration of statutory interpretation issues.

Example 3

The Fair Labor Standards Act (FLSA) imposes minimum wage and maximum hours requirements on employers, *see* 29 U.S.C. §§206-207, but those requirements do not apply to workers employed "in the capacity of outside salesman," §213(a)(1). Congress did not define the term "outside salesman," but it delegated authority to the Department of Labor to issue regulations "from time to time" to "defin[e] and delimi[t]" the term. The DOL promulgated such regulations in 1938, 1940, and 1949. In 2004, following notice-and-comment procedures, the DOL reissued the regulations with minor amendments. The current regulations are nearly identical in substance to the regulations issued in the years immediately following the FLSA's enactment.

The question before the court was whether the term "outside salesman," as defined by Department of Labor regulations, encompasses pharmaceutical sales representatives whose primary duty is to obtain nonbinding commitments from physicians to prescribe their employer's prescription drugs in appropriate cases. These representatives claim that their employer failed to pay them overtime as required by the FLSA. The employer responded that these representatives were exempt "outside salesmen."

Various DOL regulations give guidance on how to determine who counts as an "outside salesman," but none directly addresses pharmaceutical representatives. In federal district court, the representatives argued that the court must give controlling deference to the DOL's interpretation of the pertinent regulations. That interpretation had been announced in an uninvited *amicus* brief filed by the DOL in a similar action then pending in another

---

27. Eskridge & Baer, *supra*, at 1142.

court. This interpretation contradicted DOL's previous interpretation of the statute.

How much deference, if any, should the court give to the DOL's interpretation of a statute offered in the amicus brief?

Explanation

The facts above come from the Supreme Court's recent case, *Christopher v. SmithKline Beecham Corp.*[28] An agency's opinion advanced for the first time in an amicus brief does not appear to be the kind of action that would be entitled to *Chevron* deference. It is not the kind of formal rulemaking after notice-and-comment or adversarial adjudication that the Court discussed in *Mead* in drawing the *Chevron–Skidmore* line. Under *Skidmore*, the court's decision to defer to the DOL's position in an amicus brief would depend upon a number of factors, including the opinion's not being a longstanding one and its contradicting earlier DOL interpretations. It is not clear that a changed opinion coming in the context of litigation should be entitled to much deference.

However, as noted in the text before the example, the Supreme Court has developed a more complicated system of deference than just the binary *Chevron/Skidmore* choice. *Christopher* raises one of these more specific rules of deference. In *Auer v. Robbins*[29] and subsequent cases, the Court held that ordinarily courts should defer to an agency's interpretation of its own regulation, even if that interpretation is advanced in a legal brief.

I did not tell you about *Auer* before this example, so you couldn't have applied it. But knowing now the *Auer* rule, can you predict what the Supreme Court should do? If you said that the court would defer to the DOL's interpretation advanced in the *amicus* brief, you would be wrong!

Here is what Justice Alito wrote for a five-justice majority on the Supreme Court:

> Although *Auer* ordinarily calls for deference to an agency's interpretation of its own ambiguous regulation, even when that interpretation is advanced in a legal brief, this general rule does not apply in all cases. Deference is undoubtedly inappropriate, for example, when the agency's interpretation is plainly erroneous or inconsistent with the regulation. And deference is likewise unwarranted when there is reason to suspect that the agency's interpretation does not reflect the agency's fair and considered judgment on the matter in question. This might occur when the agency's interpretation conflicts with a prior interpretation or when it appears that the interpretation is nothing more than a convenient litigating position, or a *post hoc* rationalizatio[n] advanced by an agency seeking to defend past agency action against attack.

---

28. 132 S.Ct. 2156 (2012).
29. 519 U.S. 452 (1997).

In this case, there are strong reasons for withholding the deference that *Auer* generally requires. Petitioners invoke the DOL's interpretation of ambiguous regulations to impose potentially massive liability on respondent for conduct that occurred well before that interpretation was announced. To defer to the agency's interpretation in this circumstance would seriously undermine the principle that agencies should provide regulated parties fair warning of the conduct [a regulation] prohibits or requires. Indeed, it would result in precisely the kind of "unfair surprise" against which our cases have long warned. . . .

Our practice of deferring to an agency's interpretation of its own ambiguous regulations undoubtedly has important advantages, but this practice also creates a risk that agencies will promulgate vague and open-ended regulations that they can later interpret as they see fit, thereby frustrat[ing] the notice and predictability purposes of rulemaking. It is one thing to expect regulated parties to conform their conduct to an agency's interpretations once the agency announces them; it is quite another to require regulated parties to divine the agency's interpretations in advance or else be held liable when the agency announces its interpretations for the first time in an enforcement proceeding and demands deference.

Accordingly, whatever the general merits of *Auer* deference, it is unwarranted here. We instead accord the Department's interpretation a measure of deference proportional to the thoroughness evident in its consideration, the validity of its reasoning, its consistency with earlier and later pronouncements, and all those factors which give it power to persuade. *Mead* (quoting *Skidmore*).

The Court then turned to *Skidmore* deference and concluded that the agency was entitled to no *Skidmore* deference, because its statutory analysis advanced in the *amicus* brief was "wholly unpersuasive."

Ultimately, applying "traditional tools of interpretation to determine whether petitioners are exempt outside salesmen," the Court majority concluded the representatives qualified as outside salesmen and were not entitled to overtime pay.

Justice Breyer, writing for the four dissenting justices, reached a contrary conclusion on whether representatives qualified as outside salesmen, but he agreed with the Court's refusal to give deference to the DOL's position advanced in the amicus brief:

In light of important, near-contemporaneous differences in the Justice Department's views as to the meaning of relevant Labor Department regulations, I also agree that we should not give the Solicitor General's current interpretive view any especially favorable weight. Thus, I am willing to assume, with the Court, that we should determine whether the statutory term covers the detailer's job as here described through our independent examination of the statute's language and the related Labor Department regulations. But, I conclude on that basis that a detailer is not an "outside salesman."

In the end, it seems fair to note that the question of deference or not made no difference in this case, because the majority and dissent both decided that deference was inappropriate. Both sides reached this conclusion despite the earlier *Auer* case, which generally supported deference to an agency's interpretation of its own regulations even if advanced in a legal brief. A better predictor of the justice's votes in the case is not the level of deference to agency interpretation but instead his or her ideology: The five conservative justices sided with an employer to oppose overtime for pharmaceutical representatives, whereas the four liberal justices sided with the employees and in favor of overtime.

So don't get too hung up on the precise level of deference, and remember: In cases involving important public policy issues, the judges' (or justices') views may matter a whole lot more than the agency's position on the issue.

PART III

Voting Rights and Representation

The Right to Vote, Representation, and Redistricting

9.1. WHO (DECIDES WHO) VOTES?

9.1.1. Introduction: Three Questions About Literacy Tests

We turn now away from legislators, legislatures, and legislation toward the voters whom the legislators represent. This chapter considers who votes, who decides who votes, how we weigh votes, and how we divide voters up for electing representatives (the process of redistricting). The next chapter delves further into representation, redistricting, and the role of political parties in competition. Chapter 11 looks at the relationship between race and representation, again with a major focus on redistricting. Chapter 12, the last in this part, looks at how we run our elections and at the disputes that have emerged in the area of election administration since the disputed presidential election of 2000. The final part of the book turns to campaign financing.

When I teach this part of my election law course, I like to begin by giving my students an old Louisiana literacy test, which ran four single-spaced pages long. Would-be Louisiana voters who could not prove a fifth-grade education took the test. A voter had to get every answer right to avoid disenfranchisement and had only 10 minutes to complete it. One of the questions read: "Write every other word in this first line and print every third word in same line [original type smaller and first line ended at comma] but capitalize the fifth word that you write."[1] If that's a tough slog for a law student, imagine what it would be for someone without a fifth-grade education. And that's just one question of many to be completed perfectly in 10 minutes.

The Louisiana example is a nice jumping-off point for three sets of questions:

1. Should literacy be required for voting? Why, or why not?
2. If literacy should be required for voting, who should administer the test? Can we trust administrators of the test to give it fairly, especially in jurisdictions with a rich history of racial discrimination in voting?
3. To what extent is it the *courts'* role (or Congress's role) to decide the answers to these questions rather than to allow these questions to be resolved in the (state or local) political process?

The question whether literacy should be required for voting raises a fundamental point about the purpose of voting. One could defend a literacy test by arguing that voting is about choosing the best candidates to serve as representatives of the people, and the test increases the chances that those citizens doing the choosing will be educated and well-informed. A literacy test could be a proxy for being a well-informed voter under this "choose the best candidate" view of voting.

The claim is controversial on both empirical and normative grounds. Empirically, the question is whether literacy tests (even if they are fairly applied without racial animus) are a good tool for limiting the franchise to educated and well-informed voters. Some voters not literate in English could be well educated in another language, or they could be well informed even if they cannot read in English. Depending on the details of the literacy test (again, it is worth looking at the entire Louisiana literacy test posted at *Slate*), the test may be too tough even for educated and well-informed voters, meaning that some citizens who should vote would be disenfranchised.

The claim that the vote should be limited to the educated and the well-informed is also normatively questionable. If one takes the view that the purpose of voting is not to choose the best candidate but rather to provide a mechanism by which political equals (eligible voters) choose their representatives, then literacy tests are normatively objectionable. Among political

---

1. To see the entire test, and for some context, *see* Rebecca Onion, *Take the Impossible "Literacy" Test Louisiana Gave Black Voters in the 1960s*, SLATE, Jun. 28, 2013, http://www.slate.com/blogs/the_vault/2013/06/28/voting_rights_and_the_supreme_court_the_impossible_literacy_test_louisiana.html.

equals, it is not proper or fair to decide who is informed or educated enough to vote for representatives.

Although history has moved definitively against literacy tests — they are barred by the Voting Rights Act and no doubt would not be acceptable today in most places — this same debate about voter qualifications plays out in parallel ways in areas we explore in this part of the book.

The question of who administers a literacy test points out an issue that we will also examine throughout this part of the book. We count on people who administer elections to do so in a fair and neutral manner. If they don't, then lack of neutrality threatens the very core of our democracy. Consider a recent *Washington Post* headline: *Oops: Azerbaijan Released Election Results Before Voting Even Started.*[2] As we will see more in Chapter 12, our democracy is only as strong as our confidence in our system of election administration.

It was well known that in parts of the South such as Louisiana in the 1960s, literacy tests were not fairly administered. Instead, election officials and other government officials discriminated in voting against African-Americans and others. When election officials have discretion to decide who votes, and when the rules are not clear or are subject to individual interpretation, then biased election officials can skew the electorate or votes in a particular direction.

The final introductory question prompted by the literacy test issue is who decides who votes. That is, are we going to leave the question of voting rules and qualifications to state or local government, or are we going to give the courts or Congress some say?

Consider the 1959 case *Lassiter v. Northampton County Board of Elections*.[3] In *Lassiter*, an African-American woman challenged a literacy test contained in North Carolina's Constitution. North Carolina's literacy test included a "grandfather clause" that excused from the literacy test any voter whose grandfather voted in an election. However, North Carolina was no longer enforcing the grandfather clause, which the Supreme Court had held in 1915 violated the Fifteenth Amendment's prohibition on racial discrimination in voting — because many African-American citizens' grandparents could not vote due to slavery or discrimination.[4] The *Lassiter* Court also assumed for the sake of argument that North Carolina was fairly administering its literacy test to African-Americans, leaving open the possibility of unfair treatment by election officials to be proven in a later case.

---

2. Max Fisher, *Oops: Azerbaijan Released Election Results Before Voting Even Started*, Wash. Post, Oct. 9, 2013, http://www.washingtonpost.com/blogs/worldviews/wp/2013/10/09/oops-azerbaijan-released-election-results-before-voting-had-even-started/.
3. 360 U.S. 45 (1959).
4. *Guinn v. U.S.*, 238 U.S. 347 (1915).

The Court then was able to confront head-on the question whether a fairly applied literacy test was unconstitutional, violating the Fourteenth Amendment's requirement that states not deny citizens equal protection of the laws and the Seventeenth Amendment's right to vote directly for U.S. senators. The Court held literacy tests constitutional:

> We do not suggest that any standards which a State desires to adopt may be required of voters. But there is wide scope for exercise of its jurisdiction. Residence requirements, age, previous criminal record are obvious examples indicating factors which a State may take into consideration in determining the qualifications of voters. The ability to read and write likewise has some relation to standards designed to promote intelligent use of the ballot. Literacy and illiteracy are neutral on race, creed, color, and sex, as reports around the world show. Literacy and intelligence are obviously not synonymous. Illiterate people may be intelligent voters. Yet in our society where newspapers, periodicals, books, and other printed matter canvass and debate campaign issues, a State might conclude that only those who are literate should exercise the franchise. It was said last century in Massachusetts that a literacy test was designed to insure an "independent and intelligent" exercise of the right of suffrage. North Carolina agrees. We do not sit in judgment on the wisdom of that policy. We cannot say, however, that it is not an allowable one measured by constitutional standards.

Although the Court was unwilling in 1959 to declare literacy tests unconstitutional, Congress acted to outlaw the use of literacy tests as part of the 1965 Voting Rights Act. The ban was originally for 5 years but later extended indefinitely. Oregon challenged the ban as unconstitutional, but the Supreme Court in *Oregon v. Mitchell*[5] upheld it. Some justices believed it was justified under Congress's power to enforce the Fourteenth Amendment; others thought it was justified under Congress's power to enforce the Fifteenth Amendment.

This last example shows that the question of *who decides* who votes is just as important as the question of who votes. Here, the Supreme Court refused to interfere with state use of a "fairly applied" literacy test, but Congress did intervene, and eventually Congress got the Supreme Court's blessing to do so.

Example 1

Was the Supreme Court right in *Lassiter* in upholding "fairly applied" literacy tests? Why, or why not?

---

5. 400 U.S. 112 (1970).

Explanation

There is no correct answer to this normative question. Instead, my purpose in asking you this question is to get you to consider both who should be entitled to the franchise and who should decide that question. Those who believe that voting is about choosing the best candidate will be most likely to think that literacy tests are a rational and permissible way to set a voter qualification. Those who view voting as more about the allocation of power among political equals will be most likely to reject literacy tests as a rational and permissible way to set a voter qualification. Furthermore, there may be administrative problems in how the test is administered, and there could be fear over whether election officials could administer such tests in a discriminatory way.

Aside from this concern is a federalism or separation of powers question: Who should decide who votes? A Supreme Court holding or congressional legislation banning literacy tests puts the decision over such tests in the hands of the federal government rather than state or local governments. Furthermore, a court decision on this question takes the issue out of the hands of legislatures and puts it into the hands of unelected federal judges. Is this judicial power run amok? Or is this an example of the courts acting to prevent the tyranny of the majority? Check to see whether your answer remains the same as we work through the rest of the material in this chapter.

9.1.2. Voting as a Fundamental Right for Citizen, Adult, Non-felon Residents

Don't be lulled by *Lassiter* into thinking the Supreme Court has adopted a hands-off approach to questions of voter qualifications and voting rules. In fact, as we will now see, *Lassiter* represented the end of an era: Since the Warren Court in the 1960s, the Supreme Court has been deeply involved in regulating the law of politics. Today, it is fair to say that **the Supreme Court's cases have read the right to vote as a fundamental right for citizen, adult, resident non-felons, and any restriction on the right to vote in a regular election within that category is subject to strict scrutiny and likely unconstitutional.**

Let's begin with a brief history lesson of American suffrage to understand the context in which the Supreme Court acted to greatly expand voting rights beginning in the 1960s.[6] In the American colonies universal suffrage was not the norm. Women could not vote. In many places Catholics, Jews,

---

6. For greater detail, *see* J. Morgan Kousser, *Suffrage*, in 3 ENCYCLOPEDIA OF AMERICAN POLITICAL HISTORY 1236 (Jack P. Greene, ed., 1984); ALEXANDER KEYSSAR, THE RIGHT TO VOTE: THE CONTESTED HISTORY OF DEMOCRACY IN THE UNITED STATES (2009); LOWENSTEIN, HASEN, & TOKAJI, *supra*, 36-38. The history here tracks the narrative in the Lowenstein volume.

and non-property holders could not vote. Slaves, of course, could not vote, and many free African-Americans were also denied the franchise.

After the colonies became part of the United States, states remained free to set their own qualifications for voting. Article I, section 2 of the Constitution required a vote for the House of Representatives (though not for Senate or the president), and the Constitution set the requirements to vote for Congress as coextensive with the requirement to vote for "the most numerous Branch" of each state's legislature. It did not specify what those state qualifications should be.

Over time, suffrage rules changed state by state. Many states abandoned property ownership or religious tests for voting. But states still had tests or devices for voting, such as requirement of the payment of taxes to vote — the poll tax. And African-Americans remained disenfranchised not only in slave states but also in many free states. Following the Civil War, the question of African-American voting became a more immediate concern. The Fourteenth Amendment's provision of equal protection did not mean the end of discrimination in voting against African-Americans. The country then adopted the Fifteenth Amendment, which provides that "[t]he rights of citizens in the United States to vote shall not be denied or abridged by the United States or by any State on account of race, color, or previous condition of servitude." The Amendment's section 2 also gave Congress the "power to enforce this article by appropriate legislation," a key power we return to in Chapter 11 on the Voting Rights Act.

At first the Fifteenth Amendment proved greatly successful, with African-Americans voting in large numbers and African-American candidates elected to office. But then as part of the settlement of the disputed election of 1876 (a fascinating subject beyond the scope of this book), Union soldiers were withdrawn from the South, marking the end of Reconstruction. Democrats and Republicans remained competitive with each other for a while in the South, but eventually through violence and intimidation, and with the support of many white voters, Democratic forces effectively disenfranchised African-American voters again in much of the South.

Southern states used various tests or devices to stop voting, including poll taxes and literacy tests. The Democratic Party also held whites-only primaries to pick nominees, who eventually went on to win in the "solid South." Reversals came only after the Voting Rights Act of 1965, which was remarkably successful, as we will further explore in Chapter 11.

African-Americans had the toughest and most prolonged struggle to vote, but there were other struggles as well. The Seventeenth Amendment, ratified in 1913, provided for the direct election of senators; before then, senators were chosen by state legislatures. Women's suffrage did not come easily in the United States. The women's suffrage movement dates to the middle of the nineteenth century. In 1874, the Supreme Court in

9. The Right to Vote, Representation, and Redistricting

Minor v. Happersett[7] rejected the argument that the Fourteenth Amendment's Equal Protection Clause provided for the enfranchisement of women. However, further political action and organization by women's suffrage groups to led to the 1920 ratification of the Nineteenth Amendment barring discrimination in voting on the basis of gender. The Twenty-fourth Amendment eliminated poll taxes in federal elections. And the Twenty-sixth Amendment, ratified in 1971, prohibited states from setting a voting age above 18.

The subject of poll taxes makes a nice segue from this bit of history to an understanding of the Supreme Court's involvement in setting some of the basic rules for voter qualifications. In 1937, the Supreme Court upheld poll taxes, so long as they were not applied in a fairly discriminatory way.[8] As noted, the Twenty-fourth Amendment abolished poll taxes, but only in federal elections. By the 1960s, only four states still levied poll taxes in state and local elections.

In *Harper v. Virginia State Board of Elections*,[9] the Supreme Court held that the use of poll taxes violated the Equal Protection Clause. Justice Douglas, the same justice who wrote *Lassiter*, wrote *Harper*, and he concluded that poll taxes were irrational:

> We conclude that a State violates the Equal Protection Clause of the Fourteenth Amendment whenever it makes the affluence of the voter or payment of any fee an electoral standard. Voter qualifications have no relation to wealth nor to paying or not paying this or any other tax. . . . It is argued that a State may exact fees from citizens for many different kinds of licenses; that if it can demand from all an equal fee for a driver's license, it can demand from all an equal poll tax for voting. But we must remember that the interest of the State, when it comes to voting, is limited to the power to fix qualifications. Wealth, like race, creed, or color, is not germane to one's ability to participate intelligently in the electoral process. Lines drawn on the basis of wealth or property, like those of race, are traditionally disfavored. To introduce wealth or payment of a fee as a measure of a voter's qualifications is to introduce a capricious or irrelevant factor.

The dissenters, however, saw little difference between *Lassiter* and *Harper*. Justice Harlan wrote

> The final demise of state poll taxes, already totally proscribed by the Twenty-Fourth Amendment with respect to federal elections and abolished by the States themselves in all but four States with respect to state elections, is perhaps in itself not of great moment. But that fact that the coup de grace has been administered by this Court instead of being left to the affected States or to the federal political

---

7. 88 U.S. 162 (1874).
8. *Breedlove v. Suttles*, 302 U.S. 277 (1937).
9. 383 U.S. 663 (1966).

process should be a matter of continuing concern to all interested in maintaining the proper role of this tribunal under our scheme of government. . . .

Property qualifications and poll taxes have been a traditional part of our political structure. In the Colonies the franchise was generally a restricted one. Over the years, these and other restrictions were gradually lifted, primarily because popular theories of political representation had changed. Often restrictions were lifted only after wide public debate. The issue of woman suffrage, for example, raised question of family relationships, of participation in public affairs, of the very nature of the type of society in which Americans wished to live; eventually a consensus was reached, which culminated in the Nineteenth Amendment no more than 45 years ago.

Similarly with property qualifications, it is only by fiat that it can be said, especially in the context of American history, that there can be no rational debate as to their advisability. Most of the early Colonies had them; many of the States have had them during much of their histories; and, whether one agrees or not, arguments have been and still can be made in favor of them. For example, it is certainly a rational argument that payment of some minimal poll tax promotes civic responsibility, weeding out those who do not care enough about public affairs to pay $1.50 or thereabouts a year for the exercise of the franchise. It is also arguable, indeed it was probably accepted as sound political theory by a large percentage of Americans through most of our history, that people with some property have a deeper stake in community affairs, and are consequently more responsible, more educated, more knowledgeable, more worthy of confidence, than those without means, and that the community and Nation would be better managed if the franchise were restricted to such citizens. Nondiscriminatory and fairly applied literacy tests, upheld by this Court in *Lassiter*, find justification on very similar grounds.

These viewpoints, to be sure, ring hollow on most contemporary ears. Their lack of acceptance today is evidenced by the fact that nearly all of the States, left to their own devices, have eliminated property or poll-tax qualifications; by the cognate fact that Congress and three-quarters of the States quickly ratified the Twenty-Fourth Amendment; and by the fact that rules such as the "pauper exclusion" in Virginia law have never been enforced.

Property and poll-tax qualifications, very simply, are not in accord with current egalitarian notions of how a modern democracy should be organized. It is of course entirely fitting that legislatures should modify the law to reflect such changes in popular attitudes. However, it is all wrong, in my view, for the Court to adopt the political doctrines popularly accepted at a particular moment of our history and to declare all others to be irrational and invidious, barring them from the range of choice by reasonably minded people acting through the political process. It was not too long ago that Mr. Justice Holmes felt impelled to remind the Court that the Due Process Clause of the Fourteenth Amendment does not enact the laissez-faire theory of society, *Lochner*. The times have changed, and perhaps it is appropriate to observe that neither does the Equal Protection Clause of that Amendment rigidly impose upon America an ideology of unrestrained egalitarianism.

How to square *Harper* and *Lassiter*? Is it really true that literacy tests are rational but poll taxes are not? A little of the backstory of *Harper* sheds some light. As I explained in an earlier book,[10]

> Although *Harper* . . . stated its principles as self-evident, the result in the 6-3 case reversing the lower court was hardly inevitable. The case began as a proposed 6-3 *per curiam* summary affirmance (that is, without a written opinion) of the lower court decision upholding the poll tax. Justice Goldberg, joined by Chief Justice Warren and Justice Douglas, circulated a proposed dissent. Relying on [other recent Warren Court voting rights cases] along with the Virginia poll tax's legislative history evincing intent to discriminate against both African-Americans and poor whites, Justice Goldberg would have held that "no reasonable state interest is served by barring from voting those citizens who desire to vote but who lack the requisite funds."
>
> Justice Goldberg sought to explain the limits of the equal protection principle that would bar the use of a poll tax in elections:
>
>> The application of these principles obviously does not mean that Government — State or Federal — must equalize all economic inequalities among citizens. Nor does it mean that the Government cannot impose burdens or exactions which by reason of economic circumstances fall more heavily upon some than others. Nor, however desirable it may be as a matter of social and legislative policy, does it require the State affirmatively to provide relief for all the incidents of poverty. The Constitution does not command absolute equality in all areas. It does mean, however, that a State may not frustrate or burden the exercise of the basic and precious right to vote by imposing substantial obstacles upon that exercise by a class of citizens not justified by any legitimate state interest. In particular it means that with respect to the fundamental right to vote, a reverse means test cannot be applied. A classification based upon financial means embodied in a voting statute is inherently not "reasonable in light of . . . [the statute's] purpose."
>
> Justice Goldberg further rejected the long American history of tolerance for property qualifications and poll taxes as irrelevant for contemporary application of constitutional principles. "[W]e must consider voting rights in light of their full development, their 'present place in American life throughout the nation,' cf. *Brown v. Board of Education*, and our present conception of the meaning and application of the Equal Protection Clause."
>
> Only one day after Justice Goldberg's dissent circulated, Justice Black circulated a memorandum to the other Justices asking that the case be put for a full hearing. Justice Black perhaps expected from the initial 6-3 vote for summary affirmance that the case would lead to a similar 6-3 vote on an opinion affirming the validity of the poll tax and distinguishing the cases cited by Justice Goldberg. If so, his expectations were dashed, because Justices Brennan, Clark, and White changed positions. Justice Black ultimately issued a dissent arguing

10. RICHARD L. HASEN, THE SUPREME COURT AND ELECTION LAW 37-38 (2003).

the question of poll taxes should be left to the states unless Congress wanted to use its enforcement powers to ban the practice. . . .

The Constitution was not amended in 1965; three Justices simply changed their minds about its meaning. Justice Black in his *Harper* dissent protested that the Court had overruled prior precedent "not by using its limited power to interpret the original meaning of the Equal Protection Clause, but by giving that clause a new meaning which it believes represents a better governmental policy." Two days before the opinion issued, Justice Douglas added a sentence to the *Harper* majority opinion responding to Justice Black's point: "Our conclusion, like that in *Reynolds v. Sims*, is founded not on what we think governmental policy should be, but on what the Equal Protection Clause requires."

Harper shows the Court as it transitioned toward treating voting as a fundamental right and subjecting many limitations to strict scrutiny. Although Justice Douglas continued to use the language of "rationality" in *Harper*, many of the other cases decided in this same time period began using the language of strict scrutiny: requiring the government to come forward with a *compelling interest* for a voting restriction and requiring that the means be *narrowly tailored* to that interest. The Court treated voting as a fundamental right, reasoning that it is "preservative of all other rights":[11] Without the franchise, why would legislators who pass the laws listen to a citizen's concerns?

Around the same time as *Harper*, the Court required that each voter's votes be weighed equally — a topic we turn to in the next section. Furthermore, the Court held that states could not limit the franchise only to long-time residents. In *Dunn v. Blumstein*,[12] the Court rejected a one-year residency requirement in a state and a three-month residency in a county, suggesting that 30 days was a long enough residency period. The Court later upheld residency periods as long as 50 days.[13] Most jurisdictions these days use a 30-day residency period, a requirement for presidential elections contained in Section 202 of the Voting Rights Act.

Aside from preventing discrimination against recent residents, the Court also prevented discrimination against residents who may not have the same views or subjective interests as other residents. In *Carrington v. Rash*,[14] the Court held that people who moved to a jurisdiction while serving in the military could not be denied the right to vote. In *Evans v. Cornman*,[15] the Court rejected a law denying voting rights to otherwise eligible persons living on the grounds of the National Institutes of Health (NIH), a federal reservation or enclave located within the geographical boundaries of Montgomery

---

11. *Yick Wo v. Hopkins*, 118 U.S. 356 (1886).
12. 405 U.S. 330 (1972).
13. *Marston v. Lewis*, 410 U.S. 679 (1973); *Burns v. Fortson*, 410 U.S. 686 (1973).
14. 380 U.S. 89 (1965).
15. 398 U.S. 419 (1970).

County in the state of Maryland. The Supreme Court also summarily affirmed (that is, affirmed without a written opinion) a lower court case establishing the right of college students to vote in the jurisdiction to which they moved to in order to attend college.[16]

In perhaps the most far-reaching of these decisions, the Court in *Kramer v. Union Free School District No. 15*[17] held that New York State could not limit the vote in a school board election to those who either had school-aged children or rented or owned property in the district. The state had defended this requirement on grounds that it targeted those with the greatest objective interest in the outcome of the elections (parents of children and taxpayers supporting (or in the case of renters indirectly supporting) the school system). Although the Court's reasoning was a bit slippery,[18] the Court held that a 31-year-old bachelor stockbroker who lived with his parents, paid no rent, and had no children in the district had the constitutional right to vote in the school board election. The dissenters thought it enough that the plaintiff could vote in state elections and could work to get the state legislature to change the local voting rule.

Although all this talk about voting as a fundamental right may make it sound as though *any* franchise restriction is going to be subject to strict scrutiny and likely struck down, this is not the case. The fundamental right to vote applies only to *citizen, adult, resident non-felons.* The Court has held that it does not violate the Constitution's equal protection clause to exclude felons[19] or non-residents[20] from voting. There also seems little doubt that the Court would uphold a challenge by a noncitizen[21] or 16-year-old to a prohibition on voting. Whether it makes sense to uphold these restrictions on voting but not the others described in this chapter is an issue worth debating. But note the oddity that voting is a fundamental right — just not for everybody.

Example 2

Plaintiffs lived within the "police jurisdiction" of Tuscaloosa, Alabama, which consisted of the area outside but within three miles of the city limits. Under Alabama law, city criminal ordinances were applicable and the

---

16. *Symm v. United States*, 439 U.S. 1105 (1979), *aff'g United States v. Texas*, 445 F. Supp. 1245 (S.D. Tex. 1978).
17. 395 U.S. 621 (1969).
18. The Court shifted between talking about limiting the franchise based upon objective interests and subjective interests.
19. *Richardson v. Ramirez*, 418 U.S. 24 (1974). If the felon disenfranchisement law is administered in a racially discriminatory manner, however, then the law is unconstitutional. *Hunter v. Underwood*, 471 U.S. 222 (1985).
20. *Holt Civic Club v. City of Tuscaloosa*, 439 U.S. 60 (1978).
21. *See Skafte v. Rorex*, 553 P.2d 830 (Colo. 1976), *appeal dismissed* 430 U.S. 961 (1977).

jurisdiction of the municipal courts extended to the police jurisdiction. In addition, businesses located within the police jurisdiction had to pay a license tax half the amount they would be required to pay if they were within the city. However, the city's power of zoning, eminent domain, and ad valorem taxation did not extend to the police jurisdiction.

Is it constitutional to bar citizen, adult non-felons living outside the Tuscaloosa city limits but within its police jurisdiction from voting in Tuscaloosa city elections? Is such a claim subject to strict scrutiny? Regardless of how you predict the Supreme Court would decide the case, how would you decide the case?

Explanation

This was precisely the issue in *Holt Civic Club v. City of Tuscaloosa*. A Court majority held that the state could withhold the franchise from those living outside the city boundaries, on grounds that they were non-residents. The Court did not apply strict scrutiny to the question and held that limiting the vote to residents was rational. Although the dissenters, led by Justice Brennan, did not seem to have a problem with a rule that denied the vote to full non-residents, the dissenters believed that those citizens within the police jurisdiction of Tuscaloosa and subject to its laws should have been considered residents and given the franchise under a strict scrutiny analysis.

As far as what you might think: Consider what purpose the residency requirement serves. Would you want non-residents voting in local elections? What about people who worked in the jurisdiction, owned businesses or property in the area, or otherwise had connections to the area? What would be the danger of allowing non-residents to vote in local elections?

9.2. VOTE DILUTION AND THE ONE PERSON, ONE VOTE RULE

9.2.1. *Baker, Reynolds,* and the Emergence of the One Person, One Vote Rule

When someone is denied the franchise, it is easy to see the loss in voting rights: Mr. Kramer didn't get to vote in the school board election; Louisiana residents who could not pass the tough literacy test lost the franchise; people who couldn't afford a $1.50 poll tax in Virginia similarly were denied access to the ballot box.

These are *vote denial* cases: Someone is literally disenfranchised. But vote denial is not the only way to adversely affect someone's voting rights. Imagine a professor announcing to the class that the class will vote on whether to have an open-book or closed-book final exam. Each of the 30 students in the class is given one vote, but the professor gives herself 40 votes. It is not true that the students have been literally disenfranchised: Each gets to vote on the question of the format of the examination, but the votes are weighted in such a way that the professor's choice is decisive and the students' choices are inconsequential. Even if all 30 students vote the same way, the professor's vote is all that matters.

We will call this type of claim a *vote dilution* claim because the value or weight of the votes are not equal even though everyone has the franchise. Dilution is not literal disenfranchisement because people still vote, but dilution can cause a vote to be politically meaningless. We will see different kinds of vote dilution claims in coming chapters, but let's begin with dilution in the context of drawing legislative districts with different numbers of people.

The typical means of electing legislators to a legislative body (such as Congress or a state legislature) is through the use of districts. That is, rather than having all members of a state vote for all members of a legislature (or vote for a party to be represented in a legislature, as is done in some parliamentary democracies), district-based elections have legislators elected from defined geographic areas to "represent" those areas. District-based elections were used in England, and they are often used in the United States to provide local representation of interests in a larger body.

There is nothing inevitable about having district-based elections, or even about using single-member districts when we elect representatives. We could, for example, draw larger ("multimember") districts and have voters choose three or four candidates. Most typical in the United States, however, is the use of single-member districts: Voters in a defined geographical area chose one legislator to represent that area. By statute, members of Congress must be elected from single-member districts.[22]

If legislative districts are drawn with unequal populations, then votes can be diluted in the same way as in the professor-students example. California, for example, has 58 counties. Some, such as Los Angeles County, are very heavily populated. Others, such as Mono County, are sparsely populated. Imagine that the California legislature elected its members from counties—one from each county. In that case, Los Angeles and Mono counties would have the same representation in the state legislature even though it would take many, many more people to elect a Los Angeles representative than a Mono county representative. The votes of Los Angeles County voters would be diluted.

---

22. 2 U.S.C. §2c.

This was very much the situation in the United States until the 1960s. Legislative district lines in many places had vastly unequal populations in them (a condition that came to be known as *malapportionment*). The lines may not have started out that way, but as populations grew in some areas, legislative bodies did not redraw the lines (*redistrict*). This should hardly be a surprise: Legislators often act in their own self-interest, and so why would legislators in malapportioned districts vote themselves out of a job?

If legislators could not be counted on to fix the unequal weighting of votes, what about the courts? For a long time, the Supreme Court refused to get involved in these cases. In *Colegrove v. Green*,[23] the Supreme Court refused to enter the "political thicket": It held that a claim that malapportioned districts violated the U.S. Constitution was an unreviewable (or "nonjusticiable") *political question*.

Under the political question doctrine, courts sometime refuse to decide issues, leaving them to the political branches of government — the president and Congress.[24] The Court in *Colegrove* rejected a challenge to unequal districts brought under the "Guaranty Clause" of the Constitution (contained in Article IV) in which Congress guarantees that each state shall have a "Republican form of government."

With the advent of the Warren Court, the Supreme Court changed its position on the justiciability of malapportionment claims. In *Baker v. Carr*,[25] the Court distinguished *Colegrove* on grounds that the earlier case involved a challenge under the Guaranty Clause, whereas *Baker* presented a claim under the Equal Protection Clause:

> We come, finally, to the ultimate inquiry whether our precedents as to what constitutes a nonjusticiable "political question" bring the case before us under the umbrella of that doctrine. A natural beginning is to note whether any of the common characteristics which we have been able to identify and label descriptively are present. We find none: the question here is the consistency of state action with the Federal Constitution. We have no question decided, or to be decided, by a political branch of government coequal with this Court. Nor do we risk embarrassment of our government abroad, or grave disturbance at home if we take issue with Tennessee as to the constitutionality of her action here challenged. Nor need the appellants, in order to succeed in this action, ask the Court to enter upon policy determinations for which judicially manageable standards are lacking. Judicial standards under the Equal Protection Clause are well developed and familiar, and it has been open to courts since the enactment of the Fourteenth Amendment to determine, if, on the particular facts, they

---

23. 328 U.S. 549 (1946).
24. *See* ERWIN CHEMERINSKY, CONSTITUTIONAL LAW: PRINCIPLES AND POLICIES §2.8 (2011).
25. 369 U.S. 186 (1962).

must, that a discrimination reflects no policy, but simply arbitrary and capricious action.

The reasoning was pretty flimsy: There was no reason to think that deciding whether malapportionment violates the Constitution was easier to discern under the Fourteenth Amendment's Equal Protection Clause than under Article IV's Guaranty Clause. The key change here was not the constitutional provision but the Court's willingness to entertain the challenge.

The Court's decision in *Baker* was very controversial at the time, and Justice Frankfurter warned of threats to the Court's legitimacy from entering the political thicket. And indeed the Court moved slowly at first, perhaps fearing that the public would see the intrusion into political affairs as inappropriate. In *Baker* the Court did not hold that malapportionment violated the Equal Protection Clause of the Constitution, only that the courts were open to hearing such claims.

But with the justiciability barrier removed, the courts soon started striking down unequally weighted districts, leaving to the emergence of what we now refer to as the "one person, one vote rule."[26] In *Gray v. Sanders*,[27] the Court struck down the unequal weighting of votes within a single jurisdiction. In *Wesberry v. Sanders*,[28] the Court held that Article I, sections 2 and 4 of the Constitution,[29] required the equal weighting of votes in *congressional* districts. Finally, in *Reynolds v. Sims*,[30] the Court held that *a state's legislative apportionment* violated the Equal Protection Clause if it did not comply with the one person, one vote rule.

Chief Justice Warren wrote *Reynolds v. Sims*, including this key passage:

> Undoubtedly, the right of suffrage is a fundamental matter in a free and democratic society. Especially since the right to exercise the franchise in a free and unimpaired manner is preservative of other basic civil and political rights, any alleged infringement of the right of citizens to vote must be carefully and meticulously scrutinized. Almost a century ago, in *Yick Wo v. Hopkins*, the Court referred to "the political franchise of voting" as "a fundamental political right, because preservative of all rights."

---

26. Some of the older cases, apparently unaware of the earlier passage of the Nineteenth Amendment, used the term "one man, one vote."

27. 372 U.S. 368 (1963).

28. 376 U.S. 1 (1964).

29. Article I, section 2 states in part that "The House of Representatives shall be composed of members chosen every second year by the people of the several states, and the electors in each state shall have the qualifications requisite for electors of the most numerous branch of the state legislature." Article I, section 4 states in part that "[t]he times, places and manner of holding elections for Senators and Representatives, shall be prescribed in each state by the legislature thereof; but the Congress may at any time by law make or alter such regulations, except as to the places of choosing Senators."

30. 377 U.S. 533 (1964).

Legislators represent people, not trees or acres. Legislators are elected by voters, not farms or cities or economic interests. As long as ours is a representative form of government, and our legislatures are those instruments of government elected directly by and directly representative of the people, the right to elect legislators in a free and unimpaired fashion is a bedrock of our political system. It could hardly be gainsaid that a constitutional claim had been asserted by an allegation that certain otherwise qualified voters had been entirely prohibited from voting for members of their state legislature. And, if a State should provide that the votes of citizens in one part of the State should be given two times, or five times, or 10 times the weight of votes of citizens in another part of the State, it could hardly be contended that the right to vote of those residing in the disfavored areas had not been effectively diluted. It would appear extraordinary to suggest that a State could be constitutionally permitted to enact a law providing that certain of the State's voters could vote two, five, or 10 times for their legislative representatives, while voters living elsewhere could vote only once. And it is inconceivable that a state law to the effect that, in counting votes for legislators, the votes of citizens in one part of the State would be multiplied by two, five, or 10, while the votes of persons in another area would be counted only at face value, could be constitutionally sustainable. Of course, the effect of state legislative districting schemes which give the same number of representatives to unequal numbers of constituents is identical. Overweighting and overvaluation of the votes of those living here has the certain effect of dilution and undervaluation of the votes of those living there. The resulting discrimination against those individual voters living in disfavored areas is easily demonstrable mathematically. Their right to vote is simply not the same right to vote as that of those living in a favored part of the State. Two, five, or 10 of them must vote before the effect of their voting is equivalent to that of their favored neighbor. Weighting the votes of citizens differently, by any method or means, merely because of where they happen to reside, hardly seems justifiable. One must be ever aware that the Constitution forbids "sophisticated, as well as simple-minded, modes of discrimination. *Lane v. Wilson; Gomillion v. Lightfoot*. As we stated in *Wesberry v. Sanders*:

> "We do not believe that the Framers of the Constitution intended to permit the same vote-diluting discrimination to be accomplished through the device of districts containing widely varied numbers of inhabitants. To say that a vote is worth more in one district than in another would . . . run counter to our fundamental ideas of democratic government. . . ."

Justice Stewart wrote one of the dissents,[31] rejecting the equal population requirement for legislative districts:

It is important to make clear at the outset what these cases are not about. They have nothing to do with the denial or impairment of any person's right to vote.

---

31. His dissent appeared in a companion case, *Lucas v. 44th General Assembly of Colorado*, 377 U.S. 713 (1964).

Nobody's right to vote has been denied. Nobody's right to vote has been restricted. Nobody has been deprived of the right to have his vote counted. The voting right cases which the Court cites are, therefore, completely wide of the mark. . . . The question involved in these cases is quite a different one. Simply stated, the question is to what degree, if at all, the Equal Protection Clause of the Fourteenth Amendment limits each sovereign State's freedom to establish appropriate electoral constituencies from which representatives to the State's bicameral legislative assembly are to be chosen. The Court's answer is a blunt one, and, I think, woefully wrong. The Equal Protection Clause, says the Court, "requires that the seats in both houses of a bicameral state legislature must be apportioned on a population basis."

After searching carefully through the Court's opinions in these and their companion cases, I have been able to find but two reasons offered in support of this rule. First, says the Court, it is "established that the fundamental principle of representative government in this country is one of equal representation for equal numbers of people. . . . " With all respect, I think that this is not correct, simply as a matter of fact. It has been unanswerably demonstrated before now that this "was not the colonial system, it was not the system chosen for the national government by the Constitution, it was not the system exclusively or even pre-dominantly practiced by the States at the time of adoption of the Fourteenth Amendment, it is not predominantly practiced by the States today." Secondly, says the Court, unless legislative districts are equal in population, voters in the more populous districts will suffer a "debasement" amounting to a constitutional injury. As the Court explains it, "To the extent that a citizen's right to vote is debased, he is that much less a citizen." We are not told how or why the vote of a person in a more populated legislative district is "debased," or how or why he is less a citizen, nor is the proposition self-evident. I find it impossible to understand how or why a voter in California, for instance, either feels or is less a citizen than a voter in Nevada simply because, despite their population disparities, each of these States is represented by two United States Senators.

To put the matter plainly, there is nothing in all the history of this Court's decisions which supports this constitutional rule. The Court's draconian pro-nouncement, which makes unconstitutional the legislatures of most of the 50 States, finds no support in the words of the Constitution, in any prior decision of this Court, or in the 175-year political history of our Federal Union. With all respect, I am convinced these decisions mark a long step backward into that unhappy era when a majority of the members of this Court were thought by many to have convinced themselves and each other that the demands of the Constitution were to be measured not by what it says, but by their own notions of wise political theory. The rule announced today is at odds with long estab-lished principles of constitutional adjudication under the Equal Protection Clause, and it stifles value of local individuality and initiative vital to the character of the Federal Union which it was the genius of our Constitution to create. . . .

What the Court has done is to convert a particular political philosophy into a constitutional rule, binding upon each of the 50 States, from Maine to Hawaii, from Alaska to Texas, without regard and without respect for the many indi-vidualized and differentiated characteristics of each State, characteristics stemming from each State's distinct history, distinct geography, distinct distribution of population, and distinct political heritage. My own understanding of the various theories of representative government is that no one theory has ever commanded unanimous assent among political scientists, historians, or others who have considered the problem. But even if it were thought that the rule announced today by the Court is, as a matter of political theory, the most desirable general rule which can be devised as a basis for the makeup of the representative assembly of a typical State, I could not join in the fabrication of a constitutional mandate which imports and forever freezes one theory of political thought into our Constitution, and forever denies to every State any opportunity for enlightened and progressive innovation in the design of its democratic institutions, so as to accommodate within a system of representative government the interests and aspirations of diverse groups of people, without subjecting any group or class to absolute domination by a geographically concentrated or highly organized majority.

Representative government is a process of accommodating group interests through democratic institutional arrangements. Its function is to channel the numerous opinions, interests, and abilities of the people of a State into the making of the State's public policy. Appropriate legislative apportionment, therefore, should ideally be designed to insure effective representation in the State's legislature, in cooperation with other organs of political power, of the various groups and interests making up the electorate. In practice, of course, this ideal is approximated in the particular apportionment system of any State by a realistic accommodation of the diverse and often conflicting political forces operating within the State.

I do not pretend to have any specialized knowledge of the myriad of individual characteristics of the several States, beyond the records in the cases before us today. But I do know enough to be aware that a system of legislative apportionment which might be best for South Dakota, might be unwise for Hawaii, with its many islands, or Michigan, with its Northern Peninsula. I do know enough to realize that Montana, with its vast distances, is not Rhode Island, with its heavy concentrations of people. I do know enough to be aware of the great variations among the several States in their historic manner of distributing legislative power — of the Governors' Councils in New England, of the broad powers of initiative and referendum retained in some States by the people, of the legislative power which some States give to their Governors, by the right of veto or otherwise of the widely autonomous home rule which many States give to their cities. The Court today declines to give any recognition to these considerations and countless others, tangible and intangible, in holding unconstitutional the particular systems of legislative apportionment which these States have chosen. Instead, the Court says that the requirements of the Equal Protection Clause can be met in any State only by the uncritical, simplistic, and heavy-handed application of sixth-grade arithmetic.

But legislators do not represent faceless numbers. They represent people, or, more accurately, a majority of the voters in their districts — people with identifiable needs and interests which require legislative representation, and which can often be related to the geographical areas in which these people live.

The very fact of geographic districting, the constitutional validity of which the Court does not question, carries with it an acceptance of the idea of legislative representation of regional needs and interests. Yet if geographical residence is irrelevant, as the Court suggests, and the goal is solely that of equally "weighted" votes, I do not understand why the Court's constitutional rule does not require the abolition of districts and the holding of all elections at large.

The fact is, of course, that population factors must often to some degree be subordinated in devising a legislative apportionment plan which is to achieve the important goal of ensuring a fair, effective, and balanced representation of the regional, social, and economic interests within a State. And the further fact is that, throughout our history, the apportionments of State Legislatures have reflected the strongly felt American tradition that the public interest is composed of many diverse interests, and that, in the long run, it can better be expressed by a medley of component voices than by the majority's monolithic command. What constitutes a rational plan reasonably designed to achieve this objective will vary from State to State, since each State is unique in terms of topography, geography, demography, history, heterogeneity, and concentration of population, variety of social and economic interests, and in the operation and interrelation of its political institutions. But so long as a State's apportionment plan reasonably achieves, in the light of the State's own characteristics, effective and balanced representation of all substantial interests without sacrificing the principle of effective majority rule, that plan cannot be considered irrational.

Reynolds's effect was dramatic and nearly immediate: Most states had to redraw district lines to comply with the one person, one vote rule. Now, every decade after new population data becomes available from the United States census, states engage in the prospect of drawing district lines to ensure districts with equal populations.

Example 3

At the November 1962 general election, Colorado voters voted on two competing initiatives providing plans for allocating seats in the Colorado legislatures. Voters adopted proposed Amendment No. 7 by a vote of 305,700 to 172,725 and defeated proposed Amendment No. 8 by a vote of 311,749 to 149,822. Amendment No. 8, rejected by a majority of the voters, prescribed an apportionment plan pursuant to which seats in both houses of the Colorado legislature would purportedly be apportioned on a population basis. Amendment No. 7, on the other hand, provided for the apportionment of the House of Representatives on the basis of population but essentially maintained the existing apportionment in the Senate, which was based on a combination of population and various other factors.

Would the *Reynolds* majority uphold Amendment No. 7? Would Justice Stewart? Aside from precedent, how would you vote in this case?

Explanation

The facts of this case come from the *Lucas* companion case to *Reynolds*, the source of the Justice Stewart dissent above.

The majority in *Reynolds* voted the same way in *Lucas*, holding that an unequally apportioned Senate violated the Equal Protection Clause. The big difference between *Reynolds* and *Lucas* is the means of adoption. In *Reynolds*, the Court considered a plan adopted by a legislature. If the legislature is seriously malapportioned, the political process may be stuck, because legislators from the existing districts could hardly be expected to vote themselves out of a job. In *Lucas*, however, all of the voters in an initiative vote in which each person has equal voting power opted for a system that does not fully comply with the one person, one vote system. The majority in *Lucas* did not find this difference constitutionally significant, ruling that the people may no more violate the Constitution than the state legislature may. But if the main rationale for the one person, one vote rule is a concern that the legislature will not self-correct, the presence of the initiative in *Lucas* should matter.

Justice Stewart of course dissented in *Lucas* and believed that Amendment No. 7 appeared to be a rational plan. After all, the U.S. Senate is unequally apportioned — large and small states each get the same number of seats. But that malapportionment is enshrined in the Constitution. Justice Stewart did not understand why a system that is good enough to use on the national level was not good for the state level.

The big question about how Justice Stewart's rejected rationality standard would have worked in practice is how lower courts would have applied the rationality standard. In other words, after we move away from "sixth-grade arithmetic" and a mathematical application of one person, one vote, there could be great variation in how courts would decide how much malapportionment is unconstitutional malapportionment.

As far as your own views are concerned, I hope by now you have enough information to have an informed opinion either way.

9.2.2. One Person, One Vote: Extensions and Complications

Reynolds required equally populated legislative districts on the *state* level, whereas *Wesberry* required equally populated *congressional* districts. In *Avery v. Midland County*,[32] the Supreme Court extended the one person, one vote requirement to *local* elections.

---

32. 390 U.S. 474 (1968).

Now it might seem that the extension to the local level is a no-brainer following *Reynolds* and *Wesberry*, but there is a potentially significant difference: Local redistricting is subject to state control, and if state legislatures are composed of legislators elected from equally populated districts, then it may not be objectionable for that legislature to choose a different rule on the local level.[33] Justice White, for the majority, did not find this argument persuasive:

> That the state legislature may itself be properly apportioned does not exempt subdivisions from the Fourteenth Amendment. While state legislatures exercise extensive power over their constituents and over the various units of local government, the States universally leave much policy and decisionmaking to their governmental subdivisions. Legislators enact many laws but do not attempt to reach those countless matters of local concern necessarily left wholly or partly to those who govern at the local level. What is more, in providing for the governments of their cities, counties, towns, and districts, the States characteristically provide for representative government — for decisionmaking at the local level by representatives elected by the people. And, not infrequently, the delegation of power to local units is contained in constitutional provisions for local home rule which are immune from legislative interference. In a word, institutions of local government have always been a major aspect of our system, and their responsible and responsive operation is today of increasing importance to the quality of life of more and more of our citizens. We therefore see little difference, in terms of the application of the Equal Protection Clause and of the principles of *Reynolds v. Sims*, between the exercise of state power through legislatures and its exercise by elected officials in the cities, towns, and counties.

Justice Fortas, one of the Court's liberals, saw things differently and was among the dissenters:

> [The one person, one vote] rule is appropriate to the selection of members of a State Legislature. The people of a State are similarly affected by the action of the State Legislature. Its functions are comprehensive and pervasive. They are not specially concentrated upon the needs of particular parts of the State or any separate group of citizens. As the Court in *Reynolds* said, each citizen stands in "the same relation" to the State Legislature. Accordingly, variations from substantial population equality in elections for the State Legislature take away from the individual voter the equality which the Constitution mandates. They amount to a debasement of the citizen's vote and of his citizenship.
>
> But the same cannot be said of all local governmental units, and certainly not of the unit involved in this case. Midland County's Commissioners Court has

---

33. Note how this argument parallels the argument in *Kramer*: Although it was true that Kramer was excluded from the local school board election, he did have the right to vote for a state legislator, and the legislature could control access to the franchise in local elections.

special functions — directed primarily to its rural area and rural population. Its powers are limited and specialized, in light of its missions. Residents of Midland County do not by any means have the same rights and interests at stake in the election of the Commissioners. Equal protection of their rights may certainly take into account the reality of the rights and interests of the various segments of the voting population. It does not require that they all be treated alike, regardless of the stark difference in the impact of the Commissioners Court upon them. "Equal protection" relates to the substance of citizens' rights and interests. It demands protection adapted to substance; it does not insist upon, or even permit, prescription by arbitrary formula which wrongly assumes that the interests of all citizens in the elected body are the same.

Justice Fortas's dissent points out the differences and wide variation in forms of county and local government. Midland County, for example, dealt mostly with rural issues and not with issues within the city of Midland, Texas. The Supreme Court imposed a one-size-fits-all rule for local and regional government; as a result, it has become harder to create some regional governmental units, such as transportation entities. Smaller cities and towns might not want to join with a larger city in creating a transportation entity with an elected board out of fear that large city voters could dominate the voting process.

After *Avery*, congressional, state, and local redistricting all must comply with the one person, one vote rule. Indeed, the only exceptions to this rule are (1) the U.S. Senate, which uses an equal state rule (two senators from each state, regardless of the state's population); (2) special-purpose election districts, described in the next section; and (3) elections in which there are no districts, such as elections for a single office (such as governor) or at-large elections (in which all voters vote for all representatives in a legislative body). The rule does not apply to the *appointment* of members of a body. So long as the appointing authority is elected using a one person, one vote rule, then the appointment of members representing different interests should be valid.

Despite the near-universal use of the one person, one vote rule in U.S. elections, the Supreme Court has not treated the rule the same for each type of election. For *congressional elections*, the Court has required perfect population equality among districts. That is, based upon census data, states must draw congressional districts so that there are exactly the same number of people or eligible voters in each district.[34] For example, a federal court held

---

34. The Court has not required that states must use the number of people — as opposed to equal numbers of citizens, or the voting age population in each district. *Burns v. Richardson*, 384 U.S. 73 (1966). It can make a big difference: districts with many children, non-citizens, felons, and others may have many fewer voters than other districts. Most jurisdictions use total population in redistricting. Nathaniel Persily, *The Law of the Census: How to Count, What to Count, Whom to Count, and Where to Count Them*, 32 CARDOZO L. REV. 755, 775 (2011). We will return to this issue in Chapter 11, discussing Voting Rights Act litigation.

that a state would have to redraw congressional districts after there was a 19-vote difference in one district![35] The ruling is absurd on one level, given that the margin of error in census data is going to be many times that.

But the greater absurdity is that while the Court has required strict mathematical equality when it comes to drawing congressional districts, it has allowed for some variation in population when it comes to drawing state or local districts. Jurisdictions may have all sorts of reasons for deviating from perfect population, ranging from adhering to city or county boundary lines, to group communities of interest together, to more self-interested reasons such as helping incumbents or a political party stay in power.

The conventional thinking until the last decade had been that courts would allow any deviations in population between state and local districts that fell below 10 percent, and that courts would uphold deviations between 10 and 17 percent if the government could point to a legitimate reason for the deviation.[36]

However, in *Larios v. Cox*,[37] the Supreme Court summarily affirmed a lower court ruling striking down a Georgia redistricting plan that contained less than a 10 percent deviation. The lower court held that the reasons for the deviations were not valid: to protect Democrats[38] and to help rural areas. The Supreme Court's summary affirmance means that the Court agrees the lower court got it right, although not necessarily for the right reasons. "Most lower courts seem to have interpreted the Supreme Court's action in *Larios* as meaning that a maximum population deviation under ten percent places the burden of proof on the plaintiff to show arbitrariness or discrimination, but does not create a safe harbor."[39] But the upshot is that state and local redistricters are now much more apt to stick with mathematical equality to lower the risk of litigation.

Example 4

Big City hires you as its lawyer to devise a plan for creating a regional transportation authority. Big City faces great traffic problems, as commuters from the suburbs jam the roads into Big City in the morning and jam the roads out of Big City at night. Big City wants you to come up with a plan for an elected regional transportation board to propose bus, train, and other solutions to the problem. Big City advises you that the suburbs are nervous to join such a transportation authority if the election for members must be

---

35. *Vieth v. Pennsylvania*, 195 F. Supp. 2d 672 (M.D. Pa. 2002).
36. Lowenstein, Hasen, & Tokaji, *supra*, at 73-74.
37. 300 F. Supp. 2d 1320 (N.D. Ga. 2004), *aff'd*, 542 U.S. 947 (2004).
38. We will return to this reason in the next chapter, when we discuss partisan gerrymandering.
39. Lowenstein, Hasen, & Tokaji, *supra*, at 74.

conducted on a one person, one vote basis. What can you advise Big City as to its options?

Explanation

Avery requires compliance with the one person, one vote rule for local elections, even if this stymies some regional solutions to problems. There may be room for some relatively minor deviations in total population equality as allowed on the local level, but after *Larios* the government will have to come forward with good reasons for the deviation: They cannot be to promote one political party over another, for example.

An alternative might be to have the state set up the regional authority, and *appoint* rather than elect members of the board. So long as the appointing authority is elected using a one person, one vote rule, the appointment should be valid.

9.3. SPECIAL PURPOSE ELECTION DISTRICTS

Consider the rules for election to the board of the Tulare Lake Basin Water Storage District in the heart of California's farm country, as described in the Supreme Court's 1973 *Salyer Land* case:[40] The "district consists of 193,000 acres of intensively cultivated, highly fertile farm land located in the Tulare Lake Basin. Its population consists of 77 persons, including 18 children, most of whom are employees of one or another of the four corporations that farm 85% of the land in the district." Only landowners (including corporate landowners) were allowed to vote, and landowners' votes were allocated based on the amount of taxable land that they owned.

Such an election appears to violate the rules from each of the last two sections. First, non-landowning residents of the district are denied the vote. Second, voting is not done on a one person, one vote basis: Voting is based upon the amount of taxable land they owned. On top of that, the election rules gave corporations the right to vote. A clear Equal Protection violation, right?

Perhaps surprisingly, the Supreme Court said no. In the *Salyer Land* case, it carved out a small set of "special purpose" election districts in which neither the one person, one vote rule nor the rules treating voting as a fundamental right for citizen, adult, resident non-felons would apply.

What made the water district different? The Court's earlier *Avery* decision set forth the relevant test for types of districts to be exempt from the usual voting protections:

_____
40. The facts here come from *Salyer Land Co. v. Tulare Lake Basin Water Storage District*, 410 U.S. 719 (1973).

It is of course possible that there might be some case in which a State elects certain functionaries whose duties are so far removed from normal governmental activities and so disproportionately affect different groups that a popular election in compliance with *Reynolds, supra*, might not be required, but certainly we see nothing in the present case that indicates that the activities of these trustees fit in that category. Education has traditionally been a vital governmental function, and these trustees, whose election the State has opened to all qualified voters, are governmental officials in every relevant sense of that term.

The Court rejected the exemption for a junior college district in *Hadley v. Junior College District*,[41] but a Court majority in *Salyer Land* held that the Tulare water district fit the bill:

We conclude that the appellee water storage district, by reason of its special limited purpose and of the disproportionate effect of its activities on landowners as a group, is the sort of exception to the rule laid down in *Reynolds* . . . and the decision in *Avery* contemplated.

The appellee district in this case, although vested with some typical governmental powers, has relatively limited authority. Its primary purpose, indeed the reason for its existence, is to provide for the acquisition, storage, and distribution of water for farming in the Tulare Lake Basin. It provides no other general services such as schools, housing, transportation, utilities, roads, or anything else of the type ordinarily financed by a municipal body. There are no towns, shops, hospitals or other facilities designed to improve the quality of life within the district boundaries, and it does not have a fire department, police, buses, or trains.

Not only does the district not exercise what might be thought of as "normal governmental" authority, but its actions disproportionately affect landowners. All of the costs of district projects are assessed against land by assessors in proportion to the benefits received. Likewise, charges for services rendered are collectible from persons receiving their benefit in proportion to the services. When such persons are delinquent in payment, just as in the case of delinquency in payments of assessments, such charges become a lien on the land. In short, there is no way that the economic burdens of district operations can fall on residents qua residents, and the operations of the districts primarily affect the land within their boundaries.

Under these circumstances, it is quite understandable that the statutory framework for election of directors of the appellee focuses on the land benefited, rather than on people as such. California has not opened the franchise to all residents, as Missouri had in *Hadley*, nor to all residents with some exceptions, as New York had in *Kramer*. The franchise is extended to landowners, whether they reside in the district or out of it, and indeed whether or not they are natural persons who would be entitled to vote in a more traditional political

41. 397 U.S. 50 (1970).

233

election. Appellants do not challenge the enfranchisement of nonresident land-owners or of corporate landowners for purposes of election of the directors of appellee. Thus, to sustain their contention that all residents of the district must be accorded a vote would not result merely in the striking down of an exclusion from what was otherwise a delineated class, but would instead engraft onto the statutory scheme a wholly new class of voters in addition to those enfranchised by the statute.

We hold, therefore, that the popular election requirements enunciated by *Reynolds* and succeeding cases are inapplicable to elections such as the general election of appellee Water Storage District.

Justice Douglas, for three dissenters, saw things more than a bit differently:

The majority concludes that "there is no way that the economic burdens of district operations can fall on residents qua residents, and the operations of the districts primarily affect the land within their boundaries."

But, with all respect, that is a great distortion. In these arid areas of our Nation a water district seeks water in time of drought and fights it in time of flood. One of the functions of water districts in California is to manage flood control. That is general California statutory policy. It is expressly stated in the Water Code that governs water districts. The California Supreme Court ruled some years back that flood control and irrigation are different but complementary aspects of one problem.

From its inception in 1926, this district has had repeated flood control problems. Four rivers, Kings, Kern, Tule, and Kaweah, enter Tulare Lake Basin. South of Tulare Lake Basin is Buena Vista Lake. In the past, Buena Vista has been used to protect Tulare Lake Basin by storing Kern River water in the former. That is how Tulare Lake Basin was protected from menacing floods in 1952. But that was not done in the great 1969 flood, the result being that 88,000 of the 193,000 acres in respondent district were flooded. The board of the respondent district — dominated by the big landowner J. G. Boswell Co. — voted 6-4 to table the motion that would put into operation the machinery to divert the flood waters to the Buena Vista Lake. The reason is that J. G. Boswell Co. had a long-term agricultural lease in the Buena Vista Lake Basin and flooding it would have interfered with the planting, growing, and harvesting of crops the next season.

The result was that water in the Tulare Lake Basin rose to 192.5 USGS datum. Ellison, one of the appellants who lives in the district, is not an agricultural landowner. But his residence was 15 1/2 feet below the water level of the crest of the flood in 1969.

The appellee district has large levees; and if they are broken, damage to houses and loss of life are imminent. Landowners — large or small, resident or nonresident lessees or landlords, sharecroppers or owners — all should have a say. But irrigation, water storage, the building of levees, and flood control, implicate the entire community. All residents of the district must be granted the franchise.

This case . . . involves the performance of vital and important governmental functions by water districts clothed with much of the paraphernalia of government. The weighting of votes according to one's wealth is hostile to our system of government. As a nonlandowning bachelor was held to be entitled to vote on matters affecting education, *Kramer v. Union School District*, so all the prospective victims of mismanaged flood control projects should be entitled to vote in water district elections, whether they be resident nonlandowners, resident or nonresident lessees, and whether they own 10 acres or 10,000 acres. Moreover, their votes should be equal regardless of the value of their holdings, for when it comes to performance of governmental functions all enter the polls on an equal basis.

The special purpose election district raises both a normative question and a line-drawing question. Normatively, are these special districts so different that it makes sense to say they are not really governmental at all, and therefore our usual protections for voting rights do not apply? The line-drawing question is different: How does one identify an election district in which the district does not have "*normal government functions*" and the district's functions "*disproportionately*" affect those given the vote more than others? Both these factors were debatable in the *Salyer Land* case, as they were in a Supreme Court follow-up case, *Ball v. James*,[42] involving another water district that ended up becoming a major electricity provider in Phoenix.

The most common type of election conducted under these election rules may be for business improvement districts, which exist in a given area to promote shopping and business in a defined area. These districts may be used to spruce up a downtown and issue assessments on business owners and award them voting rights based upon their taxable land.

Example 5

The Chicago school board (which includes members elected in elections complying with the one person, one vote rule) sets up a local school council for each of the more than 500 schools in the district. The council selects the school's principal and approves certain spending. Membership on the council includes the principal (ex officio), two teachers, six parents, and two residents of the area who are not parents of children in the district. The parent and non-parent resident members of the council are elected by the residents, with the ability to vote for up to five candidates. The teachers are chosen by the district. The principals complain that the rules about who can run for office and who votes violate the one person, one vote principle. Do the councils qualify for the special purpose election district exception?

---

42. 451 U.S. 355 (1981).

Explanation

The facts of this case come from *Pittman v. Chicago Board of Education*,[43] a Seventh Circuit case. It sure looks as if the provision of education is a public function, and earlier cases such as the *Hadley* required the use of one person, one vote principles in elections for junior college districts. Think also of the *Kramer* case, which involved a school board election. Still, the Chicago councils have much less power than the power of normal school boards, and it could be said that the decisions affect parents and their children in the area disproportionately.

In an unusual opinion, Judge Richard A. Posner, writing for the Court, held the *Salyer Land* exception applied — but for different reasons than those offered by the Supreme Court:

> The line between a general-purpose governmental body and a special-purpose . . . one is wavering and indistinct. We are not even certain that it is the correct line. . . . [T]here is an important distinction between *Kramer* and *Hadley* on the one hand and our case on the other hand. The school board in *Kramer* and the board of trustees of the junior college district in *Hadley* had the power to tax. The local school councils in our case do not. Taxation without representation is abhorrent to Americans, but these local school councils have no power to tax directly and they also have no power to tax indirectly, for they do not have the power to raise revenues through the sale of bonds or to increase the total spending on the schools. . . . [T]he writ of each [council] runs no farther than a single school. Basically they select a principal and determine school expenditures but within budgetary limits set by the board of education. They have less power than the board of trustees of a private school.
>
> We are mindful that in neither *Kramer* nor *Hadley* did the Supreme Court single out the power to tax as critical to the decision; and when it came to distinguish these cases in the later irrigation-district decisions the basis for distinction that the Court offered was that nowadays education unlike irrigation is regarded as a vital government function — a point that had been stressed in *Hadley* itself. But the point has to be considered in context. The boards involved in *Kramer* and *Hadley* were the governing bodies of the schools and colleges, respectively, in the districts. . . . The governing body of the public schools of Chicago is the Board of Education of the City of Chicago, not these local councils. Vital public education may be, but these councils, unlike the boards in *Kramer* and *Hadley*, do not control it. The interest of the public at large in the councils is therefore attenuated.

The Supreme Court declined to hear the case. Why?

---

43. 64 F.3d 1098 (7th Cir. 1995), cert. denied 517 U.S. 1243 (1996).

9.4. INTRODUCTION TO REDISTRICTING

We have already seen that the Supreme Court's one person, one vote rule requires states and local governments to redistrict every ten years to ensure (either rough or strict) population equality across districts.

But equal populations are the beginning, not the end, of the redistricting process in the United States. Let's start with a simplified example. Imagine a jurisdiction with 210 voters (assume all residents are eligible voters), with 110 voters from the Blue Team and 100 voters from the Red Team. Now consider three proposed district plans, each of which perfectly complies with the one person, one vote rule by placing 70 voters in each district:

	Districting Plan A	Districting Plan B	Districting Plan C
Dist. 1	70 Red	32 Red, 38 Blue	40 Red, 30 Blue
Dist. 2	30 Red, 40 Blue	33 Red, 37 Blue	40 Red, 30 Blue
Dist. 3	70 Blue	35 Red, 35 Blue	20 Red, 50 Blue

Which is the best plan? The answer, of course, depends upon what your goal is with the districting process. If your goal is to maximize Blue power, you would like Districting Plan A. If your goal is to maximize Red voting power, you would like Districting Plan C. Districting Plan C is especially attractive for Red supporters because Red supporters seem likely to control two of three districts even though there are fewer Red than Blue voters. If you like competitive elections, then you might prefer Districting Plan B. Plan B has one perfectly competitive district, and the other two could be competitive depending upon turnout and other factors.

Before jumping to the conclusion that Plan B is the best, consider this. District B's elections are going to be closely contested, and in swing elections the seat could swing Red, then swing Blue. The district groups together Red and Blue people who may have little in common and who indeed could be antagonistic to each other. Contrast that with Plan A. Under Plan A, the people in Districts 1 and 3 could be quite happy with their representatives (although the Blue folks are more likely to be happy with the legislature as a whole than the Red folks).

Already this simple example shows trade-offs in redistricting. Indeed, by presenting you with the partisan breakdown of the district to start, I have already prioritized one way of thinking about redistricting compared to others. Rather than focus on outputs, we might instead focus on inputs. Why not ask first who draws the lines? We might have a different view of Plan A if it were driven by a nonpartisan redistricting commission or an automated computer system than the state legislature. Or we might think more or less of Plan B if we know that those drawing the lines complied with certain rules, such as adhering to city or county boundaries as much as possible (given the one person, one vote rule).

Other factors that redistricters might consider is the *compactness* of the district, by which we mean how regular the district lines are (much more on this in the next chapter). We also might care if districts are *contiguous*, meaning that that all the parts of the district are connected to one another (aside from the possibility of natural breaks, such as islands or rivers). There is debate over whether these criteria in fact help Republicans (because Democrats are concentrated in cities, and can get packed into compact urban districts).

Districting goals also sometimes include keeping *communities of interest* together. Grouping all farmers together, for example, could lead to election of a representative attuned to agricultural interests. Who does/should count as a community of interest? Federal voting rights law also imposes certain requirements on redistricting, as we will see in Chapter 11.

This is a knotty area. There are disputes over what redistricting should accomplish and who should accomplish it. Furthermore, when redistricting is done to favor incumbents or parties, or to minimize the voting strength of voters on the basis of race, the redistricting plan may violate federal law. We will consider those issues in the next few chapters. In the meantime, go back and look at the three plans, and see if you can articulate why you might favor one or the other, or what information (about compactness, incumbency or anything else) you would want to know before deciding which district to favor.

Example 6

To what extent does the one person, one vote rule constrain those who draw district lines in reaching their goals?

Explanation

The one person, one vote rule is certainly a constraint upon how redistricters draw district lines. Congressional redistricting must be using perfect population equality, and even state and local redistricting cannot have more than minor population variances.

That said, it is possible to draw very many different district formations even complying with the one person, one vote rule (as well as rules on contiguity). The question is much less one of constraint than of the goals to be achieved: It may be possible to draw districts that favor or hurt various groups (perhaps diluting their votes), to promote political competition, to protect incumbents, or to accomplish many other goals, such as preserving communities of interest. Those who control the drawing of district lines will not have a totally free hand thanks to the one person, one vote constraint. But if they are to be meaningfully constrained in how they draw district lines, more than one person, one vote is necessary.

Political Parties, Partisan Gerrymandering, and Political Competition

10.1. WHY PARTIES? POLITICAL COMPETITION IN POLITICAL SCIENCE AND LAW

The U.S. Constitution does not mention political parties, and the Founding Fathers didn't seem to think much of them, judging by James Madison's famous writing in *Federalist No. 10* raging against the "dangers of faction." Today we understand the centrality of political parties to both governance (as we saw in Part I of this book) and to elections, as we will see in this chapter and the rest of this book. But the absence of political parties in the Constitution raises some interesting questions about how to fit parties into the political scheme. Are parties part of the government? Are they private associations entitled to assert First Amendment (and other) rights? To what extent should courts consider the role of political parties in crafting constitutional doctrine?

We begin with a bit of political science concerning why parties have emerged, as well as a debate among legal scholars over how courts should handle disputes involving political parties, analysis that will help in the material that follows. Here we will focus on the two major political parties, the Democratic and Republican parties. We will consider minor parties in the last section of this chapter.

The traditional understanding of political parties, drawn from the work of political scientist V.O. Key, is to think of political parties as having three distinct aspects:[1]

---

1. V.O. KEY, POLITICS, PARTIES, & PRESSURE GROUPS 163-165 (5th ed., 1964).

- *The party organization.* Political parties have formal organized groups that do things like recruit candidates, fundraise, endorse candidates, get out the vote, and organize for political action. Today there are three main organized branches of each of the main political parties on the national level (Democratic National Committee, Republican National Committee, and Democratic and Republican senatorial and congressional campaign committees), as well as state and local party organizations.
- *The party in government.* Political parties are the key groups organizing politics in Congress and in most state legislatures. As we have seen in Part I of this book, much political competition and polarization in Congress cleaves along the Democratic–Republican divide.
- *The party in the electorate.* Voters traditionally form attachments to political parties from an early age, often from socialization by parents. Traditionally parties mobilized voters for political action. This aspect of party has changed the most over time, as we will soon see. Still today, parties provide a valuable *voting cue* for busy voters. A voter knowing nothing about a particular candidate or particular race may have enough information to vote simply by seeing a "D" or "R" next to a candidate's name.

Despite the absence of political parties in the U.S. Constitution, the three faces of parties quickly emerged in the new United States, both for electing and governing purposes.[2] E. E. Schattschneider, writing in 1942, made the oft-quoted claim that "modern democracy is unthinkable save in terms of the parties."[3]

Through the late 1800s, elections were party-centered affairs. Before 1889 parties printed up ballots for individuals to cast. Each party used a different color ballot, making it easy to determine the party allegiance of each voter and making voting for any combination of candidates other than a straight party ticket exceedingly difficult. Bribery and intimidation were common. Not until 1889 did Massachusetts first introduce the Australian (or secret) ballot for elections; other states quickly followed suit. Voter turnout declined with the secret ballot's arrival.

Even after the rise of the secret ballot, campaigns remained party-centered and labor-intensive. Get-out-the-vote drives in major cities often depended upon the workings of political machines. Party bosses doled out favors (most important among them, government jobs) in exchange for party work. In the first Mayor Daley's Chicago, for example, the Democratic

---

2. Portions of the material here and in section 10.4 appeared in Richard L. Hasen, *Entrenching the Duopoly: Why the Supreme Court Should Not Allow the States to Protect the Democrats and Republicans from Political Competition*, 1997 SUP. CT. REV. 331.

3. E. E. SCHATTSCHNEIDER, PARTY GOVERNMENT 1 (1942).

Organization took a 2% deduction from each city employee's paycheck and required city workers to work for the election of the party's candidates.

Though some significant changes in the nature of parties may be traced to party reform beginning in the Progressive era, the most drastic changes in party structure coincide with the arrival of television. Television provided a method by which candidates could take their message directly and easily to voters. It also challenged the parties' ability to lay exclusive claim to political legitimacy. Voters no longer needed to rely upon a party cue to know whether they agreed with the candidate's views. Television advertising became a major method for conducting statewide and many national campaigns. Advertising was (and remains) expensive. As candidates began having a greater need to raise funds and a lesser need for party faithful (including patronage employees) to get out the vote, the mass political party (the "party in the electorate") declined. New Deal legislation that provided financial support for individuals who had previously relied upon political machine patronage for such support also precipitated the decline.

Reforms of internal party electoral processes, particularly the presidential nomination processes, also have changed the orientation of campaigns away from the party and toward the candidate. Since 1968, presidential primaries are the norm, and states have moved away from caucuses and conventions. These changes moved the power to choose the major parties' nominees from the hands of local bosses into the hands of party-affiliated voters, the party-in-the-electorate, thereby weakening the link between the party-in-the-electorate and the party organization and strengthening the direct relationship between candidate and voter.

With the demise of most patronage positions and with the predominance of mass media advertising, there is less need for a mass political party. The decline in demand has been coupled with a decline in party identification by the voters. It is not so much that voters have negative attitudes toward parties as that they find the parties irrelevant to their political lives. It is therefore no longer correct to conceive of a "party-in-the-electorate." As political scientist John Aldrich has put it, the "party-in-the-electorate" has been transformed simply into the "parties-in-elections."[4]

Although some expected this change in the nature of American political campaigns to spell the demise of formal party organizations, this has not been the case. As Aldrich explains, party organizations play an increasingly important role as "party in service to its candidates." The capital-intensive, television-driven campaign requires both fundraising expertise and media savvy. Party organizations have filled this role, revitalizing their role in campaigns. Parties provide the tools for candidates to run successfully under the

---

4. JOHN H. ALDRICH, WHY PARTIES? THE ORIGIN AND TRANSFORMATION OF POLITICAL PARTIES IN AMERICA 260 (1995).

party's banner, providing the needed expertise and cash. Political parties raise loads of cash, and as we saw in Part I, political parties in Congress are now ideologically divided and united in voting on contentious issues.

There remains a growing debate as to whether parties are not strong enough or too strong for American democracy, and whether strong parties may contribute to polarization (by making all issues partisan issues) or decrease it (by acting as big tents to diffuse the special interest politics of groups such as labor unions, evangelicals, minority voters, and others).

While political scientists and legal scholars are divided on the strength or weakness of political parties, legal scholars have divided on how courts should approach political parties. In recent years some scholars have called for judicial intervention in the political process to ensure adequate political competition. The leading work calling for this "political markets" or "structural" approach to election administration is by Professors Samuel Issacharoff and Richard H. Pildes:[5]

> In cases involving the regulation of politics, we argue that courts should shift from the conventional first-order focus on rights and equality to a second-order focus on the background markets in partisan control. Rather than seeking to control politics directly through the centralized enforcement of individual rights, we suggest courts would do better to examine the background structure of partisan competition. Where there is an appropriately robust market in partisan competition, there is less justification for judicial intervention. Where courts can discern that existing partisan forces have manipulated these background rules, courts should strike down those manipulations to ensure an appropriately competitive political environment.

It is easy to see the impetus for the political markets approach. Think of the Supreme Court's decisions in the one person, one vote cases from the last chapter, beginning with *Baker v. Carr*. If the Court did not intervene in the political process, it is hard to see how to get redistricting reform. The legislature controlled the redistricting process, and self-interested legislators would be unlikely to legislate themselves out of a job.

One potential problem, however, with the political markets approach, is determining the right amount of political competition.[6] Is a two-party

---

5. Samuel Issacharoff & Richard H. Pildes, *Politics as Markets: Partisan Lockups of the Democratic Process*, 50 Stan. L. Rev. 643 (1998).
6. For some critiques of the structural approach, *see* Richard L. Hasen, *The "Political Market" Metaphor and Election Law: A Comment on Issacharoff and Pildes*, 50 Stan. L. Rev. 719 (1998); Daniel H. Lowenstein, *The Supreme Court Has No Theory of Politics — and Be Thankful for Small Favors*, in The U.S. Supreme Court and the Electoral Process 283 (David K. Ryden ed., 2002); Bruce E. Cain, *Garrett's Temptation*, 85 Va. L. Rev.1589 (1999); Nathaniel Persily, Reply, *In Defense of Foxes Guarding Henhouses: The Case for Judicial Acquiescence to Incumbent-Protecting Gerrymanders*, 116 Harv. L. Rev. 649 (2002); Richard L. Hasen, The Supreme Court and Election Law, 138-156 (2003).

system sufficiently competitive? If it turns out (as we will see in the last part of this chapter) that the U.S. use of first-past-the-post plurality election systems led to the creation of only two strong parties, does that mean there is a constitutional requirement to use proportional representation for elections? If not, what is the stopping point?

Furthermore, competitiveness is only one of a number of competing values in an electoral system. Is it better to have a highly competitive system of districts that frequently change hands and in which many voters in the district are strongly at odds with the view of their representative, as opposed to having homogenous districts in which elected officials can represent the views of a large number of their constituents? Putting this question in the hands of the courts gives the courts the power to decide the right form of political competition.

The main alternative approach to the political market approach is one based upon the traditional court balancing of rights and interests. The approach considers whether particular sets of election rules violate the constitutional rights of individuals or groups of individuals and generally finds less room for judicial intervention in the political process. To those in the political market camp, this approach is "sterile" and obfuscates the true structural work of the courts in ensuring adequate political competition. Furthermore, some argue that a rights-based approach that considers the rights of groups in addition to individuals actually contains some structural elements within it.[7]

We will return to this issue throughout the chapter as we consider whether courts should break up partisan (or bipartisan) gerrymanders and help third parties gain access to the ballot.

The Supreme Court has not directly addressed the rights–structure debate among election law scholars. However, a few cases have suggested different approaches to the question. In the campaign finance case *Randall v. Sorrell*[8] in which Justice Breyer spoke for himself, Chief Justice Roberts, and Justice Alito, Justice Breyer pointed to competition concerns as a reason to strike down a campaign finance law: "contribution limits that are too low can . . . harm the electoral process by preventing challengers from mounting effective campaigns against incumbent officeholders, thereby reducing democratic accountability." In contrast, in *New York State Board of Elections v. López Torres*[9] Justice Scalia's opinion for the majority reasoned against the right to adequate political competition in judicial elections:

> None of our cases establishes an individual's constitutional right to have a "fair shot" at winning the party's nomination. And with good reason. What constitutes a "fair shot" is a reasonable enough question for legislative judgment,

---

7. Guy-Uriel Charles, *Judging the Law of Politics*, 103 Mich. L. Rev. 1099 (2005).
8. 548 U.S. 230 (2006).
9. 552 U.S. 196 (2008).

which we will accept so long as it does not too much infringe upon the party's associational rights. But it is hardly a manageable constitutional question for judges — especially for judges in our legal system, where traditional electoral practice gives no hint of even the existence, much less the content, of a constitutional requirement for a "fair shot" at party nomination. Party conventions, with their attendant "smoke-filled rooms" and domination by party leaders, have long been an accepted manner of selecting party candidates. National party conventions prior to 1972 were generally under the control of state party leaders who determined the votes of state delegates. Selection by convention has never been thought unconstitutional, even when the delegates were not selected by primary but by party caucuses. . . .

Respondents put forward, as a special factor which gives them a First Amendment right to revision of party processes in the present case, the assertion that party loyalty in New York's judicial districts renders the general-election ballot "uncompetitive." They argue that the existence of entrenched "one-party rule" demands that the First Amendment be used to impose additional competition in the nominee-selection process of the parties. . . . This is a novel and implausible reading of the First Amendment. . . .

The reason one-party rule is entrenched may be (and usually is) that voters approve of the positions and candidates that the party regularly puts forward. It is no function of the First Amendment to require revision of those positions or candidates. The States can, within limits (that is, short of violating the parties' freedom of association), discourage party monopoly — for example, by refusing to show party endorsement on the election ballot. But the Constitution provides no authority for federal courts to prescribe such a course. The First Amendment creates an open marketplace where ideas, most especially political ideas, may compete without government interference. It does not call on the federal courts to manage the market by preventing too many buyers from settling upon a single product.

Limiting respondents' court-mandated "fair shot at party endorsement" to situations of one-party entrenchment merely multiplies the impracticable lines courts would be called upon to draw. It would add to those alluded to earlier the line at which mere party popularity turns into "one-party dominance." In the case of New York's election system for Supreme Court Justices, that line would have to be drawn separately for each of the 12 judicial districts — and in those districts that are "competitive" the current system would presumably remain valid. But why limit the remedy to one-party dominance? Does not the dominance of two parties similarly stifle competing opinions? Once again, we decline to enter the morass.

Example I

The U.S. Constitution does not mention political parties. Should it? What should it say, if anything, about the rights or obligations of political parties?

Explanation

There is of course no right answer to this normative question. But it should get you thinking about the role that political parties play in U.S. democracy and whether the parties' rights or obligations should appear in the Constitution.

Among the things a constitutional provision might consider,

- What kind of free speech and association protections should be given to political parties?
- Can political parties decide on their membership? Their nominees?
- Should political scientists be entitled to government funding for their activities in nominating candidates? Should their funding be disclosed?
- How do political parties relate to the government? Will elections be conducted based upon party primaries or some other means?

Here is a look at how the current German Constitution treats political parties:[10]

Article 21
[Political parties]
(1) Political parties shall participate in the formation of the political will of the people. They may be freely established. Their internal organisation must conform to democratic principles. They must publicly account for their assets and for the sources and use of their funds.
(2) Parties that, by reason of their aims or the behaviour of their adherents, seek to undermine or abolish the free democratic basic order or to endanger the existence of the Federal Republic of Germany shall be unconstitutional. The Federal Constitutional Court shall rule on the question of unconstitutionality.
(3) Details shall be regulated by federal laws.

10.2. PARTISAN GERRYMANDERING

We turn now from talking about political parties in the abstract to turning to particular legal issues concerning political parties, beginning with the issue of parties and redistricting.

Recall this example from the end of the last chapter: A state has 110 voters from the Blue Team and 100 voters from the Red Team. Now consider three proposed district plans, each of which perfectly complies with the one person, one vote rule by placing 70 voters in each district:

---

10. http://www.gesetze-im-internet.de/englisch_gg/englisch_gg.html#p0114.

	Districting Plan A	Districting Plan B	Districting Plan C
Dist. 1	70 Red	32 Red, 38 Blue	40 Red, 30 Blue
Dist. 2	30 Red, 40 Blue	33 Red, 37 Blue	40 Red, 30 Blue
Dist. 3	70 Blue	35 Red, 35 Blue	20 Red, 50 Blue

We saw in the last chapter that these three district plans involve trade-offs: Some plans are more competitive than others; some make districts in which voters are more likely to agree with one another.

Whatever might be the best plan in the abstract world, it is pretty clear which plan the Red (that is Republican) party would favor and which plan the Blue (that is Democratic) party would favor: Republicans would like Plan C best, because they control two-thirds of the districts even though they make up just under half the voters. Democrats would like Plan A best, because they control two districts and pack as many Republicans as possible into a single district, ensuring their dominance in the state even though they are just slightly over a majority of the voters in the state.

What, if anything, should be done by courts if a Republican legislature enacts Plan C or a Democratic legislature enacts Plan A? Does the political markets approach or concern about parties' having too much power to draw districts (sometimes framed as "candidates choosing their voters rather than voters choosing their candidates") justify judicial intervention? That is the issue of "partisan gerrymandering": the drawing of legislative districts for partisan gain.

The term "gerrymander" comes from a district drawn in Massachusetts in the early nineteenth century by the state's governor, Elbridge Gerry. Commenting on the shape of the district, a political cartoonist of that day drew a salamander-shaped district known as the "gerrymander." Today we use the term to describe a district that someone objects to as drawn on an improper or self-interested basis.

We might all agree that there is an inherent self-interest problem if legislators can draw their own districts, much like the problem we saw before *Baker v. Carr* with malapportioned districts. We might also agree that it is good public policy to keep people in the same party together in the same district — doing so helps ensure that a representative can express the values of a more homogeneous set of voters in the district.

So what's the dividing line between proper consideration of party affiliation in drawing districts and unconstitutional partisan gerrymandering? The Supreme Court has struggled with this question for decades, and so far it has not come to any definitive conclusion.

The first case in which the Supreme Court addressed partisan gerrymandering directly was the 1986 case, *Davis v. Bandemer*.[11] *Bandemer* concerned a claim by Indiana Democrats that they were the victims of a Republican party gerrymander. Democrats said that the line-drawing violated the Equal Protection Clause of the Fourteenth Amendment of the Constitution.

The Court agreed the case was justiciable (that is, as in *Baker v. Carr*, that courts were open to entertain constitutional claims). But there was no majority opinion on the merits. The Court's decision that partisan gerrymandering claims were justiciable resulted in virtually no successful claims in the lower courts,[12] in part because the standard announced by a plurality of justices in *Bandemer* was apparently impossible to meet: A major party, which is to say the Democratic or Republican Party of a state, would have to show that it "had essentially been shut out of the political process."

The Supreme Court returned to the question of partisan gerrymandering in the 2004 case *Vieth v. Jubelirer*.[13] We will focus on *Vieth*, because it represents the Court's current thinking on the partisan gerrymander question.

After the 2000 census, Pennsylvania was entitled to 19 representatives, a decrease of two from the 1990 allocation. The Pennsylvania General Assembly drew new congressional district maps at a time when the Republican Party controlled a majority of both state houses and the governor's office. Democratic voters in Pennsylvania filed suit, alleging that the new congressional districts violated the one person, one vote requirement of Article I, Section 2, of the United States Constitution and that the districting scheme constituted a political gerrymander against Democrats violating the Equal Protection Clause of the Fourteenth Amendment, following *Bandemer*.

When the case reached the Supreme Court, it split on a 4-1-4 basis, with Justice Kennedy writing the controlling opinion for himself only. Justice Scalia (writing for himself and three other justices) took the position that partisan gerrymandering claims should be nonjusticiable. After tracing the history of the political gerrymander in Pennsylvania and the colonies back to the early eighteenth century, and after noting that Congress has the power to limit the ability of states "to restrain the practice of political gerrymandering," Justice Scalia advanced the plurality's main argument that the question of partisan gerrymandering constituted a nonjusticiable political question because of the absence of "judicially manageable" standards. (Recall that that issue got considerable play in the *Baker v. Carr* case.)

The Scalia opinion rejected a variety of possible tests for separating permissible consideration of party in redistricting from an unconstitutional partisan gerrymander. It first rejected the *Bandemer* standard as unmanageable because the *Bandemer* Court produced no workable test for judging partisan

---

11. 478 U.S. 109 (1986).
12. *See Vieth v. Jubelirer*, 541 U.S. 267, 280 n.6 (2004) (listing cases).
13. *Id.*

gerrymandering and because lower courts in the 18 years since *Bandemer* had been unable to "shap[e] [a] standard that this Court was initially unable to enunciate." The Court further noted it was at a "loss to explain why the *Bandemer* line . . . should not have embraced several districting plans that were upheld despite allegations of extreme partisan discrimination, bizarre shaped districts, and disproportionate results. To think that this lower-court jurisprudence has brought forth 'judicially discernible and manageable standards' would be fantasy."

The plurality rejected the other proposed standards, too. It rejected plaintiffs' proposed alternative standard: one that would couple a "predominant intent to achieve partisan advantage" with an effects test that "would invalidate the districting only when it prevents a majority of the electorate from electing a majority of representatives [statewide]." Justice Scalia thought of the proposed effects test as a right to proportional representation, nowhere guaranteed in the Constitution. The Court also found the test unmanageable, in part because it was unclear how a party's majority status was established, especially in a state such as Pennsylvania in which some Republicans won statewide office and some Democrats did. It then rejected all of the other intent and effect tests proposed by the dissenters in *Vieth*.

Justice Stevens's dissent suggested that partisan gerrymandering could constitute an *expressive harm* in the same way that racial gerrymandering may do so (a concept we will explore in the next chapter). He also offered an *improper motive* test for judging partisan gerrymandering, much like the "predominant intent" standard proposed by the *Vieth* plaintiffs. He also raised a *conflict of interest* argument, though in a milder form than Professor Issacharoff's proposal to take redistricting decisions completely out of the hands of partisan decision makers. Justice Souter, joined by Justice Ginsburg, offered a relatively straightforward *vote dilution* approach to partisan gerrymandering claims. Finally, Justice Breyer offered his own vote dilution test. His test differed from Justice Souter's test primarily in focusing on statewide, rather than district-by-district, problems.

This left the question in Justice Kennedy's hands. Justice Kennedy split the baby. He rejected the idea that redistricting for partisan reasons is always unconstitutional. He also agreed with Justice Scalia's plurality opinion that the various standards that had been proposed — in *Bandemer*, by the *Vieth* plaintiffs, and in the three dissenting opinions — were "either unmanageable, or inconsistent with precedent, or both." But Justice Kennedy parted company with the plurality over the question of the continued justiciability of partisan gerrymandering claims. "That no such standard has emerged in this case should not be taken to prove that none will emerge in the future. . . . [B]y the timeline of the law 18 years [since *Bandemer*] is rather a short period." Nonetheless, Justice Kennedy joined the plurality in voting to dismiss plaintiffs' case for lack of a manageable partisan gerrymandering standard.

The opinion was an odd one, because Justice Kennedy invited litigants to raise these claims, only to have them lose under any standard that he and the four plurality justices rejected. Justice Kennedy said he did so to leave open room for the development of judicially manageable standards to separate permissible from impermissible consideration of party in redistricting. He suggested looking to "helpful discussions on the principles of fair districting discussed in the annals of parliamentary or legislative bodies[,]" that is, to "statements of principled, well-accepted rules of fairness that should govern redistricting, or [] helpful formulations of the legislator's duty in drawing district lines." Justice Kennedy also raised the possibility that the computer technology that has become "routine and sophisticated" for redistricting "may produce new methods of analysis that make more evident the precise nature of the burdens gerrymanders impose on the representational rights of voters and parties."

Justice Kennedy's mention of the "burdens" of gerrymanders on "representational rights of voters and parties" is especially noteworthy. In the most significant portion of his opinion, Justice Kennedy suggested that analysts and litigants shift to a First Amendment model for conceptualizing the partisan gerrymandering injury. In particular, Justice Kennedy wrote of "the First Amendment interest of not burdening or penalizing citizens because of their participation in the electoral process, their voting history, their association with a political party, or their expression of political views[,]"[14] noting that "under general First Amendment principles those burdens in other contexts are unconstitutional absent a compelling government interest."[15] Whatever Justice Kennedy meant by "burdening" the First Amendment, he did not equate "burdening" with a test of "excessiveness":

> [C]ourts must be cautious about adopting a standard that turns on whether the partisan interests in the redistricting process were excessive. Excessiveness is not easily determined. Consider these apportionment schemes: In one State, Party X controls the apportionment process and draws the lines so it captures every congressional seat. In three other states, Party Y controls the apportionment process. It is not so blatant or egregious, but proceeds by a more subtle effort, capturing less than all the seats in each State. Still, the total effect of Party Y's effort is to capture more new seats than Party X captured. Party X's gerrymander was more egregious. Party Y's gerrymander was more subtle. In my view, however, each is culpable.

What to make of all this? Whatever Justice Kennedy was thinking in *Vieth*, this much is certain: We still have seen no successful partisan gerrymandering cases brought by litigants in the period after *Vieth*. Furthermore, in *League of United Latin American Citizens v. Perry* ("LULAC"),[16] the Supreme

---

14. *Id.* at 314 (Kennedy, J., concurring in the judgment).
15. *Id.*
16. 548 U.S. 399 (2006).

Court rejected a partisan gerrymandering challenge to Texas's mid-decade congressional redistricting plan. The Republican Texas legislature enacted a redistricting plan in the middle of the decade after the enactment of an earlier court-ordered redistricting plan. To Republicans, the mid-decade redistricting was warranted to correct an earlier Democratic partisan gerrymander, which was essentially extended by the court-ordered redistricting. To Democrats, the mid-decade redistricting was a power grab to enhance Republican majorities in the U.S. House of Representatives.

Justice Kennedy rejected the "sole intent" standard put forward by Democrats and others challenging the law. To begin with, Justice Kennedy did not agree that the sole intent of the Texas legislature in passing its new redistricting plan was to further Republican political aims. Furthermore, he rejected the idea that a mid-decade redistricting would always be presumptively unconstitutional as motivated by partisan considerations. Finally, Justice Kennedy saw the redistricting as an attempt by the Texas legislature to move party representation closer to the proportional representation of the parties in the state, a permissible state objective. (The then two newest members of the Court, Chief Justice Roberts and Justice Alito, did not express any opinion on the justiciability of partisan gerrymandering claims.)

Since LULAC, guess what? The court doors remain open to partisan gerrymandering claims. And plaintiffs keep losing them because there are no judicial standards acceptable to Justice Kennedy.

There is one aspect of partisan gerrymandering that does seem to have led to judicial policing, and we saw it in the last chapter: In Larios v. Cox,[17] the Supreme Court summarily affirmed a lower court ruling striking down a Georgia redistricting plan that contained less than a 10 percent deviation. The lower court held that the reasons for the deviations were not valid: to protect Democrats and to help rural areas. The Supreme Court's summary affirmance means that the Court agrees the lower court got it right, although not necessarily for the right reasons.

Larios has had an effect. Redistricters are now skittish to draw somewhat unequally populated districts in order to gain partisan advantage. Courts sometimes strike such unequally populated districts down. So the message for partisan gerrymanders is to stick with equal population — and then there's pretty much free rein to stick it to the other party!

Example 2

You are the lawyer advising the Red Party, which controls the state legislature but has fewer overall supporters than the Blue Party in the state. There are 110 Blue Voters, 110 Red voters, and three seats. The party is planning

---

17. 300 F. Supp. 2d 1320 (N.D. Ga. 2004), aff'd, 542 U.S. 947 (2004).

on passing a redistricting plan for the state legislature. It is considering three plans:

	Districting Plan B	Districting Plan C	Districting Plan D
Dist. 1	29 Red, 41 Blue	40 Red, 30 Blue	34 Red, 30 Blue
Dist. 2	36 Red, 34 Blue	40 Red, 30 Blue	34 Red, 30 Blue
Dist. 3	35 Red, 35 Blue	20 Red, 50 Blue	33 Red, 50 Blue

What do you advise them about legal challenges to the three potential plans? (Ignore any Voting Rights Act issues.) Which would you recommend that the legislature adopt?

Explanation

The plans here are a variation on the plans we saw earlier in the chapter. Roughly speaking, Plan B creates two competitive districts that the Red Party could perhaps win, along with a solid Blue district. Plan C looks like a solid Red gerrymander: The Red party easily wins two seats by packing lots of Blue voters into District 3. It is a classic gerrymander in that there are more Blue voters but the Red Party controls the legislature. Plan D is similar in partisan power to Plan C (the Red party controls two districts and District 3 packs in the Blue voters). But Plan D deviates from the one person, one vote rule: The district populations are 68, 64, and 83. Even under the old rules allowing some variation this districting plan could violate the one person, one vote rule of *Reynolds*. Furthermore, under *Larios*, deviations even below 10% across districts may be struck down if the court believes the reason for the deviation is partisanship and not sound districting principles (such as adhering to city boundaries).

In terms of legal advice, you should advise that Plan D should be taken out of contention, leaving Plans B and C. While Plan B may be "fairer" in the sense of assuring more proportional representation of parties (but not fully proportional, given that no plan that the Red Party is considering gives control to the Blue party, which has more voters), there is no constitutional requirement for the legislature to adopt Plan B.

If the legislature adopts Plan C, it is possible the Blue party will attack it as an unconstitutional partisan gerrymander. Such a claim is justiciable and will be heard in federal court. However, it is so difficult to prove a partisan gerrymander that it is not much of a risk to adopt Plan C. Justice Kennedy, the controlling vote in these cases, has rejected a number of intent and effect tests to judge when taking party into account crosses the line into unconstitutionality. So you can advise the legislature to choose between Plans B and C based upon their preferences, with a low litigation risk.

10.3. OBLIGATIONS AND ASSOCIATIONAL RIGHTS OF POLITICAL PARTIES

To be sure, political parties are private associations, not government entities. After all, as we have seen, parties are not even mentioned in the U.S. Constitution. But parties play two important roles closely connected to government and governance. First, in most places elections are conducted in two stages, with that first stage being a party primary (or convention or caucus), and the second stage being a general election. This entangles parties deeply into the election process, more than any other kind of private association. Second, as we have seen from V.O. Key's concept of "party-in-government," today the best way to understand how Congress works and passes laws is through partisan competition. That is, it is separation of parties, not separation of powers.[18]

Given the key role of parties in U.S. democracy, what obligations do parties have? What rights do they have? This section explores those questions.

The key moment on party obligations in the U.S. comes in what has come to be known as the *White Primary Cases*. Party primaries — with party voters choosing the party's nominee to run in a general election contest — date back to the end of the nineteenth century. In the South, primaries became a means for whites to control election outcomes. Although black voters initially supported the Republican Party (Lincoln's party, which freed the slaves), by the 1930s the Democratic Party dominated state elections, and so the winner of the Democratic primary virtually always won the general election. African-Americans then wanted to vote in the Democratic primary, to influence the party's choice of candidates. In many Southern states, however, Democrats excluded African-Americans from voting in their primaries. Could the Democratic party do so?

To answer that question, we need to back up a bit and recognize that ordinarily, under the *state action doctrine*, only a government body or entity can violate someone's constitutional rights. If a private club refuses entry to Jews, for example, that cannot be a constitutional violation (although it might violate an anti-discrimination statute). If the party primary is a private associational action, then, like the discriminatory private club, the party through its discriminatory primary could not be violating anyone's constitutional rights. If the party is acting as an arm of the government in its primary, however, then its actions could potentially be a violation of the Fifteenth Amendment's prohibition on racial discrimination in elections. But not if primaries did not count as "elections."

---

18. Daryl J. Levinson & Richard H. Pildes, *Separation of Parties, Not Powers*, 119 HARV. L. REV. 2311 (2006).

In *Newberry v. United States*,[19] a divided Supreme Court could not agree on whether primaries could be considered elections subject to the Fifteenth Amendment. A plurality there reasoned that primaries were not elections. In *Nixon v. Herndon*,[20] the Court held that Texas's law barring African-Americans from voting in the state's Democratic Party violated the Fourteenth Amendment's Equal Protection Clause (it did not reach the Fifteenth Amendment issue). Texas responded by repealing the statute but giving the Democratic Party the right to set qualifications for voters. A party rule then specified a whites-only primary.

In *Nixon v. Condon*,[21] the Supreme Court struck down the new Democratic Party rule, reasoning that Texas had simply deputized the Democratic Party to discriminate. The Texas Democratic Party then acted again to have a whites-only primary, this time without any official delegation of power from the state of Texas. The Supreme Court held that this was constitutional in *Grovey v. Townsend*,[22] but the decision did not last long.

In *United States v. Classic*,[23] the Court held that political primaries were "elections" for purposes of Congress's power to regulate congressional elections. Then, in *Smith v. Allwright*,[24] the Court essentially reversed *Grovey*, ruling that Texas's involvement in the primary process rendered it a state function and accordingly struck down the Democrats' rules for a whites-only primary.

Going even further, in *Terry v. Adams*,[25] the Court held that a private association that made endorsements in the Democratic Primary, the Jaybird Democratic Association of Ford Bend County, could not exclude non-whites from its non-binding straw poll. Important for the Court was the fact that the Jaybird election in practice always went on to win the primary and general election in this area. The Court's reasoning was splintered, but the result was clear: Whether parties were private associations or not, they could not use racially discriminatory methods to choose their nominees.

Party obligation cases are rare today, thankfully, as this kind of racial discrimination has faded into the past. But occasionally issues about party obligations do arise. Consider for example the question whether a state Republican Party can exclude a gay Republican group from a booth at its state convention. A court held that it could, reasoning that who could have a booth at the state convention to influence the party's platform was not part of the electoral process. That is, the Republican Party was not a state actor

---

19. 256 U.S. 232 (1921).
20. 273 U.S. 536 (1927).
21. 286 U.S. 73 (1932).
22. 295 U.S. 45 (1935).
23. 313 U.S. 299 (1941).
24. 321 U.S. 649 (1944).
25. 345 U.S. 461 (1953).

when it came to deciding who could participate in the party's internal debates over policy.[26]

Instead, much major party litigation today involves party *rights*, not party obligations. In particular, parties sometimes object to the type of primary state law requires, and generally speaking the Supreme Court has held that the party has the final word on the choice of primary.

There are different types of primaries. Roughly speaking, in a *closed* primary, only those voters who have registered with the political party are allowed to vote in the party primary. In an *open* primary, voters who have no party affiliation (sometimes called "independent" voters) are also allowed to vote in a party primary. Why might a party care about whether a party is open or closed? The common wisdom is that open primaries are more likely to produce more moderate candidates, because voters in the party tend to be more extreme (more conservative in Republican primaries and more liberal in Democratic primaries). Bringing in independents dilutes ideological purity, but it could make the party's candidates more competitive in a general election, which features voters from across the political spectrum.

In *Tashjian v. Republican Party of Connecticut*,[27] Connecticut law imposed a closed primary for choosing party nominees to run in the general election. The state Republican Party wanted to open the primary to independent voters. The Connecticut legislature, at that point with a Democratic majority, defeated a proposal to allow parties to open up their primaries to independent voters. The Supreme Court held Connecticut's law violated the associational rights of the Republican Party.

> Were the State to restrict by statute financial support of the Party's candidates to Party members, or to provide that only Party members might be selected as the Party's chosen nominees for public office, such a prohibition of potential association with nonmembers would clearly infringe upon the rights of the Party's members under the First Amendment to organize with like-minded citizens in support of common political goals. As we have said, any interference with the freedom of a party is simultaneously an interference with the freedom of its adherents. The statute here places limits upon the group of registered voters whom the Party may invite to participate in the "basic function" of selecting the Party's candidates. The State thus limits the Party's associational opportunities at the crucial juncture at which the appeal to common principles may be translated into concerted action, and hence to political power in the community.

The Court rejected Connecticut's stated interests in keeping its administrative burden low, in preventing party "raiding" (whereby voters of

---

26. *Republican Party of Texas v. Dietz*, 940 S.W.2d 86 (Tx. 1997).
27. 479 U.S. 208 (1986).

another party vote to influence the outcome of the primary), and in keeping the two-party system strong through differentiated ideological parties. It held that the administrative interest was not strong enough against First Amendment rights, that there was no good evidence open primaries facilitated party raiding,[28] and that there was considerable dispute over whether open or closed primaries were better for the stability of the political system. On this last point, the Court wrote

> Under these circumstances, the views of the State, which to some extent represent the views of the one political party transiently enjoying majority power, as to the optimum methods for preserving party integrity lose much of their force. The State argues that its statute is well designed to save the Republican Party from undertaking a course of conduct destructive of its own interests. But on this point even if the State were correct, a State, or a court, may not constitutionally substitute its own judgment for that of the Party. The Party's determination of the boundaries of its own association, and of the structure which best allows it to pursue its political goals, is protected by the Constitution.

Justice Scalia and two other justices dissented, reasoning that there is not much of an associational interest in a party leaving "the selection of its candidate to persons who are not members of the Party, and are unwilling to become members. It seems to me fanciful to refer to this as an interest in freedom of association between the members of the Republican Party and the putative independent voters."

Tashjian does not stand for the principle that an open primary is constitutionally required. Instead, it means that a party can override a state law closing a primary as to that party's primary.

In 2000, the Supreme Court considered a case somewhat similar to *Tashjian*. California voters passed a voter initiative establishing a "blanket primary" to be used for primary elections. Under the blanket primary, all candidates for office are listed on a primary ballot along with each candidate's party. All voters choose one candidate (from any party or no party) in each race, with the top two vote-getters in each race going on to the general election. There was no party ballot, and a voter could choose a Democrat in the governor's race, a Republican in the Senate race, and an independent candidate in the state Assembly race.

In *California Democratic Party v. Jones*,[29] the Supreme Court, in an opinion by Justice Scalia, held that the blanket primary violated the First Amendment associational rights of political parties. The blanket primary gave non-party

---

28. The Court noted that under the closed primary, someone could change party registration just before voting.
29. 530 U.S. 567 (2000).

members influence over the choice of party nominees over the objections of the parties, Justice Scalia reasoned, making the case very different from *Tashjian*. The state of California defended the measure as a means of assuring more moderate voters (along with raising other arguments), but the Court was not persuaded:

> Finally, we may observe that even if all these state interests were compelling ones, [California's law] is not a narrowly tailored means of furthering them. Respondents could protect them all by resorting to a nonpartisan blanket primary. Generally speaking, under such a system, the State determines what qualifications it requires for a candidate to have a place on the primary ballot — which may include nomination by established parties and voter-petition requirements for independent candidates. Each voter, regardless of party affiliation, may then vote for any candidate, and the top two vote getters (or however many the State prescribes) then move on to the general election. This system has all the characteristics of the partisan blanket primary, save the constitutionally crucial one: Primary voters are not choosing a party's nominee. Under a nonpartisan blanket primary, a State may ensure more choice, greater participation, increased "privacy," and a sense of "fairness" — all without severely burdening a political party's First Amendment right of association.

The *Jones* case not only struck down California's law but also doomed Washington state's longstanding blanket primary. In response to *Jones*, Washington state passed a new law that was like the old blanket primary with a two-stage voting process after which the top two vote-getters advanced to the general election. The difference was that the ballots did not list the candidate's party affiliations — instead it listed the party "pre-ferences" of each candidate. The ballot further explained that this was not a party primary.

You should see what Washington state was trying to do: It wanted to take advantage of the non-partisanship opening Justice Scalia mentioned in *Jones* but still give voters the party cue information to help voters choose candidates in line with their ideology or interests. Unsurprisingly, Washington state political parties complained that this form of primary was really still a party primary and that it thus infringed on the parties' First Amendment rights. In *Washington State Grange v. Washington State Republican Party*,[30] the Supreme Court rejected a facial challenge to the state's law: By its terms, the Washington state primary was not a party primary. But the parties also argued that voters might be confused into thinking Washington was running a party primary: "This, they say, compels them to associate with candidates they do not endorse, alters the messages they wish to convey, and forces them to engage in counterspeech to disassociate themselves from the

---

30. 552 U.S. 442 (2008).

candidates and their positions on the issues." The Court expressed doubts that voters would be confused but remanded the case for the parties to argue about confusion. On remand, lower courts rejected the confusion arguments. Recently, California adopted a top-two primary modeled after the Washington state primary system.

Example 3

The state of Oklahoma uses a "semiclosed" primary in which only voters registered with a political party may vote in that party's primary. The Libertarian Party of Oklahoma wants to allow not only independent voters, but also voters registered with other parties, to vote in its primary. It sues the state of Oklahoma, claiming that Oklahoma's rule violates its First Amendment associational rights.

How should a court rule on the Libertarian Party's challenge?

Explanation

The facts of this question are based upon the Supreme Court's decision in *Clingman v. Beaver*.[31] At first glance this case looks a lot like *Tashjian*: A party wants to go broader in seeking primary voters than state law allows. But there is a major difference between the two cases. In *Tashjian*, Republican party voters were seeking only independent voters who otherwise would not be voting in a party primary (or could, after *Tashjian*, choose to vote in any party's primary in which the party opened up the primary to independent voters). In *Clingman*, Libertarian voters were seeking the votes of *other party members*. This could affect the outcome of other party primaries. For example, if many Libertarian-oriented Republicans ended up voting in the Libertarian primary, then the Republican Party nominee could be less Libertarian, and perhaps less likely to win in the general election. Thus, *Clingman* presented a clash between parties, and not just one party against the state. It is not surprising that the Court sided with Oklahoma and against the Libertarian Party. The Court pointed to the state's interest in preventing confusion (which the Court later found to be insufficient in the *Washington State Grange* case), as well as its interest in facilitating efficient campaigning and party building.

Perhaps the most interesting aspect of *Clingman* is Justice Thomas's discussion (for a plurality, not for a majority, of the Court in this portion of his opinion) of the level of scrutiny applicable to the challenge. Justice Thomas wrote that the Libertarian Party's inability to have members of other parties vote in the Libertarian Party primary did not severely burden the party's

---

31. 544 U.S. 581 (2005).

rights. Accordingly, he wrote that strict scrutiny should not apply, a holding that seems somewhat inconsistent with *Tashjian* and more in line with Justice Scalia's *Tashjian* dissent. It remains to be seen whether the Court will change the level of scrutiny in other cases in which a party wants the right to allow more non-members to influence the party primary.

10.4. MINOR PARTIES AND INDEPENDENT CANDIDATES

Finally, we turn to minor parties and independent candidates. Some of the issues facing minor parties and independent candidates are similar to those faced by major parties. In *Clingman*, as we just saw, it was the Libertarian Party complaining about the form of primary. But minor political parties and independent candidates face more serious issues: Often they have difficulty making it to the general election ballot, and sometimes government benefits that go to major parties are not available (or not as generously available) for minor party candidates.

Before we get into the law related to minor parties, let's again visit the political science surrounding parties. The key insight from political science is that first-past-the-post (plurality) election systems, such as we have in the United States, tend to produce only two major political parties. In contrast, more proportional systems, more popular in Europe, tend to produce multi-party systems. This observation is sometimes referred to as "Duverger's Law," after a French political scientist, Maurice Duverger.[32] However, E. E. Schattschneider, writing the decade before Duverger, observed that second parties in single-member-district systems survive because they have a "monopoly of the opposition" and win almost all the seats not won by the most popular party.[33]

Thus, if we really wanted to use law to prevent "lockups" or "entrenchment" and to promote political competition (as suggested by the political markets/structural approach described in the first section of this chapter), courts should perhaps declare single-member district plurality elections to be unconstitutional. No one expects that to happen, and the political markets adherents do not call for that, and so many of the lawsuits involving third parties occur on the margins: Few of these suits, if successful, are likely to lead to the actual election of third party or independent candidates in large numbers. Many of the suits involve the number of signatures required or other procedures that minor party candidates must follow to earn a place on the general election ballot.

---

32. MAURICE DUVERGER, POLITICAL PARTIES 216-228 (2d English ed., 1959).
33. E. E. SCHATTSCHNEIDER, PARTY GOVERNMENT 81-83 (1942).

The Supreme Court early on declared that laws regulating ballot access cannot ensure that only the Democratic and Republican parties may have candidates appearing on the ballot.[34] However, the Court has allowed some pretty tough ballot access rules to stand against equal protection challenges brought by minor parties and independent candidates.

In *Jenness v. Fortson*,[35] the Court upheld a requirement in Georgia that independent candidates get signatures equal to 5 percent of the number of registered voters in a jurisdiction. Getting 5 percent of registered (as opposed to actual) voters is not easy, and few candidates have been successful under such standards.[36] In *Munro v. Socialist Workers Party*,[37] the Court rejected a challenge to a rule under Washington state's old blanket primary (before *Jones*) that said that candidates who did not get 1 percent of votes for the office on the first round of the blanket primary could not go on to the second round of the primary.

The Court has been similarly stingy concerning minor party rights in cases involving other election laws. In *Timmons v. Twin Cities Area New Party*,[38] the court rejected a challenge by a minor party that wanted to put up for nomination the same candidate as a major party. This practice, known as "fusion," is allowed in some jurisdictions (most notably New York), and it helps minor parties build support—people can vote for the major party candidate (thereby not "wasting" a vote) on the minor party line, helping to ensure attention and sometimes automatic ballot access for the minor party's other candidates. In *Buckley v. Valeo*,[39] the Court upheld more generous public financing grants for major party presidential candidates compared to minor party presidential candidates. And in *Arkansas Educational Television Commission v. Forbes*,[40] the Court upheld a public television station's decision to exclude a minor party candidate from a televised debate.

In each of these cases, the minor party or independent candidate asserted equal protection and First Amendment claims, and in most of these cases the claims failed. Part of the reason for the usual failure was the Court's view of the purpose of minor party candidacies. For the Court majority, the purpose of all the candidacies is about winning elections. Thus in *Anderson v. Celebrezze*,[41] the Court struck down Ohio's ballot access rules for an independent candidate who had a real chance of winning election. But

---

34. *Williams v. Rhodes*, 393 U.S. 23 (1968).
35. 403 U.S. 471 (1971).
36. Richard Winger, *The Supreme Court and the Burial of Ballot Access: A Critical Review of* Jenness v. Fortson, 1 ELECTION L.J. 235 (2002).
37. 479 U.S. 189 (1986).
38. 520 U.S. 351 (1997).
39. 424 U.S. 1 (1976). *Buckley* is the most important U.S. campaign finance case, and each of the four chapters in Part IV of this book discusses some aspects of the case.
40. 523 U.S. 666 (1998).
41. 460 U.S. 780 (1983).

most of these candidates were not going to be successful. In *Munro* the challenging candidate received 596 of the 681,690 votes cast in the primary. Justice Marshall, dissenting in *Munro*, did not believe these candidates had a real chance to win elections, but he saw minor party candidates as playing a more important role in the debate:

> The minor party's often unconventional positions broaden political debate, expand the range of issues with which the electorate is concerned, and influence the positions of the majority, in some instances ultimately becoming majority positions. And its very existence provides an outlet for voters to express dissatisfaction with the candidates or platforms of the major parties.

The other reason minor party claims fare so poorly at the Supreme Court is the standard of review. The Court in this area has said that "no litmus paper" test exists to separate permissible from impermissible regulation of elections, which are necessary for the state to run an efficient election. In what has come to be known as "the *Anderson-Burdick* test" coming from *Anderson v. Celebrezze* and a 1992 case, *Burdick v. Takushi*,[42] the Court has adopted a varying scale for judging the constitutionality of garden-variety election laws. Here is how the Court phrased the test in *Timmons*:

> When deciding whether a state election law violates First and Fourteenth Amendment associational rights, we weigh the "character and magnitude" of the burden the State's rule imposes on those rights against the interests the State contends justify that burden, and consider the extent to which the State's concerns make the burden necessary. Regulations imposing severe burdens on plaintiffs' rights must be narrowly tailored and advance a compelling state interest. Lesser burdens, however, trigger less exacting review, and a State's "important regulatory interests" will usually be enough to justify "reasonable, nondiscriminatory restrictions." No bright line separates permissible election-related regulation from unconstitutional infringements on First Amendment freedoms.

The Court in practice often has not found burdens on third parties or independent candidates to be severe, and in cases involving non-severe burdens, the Court has allowed states to assert, without having to prove, which interests justify its law. For example, in *Munro*, the state did not need to prove that the 1 percent threshold for moving candidate names from the primary ballot to the general election ballot was actually necessary to prevent voter confusion. Furthermore, the Court in *Timmons* allowed the state's interest in promoting a "healthy two-party system" to trump rules making it easier for third party candidates to compete. If anti-competition can be an

---

42. 504 U.S. 428 (1992).

acceptable interest for these laws, it will be very hard for minor parties and independent candidates to mount successful defenses unless they can show that the laws impose severe burdens on the candidacies.[43]

As we will see in Chapter 12, the *Anderson-Burdick* test has become important in election administration challenges as well, and recent cases there have cast some doubt as to how the test is to work in practice.

Example 4

A state allows fusion candidacies in local elections for major parties but not for minor parties. A minor party brings a First Amendment and Equal Protection challenge to the law. How should a court rule on the challenge?

Explanation

Although the Supreme Court has hardly been protective of minor parties, and *Timmons* viewed an anti-fusion law as a minor burden under the *Anderson-Burdick* balancing test, this law seems unconstitutional unless the state can actually point to anti-competitiveness (promoting a "healthy two-party system") as an acceptable state interest. After all, why allow fusion for major parties but not minor parties?

In *Reform Party of Allegheny County v. Department of Elections*,[44] the U.S. Court of Appeals for the Third Circuit struck down the Pennsylvania law:

> The statutory scheme in *Timmons* differs from the Pennsylvania scheme in a manner crucial for the equal protection analysis. *Timmons* involved an across-the-board ban on fusion by both major and minor parties. In contrast, the Pennsylvania statutes involve a ban on cross-nomination that facially discriminates against minor parties by allowing major parties, but not minor parties, to cross-nominate in certain circumstances. The Supreme Court in *Timmons* did not hold that states can treat minor parties in a discriminatory way.

---

43. Richard L. Hasen, *Entrenching the Duopoly: Why the Supreme Court Should Not Allow the States to Protect the Democrats and Republicans from Political Competition*, 1997 Sup. Ct. Rev. 331.
44. 174 F.3d 305 (3rd Cir. 1999).

CHAPTER

11

The Voting Rights Act, Race, and Redistricting

11.1. ORIGINS OF THE VOTING RIGHTS ACT AND THE WORKINGS OF SECTION 5 PRECLEARANCE

As we saw in Chapter 9, despite the Thirteenth, Fourteenth, and Fifteenth Amendments (the "Reconstruction Amendments"), African-Americans faced tremendous barriers to voting, especially in the South, until the passage of the 1965 Voting Rights Act.[1] Among the obstacles black voters faced were poll taxes, literacy tests, violence, and intimidation. If you haven't read Chapter 9 yet, you should go back and review this important history, which provides background to the passage of the Voting Rights Act.

In the decade before the 1965 act, there was some progress on voting rights. Congress passed voting rights legislation in 1957 and 1960. The U.S. Department of Justice in the 1950s and 1960s challenged various voting rules in the South, proving them unconstitutional. After the DOJ lawyers left, discriminating states and localities introduced new restrictions.

Although there was gradual improvement in African-American voting rights, it was not nearly enough. Civil rights protests in Alabama turned violent as police turned on protesters. President Lyndon Johnson then pushed for passage of the Voting Rights Act a year after the Civil Rights Act of 1964.

---

1. The discussion here draws from LOWENSTEIN, HASEN, & TOKAJI, *supra*, at 34-36.

The VRA included many provisions to secure voting rights for all, the most important of which were limited by both geography and time. Geographically, the VRA in Section 4 singled out for special treatment jurisdictions that had used a literacy test or other test or device for voting in 1964 and in which less than half of the voting population voted in the most recent presidential election. This geographic limit of "covered jurisdictions" apparently was reverse-engineered to cover most of the deep South: Alabama, Georgia, Louisiana, Mississippi, South Carolina, Virginia, and 40 of 100 counties in North Carolina. Temporally, the new rules were to be put in effect for only five years.

Covered jurisdictions:

- Could not use a literacy test or other device for voting
- Were subject to the federal government's sending in its own registrars to register voters and election observers to make sure that voters could vote free of violence and intimidation
- Had to submit any changes in voting rules for federal approval, or "preclearance," before those changes could go into effect; these requirements appear in Section 5 of the VRA

These three provisions together had a profound effect on African-American voter turnout and electoral opportunities. The first two provisions removed most of the formal barriers to voting. Section 5's preclearance provision ensured that jurisdictions did not implement new tests or devices. Preclearance shifted the burden from the federal government to these jurisdictions to prove any voting changes were nondiscriminatory. Eventually, it provided a seat at the bargaining table for representatives of minority communities to have their views taken into account before covered jurisdictions could implement election changes.

Rather than let these temporary provisions expire in 1970, Congress renewed them for another five years, adding additional jurisdictions tied to 1968 turnout, and making the ban on literacy tests nationwide. In 1975, Congress renewed the VRA for another seven years and added still more jurisdictions, this time protecting language minorities: Asian Americans, Native Americans, Latinos, and Native Alaskans. The new jurisdictions became covered based upon voter turnout data from 1972.

In 1982, Congress renewed the VRA without adding any new covered jurisdictions, for 25 more years, then again in 2006, for another 25 years. However, as we will see in the next section, the Supreme Court recently rejected the continuation of the Section 5 preclearance regime as unconstitutional in a 2013 case, *Shelby County v. Holder*. The nationwide ban on literacy tests and other provisions of the VRA remain in place.

Even though the Section 5 preclearance regime is no longer in current operation, it is important to understand how preclearance worked for three reasons: (1) One cannot understand the history and current controversy over the VRA generally and *Shelby County* in particular without understanding how preclearance worked; (2) another provision of the VRA, Section 3, allows courts to "bail in" more jurisdiction for preclearance, and so preclearance rules still matter; and (3) there are proposals for Congress to create a new preclearance regime, and you need to understand how new preclearance rules would differ from old preclearance rules.

Here is how the Department of Justice's website has described the basic workings of preclearance in the period before *Shelby County*:[2]

> Under Section 5, any change with respect to voting in a covered jurisdiction — or any political subunit within it — cannot legally be enforced unless and until the jurisdiction first obtains the requisite determination by the United States District Court for the District of Columbia or makes a submission to the Attorney General. This requires proof that the proposed voting change does not deny or abridge the right to vote on account of race, color, or membership in a language minority group. If the jurisdiction is unable to prove the absence of such discrimination, the District Court denies the requested judgment, or in the case of administrative submissions, the Attorney General objects to the change, and it remains legally unenforceable. . . .
>
> Section 5 provides two methods for a covered jurisdiction to comply with Section 5. The first method mentioned in the statute is by means of a declaratory judgment action filed by the covered jurisdiction in the United States District Court for the District of Columbia. A three-judge panel is convened in such cases. The defendant in these cases is the United States or the Attorney General, represented in court by attorneys from the Voting Section of the Civil Rights Division. Appeals from decisions of the three-judge district court go directly to the United States Supreme Court.
>
> The jurisdiction must establish that the proposed voting change "does not have the purpose and will not have the effect of denying or abridging the right to vote on account of race or color or [membership in a language minority group]." The status of a voting change that is the subject of a declaratory judgment review action is that it is unenforceable until the declaratory judgment action is obtained and the jurisdiction may not implement or use the voting change. . . .
>
> The second method of compliance with Section 5 is known as administrative review. A jurisdiction can avoid the potentially lengthy and expensive litigation route by submitting the voting change to the Civil Rights Division of the Department of Justice, to which the Attorney General of the United States has delegated the authority to administer the Section 5 review process. The jurisdiction can implement the change if the Attorney General affirmatively indicates no objection to the change or if, at the expiration of 60 days, no objection to the submitted change has been interposed by the Attorney

---

2. *About Section 5 of the Voting Rights Act*, DEPARTMENT OF JUSTICE, http://www.justice.gov/crt/about/vot/sec_5/about.php (page as of Feb. 16, 2014). This explanation has been removed since the *Shelby County* decision.

General. . . . Well over 99 percent of the changes affecting voting are reviewed administratively, no doubt because of the relative simplicity of the process, the significant cost savings over litigation, and the presence of specific deadlines governing the Attorney General's issuance of a determination letter.

In a typical year, the Voting Section receives between 4,500 and 5,500 Section 5 submissions, and reviews between 14,000 and 20,000 voting changes. Since the release of the 2000 Census, the Attorney General has reviewed under Section 5 approximately 3,000 redistricting plans, districting plans, and limited redistricting plans.

The preclearance regime started out slowly until the Supreme Court decided *Allen v. State Board of Elections*[3] in 1969. In *Allen*, the Supreme Court read the term "any voting qualification or prerequisite to voting, or standard, practice, or procedure with respect to voting" in Section 5 quite broadly. This meant that jurisdictions not only had to submit for preclearance changes to the mechanics of voting, such as moving the location of a polling place or making changes for the form to register voters, but also had to preclear changes made that affected the allocation of political power, such as a decision to change district lines in a redistricting process, to change from election to appointment of election officials, or to move from districts to at-large voting. Section 5 preclearance was not required for "changes in the decision-making authority of the elected members" of a legislative body.[4]

Although *Allen's* statutory interpretation of the language of Section 5 was somewhat questionable (is a districting plan a voter "qualification," "prerequisite to voting, or standard, practice or procedure with respect to voting"?), Congress reenacted the VRA many times without ever changing that standard.[5] Eventually DOJ reviewed thousands of changes large and small. Initial court review was rare; more commonly covered jurisdictions sued DOJ if DOJ objected to a proposed change. (When DOJ *approved* a proposed change, that decision could not be appealed by voters unhappy with the decision.[6])

The standard required the covered jurisdiction to prove that its proposed change would not have a discriminatory *purpose* or discriminatory *effect*. We consider discriminatory effect first.

The key standard for discriminatory effects comes from the case of *Beer v. United States*.[7] When I tell my students they have to master "the *Beer* test," they get unjustifiably excited. It would perhaps be better to refer to it by its technical name, "non-retrogression." As the Supreme Court wrote, "the

---

3. 393 U.S. 544 (1969).
4. *Presley v. Etowah Cnty. Comm'n,* 502 U.S. 491 (1992).
5. See Chapter 7.2 of this book on whether it is appropriate to infer congressional acquiescence in Court interpretation from congressional silence.
6. *Morris v. Gressette,* 432 U.S. 491 (1977).
7. 425 U.S. 130 (1976).

purpose of §5 has always been to insure that no voting-procedure changes would be made that would lead to a retrogression in the position of racial minorities with respect to their effective exercise of the electoral franchise."

In *Beer*, the Supreme Court held it was not retrogression for the city of New Orleans to enact a redistricting plan that increased the number of districts in which minority voters had a realistic chance of electing candidates of their choice from 0 to 1. The Court wrote

> The District Court concluded that Plan II would have the effect of abridging the right to vote on account of race or color. It calculated that if Negroes could elect city councilmen in proportion to their share of the city's registered voters, they would be able to choose 2.42 of the city's seven councilmen, and, if in proportion to their share of the city's population, to choose 3.15 councilmen. But under Plan II the District Court concluded that, since New Orleans' elections had been marked by bloc voting along racial lines, Negroes would probably be able to elect only one councilman—the candidate from the one councilmanic district in which a majority of the voters were Negroes. This difference between mathematical potential and predicted reality was such that "the burden in the case at bar was at least to demonstrate that nothing but the redistricting proposed by Plan II was feasible." The court concluded that "[t]he City has not made that sort of demonstration; indeed, it was conceded at trial that neither that plan nor any of its variations was the City's sole available alternative."

The redistricting plan adopted by New Orleans (Plan II) had to be precleared, the Supreme Court concluded, because it did not *decrease* the number of majority-minority districts. The old plan had 0 majority-minority districts; Plan II had 1 such district. It therefore was "non-retrogressive" (also referred to as an "ameliorative" plan).

For many years, people understood the discriminatory effects prong of Section 5 (at least in the context of redistricting) as comprising a mechanical non-retrogression test: Count up the number of majority-minority districts: If the new plan has at least as many such districts as the old plan, it is not retrogressive. There is no requirement, for example, that minority voters have any kind of proportional representation in legislative bodies.

In 2003, however, the Supreme Court decided a case out of Georgia, *Georgia v. Ashcroft*,[8] in which Democrats drew legislative districts to decrease the number of majority-minority districts but increase the number of "influence" districts—where minority voters, with crossover white voters, could elect minority-preferred candidates. Although the 5-4 opinion was not crystal-clear, it rejected a mechanical *Beer*-like approach to retrogression. In the 2006 reauthorization of the VRA, Congress "reversed" *Georgia v.*

---

8. 539 U.S. 461 (2003).

Ashcroft, although precisely what that meant was anyone's guess[9] (and was never tested thanks to *Shelby County*).

While the *Beer* test for non-retrogression was pretty straightforward in the context of redistricting, it was less clear in other types of cases. Indeed, in such cases the burden of proof on covered jurisdictions seemed to matter a great deal. For example, just before the Supreme Court nixed the preclearance regime, a three-judge court in Washington, D.C. agreed with DOJ that Texas could not implement a new strict voter identification law. (Much more about voter identification laws later in this chapter and in the next chapter.) Although both Texas and the federal government put on expert testimony as to the racial impact of the state's law, the court found the evidence weak for both sides. Instead, the court decided the case more simply:[10]

> We pause to summarize the evidentiary findings we have made so far. Contrary to Texas's contentions, nothing in existing social science literature speaks conclusively to the effect of photo ID requirements on voter turnout. More-over, scant lessons, if any, can be drawn from Indiana and Georgia, largely because [Texas's law] is more restrictive than the photo ID laws adopted by either of those states. Finally, no party has submitted reliable evidence as to the number of Texas voters who lack photo ID, much less the rate of ID possession among different racial groups.
>
> Given this, we could end our inquiry here. Texas bears the burden of proving that nothing in SB 14 "would lead to a retrogression in the position of racial minorities with respect to their effective exercise of the electoral franchise." *Beer*. Because all of Texas's evidence on retrogression is some com-bination of invalid, irrelevant, and unreliable, we have little trouble concluding that Texas has failed to carry its burden.
>
> Significantly, however, this case does not hinge merely on Texas's failure to "prove a negative." To the contrary, record evidence suggests that [Texas's law], if implemented, would in fact have a retrogressive effect on Hispanic and African American voters. This conclusion flows from three basic facts: (1) a substantial subgroup of Texas voters, many of whom are African American or

---

9. For an exhaustive inquiry, *see* Nathaniel Persily, *The Promise and Pitfalls of the New Voting Rights Act*, 117 YALE L.J. 174 (2007). The language of the *"Georgia v. Ashcroft* fix" reads

> Any voting qualification or prerequisite to voting, or standard, practice, or procedure with respect to voting that has the purpose of or will have the effect of diminishing the ability of any citizens of the United States on account of race or color, or in contra-vention of the guarantees set forth in section 4(f)(2), to elect their preferred candidates of choice denies or abridges the right to vote within the meaning of subsection (a) of this section.

The text of the 2006 amendments appears at https://www.govtrack.us/congress/bills/109/hr9/text.

10. *Texas v. Holder*, 888 F. Supp. 2d 113 (D.D.C. 2012), *vacated*, 133 S.Ct. 2886 (2013) (mem.).

Hispanic, lack photo ID; (2) the burdens associated with obtaining ID will weigh most heavily on the poor; and (3) racial minorities in Texas are disproportionately likely to live in poverty. Accordingly, SB 14 will likely "lead to a retrogression in the position of racial minorities with respect to their effective exercise of the electoral franchise." *Beer*.

The Supreme Court vacated this Texas decision as moot rather than review its merits after it decided *Shelby County*.

One other important point about preclearance is worth considering. Section 5 put the burden on covered jurisdictions to prove not just an absence of a discriminatory *effect* on minority voters, but also absence of discriminatory *purpose*. Over the years, DOJ blocked a number of proposed voting changes from covered jurisdictions on discriminatory purpose grounds, including redistricting plans that showed no retrogressive effect (in other words, meaning that the plans did not decrease the number of majority-minority districts). Among other things, DOJ took the position that a plan that (in DOJ's view) violated Section 2 of the VRA could not be precleared, because failure to comply with Section 2 showed discriminatory purpose or effect. This aggressive use of preclearance led to the creation of the "racial gerrymandering" cause of action discussed in the last section of this chapter.

The Supreme Court held in the *Bossier Parish* cases that failure to comply with Section 2 could not be the basis to deny preclearance under Section 5 and that discriminatory purpose as used in Section 5 referred only to the purpose to retrogress, and not some other purpose.[11] This led to a great narrowing of the purpose prong of the preclearance standard: After all, most jurisdictions that would have a purpose to retrogress would also pass a plan with a retrogressive effect (the Court acknowledged that only the "incompetent retrogressor" would get caught under the purpose test as the Court understood it).

Thus, a covered jurisdiction that had no majority-minority legislative districts and that blocked such districts for racially discriminatory reasons could not have its legislative plan blocked on discriminatory purpose grounds, because there would be no purpose shown to decrease the number of majority-minority districts (going from 0 to 0 is not retrogression!).

In the 2006 VRA amendments, Congress purported to reverse this meaning of discriminatory purpose. The legislation declared that "the effectiveness of the Voting Rights Act of 1965 has been significantly weakened by the United States Supreme Court decisions in *Reno v. Bossier Parish II* and *Georgia v. Ashcroft*, which have misconstrued Congress' original intent in enacting the Voting Rights Act of 1965 and narrowed the protections

---

11. *Reno v. Bossier Parish School Bd.*, 520 U.S. 471 (1997) (*Bossier Parish I*); *Reno v. Bossier Parish School Bd.*, 528 U.S. 320 (2000) (*Bossier Parish II*).

afforded by section 5 of such Act." On the *Bossier Parish* question, Congress added a provision to Section 5 reading: "The term 'purpose' in subsections (a) and (b) of this section shall include any discriminatory purpose." Exactly what this language meant was not tested in the Supreme Court because of the *Shelby County* case.

Example 1

The state of Pacifica was a covered jurisdiction before the *Shelby County* case. Its state assembly has 3 majority-minority districts, 1 Latino majority district, and 2 African-American majority districts. The Pacifica legislature passes a legislative redistricting plan that increases the number of majority Latino districts to 2 and decreases the number of African-American majority districts to 1. The legislature in passing the redistricting plan points to population shifts: There has been a large increase in Latinos in the state and a decrease in the number of African-Americans. The legislature rejected plans that had 2 majority Latino districts and 2 majority African-American districts, that had 1 Latino majority district and 2 African-American majority districts, and that had 2 Latino majority districts and 0 African-American majority districts.

Before *Shelby County*, should DOJ have precleared the legislature's redistricting plan?

Explanation

This is a difficult question, and nothing in the Supreme Court's retrogression jurisprudence answers it. To begin with, it is not clear whether DOJ should lump together minority voters from two different communities for the purpose of retrogression. If so, at least under the traditional understanding of retrogression from *Beer*, there would be no retrogression, because the old and new plans each have three majority-minority districts.[12] Going from 3 to 3 districts would not constitute a retrogressive effect. Nor is there any evidence of any discriminatory purpose, at least in this fact pattern — neither an intent to retrogress nor any unconstitutional intent to discriminate against voters on the basis of race.[13]

However, if we do not treat Latino and African-American voters together, then it looks like there is a claim for retrogression, as the number of African-American majority districts went from 2 under the old plan to 1

---

12. We are considering the old *Beer* test rather than the more nuanced test from *Georgia v. Ashcroft*, because Congress purported to "reverse" *Georgia v. Ashcroft* in the 2006 amendments to the VRA.

13. Again, we would apply a broader definition of discriminatory purpose because Congress purported to "reverse" *Bossier Parish II* in the 2006 amendments to the VRA.

under the new plan. This looks to be a plan with a retrogressive effect. Although the African-American population has decreased, we know from the rejected plans that it was still possible to create a plan drawing two African-American majority districts (and even to do so while increasing the number of Latino districts).

The open question (not answered by *Beer* or *Georgia v. Ashcroft*) is whether a decline in population in a covered jurisdiction would be a reason to allow for the decline in the number of majority-minority districts. The Court never reached this question because of *Shelby County*.

11.2. *SHELBY COUNTY* AND THE END OF SECTION 5 PRECLEARANCE[14]

The preclearance requirement for covered jurisdictions in the 1965 Voting Rights Act was a major infringement on state sovereignty. States and local jurisdictions had to ask the federal government for permission before enforcing their own laws. Unsurprisingly, some covered jurisdictions challenged parts of the VRA as exceeding congressional power. In the 1966 *South Carolina v. Katzenbach* case,[15] the Court rejected South Carolina's argument that the Section 5 preclearance provision and other challenged parts of the VRA "exceed[ed] the powers of Congress and encroach[ed] on an area reserved to the States by the Constitution." On an 8-1 vote (with Justice Black dissenting) the Court held that Congress had acted appropriately under its powers granted in Section Two of the Fifteenth Amendment. In so holding, the Court gave considerable deference to congressional determinations about the means necessary to "enforce" the Fifteenth Amendment prohibition by states in discriminating in voting on the basis of race and applied a rationality standard of review.

As noted in the last section, over the years, Congress continued to renew Section 5, adding in additional coverage areas pegged to a formula tied to data from 1964, 1968, and 1972. In 1982, Congress renewed the provision for a 25-year period, expiring in 2007. The city of Rome, Georgia, challenged the renewed preclearance provision, and the Court again rejected the challenge.[16] Then-Justice Rehnquist, joined by Justice Stewart, dissented, raising federalism concerns, as did Justice Powell.

In the years since *City of Rome*, the Supreme Court underwent a federalism revolution, narrowing congressional power over the states. Beginning with

---

14. This section draws from Richard L. Hasen, Shelby County and the Illusion of Minimalism, 22 WM. & MARY BILL OF RTS. J. 713 (2014).
15. 383 U.S. 301 (1966).
16. *City of Rome v. United States*, 446 U.S. 156 (1980).

City of Boerne v. Flores,[17] the Court has limited Congress to passing "remedial" statutes. It has rejected congressional attempts to expand the scope of constitutional rights through legislation beyond that which is "congruen[t] and proportional[]" to remedy intentional unconstitutional discrimination by the states. In Board of Trustees v. Garrett,[18] the Court indicated that it will search for an adequate evidentiary record to support a congressional determination that states are engaging in sufficient intentionally unconstitutional conduct so as to justify congressional regulation. Importantly, the Boerne line of cases cited Katzenbach as correct, noting that Congress was within its power to require preclearance especially given the law's limited temporal and geographic scope.

Because of the new federalism cases, election law scholars worried that unless Congress made changes to the existing Section 5 regime when the act was due to expire in 2007, a renewed Section 5 could be struck down as unconstitutional under these new standards.[19] As we saw in the last section, Congress did make some changes to Section 5 when it renewed the act in 2006, such as rejecting earlier, stingier Supreme Court interpretations of the applicable Section 5 standards in Georgia v. Ashcroft and Bossier Parish II. But these changes, which had the effect of making it more difficult for covered jurisdictions to obtain preclearance, made the constitutional case harder not easier. Congress, however, did not change the coverage formula for which jurisdictions must engage in preclearance or otherwise make it easier for states to get out of preclearance. That formula used data from the 1964, 1968, or 1972 elections.

Soon after Congress passed the renewed Section 5, an obscure Austin utility district, the Northwest Austin Municipal Utility District Number One, brought suit against the renewal of preclearance. Though its main argument was against the continued constitutionality of the preclearance provision of Section 5, the utility district also argued it should be entitled to bail out from coverage under the act as a "political subdivision" covered by Section 5. The lower court in NAMUDNO v. Mukasey rejected both arguments.[20] In a surprising and relatively short opinion, however, the Court on an 8-1 vote decided NAMUDNO v. Holder on statutory grounds, ruling that the utility district was

---

17. 521 U.S. 507 (1997).
18. 531 U.S. 356 (2001).
19. Richard L. Hasen, Congressional Power to Renew the Preclearance Provisions of the Voting Rights Act After Tennessee v. Lane, 66 Ohio St. L.J. 177 (2005); Samuel Issacharoff, Is Section 5 of the Voting Rights Act a Victim of Its Own Success?, 104 Colum. L. Rev. 1710 (2004); The Continuing Need for Section 5 Pre-Clearance: Hearing Before the Senate Committee on the Judiciary, 109th Cong., 2d Sess. 10 (2006) (statement of Richard H. Pildes). See generally The Future of the Voting Rights Act (David Epstein et al., eds. 2006).
20. Northwest Austin Municipal Utility District Number One v. Mukasey, 573 F. Supp. 2d 221 (D.D.C. 2008) (three-judge court).

entitled to bail out.[21] Although the Court did not resolve the constitutional question, it offered five pages of dicta on the question of Section 5's constitutionality, casting strong constitutional doubts on preclearance. The Court began by noting the great strides in minority voter registration and otherwise for minorities in covered jurisdictions since the 1965 VRA enactment. It then noted the "substantial" federalism costs and how those costs had caused members of the Court in the past "to express serious misgivings about the constitutionality of §5." The Court commented that some of the improvements in conditions for minority voters "are no doubt due in significant part to the Voting Rights Act itself. . . . Past success alone, however, is not adequate justification to retain the preclearance requirements." "[T]he Act imposes current burdens and must be justified by current needs." Furthermore, VRA "differentiates between the States, despite our historic tradition that all states enjoy 'equal sovereignty.'" The Court then noted that the coverage formula may be outdated: "The statute's coverage formula is based on data that is now more than 35 years old, and there is considerable evidence that it fails to account for current political conditions." "Congress heard warnings from supporters of extending §5 that the evidence in the record did not address 'systematic differences between the covered and non-covered areas of the United States[,] . . . and, in fact, the evidence that is in the record suggests there is more similarity than difference.'"

Congress did nothing to reconsider the coverage formula or otherwise change the VRA for four years after *NAMUDNO*. Shelby County, Alabama, a jurisdiction not entitled to bail out of coverage under the act because there had been recent objections to the county's proposed voting changes, then brought suit against preclearance's constitutionality. A federal district court in a lengthy opinion rejected Shelby County's facial constitutional attack on preclearance.[22] A divided panel of the United States Court of Appeals for the D.C. Circuit affirmed.[23] In *Shelby County v. Holder*,[24] the Supreme Court on a 5-4 vote held that the extension of preclearance for another 25 years without updating the coverage formula exceeded congressional power.

The Court, in an opinion by Chief Justice Roberts for the conservative justices,[25] wrote that "[o]utside the strictures of the Supremacy Clause, States retain broad autonomy in structuring their governments and pursuing legislative objectives. Indeed, the Constitution provides that all powers not specifically granted to the Federal government are reserved to States or

---

21. *NAMUDNO*, 557 U.S. 193 (2009).
22. *Shelby County v. Holder*, 811 F. Supp. 2d 424 (D.D.C. 2011).
23. *Shelby County v. Holder*, 679 F.3d 848 (D.C. Cir. 2012).
24. 133 S.Ct. 2612 (2013).
25. Justice Thomas wrote separately to indicate that he would not only strike the coverage formula of VRA Section 4(b) but also the preclearance regime of Section 5.

citizens. Amdt. 10." The opinion declared the Framers' intent to have the states maintain power over elections through the Tenth Amendment, while noting that the Elections Clause of Article I, section 4 gives Congress the power to set the time and manner for congressional elections. The Court further held that state sovereignty protected through the Tenth Amendment against federal government encroachment includes a principle of "*equal sovereignty*" among the states.

The *Shelby County* majority then held that the Voting Rights Act "sharply departs from" these Tenth Amendment principles by making covered states "beseech the Federal government for permission to implement laws they would otherwise have the right to enact and execute on their own." The law further violates "equal sovereignty" principles because covered states can wait "months or years and expend[] funds to implement a validly enacted law [while] its neighbor can typically put the same law into effect immediately." Covered states are also subject to different substantive standards under the act, including a shifting of the burden of proof to covered jurisdictions to prove an absence of discriminatory purpose and effect.

The majority conceded that the coverage formula initially adopted "made sense" to deal with areas where discrimination was most prevalent, and that the Voting Rights Act itself "in large part" was responsible for improvements in voting conditions for minority voters. But it concluded that the decline in racial discrimination in voting (as measured by objections in the covered jurisdictions) and the increase in minority voting statistics and minority representation in Congress showed a coverage formula now constitutionally impermissible. The formula was made even more problematic when Congress made preclearance more difficult by reversing *Georgia v. Ashcroft* and *Bossier II*. The Court rejected the argument that the improvements on the ground could be attributable to Section 5's deterrent effect, which justified continuation of the law: "Under this theory . . . §5 would be effectively immune from scrutiny; no matter how 'clean' the record of covered jurisdictions, the argument could always be made that it was deterrence that accounted for the good behavior."

Finally, the Court majority rejected counterarguments of the federal government and dissent. It disagreed with the government that the original coverage formula was "reverse-engineered" back in the 1960s and that the government need not show a "logical relationship between the criteria in the formula and the reason for coverage." It held that *Katzenbach* in fact recognized a rational relationship between the coverage formula and the aims of preclearance in 1965, and that the failure to show "even relevance [between the coverage formula and current conditions] is fatal." The Court characterized the government as ignoring history after 1965; for preclearance to remain constitutional, Congress must use "current data reflecting current needs."

The Court in a single paragraph then dismissed as irrelevant thousands of pages of congressional evidence supporting the continuing need for preclearance. "Contrary to the dissent's contention, we are not ignoring the record; we are simply recognizing that it played no role in shaping the statutory formula before us today." "Regardless of how to look at the record, however, no one can fairly say it shows anything approaching the 'pervasive,' 'flagrant,' 'wide-spread,' and 'rampant' discrimination that faced Congress in 1965 and that clearly distinguished the covered jurisdictions from the rest of the Nation at that time." The Court also dismissed in a short paragraph the dissent's argument that Shelby County cannot complain about the coverage formula because under any rational coverage formula Shelby County and the state of Alabama, with their recent histories of race discrimination in voting, deserved to be covered. "But that is like saying that a driver pulled over pursuant to a policy of stopping all redheads cannot complain about that policy, if it turns out his license has expired."

The Court concluded by protesting that the dissent "analyzes the question presented as if our decision in *Northwest Austin* never happened," noting that "four years ago, in an opinion joined by two of today's dissenters, the Court expressly stated that '[t]he Act's preclearance requirement and its coverage formula raise serious constitutional questions." It then sought to minimize its holding: Congress "leaves us today with no choice." "Striking an Act of Congress 'is the gravest and most delicate duty that this Court is called on to perform.'"[26] "[T]hat is why, in 2009, we took care to avoid ruling on the constitutionality of the Voting Rights Act when asked to do so, and instead resolved the case then before us on statutory grounds."[27] Rather than strike down Section 5, the Court "issue[s] no holding on §5 itself, only on the coverage formula. Congress may draft another formula based on current conditions."[28]

The dissenters, led by Justice Ginsburg for the four more liberal members of the Court, believed that renewing preclearance for another 25 years was within Congress's power. The Court stressed the deferential standard of review that it believed the Court should use when Congress acted pursuant to its powers under the reconstruction amendments:

> The stated purpose of the Civil War Amendments was to arm Congress with the power and authority to protect all persons within the Nation from violations of their rights by the States. In exercising that power, then, Congress may use "all means which are appropriate, which are plainly adapted" to the constitutional ends declared by these Amendments. *McCulloch.* So when Congress acts to enforce the right to vote free from racial discrimination, we ask not whether

---

26. *Id.* (quoting *Blodgett v. Holden*, 275 US 142, 148 (1927)).
27. *Id.*
28. *Id.* at 2631.

Congress has chosen the means most wise, but whether Congress has rationally selected means appropriate to a legitimate end. "It is not for us to review the congressional resolution of [the need for its chosen remedy]. It is enough that we be able to perceive a basis upon which the Congress might resolve the conflict as it did." *Katzenbach v. Morgan*, 384 U.S. 641 (1966).

Until today, in considering the constitutionality of the VRA, the Court has accorded Congress the full measure of respect its judgments in this domain should garner. *South Carolina v. Katzenbach* supplies the standard of review: "As against the reserved powers of the States, Congress may use any rational means to effectuate the constitutional prohibition of racial discrimination in voting." Faced with subsequent reauthorizations of the VRA, the Court has reaffirmed this standard. *E.g.*, *City of Rome*. Today's Court does not purport to alter settled precedent establishing that the dispositive question is whether Congress has employed "rational means."

In supporting the rationality of Congress's readoption of the coverage formula, the dissent pointed to numerous recent instances of racial discrimination in voting rules occurring in covered jurisdictions. For example, "[i]n 2001, the mayor and all-white five-member board of aldermen of Kilmichael, Mississippi, abruptly canceled the town's election after 'an unprecedented number' of African–American candidates announced they were running for office. DOJ required an election, and the town elected its first black mayor and three black aldermen." The dissent also noted that the Court itself in a 2006 case held that the state of Texas engaged in intentional racial discrimination against Latino voters in its mid-decade congressional redistricting.

The dissent further argued that the Court should apply a more deferential standard of review when it considers the constitutionality of a law being renewed compared to when it considers the constitutionality of a new law. Assuming that Section 5 worked successfully at least as a partial deterrent, no one would expect to see continued "flagrant," "wide-spread," or "rampant" racial discrimination in voting occurring in covered jurisdictions. Nonetheless, evidence submitted to Congress demonstrated that despite the preclearance requirement, covered jurisdictions as a whole had more successful VRA Section 2 suits against them than non-covered jurisdictions. The dissent concluded that under the broad *Katzenbach* rationality standard of review, the continued preclearance regime should pass constitutional muster.

The dissenters also responded to the majority's deterrence argument: "the Court strikes §4(b)'s coverage provision because, in its view, the provision is not based on 'current conditions.' It discounts, however, that one such condition was the preclearance remedy in place in the covered jurisdictions, a remedy Congress designed both to catch discrimination before it causes harm, and to guard against return to old ways. Volumes of evidence supported Congress' determination that the prospect of retrogression was real. Throwing out preclearance when it has worked and is continuing to work to stop discriminatory changes is like throwing away your umbrella in a rainstorm because you are not getting wet."

Because the Court did not strike down preclearance itself, but only the coverage formula of VRA section 4(b), jurisdictions could still be "bailed in" to preclearance coverage at the discretion of a court under Section 3 of the VRA. A court has such discretion after it has determined that a jurisdiction has engaged in voting discrimination in violation of the Fourteenth or Fifteenth Amendment. Furthermore, the Supreme Court's opinion contemplates that Congress could pass a new coverage formula updated to "covered conditions." Although a bill has been introduced with a new coverage formula, it is not clear if there will be any movement in Congress to pass it and, if it passes, whether it would be constitutional according to the Supreme Court under the *Shelby County* standards.

Example 2

Congress considers a law reinstituting preclearance for any state that had five successful voting rights lawsuits and/or Section 5 objections in the last five years, counting suits in smaller jurisdictions within a state, but not counting suits involving voter identification laws. Under this standard, as of now, only Georgia, Louisiana, Mississippi, and Texas would be covered jurisdictions under the new law. The voting rights lawsuits would include claims under Section 2 of the Voting Rights Act, which do not require proof of intentional racially discriminatory conduct in violation of the Constitution.

If Congress passes this law, would the Supreme Court uphold it as a permissible exercise of congressional power under the Fourteenth or Fifteenth Amendments?

Explanation

The hypothetical statute is based upon legislation introduced in Congress, the Voting Rights Amendments Act.[29] Representative Jim Sensenbrenner, a Republican co-sponsor of the legislation, is a fan of voter identification laws, which explains the voter identification aspect of the bill.

It is unclear whether, if this bill passed, the Supreme Court would uphold it as a permissible exercise of congressional power. The formula would grandfather in both objections under the old (now unconstitutional under *Shelby County*) preclearance regime. It would also count Section 2 violations, which are not necessarily based upon unconstitutional conduct

---

29. H.R. 3899, 113th Cong. (2d Sess. 2014), http://beta.congress.gov/bill/113th-congress/house-bill/3899.

by the states. This means that the states might not be punished in a "congruent and proportional" way for unconstitutional conduct. Furthermore, it looks like states as a whole might be punished even if there were only one or a few smaller municipalities that engaged in voting rights violations. Thus, although the new coverage formula would be tied more to "current conditions," it might not be a permissible exercise of congressional power respecting state sovereignty and "equal sovereignty" guaranteed to the states under the Tenth Amendment.

11.3. SECTION 2 OF THE VOTING RIGHTS ACT: REDISTRICTING AND BEYOND

11.3.1. Section 2 and Redistricting

Although Section 5 preclearance is among the most important parts of the Voting Rights Act, it is not the only one. Section 203 of the act has required jurisdictions, since 1975, to provide for certain ballot materials translated into other languages. Section 203 arose at the time that the VRA was expanded from primarily protecting African-American voters to protecting Latinos, Native Americans, Asian Americans, and Alaskan Native voters.[30]

When Congress initially enacted Section 2 of the Voting Rights Act, it was basically a codification of the Fifteenth Amendment's prohibition on racial discrimination in voting. Impetus to change Section 2 came from the Supreme Court's decision in *City of Mobile v. Bolden*.[31] Before *City of Mobile*, when minority voters challenged arrangements such as at-large voting plans as unconstitutionally discriminatory, the courts seemed to allow such challenges to go forward without proof that the at-large voting plans were passed with the intent to discriminate against minority voters.[32] The court would look at the "totality of the circumstances."

In *City of Mobile*, plaintiffs challenged the system that the city of Mobile, Alabama, used for electing members of its three-member city commission. Because all the commissioners were elected at large, there were more whites than African-Americans voting in city elections, and voting was racially polarized, African-Americans had no representation on the commission. The Supreme Court held that proof of a discriminatory impact of the at-large

---

30. For a basic introduction to how Section 203 works, *see* United States Department of Justice, Section 203 of the Voting Rights Act, http://www.justice.gov/crt/about/vot/sec_203/203_brochure.php.

31. 446 U.S. 55 (1980).

32. *White v. Regester*, 412 U.S. 755 (1973); *Whitcomb v. Chavis*, 403 U.S. 124 (1971); *Zimmer v. McKeithen*, 485 F.2d 1297 (5th Cir. 1973).

system was not good enough under either Section 2 of the Voting Rights Act or the Constitution; plaintiffs had to prove that the city adopted the at-large system with an intent to discriminate against minority voters. (You should see why Section 5 would not have helped minority voters: At-large elections comply with one person, one vote, and thus there would be no need to draw districts and thus no involvement of the Department of Justice or a three-judge court in a preclearance process.)

In response to *City of Mobile*, Congress amended Section 2 of the Voting Rights Act when Section 5 came up for renewal in 1982. The old language read

> No voting qualification or prerequisite to voting, or standard, practice, or procedure shall be imposed or applied by any State or political subdivision to deny or abridge the right of any citizen of the United States to vote on account of race or color.

The revised language of Section 2 reads

> (a) No voting qualification or prerequisite to voting or standard, practice, or procedure shall be imposed or applied by any State or political subdivision in a manner which results in a denial or abridgement of the right of any citizen of the United States to vote on account of race or color, or in contravention of the guarantees set forth in section 1973b(f)(2) of this title, as provided in sub-section (b) of this section.
>
> (b) A violation of subsection (a) of this section is established if, based on the totality of circumstances, it is shown that the political processes leading to nomination or election in the State or political subdivision are not equally open to participation by members of a class of citizens protected by subsection (a) of this section in that its members have less opportunity than other members of the electorate to participate in the political process and to elect representatives of their choice. The extent to which members of a protected class have been elected to office in the State or political subdivision is one circumstance which may be considered: Provided, That nothing in this section establishes a right to have members of a protected class elected in numbers equal to their proportion in the population.

Let's take this apart. Subsection (a) looks somewhat like the older version of Section 2, with the addition of reference to now-protected language minorities (in section 1973b(f)(2)). But note how the language "to deny or abridge" the right to vote was changed to "in a manner which results in a denial or abridgement" of the right to vote. This "results test" was meant to broaden Section 2 to allow for violations when there was discriminatory effect only. The legislative history shows that Congress wanted to reverse the outcome in *City of Mobile* regarding violations of the Voting Rights Act.[33]

---

33. Of course, Congress in a statute could not reverse the Court's constitutional holding.

Subsection (b) of the new Section 2 relied upon the pre-*Mobile* cases to put a "totality of the circumstances" test into the law. The key question about a challenged voting practice is whether "the political processes leading to nomination or election in the State or political subdivision are not equally open to participation by members of a class of citizens protected by subsection (a) of this section in that its members have less opportunity than other members of the electorate to participate in the political process and to elect representatives of their choice."

This language is pretty vague, and there was disagreement in Congress over whether the courts would interpret the language to require some kind of proportional representation in redistricting. For example, if African-Americans made up about one-third of the eligible voters in Mobile, would they be entitled to one seat on the three-member commission? To deal with this problem, Senator Bob Dole, a Republican from Kansas, crafted the compromise to include the language at the end of subsection (b) clarifying that the new section does not establish a right to proportional representation.

Even with that clarification, however, the language of the revised Section 2 was quite opaque. Note how different the question Section 2 asks courts to resolve is from the Section 5 question. The Section 5 question compares a new law against an old law as a baseline; it does not require value judgments to decide if a law has a discriminatory effect. But Section 2 does require such a qualitative judgment (and does not require any change in the law). Thus, there is a Section 2 violation when it "results" in "denial" or "abridge[ment]" of the right to vote on race or language minority grounds, looking at the "totality of the circumstances." Those words do not define themselves, my friends.

The Supreme Court in 1986 first construed the Section 2 language in a case called *Thornburg v. Gingles*,[34] stemming from a dispute over redistricting of North Carolina's legislative districts. Justice Brennan wrote the main opinion of the Court, which was a majority opinion in parts but only a plurality opinion in other parts. Plaintiffs attacked the use of multi-member districts, which the plaintiffs claimed diluted minority votes. Multi-member districts are like miniature at-large elections. A larger group of voters will get to vote for two, three, or more representatives in a single district.[35]

Gingles established a two-stage process for determining whether a multi-member or at-large districting plan violates Section 2 of the VRA.[36] In step

---

34. 478 U.S. 30 (1986).

35. Properly constructed, multi-member districts do not violate one person one vote if the voting power across districts remain the same. For example, a plan could have a number of single-member districts with a 60,000 person population and a number of triple-member districts with 180,000 person populations.

36. The same test has later been applied to vote dilution claims involving single-member districts, where minority plaintiffs allege the district lines could be redrawn so as not to dilute minority voting rights. *Johnson v. De Grandy*, 512 U.S. 997 (1994).

one (sometimes referred to as a "threshold" test), the court applies a three-part test:

> First, the minority group must be able to demonstrate that it is sufficiently large and geographically compact to constitute a majority in a single-member district. If it is not, as would be the case in a substantially integrated district, the multi-member form of the district cannot be responsible for minority voters' inability to elect its candidates. Second, the minority group must be able to show that it is politically cohesive. If the minority group is not politically cohesive, it cannot be said that the selection of a multimember electoral structure thwarts distinctive minority group interests. Third, the minority must be able to demonstrate that the white majority votes sufficiently as a bloc to enable it — in the absence of special circumstances, such as the minority candidate running unopposed — usually to defeat the minority's preferred candidate. In establishing this last circumstance, the minority group demonstrates that submergence in a white multimember district impedes its ability to elect its chosen representatives.

If this threshold test is met, then the court is to turn to the "totality of the circumstances" to determine whether the Section 2 claim is successful. In determining the totality of the circumstances, *Gingles* directed courts to consider factors listed in the Senate report accompanying the passage of the 1982 VRA amendments, factors referred to as the "Zimmer factors" because they appeared in the *Zimmer* case and other pre-City of Mobile constitutional vote dilution cases:[37]

> 1. the extent of any history of official discrimination in the state or political subdivision that touched the right of the members of the minority group to register, to vote, or otherwise to participate in the democratic process;
> 2. the extent to which voting in the elections of the state or political subdivision is racially polarized;
> 3. the extent to which the state or political subdivision has used unusually large election districts, majority vote requirements, anti-single shot provisions, or other voting practices or procedures that may enhance the opportunity for discrimination against the minority group;
> 4. if there is a candidate slating process, whether the members of the minority group have been denied access to that process;
> 5. the extent to which members of the minority group in the state or political subdivision bear the effects of discrimination in such areas as

---

37. As *Gingles* explained: "These factors were derived from the analytical framework of *White* v. *Regester*, 412 U. S. 755 (1973), as refined and developed by the lower courts, in particular by the Fifth Circuit in *Zimmer* v. *McKeithen*, 485 F. 2d 1297 (1973) (en banc), aff'd *sub nom. East Carroll Parish School Board v. Marshall*, 424 U. S. 636 (1976) (*per curiam*). S. Rep., at 28, n. 113."

education, employment and health, which hinder their ability to participate effectively in the political process;

6. whether political campaigns have been characterized by overt or subtle racial appeals.

7. the extent to which members of the minority group have been elected to public office in the jurisdiction.

Additional factors that in some cases have had probative value as part of plaintiffs' evidence to establish a violation are:

whether there is a significant lack of responsiveness on the part of elected officials to the particularized needs of the members of the minority group.

whether the policy underlying the state or political subdivision's use of such voting qualification, prerequisite to voting, or standard, practice or procedure is tenuous.

The First Gingles Factor. The first *Gingles* factor requires evidence on the size of the minority voting population in the district. Although *Gingles* did not foreclose the possibility of a claim based upon a smaller minority population in which minority voters could *influence*, but not determine, the choice of candidate, in *Bartlett v. Strickland*[38] the Court rejected the argument that minority voters could press an influence district claim under Section 2.[39]

One question left open after *Gingles* and not yet considered by the Supreme Court is whether the Court can consider different minority populations together (for example, African-Americans and Latinos) for purposes of satisfying this requirement. It may be possible to show in some circumstances that minority voters from different groups prefer many of the same candidates.[40]

Another issue left open after *Gingles* is how compact the group of minority voters would have to be to satisfy this first prong. For many years, the compactness requirement did not have much bite. But thanks to the "racial gerrymandering" cases we will consider in the next section, courts now seem to require that the districts that could be drawn to remedy a Section 2 violation need to be "reasonably compact." Furthermore, in *League of United Latin American Citizens v. Perry*,[41] the Court seemed to require that the minority voters to be joined in a district be culturally or economically compact as well. In other words, one could not draw a majority-minority district (sometimes called "minority opportunity district") to remedy a Section 2 violation if it would join groups of minority voters who have little in common besides race or ethnicity—such as a district combining urban

---

38. 556 U.S. 1 (2009).

39. This is different from how the Court saw the role of influence districts in a Section 5 claim, at least for a time. As noted in the last section, in *Georgia v. Ashcroft* the Court viewed influence districts as relevant to assessing retrogression of minority voting power.

40. *See Growe v. Emison*, 507 U.S. 25, 41 (1993) (noting the issue).

41. 548 U.S. 399 (2006).

and rural African-American voters across a large expanse of a jurisdiction. More on this idea in the next section.

The Second and Third Gingles Factors.   Although the Supreme Court treated the second and third factors as separate, most people today think of them as a single factor: *racially polarized voting*. When voting is racially polarized, white voters and minority voters tend to vote for different sets of candidates, and the candidates favored by majority white voters usually win. Usually courts consider social science evidence on how much racially polarized voting exists in a jurisdiction.

In some parts of the country, especially in the South, rates of racially polarized voting were very high. This meant that as a Section 2 remedy, courts would have to draw districts with large minority populations, especially if turnout among minority voters was lower than among whites. As more whites were willing to vote for minority-preferred candidates (these whites are sometimes referred to as "crossover" voters), the number of minority voters in a district could be made lower while keeping it a majority-minority district. Of course, if there is a great deal of crossover voting, then that means that racially polarized voting is diminishing, and there may not be a Section 2 violation.

The Totality of the Circumstances.   Even when plaintiffs can meet the three *Gingles* threshold factors, they can still lose under a totality of the circumstances. One key factor here is proportionality: If members of protected minority groups can elect candidates consistent with their proportion of the population, courts will generally say there is no Section 2 violation.[42] This does not violate the "Dole compromise"; that compromise says that minority voters have no right to proportionality. The idea here is that if there *is* proportionality there is no Section 2 violation. Whether the *Gingles* test improperly leads to proportionality is an issue that is often debated.

Causation.   Look back at the language of the amended Section 2 requiring that the voting rule must *result* in the denial or abridgement of voting *on account of* race, color, or membership in a language minority. Although Justice Brennan, speaking for a plurality in *Gingles*, read this language to include only an effects (or results) test and not an intent test, lower courts sometimes bring the issue of intent through the back door thanks to the "results . . . on account of" language. That is, some courts require proof that intentional racial discrimination by the state *caused* the vote dilution.[43] The Supreme

---

42. *Johnson v. DeGrandy*, 512 U.S. at 1013-1014.
43. For example, *see Goosby v. Town of Hempstead*, 180 F.3d 476, 500 (2d Cir. 1999).

Court has not since clarified the answer to how causation might relate to the effects standard.

The Remedy. Plaintiffs may complain in a Section 2 suit about the failure to draw districts at all (the at-large or multi-member problem), about "packing" too many minority voters in too few districts, or about spreading out minority voters across districts ("cracking"). The remedy is usually to draw reasonably compact single-member majority-minority districts, roughly proportional to the possible number of reasonably compact majority-minority districts that can be drawn. As noted above, recently the Supreme Court indicated that a Section 2 remedy (or districts drawn to avoid Section 2 liability) cannot join together culturally or economically disparate groups of minority voters. Within these guidelines, courts will often defer to the plans put forward by the state or local defendants.

Although the usual remedy for a Section 2 violation is the creation of majority-minority single member districts, some cases end with the use of alternative voting systems, such as the use of cumulative voting.[44] A cumulative voting system might create multi-member districts and give voters a number of votes equal to the total number of seats up for a vote in the district. In the *City of Mobile* example, each voter would have three votes (for the three-member commission). Voters could "plump" all three votes on a single candidate if desired. Such plumping by a minority (of any type) of the population can be an effective way to elect a representative in a multi-member district.

The Politics. For a while, Republicans saw a great benefit to the creation of majority-minority districts, especially African-American majority districts. African-American voters tend to overwhelmingly vote Democratic, and if Republicans create districts that can put as many reliably Democratic voters in as few districts as possible, doing so could help Republicans create more Republican districts. Democrats, of course, attacked this as "packing" in violation of Section 2, and for partisan reasons Democrats tried to spread out reliably Democratic minority voters across districts to maximize Democrats' chance of success. (This dynamic led to the *Georgia v. Ashcroft* Section 5 litigation, in which Republicans and African-American incumbents were pitted against Democrats.) Today, given the significant overlap between race and party, VRA claims and remedies often have serious implications for the partisan politics of the jurisdiction.

---

44. The U.S. Court of Appeals for the Fourth Circuit rejected such a remedy in *Cane v. Worcester County*, 35 F.3d 921 (4th Cir. 1994). In *United States v. Village of Port Chester*, 704 F. Supp. 2d 411 (S.D.N.Y. 2010), the court adopted cumulative voting as a remedy, which was favored by the defendant village and opposed by the U.S. government.

Example 3

Consider the following portion of a challenge to California's 2000 round of redistricting for its state senate:[45]

> Senate District 27 is located in southeast Los Angeles County, and includes the communities of Downey, Paramount, Cerritos, Artesia, Hawaiian Gardens, Signal Hill, Lakewood, and Lynwood, as well as parts of Long Beach and South Gate. The seat is currently held by Sen. Betty Karnette, who was first elected in 1990. Plaintiffs do not dispute that Sen. Karnette was the Latino candidate of choice; although herself white, she received the majority of Latino support within the district during the 1990 primary election, in which there was no incumbent Senator. It is also undisputed that Sen. Karnette voted in accordance with the Senate Latino caucus 95% of the time in the 1997-98 session, and 85% in the 1998-99 session. Due to the limits on state legislative terms in California, Sen. Karnette will be unable to run for re-election in 2004.
>
> The essence of plaintiffs' traditional §2 claim regarding Senate District 27 is that the redistricting statute packs Latinos into neighboring Senate District 30, a majority-Latino district, and that the challenged district could and should have been drawn as an additional majority-Latino seat. Latinos constitute a plurality of the voting-age population ("VAP") in SD 27: 40% of the VAP is Latino, 36% is white, 12% is Asian and 9% is black. In SD 30, Latinos constitute the overwhelming majority of the district: 76% of the total population and 71% of the VAP is Latino. [T]he legislature could have moved some Latino voters from the Latino-dominated SD 30 to SD 27 in order to construct an additional majority-minority district . . . . The evidence in the record is overwhelming that Latinos in Los Angeles County vote monolithically for Latino candidates, regardless of the ideology of that candidate. . . .
>
> Every set of election returns presented by either party demonstrates that Latinos win elections, aided by substantial white cross-over voting, in the areas comprising SD 27. For instance, the evidence submitted by plaintiffs' expert shows that in the two Assembly districts that constitute a substantial portion of SD 27, Latino candidates received large numbers of white votes. In the 50th Assembly District . . . 57% and 59% of whites voted for the Latino Assembly candidate in the 2000 primary and general elections respectively. In AD 56, "less than 50% of the Anglo vote"—but evidently a still-substantial percentage—went to the Latino candidate for that post. Moreover, *Latino candidates won both elections.* In addition . . . Latino candidates have in fact won the sets of precincts in the two Assembly districts that overlap with SD 27. For instance, in the 2000 general election for AD 56, Latina Assembly Member Sally Havice won 59% of the vote in the portion of her district that is contained within SD 27. The overlapping area has a *lesser* percentage of Latino voters than does SD 27 as a whole: SD 27 has a 45.1% Latino population and 39.8% VAP,

---

45. *Cano v. Davis,* 211 F. Supp. 2d 1208 (C.D. Cal. 2002) (three-judge court).

whereas the area contained in both SD 27 and AD 56 is 37.2% Latino overall, and includes a Latino VAP of 33.2%

Can plaintiffs meet the *Gingles* threshold test in a VRA Section 2 case as to SD 27? If so, can plaintiffs prove a violation under a totality of the circumstances?

Explanation

Now we are getting in the weeds. Could plaintiffs make out the *Gingles* three threshold factors?

- "First, the minority group must be able to demonstrate that it is sufficiently large and geographically compact to constitute a majority in a single-member district." The facts tell us that "the legislature could have moved some Latino voters from the Latino-dominated SD 30 to SD 27 in order to construct an additional majority-minority district." So the Latino population is large enough. If there is enough evidence that SD 27 could be drawn in a reasonably compact way while including Latinos, the first *Gingles* threshold factor would be met.
- "Second, the minority group must be able to show that it is politically cohesive." This, too, looks easily met. The facts from *Cano* tell us that "[t]he evidence in the record is overwhelming that Latinos in Los Angeles County vote monolithically for Latino candidates, regardless of the ideology of that candidate."
- "Third, the minority must be able to demonstrate that the white majority votes sufficiently as a bloc to enable it—in the absence of special circumstances, such as the minority candidate running unopposed—usually to defeat the minority's preferred candidate." This factor is a problem for plaintiffs. There appears to be significant white crossover voting, and not strong evidence that in this area white voters usually vote together to defeat Latino-preferred candidates. For this reason, the *Cano* court concluded that the Section 2 challenge to SD 27 failed and that there was no reason to go on to consider the "totality of the circumstances" analysis that follows the *Gingles* threshold.

11.3.2. Section 2 Beyond Redistricting

The analysis of Section 2 in the last section concerned claims about districts: Either a jurisdiction was using at-large or multi-member districts and the plaintiffs wanted the creation of majority-minority districts, or the jurisdiction already used single-member districts and the plaintiffs wanted districts redrawn to create majority-minority districts.

But districting claims are not the only possible claims. Consider, for example, *Holder v. Hall*.[46] Bleckley County, Georgia, used a single-commissioner system for governance. African-American voters, making up about 20% of the county brought suit under Section 2 arguing, among other things, that the court should order the county to use a five-member commission so that African-Americans could get some representation in local government. The Supreme Court on a 5-4 vote rejected the argument that Section 2 required the creation of more offices. There was no majority opinion. Justice Kennedy's plurality opinion argued

> In certain cases, the benchmark for comparison in a §2 dilution suit is obvious. The effect of an anti-single-shot voting rule, for instance, can be evaluated by comparing the system with that rule to the system without that rule. But where there is no objective and workable standard for choosing a reasonable benchmark by which to evaluate a challenged voting practice, it follows that the voting practice cannot be challenged as dilutive under §2.
>
> As the facts of this case well illustrate, the search for a benchmark is quite problematic when a §2 dilution challenge is brought to the size of a government body. There is no principled reason why one size should be picked over another as the benchmark for comparison.

Justice O'Connor agreed, but Justice Thomas, joined by Justice Scalia, went much further. Among other things, Justice Thomas took the position that Section 2 did not cover cases of vote dilution.

Justice Blackmun, for the dissenters, argued there was a benchmark in a case involving single-member offices as in this Georgia county:

> By all objective measures, the proposed five-member Bleckley County Commission presents a reasonable, workable benchmark against which to measure the practice of electing a sole commissioner. First, the Georgia Legislature specifically authorized a five-member commission for Bleckley County. Moreover, a five-member commission is the most common form of governing authority in Georgia. Bleckley County, as one of a small and dwindling number of counties in Georgia still employing a sole commissioner, markedly departs from practices elsewhere in Georgia. . . . Finally, the county itself has moved from a single superintendent of education to a school board with five members elected from single-member districts, providing a workable and readily available model for commission districts. Thus, the proposed five-member baseline is reasonable and workable.

---

46. 512 U.S. 874 (1994).

As difficult as the dilution question is in *Holder v. Hall*, the question of Section 2's application to vote denial cases is even more difficult.[47] Consider the issue of felon disenfranchisement. Minorities are disproportionately affected by felon disenfranchisement laws. Is that enough? How should courts judge the "totality of the circumstances" in a Section 2 vote denial case?

Perhaps surprisingly, the Supreme Court has not considered Section 2 vote denial cases. A number of lower courts have considered whether felon disenfranchisement laws violate Section 2, but those claims have failed. Sometimes courts have said that Congress did not intend Section 2 to cover felon disenfranchisement laws, or at least that principles of constitutional avoidance suggest this interpretation.[48] Other courts, relying on the causation issue described in the last subsection, concluded that felon disenfranchisement cannot violate Section 2 absent proof that the disenfranchisement itself was caused by (the result of) intentional racial discrimination.[49]

It is not clear how vote denial claims will fare under Section 2, when it is impossible to mechanically apply the *Gingles* test (there are no districts at issue, to begin with). It also appears likely that the causation/results question will loom large: Many things are correlated with race in the United States, especially because many minority voters tend to be poorer. If all that plaintiffs must show is correlation, could election practices such as Internet voting or voting on Tuesday be subject to Section 2 claims if there is a racially disparate impact?[50] Or is more required? If no more is required, will the Supreme Court consider whether Section 2 is not (always) constitutional? The argument would be that a broad Section 2 would exceed congressional power and infringe on state sovereignty under the new federalism cases and *Shelby County*.

We may get a sense of the scope of Section 2 in the vote denial context in two high-profile cases recent brought by the Department of Justice. In one case, DOJ challenged Texas's voter ID law. That law had been put on hold under Section 5, but the hold lifted after the Supreme Court decided *Shelby County*. In the same lawsuit, DOJ is also trying to get Texas bailed back into coverage under the Section 3 bail in provision. In the other lawsuit, DOJ has brought Section 2 and Section 3 claims against North Carolina, whose legislature passed a large voting bill that imposed voter identification,

---

47. On this question, *see* Daniel P. Tokaji, *The New Vote Denial: Where Election Reform Meets the Voting Rights Act*, 57 S. C. L. Rev. 689 (2006).

48. *Simmons v. Galvin*, 575 F.3d 24 (1st Cir. 2009), *cert. denied* 131 S.Ct. 412 (2010); *Johnson v. Gov. of State of Fla.*, 405 F.3d 1214 (11th Cir. 2005) (en banc); *Hayden v. Pataki*, 449 F.3d 305 (2d Cir. 2006) (en banc).

49. *Farrakhan v. Gregoire*, 623 F.3d 990 (9th Cir. 2010) (en banc).

50. *See Farrakhan v. Washington*, 359 F.3d 1116, 1116-1127 (9th Cir. 2004) (Kozinski, J., dissenting from denial of rehearing en banc).

eliminated same-day voter registration, and cut back on the number of days (but not the number of hours) of early voting, among other changes.

One of the interesting questions in the lawsuit is whether it will be any defense if courts conclude that the laws were motivated by party, and not race. In both cases, Republican legislatures passed the laws over the objections of Democrats. Because these days minority voters are overwhelmingly Democrats, it is not clear how courts should decide the "race or party" question.[51]

As this book went to press, a federal district court in Wisconsin held in *Frank v. Walker* that Wisconsin's voter identification law violated Section 2 of the Voting Rights Act because the identification burden fell disproportionately on racial minorities.[52] The court rejected application of the *Gingles* factors as not being particularly relevant to a vote dilution claim. Instead, the judge defined the operative test through a focus on the language of the statute:

> The meaning of this language is clear: "Section 2 requires an electoral process 'equally open' to all, not a process that favors one group over another." Justice Scalia, in a dissent in a vote dilution case, provided the following illustration of the meaning of Section 2: "If, for example, a county permitted voter registration for only three hours one day a week, and that made it more difficult for blacks to register than whites, blacks would have less opportunity 'to participate in the political process' than whites, and Section 2 would therefore be violated. . . . " *Chisom*, 501 U.S. at 407–08 (Scalia, J., dissenting). Based on the text, then, I conclude that Section 2 protects against a voting practice that creates a barrier to voting that is more likely to appear in the path of a voter if that voter is a member of a minority group than if he or she is not. The presence of a barrier that has this kind of disproportionate impact prevents the political process from being "equally open" to all and results in members of the minority group having "less opportunity" to participate in the political process and to elect representatives of their choice.

The court did not grapple with the limitations of this standard, and whether it would mean that a large number of other election practices, such as normal rules for voter registration, could then be subject to Section 2 challenge. We shall see how this standard fares on appeal and whether other courts follow it or use a different standard.

---

51. Richard L. Hasen, *Race or Party? How Courts Should Think About Republican Efforts to Make It Harder to Vote in North Carolina and Elsewhere*, 127 HARV. L. REV. FORUM 58 (2014), http://www.harvardlawreview.org/issues/127/january14/forum_1022.php./
52. *Frank v. Walker*, ___ F.Supp.2d ___, 2014 WL 1775432 (E.D. Wis, 2014).

Example 4

The state of Ohio passes a law cutting back the dates of early voting in the state, and the secretary of state issues regulations barring the use of early voting on Sundays. Both the Ohio legislature majority and the secretary of state are Republicans. African-American voters in the state engaged in a "Souls to the Polls" program to take worshippers after church services to go vote, a program that can no longer work during the early voting period.

Can African-American voters bring a successful Section 2 claim against the early voting cutback?

Explanation

The answer is not clear, but it would be a tough claim to bring. The standard from Section 2 should be whether "based on the totality of circumstances, it is shown that the political processes leading to nomination or election in the State or political subdivision are not equally open to participation by members of a class of citizens protected by subsection (a) of this section in that its members have less opportunity than other members of the electorate to participate in the political process and to elect representatives of their choice." That seems a pretty demanding standard. Even with the cutback of early voting, it would be hard to show a significant decrease in minority voting rights in Ohio simply by such a cutback.

Furthermore, there may well be a causation question. Did this cutback *result* from racial discrimination? If it resulted from partisan considerations, it is not clear how the courts will approach this question.

We have very little experience thus far with Section 2 vote denial claims outside of felon disenfranchisement claims. But there are reasons for doubting such claims' broad success.

11.4. RACIAL GERRYMANDERING CLAIMS AND THE FUTURE OF THE VOTING RIGHTS ACT

During the 1980s and 1990s, the Department of Justice was aggressive in enforcing Section 5 of the Voting Rights Act in the redistricting context. Among other things, as noted earlier in this chapter, DOJ, sometimes using the "purpose" prong of Section 5, denied preclearance to plans that it judged would violate Section 2 of the Voting Rights Act. DOJ would push to create as many majority-minority districts in covered jurisdictions as was feasible, but DOJ did not express strong opinions about *where* in a jurisdiction these districts had to be drawn.

In North Carolina, Democrats reacted to DOJ's demands the way you would expect self-interested politicians to do so: They passed a plan creating the number of majority-minority districts required by DOJ but did so in a way to protect Democratic incumbents and to maximize the number of Democratic seats. This led to the creation of some very oddly shaped majority-minority districts, including one that tied together disparate populations of African-American voters along the I-85 corridor.

Republicans initially challenged the legislative districting plan as a partisan gerrymander. For reasons given in the last chapter, the claim failed. Opponents of the redistricting plan then filed a new claim, claiming that the redistricting was an unconstitutional "racial gerrymander." Importantly, the claim was not that the plan diluted the white vote or anyone else's vote. Instead, the claim was that the plan separated voters on the basis of race in violation of the Equal Protection Clause of the Constitution.

In *Shaw v. Reno*,[53] a closely divided Supreme Court accepted the argument, creating a cause of action for an unconstitutional racial gerrymander. Justice O'Connor's decision for the Court stressed the odd shape of the district, and said that the odd shape of the districting showed voters being separated on the basis of race, in violation of the Constitution:

> Put differently, we believe that reapportionment is one area in which appearances do matter. A reapportionment plan that includes in one district individuals who belong to the same race, but who are otherwise widely separated by geographical and political boundaries, and who may have little in common with one another but the color of their skin, bears an uncomfortable resemblance to political apartheid. It reinforces the perception that members of the same racial group — regardless of their age, education, economic status, or the community in which they live — think alike, share the same political interests, and will prefer the same candidates at the polls. We have rejected such perceptions elsewhere as impermissible racial stereotypes. By perpetuating such notions, a racial gerrymander may exacerbate the very patterns of racial bloc voting that majority-minority districting is sometimes said to counteract.
>
> The message that such districting sends to elected representatives is equally pernicious. When a district obviously is created solely to effectuate the perceived common interests of one racial group, elected officials are more likely to believe that their primary obligation is to represent only the members of that group, rather than their constituency as a whole. This is altogether antithetical to our system of representative democracy.

The Court held such separation could not be sustained unless it satisfied strict scrutiny, and the case was remanded for further consideration of that question.

---

53. 509 U.S. 630 (1993).

Shaw was harshly criticized by some liberals and others. Why should there be a cause of action without evidence of vote dilution? Why should the shape of the district matter? Where was the evidence that the shape of the district affected representation in the way suggested by the majority? In any case, the districts at issue in *Shaw* had many white and African-American voters in them — they were not districts containing only African-Americans.

Subsequent cases in the 1990s fleshed out the theory and workings of the new racial gerrymandering claim. Justice O'Connor explained in a later case that the interest she was protecting was against an "expressive harm." As Professors Pildes and Niemi explained,[54]

> One can only understand Shaw, we believe, in terms of a view that what we call expressive harms are constitutionally cognizable. An expressive harm is one that results from the ideas or attitudes expressed through a governmental action, rather than from the more tangible or material consequences the action brings about. On this view, the meaning of a governmental action is just as important as what that action does. Public policies can violate the Constitution not only because they bring about concrete costs, but because the very meaning they convey demonstrates inappropriate respect for relevant public values. On this unusual conception of constitutional harm, when a governmental action expresses disrespect for such values, it can violate the Constitution.

Although Justice O'Connor continued to focus on the shape of the district, the Court conservatives moved in a different direction, focusing on motive. In *Miller v. Johnson,*[55] the Court held that race could not be the "predominant factor" in redistricting without compelling justification. This led the Court to focus on motive. In *Miller,* the Court held that the Georgia legislature had such an impermissible motive to make race the "predominant factor" in redistricting, thereby setting up the state for a possible racial gerrymandering claim.

To talk of the state's predominant factor in redistricting was odd, because the state of Georgia, subject to preclearance, was only drawing the number of majority-minority districts required by DOJ. The placement of the districts was motivated not by race but by party and incumbency considerations. Nonetheless, the Court found race the predominant factor in redistricting.

In a few of the cases, jurisdictions defended their districts by arguing that the districts were created in order to avoid Section 2 VRA liability (for failure to create enough majority-minority districts). This led to some question whether the conservatives would hold Section 2 unconstitutional,

---

54. Richard H. Pildes and Richard G. Niemi, *Expressive Harms, "Bizarre Districts," and Voting Rights: Evaluating Election-District Appearances After* Shaw v. Reno, 92 Mich. L. Rev. 483, 506-507 (1993).
55. 515 U.S. 900 (1995).

if indeed it required the creation of these districts. Eventually, Justice O'Connor agreed compliance with Section 2 could be a compelling interest, but the Court has never found that Section 2 justified what would otherwise be a "racial gerrymander." The reason went back to *Gingles*.

Recall in *Gingles* that the first prong of the threshold test was that the minority group bringing a claim is large and *compact* enough to be a majority in a single member district. Although the compactness requirement did not have much bite before the racial gerrymandering cases, it does now: Section 2 does not require those drawing district lines to draw a majority-minority district if the only way to do so is to draw a non-compact district. In other words, it would be hard to show one was compelled to draw a majority-minority district in an odd shape to comply with Section 2, if Section 2 itself requires the creation of such districts only when the minority population is reasonably compact.

In 2001, the Court decided *Easley v. Cromartie*,[56] the fourth time North Carolina districting got to the Supreme Court in a decade. In *Easley*, the Court (Justice O'Connor and the four more liberal members of the Court) rejected a challenge to North Carolina's latest redistricting plan after concluding that *party*, not race, was the predominant factor in drawing district lines.

Since *Easley*, racial gerrymandering cases have become far less frequent. One reason may be that redistricters got smart and started drawing more compact majority-minority districts (and hiding any evidence of a predominant motive in using race in redistricting). Another key factor is likely the changed role of the DOJ. Because of a number of cases reining in the DOJ's preclearance powers, DOJ was no longer pushing jurisdictions to create more majority-minority districts. Without such pressure, jurisdictions could avoid both DOJ liability and potential problems in the courts.

The most recent Supreme Court case touching on racial gerrymandering claims is *League of United Latin American Citizens v. Perry*, mentioned earlier this chapter. This case concerned a Texas redistricting plan. Challengers raised both racial gerrymandering and Section 2 claims against the plan. In a portion of the majority opinion written by Justice Kennedy and joined by the four liberal justices, Justice Kennedy found that one of the districts, District 23, violated Section 2 of the VRA because it drew together Latinos from different parts of the state that had little culturally or socioeconomically in common. This kind of "cultural compactness" seemed to make the *Gingles* compactness requirement even stronger, and it appeared to borrow concepts from the racial gerrymandering cases into the Section 2 analysis. It is not clear to what extent courts will continue to merge Section 2 and racial gerrymandering concepts in considering districting claims.

---

56. 532 U.S. 234 (2001).

Example 5

What is your assessment of how the Voting Rights Act and the racial gerrymandering cases regulate the role of race in the U.S. political process? What would you change, if anything, and why?

Explanation

I thought it useful to end not with a discussion of the intricacies of the racial gerrymandering claim (which now appears to be less important in redistricting cases, especially with the demise of Section 5), but rather with an attempt to get the bigger picture on the role of regulating race in U.S. politics.

Few today would quarrel with the notion that the Voting Rights Act was a tremendous success in fulfilling the promise of the Reconstruction amendments, especially the Fifteenth Amendment. But beyond that, there is much dispute over both the Voting Rights Act and the Supreme Court's constitutional and statutory cases in this area. Some believe the Court was wrong in striking down the coverage formula of Section 5, that its Section 2 cases have read the protection for minority voters too narrowly, and that its racial gerrymandering cases are wrongheaded. Others believe the Court was right in striking the coverage formula as not updated to current conditions, that the Court, if anything, has been too generous to plaintiffs interpreting Section 2 (recall Justice Thomas's concurrence in *Holder v. Hall*, in which he would have interpreted the law to apply only to narrow election procedure cases), and that the racial gerrymandering cases were necessary to stop states from making race the predominant factor in redistricting. Of course, there are many intermediate positions between these two poles.

Furthermore, regardless of where you fall on the continuum in these cases, consider whether the division of authority between the Congress and courts (and to some extent, the states) on these questions makes sense. Would it make more sense for the country to decide on the appropriate role of race in redistricting and the political process and to put those commitments in the Constitution, as many other democracies with more recent constitutions do? Or do we trust the incrementalism that comes with court adjudication and congressional tinkering?

CHAPTER 12

Election
Administration

12.1. INTRODUCTION: FLORIDA 2000 AS THE MODERN START OF THE VOTING WARS

Before the disputed presidential election in 2000, election law courses did not spend much time (if any) on the nuts-and-bolts of how elections are run: rules for counting (or recounting ballots), registration standards, ballot design, or theories of statutory interpretation of election law issues. The issues were less sexy than campaign finance and redistricting.[1]

All of that changed in 2000, when the U.S. presidential election between Republican George W. Bush and Democrat Al Gore came down to a very close election in Florida for Florida's decisive electoral votes: On election night the parties were 1,784 votes apart. Through recounts, an election "protest" and "contest," and dozens of separate legal actions, at one point only a few hundred votes out of millions of votes cast separated the candidates. It ended with the Supreme Court's controversial decision in Bush v. Gore[2] halting a statewide recount of some presidential ballots and assuring the election of Bush over Gore.

---

1. It tells you a lot about election law professors that we thought campaign finance and redistricting were sexy issues.
2. 531 U.S. 98 (2000).

The story of Florida 2000 is a fascinating one told in many places, but I won't repeat it here.[3] Among the salient lessons of the election and the month-long recount and litigation that ensued are the following:

- **U.S. elections often are partisan affairs.** The secretary of state, Katherine Harris, served as chief elections officer of the state. But she also served as honorary co-chair of Bush's election committee in Florida and ran for office as a Republican. This kind of dual hat wearing is common, with at least 33 state chief election officers chosen in partisan elections. (After the Florida controversy the state changed its selection process to appointment by the state's governor — arguably a more partisan process.) Partisan election officials existed throughout Florida's system of running elections. County election boards were chosen based on partisan affiliation as well. Partisanship seemed to have an effect on decisionmaking. Republican election officials made some discretionary decisions that seemed to help Republicans, and Democratic election officials made some discretionary decisions which seemed to help Democrats. For example, Harris interpreted deadlines strictly in the code to favor Bush over Gore. However, she interpreted rules for accepting late-arriving military ballots in a lax manner, also helping Bush over Gore. When county canvassing boards had to recount ballots, Democratic boards used much more forgiving standards (which helped Gore) than Republican boards did. Democratic election administrators were much less likely than Republican election administrators to use a flawed list of potential felons to be purged from registration lists. The result? More ineligible felons mistakenly left on the voting rolls in Democratic counties and more eligible voters mistakenly removed (or "purged") as felons from the voting rolls in Republican counties.

- **U.S. election administration is decentralized.** Katherine Harris served as the chief elections officer of the state of Florida in 2000, but it turns out that Harris had very little authority over many of the decisions made about how votes would be cast and counted. Instead, a great deal of the authority was in the hands of local election officials, who made decisions about ballot design, ballot machinery, voter registration and purging, and many aspects of the recount process. Indeed, there are over 8,000 election jurisdictions in the U.S. conducting elections. Power is split between the state and local level, with various federal laws regulating aspects of the political process (*see* section 12.3). The result is a surprising lack of uniformity in the rules for running

---

3. For my narrative take on the dispute, see RICHARD L. HASEN, THE VOTING WARS ch. 1 (2012) (and see LOWENSTEIN, HASEN, & TOKAJI, at 268-270 for a briefer account), but there are many books and articles available. *See* the bibliographical note in *id.* at 292-293.

elections. In this regard, the United States is noteworthy among modern democracies, most of which have national nonpartisan agencies running elections using a centralized voting registry, national identification cards, and uniform technology throughout the country.

- **U.S. election and voting technology is full of problems.** Litigation and journalistic investigations in Florida revealed the extent of technical problems with U.S. election administration. In Florida, thousands of votes were lost because of poor technology, such as old "punch card" voting machines. Voters cast votes on these machines using a small pin or "stylus" to punch out a piece of perforated cardboard from a card. The card was fed into a machine that counted the number of holes corresponding to various votes cast by voters. The machinery was unreliable, and much of the dispute over the 2000 election concerned whether, and how, to recount the cards with partially perforated holes in them (so called "hanging chads"). Problems were even worse in Palm Beach County, which combined punch card voting with a confusing ballot layout (the "butterfly ballot") which caused many voters either to vote for too many candidates (overvote) or to vote for a candidate who was not a voter's first choice. Bad instructions also were a problem, with many voters in Duvall County casting too many votes for a presidential candidate after instructional materials told voters to vote for a candidate on every page. Investigations after Florida revealed the problems with voting technology were widespread.

The Bush v. Gore case was part of the partisan battle over the election outcome. Many Democrats believe the conservatives on the U.S. Supreme Court decided the case in a disingenuous way to ensure the election of Bush. Many Republicans believe the U.S. Supreme Court was justified in intervening in the election and stopping the recount because the Florida Supreme Court, dominated by state supreme court justices elected as Democrats, bent (or broke) Florida election rules to give Gore a chance to steal the election from Bush.

The case did not involve all the myriad issues that arose in the month-long Florida controversy, from the butterfly ballot to the felon purge to the counting of late-arriving military ballots. Instead, the case more narrowly concerned the Florida Supreme Court's order stemming from Gore's election contest of a statewide recount of ballots that were recorded as "undervotes" — that is, ballots containing no valid votes for president.

The order was controversial. To begin with, the U.S. Supreme Court had already sent one case arising from the Florida controversy back to the Florida Supreme Court for clarification. The Florida Supreme Court had extended the time for conducting recounts beyond that allowed by the secretary of state and also allowed for a manual recount of ballots to look for voter errors.[4] Bush argued that this ruling violated Article II of the U.S. Constitution, which gives each state *legislature* the right to determine the rules for choosing presidential electors. The U.S. Supreme Court remanded the case to the Florida Supreme Court to clarify whether its ruling was consistent with the Florida legislature's rules for choosing presidential electors.[5]

Republicans were concerned that the Florida high court was manipulating the rules to favor Gore. Gore had asked for a recount of undervoted ballots in only four of Florida's counties, counties in which he expected to pick up votes to make up the difference with Bush. A lower court rejected the request. On appeal, the Florida supreme court ordered a statewide recount (not one of just four counties), but it did not order a recount of *all* ballots, only the undervoted ones. (Ironically, a later study determined that Gore might have been able to win only if he had asked for *all* ballots to be recounted;[6] there were a fair number of ballots that counted as illegal overvotes that were really votes for Gore, such as ballots on which voters had written Gore's name in the box for write-in ballots and also marked Gore's name on the ballot.) The vote was 4-3, with the chief justice writing a strong dissent that the Florida courts lacked the power to order this recount.

The U.S. Supreme Court intervened, first granting a controversial stay on a 5-4 vote that stopped the counting just days before a statutory deadline for states to certify their electoral college votes. After a very expedited briefing and hearing schedule, the Court on the same 5-4 vote held the recount unconstitutional. The *per curiam* opinion held that the inconsistent standards for the counting and recounting violated the Equal Protection Clause of the Fourteenth Amendment of the U.S. Constitution. Here is the key language from the Court's opinion:

> The right to vote is protected in more than the initial allocation of the franchise. Equal protection applies as well to the manner of its exercise. Having once granted the right to vote on equal terms, the State may not, by later arbitrary and disparate treatment, value one person's vote over that of another. *See, e.g., Harper v. Virginia Bd. of Elections* ("[O]nce the franchise is granted to the electorate, lines may not be drawn which are inconsistent with the Equal Protection Clause of the Fourteenth Amendment"). It must be remembered that "the right of suffrage can be denied by a debasement or dilution of the weight of a citizen's vote just as effectively as by wholly prohibiting the free exercise of the franchise." *Reynolds v. Sims.*
>
> There is no difference between the two sides of the present controversy on these basic propositions. Respondents say that the very purpose of vindicating

---

4. *Palm Beach Cnty. Canvassing Bd. v. Harris,* 772 So.2d 1220 (Fla. 2000).
5. *Bush v. Palm Beach Cnty. Canvassing Bd.,* 531 U.S. 70 (2000).
6. Ford Fessenden and John M. Broder, *Study of Disputed Florida Ballots Finds Justices Did Not Cast the Deciding Vote,* N.Y. Times, Nov. 12, 2001, http://www.nytimes.com/2001/11/12/politics/recount/12VOTE.html.

the right to vote justifies the recount procedures now at issue. The question before us, however, is whether the recount procedures the Florida Supreme Court has adopted are consistent with its obligation to avoid arbitrary and disparate treatment of the members of its electorate.

Much of the controversy seems to revolve around ballot cards designed to be perforated by a stylus but which, either through error or deliberate omission, have not been perforated with sufficient precision for a machine to count them. In some cases a piece of the card — a chad — is hanging, say by two corners. In other cases there is no separation at all, just an indentation.

The Florida Supreme Court has ordered that the intent of the voter be discerned from such ballots. For purposes of resolving the equal protection challenge, it is not necessary to decide whether the Florida Supreme Court had the authority under the legislative scheme for resolving election disputes to define what a legal vote is and to mandate a manual recount implementing that definition. The recount mechanisms implemented in response to the decisions of the Florida Supreme Court do not satisfy the minimum requirement for nonarbitrary treatment of voters necessary to secure the fundamental right. Florida's basic command for the count of legally cast votes is to consider the "intent of the voter." This is unobjectionable as an abstract proposition and a starting principle. The problem inheres in the absence of specific standards to ensure its equal application. The formulation of uniform rules to determine intent based on these recurring circumstances is practicable and, we conclude, necessary. . . .

The recount process, in its features here described, is inconsistent with the minimum procedures necessary to protect the fundamental right of each voter in the special instance of a statewide recount under the authority of a single state judicial officer. Our consideration is limited to the present circumstances, for the problem of equal protection in election processes generally presents many complexities.

The question before the Court is not whether local entities, in the exercise of their expertise, may develop different systems for implementing elections. Instead, we are presented with a situation where a state court with the power to assure uniformity has ordered a statewide recount with minimal procedural safeguards. When a court orders a statewide remedy, there must be at least some assurance that the rudimentary requirements of equal treatment and fundamental fairness are satisfied. . . .

Upon due consideration of the difficulties identified to this point, it is obvious that the recount cannot be conducted in compliance with the requirements of equal protection and due process without substantial additional work. It would require not only the adoption (after opportunity for argument) of adequate statewide standards for determining what is a legal vote, and practicable procedures to implement them, but also orderly judicial review of any disputed matters that might arise. In addition, the Secretary [of State] has advised that the recount of only a portion of the ballots requires that the vote tabulation equipment be used to screen out undervotes, a function for which the machines were not designed. If a recount of overvotes were also required, perhaps even a second screening would be necessary. Use of the equipment for this purpose, and any new software developed for it, would have to be evaluated for accuracy by the Secretary of State, as required by Fla. Stat. §101.015 (2000).

The majority opinion was controversial for a few reasons. First, it was the first time the Court had expanded equal protection principles to election administration. Chapter 9 covered *Reynolds* and *Harper*, the principal precedents the *Bush v. Gore* majority relied upon in its equal protection holding. The conservative justices' expansion of equal protection in this context was also somewhat incongruous with the general expansion of equal protection of voting rights, something usually more associated with the liberal justices. Furthermore, the remedial aspect of the Court's decision was the most controversial; the Court held that with the statutory time arriving for states to certify their electoral votes without facing a possible challenge in Congress, there was no time left to do a full recount of the ballots. Thus, the Court's order not only stopped the existing recount but prevented a further recount from taking place.

Chief Justice Rehnquist, joined by Justices Scalia and Thomas, signed the majority opinion (which presumably was written by Justice Kennedy or Justice O'Connor).[7] But the three also wrote a separate opinion arguing that the court-ordered recount violated Article II of the Constitution giving the state legislature the power to set the rules for choosing presidential electors.

The four more liberal justices dissented. All disagreed with the Article II theory. Justices Breyer and Souter believed that there were equal protection (or perhaps due process) problems with how the Florida supreme court ordered the recount to take place. But these justices disagreed with the Court's decision to foreclose a recount under uniform standards. The other two justices, Ginsburg and Stevens, rejected the equal protection claims as well. One might have expected these justices to be most likely to embrace expansive equal protection claims.

Example 1

The state of Ohio uses punch card voting machines in some counties in the state and not in others. Such voting machines are much more likely to fail to record valid votes than the other machinery.

Does the use of punch card voting technology in part of the state violate the Equal Protection Clause of the Fourteenth Amendment under *Bush v. Gore*?

---

7. Perhaps these justices signed the equal protection opinion because otherwise there would have been a majority of justices not agreeing with either the equal protection or Article II theories.

Explanation

One of the great debates about the *Bush v. Gore* majority opinion is whether the case has any precedential value and if so, how it would affect election disputes. The next section of this chapter addresses this issue, among others, regarding the voting wars since 2000. But before turning to what the courts did, it is useful for you to give your own take based upon reading the key paragraphs from *Bush v. Gore*.

At its narrowest, *Bush v. Gore* is a holding about using different standards to conduct a jurisdiction-wide recount of ballots. If *Bush v. Gore* applies to any other cases at all (and liberal critics say that perhaps it was a "one-day only ticket" to hand Bush the presidency), presumably one cannot have different and changing counting standards for ballots being recounted.

It may not be much of an expansion of the *Bush* holding to argue that a state violates equal protection when some voters have a much greater chance of casting a ballot that won't count than other voters in the same state. Could it be that this disparity violates *Bush*'s admonition against "arbitrary and disparate treatment [which] value[s] one person's vote over that of another"? On the other hand, the Court was explicit in *Bush* that the question before it was not "whether local entities, in the exercise of their expertise, may develop different systems for implementing elections." That language and the "many complexities" language seemed to indicate a narrow reading of the case.

Furthermore, it is not clear what level of scrutiny would apply to a *Bush* claim. Does the "arbitrary and capricious" language suggest rational basis? But note that the two main cases relied upon by the Court, *Reynolds* and *Harper*, are now thought of as the cases establishing strict scrutiny for voting as a fundamental right.

Now that you have thought this through on your own, the next section describes how *Bush* has fared in the courts since 2000. (Shortcut answer: so far, not well.)

12.2. THE FIGHT OVER VOTER IDENTIFICATION LAWS, AND BROADER DISPUTES OVER ELECTION ADMINISTRATION LAWS SINCE 2000

The Florida controversy had a number of important ramifications for U.S. elections. In 2002, Congress passed the Help America Vote Act to provide money to replace old and poor voting technology and to set up a bipartisan agency, the U.S. Election Assistance Commission ("EAC"), to certify voting technology and provide research and best practices information for state and local election officials. Election administrators and others worked on improving ballot design. Reformers filed lawsuits to try to force further improvements in the rules and technology for running elections.

Partisanship and localism did not disappear, however. No states used the Florida dispute as a reason to abandon partisan election administration, or to take primary power for election administration away from local bodies. Instead, races for secretaries of state became more partisan, and fights on the state and local levels over election rules became more common. People now pay more attention to changes in election administration, and are quick to accuse the other side of malfeasance. The EAC became mired in partisan controversy, and since before the 2012 elections it has had no confirmed commissioners, because many Republican senators believe the EAC should be disbanded.

Parties and others became more willing to sue over election rules and to use election law as part of a political strategy. The rate of election litigation more than doubled in the period since Florida 2000 compared to before it.[8] Part of the reason for the increased litigation is that people are more willing to sue to gain political advantage. Part of the reasons for the increase is the passage of new laws, which raise new ambiguities and in some cases constitutional challenges. Increasingly, Republican-dominated legislatures are passing laws that make it harder to register or cast ballots, whereas Democratic-dominated legislatures are passing laws that make it easier to register and cast ballots. Defenders say the laws are necessary to prevent voter fraud (Republican talking point), empower voters (Democratic talking point), and instill public confidence in the electoral process (both parties' talking point). Cynics say that both sides pass these laws with the aims of attaining partisan advantage at the polls. Empirical evidence over the effect of these laws on overall turnout and on party advantage remains uncertain. But the trend toward continued "voting wars" seems clear.

In the face of all of this partisan wrangling, one question has been about the role courts will play in policing election administration rules. After *Bush v. Gore*, some scholars and lawyers believed that its equal protection holding would lead to court-forced improvements to election administration. There was a vigorous scholarly debate on whether the opinion had precedential value and, if so, what the case meant and which standard of review applied.[9]

---

8. LOWENSTEIN, HASEN, & TOKAJI, at 287.
9. Edward B. Foley, *The Future of Bush v. Gore?*, 68 OHIO ST. L.J. 925 (2007); Richard L. Hasen, *Bush v. Gore and the Future of Equal Protection Law in Elections*, 29 FLA. ST. U. L. REV. 377 (2001); Daniel H. Lowenstein, *The Meaning of Bush v. Gore*, 68 OHIO ST. L.J. 1007 (2007); Nelson Lund, *The Unbearable Rightness of Bush v. Gore*, 23 CARDOZO L REV. 1219 (2002); Daniel P. Tokaji, *Leave It to the Lower Courts: On Judicial Intervention in Election Administration*, 68 OHIO ST. L.J. 1065, 1068-1072 (2007).

There were some initial judicial successes, particularly cases in which public interest lawyers challenged the use of punch card voting machines in some parts of a jurisdiction but not the entire jurisdiction as a Bush v. Gore violation. However, within a few years, federal appellate courts limited or reversed those holdings, ruling that Bush did not compel uniformity in the use of election machinery or election rules.[10] Bush claims arose in a host of cases involving recounts as well, but the case never seemed to play a major role in court decisions involving these recounts. Until the 2012 election, it looked as if Bush claims were all but dead. The Supreme Court has never cited Bush v. Gore in a majority or dissenting opinion since it was decided, even in other cases involving election administration.[11] It has been unclear when, if ever, Bush compels uniformity or a minimal level of competency in election administration.

In 2012, however, there was something of a revival of Bush v. Gore claims in the Sixth Circuit in two important cases.[12] In one case, a conservative panel of the United States Court of Appeals for the Sixth Circuit — a court that had shown itself bitterly divided along party and ideological lines on election issues in 2008 — unanimously held that Ohio's disenfranchisement of voters for voting in the wrong polling location because of poll worker error likely violated the Equal Protection Clause.[13] In the other case, the Obama campaign argued that Ohio's contraction of the early voting period to exclude the weekend before the election for all voters except certain military voters violated the Equal Protection Clause under Bush v. Gore.[14] The campaign made this argument despite the fact that Ohio provided 23 days of early voting and had for the first time sent all Ohio voters a no-excuse absentee ballot application. It remains to be seen whether this expansion will go beyond the Sixth Circuit or even whether it will have broader applications in the Sixth Circuit.

Although Bush v. Gore itself has not played a major role in post-2000 litigation over election rules, federal courts have been deeply involved in resolving election administration disputes. The most important post-Bush election administration case to reach the Supreme Court, Crawford v. Marion County Election Board,[15] concerned the most high-profile election administration issue since 2000: voter identification laws.

---

10. For a chronicling of these cases, see Richard L. Hasen, The Untimely Death of Bush v. Gore, 60 STAN. L. REV. 1 (2007).

11. Justice Thomas cited Bush v. Gore in a 2013 concurring opinion involving the Elections Clause on an issue having nothing to do with Bush v. Gore's equal protection holding. Arizona v. Inter Tribal Council, 133 S.Ct. 2247, 2268 n.2 (2013) (Thomas, J., concurring). More on that case in the final section of this chapter.

12. This paragraph draws on Richard L. Hasen, The 2012 Voting Wars, Judicial Backstops, and the Resurrection of Bush v. Gore, 81 GEO. WASH. L. REV. 1865 (2013).

13. Ne. Ohio Coal. for the Homeless v. Husted, 696 F.3d 580, 597-598 (6th Cir. 2012).

14. Obama for Am. v. Husted, 697 F.3d 423, 428-429, 436-437 (6th Cir. 2012).

15. 553 U.S. 181 (2008).

States use various means to identify voters casting votes at the polls or via absentee/vote-by-mail ballots, from signature matching to requiring some proof of identification at the polls such as a utility bill or driver's license number. Beginning in the mid-2000s, Republican legislators started pushing for stricter voter identification laws, on grounds that such laws would prevent voter fraud and keep public confidence in the fairness of the electoral process. Democrats contended that such laws were designed to suppress the votes of Democratic voters, and that they would not have an effect on voter confidence. All but one of the states passing new voter identification laws had Republican legislatures (the exception was Democratic-majority Rhode Island, but its law was considerably less strict than the laws passed in other states).

One of the first states to pass a strict law was Indiana. The ACLU and other organizations brought suit in federal court, arguing that the law violated the Equal Protection Clause of the Fourteenth Amendment. The case was a *facial challenge* — that is, a challenge to the law as applied to everyone. This is in contrast to an *as-applied challenge*, which argues that the law is unconstitutional as applied to a person or class of people.

The case proceeded without much evidence on both sides. The state could point to no evidence that impersonation fraud (where one person goes to the polls claiming to be someone else) was a problem. Indeed, the state conceded there were no cases of such impersonation fraud in Indiana. But the plaintiffs could not produce many voters who (1) lacked identification; (2) would have a difficult time getting identification; and (3) wanted to vote. Plaintiffs claimed they did not need to produce such evidence because they were bringing a facial challenge.

A federal district court rejected plaintiffs' challenge, citing a lack of evidence on plaintiffs' side. The United States Court of Appeals for the Seventh Circuit affirmed in a divided opinion. Judge Richard A. Posner, writing for the majority, believed the law was targeted at Democrats but believed the law did not impose a large burden:[16]

> Even though it is exceedingly difficult to maneuver in today's America without a photo ID (try flying, or even entering a tall building such as the courthouse in which we sit, without one), and as a consequence the vast majority of adults have such identification, the Indiana law will deter some people from voting. A great many people who are eligible to vote don't bother to do so. Many do not register, and many who do register still don't vote, or vote infrequently. The benefits of voting to the individual voter are elusive (a vote in a political election rarely has any *instrumental* value, since elections for political office at the state or federal level are never decided by just one vote), and even very slight costs in time or bother or out-of-pocket expense deter many people from

---

16. *Crawford v. Marion County Election Bd.*, 472 F.3d 949 (7th Cir. 2007).

voting, or at least from voting in elections they're not much interested in. So some people who have not bothered to obtain a photo ID will not bother to do so just to be allowed to vote, and a few who have a photo ID but forget to bring it to the polling place will say what the hell and not vote, rather than go home and get the ID and return to the polling place.

Judge Terence Evans dissented:

> Let's not beat around the bush: The Indiana voter photo ID law is a not-too-thinly-veiled attempt to discourage election-day turnout by certain folks believed to skew Democratic. We should subject this law to strict scrutiny — or at least, in the wake of *Burdick v. Takushi*, something akin to "strict scrutiny light" — and strike it down as an undue burden on the fundamental right to vote.

When the case made it to the Supreme Court, the Court divided 3-3-3. Justice Stevens, writing for himself, Chief Justice Roberts, and Justice Kennedy, rejected the facial challenge to the law but left open the possibility of plaintiffs facing significant burdens from the law (such as those who could not afford the underlying documents to get a free voter identification card) to bring an as-applied challenge to the law. The Stevens opinion applied the *Anderson-Burdick* flexible balancing test (described in Chapter 10.4 in relation to minor party challenges to ballot access and related restrictions[17]) to the challenged law. The plurality did not apply *Bush v. Gore*'s "arbitrary and disparate treatment" standard, nor did it apply strict scrutiny. Instead, it found the burden under the *Anderson-Burdick* test to be minor for most voters and the law justified by important enough state interests in preventing voter fraud and instilling state confidence. "For most voters who need them, the inconvenience of making a trip to the [Bureau of Motor Vehicles], gathering the required documents, and posing for a photograph surely does not qualify as a substantial burden on the right to vote, or even represent a significant increase over the usual burdens of voting."

---

17. As explained in that chapter,

> Here is how the Court phrased the test in *Timmons*:

> > When deciding whether a state election law violates First and Fourteenth Amendment associational rights, we weigh the "character and magnitude" of the burden the State's rule imposes on those rights against the interests the State contends justify that burden, and consider the extent to which the State's concerns make the burden necessary. Regulations imposing severe burdens on plaintiffs' rights must be narrowly tailored and advance a compelling state interest. Lesser burdens, however, trigger less exacting review, and a State's "important regulatory interests" will usually be enough to justify "reasonable, nondiscriminatory restrictions." No bright line separates permissible election-related regulation from unconstitutional infringements on First Amendment freedoms.

Regarding the lack of evidence that impersonation fraud posed a significant problem to justify the law, Justice Stevens wrote

> The only kind of voter fraud that [Indiana's law] addresses is in-person voter impersonation at polling places. The record contains no evidence of any such fraud actually occurring in Indiana at any time in its history. Moreover, petitioners argue that provisions of the Indiana Criminal Code punishing such conduct as a felony provide adequate protection against the risk that such conduct will occur in the future. It remains true, however, that flagrant examples of such fraud in other parts of the country have been documented throughout this Nation's history by respected historians and journalists, that occasional examples have surfaced in recent years, and that Indiana's own experience with fraudulent voting in the 2003 Democratic primary for East Chicago Mayor — though perpetrated using absentee ballots and not in-person fraud — demonstrate that not only is the risk of voter fraud real but that it could affect the outcome of a close election.

One footnote to the section pointed to evidence from Boss Tweed's corrupt New York machine in 1868 and another footnote pointed to a single case of impersonation fraud in a 2004 Washington state gubernatorial election.

Justice Scalia, writing for himself, Justice Alito, and Justice Thomas, took a different view of the *Anderson-Burdick* balancing test. While Justice Stevens and the dissenters seemed to view the balancing test as a flexible one, much like a dimmer switch,[18] Justice Scalia viewed it as an on/off switch: Significant burdens are subject to strict scrutiny, and minor burdens get something like rational basis review. There is no middle ground. Justice Scalia, believing the law imposed little burden on most voters, would have upheld the law against a rational basis review. Unlike the Stevens opinion, the Scalia opinion seems to leave no opening for as-applied challenges.

The three dissenting justices, Justices Souter, Ginsburg, and Breyer, agreed with the Justice Stevens plurality that the *Burdick-Anderson* flexible standard applied. The dissenters believed that the law imposed greater burdens on voters, and that the state failed to demonstrate that its interests were strong enough to defeat the voters. The dissenters would have struck down the law facially — for all voters in Indiana.

Developments after *Crawford* have been quite interesting. Federal courts generally continue to reject facial federal Equal Protection challenges to voter identification laws. Few as-applied challenges have been brought. States have made voter identification laws even tougher, with some of the newest ones in North Carolina and Texas not allowing student identifications to count. These laws have been challenged under Section 2 of the Voting Rights

---

18. Justin Levitt, *Crawford — More Rhetorical Bark Than Legal Bite?*, Brennan Center, May 2, 2008, http://www.brennancenter.org/blog/archives/crawford_more_rhetorical_bark_than_legal_bite/.

Act. As explained in the last chapter, those challenges have only a moderate chance of success. Challenges in state court, often under state constitutions, have had greater success, with laws blocked (at least temporarily) in Missouri, Pennsylvania, and Wisconsin. As this book went to press, a federal district court, purportedly applying the *Anderson-Burdick* standard in *Crawford*, struck down Wisconsin's voter identification law.[19] It is not clear whether this ruling will survive appeal.

Judge Posner wrote in a recent book that he may have been wrong in the *Crawford* case: "I plead guilty to having written the majority opinion (affirmed by the Supreme Court) upholding Indiana's requirement that prospective voters prove their identity with a photo ID—a type of law now widely regarded as a means of voter suppression rather than fraud prevention."[20] Many people now seem skeptical, too, that voter identification laws stop much fraud[21] or promote voter confidence in the fairness of the electoral process.[22] But Democratic predictions that the law would disenfranchise thousands of voters also seems not to have materialized. *New York Times* correspondent Ethan Bronner summed up the fight this way: "To quote Jorge Luis Borges on the Falklands war, 'It's a fight between two bald men over a comb.'"[23] Nonetheless, in the most recent cases out of Wisconsin and Pennslvania, judges found that there were hundreds of thousands of voters lacking identification and without easy access to state-issued "free" identifications (usually to get the identification one must produce a birth certificate or other documentation which costs time and money to obtain). The empirical debate continues to rage.

---

19. *Frank v. Walker*, ___ F.Supp.2d ___, 2014 WL 1775431 (E.D. Wis, 2014).
20. Richard A. Posner, Reflections on Judging (2013); Richard L. Hasen, *Why Judge Posner Changed His Mind on Voter ID Laws*, Daily Beast, Oct. 23, 2013, http://www.thedailybeast.com/articles/2013/10/23/why-judge-posner-is-right-on-voter-id-laws.html; John Schwartz, *Judge in Landmark Case Disavows Support for Voter ID*, N.Y. Times, Oct. 15, 2013, at A16, http://www.nytimes.com/2013/10/16/us/politics/judge-in-landmark-case-disavows-support-for-voter-id.html. He has since moved away from that claim, saying only he is sure he "may" have been wrong. Richard A. Posner, *I Did Not "Recant" on Voter ID Laws*, New Republic (Oct. 27, 2013), http://www.newrepublic.com/article/115363/richard-posner-i-did-not-recant-my-opinion-voter-id.
21. I make the point that these laws stop virtually no fraud in chapter 2 of The Voting Wars.
22. The Supreme Court in an earlier case, *Purcell v. Gonzalez*, 549 U.S. 1 (2006), expressed the view that voter fraud could suppress turnout and therefore voter identification laws could boost turnout. A subsequent study demonstrated that voter confidence in the electoral process is not correlated with the presence or absence of a voter identification law in a state. Stephen Ansolabehere & Nathaniel Persily, *Vote Fraud in the Eye of the Beholder: The Role of Public Opinion in the Challenge to Voter Identification Requirements*, 121 Harv. L. Rev. 1737 (2008).
23. Margaret Sullivan, *Ethan Bronner Discusses "Core Issue" About Voting*, N.Y. Times, Public Editor's Journal, Sept. 24, 2012, http://publiceditor.blogs.nytimes.com/2012/09/24/ethan-bronner-discusses-the-core-issue-about-voting/.

The broader implications of *Crawford* and the voter identification debate are unclear. Exactly how and when the *Anderson-Burdick* balancing test should apply instead of a *Bush v. Gore* or otherwise "strict scrutiny" standard remain uncertain.[24] Critics such as me argue that the Court needs to follow Judge Evans and apply something like "strict scrutiny lite" or at least require the state to come forward with real evidence that laws serve important state interests — rather than simply listing possibilities such as preserving voter confidence or preventing voter fraud.[25] The issues are especially difficult to analyze when there is both a partisan and racial dimension to some of these laws. North Carolina's strict set of voting rules has been attacked in court under the Voting Rights Act as well as under state and federal constitutional provisions protecting all voters.

New lawsuits have targeted cutbacks in early voting and same-day voter registration, rules regarding the counting of provisional ballots cast in the wrong precinct, and a variety of other election law changes. It is hard to see how a cutback on the number of early voting days counts as a severe burden, especially because some states offer no early voting opportunities. (Are states that require voting in person only on election day and absentee balloting only with a proven excuse imposing severe burdens on voters?) One fascinating question is whether courts will adopt something of a "nonretrogression" principle in election law cases:[26] After a state enacts a voter-friendly measure such as early voting, may it then cut back on such measures for partisan reasons?[27] That might discourage the expansion of voting rights to begin with.

This is a fertile and uncertain area of the law, and I have little doubt that some of the courts' most interesting and controversial election law cases in the next decade will be in this area.

Example 2

The state of Pacifica lets each county pick its voting technology for use in elections. Some counties in the state use optical scan voting technology, in which a voter uses a pencil to bubble in choices on a piece of paper. The paper is then fed into a machine and the votes counted by a computer. Any recounts are done manually with a visual inspection of the ballot to

---

24. Christopher S. Elmendorf & Edward B. Foley, *Gatekeeping vs. Balancing in the Constitutional Law of Elections: Methodological Uncertainty on the High Court*, 17 Wm. & Mary Bill of Rts. J. 507 (2008).
25. Richard L. Hasen, *Race or Party? How Courts Should Think About Republican Efforts to Make It Harder to Vote in North Carolina and Elsewhere*, 127 Harv. L. Rev. F. 58 (2014).
26. For the original meaning of nonretrogression in the Voting Rights Act context, *see* Chapter 10.1.
27. On this point, *see* Richard L. Hasen, *The 2012 Voting Wars, Judicial Backstops, and the Resurrection of Bush v. Gore*, 81 Geo. Wash. L. Rev. 1865 (2013).

determine the intent of the voter. Other counties in the state use "ATM"-style touchscreen voting machines in which voters select their choices by touching a computer screen, which records their voices. Each machine's recorded votes are later sent as a "ballot image report" to a central location electronically for counting. In the event of a recount involving touch screen voting machines, each machine's "ballot image report" is generated again and sent to a central location electronically for counting.

Plaintiffs, who oppose electronic voting machines because they believe they are susceptible to hacking and manipulation, file a lawsuit arguing, among other things, that the different manual recount procedures for optically scanned ballots and touchscreen-recorded ballots violate Equal Protection.

What level of scrutiny should the court use to evaluate this claim? How should the court decide this claim?

Explanation

The facts in this case are based upon *Wexler v. Anderson*, 452 F.3d 1226 (11th Circ. 2006), involving Florida's voting machines. The court, applying the flexible *Anderson-Burdick* balancing test, rejected the challenge. This seems to be the right result under existing law: It does not appear that these recount rules impose severe burdens on voters, and thus under the flexible balancing test something like rational basis scrutiny should apply. Nor have courts so far read *Bush v. Gore* to require uniformity in voting machinery throughout a state.

The reason for differing recount rules in this case stems from the use of different technology. Note that the claim here is not, as in the punch card litigation, that the touchscreen machines are less reliable than the other machines in counting votes. The claim instead is that the machines are untrustworthy during a recount in some undefined way. *Wexler*'s result is typical; constitutional challenges to electronic voting technology have failed in the lower courts.[28] This is a function of both the low level of scrutiny as well as the lack of evidence that the electronic machinery is unreliable.

Still, just because something is constitutional does not make it a good idea. Florida, facing controversy over the use of its touchscreen machines in a 2006 congressional election in which thousands of voters apparently failed to vote in a tight congressional race thanks to poor ballot design, no longer uses this technology.[29]

---

28. Lowenstein, Hasen, & Tokaji, at 298.
29. Laurin Frisina et al., *Ballot Formats, Touchscreens, and Undervotes: A Study of the 2006 Midterm Elections in Florida*, 7 Election L.J. 25 (2008), http://www.liebertonline.com/doi/abs/10.1089/elj.2008.7103; on voting technology issues generally, *see* Charles Stewart III, *Voting Technologies*, 14 Annual Rev. of Pol. Sci. 353 (2011), http://www.annualreviews.org/doi/pdf/10.1146/annurev.polisci.12.053007.145205.

12.3. NVRA, HAVA, UOCAVA, AND LIMITS ON THE FEDERAL POWER TO REGULATE ELECTIONS

The last two sections of this chapter illustrate the central role that state and local governments play in U.S. election administration. Local election administrators make many of the key decisions about how to run elections, supplemented and to some extent supervised by state law and state election officials.

Yet the federal government has come to play a key role as well in election administration, and as we will see, in recent years the federal role in elections has come under attack by state officials seeking to prevent what they see as national encroachment on state and local prerogatives.

Sources of Federal Power. Congress cannot legislate absent an express grant of power in the Constitution. The three main grants of power relevant to elections are the power to enforce the Equal Protection Clause of the Fourteenth Amendment,[30] the power to enforce the ban on racial discrimination in voting in the Fifteenth Amendment,[31] and the Elections Clause of Article I, section 4, which provides that "[t]he times, places and manner of holding elections for Senators and Representatives, shall be prescribed in each state by the legislature thereof; but the Congress may at any time by law make or alter such regulations, except as to the places of choosing Senators."[32] Note that the Elections Clause gives Congress the power to regulate congressional elections but not state and local elections.[33]

Major Federal Election Legislation. Congress has passed some major election legislation in the last 50 years, including the Voting Rights Act (discussed in Chapter 11) and various campaign finance laws (discussed in Chapters 13-16). In addition, the most important pieces of congressional legislation in this area are the National Voter Registration Act (NVRA), the Help America Vote Act (HAVA), and the Uniform Overseas Citizen Absentee Voting Act (UOCAVA).

---

30. U.S. Const. Amend. XIV, §5.
31. U.S. Const. Amend. XV, §2.
32. Congress may have additional powers to regulate elections as well that are mainly untested in the courts, such as its Article IV power to guarantee that states have a "Republican form of government."
33. Presidential elections take place with congressional elections, so one might think that the powers are co-extensive. However, there is a question whether Congress could, for example, establish the dates for presidential primaries. Richard L. Hasen, *"Too Plain for Argument?" The Uncertain Congressional Power to Require Parties to Choose Presidential Nominees Through Direct and Equal Primaries*, 102 Nw. U. L. Rev. 2009 (2008).

- **NVRA.**[34] Congress passed this law in 1993, and it is commonly known as the "motor voter law" because of Section 5 of the act, which requires state departments of motor vehicles to offer voter registration for federal elections to people getting new or renewed drivers licenses. Section 6 provides that voters must be allowed to register for elections by mail using a form approved by the U.S. Election Assistance Commission (EAC).[35] Section 7 of the act requires that offices of public assistance and those providing services to persons with disabilities need to offer voter registration materials to clients. Section 8 of the act contains various provisions regarding how states must maintain their voter registration database, including a provision for purging ineligible voters from the rolls. Perhaps unsurprisingly, the DOJ under Democratic administrations has been more concerned with enforcing Section 7's provisions on making voter registration materials available at public assistance agencies, whereas DOJ under Republican administrations has been more concerned with the voter purge provisions of Section 8.
- **HAVA.**[36] Congress passed HAVA in 2002 in response to the 2000 Florida debacle. As already noted in this chapter, HAVA provided funding to states to replace outdated voting machinery. It also created the EAC with responsibilities for maintaining the federal mail-in voter registration form, certifying various voting technology, and providing resources and best practices for election administration. The EAC maintains a staff, but it has been hobbled in acting for the last few years because Senate Republicans have refused to approve Democratic commissioners or to nominate the two Republican commissioners to the commission. HAVA was compromise legislation between Democrats, who were concerned primarily with issues of voter access, and Republicans, who were concerned more with voter integrity. Accordingly, one key part of HAVA requires states to update and maintain statewide voter registration databases, a provision that shifted some power away from local governments and toward states. Another part required that anyone showing up asking to vote at an election must be given a "provisional ballot" to cast; the law does not require states to accept the provisional ballot for counting, but only to accept it (for possible administrative or court action later).[37]

---

34. 42 U.S.C.§1973gg. et seq.

35. The Federal Election Commission initially had this responsibility, but HAVA transferred it to the EAC, an issue to which we return later in this chapter.

36. 42 U.S.C.§15301 et seq.

37. Some early HAVA cases considered whether the law requires states to accept for counting in races for which a voter is eligible to vote ballots that were cast by voters in the wrong precinct. Courts ruled that HAVA does not require voters to count such ballots. *Sandusky Cnty. Dem. Party v. Blackwell*, 387 F.3d 565 (6th Cir. 2004).

- **UOCAVA.**[38] This 1986 act, supplemented by the 2009 Military and Overseas Voters Empowerment Act (MOVE Act), provides protections for military and overseas voters. Among other things, it provides a postcard to be used by this population for voter registration and requesting an absentee ballot, as well as for a "fail safe" federal ballot to be able to vote in federal races in the event the overseas person fails to receive a state absentee ballot. The MOVE Act adds electronic transmissions of certain documents to facilitate voting. One of the key provisions of the law requires overseas and military ballots to be transmitted at least 45 days before an election. This means that disputes over ballot access and other issues — disputes that often get resolved at the last minute — need to be resolved sooner thanks to this law.

One of the key unanswered questions under these statutes is where Congress's power under the Elections Clause ends and a state's power to set voter qualifications begin. A recent Supreme Court case, *Arizona v. Inter Tribal Council of Arizona*,[39] raises more questions than it answers on this question.

Inter Tribal involves that federal form for voter registration, which the NVRA specifies that states are required to "accept and use" for registration in federal elections. The form does not require registrants to provide citizenship information to register. Arizona law did require such information, and Arizona did not want to accept the federal form without such information being included for those who tried to register in Arizona. Justice Scalia, in a 7-2 opinion for the Court, held that Congress's Elections Clause power is broad, and that states must accept and use the federal form for federal elections and cannot reject it for lack of citizenship information:

> When Congress legislates with respect to the "Times, Places and Manner" of holding congressional elections, it *necessarily* displaces some element of a preexisting legal regime erected by the States. Because the power the Elections Clause confers is none other than the power to pre-empt, the reasonable assumption is that the statutory text accurately communicates the scope of Congress's pre-emptive intent. Moreover, the federalism concerns underlying the presumption in the Supremacy Clause context are somewhat weaker here. Unlike the States' "historic police powers," the States' role in regulating congressional elections — while weighty and worthy of respect — has always existed subject to the express qualification that it "terminates according to federal law." In sum, there is no compelling reason not to read Elections Clause legislation simply to mean what it says.

---

38. 42 U.S.C. §1973ff et seq.
39. 133 S.Ct. 2247 (2013).

We conclude that the fairest reading of the statute is that a state-imposed requirement of evidence of citizenship not required by the Federal Form is "inconsistent with" the NVRA's mandate that States "accept and use" the Federal Form. If this reading prevails, the Elections Clause requires that Arizona's rule give way.

Although that may sound like a rousing win for the federal government's power of the states when it comes to elections, the rest of the opinion explained that it was not so simple. Recall that the Constitution gives the states the power to set voter *qualifications*, such as the choice whether or not felons are allowed to vote. Justice Scalia, for the majority, wrote that "it would raise serious constitutional doubts if a federal statute precluded a State from obtaining the information necessary to enforce its voting qualifications." Justice Scalia then suggested that Arizona seek permission from the EAC to change the federal form to include citizenship information for Arizona, and that Arizona sue if the EAC did not give such permission.

How courts would resolve the constitutional dispute if EAC commissioners would have refused to change the federal form to include citizenship information for Arizona residents is a complicated enough question. But the question is further muddied because (as of the writing of this book) the EAC has no commissioners. Arizona and Kansas (which also wants the citizenship information) sued the EAC. The EAC executive director issued an opinion rejecting Arizona's request to include citizenship information. A federal district court held that the EAC's director likely did not have authority to speak for the EAC, but even if he did, the EAC was required to include a request for citizenship information on the form for use in Arizona and Kansas.[40] The case is currently on appeal.

While the case was pending, Arizona and Kansas took steps to establish "dual" registration systems: one for congressional elections, in which voters registered using the federal form would be included on the registration rolls, and one for state and local elections excluding those voters because they failed to provide citizenship information. Congress's Elections Clause power, you will recall, applies only to federal elections. Voting rights groups have now challenged the dual registration system as a violation of the Equal Protection Clause.

Inter Tribal raises broader questions about the distinction between a rule setting the "time, place, and manner" of an election and a rule setting a "voter qualification."

---

40. *Kobach v. U.S. Elec. Assist. Comm'n*, ___ F. Supp. 2d ___, 2014 WL 1094957 (D. Kansas, Mar. 19, 2014).

Example 3

Congress passes a statute barring a state from imposing a photographic voter identification requirement for voting in federal elections, unless the state agrees to accept, among other forms, drivers licenses, passports, student identifications issued by colleges, and a utility bill and sworn affidavit from a voter in lieu of a voter id.

The state of Pacifica challenges such a law as impinging on its right to set voter qualifications. Is such a law unconstitutional?

Explanation

The congressional statute is fictional. The answer to this question is unclear after *Inter Tribal*. On the one hand, a law setting the rules for voter identification in federal elections looks like a permissible exercise of Congress's power under the Elections Clause to set the "manner" for voting in federal elections. On the other hand, the state could argue that it has the right to set voter qualifications, and embedded in that right is the right to verify identity to ensure that persons showing up to vote are actually qualified to vote.

Inter Tribal does not define what a voter qualification is, but it does express doubts about whether the federal government can keep a state from getting the "information necessary to enforce its voter qualifications." If that's right, it means that Congress actually lost power in the *Inter Tribal* case rather than gaining it. This in turn raises another question: Why would the four liberal Supreme Court justices sign onto this part of Justice Scalia's opinion that increases state power over elections against Congress?[41]

In the meantime, we must consider what steps can be taken to encourage states to improve their election administration practices, short of federal mandates to do so.[42]

---

41. *See* Richard L. Hasen, *Are the Liberal Justices Savvy or Suckers? They Are Playing to Beat John Roberts at His Long Game*, SLATE, July 1, 2013, http://www.slate.com/articles/news_and_politics/ jurisprudence/2013/07/are_the_liberals_on_the_supreme_court_savvy_or_suckers.html.
42. HEATHER K. GERKEN, THE DEMOCRACY INDEX (2012), considers use of a ratings system to motivate states to improve their election administration.

PART IV

Campaign Finance

Introduction to Campaign Finance: Spending Limits from *Buckley* to *Citizens United*

13.1. INTRODUCTION

We turn now in the final part of this book to the large and complex question of whether and how to regulate money in politics. Campaign strategist Mark Hanna once said: "There are two things that are important in politics. The first is money, and I can't remember what the second one is."[1] In any privately financed electoral system, candidates and others attempting to influence voters' choices need money for the campaign. Money rents office space; funds flyers; pays for television, radio, and Internet advertising; bankrolls campaign travel; and covers other campaign expenses. Campaigns are expensive, especially for major offices in larger states: Total campaign spending in the United States runs into the billions of dollars in election years.

But privately financed campaigns raise potential problems. When campaign contributions are exchanged for official action, that constitutes a bribe (as described in Chapter 3). Even when there is no bribery, money may still influence official action, which some people find improper. Time spent fundraising by elected officials takes time away from officials to do government business. If wealth affects the outcome of elections or legislative policy, then the wealthy may have more influence than others, raising

---

1. Jacob S. Hacker & Nathaniel Loewentheil, *How Big Money Corrupts the Economy*, DEMOCRACY: A JOURNAL OF IDEAS, Winter 2013, http://www.democracyjournal.org/27/how-big-money-corrupts-the-economy.php.

equality concerns. The public's confidence also could be negatively affected if people believe that money is driving political outcomes. We can summarize these main interests in regulation as follows:

- **Preventing corruption**
- **Preserving elected officials' time for legislative activities**
- **Promoting political equality**
- **Instilling public confidence**

Behind these generalized labels are many nuances we will explore later in this part of the book.

Some have long favored campaign finance laws to serve these and other interests. The main types of laws that governments have adopted regulating campaign financing are

- **Spending limits:** These laws limit the amount that an individual, entity, or candidate may spend on an election. For instance, until recently, federal law prevented business corporations from spending their general treasury funds in federal candidate elections.
- **Contribution limits:** These laws limit how much an individual or entity may give to a candidate, party, committee, or other entity for election related purposes. For instance, in the 2014 election season, an individual may give no more than $2,600 per candidate per election.
- **Disclosure laws**: These laws require donors or the recipients of donations to disclose information about contributions and/or spending. For example, federal campaign committees must disclose the name, address, employer, and amount of contribution for each contributor who contributes at least $200 in the aggregate to a campaign.
- **Public financing:** These laws provide funding to candidates for office in exchange for the candidates agreeing to abide by certain rules. For example, major party presidential candidates participating in the federal government's voluntary public financing program receive tens of millions of dollars for use in the general election in exchange for an agreement not to raise private funds for the campaign.

Each of these types of law is controversial. Opponents argue that some or all campaign finance regulation is unnecessary, counterproductive, or otherwise bad public policy. Limits may entrench incumbents and public financing can fund fringe candidates. Disclosure may subject contributors to unpopular candidates to ridicule.

By far the most important criticism of U.S. campaign finance regulation is that campaign finance laws infringe on the rights of free speech and association guaranteed by the First Amendment of the United States Constitution. The story of the last 40 years of campaign finance law in the United

States has been one of regulation, litigation, and Supreme Court adjudication of numerous First Amendment claims. The Court's approach has been inconsistent, vacillating between periods of great deference to legislatively enacted laws and deep skepticism of such limits as a First Amendment infringement.

This chapter considers the basic constitutional framework for campaign finance laws and constitutional issues concerning spending limits. The next three chapters consider contribution limits, disclosure laws, and public financing.

Example 1

A medium-sized city passes a new law limiting contributions to city council candidates to $100 per person per election. Does such a law promote the interests behind campaign finance regulation? What are the dangers of such a law?

Explanation

As noted above, campaign finance limits could serve various government interests: anti-corruption, time preservation, political equality, and public confidence. The point of this question is to demonstrate that such laws might not serve all interests simultaneously. That is, one could make a case that low contribution limits might prevent corruption (by limiting the amount any one individual could give to a city council member), promote political equality (by ensuring many more people could give a maximum $100 campaign contribution, compared to the number of people who could comfortably max out with a $1,000 or $10,000 limit) and instill public confidence (if the public believes that low contributions minimize the risk of corruption or undue influence and promote political equality). These points are controversial and we will explore them more later, but the claims are plausible.

A very low limit, such as the $100 limit, however, would not serve the goal of time preservation for elected officials. If elected officials can only raise funds in $100 chunks, they will spend much of their time fundraising from as many people as possible, which will take away time from pursuing government business.

Of course, those who propose low limits likely do not want to take elected officials away from their legislative duties. But many proposed campaign finance laws can have unintended consequences. The example shows the difficulty of designing a campaign finance law that serves multiple interests simultaneously.

Furthermore, low limits present other possible dangers. What about the rights of those people who wish to give more to candidates? Some believe that it is a major infringement on First Amendment rights of speech and association to limit contributions, especially to such a low level. Very low limits could also benefit incumbents: Incumbents already have great name recognition and are likely to find it easier to raise funds than many challengers. A low limit could make fundraising tilt in favor of incumbents, which could help those incumbents win election.

The point of the example is to show you that even the simplest type of campaign finance law raises difficult empirical and theoretical questions — questions we will explore in this chapter.

13.2. THE *BUCKLEY v. VALEO* FRAMEWORK

13.2.1. Before *Buckley*: The History of U.S. Campaign Finance Law[2]

Modern federal campaign finance law dates back to the early 20th century, when through the Tillman Act Congress barred corporations from making contributions to federal candidates.[3] Congress periodically changed and updated its laws, such as when it imposed tougher disclosure regulations on political committees in the 1920s following the Teapot Dome scandal.[4] Notably, in the 1940s, Congress extended to labor unions the bar on corporate contributions to candidates;[5] the new law also prevented both kinds

---

2. This section draws from Richard L. Hasen, *The Nine Lives of* Buckley v. Valeo, in First Amendment Stories 345 (Richard Garnett & Andrew Koppelman, eds., 2011).

3. *See* Robert E. Mutch, Campaigns, Congress and the Courts: The Making of Federal Campaign Finance Law 1-23 (1988) and Adam Winkler, *"Other People's Money": Corporations, Agency Costs, and Campaign Finance Law*, 92 Geo. L.J. 871 (2004) for an overview on the origin of federal and state campaign contribution bans. *See also* Robert E. Mutch, *The First Federal Campaign Finance Bills*, 14 J. Pol'y Hist. 30 (2002) for a look at proposed federal campaign finance bills in the nineteenth century.

4. *See* Mutch, *supra*, at 24. The Teapot Dome scandal involved large contributions given to the Republican Party by Harry F. Sinclair of Sinclair Oil Corporation. The corporation "had leased Wyoming's Teapot Dome Oil reserve from the Interior Department. A Senate committee investigating these transactions, acting on rumors of a link between the Teapot Dome lease and developer's contributions to the Republican Party, discovered that Sinclair had indeed given sizeable sums to the GOP. . . . Although RNC officials denied any connection between the oil leases and the retiring of the 1920 party dept, their testimony . . . led Congress to require political committees to report financial activity for all years, even those in which no election is held." *Id.*

5. Congress did so for the duration of World War II in the Smith-Connally Act, in effect through the war, and then permanently in 1947 in the Taft-Hartley Act. Mutch, *supra*, at 152-153.

of organizations from independently spending their entity's funds supporting or opposing candidates to federal office.[6] Labor unions responded by setting up separate segregated funds, or political action committees (PACs), to engage in such spending through political contributions from union members rather than from the union's own coffers.

Although a number of federal campaign finance laws were on the books, through the first six decades of the twentieth century, they were rarely enforced.[7] Disclosure reports were often missing, incomplete, or wrong, and when filed they were difficult even for experts to inspect.[8] Enforcement was so lax that the Justice Department refused to prosecute 20 Nixon fundraising committees that had not filed a single report in the 1968 presidential campaign, or 107 congressional candidates who had violated disclosure rules, on grounds that "fair play" required adequate notice that violators of the law would actually be prosecuted.[9] From the 1920s until the 1970s, in the rare cases in which prosecutors went after those accused of corporate spending or disclosure violations, the prosecutions did not always lead to convictions.[10] The Supreme Court considered some First Amendment challenges to these laws over the years but mostly avoided deciding the constitutional questions.[11]

Although Congress considered a variety of additional campaign finance laws in the 1950s and 1960s, including contribution limitations, spending limitations, improved disclosure, public financing, and the creation of an independent agency to enforce campaign finance laws,[12] Congress did not pass any significant legislation in the area until the 1970s,[13] when it passed the Federal Election Campaign Act (FECA) of 1971 (which was actually signed into law in early 1972) and amendments to the FECA in 1974. What changed to allow for the passage of such legislation?

Great social upheavals beginning in the 1960s, including controversies over the Vietnam War and civil rights, contributed to a marked decline in

---

6. Id. at 155-157.

7. Julian E. Zelizer, Seeds of Cynicism: The Struggle over Campaign Finance, 1956-1974, 14 J. POL'Y HIST. 73, 76 (2002).

8. See MUTCH, supra, at 25-26 (reporting that Louise Overacker, a political scientist, was led to a tiny washroom near a congressional office, where party committee reports were stored, unlabeled in dusty paper-covered bundles on a top shelf).

9. Id. at 28 (citation omitted).

10. Allison Hayward, The Michigan Auto Dealers Prosecution: Exploring the Department of Justice's Mid-Century Posture Toward Campaign Finance Violations, 9 ELECTION L.J. 177 (2010); MUTCH, supra, at 28.

11. See MUTCH, supra, at 158-165.

12. MUTCH, at 29-42; Zelizer, supra, at 78-88; JULIAN E. ZELIZER, ON CAPITOL HILL: THE STRUGGLE TO REFORM CONGRESS AND ITS CONSEQUENCES, 1948-2000 51-52 (2004).

13. In 1966, Congress passed a bill providing for the public financing of presidential elections but repealed its implementation a year later. KURT HOHENSTEIN, COINING CORRUPTION: THE MAKING OF THE AMERICAN CAMPAIGN FINANCE SYSTEM 207 (2007).

public trust in the government.[14] In this environment, a coalition of "legislators, experts, philanthropists, foundations, and public interest groups" emerged who believed that the system of representative government could be improved through campaign finance reform.[15] In the 1970s the reform coalition found Congress more receptive to its message, in part because the increasing costs of campaigns[16] and the decline in the power of political parties[17] made some reforms in Congress's self-interest. For this reason, reform proposals in the 1970s began as those aimed at dealing with campaign costs.[18] Thus, in 1970, Congress passed a bill that, among other things, provided discount television airtime rates to candidates; President Nixon vetoed the law, claiming it was full of loopholes.[19]

In the early 1970s, Common Cause, a new group headed by John Gardner, a liberal Republican and a former member of Democratic president Lyndon B. Johnson's cabinet, spearheaded reform efforts.[20] The group built on public distrust to create an interest group aimed at reforming the political system and rooting out political corruption.[21] It relied heavily upon direct mail aimed at "well-educated people in the upper reaches of the income distribution."[22] By 1972 it had nearly 250,000 members.[23]

Common Cause's strategy was a mixture of lobbying Congress for reform, litigating over enforcement of existing campaign finance laws, and engaging the press in a sophisticated public relations strategy. The media covered stories of possible corruption with relish, drawing on the data mined by Common Cause and other groups.[24] Democrats walked a fine line between supporting the goals of Common Cause, which were popular with their constituents, and placating organized labor, which was suspicious of proposed campaign finance legislation.[25]

---

14. See MUTCH, *supra*, at 42-44 (citing ANDREW S. McFARLAND, COMMON CAUSE: LOBBYING IN THE PUBLIC INTEREST (1984)).

15. Zelizer, *supra*, at 74.

16. Id. at 74.

17. Id. at 77.

18. Id. at 88.

19. Id. at 89.

20. ZELIZER, *supra*, at 100.

21. Zelizer, *supra*, at 90; ZELIZER, *supra*, at 101-103.

22. MUTCH, *supra*, at 44; *see also* ZELIZER, *supra*, at 100.

23. MUTCH, *supra*, at 44.

24. See id. at 46; ZELIZER, *supra*, at 104.

25. Zelizer, *supra*, at 90. Labor had good reason to be concerned. As Congress debated the 1971 FECA bill, Republicans turned their attention to limiting the political activities of labor unions. In 1968, a St. Louis union, the Pipefitters Local Union 562, had been prosecuted for violating the prohibition on labor contributions to federal candidates. The union claimed that it had a constitutional right to contribute the funds, because they came not from the union's general treasury funds but from segregated PAC funds. *See* MUTCH, *supra*, at 160-163. A jury convicted the union, and the union's prosecution was upheld by the United States Court of Appeals for the Eighth Circuit. *U.S. v. Pipefitters Local*

The strategy worked, helped by Democrats' increasing interest in campaign finance reform as large donor money shifted from Democrats to Republicans after Nixon's 1968 election[26] and as Democrats endured Democratic presidential nominee Hubert Humphrey's lackluster fundraising in 1968. President Nixon signed the FECA in January 1972, strengthening disclosure requirements, expressly allowing for the creation of political action committees, repealing some ineffective contribution limitations, and forcing broadcasters to sell advertising to candidates at reduced rates.[27] One of its more controversial provisions limited federal candidate spending on media to $50,000 or less per election.[28] A related bill revived the plan for the public financing of presidential elections, but it was not to go into effect until the 1976 elections.[29]

After FECA passed, the reform community continued to push for greater regulation as allegations of improprieties involving the Nixon campaign came to light in the Watergate scandal. The group Public Citizen "filed a lawsuit claiming that the president accepted money from . . . milk co-ops in exchange for reversing a decision by the Department of Agriculture that had lowered milk prices."[30] Common Cause engaged in a concerted effort to gather and disseminate disclosure data mandated by the new law.[31] Common Cause also publicly pressured candidates to voluntarily reveal contributions received before the FECA disclosure provisions went into effect in April 1972. When Nixon finally relented in the face of public pressure and litigation by Common Cause and others, the campaign's disclosures revealed million-dollar contributions from some individuals, as well as millions of dollars in illegal contributions from corporations.[32]

Watergate revealed all kinds of abuses connected to the campaign finance system. Major corporations gave large sums to the Nixon campaign — the

---

Union No. 562, 434 F.2d 1116 (8th Cir. 1970). The Supreme Court agreed to hear the case while Congress was debating the FECA.

Some Republican members of Congress proposed including in the FECA limitations on union political activity, but Republican Representative Hansen, fearful of losing labor's support for the FECA, supported an amendment which allowed union political spending on communications with members, nonpartisan voter registration and get-out-the-vote activities, and contributions collected through a separate segregated fund. MUTCH, *supra*, at 162-163. After the FECA passed with the Hansen amendment, the Supreme Court struck down the union's conviction, holding it had a constitutional right to spend money collected from members through a separate PAC. *Pipefitters Local Union No. 562 v. U.S.*, 407 U.S. 385 (1972).

26. Zelizer, *supra* 8, at 92.
27. For a detailed description of the legislative history of the FECA, *see generally Campaign Spending: Major Reform Bill Neared Passage*, in CQ ALMANAC 1971, at 05-875-05-896 (27th ed., 1972), http://library.cqpress.com/cqalmanac/cqal71-1252749.
28. HOHENSTEIN, *supra*, at 208.
29. Zelizer, *supra*, at 94-95.
30. *Id.* at 95.
31. *See* MUTCH, *supra*, at 45; Zelizer, *supra*, at 95-96.
32. MUTCH, *supra*, at 45-46.

usual request was for $100,000[33] — despite the longstanding prohibition on corporate giving to federal candidates. American Airlines was the first corporation to plead guilty to funneling $55,000 in illegal corporate cash, laundered through a Lebanese agent and a Swiss bank, to the 1972 Nixon re-election effort.[34] Cash also arrived to the campaign in paper bags from millionaires. The secret cash allowed for all kinds of out-of-sight dirty tricks, such as breaking into offices of rivals, planting spies with opposition campaigns, and attempts at outright bribery of officials.[35]

Though Watergate brought unprecedented attention to illegal campaign activities of the Nixon reelection campaign, such activities were hardly so confined. An internal review of the activities of one major corporation, the Gulf Oil Company, revealed a pattern of the company making "domestic political contributions with corporate funds . . . . The activity was generally clandestine and in disregard of federal, as well as a number of state, statutes."[36] The Ervin commission investigating Watergate found evidence of illegal campaign contributions to Nixon and other candidates, including 1972 Democratic presidential nominee George McGovern.[37]

The Watergate scandal created momentum for further campaign finance reform: The public, for a time, became intensely interested in the issue, with "well over 25 percent of all mail [sent to members of Congress] in the post-Watergate period . . . on campaign finance, far more than on any other issue."[38] Democrats saw it as "a defining issue in 1974."[39]

The 1974 FECA amendments were debated at the same time as the Watergate hearings, trials, and investigations.[40] Facing public pressure to tighten campaign finance laws, Republicans joined Democrats in Congress in agreeing to strict contribution and spending limits in federal campaigns,

---

33. HERBERT E. ALEXANDER, FINANCING THE 1972 ELECTION 514 (1976).

34. Id. at 514.

35. Id. at 54-62, 489-493.

36. JOHN J. McCLOY, THE GREAT OIL SPILL: THE INSIDE REPORT: GULF OIL'S BRIBERY AND POLITICAL CHICANERY 31 (1976); see also Zelizer, supra, at 79 (recounting ways in which corporations violated federal law during the 1950s and 1960s).

37. Zelizer, supra, at 97.

38. MUTCH, supra, at 46.

39. Zelizer, supra, at 100. Professor Fleishman concludes that "[b]ut for the embarrassing and widening wake of Watergate — the plethora of illegal corporate campaign contributions, the illegal sale of high office in return for contributions, among others — there would very likely have been no new campaign finance reforms in 1974." Joel L. Fleishman, The 1974 Federal Election Campaign Act Amendments: The Shortcomings of Good Intentions, 1975 DUKE L.J. 851, 852 (1975).

40. See MUTCH, supra, at 48-50. For a detailed description of the legislative history of the 1974 FECA Amendments, see generally Congress Clears Campaign Financing Reform, in CQ ALMANAC 1974, at 611-633 (30th ed., 1975), http://library.cqpress.com/cqalmanac/cqal74-1221728.

public financing for presidential campaigns, and the creation of an independent agency, the Federal Election Commission (FEC), to administer the laws. As Congress considered the 1974 Amendments, much of the disagreement in Congress concerned whether public financing should be extended to congressional campaigns or be limited to presidential campaigns.[41] The final version of the FECA amendments reaching the president contained public financing for only presidential campaigns. President Nixon had threatened to veto the bill if it contained any public financing provisions, but he resigned before the FECA passed. President Ford, fearing political consequences and a congressional override if he vetoed the bill, signed the bill despite his dislike for it.[42] Among other things, the law imposed strict contribution and spending limits.

Not everyone was happy with the new campaign finance laws, especially those skeptical about government power, skepticism also nourished by the Vietnam War and corruption scandals. To opponents of the FECA, including the liberal American Civil Liberties Union, the Common Cause folks were "goo goos" (good government advocates) who were duped by self-interested incumbent politicians to urge the passage of laws aimed at squelching political competition. The ACLU saw prosecutions under the original 1971 FECA as the Nixon Justice Department targeting opponents for political motivations.[43]

Upon the passage of the 1974 Amendments, Senator James Buckley, one of the principal opponents of the law, "labeled the bill an incumbent protection measure because of its low spending limits. 'To offer this bill in the name of reform is an act of cynicism,' he said."[44] Key opposition to the law also came from Buckley and from Senator Eugene McCarthy, two senators who depended upon seed money from wealthy contributors to launch insurgent campaigns. Buckley was "a political newcomer who had won a Senate seat [as a third party candidate] from New York by being able to raise a significant amount of money from relatively few supporters; Senator Eugene McCarthy['s] 1968 presidential campaign [in the Democratic presidential primary against Lyndon Johnson] was funded in a similar way and managed to bring down a sitting president over the issue of the war in Vietnam."[45]

Opponents brought suit against the 1974 amendments in a case known as *Buckley v. Valeo* (Francis Valeo was the secretary of the Senate sued in his

---

41. Zelizer, *supra*, at 100-102.
42. *See* Mutch, *supra*, at 49; Zelizer, *supra*, at 123; John Samples, The Fallacy of Campaign Finance Reform 219 (2006); Christopher Lydon, *Campaign Reform Nears Court Test*, N.Y. Times, May 25, 1975, at 24.
43. Joel M. Gora, *Campaign Finance Reform: Still Searching Today for a Better Way*, 6 J. L. & Pol'y 137, 137-138 (1997) (footnotes omitted).
44. 1974 CQ Almanac, *supra*, at 633; Samples, *supra*, at 217.
45. Joel M. Gora, *The Legacy of* Buckley v. Valeo, 2 Election L.J. 55, 58 (2003).

official capacity). The *Buckley* plaintiffs were a group of "political underdogs and outsiders."[46] The coalition included Senators Buckley and McCarthy, "Stewart Mott, one of McCarthy's main backers; and an unusual assortment of groups like the Libertarian Party, the Mississippi Republican Party, the American Conservative Union, and the New York Civil Liberties Union."[47]

While the ACLU had been motivated primarily by a belief that campaign finance laws impinged on the right to criticize the government, many of the *Buckley* plaintiffs appeared more concerned with how such laws might benefit incumbents. "What united the various challengers was a belief that Congress' comprehensive regulations would make it more difficult for challengers to defeat incumbents, and for minor parties and independents to challenge the hegemony of the two major parties."[48] As Senator Buckley explained: "What we had in common was a concern that the restrictions imposed by the new law would squeeze independent voices out of the political process by making it even more difficult than it already was to raise effective challenges to the political status quo."[49] Though they were odd political bedfellows, the plaintiffs' lawyers believed that their unity against the FECA gave them "an even stronger bond."[50] Despite coming from the left and right side of the political spectrum, however, they "generally shared a libertarian ideological stance."[51]

Example 2

What role did the Watergate scandal of the 1970s play in lead up to *Buckley v. Valeo?*

Explanation

This question simply tests your ability to read a few pages of historical context leading up to the *Buckley* decision. The Watergate scandal involving President Nixon and related scandals energized both supporters and opponents of campaign finance reform. For supporters, the scandals showed that

---

46. James L. Buckley, *Bucks and Buckley: The Plaintiff Makes His Case*, NAT'L REV., Sept. 27, 1999, at 40.
47. Gora, *The Legacy, supra*, at 58.
48. BURT NEUBORNE, CAMPAIGN FINANCE REFORM & THE CONSTITUTION: A CRITICAL LOOK AT BUCKLEY V. VALEO 10 (1998), http://brennan.3cdn.net/f124fc7ebf928fb019_hqm6bn3w0.pdf.
49. JAMES L. BUCKLEY, GLEANINGS FROM AN UNPLANNED LIFE: AN ANNOTATED ORAL HISTORY 149 (2006).
50. MUTCH, *supra*, at 50 (quoting Joel Gora).
51. Ralph K. Winter, *The History and Theory of* Buckley v. Valeo, 6 J. L. & POL'Y 93, (1997-1998).

money was being used to buy influence in elections, often blatantly ignoring the weak set of campaign finance laws on the books. But to detractors of the new laws, Watergate revealed the abuses of government power and the steps that incumbents would take to protect their own interests. Both sides viewed the 1974 FECA amendments as the government's main response to Watergate, but they differed strongly over whether this response should be celebrated or condemned.

13.2.2. *Buckley*'s Major Holdings on Contributions and Expenditures[52]

The Supreme Court's 1976 *Buckley* case considered the constitutionality of much of the 1974 FECA Amendments. The FECA Amendments were complex, establishing (among other things) limits on the amounts that individuals or organizations could contribute to candidates (contribution limits), limits on the amounts that individuals or organizations could spend to support or oppose candidates for federal office independent of candidates (independent expenditure limits),[53] public financing for major presidential candidates, and the creation of the Federal Election Commission (FEC). One of the spending limits provisions made it illegal to spend more than $1,000 "relative to a clearly identified candidate" for federal office, which would have made it a felony to take out a reasonably sized advertisement in a newspaper supporting or opposing a candidate for office.

The *Buckley* plaintiffs challenged many of these decisions as violating the First Amendment. The Court upheld the FECA's contribution limits, struck down the expenditure limits, upheld the public financing system, and struck down the means for the appointment of members of the FEC.

Most notable is the Court's decision to uphold the campaign contribution limits but to strike down the expenditure limits. Although recognizing that any law regulating campaign financing was subject to the "exacting scrutiny required by the First Amendment,"[54] the Court mandated divergent treatment of contributions and expenditures for two reasons. First, the Court held that campaign expenditures were core political speech, but a limit on the amount of campaign contributions only marginally restricted a contributor's ability to send a message of support for a candidate.[55] Thus,

---

52. This section draws from Richard L. Hasen, Buckley *is Dead: Long Live* Buckley: The New Campaign Finance Incoherence *of* McConnell v. Federal Election Commission, 153 U. Pa. L. Rev. 31 (2004).

53. The FECA treats spending done in coordination with candidates as a contribution, not an expenditure. *See* 2 U.S.C. §441a(a)(7)(B)(i).

54. *Buckley*, 424 U.S. at 16.

55. *Id.* at 21.

expenditures were entitled to greater constitutional protection than contributions. Contribution limits would be subject to "exacting scrutiny" and spending limits to "strict scrutiny." Second, the Buckley Court recognized only the interests in prevention of corruption and the appearance of corruption as justifying infringement on First Amendment rights.

The Court held that large contributions raise the problem of corruption "[t]o the extent that large contributions are given to secure a political quid pro quo from current and potential officeholders."[56] But truly independent expenditures do not raise the same danger of corruption, because a quid pro quo is more difficult if politician and spender cannot communicate about the expenditure.[57]

With the corruption interest having failed to justify a limit upon independent expenditures, the Court considered the alternative argument that expenditure limits were justified by "the ancillary governmental interest in equalizing the relative ability of individuals and groups to influence the outcome of elections . . . ."[58] In one of the most famous (some would say notorious) sentences in Buckley, the Court rejected this equality rationale for campaign finance regulation, at least in the context of expenditure limits: "[T]he concept that government may restrict the speech of some elements of our society in order to enhance the relative voice of others is wholly foreign to the First Amendment."[59]

Portions of Buckley show some deference to legislative judgments. For example, the Court refused to consider whether the amount of the individual contribution limits (set at $1,000 per election) was too low.[60] The amount of contribution limitations would raise constitutional problems only when they prevented candidates and committees from "amassing the resources necessary for effective advocacy."[61] But the overall tenor and tone of Buckley was one of skepticism of legislative judgments about the need for campaign finance regulation.

Thus, the Court rejected expenditure limits not only because they interfered with free speech and association rights, but also because in light of the Court's narrowing interpretation of the FECA's reach only to cover

---

56. Id. at 26-27.
57. Id. at 46-47.
58. Id. at 48.
59. Id. at 48-49.
60. Buckley, 424 U.S. at 30. The Court also upheld an aggregate annual $25,000 individual contribution limit to federal candidates, parties, and political committees. Id. at 38. See also California Medical Association v. Federal Election Commission, 453 U.S. 182 (1981) (CMA) (upholding $5,000 limit on annual contributions by individuals and unincorporated associations to multicandidate political committees supporting federal candidates).
61. Buckley, 424 U.S. at 21.

advertisements containing express words of advocacy (such as "Vote for Smith"),[62] the limits could be circumvented easily, meaning that such limits would serve "no substantial societal interest."[63] Indeed, the Court even applied its narrowing construction to FECA's disclosure rules,[64] leaving many election-related campaign expenditures lacking any regulation whatsoever. (We will return to the Court's narrow interpretation of FECA's reach — and Congress's response to that interpretation — later in this chapter.)

Three justices disagreed with the Court's split over the constitutionality of contributions and expenditures. Chief Justice Burger thought the contribution limitations were unconstitutional as well:[65] "For me contributions and expenditures are two sides of the same First Amendment coin."[66] Justice White would have sustained the spending limits. He wrote that the limit on independent spending "is essential to prevent transparent and widespread evasion of the contribution limits."[67] He also would have upheld the limit on spending of personal funds, which he said "helps to assure that only individuals with a modicum of support from others will be viable candidates."[68] He supported candidate spending limits on grounds that they would "ease the candidate's understandable obsession with fundraising, and so free him. . . . from the influence inevitably exerted by the endless job of raising increasingly large sums of money. I regret that the Court has returned them all to the treadmill."[69] Justice Marshall wrote of his support for the constitutionality of the limit on personal and family funds, noting that "the interest [in promoting equality that has been derided by the Court] is more precisely the interest in promoting the reality and appearance of equal access to the political arena."[70]

Example 3

The state of Pacifica passes a new campaign finance law limiting the total amount that individuals may contribute to all candidates for state office to $25,000 per year and limiting spending made in coordination with a candidate to $1,000. These limits are in addition to an individual $1,000 contribution limit to candidates for state office. Opponents of the law sue in court, claiming that the $25,000 aggregate (or total) contribution limit and

---

62. *See id.* at 44 n.52.
63. *Id.* at 45.
64. *Id.* at 67.
65. *Buckley,* 424 U.S. at 235 (Burger, C.J., concurring in part and dissenting in part).
66. *Id.* at 241.
67. *Id.* at 262 (White, J., concurring in part and dissenting in part).
68. *Id.* at 266.
69. *Id.* at 265.
70. *Id.* at 287 (Marshall, J., concurring in part and dissenting in part).

the spending limit for coordinated spending violate the First Amendment. According to *Buckley*, under what level of scrutiny should the Supreme Court consider the constitutionality of the aggregate limit and the coordinated spending limit? According to *Buckley*, are the aggregate contribution limits and coordinated spending limits constitutional?

Explanation

This question is very hard, and it rewards you if you read the last section (including the footnotes) very carefully.

Let us take the two provisions separately. First, we consider the aggregate contribution limits. An aggregate contribution limit appears to be a contribution limit because it limits the total amount that an individual can give to candidates.[71] According to *Buckley*, contribution limits are subject to "exacting scrutiny," which is something much less than strict scrutiny. How much less than strict scrutiny was unclear in *Buckley*, but we do know that the Court sustained all the challenges to contribution limits in the case, including a challenge to the federal $25,000 aggregate limits (as noted in the footnotes above).

The *Buckley* Court's analysis of the constitutionality of the aggregate limits was quite brief. Here is the full discussion:

> 4. The 25,000 Limitation on Total Contributions During any Calendar Year
>
> In addition to the $1,000 limitation on the nonexempt contributions that an individual may make to a particular candidate for any single election, the Act contains an over-all $25,000 limitation on total contributions by an individual during any calendar year. §608(b)(3). A contribution made in connection with an election is considered, for purposes of this subsection, to be made in the year the election is held. Although the constitutionality of this provision was drawn into question by appellants, it has not been separately addressed at length by the parties. The overall $25,000 ceiling does impose an ultimate restriction upon the number of candidates and committees with which an individual may associate himself by means of financial support. But this quite modest restraint upon protected political activity serves to prevent evasion of the $1,000 contribution limitation by a person who might otherwise contribute massive amounts of money to a particular candidate through the use of unearmarked contributions to political committees likely to contribute to that candidate, or huge contributions to the candidate's political party. The limited, additional restriction on associational freedom imposed by the overall ceiling is thus no more than a corollary of the basic individual contribution limitation that we have found to be constitutionally valid.

---

71. One might argue that an aggregate limit is really a limit on spending, because it limits the total amount that someone can give to all candidates in a given year, and that such a limit incidentally affects total spending. However, in *Buckley*, the Court rejected such logic.

Although *Buckley*'s analysis of this issue was quite limited, the Supreme Court recently reached a contrary conclusion in *McCutcheon v. Federal Election Commission*, a case you will learn more about in the next chapter.

Now let us turn to the second part of the question: the coordinated spending limits. This law limits how much someone may spend in coordination with a candidate (or through "in kind" contributions of goods or services to a candidate). As noted in footnote 53, the law treats spending done in coordination with candidates as a contribution, not as an expenditure. Thus, although spending limits are subject to strict scrutiny and the *Buckley* Court struck the challenged spending limits down, the holding was premised on the idea that the spending was independent of the candidates. Coordinated spending is just like a contribution: It involves coordination between a candidate and party, and raises the same dangers of corruption. Accordingly, *Buckley* would treat a coordinated spending limit as a contribution limit and subject the law to exacting scrutiny. Furthermore, given that the *Buckley* Court upheld a $1,000 contribution limitation, it likely would uphold a $1,000 coordinated spending limit on the same anticorruption basis.

13.3. SPENDING LIMITS AFTER *BUCKLEY*[72]

13.3.1. Before *Citizens United*

In *First National Bank of Boston v. Bellotti*, the Supreme Court, following *Buckley*'s rejection of individual spending limits in candidate elections, struck down a Massachusetts limit on spending by corporations in ballot measure elections.[73] Without a candidate to corrupt in a ballot measure election, the anticorruption interest could not justify a spending limit. The Court suggested that public confidence might justify a restriction on corporate spending in ballot measure elections if the state could demonstrate that such spending in fact negatively affected public confidence, but it held that the state presented no such evidence. The Court also rejected the argument that the law was justified to protect corporate shareholders.

Although the Court took an expansive view of corporate free speech rights, it added an important footnote, Footnote 26, stating that "Congress might well be able to demonstrate the existence of a danger of real or

---

72. This section draws from Richard L. Hasen, Citizens United *and the Illusion of Coherence*, 109 Mich. L. Rev. 581 (2011).
73. 435 U.S. 765, 767-770, 795 (1978).

apparent corruption in independent expenditures by corporations to influence candidate elections."[74] Footnote 26 stood in tension with *Buckley's* statement that independent spending by individuals cannot corrupt candidates because of the absence of the possibility of a quid pro quo.

Eight years later, the Court in *FEC v. Massachusetts Citizens for Life* (MCFL) first confronted the question of corporate spending limits in *candidate* elections. The MCFL Court held that nonprofit ideological corporations (later known as "MCFL corporations") that do not take corporate or union money cannot be limited in spending their treasury funds in candidate elections.[75] But in so doing, the Court added dicta suggesting that for-profit corporations could be limited in their independent spending to prevent corporations from spending money on campaigns out of line with the public's support for the corporations' political ideas.[76]

In *Austin v. Michigan Chamber of Commerce*, the Court more directly addressed the constitutionality of electoral spending limits imposed upon for-profit corporations in candidate elections.[77] At issue was a Michigan state law, that, like federal law, prevented corporations from spending money on candidate elections.[78] (Federal law prevented labor unions from engaging in such spending, too, but Michigan's law did not.) If a Michigan corporation wanted to be involved in state candidate campaigns, it could set up a political action committee (or "PAC") for this purpose. The PAC could accept individual contributions, and not use money from general treasury funds. The corporation could solicit only officers, managers, and shareholders to contribute to the PAC.

---

74. *Id.* at 788 n.26 ("our consideration of a corporation's right to speak on issues of general public interest implies no comparable right in the quite different context of participation in a political campaign for election to public office. Congress might well be able to demonstrate the existence of a danger of real or apparent corruption in independent expenditures by corporations to influence candidate elections.").

75. 479 U.S. 238, 241, 263 (1986).

76. Justice Brennan wrote

> This concern over the corrosive influence of concentrated corporate wealth reflects the conviction that it is important to protect the integrity of the marketplace of political ideas. . . . Direct corporate spending on political activity raises the prospect that resources amassed in the economic marketplace may be used to provide an unfair advantage in the political marketplace. Political "free trade" does not necessarily require that all who participate in the political marketplace do so with exactly equal resources. Relative availability of funds is after all a rough barometer of public support. The resources in the treasury of a business corporation, however, are not an indication of popular support for the corporation's political ideas. They reflect instead the economically motivated decisions of investors and customers. The availability of these resources may make a corporation a formidable political presence, even though the power of the corporation may be no reflection of the power of its ideas.

Id. at 257-258.

77. 494 U.S. 652, 654-655, 668-669 (1990).

78. Although the First Amendment by its literal terms applies just to the federal government, the Supreme Court has held that its restrictions apply against the states as well.

The Court did not address *Bellotti*'s suggestion in footnote 26 that Michigan's corporate limits might be justified to prevent corruption of candidates. Instead, building on *MCFL*'s dicta, the Court held the law was justified to prevent a "different type of corruption in the political arena: the corrosive and distorting effects of immense aggregations of wealth that are accumulated with the help of the corporate form and that have little or no correlation to the public's support for the corporation's political ideas." The case drew very strong dissents from Justice Kennedy and Justice Scalia, who called it "Orwellian" and the "rawest form of censorship."

Although cast as an anti-"corruption" rationale,[79] *Austin*'s emphasis on preventing distortion of the electoral process through large corporate spending suggested the Court in fact was espousing an equality rationale,[80] which the Court had rejected as applied to individuals in *Buckley*. After all, the problem with large corporate wealth described in *Austin* was not one of dollars for political favors but instead about oversized influence of wealthy corporations.

The Court retreated even further from *Bellotti*'s recognition of corporate First Amendment rights in *FEC v. Beaumont*, another case from its deferential post-2000 period (and discussed in more detail below). The Court in *Beaumont* wrote that

> corporate contributions are furthest from the core of political expression, since corporations' First Amendment speech and association interests are derived largely from those of their members, and of the public in receiving information. A ban on direct corporate contributions leaves individual members of corporations free to make their own contributions, and deprives the public of little or no material information.[81]

The struggle over corporate spending limits heated up again when Congress passed the Bipartisan Campaign Reform Act of 2002 ("BCRA," more commonly referred to as "McCain-Feingold").[82] BCRA aimed to strengthen what its supporters characterized as "loopholes" in existing campaign finance law. Its "electioneering communications" provision was one of its most significant changes.

Federal law, like the Michigan law at issue in *Austin*, barred corporations and unions from spending general treasury funds on certain election-related activities.[83] FECA blessed the PAC alternative: Corporations and unions could

---

79. *Id.* at 660.
80. *See* RICHARD L. HASEN, THE SUPREME COURT AND ELECTION LAW 111-114 (2003).
81. 539 U.S. 146, 161 n.8 (2003) (citations omitted).
82. Bipartisan Campaign Reform Act of 2002 §101, 2 U.S.C. §441i(a).
83. 2 U.S.C. §441b.

establish separate political committees to spend money on these campaigns, but these PACs were limited in both the amount that could be contributed to candidates and who could be solicited to contribute.

The general treasury fund limitation proved ineffective, thanks to an interpretation of the statute by the Court in *Buckley* (as mentioned in the last section).[84] The *Buckley* Court held that to avoid vagueness and overbreadth problems within FECA, its provisions should be interpreted to reach only election-related activity containing "express advocacy" such as "Vote against Jones."[85] "Issue ads," paid for by corporations, labor unions, and wealthy individuals began appearing in the 1990s. These ads appeared to be aimed at influencing federal elections but escaped FECA regulation through avoidance of express advocacy. "Call Senator Jones and tell her what you think of her lousy vote on the stimulus bill" went unregulated, even though the person running the ad certainly wanted to defeat Senator Jones for reelection. Spending on such ads skyrocketed in the 1990s.[86]

BCRA responded to the issue advocacy problem through the "electioneering communications" provision. Electioneering communications are television or radio (not print or Internet) advertisements that feature a candidate for federal election and are capable of reaching 50,000 people in the relevant electorate 30 days before a primary or 60 days before a general election. The definition applied to both *disclosure rules* and *spending limitations*. Under BCRA §201, anyone making electioneering communications over a certain dollar threshold must disclose contributions funding the ads and spending related to the ads to the FEC.[87] In addition, under BCRA §203 corporations and unions could not fund such ads from general treasury funds but had to rely on their PACs.[88] (The Court later interpreted §203 in such a way as not to apply to MCFL corporations.[89])

In *McConnell v. FEC*,[90] the Court on a 5-4 vote upheld BCRA §203 against facial challenge. Reaffirming *Austin*,[91] the *McConnell* Court upheld the rules because most of the ads covered by the statute were the "functional equivalent of express advocacy."[92] The Court upheld the provision against labor unions, too, without explaining how labor unions could "distort" the political process like corporations.[93]

---

84. *See McConnell v. FEC*, 540 U.S. 93, 126 (2003).
85. *Buckley*, 424 U.S. at 44 n.51.
86. *See McConnell v. FEC*, 540 U.S. at 126-127.
87. *See* Bipartisan Campaign Reform Act of 2002 §201, 2 U.S.C. §434(f)(1).
88. *See id.* §203, 2 U.S.C §441b(b)(2).
89. McConnell, 540 U.S. at 210-211.
90. 540 U.S. 93 (2003).
91. 494 U.S. 652 (1990).
92. *McConnell*, 540 U.S. at 206. By an 8-1 vote, the Court also upheld BCRA §201 and §311 against facial challenge.
93. *Id.*

Example 4

The state of Pacifica passes a law barring corporations from spending money in state candidate elections. Unlike federal law or Michigan law, Pacifica does not allow corporations to set up a PAC to support Pacifica candidates. Under the Supreme Court's constitutional jurisprudence through the *McConnell* case, would such a law be constitutional?

Explanation

The answer to this question is not clear, because both the Michigan law at issue in *Austin* and the federal law at issue in *McConnell* afforded the PAC option for corporations (and for labor unions under federal law). It is not clear whether the Court would have struck the balance differently in either case had the Court faced the question.

But the question should get you to think about some basic issues involving First Amendment speech and expression issues. The PAC option allows the corporation to "speak" through an affiliated committee so that the corporations' views on candidates and issues are known to the public. To the *Austin* and *McConnell* dissenters, the PAC option was not enough. But to the majority, it was clearly sufficient. Note the statement in *Beaumont* about how political speech of corporations is farthest from the core of the First Amendment. Corporations are made up of individuals who are owners, managers, shareholders, employees, and others. Is it enough that these individuals have First Amendment rights, or should the law recognize corporations as having a speech right apart and not wholly derivative of those affiliated with the corporation?

If the state takes away the PAC option, the possibility of the corporation as corporation speaking becomes impossible. We do not know how the *Austin* and *McConnell* justices in the majority would have answered that question.

13.3.2. *Citizens United* and Beyond

The Supreme Court's campaign finance jurisprudence shifted dramatically when Justice Alito replaced Justice O'Connor in 2006. The Court, which upheld extended corporate and labor union spending limits in *McConnell* and which minimized corporate free speech rights in *Beaumont*, turned 180 degrees with the arrival of Justice Alito, from a 5-4 Court apt to uphold campaign finance limits to a 5-4 Court apt to strike limits down. In fact, so far, the Supreme Court with Justice Alito has struck down or narrowed every campaign finance limit it has considered.

In *Wisconsin Right to Life v. Federal Election Commission (WRTL I)*,[94] decided as Justice O'Connor was leaving the Court, the Court held that *McConnell* did not prevent a corporation or union from bringing an "as applied" challenge to BCRA §203 on the basis that their ads were not the "functional equivalent of express advocacy." *WRTL I* concerned an electioneering communication discussing Senator Feingold's and Senator Kohl's position on judicial filibusters. The group wanted to broadcast the ad in Wisconsin during the period of Senator Feingold's reelection campaign. The case returned to the Supreme Court after the lower court, on remand, held that the ads were not the functional equivalent of express advocacy and thus were not entitled to an as-applied exemption. In another 5-4 vote, the Court in *Federal Election Commission v. Wisconsin Right to Life (WRTL II)*[95] reached a conclusion contrary to the lower court. Three justices in the majority (Justices Kennedy, Scalia, and Thomas), echoing their dissenting opinions in *McConnell*, took the position that BCRA §203 was unconstitutional as applied to *any* corporate spending. They contended that that *McConnell* and *Austin* should be overruled.[96] Chief Justice Roberts and Justice Alito wrote a narrower (and therefore controlling) opinion, which did not reach the question whether *McConnell* and *Austin* should be overruled. They instead concluded that the only corporate-funded advertisements that BCRA could bar constitutionally were those that were the "functional equivalent of express advocacy,"[97] and they read "functional equivalency" very narrowly.[98] Otherwise, it would be unconstitutional to apply BCRA §203 to bar corporate funding for an election-related advertisement. Applying this new test, the controlling opinion held that the WRTL ad was not the "functional equivalent" of an express advocacy against Senator Feingold: It did not mention Senator Feingold's character or fitness for office, and had no other clear indicia of the functional equivalent of express advocacy.[99] The new functional equivalency test appeared likely to eviscerate BCRA §203.

WRTL II's reach was never fully tested because the Supreme Court soon turned to decide *Citizens United v. FEC*. Though *Citizens United* ultimately brought down *Austin* and part of *McConnell*, the case did not begin as such an audacious

---

94. 546 U.S. 410 (2006).
95. 551 U.S. 449 (2007).
96. *See id.* at 483-504 (Scalia, J., concurring). Justice Scalia was quite critical of the limited nature of the controlling opinion, calling it "faux judicial restraint" that was "judicial obfuscation." *Id.* at 498 n.7 (Scalia, J., concurring).
97. *Id.* at 454-482 (principal opinion).
98. More specifically, Roberts and Alito determined that in making the "functional equivalency" determination, one must consider whether, without regard to context (such as the fact that the filibuster issue was one that conservatives were using to attack liberal Democrats) and without detailed discovery of the intentions of the advertisers, an advertisement was susceptible of "no reasonable interpretation" other than as an advertisement supporting or opposing a candidate for office. *Id.* at 469-470.
99. *Id.* at 480-481.

challenge. Like *WRTL II, Citizens United* began as a suit to weaken existing campaign finance precedent. Citizens United, a nonprofit ideological corporation that took some for-profit corporate funding,[100] produced a feature-length documentary entitled *Hillary: The Movie*.[101] Though the documentary was available in theaters and on DVD during the 2008 primary season, Citizens United also wished to distribute the movie through a cable television "video-on-demand" service. Citizens United wanted to use its general treasury funds to pay a $1.2 million fee to a cable television operator consortium to make the documentary available to be downloaded by cable subscribers for free "on demand."[102]

The documentary contained no express advocacy, but unlike the *WRTL II* ad, it did contain a great deal of negative statements about a candidate for office,[103] including statements that the candidate, Hillary Clinton, was a "European socialist not fit to be commander-in-chief." The FEC argued that the documentary met *WRTL II*'s "functional equivalency" test. Though the group's PAC had ample resources, it did not wish to pay for the broadcasts with PAC funds.

Citizens United advanced numerous arguments, both statutory and constitutional. Most narrowly, it argued that the FEC regulations should not be construed to apply to "video-on-demand" cable broadcasts. Most broadly, it argued that *Austin* was wrongly decided and should be overruled.

The case was first argued in March 2009, and at this point it grew to a case with broader significance. The deputy solicitor general had trouble answering a hypothetical question about whether the government could ban payment from corporations for books that contain the "the functional equivalent of express advocacy."[104] On the last regular day of the Court's term in June 2009, the Court announced a rehearing of the case for September. Surprisingly, the Court asked for supplemental briefing on the following question: "For the proper disposition of this case, should the Court overrule either or both *Austin v. Michigan Chamber of Commerce*, 494 U.S. 652 (1990), and the part of *McConnell v. Federal Election Comm'n*, 540 U.S. 93 (2003), which addresses the facial validity of Section 203 of the Bipartisan Campaign Reform Act of 2002, 2 U.S.C. §441b?" The Court reheard argument in September 2009, and struck down the corporate spending limits in January 2010.

---

100. By taking some for-profit corporate money, the corporation appeared ineligible for the MCFL exemption.
101. *Citizens United*, 558 U.S. at 319.
102. *Id.* at 320.
103. *Id.*
104. Adam Liptak, *Justices Consider Interplay Between First Amendment and Campaign Finance Laws*, N.Y. Times, Mar. 25, 2009, at A16, http://www.nytimes.com/2009/03/25/washington/25scotus.html.

Justice Kennedy wrote the majority opinion on the corporate spending limits question for himself, Chief Justice Roberts, and Justices Alito, Scalia, and Thomas.[105] Justice Stevens, for himself and Justices Breyer, Ginbsurg, and Sotomayor, dissented on the spending limits question.[106] Justice Kennedy's majority opinion began by rejecting arguments to resolve Citizens United's complaint against corporate spending limits on statutory grounds or to issue a narrow constitutional ruling. It also rejected an extension of the MCFL exemption to nonprofit corporations who take some corporate or labor union money but whose "political speech [is] funded overwhelmingly by individuals."[107]

On the merits, the Court characterized federal law as a "ban" on corporate political speech, rejecting the argument that the law merely imposed a requirement that non-MCFL corporations use PAC funds rather than general treasury funds for election-related communications. The Court stated that a PAC does not "allow a corporation to speak"[108] and that PACs are "burdensome alternatives . . . expensive to administer and subject to extensive regulations."[109] Having found the law's "prohibition on corporate independent expenditures . . . a ban on speech,"[110] the Court then explained the First Amendment interests at stake: "Were the Court to uphold these restrictions, the Government could repress speech by silencing certain voices at any of the various points in the speech process."[111] Recognizing political speech as central to the First Amendment, the Court stated that the law would have to survive strict scrutiny.[112]

The First Amendment, "[p]remised on mistrust of government power[,]" "stands against attempts to disfavor certain subject or viewpoints. Prohibited too are restrictions distinguishing among different speakers, allowing speech by some but not others."[113] A government decision to privilege some speakers over others "deprive[s] the public of the right and privilege to determine for itself what speech and speakers are worthy of consideration. The First Amendment protects speech and speaker, and the ideas that flow from each."[114] The Court then canvassed its pre-*Austin* caselaw on the topic of corporate spending in elections,[115] including *Buckley* and *Bellotti*. It stated that prior caselaw contradicted *Austin*,[116] and the question

---

105. *Citizens United*, 558 U.S. at 318-372.
106. Id. at 393-485 (Stevens, J., concurring in part and dissenting in part).
107. *Citizens United*, 558 U.S. 327.
108. Id. at 337.
109. Id.; *see also* id. at 337-339 (describing PAC regulations).
110. Id. at 339.
111. Id.
112. Id. at 340.
113. Id. (citation omitted).
114. Id. at 341.
115. Id. at 341-347.
116. Id. at 348.

before the Court was whether *Austin* should be overruled. It then turned to the three arguments made in support of *Austin*, antidistortion, anticorruption, and shareholder protection.

Antidistortion. Noting that the government "all but abandon[ed] reliance" on *Austin*'s antidistortion interest,[117] the Court strongly and equivocally rejected antidistortion as a permissible governmental interest. The Court said that the interest could justify the banning of books and was an equalization rationale inconsistent with *Buckley* and other cases.[118] The special advantages that the state conferred on corporations, such as limited liability and perpetual life, "do[] not suffice" to prohibit speech under the First Amendment,[119] and it is irrelevant whether the speech of corporations has "little or no correlation" with public support.[120] The Court stated that the antidistortion rationale "would produce the dangerous, and unacceptable, consequence that Congress could ban political speech of media corporations."[121] It concluded that *Austin* "permits the Government to ban the political speech of millions of associations of citizens. . . . The censorship we now confront is vast in its reach."[122] *Austin* was "all the more an aberration" because the law included both small and nonprofit corporations,[123] neither of which had vast accumulations of wealth.

Anticorruption. The Court then rejected the argument that a corporate spending limit could be justified on anticorruption grounds. It cited to those portions of *Buckley* rejecting a similar argument[124] and brushed aside footnote 26 of *Bellotti*, in which the Court had left the issue open: "For the reasons explained above, we now conclude that independent expenditures, including those made by corporations, do not give rise to corruption or the appearance of corruption."[125]

In a key part of the opinion, the Court then explained its understanding of the meaning of the term "corruption": "When *Buckley* identified a sufficiently important governmental interest in preventing corruption or the appearance of corruption, that interest was limited to *quid pro quo* corruption."[126] The Court quoted Justice Kennedy's partial dissent in the *McConnell*

---

117. *Id.*
118. *Id.* at 349-350.
119. *Id.* at 351.
120. *Id.* (quoting *Austin*).
121. *Id.*
122. *Id.* at 354.
123. *Id.* at 355.
124. *Id.* at 356-357.
125. *Id.* at 357. The Court stated that the *Bellotti* footnote was "supported only by a law review student comment, which misinterpreted *Buckley*." *Id.* at 358.
126. *Id.* at 359.

case[127] for the proposition that "[t]he fact that speakers may have influence over or access to elected officials does not mean that these officials are corrupt."[128] "Favoritism and influence" are unavoidable in representative politics, and a "substantial and legitimate reason" to cast a vote or make a contribution to one candidate or another "is that the candidate will respond by producing those political outcomes the supporter favors."[129] The Court further stated that "[t]he appearance of influence or access . . . will not cause the electorate to lose faith in our democracy," and independent spending which is uncoordinated with a candidate cannot give rise to an appearance of corruption because the additional political speech simply seeks to persuade voters who have "the ultimate influence over elected officials."[130]

Shareholder Protection. Though the government put most of its eggs into the shareholder protection basket, the Court disposed of the argument in two short paragraphs. First, the Court said, the argument was an impermissible basis for limiting corporate spending, because like the antidistortion argument, it would allow the government to apply the ban to media corporations.[131] There was also "little evidence of abuse that cannot be corrected by shareholders" through corporate democracy.[132] The statute also suffered from being underinclusive in serving the shareholder protection interest, because it covered certain media ads in the short period before the election, and overinclusive, because it covered nonprofit corporations and for-profit corporations with single shareholders.[133] The Court concluded by quickly noting that it did not reach the question "whether the Government has a compelling interest in preventing foreign individuals or associations from influencing our Nation's political process."[134]

Justice Stevens, for the four dissenters on the corporate spending limits question, issued a lengthy dissenting opinion.[135] He began with two sections addressing why the Court should have decided the case on narrower statutory grounds, as well as why the Court should have affirmed *Austin* under principles of *stare decisis*. Justice Stevens then turned to a lengthy discussion of the merits. He disagreed with the majority's repeated insistence that the PAC requirement "banned" political speech, calling the

---

127. 540 U.S. at 297.
128. *Citizens United*, 558 U.S. at 359.
129. *Id.* (quoting Justice Kennedy's opinion in *McConnell*).
130. *Id.* at 360.
131. *Citizens United*, 558 U.S. at 361.
132. *Id.* at 361-362.
133. *Id.* at 362.
134. *Id.*
135. The opinion runs 50 pages in the Supreme Court Reporter. Justice Stevens even apologized for the length of the dissent: "I regret the length of what follows, but the importance and novelty of the Court's opinion require a full response." *Id.* at 395 (Stevens, J., concurring in part and dissenting in part).

characterization "highly misleading, and need[ing] to be corrected."[136] The idea that corporate speech would be banned is "nonsense."[137] Justice Stevens defended the media exemption, noting the "unique role played by the institutional press in sustaining public debate."[138] The dissent rejected the "identity-based" distinctions of the majority, noting that in the election context laws ban political activities of foreigners and government employees.[139] It then turned to a very long discussion of the "original understandings" of the First Amendment,[140] the pre-*Austin* campaign finance cases,[141] and the post-*Austin* cases that "reaffirmed" its holding.[142] The dissent also disagreed with the majority's reading of *Buckley* and *Bellotti*, stating that *Austin* did not conflict with *Buckley*'s rejection of the equalization rationale,[143] and noting that *Bellotti* footnote 26 expressly left the anticorruption rationale open as to corporate spending limits in candidate elections.[144] Finally, the dissent turned to discuss the anticorruption, antidistortion, and shareholder protection rationales.

Anticorruption. The dissent began by disagreeing with the narrow view of corruption embraced by the majority: "[T]he difference between selling a vote and selling access is a matter of degree, not kind."[145] Setting forth a broad view of "undue influence" that could justify campaign finance regulations, the dissent rejected the idea that *Buckley* compelled a conclusion that independent spending can never corrupt a candidate.[146] It then concluded that corporations raised a special problem of *quid pro quo* corruption because corporations as a class "tend to be more attuned to the complexities of the legislative process and more directly affected by tax and appropriation measures that receive little public scrutiny; they also have vastly more money with which to try to buy access and votes."[147]

---

136. *Id.* at 415.

137. *Id.* at 418.

138. *Id.* at 417; *see also id.* at 473-374 (discussing role of the press and media exemption). Justice Stevens added that "with a media corporation there is also a lesser risk that investors will not understand, learn about, or support the advocacy messages that the corporation disseminates." *Id.* at 417 n.32. He also stated that the majority "[r]oam[ed] far afield from the case at hand" by worrying "that the government will use §203 to ban books, pamphlets, and blogs." *Id.* at 417 n.31.

139. *Id.* at 419-425.

140. *Id.* at 425-432.

141. *Id.* at 432-438.

142. *Id.* at 439-441.

143. *Id.* at 441-446.

144. *Id.* at 443.

145. *Id.* at 447.

146. *Id.* at 453-454.

147. *Id.* at 454.

Antidistortion. While acknowledging "that *Austin* can bear an egalitarian reading,"[148] the dissent disputed the claim that it was "just" an equalization rationale "in disguise."[149] Instead, "understood properly" the argument "is simply a variant on the classic governmental interest in protecting against improper influences on officeholders that debilitate the democratic process."[150] According to the dissent, corporations do not engage in self-expression the way human beings do.[151] In any case, some corporations actually wanted limits on spending to prevent officeholders from "shak[ing] them down for supportive ads."[152] Finally, large corporate spending could "marginalize[]" the opinions of "real people" by "drowning out non-corporate voices."[153] This in turn "can generate the impression that corporations dominate our democracy"[154] and give corporations "special advantages in the market for legislation."[155]

Shareholder Protection. The dissent further stated that the law can "serve First Amendment values" by protecting the rights of shareholders from a "kind of coerced speech: electioneering communications that do not reflect their support."[156] The PAC mechanism prevents managers from advancing personal agendas, limiting the "rent seeking behavior of executives and respects views of dissenters."[157]

The *Citizens United* case was controversial when the Court decided it, and some wondered whether the justices might change their minds after seeing the rise in outside money in elections (more about that in the next chapter). Critics focused upon a case in which the Montana Supreme Court held that Montana's history demonstrated corporate corruption of candidates through independent spending. Montana had a 100-year history of corporate influence over the Montana legislature. The Montana Supreme Court used these facts to distinguish *Citizens United* and uphold the state's corporate spending ban. *Western Tradition Partnership v. Attorney General.*[158] Hopes for a Supreme Court turnaround were quickly dashed in *American Tradition Partnership v. Bullock,*[159] in an opinion the Court issued summarily from a certiorari petition without oral argument: "The question presented in this case is whether the holding of *Citizens United* applies to the Montana state law.

---

148. Id. at 464 n.69.
149. Id. at 464.
150. Id.
151. Id. at 466.
152. Id. at 468.
153. Id. at 470.
154. Id.
155. Id. at 471.
156. Id. at 475 (brackets omitted).
157. Id. at 476.
158. 271 P.3d 1 (Mont. 2011).
159. 132 S.Ct. 2490 (2012).

There can be no serious doubt that it does. *See* U.S. Const., Art. VI, cl. 2. Montana's arguments in support of the judgment below either were already rejected in *Citizens United*, or fail to meaningfully distinguish that case." Justice Kagan, who joined the Court upon the retirement of Justice Stevens, dissented along with the constitutionality of *Citizens United* dissenters in this case. The Court is still divided 5-4 against the constitutionality of corporate spending limits.

Example 4

Federal law, 2 U.S.C. §441e, bars foreign individuals, entities and corporations from contributing to or spending money in federal elections. The majority in *Citizens United* declined to decide whether bans on spending on elections by foreign individuals, entities, or governments would be constitutional.[160]

Is such a ban constitutional after *Citizens United*?

Explanation

At first glance, it looks as if a ban on foreign spending would be inconsistent with the understanding of the First Amendment the Supreme Court put forward in *Citizens United*. After all, if the identity of the speaker does not matter when the speaker is a corporate entity, why should it matter whether the speaker is a foreign individual or entity? Furthermore, all of the arguments one might raise against foreign spending in U.S. elections — that it can corrupt the system, lower public confidence, or lessen political equality — appear to be interests the Court in *Citizens United* rejected as inadequate justifications for the corporate campaign finance ban.

Yet two years after *Citizens United*, the Supreme Court summarily affirmed a lower court opinion upholding the ban on foreign spending in elections. *Bluman v. FEC*.[161] A "summary affirmance" is a decision on the merits that the lower court got the result right, although perhaps not for the same reasons as the Court would have given.

Here are the reasons the lower court gave for upholding the ban on foreign spending in elections:

> [T]he Supreme Court has drawn a fairly clear line: The government may exclude foreign citizens from activities "intimately related to the process of democratic self-government." As the Court has written, "a State's historical power to exclude aliens from participation in its democratic political institutions [is] part of the sovereign's obligation to preserve the basic conception

---

160. *Citizens United*, 558 U.S. at 362.
161. 132 S.Ct. 1087 (2012) (mem.), *affirming* 800 F. Supp. 2d 281 (D.D.C. 2011) (three-judge court).

of a political community." In other words, the government may reserve "participation in its democratic political institutions" for citizens of this country. When reviewing a statute barring foreign citizens from serving as probation officers, the Court explained that the "exclusion of aliens from basic governmental processes is not a deficiency in the democratic system but *a necessary consequence of the community's process of political self-definition.*" Upholding a statute barring aliens from teaching in public schools, the Court reasoned that the "distinction between citizens and aliens, though ordinarily irrelevant to private activity, is *fundamental to the definition and government of a State. . . .* It is because of this special significance of citizenship that governmental entities, when exercising the functions of government, have wider latitude in limiting the participation of noncitizens." And in upholding a ban on aliens serving as police officers, the Court stated that, "although we extend to aliens the right to education and public welfare, along with the ability to earn a livelihood and engage in licensed professions, the right to govern is reserved to citizens."

We read these cases to set forth a straightforward principle: It is fundamental to the definition of our national political community that foreign citizens do not have a constitutional right to participate in, and thus may be excluded from, activities of democratic self-government. It follows, therefore, that the United States has a compelling interest for purposes of First Amendment analysis in limiting the participation of foreign citizens in activities of American democratic self-government, and in thereby preventing foreign influence over the U.S. political process.

Applying the Supreme Court's precedents, the question here is whether political contributions and express-advocacy expenditures — including donations to outside groups that in turn make contributions or express-advocacy expenditures — constitute part of the process of democratic self-government. In our view, the answer to that question is straightforward: Political contributions and express-advocacy expenditures are an integral aspect of the process by which Americans elect officials to federal, state, and local government offices. Political contributions and express-advocacy expenditures finance advertisements, get-out-the-vote drives, rallies, candidate speeches, and the myriad other activities by which candidates appeal to potential voters. We think it evident that those campaign activities are part of the overall process of democratic self-government. Moreover, it is undisputed that the government may bar foreign citizens from voting and serving as elected officers. It follows that the government may bar foreign citizens (at least those who are not lawful permanent residents of the United States) from participating in the campaign process that seeks to influence how voters will cast their ballots in the elections. Those limitations on the activities of foreign citizens are of a piece and are all "part of the sovereign's obligation to preserve the basic conception of a political community."

Convincing?

CHAPTER 14

Campaign Contribution Limits from *Buckley* to *Citizens United* and Beyond

14.1. THE PATH FROM *BUCKLEY* TO DEFERENCE[1]

As we saw in the last chapter, the Supreme Court's decision in *Buckley v. Valeo* mandated different constitutional review of contribution limits and spending limits. The Court subjected spending limits to strict scrutiny because the Court viewed such limits as imposing a direct restriction on speech. In contrast, the Court subjected contribution limits to lesser "exacting" scrutiny. The Court held that a limit on the amount of campaign contributions only marginally restricted a contributor's ability to send a message of support for a candidate.[2] Furthermore, the Court held that contribution limits could be justified to prevent corruption and the appearance of corruption.[3] Finally, the Court refused to consider whether the amount of the individual contribution limits (set at $1,000 per election) was too low.[4] The amount of contribution limitations would raise constitutional problems only when they prevented candidates and committees from "amassing the resources necessary for effective advocacy."[5]

---

1. This section draws from Richard L. Hasen, *Rethinking the Unconstitutionality of Contribution and Expenditure Limits in Ballot Measure Campaigns*, 78 S. CAL. L. REV. 885 (2005).
2. *Buckley*, 424 U.S. at 21.
3. *Id.* at 26-27.
4. *Id.* at 30.
5. *Id.* at 21.

Buckley left many unanswered questions, however, about the constitutionality of contribution limits. What about limits in ballot measure elections? What about contributions to political parties, or to groups that make only independent expenditures? When would the Court say that a contribution limit is so low as to be unconstitutional by its preventing candidates from amassing the resources necessary for effective advocacy?

The pattern that emerges in this chapter about contribution limits mirrors the pattern in the last chapter on spending limits: a Supreme Court vacillating between periods of deference and skepticism to such laws when challenged under the First Amendment. As we shall see, in the Court's most recent contributions case, *McCutcheon v. FEC*, the Court appeared to import parts of *Citizens United*, and especially its narrowed definition of corruption, into review of the constitutionality of contribution limits.

Despite *Buckley*'s holding that lower "exacting scrutiny" applied to review of contribution limits,[6] the Court held that limits on contributions to a local ballot measure committee were unconstitutional because the anticorruption interest did not apply to incorruptible ballot measures.[7] This 1981 holding in *Citizens Against Rent Control v. City of Berkeley* mirrored the holding of *Bellotti* (discussed in the last chapter) regarding the unconstitutionality of corporate spending limits in ballot measure campaigns.

In the 2000s, as the Court entered its period of greatest deference to legislative judgments about the need for campaign contribution limits, the Court in *Nixon v. Shrink Missouri Government PAC* upheld a $1,075 contribution limit in Missouri state elections against a challenge that the amount was too low for challengers to mount an effective campaign.[8] The Court did so even though the $1,075 limit was much lower in 1976 dollars than the value of $1,000 contribution limit upheld in *Buckley*.[9]

In four ways, *Shrink Missouri* showed remarkable deference toward legislative judgments. First, the Court ratcheted down the level of scrutiny for reviewing contribution limits from *Buckley*'s "exacting" level of scrutiny to one in which interests need only be "sufficiently important"[10] and not narrowly tailored to the government's interest.[11] Second, the Court expanded the definition of corruption and the appearance of corruption sufficient to justify campaign finance regulation. The Court explained that corruption extended beyond quid pro quo arrangements to embrace "the broader threat from

---

6. *See id.* at 16.
7. *Citizens Against Rent Control v. City of Berkeley*, 454 U.S. 290, 299-300 (1981) ("Whatever may be the state interest . . . in regulating and limiting contributions to or expenditures of a candidate[,] . . . there is no significant state or public interest in curtailing debate and discussion of a ballot measure.").
8. *Nixon v. Shrink Mo. Gov't PAC*, 528 U.S. 377, 382-383, 397-398 (2000).
9. *See id.* at 382, 395-397.
10. *Id.* at 388.
11. *Id.* ("the dollar amount of the limit need not be 'fine tun[ed]'.")

politicians too compliant with the wishes of large contributors."[12] As for the appearance of corruption, the Court remarked, "Leave the perception of impropriety unanswered, and the cynical assumption that large donors call the tune could jeopardize the willingness of voters to take part in democratic governance."[13]

Third, and perhaps most significantly, the Court lowered the evidentiary burden for proving corruption or its appearance. The Court began by noting that the "quantum of empirical evidence needed to satisfy heightened judicial scrutiny of legislative judgments will vary up or down with the novelty and plausibility of the justification raised."[14] Although the Court insisted that "mere conjecture"[15] was not enough to support a campaign limit, it held that Missouri could justify the need for its contribution limits to fight corruption or the appearance of corruption by some pretty flimsy evidence: the affidavit from a Missouri legislator who had supported the legislation stating that "large contributions 'have the real potential to buy votes,'"[16] newspaper accounts suggesting possible corruption in Missouri politics, and the passage of an earlier Missouri voter initiative establishing campaign contribution limits. Fourth, the Court created a difficult test for challenging the constitutionality of a contribution limit as too low to prevent effective advocacy. Refining (or changing) the effective advocacy test from *Buckley*, the Court stated: "We asked, in other words, whether the contribution limitation was so radical in effect as to render political association ineffective, drive the sound of a candidate's voice below the level of notice, and render contributions pointless."[17] In an era of faxes, websites, social media, and e-mails, it is hard to imagine any contribution limit that would fail that test of constitutionality.

Three other opinions continued in *Shrink Missouri*'s deferential mode. *Federal Election Commission v. Colorado Republican Federal Campaign Committee (Colorado II)*[18] concerned whether political parties had a constitutional right to spend unlimited sums in coordination with the parties' candidates. As discussed in the last chapter, FECA treats a coordinated expenditure as a contribution, and limits the amount of coordinated expenditures that a party may make with a party's candidate.[19] By a 5-4 vote, the Court upheld the FECA provision, primarily on grounds that parties may serve as conduits for corruption: "[W]hether they like it or not, [parties] act as agents for spending on behalf

---

12. *Id.* at 389.
13. *Id.* at 390.
14. *Id.* at 391.
15. *Id.* at 392.
16. *Id.* at 393.
17. *Id.* at 397.
18. 533 U.S. 431 (2001).
19. 2 U.S.C. §441a(a)(7)(B)(i); §441a(d)(3).

of those who seek to produce obligated officeholders."[20] In support of this conclusion, the Court once again relied upon some rather casual empirical evidence.[21]

Then, in *Federal Election Commission v. Beaumont*[22] (discussed briefly in the last chapter) the Supreme Court held it permissible to ban contributions by MCFL corporations (those non-ideological corporations that were entitled to an exemption from the corporate spending limit ban during the *Austin* era). As noted in the last chapter, *Beaumont* called into question *Bellotti*'s statement that the corporate form of the speaker is irrelevant for purposes of determining the degree of First Amendment protection.

The final major deferential contributions case is *McConnell v. Federal Election Commission*,[23] the mammoth 2003 decision upholding the major provisions of the federal McCain-Feingold law. In the last chapter, we saw how the Court upheld McCain-Feingold's expansion of the corporate and labor union ban on spending general treasury funds on "electioneering communications." But the Court also upheld a ban on political parties collecting "soft money." Before McCain-Feingold, parties would collect large contributions from individuals, corporations and labor unions to fund "issue advertisements" promoting the party's candidates (and opposing the other parties' candidate). Large party donors bought extensive access to elected officials, including the president and congressional leaders. Because the funds collected for these ads were not used for express advocacy, the parties took the position that contributions did not count against the federal limits (known as the "hard money" limits). McCain-Feingold banned the practice of parties' collecting soft money, and the Supreme Court, on a 5-4 vote, upheld the soft money contribution ban on grounds it was necessary to prevent corruption and the appearance of corruption. The case relied upon a broad definition of corruption — to prevent the sale of access and to limit ingratiation of donors with elected officials. Justice Kennedy, one of the dissenters, argued against this broader definition of corruption and said that ingratiation and access are not corruption (which later became the majority position in *Citizens United*).

Example I

Vermont passes one of the strictest campaign finance laws in the country. Among other things, the law limits the amount that may be contributed to some state offices to $400 per two-year election cycle (not per election).

---

20. *Colorado II*, 533 U.S. at 452.
21. *See* Richard L. Hasen, *The Constitutionality of a Soft Money Ban After* Colorado Republican II, 1 ELECTION L.J. 195, 203 (2002).
22. 539 U.S. 146 (2003).
23. 540 U.S. 93 (2003).

The amount is not indexed to inflation. While the value of volunteer time does not count toward the contribution limit, expenses associated with volunteer time does (such as providing coffee and donuts to voters who come to meet with a candidate at the volunteer's home). Political parties are subject to the same contribution limit. Is the Vermont contribution limit constitutional under the Supreme Court's cases through *McConnell*?

Explanation

The amount of the contribution limits looks quite low, much lower than the limits in Buckley ($1,000 in 1976 dollars per election) or in *Shrink Missouri* ($1075 per election). This is $400 for use in both a primary and a general election. Now it may be that because Vermont is a smaller state, the amount per voter is not that low. But combined with the other restrictions (such as the counting of expenses connected with volunteer time), this looks like a low limit indeed.

Nonetheless, following *Shrink Missouri* and other cases it looks as if such a limit would be constitutional. A $400 contribution limit would not be "so radical in effect as to render political association ineffective, drive the sound of a candidate's voice below the level of notice, and render contributions pointless." The *Shrink Missouri* standard requires deference to the legislature and requires little or no evidence showing that a $400 limit serves anticorruption purposes and prevents the appearance of corruption. Such a claim is "neither novel nor implausible." Limiting political party contributions, as in *Colorado Republican II* and *McConnell*, could be justified by anticorruption and anticircumvention interests — in particular, the desire to prevent political parties from becoming conduits for ingratiation and access.

14.2. NEW SKEPTICISM ABOUT CONTRIBUTION LIMITS

Soon after *Shrink Missouri* and these other deferential cases, the Court abruptly changed course when Chief Justice Roberts and Justice Alito replaced Chief Justice Rehnquist and Justice O'Connor. We saw the results of this personnel change on the spending limits side of campaign finance jurisprudence in the last chapter. Parallel change is now occurring on the contributions side.

We begin with the 2006 opinion in *Randall v. Sorrell*,[24] the basis for Example 1 above. Vermont's Act 64 imposed both candidate spending limits and contribution limits. As for spending limits, Act 64

---

24. *Randall v. Sorrell*, 548 U.S. 230, 262 (2006). This section draws from Richard L. Hasen, *The Newer Incoherence: Competition, Social Science, and Balancing in Campaign Finance Law After* Randall v. Sorrell, 68 Ohio St. L.J. 849 (2007).

imposes mandatory expenditure limits on the total amount a candidate for state office can spend during a "two-year general election style," i.e., the primary plus the general election, in approximately the following amounts: governor, $300,000; lieutenant governor, $100,000; other statewide offices, $45,000; state senator, $4,000 (plus an additional $2,500 for each additional seat in the district); state representative (two-member district), $3,000; and state representative (single member district), $2,100. These limits are adjusted for inflation in odd-numbered years based on the consumer price index.[25]

The act also imposed additional limits on incumbents seeking election, and defined "expenditures" broadly.[26] Moreover, Act 64 treated certain expenditures made by others against the candidates limit. "These provisions apply so as to count against a campaign's expenditure limit any spending by political parties or committees that is coordinated with the campaign and benefits the candidate."[27]

As for the contribution limits,

> Act 64 also imposes strict contribution limits. The amount any single individual can contribute to the campaign of a candidate for state office during a "two-year general election cycle" is limited as follows: governor, lieutenant governor, and other statewide offices, $400; state senator, $300; and state representative, $200. Unlike its expenditure limits, Act 64's contribution limits are not indexed for inflation.
>
> A political committee is subject to these same limits. So is a political party, defined broadly to include "any subsidiary, branch or local unit" of a party as well as any "national or regional affiliates" of a party (taken separately or together). Thus, for example, the statute treats the local, state, and national affiliates of the Democratic Party as if they were a single entity and limits their total contribution to a single candidate's campaign for governor (during the primary and general election together) to $400.[28]

In considering the constitutionality of both the expenditure and contribution limits, the nine justices issued six opinions. Unsurprisingly, a majority of the Court held that the candidate *spending limits* were unconstitutional under *Buckley*.

The Court's treatment of the *contribution limits* question, however, was far more fractured. Three justices (Ginsburg, Souter, and Stevens) would have upheld the Vermont contribution limits under *Shrink Missouri*, holding that campaign contribution should be struck down only when they are "laughabl[y]"[29] low and when they would depress candidates' voices "to the level

---

25. *Randall*, 548 U.S. at 237 (citations omitted).
26. Id. at 238.
27. Id.
28. Id. at 238-239.
29. *Randall*, 548 U.S. at 286 (Souter, J., dissenting).

of political inaudibility."[30] For these justices, deference remained the appropriate legal standard.

Two justices (Scalia and Thomas) would have struck down the Vermont contribution limits not because they were unconstitutionally low, but out of a belief that *all* contribution limits should be subject to strict scrutiny and struck down as a violation of the First Amendment.[31] Justice Kennedy was a bit less categorical than Justices Scalia and Thomas, but he agreed that the Vermont contribution limits were unconstitutional, being "even more stifling than the ones that survived *Shrink*'s unduly lenient review."[32]

The key was the plurality of three justices in the middle: Alito, Breyer, and Chief Justice Roberts. These justices purported to apply existing precedent, including *Buckley* and *Shrink Missouri*, to reach the conclusion that the Vermont contribution limits, unlike the limits upheld in other cases including *Shrink Missouri*, were too low.[33] Because this plurality forms the controlling bloc of votes on the Court on the question of low contribution limits, it is worth examining its analysis in some detail.

The plurality drew its constitutional test from the concern noted in *Buckley* over contribution limits' being so low as to prevent candidates from amassing resources necessary to engage in effective advocacy. The plurality opinion notes: "At some point the constitutional risks . . . [from low contribution limits] become too great. . . . [C]ontribution limits that are too low can also harm the electoral process by preventing challengers from mounting effective campaigns against incumbent officeholders, thereby reducing democratic accountability."[34] Citing his own concurring opinion in *Shrink Missouri* setting forth the participatory self-government rationale, Justice Breyer for the plurality added: "[I]ndividual Members of the Court have expressed concern lest too low a limit magnify the 'reputation-related or media-related advantages of incumbency and thereby insulat[e] legislators from effective electoral challenge.'"[35]

The plurality set forth a two-part test for judging the constitutionality of the *amount* of a campaign contribution limit in the "exercise of independent judicial judgment."[36]

(1) Are there "danger signs" that the risks to the political process in terms of decreased political competition are too high?[37]

---

30. *Id.* at 290.
31. *Id.* at 266-267 (Thomas, J., concurring).
32. *Id.* at 264 (Kennedy, J., concurring).
33. *Id.* at 262 (plurality opinion).
34. *Id.* at 248-249.
35. *Id.* at 248.
36. *Id.* at 249.
37. *Id.*

(2) If so, based on a review of the record, is the measure "closely drawn," or is it too restrictive given the anticorruption goals it is trying to accomplish?[38]

Applying this two-part test, the plurality held that Vermont's $200 to $400 contribution limits per election cycle were unconstitutional. Under the first part of the test, the plurality concluded: "As compared with the contribution limits upheld by the Court in the past, and with those in force in other States, Act 64's limits are sufficiently low as to generate suspicion they are not closely drawn."[39] The plurality pointed to the following factors:

- Vermont's limits apply per election cycle (that is, a single limit applied to contributions made during both the primary and general election), not per election — so they are essentially half the size they appear to be.[40]
- The limits are very low, especially compared to amounts the Court has upheld in the past, as adjusted for inflation.[41]
- The amounts are very low when compared to other state limits (seven states have contribution limits at or below $500 per election, twice the Act 64 limits).[42]
- No state has a limit lower than $200 on contributions from political parties to candidates.[43]
- The amount is well below any limit previously upheld. In making this comparison, the Court looked at the amount of contributions per citizen ("As of 2006, the ratio of the contribution limit to the size of the constituency in Vermont is .00064, while Missouri's ratio is .00044, 31% lower."), as well as the type of race involved ("A campaign for state auditor is likely to be less costly than a campaign for governor; campaign costs do not automatically increase or decrease in precise proportion to the size of an electoral district.").[44]

Once the plurality determined that there were "danger signs,"[45] it moved to the second part of the test. Under this part, the court must "independently and carefully . . . determine whether . . . [the measure's] contribution limits

---

38. Id.; *see also* id. at 253.
39. Id. at 249.
40. Id.
41. Id. at 250.
42. Id. at 250-251.
43. Id.
44. Id. at 251-252.
45. Id. at 253.

are 'closely drawn' to match the State's interests."[46] For five reasons, the plurality held that the Vermont limit was not closely drawn and was thus unconstitutional:

- "First, the record suggests, though it does not conclusively prove, that Act 64's contribution limits . . . [are too] . . . restrict[ive]."[47] Much of this analysis depended upon the testimony of expert witnesses.[48]
- "Second, Act 64's insistence that political parties abide by *exactly* the same low contribution limits that apply to other contributors threatens harm to a particularly important political right, the right to associate in a political party."[49] The plurality also detailed other ways in which the law hampers political parties.[50]
- "Third, the Act's treatment of volunteer services aggravates the problem. . . . [T]he act does not exclude the expenses those volunteers incur, such as travel expenses, in the course of campaign activities. . . . That combination, low limits and no exceptions" means volunteers could easily exceed the contribution limit through minimal activity such as travel or giving doughnuts to neighbors.[51]
- "Fourth, unlike the contribution limits we upheld in *Shrink*, . . . Act 64's contribution limits are not adjusted for inflation."[52]
- "Fifth, we have found nowhere in the record any special justification that might warrant a contribution limit so low or so restrictive as to bring about the serious associational and expressive problems that we have described."[53]

The Court concluded that the limits "violate the First Amendment, for they burden First Amendment interests in a manner that is disproportionate to the public purposes they were enacted to advance."[54]

It is not clear how much significance to attribute to *Randall*. To date, there has not been a single case in the lower courts since *Randall* to strike down another campaign contribution limit as too low; courts have rejected those challenges so far. *Randall* presents a non-binding (because there is no majority opinion), multi-factor test that has been hard for plaintiffs to

---

46. Id.
47. Id.
48. Id. at 254.
49. Id. at 256.
50. For example, the plurality noted that "the Act would severely inhibit collective political activity by preventing a political party from using contributions by small donors to provide meaningful assistance to any individual candidate." Id. at 258.
51. Id. at 259-260.
52. Id. at 261.
53. Id.
54. Id. at 262.

meet — and few jurisdictions had contribution limits as low (and with such strict rules) as Vermont did.

Justice Alito and Chief Justice Roberts decided the case early in their tenure, and they may have signed on to Justice Breyer's cautious fact-intensive opinion to avoid making any major decisions on campaign finance questions. Now, with more years — and *Citizens United* and other campaign finance cases behind them — these justices have shown themselves willing to move more boldly in reining in contribution limits. At some point they could join Justices Scalia and Thomas in believing that strict scrutiny should apply to review of contribution limits.

In *Davis v. Federal Election Commission*,[55] the Court struck down a provision of the McCain-Feingold campaign finance law giving U.S. House candidates the right to collect increased individual contributions for their campaigns when they faced a self-financed opponent spending large sums. The Court held that the law was not a permissible anticorruption measure but rather a measure premised on an impermissible equality rationale to level the playing fields for candidates.

Most recently, in *McCutcheon v. FEC*,[56] the Supreme Court on a 5-4 vote struck down federal aggregate contribution limits. Federal law capped at $48,600 the total amount that an individual can give to all federal candidates for office during a two-year election cycle. It also limited to $74,600 the total amount an individual can give to political committees that make contributions to candidates and set a total cap of $123,200 for contributions in the two-year cycle.

Although the Supreme Court in *Buckley* upheld FECA's $25,000 aggregate limit in a brief discussion (reprinted in full on page 332 of this book), Chief Justice Roberts, writing for a plurality of justices, held that *Buckley*'s analysis was distinguishable and its three-sentence analysis of the aggregate limits insufficient. The plurality did not decide to apply strict scrutiny to contribution limits, finding the issue unnecessary to reach in this case. Only Justice Thomas, in a separate opinion, urged application of strict scrutiny. (Interestingly, Justices Scalia and Kennedy, who had in the past agreed with Justice Thomas on strict scrutiny, did not join the opinion.) Four justices, in an opinion by Justice Breyer, dissented.

Despite the Court's failure to adopt strict scrutiny for review of campaign contribution limitations in *McCutcheon* (something the Court left the door open to in a future case), the plurality opinion is doctrinally very significant and makes it much more likely that other campaign contribution limits could be struck down as unconstitutional going forward. To begin with, the opinion incorporated the narrow definition of corruption from the

---

55. 554 U.S. 724, 740 (2008).
56. 134 S.Ct. 1434 (2014).

spending limits case, *Citizens United*, ignoring the much broader definition in cases such as *Shrink Missouri*.[57] "Ingratiation and access" or "undue influence" do not count as "corruption" for purposes of determining the constitutionality of contribution limits. Similarly, the opinion read "appearance of corruption" narrowly, to apply only to an "appearance of quid pro quo corruption," much narrower than *Buckley*'s language about "appearance of improper influence."[58] Finally, the Court ratcheted up the meaning of "exact scrutiny" so that it is apparently a much more "rigorous" test for reviewing the constitutionality of contribution limits.[59] How close it is to strict scrutiny is uncertain.

Also of note is dicta appearing in *McCutcheon* extolling the virtues of money flowing through political parties, perhaps laying the groundwork for a renewed attack on the soft money limitations in the McCain-Feingold law. The chief justice wrote

> Of course a candidate would be pleased with a donor who contributed not only to the candidate himself, but also to other candidates from the same party, to party committees, and to PACs supporting the party. But there is a clear, administrable line between money beyond the base limits funneled in an identifiable way to a candidate — for which the candidate feels obligated — and money within the base limits given widely to a candidate's party — for which the candidate, like all other members of the party, feels grateful.
>
> When donors furnish widely distributed support within all applicable base limits, all members of the party or supporters of the cause may benefit, and the leaders of the party or cause may feel particular gratitude. That gratitude stems from the basic nature of the party system, in which party members join together to further common political beliefs, and citizens can choose to support a party because they share some, most, or all of those beliefs. *See Tashjian.* To recast such shared interest, standing alone, as an opportunity for *quid pro quo* corruption would dramatically expand government regulation of the political process. *Cf. California Democratic Party v. Jones* (recognizing the Government's "role to play in structuring and monitoring the election process," but rejecting "the proposition that party affairs are public affairs, free of First Amendment protections").
>
> The Government suggests that it is the *solicitation* of large contributions that poses the danger of corruption, but the aggregate limits are not limited to any direct solicitation by an officeholder or candidate. *Cf. McConnell* (opinion of KENNEDY, J.) (rejecting a ban on "soft money" contributions to national

---

57. *Id.* at 1450-51.
58. *Id.*; *Buckley v. Valeo*, 424 U.S. 1, 27 (1976); *see also* Richard L. Hasen, *Opening the Political Money Chutes*, Reuters, (Apr. 7, 2014), http://blogs.reuters.com/great-debate/2014/04/07/opening-the-political-money-chutes/.
59. *See McCutcheon*, 134 S.Ct. at 1446 ("[I]f a law that restricts political speech does not 'avoid unnecessary abridgement' of First Amendment rights, it cannot survive 'rigorous' review." (citing *Buckley*, 424 U.S. at 25)).

parties, but approving a ban on the solicitation of such contributions as "a direct and necessary regulation of federal candidates' and officeholders' receipt of *quids*"). We have no occasion to consider a law that would specifically ban candidates from soliciting donations — within the base limits — that would go to many other candidates, and would add up to a large sum. For our purposes here, it is enough that the aggregate limits at issue are not directed specifically to candidate behavior.

There was a lot at stake in the *McCutcheon* ruling. With the aggregate limits gone, a member of Congress would be able ask for a single $3.6 million contribution (through a "joint fundraising committee" — essentially an arrangement to take a check to be disbursed to more than one campaign) to distribute to all federal congressional candidates and to national and local political parties. He or she could keep from that check only $5,200 ($2,600 for the primary and another $2,600 for the general election), but the parties and PACs could then use the passed-on funds to run ads attacking his or her opponent. As a big bundler, this member of Congress would have great influence over other members. And, of course, the $3.6 million donor would have the most influence of all. The majority opinion by Chief Justice Roberts disagreed strongly with the dissenting opinion by Justice Breyer over how likely it is that politicians and parties will begin raising large sums through joint fundraising committees.

Example 2

The city of Pacificana imposes a $500 per election individual contribution limitation on contributions to city candidates, which is indexed to inflation. The city also imposes a $1,000 contribution limitation on contributions from political parties to individuals. Assess the constitutionality of both contribution limitations under current Supreme Court jurisprudence.

Explanation

Let's consider the individual $500 contribution limitation first. Under the old *Shrink Missouri* test, there would seem to be little question that the limitation would be constitutional. The amount does not seem so low as to make a candidate's voice inaudible. However, things are more uncertain under *Randall* and *McCutcheon*. There is no majority opinion, and so lower courts are not necessarily bound by the Justice Breyer plurality decision. Nonetheless, most courts that have considered the constitutional question of these limits have applied the framework from the plurality in *Randall*. Also, as noted in the text above, no court applying the *Randall* plurality framework has ever found a limit aside from Vermont's unconstitutionally low. Indeed, federal courts have rejected a challenge to the city of San Diego's $500 contribution limit.[60] Among other things, the district court noted that the limit was more than double the amount struck down in Vermont; it was indexed to inflation; and it did not count volunteer expenses toward contribution limits. The court also considered evidence whether the $500 limit inhibited political competition.

It is unclear whether and how *McCutcheon* would change this *Randall* analysis. We do not know, for example, what more "rigorous" scrutiny looks like, or whether the narrowed definitions of corruption or the appearance of corruption would lead courts to strike down more individual contribution limitations as unconstitutionally low.

Consider now the $1,000 contribution limitation imposed on political party contributions to city candidates. *Randall* did not directly address the constitutionality of such a limit. However, the *Randall* plurality, in assessing the many factors relevant to deciding the constitutionality of the individual contribution limits, noted that the law limited political parties to exactly the same amount of contributions as individuals, even if parties got their money through collecting many small contributions from many contributors. Furthermore, the language about political parties in *McCutcheon* suggests that courts may begin recognizing special First Amendment rights for political parties when it comes to campaign contribution limitations.

In the San Diego case (decided after *Randall* but before *McCutcheon*), the district court held that the party contribution limitation was likely unconstitutional for the city to prevent political parties from making direct contributions to candidates. After the city enacted a $1,000 contribution limitation for political party contributions to candidates in response to the court's ruling, the court then struck down that $1,000 limit as well, holding it was too low under *Randall*. So far this ruling is the only court ruling recognizing that political parties have the right to make direct contributions to candidates and that the amount of such contributions can be unconstitutionally low. Crucially, San Diego law limited the amount people could contribute to parties for use in contributing to candidates to $500. After the litigation ended, the city enacted $20,000 contribution limitations to political parties, which so far have not been challenged. It is unclear whether other courts would follow the San Diego case should the issue arise again, although the language in *McCutcheon* appears to make it more likely.

---

60. *Thalheimer v. City of San Diego*, 09-CV-2862-IEG BGS, 2012 WL 177414 (S.D. Cal. Jan. 20, 2012); *Thalheimer v. City of San Diego*, 645 F.3d 1109 (9th Cir. 2011). Disclosure: I was one of the lawyers for the city of San Diego defending their campaign finance laws against constitutional challenge.

Example 3

The city of Pacificana enacts a law barring labor unions and corporations, including MCFL corporations, from making direct campaign contributions to city candidates. As authority for this law, the city's attorneys cite to the U.S. Supreme Court's decision in FEC v. *Beaumont*, which upheld such a limitation against corporations. Challengers to the law take the case against the city to the Supreme Court, arguing that the Court should overturn *Beaumont*. How will the Supreme Court rule?

Explanation

This is a very difficult question. In *Beaumont*, the Supreme Court held such a ban was constitutional, applying lower "exacting scrutiny" even though the law was a ban, rather than a limit, on contributions. You will recall that the reason the Court had applied lower exacting scrutiny in *Buckley* was because the Court said that the main First Amendment act in a contribution was the associational act of contributing, and it was all right to limit the *amount* of that contribution. With a ban, however, a corporate entity cannot even engage in the symbolic act of making a small contribution.

Beaumont was one of the cases decided at the height of the Supreme Court's deference to campaign finance regulation — the period that also included *Shrink Missouri*, *Colorado II*, and *McConnell*. Among the rationales the Court accepted for the corporate contribution ban was an interest in preventing corporate distortion of political outcomes, an interest first recognized in *Austin*.

Lower courts so far, including the courts considering San Diego's ban on entity contributions to candidates, have upheld the bans, viewing themselves as bound by the Supreme Court's decision in *Beaumont*. This remains true even after *McCutcheon*, which did not overrule *Beaumont*. But the Supreme Court would not be so bound, and it is hard to see the current Court simply endorsing *Beaumont* if it chose to revisit the issue. (The Court so far has turned down two cases raising the issue.[61]) It might follow *Beaumont* for reasons of *stare decisis*. But the five justices in the *Citizens United* majority could well choose to overturn *Beaumont*.

The justices might conclude that contribution bans should be subject to strict scrutiny because they bar even symbolic contributions. Even without strict scrutiny, under the *McCutcheon* case the Court will look more skeptically about anything that limits contributions. Furthermore, part of the rationale of *Beaumont* has been discredited: The Court no longer subscribes to the view

---

61. *United States v. Danielczyk*, 683 F.3d 611 (4th Cir. 2012) *cert. denied*, 133 S.Ct. 1459 (2013), *Iowa Right to Life v. Tooker*, 717 F.3d 576 (8th Cir. 2013), *cert. denied*, 134 S.Ct. 1787 (2014).

that corporate money may be limited to prevent distortion of the electoral process (as *Citizens United* overturned *Austin*).

Nonetheless, the question is whether a corporate (and labor union) contribution ban might be justified on anticircumvention grounds. As an individual, I can give contributions only to the legal limit. But if corporations could also do so, it would be possible to set up a very large number of corporations to make contributions to a set of candidates from a set of individuals. This would allow, through creative accounting and careful avoidance of rules that prevent individuals from "earmarking" contributions to others toward specific candidates, a way to circumvent the contribution limitation.

It is certainly possible that the Court could accept this rationale. But it is also possible for the Court to rely on *McCutcheon*'s holding that ingratiation and access are not corruption, and use that to strike a corporate ban. The Court had an opportunity to address the issue in a case being held for *McCutcheon* but declined to hear the case. So we will have to wait a while longer for the answer to this question.

14.3. THE RISE OF SUPER PACS AND OTHER OUTSIDE GROUPS

Finally, we turn to the major development in campaign finance law since *Citizens United*: the rise of "Super PACs" and other outside groups engaged in raising very large (and sometimes undisclosed) campaign contributions. These groups do not donate to candidates (or if they do, they have a separate fund that does so), and they do not coordinate campaign strategy with candidates.

As we saw in the last chapter, in *Citizens United* the Supreme Court resolved what appeared to be an empirical question about independent spending and corruption: "We now conclude that independent expenditures, including those made by corporations, do not give rise to corruption or the appearance of corruption."

The statement of fact is controversial. If the court believes that the government may limit a $3,000 contribution to a candidate because of its corruptive potential, how could it not believe that the government has a similar anticorruption interest in limiting $3 million spent in an independent effort to elect that candidate? Would a federal candidate not feel much more beholden to the big spender than the more modest contributor?

Whether or not the statement is true as an empirical matter, courts and the Federal Election Commission have accepted the statement as fact for purposes of deciding other campaign finance controversies. The Court's declaration has spawned the Super PAC and the unraveling of campaign finance law. First, the United States Court of Appeals for the D.C. Circuit in *SpeechNow.Org v. FEC* struck down the $5,000 individual contribution limit on contributions to political action committees that make only independent expenditures. It held that if independent spending cannot corrupt, then an individual's contributions to an independent group cannot corrupt.[62] The case relied heavily on *Citizens United*, citing it 13 times in its ruling. The effect of *Speechnow.Org* was to eliminate the $5,000 contribution limit to political action committees — or PACs — that only spend independently to support or oppose federal candidates. The United States decided not to appeal this D.C. Circuit ruling to the Supreme Court, likely fearing that the Supreme Court could issue an opinion calling more contribution limitations into question.

Following the *SpeechNow.Org* decision allowing individuals to donate unlimited sums to independent expenditure committees, the Federal Election Commission held that corporations and unions could donate unlimited sums to these groups as well,[63] leading to the creation of "Super PACs":[64] campaign committees registered with the Federal Election Commission that accept unlimited individual, corporate, and labor union contributions to fund election ads. Finally, federal courts held that even political committees that make donations to candidates could establish a separate fund for independent spending, thereby turning every PAC into a potential Super PAC.[65] The FEC has not issued any new regulations governing Super PACs, including concerning what counts as illegal coordination with campaigns.

Scholars are still assessing how these changes in campaign finance rules, on both the spending and contributions side, have affected elections. In the 2007-2008 election season, political action committees spent just under $1.2 billion on federal election activity (equivalent to $1.28 billion in 2014 dollars).[66] In the 2011-2012 election season, the amount increased to $2.2 billion[67], an 83% increase (a 77% increase when inflation is taken into account[68]). More dramatically, the total amount spent on independent expenditures for or against presidential candidates in the 2007-2008

---

62. *SpeechNow.org v. FEC*, 599 F.3d 686 (D.C. Cir. 2010), *cert. denied sub nom Keating v. FEC*, 131 S.Ct. 553 (2010).

63. FEC Adv. Op. 2010-09 (Club for Growth); FEC Adv. Op. 2010-11 (Commonsense 10).

64. The term originates with Eliza Newlin Carney, *FEC Rulings Open Door for "Super" PACs*, National Journal, Aug. 2, 2010, http://mobile.nationaljournal.com/columns/rules-of-the-game/fec-rulings-open-door-for-super-pacs-20100802.

65. *Carey v. FEC*, 791 F. Supp. 2d 121 (D.D.C. 2011).

66. *Table 1, PAC Financial Activity, 2007-2008*, Federal Election Commission, http://www.fec.gov/press/press2009/20090415PAC/documents/1summary2008.pdf.

67. *FEC Summarizes Campaign Activity of the 2011-2012 Election Cycle*, Federal Election Commission, http://www.fec.gov/press/press2013/pdf/20130419_2012yesummary.pdf.

68. These figures were calculated using the Bureau of Labor Statistics' Inflation Calculator at http://www.bls.gov/data/inflation_calculator.htm.

election season was about $169 million (equivalent to $185 million in 2014 dollars).[69] Each major presidential candidate was backed by at least one Super PAC (sometimes more), with some raising funds from the candidate's family members and some run by former close advisors or campaign managers for the candidates. Candidates may even make a general fundraising appeal for supportive Super PACs so long as the candidate does not ask for contributors to give the committee more than $5,000. What is prohibited is coordination between the candidate/candidate's campaign and the Super PAC on advertising or campaign strategy. (That type of coordination is really unnecessary, as the Super PAC can simply follow the advertising lead set by the campaign.)

Independent spending in the presidential election increased by 245% from 2008 to 2012 (a 224% increase when inflation is taken into account). There has been a similar explosion in outside money in House and Senate races. In 2008, total non-party independent expenditures in the House were just under $26 million, rising to almost $98 million in 2010 and $197 million in 2012. On the Senate side, total non-party independent expenditures were just under $18 million in 2008, rising to $97 million in 2010 and $259 million in 2012. That is a 662% increase in House outside funding comparing 2008 to 2012 and a 1,338% increase on the Senate side.[70]

Perhaps surprisingly, most of the large Super PAC contributions have come from individuals (such as Sheldon Adelson, who spent tens of millions of dollars supporting Republican candidates) rather than from corporations. This may be surprising in two ways: First, even before *Citizens United* and *SpeechNow.Org*, wealthy individuals could already spend unlimited sums independently supporting or opposing federal candidates (thanks to the ruling in *Buckley*). Second, some predicted a large rise in corporate contributions following *SpeechNow.Org*. What happened?

---

69. *Presidential Campaign Receipts*, Federal Election Commission, http://www.fec.gov/press/press2009/20090608Pres/1_OverviewPresFinActivity1996-2008.pdf. According to the FEC,

> Independent expenditures reported to the Commission in connection with the 2012 presidential election totaled approximately $583.8 million as of December 31, 2012, with approximately $373.5 million reported by Independent Expenditure-Only Committees, $8.3 million reported by Committees with Non-Contribution Accounts and $26.1 million reported by other PACs. Persons other than political committees and party committees report[ed] making $131.7 million and nearly $44.3 million, respectively, in independent expenditures in connection with the presidential election. Independent expenditures advocating the election of presidential candidates totaled $118.5 million, while $465.3 million was reported to advocate the defeat of presidential candidates.

FEC Summarizes Campaign Activity of the 2011-2012 Election Cycle, supra.
70. *Vital Statistics on Congress, Chapter 3, Table 3-14*, Brookings Institute, http://www.brookings.edu/~/media/Research/Files/Reports/2013/07/vital%20statistics%20congress%20mann%20ornstein/Vital%20Statistics%20Chapter%203%20%20Campaign%20Finance%20in%20Congressional%20Elections.pdf.

On the first point, it is true that before *Citizens United* people could spend unlimited sums on independent advertising directly supporting or opposing candidates. But that money had to be spent by the individual directly. It could not be given to a political action committee, which had an individual contribution cap of $5,000 and could not take corporate or union funding. In many cases, wealthy individuals did not want to spend their own money on advertising, which would say "Paid for by Sheldon Adelson" or "Paid for by George Soros," so fewer of these ads were made. The only way to avoid having your name plastered across every ad was to give to groups that were known as "527 organizations," which claimed they could take unlimited money from individuals (including, sometimes, corporate and labor union money) on grounds that they were not PACs under the FEC's definition of PACs. These organizations were somewhat successful, but a legal cloud always hung over them. After *Citizens United* and *SpeechNow.Org*, what was once of questionable legality before the court's decision was fully legal.

On the second point, contributions to Super PACs are fully disclosed, although the disclosure sometimes is delayed. Corporate contributions to Super PACs supporting particular candidates could alienate customers (you might be less likely to buy a bar of soap from a corporation supporting the other party), and it turns out there is an easy way for corporations to contribute money without triggering disclosure — through the use of 501(c)(4) and (c)(6) organizations.[71] We take up this latest trend in the next chapter on disclosure.

Example 4

The brother of a U.S. Senate candidate in your state comes to you for legal advice. The client wants to know how he can maximize support for his sister's campaign. What kind of fundraising can the client do, from whom may he raise contributions, and how will it work?

Explanation

The brother has two options: to work with the campaign or to work for an outside group such as a Super PAC. The client may devote unlimited volunteer hours for his sister's campaign, raising contributions from individuals who may give no more than the current individual federal contribution limits ($2,600 in the primary and $2,600 in the general election, subject to additional aggregate federal limits). The client may also solicit up to $5,000 in contributions for the campaign from a federally registered PAC

---

71. On the differences and similarities between Super PACs, 501(c)(4) organizations, and other organizations, *see* Richard Briffault, *Super PACs*, 96 Minn. L. Rev. 1644 (2012).

(and that PAC in turn may fund such contributions only from contributions of up to $5,000 from individuals). With aggregate limits gone thanks to *McCutcheon*, there may be new fundraising opportunities, but the money cannot be directly earmarked for the candidate.

Alternatively, the client may set up or work with an independent group supporting his sister's candidacy for Senate. Such a group could be a Super PAC or, as explained in the next chapter, a 501(c) organization. The client may devote unlimited volunteer hours working for the independent group supporting his sister's election, raising contributions from individuals, corporations, labor unions and other entities that are not foreign-owned or foreign-controlled. The amount of these contributions are unlimited so long as they are being used to fund independent spending supporting or opposing a candidate for federal office. (If the entity wishes to donate funds up to $5,000 to the sister's campaign, it must set up a separate account subject to source and dollar limitations.)

The one wrinkle with the second option is that the brother, and the outside Super PAC (or other outside organization), may not engage in illegal coordination with the campaign. The brother and others from the outside group may not discuss strategy or advertising with the sister or anyone in her campaign organization. The group may instead simply follow the lead of the sister's campaign in terms of message, advertising areas, and so forth. The sister may make a general fundraising appeal for the outside group but may not ask for donors to give more than $5,000 to the group.

If you were the client, which path would you take?

Campaign Finance Disclosure

15.1. THE PATH FROM *BUCKLEY* TO *MCINTYRE*[1]

As with the framework for analyzing constitutional questions surrounding campaign spending and contributions, campaign finance disclosure analysis begins with *Buckley v. Valeo*.[2] Since *Buckley*, things have gotten a lot more complicated, but *Buckley* set the ground rules, as it has for contributions and spending limits.

In *Buckley*, the Supreme Court considered the constitutionality of the FECA's disclosure provisions. Generally speaking, the FECA requires candidates and political committees to file periodic reports with the Federal Election Commission of contributions received and expenditures made for the purpose of influencing federal elections. Section 434(e) of the FECA requires individuals or groups to file a statement with the FEC if they make contributions or independent expenditures over $200 (it was $100 at the time of *Buckley*) that are not otherwise subject to disclosure by political committees or candidates. Challengers argued that these laws violate the First Amendment rights of individuals to keep their political contributions and spending anonymous, especially if they are from minor and unpopular political parties.

---

1. This section draws from Richard L. Hasen, *The Surprisingly Complex Case for Disclosure of Contributions and Expenditures Funding Sham Issue Advocacy*, 48 UCLA L. Rev. 265 (2000).
2. 424 U.S. 1 (1976).

After noting that "compelled disclosure, in itself, can seriously infringe on privacy of association and belief guaranteed by the First Amendment," the Buckley Court upheld the FECA's disclosure requirements under an "exacting scrutiny" standard.[3] Although this is the same standard the Court announced in reviewing contribution limits (see the last two chapters), the analysis of disclosure questions raises different government interests and balancing than we have seen in the disclosure context.

In particular, the Court recognized three "sufficiently important" government interests justifying the FECA's disclosure rules against First Amendment challenge:[4]

1. Disclosure Deters Corruption (the "anticorruption" interest). Disclosure allows interested parties to look for connections between campaign contributors or spenders and the candidates who benefit from those contributions or spending.

2. Disclosure Provides Information Helpful to Voters (the "information" interest). Voters often are rationally ignorant regarding details about the candidates or issues on the ballot. Disclosure provides information helpful to voters. For example, a voter who knows that the insurance industry or the Sierra Club backs a particular ballot measure or candidate may use that information as a proxy for whether a vote for the measure or candidate is in the voter's interest.

3. Disclosure Aids in the Enforcement of Other Campaign Finance Laws (the "enforcement" interest). For example, without effective disclosure, contributors could evade campaign contribution limits.

Even as it acknowledged these three important interests, the Buckley Court also recognized that contributors and members of some minor parties might face threats, reprisals, or harassment if their identities were disclosed. Accordingly, it held that such parties were entitled to an exemption from campaign finance disclosure laws upon proof of a "reasonable probability that the compelled disclosure of a party's contributors' names will subject them to threats, harassment, or reprisals from either Government officials or private parties."[5] Indeed, the Court in a later case recognized the right of the Ohio Socialist Workers Party to such an exemption, a case to which we return in the next section.

Significantly, the Court rejected a challenge to section 434(e)'s requirement of disclosure for "'[e]very person . . . who makes contributions or expenditures . . . for the purpose of . . . influencing' the nomination or

---

3. Id. at 64, 84.
4. Id. at 66-68.
5. Id. at 74.

election of candidates for federal office."[6] The Court did not find a problem with the requirement to report contributions. However, the Court held that the FECA's requirement to report expenditures might be vague. "Due process requires that a criminal statute provide adequate notice to a person of ordinary intelligence that his contemplated conduct is illegal, for 'no man shall be held criminally responsible for conduct which he could not reasonably understand to be proscribed.'"[7] It therefore construed the statute narrowly. "To insure that the reach of §434(e) is not impermissibly broad, we construe 'expenditure' . . . to reach only funds used for communications that expressly advocate the election or defeat of a clearly identified candidate. This reading is directed precisely to that spending that is unambiguously related to the campaign of a particular federal candidate."[8]

The Court wrote

> As narrowed, 434(e) . . . does not reach all partisan discussion for it only requires disclosure of those expenditures that expressly advocate a particular election result. This might have been fatal if the only purpose of §434(e) were to stem corruption or its appearance by closing a loophole in the general disclosure requirements. But the disclosure provisions, including §434(e), serve another, informational interest, and even as construed §434(e) increases the fund of information concerning those who support the candidates. It goes beyond the general disclosure requirements to shed the light of publicity on spending that is unambiguously campaign related but would not otherwise be reported because it takes the form of independent expenditures or of contributions to an individual or group not itself required to report the names of its contributors. By the same token, it is not fatal that §434(e) encompasses purely independent expenditures uncoordinated with a particular candidate or his agent. The corruption potential of these expenditures may be significantly different, but the informational interest can be as strong as it is in coordinated spending, for disclosure helps voters to define more of the candidates' constituencies.

The significance of this passage is that in it the Court recognized broad reasons for requiring disclosure, even though it construed the statute to leave much campaign-related activity not disclosed. For example, after *Buckley* an ad that said to "Call Bob Dole and tell him what you think of his lousy Medicare plan" would not be subject to disclosure, because it lacked words of express advocacy. As we will see in the next section, that left a large hole in disclosure provisions until the 2002 McCain-Feingold law expanded federal statutory disclosure requirements.

---

6. *Id.* at 77.
7. *Id.*
8. *Id.* at 79-80.

Although the Court discussed campaign finance disclosure in a few cases after Buckley,[9] those cases essentially continued Buckley's disclosure jurisprudence. For example, in First National Bank v. Bellotti (the corporate spending limits case considered in Chapter 13), the Court in dicta supported disclosure of corporate expenditures in ballot campaigns.

However, the jurisprudence took an uncertain turn when the Court decided McIntyre v. Ohio Elections Commission.[10] In McIntyre, the Ohio Elections Commission fined Margaret McIntyre for distributing unsigned leaflets expressing her opposition to a local referendum. McIntyre's conduct violated an Ohio law prohibiting the circulation of unsigned documents designed to influence voters in an election.

Applying an "'exacting scrutiny" standard, the Supreme Court held that Ohio could not justify its infringement of McIntyre's First Amendment right to engage in anonymous political speech. It held that the information interest "does not justify a state requirement that a writer make statements or disclosures she would otherwise omit."[11] It also rejected Ohio's interest in preventing fraud and libel because the prohibition was overbroad, "encompass[ing] documents that are not even arguably false or misleading."[12] Significantly, McIntyre distinguished laws requiring disclosure of the speaker's identity in candidate elections. The Court explained that "[r]equired disclosures about the level of financial support a candidate has received from various sources are supported by an interest in avoiding the appearance of corruption."[13] The Court further stated that "[i]n candidate elections, the Government can identify a compelling state interest in avoiding the corruption that might result from campaign expenditures. Disclosure of expenditures lessens the risk that individuals will spend money to support a candidate as a quid pro quo for special treatment."[14] The Court also placed special emphasis on the fact that McIntyre was a lone pamphleteer, acting independently and using her own modest resources. Thus, the Court distinguished its earlier dictum in Bellotti supporting disclosure of corporate spending in ballot campaigns, noting that the dictum "did not necessarily apply to independent communications by an individual like Mrs. McIntyre."[15]

Given the Court's decisions in Buckley and McIntyre, it was difficult to state the constitutional requirement for campaign finance disclosure. Buckley

---

9. See Fed. Election Comm'n v. Mass. Citizens for Life, 479 U.S. 238, 251-256 (1986); Brown v. Socialist Workers '74 Campaign Comm. (Ohio), 459 U.S. 87, 89-98 (1982); Citizens Against Rent Control v. City of Berkeley, 454 U.S. 290, 303 (1981); First Nat'l Bank v. Bellotti, 435 U.S. 765, 792 n.32 (1978).
10. 514 U.S. 334 (1995).
11. Id. at 348.
12. Id. at 351.
13. Id. at 354.
14. Id. at 356.
15. Id. at 354.

recognized three interests served by disclosure outlined above: the anticorruption interest, the information interest, and the enforcement interest. In *McIntyre*, the Court held that the anticorruption interest could not be invoked to support the Ohio disclosure law because there was no candidate to be corrupted. Ohio similarly could not rely upon the enforcement interest as the federal government did in *Buckley* because disclosure was unnecessary to support any other Ohio campaign finance regulation. Only the information interest remained, which the Court held was inadequate in McIntyre's case.

Following *McIntyre*, it was unclear whether the information interest standing alone ever constitutes adequate grounds for disclosure in a campaign finance case. If not, it would be unconstitutional to require disclosure of contributions and expenditures in any ballot measure campaign. The anticorruption interest is inapplicable because one cannot corrupt a ballot measure, and the enforcement interest is inapplicable because contribution and expenditure limits are unconstitutional in ballot measure campaigns. But the two cases were distinguishable in other ways as well. *Buckley* involved federal elections, which are among the most expensive and highly salient elections, whereas *McIntyre* involved a lone pamphleteer in a small local election. Furthermore, *Buckley* required disclosure in documents filed with a government agency after the expenditure or contribution, whereas McIntyre required disclosure on the face of the document itself.

Fortunately, as we shall see, in recent years we have a bit more clarity about how to resolve the tension between the two cases.

Example 1

The state of Pacifica enacts a provision requiring all contributors to ballot measure campaigns giving more than $100 to be disclosed in reports filed with the government. Furthermore, the law requires that television ads for or against a ballot measure include the names of the five individuals or entities who gave the most money to the committee. Would such a law be constitutional under *Buckley* and *McIntyre*?

Explanation

The law after *McIntyre* made this question somewhat uncertain. Of the three interests the *Buckley* Court recognized in disclosure, the only interest that could justify disclosure of contributors to ballot measure committees is the information interest. (There could be no anticorruption interest, because there are no candidates to corrupt in the ballot measure context and no other laws aside from disclosure to be enforced.) Yet in *McIntyre* the Supreme Court held that the disclosure interest standing alone was not sufficient to require disclosure of McIntyre's modest spending.

McIntyre, however, might be distinguished in a few ways. First, McIntyre was involved in spending very small sums, and the information interest is much stronger when it comes to revealing information about contributors who give thousands or even millions of dollars. Second, disclosure in reports is different than disclosure of identity on the face of the documents. That suggests that under McIntyre disclosure in reports could be constitutional while disclosing the identity of contributors in television advertising may not be.

For those who dislike uncertainty, there is good news: As we will see in the next section, courts have determined that disclosure applied to ballot measure elections is generally constitutional.

15.2. AFTER MCINTYRE: BROAD DISCLOSURE LAWS AND A NARROW HARASSMENT EXEMPTION

The Buckley-McIntyre tension spawned a host of cases in the lower courts over the constitutionality of campaign finance disclosure laws on the federal, state, and local level. The issue finally returned to the Supreme Court in a series of cases that put a strong majority of the justices on the Buckley pro-disclosure side of the line.

The first of these new cases was the McConnell case,[16] involving disputed provisions of the Bipartisan Campaign Reform Act (McCain-Feingold). We saw in the last two chapters that the Supreme Court in McConnell upheld the ban on parties collecting "soft money" and the extension of the ban or spending of corporate and labor union treasury funds to "electioneering communications," those television and radio advertisements featuring a candidate for federal office and broadcast close to the election. McCain-Feingold not only banned corporate and union money on those electioneering communications; it also required disclosure of the funders (entity or individual) of such communications.

In McConnell, Supreme Court upheld every challenged disclosure provision of the BCRA by at least a 5-4 vote. On the central disclosure provision involving electioneering communications, the Court's vote was 8-1. The McConnell Court first rejected plaintiffs' contention that the Constitution prohibited regulation of issue advocacy.[17]

The McConnell majority then held that BCRA section 201's disclosure requirements furthered the same three interests in deterring corruption, providing information, and facilitating enforcement of other limits recognized

16. 520 U.S. 93 (2003).
17. Id. at 193.

in *Buckley*.[18] Justice Kennedy, joined by Chief Justice Rehnquist and Justice Scalia, agreed that section 201's disclosure requirement was permissible as a means of providing information to voters—an interest Justice Kennedy could not bring himself to even name[19]—but he argued that the disclosure provision did not further interests in deterring corruption or aiding in the enforcement of other campaign finance laws.[20] Justice Scalia in his separate opinion expressed greater confidence that broad disclosure provisions—presumably including section 201—are valuable as a means of deterring corruption.[21]

Justice Thomas alone dissented on section 201. His view was that BCRA could be justified only under the information interest, and he viewed *McIntyre* as holding this an insufficient interest in all circumstances.[22] The majority did not respond to the point; the only mention of *McIntyre* it provided appeared in the cryptic footnote 88, in which the Court opined that BCRA's "fidelity" to the "imperatives" to "preserv[e] the integrity of the electoral process, [prevent] corruption, and [sustain] the active, alert responsibility of the individual citizen in a democracy for the wise conduct of the government" "sets it apart from the statute at issue in [*First National Bank of Boston v.*] *Bellotti*—and for that matter from the Ohio statute banning the distribution of anonymous campaign literature struck down in *McIntyre v. Ohio Elections Comm'n*."[23]

Even after the shift from Justice O'Connor to Justice Alito, and the rejection of *Austin* and *McConnell*'s endorsement of the antidistortion/political equality interest to justify corporate and labor union spending limits, the Court has remained firmly in favor of the constitutionality of disclosure laws.[24] Although Justice Kennedy didn't mention the information interest

---

18. *Id.* at 196.

19. "The regulation does substantially relate to the other interest the majority details, however. This assures its constitutionality." *Id.* at 321.

20. *Id.*

21. *See id.* at 258 (Scalia, J., concurring in the judgment in part and dissenting in part) ("The use of corporate wealth (like individual wealth) to speak to the electorate is unlikely to 'distort' elections—*especially* if disclosure requirements *tell* the people where the speech is coming from"); *id.* at 259 ("Evil corporate (and private affluent) influences are well enough checked (so long as adequate campaign-expenditure disclosure rules exist) by the politician's fear of being portrayed as 'in the pocket' of so-called moneyed interests.").

22. *Id.* at 275-276 (Thomas J. concurring in the judgment in part and dissenting in part). Justice Thomas also stated that *McIntyre* "overturned *Buckley* to the extent that *Buckley* upheld a disclosure requirement solely based on the governmental interest in providing information to voters." *Id.* at 276; *see also id.* at 282-283 (discussing *Buckley*'s disclosure requirement for express advocacy).

23. *Id.* at 206 n.88 (internal citations omitted).

24. Following *Citizens United* and *Doe*, lower courts generally have been rejecting constitutional challenges to campaign finance disclosure laws. *See*, for example, *National Organization for Marriage v. McKee*, 723 F. Supp. 2d 245 (D. Maine 2010); *Ctr. for Individual Freedom, Inc. v. Tennant*, 706 F.3d 270 (4th Cir. 2013); *Ctr. for Individual Freedom v. Madigan*, 697 F.3d 464 (7th Cir. 2012); *The Real Truth About Abortion, Inc. v. FEC*, 681 F.3d 544 (4th Cir. 2012), *cert. denied*, 133 S.Ct. 841 (2013).

by name in his partial concurrence in *McConnell*, here is what he wrote for the Court in *Citizens United*:

> The Court has explained that disclosure is a less restrictive alternative to more comprehensive regulations of speech. In *Buckley*, the Court upheld a disclosure requirement for independent expenditures even though it invalidated a provision that imposed a ceiling on those expenditures. In *McConnell*, three Justices who would have found [the ban on spending from corporate and labor union treasury funds] to be unconstitutional nonetheless voted to uphold BCRA's disclosure and disclaimer requirements. And the Court has upheld registration and disclosure requirements on lobbyists, even though Congress has no power to ban lobbying itself. *United States v. Harriss*, 347 U.S. 612, 625 (1954) (Congress "has merely provided for a modicum of information from those who for hire attempt to influence legislation or who collect or spend funds for that purpose"). For these reasons, we reject Citizens United's contention that the disclosure requirements must be limited to speech that is the functional equivalent of express advocacy.
>
> Citizens United also disputes that an informational interest justifies the application of [BCRA's disclosure requirements] to its ads, which only attempt to persuade viewers to see the film. Even if it disclosed the funding sources for the ads, Citizens United says, the information would not help viewers make informed choices in the political marketplace. This is similar to the argument rejected above with respect to disclaimers. Even if the ads only pertain to a commercial transaction, the public has an interest in knowing who is speaking about a candidate shortly before an election. Because the informational interest alone is sufficient to justify application of [the disclosure law] to these ads, it is not necessary to consider the Government's other asserted interests

Justice Thomas alone dissented, again arguing for a different result under *McIntyre*.

At this point, it is not clear what is left of *McIntyre*. The justices have come to recognize the importance of the information interest. To take a recent example, California voters recently turned down a ballot proposition that would have benefited Pacific Gas and Electric ("PG&E").[25] PG&E provided almost all of the $46 million to the "Yes on 16" campaign, compared with very little spent opposing the measure. Thanks to California's disclosure laws, PG&E's name appeared on every "Yes on 16" ad, and the measure narrowly went down to defeat. Campaign finance disclosure can provide

---

Some courts have, however struck down more burdensome reporting requirements. *See, e.g.,* *Minnesota Citizens Concerned for Life, Inc. v. Swanson*, 692 F.3d 864 (8th Cir. 2012). *See also* Ciara Torres-Spelliscy, *Has the Tide Turned in Favor of Disclosure? Revealing Money in Politics After* Citizens United *and* Doe v. Reed, 27 Ga. St. U. L. Rev. 1057 (2011).

25. *See* Richard L. Hasen, *Show Me the Donors: What's the Point of Campaign Finance Disclosure? Let's Review*, Slate (Oct. 14, 2010), http://www.slate.com/articles/news_and_politics/politics/2010/10/show_me_the_donors.single.html.

important shortcuts to busy voters wondering about the interests behind ballot measures and candidates.

The Court's most recent discussion of the constitutionality of disclosure laws in *Doe v. Reed* revived the question of when an individual or group might be able to get an exemption from generally applicable disclosure rules because of the potential for harassment.[26]

Recall that *Buckley* recognized the possibility of such "as applied" exemptions. Soon after *Buckley*, in *Brown v. Socialist Workers '74 Campaign Committee*,[27] the Court recognized that the Constitution mandated an exemption based upon harassment for contributors to the Socialist Workers Party ("SWP"). The harassment of SWP contributors was pervasive and egregious:

> Appellees introduced proof of specific incidents of private and government hostility toward the SWP and its members within the four years preceding the trial. These incidents, many of which occurred in Ohio and neighboring states, included threatening phone calls and hate mail, the burning of SWP literature, the destruction of SWP members' property, police harassment of a party candidate, and the firing of shots at an SWP office. There was also evidence that in the 12-month period before trial 22 SWP members, including four in Ohio, were fired because of their party membership. Although appellants contend that two of the Ohio firings were not politically motivated, the evidence amply supports the District Court's conclusion that "private hostility and harassment toward SWP members make it difficult for them to maintain employment."
>
> The District Court also found a past history of government harassment of the SWP. FBI surveillance of the SWP was "massive" and continued until at least 1976. The FBI also conducted a counterintelligence program against the SWP and the Young Socialist Alliance (YSA), the SWP's youth organization. One of the aims of the "SWP Disruption Program" was the dissemination of information designed to impair the ability of the SWP and YSA to function. This program included "disclosing to the press the criminal records of SWP candidates, and sending anonymous letters to SWP members, supporters, spouses, and employers." Until at least 1976, the FBI employed various covert techniques to obtain information about the SWP, including information concerning the sources of its funds and the nature of its expenditures. The District Court specifically found that the FBI had conducted surveillance of the Ohio SWP and had interfered with its activities within the State. Government surveillance was not limited to the FBI. The United States Civil Service Commission also gathered information on the SWP, the YSA, and their supporters, and the FBI routinely distributed its reports to Army, Navy and Air Force Intelligence,

---

26. The next few paragraphs draw from Richard L. Hasen, *Chill Out: A Qualified Defense of Campaign Finance Disclosure Laws in the Internet Age*, 27 J. L. & Pol. 557 (2012).
27. 459 U.S. 87 (1982).

the United States Secret Service, and the Immigration and Naturalization Service.[28]

In determining whether SWP supporters were entitled to a harassment-based exemption from campaign finance laws, the Court took the fact-inquiry regarding harassment seriously. The lesson of the case is that the threat of harassment must be proven, not assumed. And it must be severe, not casual or minor, such as merely being "mooned" or "flipped off" by detractors for engaging in controversial political activity.[29]

In the recent *Doe v. Reed* case,[30] the Court rejected a constitutional argument against the disclosure of the names of people signing referendum petitions in Washington State, but it remanded the case to the district court to consider whether the signers of a particular referendum opposing gay rights were entitled to an as-applied exemption based upon proof of harassment. Although the Court, in dicta, split in the *Doe* case over the precise standards for the as-applied harassment exemption to be applied on remand, the District Court examining *Doe* on remand concluded that Justice Sotomayor's standard, which mirrors the *Socialist Workers*' standard, had the support of a majority of the Court.[31] This standard requires proof of "serious and widespread harassment that the State is unwilling or unable to control."[32]

The *Doe* case is a useful lens to consider how serious a problem harassment is these days, especially in the Internet era where it is quite easy to obtain information about contributors to campaigns or signers of ballot measures. Using the *Socialist Workers* standard, evidence of harassment of campaign finance contributors and spenders these days is sparse. Violence, intimidation, and government interference with unpopular groups in this country is currently blessedly rare and even rarer among groups choosing to

---

28. *Id.* at 99-100 (footnotes omitted). Omitted footnote 18 includes the following finding from the district court:

> "The Government possesses about 8,000,000 documents relating to the SWP, YSA . . . and their members. . . . Since 1960 the FBI has had about 300 informants who were members of the SWP and/or YSA and 1,000 non-member informants. Both the Cleveland and Cincinnati FBI field offices had one or more SWP or YSA member informants. Approximately 2 of the SWP member informants held local branch offices. Three informants even ran for elective office as SWP candidates. The 18 informants whose files were disclosed to Judge Breitel received total payments of $358,648.38 for their services and expenses."

Id. at 424 n.18.
29. *Doe v. Reed*, 823 F. Supp. 2d 1195 (W.D. Wash. 2011) (hearing allegations made of signature gatherers for referendum opposing gay civil unions in Washington State).
30. 130 S.Ct. 2811 (2010).
31. *Doe v. Reed*, 823 F. Supp. 2d at 1211.
32. *Doe*, 130 S.Ct. at 2829 (Sotomayor, J., concurring). One open question is whether the exemption is available only to "minor parties" or "fringe groups." *See Doe v. Reed*, 823 F. Supp. 2d at 1203-1204.

participate in the political process through campaign contributions and expenditures. Indeed, outside the context of disputes over gay marriage-related measures, it is hard to think of examples of even credible *allegations* of harassment. As a political scientists' amicus brief in the *Doe* case noted, "[w]ith respect to the twenty-eight statewide referenda that have qualified for the ballot [nationwide] between 2000 and 2009, well over a million citizens have signed their names to petitions. Yet petitioners have identified no individual petition signer — not one — who has alleged any instance of harassment or intimidation."[33]

It is worth noting an ideological split on the empirical evidence of harassment. Judged from their recent opinions, conservative Supreme Court justices Thomas and Alito appear to believe that intimidation of conservatives for their political opinions is commonplace.[34] (I cannot help but believe that the contentious Senate confirmation hearings for these justices, especially Justice Thomas, contributed to a feeling of conservatives' being under siege.) This concern about leftist harassment appears to be widespread among staunch conservatives. As lawyer Jim Bopp (involved in the *Doe* litigation) recently put it in a posting to the Election Law listserv, "Blacks, gays and leftist[s] were harassed yesterday; conservatives and Christians are harassed today. And no one is safe from the thugs and bullies tomorrow."[35]

But courts looking at the empirical evidence of harassment have concluded otherwise. In the remand in the *Doe* case, the court found virtually no evidence that voters who signed of the referendum opposing gay rights were subject to harassment.[36] Nor did financial contributors who supported the referendum face harassment. It was true, and lamentable, that national *public leaders* of the marriage measures suffered some harassment, but mere petition

---

33. Brief for Direct Democracy Scholars as Amicus Curiae Supporting Respondents, *Doe v. Reed*, 130 S.Ct. 2811 (2010) (No. 09-559), 2010 WL 1256467 at *12.

34. *Doe*, 130 S.Ct. at 2823-2824 (Alito, J., concurring); *id.* at 2845-2847 (Thomas, J., dissenting). Justice Thomas also dissented on the disclosure issues in the *Citizens United* case. *Citizens United v. FEC*, 558 U.S. at 480-485 (2010) (Thomas, J., concurring in part and dissenting in part).

35. Posting of Jim Bopp, JBoppjr@aol.com, to law-election@department-lists.uci.edu (Oct. 17, 2011) (on file with author) (quoted with the permission of the author).

36. *Doe v. Reed*, 823 F. Supp. 2d at 1212 ("Applied here, the Court finds that Doe has only supplied evidence that hurts rather than helps its case. Doe has supplied minimal testimony from a few witnesses who, in their respective deposition testimony, stated either that police efforts to mitigate reported incidents was sufficient or unnecessary. Doe has supplied no evidence that police were or are now unable or unwilling to mitigate any claimed harassment or are now unable or unwilling to control the same, should disclosure be made. This is a quite different situation than the progeny of cases providing an as-applied exemption wherein the government was actually involved in carrying out the harassment, which was historic, pervasive, and documented. To that end, the evidence supplied by Doe purporting to be the best set of experiences of threats, harassment, or reprisals suffered or reasonably likely to be suffered by R-71 signers cannot be characterized as 'serious and widespread.'").

signers or contributors did not.[37] A federal district court judge reached the same conclusion in a challenge to the disclosure of the names of contributors to Proposition 8, California's anti–same sex marriage initiative. On the request for a preliminary injunction, the trial judge found a similar lack of evidence of harassment to meet the *Socialist Workers* standard.[38] The court recently granted summary judgment for California on the same issue, ending the case.

Part of the rhetorical divide appears to stem from conservatives' adopting a broader definition of harassment than the one allowed by *Socialist Workers*. Most important, conservatives seem to count economic boycotts as harassment. But as Elian Dashev argues in an important student note, economic boycotts are themselves protected First Amendment activity that should not be the basis for claiming a harassment exemption.[39]

The United States Chamber of Commerce has raised its own harassment objection to a proposed Obama administration executive order requiring disclosure of the campaign finance activities of federal contractors. The Chamber describes what economists would term a form of "rent extraction," whereby politicians punish companies that do not contribute to the politicians or their party (or who contribute to their rivals).[40] But public disclosure actually should minimize, not exacerbate, the dangers of rent extraction. Without public disclosure, politicians would be the only ones to know whether they are getting campaign finance support from a government contractor and could shake down those who do not support the candidate or his or her party. Public disclosure makes such retaliation by politicians much less likely, because the public can more easily see patterns of retribution. The chamber, representing the most powerful corporations in the United States, hardly seems akin to those SWP members who faced violence and intimidation. I am confident that Philip Morris and Exxon Mobil can hold their own in the public square.[41]

---

37. Id. (Plaintiffs "have developed substantial evidence that the public advocacy of traditional marriage as the exclusive definition of marriage, or the expansion of rights for same sex partners, has engendered hostility in this state, and risen to violence elsewhere, against some who have engaged in that advocacy. This should concern every citizen and deserves the full attention of law enforcement when the line gets crossed and an advocate becomes the victim of a crime or is subject to a genuine threat of violence.").

38. *ProtectMarriage.com v. Bowen*, 599 F. Supp. 2d 1197 (E.D. Cal. 2009).

39. Elian Dashev, Note, *Economic Boycotts as Harassment: The Threat to First Amendment Protected Speech in the Aftermath of* Doe v. Reed, 45 Loy. L.A. L. Rev. 207 (2011).

40. Fred S. McChesney, Money for Nothing: Politicians, Rent Extraction, and Political Extortion (1997); *see also* Fred S. McChesney, *Rent Extraction and Rent Creation in the Economic Theory of Regulation*, 16 J. Legal Stud. 101 (1987).

41. Eric Lipton et al., *Top Corporations Aid U.S. Chamber of Commerce Campaign*, N.Y. Times, Oct. 21, 2010, http://www.nytimes.com/2010/10/22/us/politics/22chamber.html ("These large donations [from major corporations] — none of which were publicly disclosed by the chamber, a tax-exempt group that keeps its donors secret, as it is allowed by law — offer a glimpse of the chamber's money-raising efforts, which it has ramped up recently in an

The bottom line is that constitutionally significant harassment is extremely rare, and in all but the most hot-button cases (perhaps these days only in the gay marriage cases), we may safely discount the danger of harassment as a reason for opposing generally applicable campaign finance laws. Of course, all such laws should include procedures for receiving an as-applied exemption upon showing the threat of serious and pervasive harassment of the *Socialist Workers* variety. But the granting of exemptions should be rare because harassment is rare.

Even though evidence of harassment is sparse, one can still make a strong argument that federal, state, and local governments still should dramatically raise the reporting thresholds for campaign finance contributions. The issue here is not harassment but the informational privacy concerns.[42] For example, I live in a neighborhood populated by a number of liberals in the entertainment industry. In the 2012 election season, I was able to go to the Huffington Post's "fundrace.huffingtonpost.com" website (which has been taken down, at least for now) and figure out which of my neighbors gave $100 to conservative candidates. Those conservative neighbors making such donations will not face harassment for making such contributions, but I would guess that there would be some whispering among the typical liberal people living in my neighborhood, who would think differently about these neighbors if they got this information. Whispering is not harassment, but the entire process is unseemly and unnecessary.

This type of snooping is a new phenomenon facilitated by the Internet. One of the pioneers of the study of money in politics, Professor Louise Overacker, reports how in the 1930s she literally had to go into the men's room at the House of Representatives to retrieve campaign finance records from dusty, unlabeled bundles above some lockers.[43] Campaign finance data was hard to come by. In the 1970s, if you wanted campaign finance records, you needed to go down to the Federal Election Commission and peruse the papers organized by campaign, not donor. By the 1990s, enterprising private organizations were digitizing the data for searching. Today, anyone with an Internet connection can have the information about federal (and many state and local) campaign contributions in seconds from either the FEC, private organizations, or good government groups such as the Center for Responsive Politics that maintains the indispensable Open Secrets website and database.

The unseemliness of Fundrace-type snooping would be worth putting up with if disclosure of very small contributions served some important

---

orchestrated campaign to become one of the most well-financed critics of the Obama administration and an influential player in this fall's Congressional elections.").

42. William McGeveran, *Mrs. McIntyre's Persona: Bringing Privacy Theory to Election Law*, 19 Wm. & Mary Bill Rts. J. 859 (2011).

43. Robert E. Mutch, Campaigns, Congress, and the Courts: The Making of Federal Campaign Finance Law 25-26 (1988).

interest. Knowing that one's Hollywood neighbor gave $100 to Herman Cain or one's Houston neighbor gave $50 to Elizabeth Warren does not do much to prevent the corruption of these candidates or give voters valuable information about choosing candidates. As Professor Mayer argues, modest contributors are engaging in a symbolic act of support for the candidate. Like voting, such modest action generally should be considered a private matter.[44]

Privacy is also advisable in light of occasional disturbing instances of serious economic boycotts against those making very small campaign contributions to anti–same sex marriage causes. The most famous victim was Majorie Christofferson, who donated only $100 in support of Proposition 8. After her donation was publicly disclosed, her family-owned establishment, popular Los Angeles restaurant El Coyote, was besieged.[45] While boycotts are constitutionally protected and do not constitute legal harassment, the state interest in disclosure of modest contributions is weak, and the cost of such disclosure can be more serious.

While the Constitution does not require raising the reporting thresholds, good policy sense does. Only contributors giving over a more significant threshold, say $1,000, should have their names disclosed publicly (though all contributions of any amount should be reported to government agencies to make sure there is no fraud, sham, or conduit contributions taking place in campaigns, and government agencies should regularly audit these campaigns).

Example 2

The state of Pacifica enacts a provision requiring all contributors to ballot measure campaigns giving more than $100 to be disclosed in reports filed with the government. Furthermore, the law requires that television ads for or against a ballot measure include the names of those top five individuals or entities who gave the most money to the committee. Would such a law be constitutional under current Supreme Court doctrine? What about as applied to a measure to legalize polygamy?

Explanation

Although there was some considerable uncertainty about the constitutionality of disclosure of information related to contributions funding ballot measure elections in the period after *McIntyre*, the recent cases of *McConnell*, *Citizens United*, and *Doe v. Reed* have generally offered strong endorsements to generally applicable disclosure laws. If the information interest standing alone is enough to justify disclosure, then disclosure of ballot measure

---

44. Lloyd Hitoshi Mayer, *Disclosures About Disclosure*, 44 IND. L. REV. 255 (2010).
45. Dashev, *supra*, at 248.

information should be fine. *McIntyre* could well be limited to cases involving actors spending very little money.

Although disclosure generally is constitutional, it might be that people promoting a particularly controversial ballot measure, such as one that would legalize polygamy, might be entitled to an "as applied" exemption to the disclosure laws. The Court recognized that groups that could face major government harassment or threats of violence, such as the Socialist Workers Party, should be entitled to an exemption. The case would turn upon those who seek an exemption to demonstrate that they face a realistic threat of harassment — something that under the Supreme Court's precedents (including *Doe v. Reed*), it may be quite difficult to do. Threats of economic boycotts are likely not enough.

Finally, although disclosure laws such as those requiring disclosure of very small contributions are likely constitutional, it does not mean they are wise policy. It is not clear that the disclosure of such information serves anticorruption, enforcement, or information purposes, and it takes away some informational privacy.

15.3. THE RISE OF 501(C) ORGANIZATIONS AND THE FAILURES OF FEDERAL DISCLOSURE LAW

In the last chapter, we saw how *Citizens United* and follow-up decisions such as the D.C. Circuit Court of Appeal's decision in *SpeechNow.Org* led to the creation of Super PACs: federal committees that accept unlimited contributions from individuals, corporations, and labor unions to make independent expenditures supporting or opposing federal candidates. These outside organizations have proven to be very important in elections, because they are not subject to contribution limitations to which candidate committees and political parties must adhere.

From the fundraiser's point of view, a major downside of Super PACs (aside from the inability to fully coordinate with the candidates being supported) is that federal law requires Super PACs to disclose their donors. Some donors, corporate and individual, may prefer to donate without their identities' being disclosed.

The desire for donor anonymity led to the emergence of social welfare organizations (organized under section 501(c)(4) of the Internal Revenue Code) and trade associations, such as the Chamber of Commerce (organized under section 501(c)(6) of the Internal Revenue Code), that function much like Super PACs. These organizations claim that their primary purpose is a social welfare purpose, and that the ads they run supporting or opposing candidates are permissible for having made up less than half of the spending of these groups (keeping the social welfare purpose) and not being express advocacy (triggering the requirement to register with the FEC as a political committee).

Political spending by 501(c)(4) and similar entities exploded in the 2012 elections. According to the Center for Responsive Politics, the amount of spending by non-disclosing 501(c)(4), (c)(5), and (c)(6) groups went from $5.2 million in the 2006 elections to over $300 million in the 2012 elections, led with spending by conservative groups.[46]

501(c)(4) spending is controversial, and groups supporting campaign finance reform have argued that the IRS should deny these groups social welfare status and that the FEC should regulate these groups as political committees. The IRS began investigating these groups, leading to a major controversy. In 2013, IRS official Lois Lerner revealed that IRS employees in the Cincinnati office (which handles applications for exempt groups) had improperly used key words for conservative groups such as "Tea Party" and "patriot" in searching the names of (c)(4) groups to be investigated further. The IRS also delayed processing a number of applications from such groups. Lerner apologized for the IRS's actions. After the revelations, IRS officials resigned and Lerner was put on administrative leave and eventually resigned. Congressional investigations focused on whether the Obama administration played any role in the targeting.[47]

As the investigation continued, the IRS proposed new rules to limit the electoral activity of 501(c)(4) organizations. Democrats also introduced legislation that would require disclosure of the funding of election-related advertising contributions regardless of the organizational form of the group. It is not clear whether any of these efforts will be successful. In the meantime, Democratic groups have begun using the 501(c)(4) structure as well to engage in anonymous fundraising.

For those who wish to have greater disclosure of campaign contributions on the federal level, the solution is political, not legal. In other words, as we saw in the last section, the Supreme Court has been quite willing to allow the government to impose strict disclosure requirements on those engaging in political activities. The problem is that Congress, the Federal

---

46. *Political Nonprofits*, OPENSECRETS.ORG, https://www.opensecrets.org/outsidespending/nonprof_summ.php.

47. Jonathan Weisman, *I.R.S. Suspends Official at Center of Storm*, N.Y. TIMES, May 13, 2013, at A17, http://www.nytimes.com/2013/05/24/us/politics/irs-official-who-refused-to-testify-is-put-on-leave.html; Nicholas Confessore & Michael Luo, *Groups Targeted by I.R.S. Tested Rules on Politics*, N.Y. TIMES, May 28, 2013, at A1, http://www.nytimes.com/2013/05/27/us/politics/nonprofit-applicants-chafing-at-irs-tested-political-limits.html; Josh Hicks, *Democrats Offer New Evidence That IRS Targeted Progressive Groups*, WASH. POST, July 12, 2013, http://www.washingtonpost.com/blogs/federal-eye/wp/2013/07/12/democrats-offer-new-evidence-that-irs-targeted-progressive-groups/. To read the inspector general's report, *see* Treasury Inspector General for Tax Administration, *Inappropriate Criteria Were Used to Identify Tax Exempt Applications for Review*, Reference Report 2013-10-053, May 14, 2013, http://www.treasury.gov/tigta/auditreports/2013reports/201310053fr.html.

Election Commission, and the Internal Revenue Service have not passed laws or regulations that would require effective disclosure. Clever campaign finance lawyers can easily avoid disclosure thorough creative accounting and legal maneuvers. It is unclear whether there will be the political will on the federal level to mandate effective disclosure.

Example 3

You are advising a billionaire who wants to help elect (and have influence over) a presidential candidate. The billionaire asks you about her options for her money: What can she legally do, how much can she give, and what are her options in terms of anonymity?

Explanation

The billionaire can give only a limited amount to the presidential candidate directly: $2,600 in the primary and $2,600 in the general election (spouses and children of the billionaire may each make their own donations). The presidential candidate has likely set up a "joint victory fund," which will allow the billionaire to give a check giving the maximum to the presidential candidate, and then more money to the candidate's national political party along with state party committees (these joint fundraising committees used to be subject to the maximum aggregate contribution limitation for political party contributions in a two-year election cycle, but that aggregate limit was recently held unconstitutional in the *McCutcheon* case). Money given to the candidate and the candidate's party is money that is most likely to be spent in accordance with the candidate's wishes.

Beyond that, the billionaire can give up to $5,000 to political committees that support the presidential candidate through direct contributions (subject to a separate aggregate contribution limit) and unlimited sums to Super PACs that can support a single presidential candidate (but not engage in illegal coordination with the candidate). These Super PAC donations are disclosed, eventually, in reports filed with the Federal Election Commission.

Furthermore, the billionaire can give unlimited sums to 501(c)(4) and (c)(6) organizations that run ads supporting the billionaire's preferred presidential candidate (or attacking her opponent). At present, such contributions are legal and are not subject to disclosure (though both of these points may change with legal and political developments). Also, such groups may not have a primarily political purpose, and for this reason some of the donated funds will have to be used for related "educational" or other "social welfare" purposes (which could well have a political purpose as well). Whether giving to these groups will ingratiate the billionaire with the presidential candidate may depend upon the candidate and the amount of the contribution. Further, lawyers are thinking up new fundraising mechanisms all the time, including the use of for-profit corporations as campaign finance launderers. The legality of new methods is always subject to question.

The billionaire therefore faces trade-offs in deciding who should get the money and how much they should get. Someone wanting anonymity above all else would be stuck using a 501(c)(4) or similar group.

Public Financing

16.1. WHY PUBLIC FINANCING?

It is no surprise that some campaign finance reformers like the idea of public financing. If the government, rather than private entities, supplies the funds for campaigns, that lessens the chances of corruption and could instill public confidence in elected officials. It also might promote political equality[1] — an interest about which the Supreme Court has been skeptical in the context of campaign limits (and, as we will see, about which it is now skeptical in the context of public financing as well). According to its supporters, public financing may make elections more competitive, increase the diversity of candidates running for office, and lead to more informative campaigns.

For reformers, an additional benefit of public financing is that it is usually coupled with spending limits or other restrictions: Candidates who opt into a public financing program promise not to raise or spend funds beyond a certain level. In the next section we will explore the constitutionality of this trade-off. But for now, it is enough to note the usual coupling of public financing and limits.

It should not surprise you that opponents of campaign finance laws generally also tend to oppose public financing plans. Aside from deriding the concept of money going to candidates as "welfare for politicians," opponents see public financing as an unnecessary interference with private

---

1. Richard Briffault, *Public Funding and Democratic Elections*, 148 U. PA. L. REV. 563, 577-578 (1999).

funding of campaigns, often enacted by politicians out of self-interest and partisan considerations, and serving to make politicians dependent on the state.[2] Some opponents also do not like the spending limits or other restrictions that often accompany public financing plans.[3]

States and localities each have their own rules about whether to have a public financing system and if so, what the rules of such a system should be. There are many issues to consider in constructing a public finance system, including how candidates may qualify for funding (jurisdictions want to avoid funding frivolous candidacies that can waste taxpayer money and distract from a campaign); what limits, if any, candidates must abide by if they take public funding; whether to favor major party candidates; whether to give all candidates the same amount of money or to use some formula pegged to popularity, outside spending, the amount of small contributions, or something else; and whether the program is funded with general funds or a special tax or assessment.

Empirical studies of the effect of state and local public financing laws on competitiveness, public confidence, diversity, and other factors have reached conflicting results.[4] And of course in light of the wide diversity of approaches to campaign financing, it is hard to draw any general conclusions. Certainly partial public financing is no cure-all for problems that plague election campaigns in the United States.

Strong supporters of public financing believe that great benefits would accrue from full public funding systems that exclude or make less relevant private money in elections (such as through the use of campaign finance vouchers[5]). Of course, if such a system excludes private money, it requires amending the Constitution or the Supreme Court's overturning some of its key rulings, beginning with *Buckley*.

On the federal level, only the presidential campaign has a public financing system; there is no program for congressional campaigns, although Congress has considered public financing proposals from time to time.[6] In recent years,

---

2. *See* Bert Brandenburg & Roy A. Schotland, *Justice in Peril: The Endangered Balance Between Impartial Courts and Judicial Election Campaigns*, 21 GEO. J. LEGAL ETHICS 1229, 1254 (2008).

3. Bradley A. Smith, *Some Problems with Taxpayer-Funded Political Campaigns*, 148 U. PA. L. REV. 591, 628 (1999).

4. MICHAEL G. MILLER, SUBSIDIZING DEMOCRACY: HOW PUBLIC FUNDING CHANGES ELECTIONS AND HOW IT CAN WORK IN THE FUTURE (2013); Kenneth R. Mayer, Timothy Werner, & Amanda Williams, *Do Public Funding Programs Enhance Electoral Competition?* in THE MARKETPLACE OF DEMOCRACY 245-267 (Michael P. McDonald & John Samples, eds. 2006); David M. Primo, Jeffrey Milyo, & Tim Groseclose, *State Campaign Finance Reform, Competitiveness, and Party Advantage in Gubernatorial Elections*, 268-285, in THE MARKETPLACE OF DEMOCRACY.

5. On campaign finance vouchers, *see* Richard L. Hasen, *Clipping Coupons for Democracy: An Egalitarian/Public Choice Defense of Campaign Finance Vouchers*, 84 CALIF. L. REV. 1 (1996); BRUCE A. ACKERMAN & IAN AYRES, VOTING WITH DOLLARS: A NEW PARADIGM FOR CAMPAIGN FINANCE (2004); LAWRENCE LESSIG, REPUBLIC, LOST (2011).

6. Congress also provided public financing to subsidize the cost of major party nominating conventions. So far the parties have willingly taken this money for their conventions.

the presidential federal system has collapsed because the serious candidates can raise so much more money outside the system that they do not participate.

Under the voluntary federal system, presidential candidates may receive public financing in both primaries and the general election. In primaries, candidates become eligible for public funding by raising $5,000 or more in contributions of $250 or less in at least 20 states. Candidates who accept public financing are subject to campaign spending limits. There is both a nationwide spending limit for presidential primaries and a spending limit for each state. Participating candidates get matching funds for the first $250 of contributions up to a set limit. In the general election, the major party candidates receive a grant but cannot raise funds for their own campaigns. Minor party candidates can receive a smaller grant and get more money retroactively and going into the next campaign if the candidates receive enough votes.

It is no surprise that the presidential public financing system collapsed given the fact that the grants did not keep up with private fundraising opportunities. In 2008, Republican candidate John McCain opted into the system, receiving a grant of $84.1 million for use during the general election period. His opponent, Barack Obama, opted out and raised almost $337 million during that period.[7] But things were not quite as lopsided as they sound: Even though McCain was not allowed to raise money for his own campaign because he took the public financing grant, he helped the Republican National Committee raise millions of dollars that were used to promote McCain's candidacy.

In the 2012 election, neither Obama (running for reelection) nor his opponent Mitt Romney participated in the public financing system. Counting the money raised by the candidates, joint fundraising committees and the major political parties, each candidate raised over $1 billion in private money.[8] No rational major party candidate will ever again participate in the presidential public financing system unless Congress revamps it in a serious way to make it attractive to candidates.[9] Participating leaves too much money lying on the table.

---

7. *Sources of Funds for Presidential Candidates, 2007-08,* CAMPAIGN FINANCE INSTITUTE, http://www.cfinst.org/pdf/federal/president/2010_0106_Table1.pdf.

8. *Presidential Campaign, National Party, and Joint Committee Fundraising Through December 31, 2012,* CAMPAIGN FINANCE INSTITUTE, http://www.cfinst.org/pdf/federal/president/2012/Presidential%20Fundraising%20byCommittee_2012.pdf.

9. Richard L. Hasen, *The Changing Nature of Campaign Financing for Presidential Primary Candidates,* in NOMINATING THE PRESIDENT: EVOLUTION AND REVOLUTION IN 2008 AND BEYOND 27, 29 (Jack Citrin and David Karol eds., 2009); Richard L. Hasen, *The Transformation of the Campaign Financing Regime for U.S. Presidential Elections,* in THE FUNDING OF POLITICAL PARTIES 225 (Keith D. Ewing, Jacob Rowbottom, and Joo-Cheong Tham eds., 2011).

Example 1

You are a legislator in the state of Pacifica, and you chair a committee considering a bill to set up a public financing program for state offices. Do you support or oppose such a program? On what basis? If there is support for such a program, what features do you believe would be important for the design of the program?

Explanation

There is of course no right answer to these normative questions. My sense is that those who support campaign finance regulation generally tend to like public financing and that those who oppose it generally tend to dislike it. Taking (some) private money out of the system could promote some of the interests behind campaign finance, such as preventing corruption, promoting public confidence (minimizing the appearance of corruption) and promoting political equality. Supporters also claim that public financing increases the competitiveness of elections and the diversity of the candidate pool. Opponents doubt the efficacy of public financing and question some of the rationales behind the laws. Opponents worry that public financing systems may be designed to make, or at least have the effect of making, it easier for incumbents to remain in office.

As far as the design of the system, it probably depends upon the goals to be achieved. A system that is going to work must be attractive to candidates. (As we will see in the next section, constitutional constraints may make that difficult.) Most supporters likely would not want to give public funds to fringe candidates, but there are fundamental choices to be made: Do all candidates get the same public money? Is it better to favor major party candidates? To use a matching system? Where should the public funds come from? Most important, one should consider unintended consequences: How might the public financing system change state elections in ways not intended by those supporting such a system?

16.2. CONSTITUTIONAL ISSUES WITH PUBLIC FINANCING PLANS

16.2.1. Discrimination Against Minor Parties and Voluntariness

As with all else concerning the constitutionality of U.S. campaign finance laws, *Buckley v. Valeo*[10] serves as the starting point for analysis of constitutional

---

10. 424 U.S. 1 (1976).

issues involving public financing plans. *Buckley* considered two primary issues related to the presidential public financing plan: Does the system discriminate against minor parties, and does the spending limits aspect of the system infringe on the First Amendment?

On the minor party issue, the Court rejected the challenge brought by minor parties that the more generous grants to major parties violated the equal protection rights of minor parties and candidates. This conclusion should not surprise you if you have already read Chapter 10 of this book discussing the constitutional rights of minor parties.

It cannot be gainsaid that public financing as a means of eliminating the improper influence of large private contributions furthers a significant governmental interest. In addition, the limits on contributions necessarily increase the burden of fundraising, and Congress properly regarded public financing as an appropriate means of relieving major party Presidential candidates from the rigors of soliciting private contributions. The States have also been held to have important interests in limiting places on the ballot to those candidates who demonstrate substantial popular support. Congress' interest in not funding hopeless candidacies with large sums of public money necessarily justifies the withholding of public assistance from candidates without significant public support. Thus, Congress may legitimately require "some preliminary showing of a significant modicum of support," as an eligibility requirement for public funds. This requirement also serves the important public interest against providing artificial incentives to "splintered parties and unrestrained factionalism." . . .

As conceded by appellants, the Constitution does not require Congress to treat all declared candidates the same for public financing purposes. As we said in *Jenness*, "there are obvious differences in kind between the needs and potentials of a political party with historically established broad support, on the one hand, and a new or small political organization on the other. . . . Sometimes the grossest discrimination can lie in treating things that are different as though they were exactly alike, a truism well illustrated in *Williams*." Since the Presidential elections of 1856 and 1860, when the Whigs were replaced as a major party by the Republicans, no third party has posed a credible threat to the two major parties in Presidential elections. Third parties have been completely incapable of matching the major parties' ability to raise money and win elections. Congress was, of course, aware of this fact of American life, and thus was justified in providing both major parties full funding and all other parties only a percentage of the major-party entitlement. Identical treatment of all parties, on the other hand, "would not only make it easy to raid the United States Treasury, it would also artificially foster the proliferation of splinter parties." The Constitution does not require the Government to "finance the efforts of every nascent political group" merely because Congress chose to finance the efforts of the major parties.

Furthermore, appellants have made no showing that the election funding plan disadvantages nonmajor parties by operating to reduce their strength below that attained without any public financing. First, such parties are free to raise money from private sources, and by our holding today new parties are freed from any expenditure limits, although admittedly those limits may be a largely academic matter to them. But since any major party candidate accepting public financing of a campaign voluntarily assents to a spending ceiling, other candidates will be able to spend more in relation to the major-party candidates. The relative position of minor parties that do qualify to receive some public funds because they received 5% of the vote in the previous Presidential election is also enhanced. Public funding for candidates of major parties is intended as a substitute for private contributions; but for minor-party candidates such assistance may be viewed as a supplement to private contributions since these candidates may continue to solicit private funds up to the applicable spending limit. Thus, we conclude that the general election funding system does not work an invidious discrimination against candidates of nonmajor parties.[11]

The Court's analysis of the spending limits issue was more cryptic. In footnote 65 of *Buckley*, the Supreme Court wrote:

> For the reasons discussed in Part III, *infra*, Congress may engage in public financing of election campaigns and may condition acceptance of public funds on an agreement by the candidate to abide by specified expenditure limitations. Just as a candidate may voluntarily limit the size of the contributions he chooses to accept, he may decide to forgo private fundraising and accept public funding.

Contrary to footnote 65, Part III of the *Buckley* opinion never explains why Congress may condition acceptance of public funds on an agreement by the candidate to accept spending limits. Why is this not an unconstitutional condition? After all, one cannot condition a government benefit, such as a payment of Social Security benefits, in exchange for requiring the beneficiary not to speak out against the government.

The key to the Court's analysis on this point appears to be the *voluntariness* of the program: If a candidate has the choice whether or not to participate in the program, then the candidate faces no coercion, only a choice. In later cases in the lower courts, judges have analyzed the specifics of particular public financing programs, making sure that the benefits of the program are not so large in comparison to the limits put on non-participating candidates so that it cannot be fairly said that the program is coercive. For example, if nonparticipating candidates may not accept contributions above $50 but participating candidates receive a large amount of public financing, it is possible a court would rule the program coercive and thus violative of *Buckley*'s prohibition on candidate spending limits.

---

11. Id. at 96-99.

A leading case on voluntariness is a First Circuit case involving Maine's public financing system, which was enacted as part of a new wave of campaign finance laws. Here is how the Court in *Daggett v. Commission on Governmental Ethics and Election Practices*[12] described the Maine system:

> Maine voters, pursuant to their authority under Part First, §1, and Part Third, §18, of Article IV of the Maine Constitution enacted the Maine Clean Election Act (MCEA) in November 1996 to take effect on January 1, 1999. The Act creates a system of optional public funding for qualifying candidates in state legislative and gubernatorial campaigns, both in primaries and the general election. It establishes public funding beginning with the 2000 elections, and requires candidates to complete qualifying actions by March 16, 2000.
>
> In order to qualify for public funding, a candidate must fulfill several requirements during the qualifying period. The candidate must file a declaration of intent that he is seeking certification. The candidate must seek "seed money contributions" in amounts not greater than $100, limited to an aggregate amount that varies depending on the office sought: gubernatorial candidates are limited to $50,000, Senate candidates to $1,500, and House of Representatives candidates to $500. With that seed money, candidates seek out "qualifying contributions," $5 donations in the form of a check or money order payable to the Maine Clean Election Fund ("Fund") in support of their candidacy from registered voters in their district. Again, the requisite number of qualifying contributions depends on the type of seat sought: gubernatorial candidates must collect 2,500 contributions, Senate candidates 150 contributions, and House candidates 50 contributions.
>
> Once certified as a "participating candidate" by the Maine Commission on Governmental Ethics and Election Practices, a candidate must agree not to accept any private contributions and not to make expenditures except from disbursements made to him from the Fund. The candidate transfers all unspent seed money to the Fund and receives an initial disbursement from the Fund.
>
> The amount of the initial distribution is the average amount of campaign expenditures in the prior two election cycles for the particular office, although for the 2000 elections that amount has been discounted by 25% in order to ensure the availability of adequate funds. For the 2000 elections, participating Senate candidates will receive an initial distribution of $4,334 for the primary ($1,785 if uncontested) and $12,910 for the general election; House candidates will receive $1,141 for the primary ($511 if uncontested) and $3,252 for the general election. Participating candidates face both civil and criminal penalties for violation of the participation rules.
>
> In addition to the initial disbursement, a participating candidate receives a dollar-for-dollar match of any monies raised by a non-participating opponent after the opponent raises more than the initial disbursement allotted to the participating candidate. Matching funds are also provided to correspond to "independent expenditures," outlays made by an independent entity endorsing

---

12. 205 F.3d 445 (1st Cir. 2000).

the participant's defeat or the non-participating opponent's election. Once the participating candidate has received double the initial distribution in matching funds, however, the matching funds cease. No matter how much additional fundraising the participant's non-participating opponent undertakes, the participant's matching funding is capped at two times the initial distribution.

Reduced limits on contributions by individuals and groups to political candidates were enacted simultaneously with the Act by the voter referendum and effectively apply only to non-participating candidates. The limit on contributions made by an individual to a candidate in an election was reduced to $500 for gubernatorial candidates and $250 for all other candidates; the limit on contributions to a candidate by a political committee, other committee, corporation, or association in a single election was reduced to $500 for gubernatorial candidates and $250 for all other candidates. In addition, a pre-existing disclosure statute requiring reporting of independent expenditures aggregating more than $50 in any election was adapted to conform to the Act.

The *Daggett* court undertook a detailed analysis of the various provisions of the Maine law to determine "whether the elements of the system, considered as a whole, create a situation where it is so beneficial to join up and so detrimental to eschew public funding that it creates coercion and renders a candidate's choice to pursue public funding essentially involuntary." The court took a close look at the facts, including testimony from campaign consultants about how candidates would react to the program, and concluded the system was not coercive:

> Turning to Maine's system, we first observe that the benefits for a participating candidate are accompanied by significant burdens. The benefits to the candidate include the release from the rigors of fundraising, the assurance that contributors will not have an opportunity to seek special access, and the avoidance of any appearance of corruption. More peripheral benefits include the ability to bypass a small number of additional reporting requirements and the opportunity to be free of the reduced contribution limits imposed on private contributions.
>
> In order to gain these benefits, however, the candidate must go through the paces of demonstrating public support by obtaining seed money contributions as well as a substantial number of $5 qualifying contributions. Additional detriments include the limited amount of public funding granted in the initial disbursement; the uncertainty of whether and when additional funds will be received based on an opponent's fundraising; the ultimate cap on matching funds; and the foreclosure of the option of pursuing any private campaign funding or spending any monies above those disbursed by the Commission.
>
> With regard to the contribution limits, we do not believe that they serve as a coercive penalty for non-participating candidates. Until the privately funded candidate reaches the funding level equivalent to the initial disbursement granted to his participating opponent, the contribution limits may serve to the disadvantage of the privately funded candidate. Nevertheless, once the privately funded candidate exceeds that initial disbursement level of his

opponent and until he reaches the level at which his opponent's matching funds run out, the contribution limits work to the detriment of both candidates because the less the privately funded candidate raises the less his participating opponent receives in matching funds.

In conclusion, the incentives for a Maine candidate, as the district court characterized them, are "hardly overwhelming." Despite appellants' contention that a participating candidate cedes nothing in exchange for public funding, there are in fact significant encumbrances on participating candidates. The constraints on a publicly funded candidate, we think, would give significant pause to a candidate considering his options. In fact, appellant Representative Elaine Fuller has attested that she will not seek certification and appellant Senator Beverly Daggett has not yet decided. We also take note of the Commission figures that, as of February 8, halfway through the qualifying period, 27.5% of 142 legislative candidates have filed declarations of intent to seek public funding; on the other hand, at least 38, or roughly 26.7%, of the candidates have received contributions or made expenditures in excess of seed money limitations, signaling a desire not to seek certification. Thus, we hold that Maine's public financing scheme provides a roughly proportionate mix of benefits and detriments to candidates seeking public funding, such that it does not burden the First Amendment rights of candidates or contributors.

We add a final call for vigilant monitoring. In this case we necessarily regard appellants' claims as facial challenges to the public funding system and contribution limits. Although we indicate no opinion as to the success that an as-applied challenge would meet in the future, that door remains open. Experience, after all, will be our best teacher.[13]

Example 2

The state of Pacifica provides public funding for legislative candidates who opt to participate. Participating candidates, however, must agree to at least three debates with their opponents in order to receive public funding. Non-participating candidates must abide by relatively low contribution limits. Is the debate requirement constitutional?

Explanation

New Jersey has imposed such a condition for public financing, but I am not aware of any First Amendment challenge to the provision. To answer this question, a court likely would need more information to determine "whether the elements of the system, considered as a whole, create a situation where it is so beneficial to join up and so detrimental to eschew public funding that it creates coercion and renders a candidate's choice to pursue

---

13. *Id.* at 471-472.

public funding essentially involuntary" (*Daggett*). On these facts it is difficult to say whether the system as a whole is unconstitutionally coercive.

But there does seem to be something different about a debate requirement. This requirement seems to *force* political speech. As we saw in the last chapter in *McIntyre*, courts are wary of compelled speech. On the other hand, the debate requirement doesn't compel any particular speech; a candidate could show up at one of these debates in order to qualify for the public financing and remain literally silent. (I would not recommend total silence at a candidate debate as an ideal campaign strategy.) It is unclear how courts would resolve such a challenge if it ever arose.

16.2.2. Impermissibility of Matching Funds Tied to Others' Campaign Spending

Let's go back for a moment to the details of the Maine program at issue in *Daggett*. Aside from the voluntariness question, there was a separate constitutional question at issue in the case: Note that the Maine program did not simply give candidates participating in the public financing system a flat grant of funds to use for the election. Instead, the program gave an initial grant, with more money going to the participating candidate that was "triggered" by spending by a non-participating opponent or outside money.

You should easily see why Maine included the trigger aspect of its public financing system: Without such a trigger, candidates would be much more reluctant to participate in the program out of fear of being greatly outspent by the other side or a Super PAC. Participating candidates agree to spend no private funds in the campaign, and so without more money that could be a disadvantage. (Note, however, that the Maine system capped the amount of extra matching funds to double the initial distribution; this means that a candidate who expected to be *far outspent* by an opponent or outside money still might opt out of such a system.)

In *Daggett* and in other cases challenging public financing plans with triggers for extra matching funds, challengers argued that the trigger was an unconstitutional infringement on the rights of participating candidates or outside spenders whose spending would be matched by the government to the spenders' participating opponents. The *Daggett* court, in a portion of the opinion not included in the excerpt in the last section, rejected this First Amendment challenge. But lower courts divided on the question, and some courts held the trigger provision to be unconstitutional.

The issue reached the Supreme Court in *Arizona Free Enterprise Club's Freedom Club PAC v. Bennett*.[14] The Court, on a 5-4 vote along the usual conservative–

---

14. 131 S.Ct. 2806 (2011).

liberal line we've seen on the Roberts Court, held that Arizona's matching provision, which worked very much like the Maine system upheld in *Daggett*, violated the First Amendment.

The majority and dissenters disagreed about almost everything at issue in the case. To begin with, the majority believed that the system violated the First Amendment rights of those whose spending would trigger matching funds, whereas the dissenters did not. The majority relied upon the Court's earlier decision in *Davis v. FEC* (discussed in Chapter 14) holding that providing higher contribution limits for candidates facing large spending by outside groups or self-financed candidates violated the First Amendment. Chief Justice Roberts wrote for the *Arizona Free Enterprise* majority: "Much like the burden placed on speech in *Davis*, the matching funds provision 'imposes an unprecedented penalty on any candidate who robustly exercises [his] First Amendment right[s].' Under that provision, 'the vigorous exercise of the right to use personal funds to finance campaign speech' leads to 'advantages for opponents in the competitive context of electoral politics.'" The majority held that application of strict scrutiny was appropriate to reviewing the provision.

In contrast, the dissenters, in a caustic dissent written by Justice Kagan (her first major campaign finance opinion as a justice), rejected the argument that the system implicated the First Amendment at all:

> This suit, in fact, may merit less attention than any challenge to a speech subsidy ever seen in this Court. In the usual First Amendment subsidy case, a person complains that the government declined to finance his speech, while bankrolling someone else's; we must then decide whether the government differentiated between these speakers on a prohibited basis — because it preferred one speaker's ideas to another's. But the candidates bringing this challenge do not make that claim — because they were never denied a subsidy. Arizona, remember, offers to support any person running for state office. Petitioners here *refused* that assistance. So they are making a novel argument: that Arizona violated *their* First Amendment rights by disbursing funds to *other* speakers even though they could have received (but chose to spurn) the same financial assistance. Some people might call that *chutzpah*.[15]

---

15. *Id.* at 2835 (Kagan, J., dissenting). On this point, the chief justice responded:

The dissent sees "*chutzpah*" in candidates exercising their right not to participate in the public financing scheme, while objecting that the system violates their First Amendment rights. The charge is unjustified, but, in any event, it certainly cannot be leveled against the independent expenditure groups. The dissent barely mentions such groups in its analysis, and fails to address not only the distinctive burdens imposed on these groups — as set forth above — but also the way in which privately financed candidates are particularly burdened when matching funds are triggered by independent group speech.

The majority and dissent also disagreed about what government interest the trigger provision served. The majority held that Arizona enacted the trigger provision to serve an equality goal, to level the electoral playing field between candidates, an interest the Court had rejected as impermissible under the First Amendment in *Buckley, Citizens United,* and *Davis.* The dissenters first disagreed about identification of the government interest. The majority had relied upon a statement about leveling the playing field that the chief justice found on the website of the Arizona Clean Elections Commission, the entity charged with enforcing Arizona's public financing law. The dissent noted that it was the intent of the voters that passed an initiative establishing the provision, and not the commission, that would control.[16] Furthermore, the dissenters stated that even if promoting political equality was *an interest* in the provision, it was not the sole interest, because the measure was justified as an anticorruption measure. "This Court, after all, has never said that a law restricting speech (or any other constitutional right) demands two compelling interests."

To the dissenters, the trigger provision was well justified on anticorruption grounds given a recent history of campaign finance and bribery scandals in the state of Arizona:

> On the heels of a political scandal involving the near-routine purchase of legislators' votes, Arizonans passed a law designed to sever political candidates' dependence on large contributors. They wished, as many of their fellow Americans wish, to stop corrupt dealing — to ensure that their representatives serve the public, and not just the wealthy donors who helped put them in office. The legislation that Arizona's voters enacted was the product of deep thought and care. It put into effect a public financing system that attracted large numbers of candidates at a sustainable cost to the State's taxpayers. The system discriminated against no ideas and prevented no speech. Indeed, by increasing electoral competition and enabling a wide range of candidates to express their views, the system "further[ed] ... First Amendment values." Less corruption, more speech. Robust campaigns leading to the election of representatives not beholden to the few, but accountable to the many. The people of Arizona might have expected a decent respect for those objectives.

The majority, however, strongly rejected the dissent's contention that the Arizona trigger could serve an anticorruption purpose:

> Burdening a candidate's expenditure of his own funds on his own campaign does not further the state's anticorruption interest. Indeed, we have said that "reliance on personal funds *reduces* the threat of corruption" and that

---

16. "Yet here the majority makes a much stranger claim: that a statement appearing on a government website in 2011 (written by who-knows-whom?) reveals what hundreds of thousands of Arizona's voters sought to do in 1998 when they enacted the Clean Elections Act by referendum. Just to state that proposition is to know it is wrong."

"discouraging [the] use of personal funds[] disserves the anticorruption interest." *Davis.* That is because "the use of personal funds reduces the candidate's dependence on outside contributions and thereby counteracts the coercive pressures and attendant risks of abuse" of money in politics. *Buckley.* The matching funds provision counts a candidate's expenditures of his own money on his own campaign as contributions, and to that extent cannot be supported by any anticorruption interest.

We have also held that "independent expenditures . . . do not give rise to corruption or the appearance of corruption." *Citizens United.* "By definition, an independent expenditure is political speech presented to the electorate that is not coordinated with a candidate." The candidate-funding circuit is broken. The separation between candidates and independent expenditure groups negates the possibility that independent expenditures will result in the sort of *quid pro quo* corruption with which our case law is concerned. Including independent expenditures in the matching funds provision cannot be supported by any anticorruption interest.

We have observed in the past that "[t]he interest in alleviating the corrupting influence of large contributions is served by . . . contribution limitations." Arizona already has some of the most austere contribution limits in the United States. See *Randall* (plurality opinion). Contributions to statewide candidates are limited to $840 per contributor per election cycle and contributions to legislative candidates are limited to $410 per contributor per election cycle. Arizona also has stringent fundraising disclosure requirements. In the face of such ascetic contribution limits, strict disclosure requirements, and the general availability of public funding, it is hard to imagine what marginal corruption deterrence could be generated by the matching funds provision.

Perhaps recognizing that the burdens the matching funds provision places on speech cannot be justified in and of themselves, either as a means of leveling the playing field or directly fighting corruption, the State and the Clean Elections Institute offer another argument: They contend that the provision indirectly serves the anticorruption interest, by ensuring that enough candidates participate in the State's public funding system, which in turn helps combat corruption. We have said that a voluntary system of "public financing as a means of eliminating the improper influence of large private contributions furthers a significant governmental interest." *Buckley.* But the fact that burdening constitutionally protected speech might indirectly serve the State's anticorruption interest, by encouraging candidates to take public financing, does not establish the constitutionality of the matching funds provision.

We have explained that the matching funds provision substantially burdens the speech of privately financed candidates and independent groups. It does so to an even greater extent than the law we invalidated in Davis. We have explained that those burdens cannot be justified by a desire to "level the playing field." We have also explained that much of the speech burdened by the matching funds provision does not, under our precedents, pose a danger of corruption. In light of the foregoing analysis, the fact that the State may feel that the matching funds provision is necessary to allow it to "find[ ] the sweetspot" and "fine-tun[e]" its public funding system (Kagan, J., dissenting), to achieve its desired level of participation without an undue drain on public resources, is not a sufficient justification for the burden.

The flaw in the State's argument is apparent in what its reasoning would allow. By the State's logic it could grant a publicly funded candidate five dollars in matching funds for every dollar his privately financed opponent spent, or force candidates who wish to run on private funds to pay a $10,000 fine in order to encourage participation in the public funding regime. Such measures might well promote participation in public financing, but would clearly suppress or unacceptably alter political speech. How the State chooses to encourage participation in its public funding system matters, and we have never held that a State may burden political speech — to the extent the matching funds provision does — to ensure adequate participation in a public funding system. Here the State's chosen method is unduly burdensome and not sufficiently justified to survive First Amendment scrutiny.

Arizona Free Enterprise was careful to say that it was not striking down public financing laws generally. Instead, the Court confirmed the voluntariness analysis from *Buckley* and added a ban on triggering provisions. It also indicated that the Court would look closely for political equality justifications and strike down campaign finance laws premised on that basis (even if there may be other rationales for the law). It is unclear whether the Court or lower courts will apply strict scrutiny to other aspects of public financing plans.

Example 3

The city of Pacificana provides voluntary public financing for city candidates. Candidates who agree to take public financing and stick with a spending limit get a 6-to-1 match on contributions from city residents, for contributions up to $175. Contribution limits for both participating and non-participating candidates are $500 per individual per election. The city's campaign finance board website says this about the purpose of its program: "The matching funds program encourages participants to seek small contributions, and reach out to a greater number of their prospective constituents."

Does the 6:1 matching funds provision violate the First Amendment?

Explanation

This example is based upon New York City's public financing system,[17] and that statement about the law's purposes appeared on the New York City Campaign Finance board web page in 2012.[18] To determine whether the city's public financing law is unconstitutional, we would begin by asking whether the law is voluntary. If the benefits to participating candidates are very great and the limits applied to non-participating candidates are very

---

17. Michael J. Malbin, Peter W. Brusoe, and Brendan Glavin, *Small Donors, Big Democracy: New York City's Matching Funds as a Model for the Nation and States*, 11 ELECTION L.J. 3 (2012).
18. *See* http://www.nyccfb.info/candidates/candidates/whyJoin.aspx.

strict, a court may conclude that the system is coercive and therefore in violation of the First Amendment. *See Buckley; Daggett.*

Nothing on these limited facts shows the law is coercive; a $500 individual contribution limit for non-participating candidates seems in line with other individual contribution limits in other cities.

The next claim might be that the measure has an unconstitutional equalizing purpose. In *Arizona Free Enterprise Club*, the Supreme Court rejected a "trigger" mechanism in Arizona's public financing plan that gave extra matching funds to candidates who faced large spending from non-participating opponents or from independent groups. Applying strict scrutiny, the Court held that the trigger violated the First Amendment rights of those non-participating candidates and independent groups and that the measure was improper because it appeared to be motivated by a purpose to level the electoral playing field — an interest the Supreme Court has repeatedly rejected as a basis for campaign finance regulations.

It is not clear how a court applying the *Arizona Free Enterprise* ruling to a system with a 6:1 match for small donations only would decide the constitutional question. On the one hand, it is even harder in such a case than in the Arizona case to find a First Amendment injury to non-participating candidates or third parties. No one's speech is squelched, and the government is not matching the speech of non-participating opponents in a way that could be seen as penalizing them.

On the other hand, why are only small contributions matched, and matched with multiple matching funds? The purpose appears to amplify the voices of some and encourage more participation. It is quite possible that a conservative Court could view this once again as an impermissible equalizing purpose and hold that the measure is unconstitutional. However, that is not certain, and matching the first $175 of all donations at a large measure could be seen as a rational way of designing a system aimed at limiting the corruptive potential of large donations.

As with much else in this part (and this book!), much depends upon the views of the current nine justices on the Supreme Court.

Correlation Table

The fields of Legislation, Statutory Interpretation, and Election Law have much overlap, but likely no single course covers all the material in this book (and no doubt, some courses in these areas cover issues that are not described in this book). On the next two pages, you will find a table that matches up the material in this book with the chapters in most of the casebooks in the Legislation and Election Law fields.

To use this table, find your course's casebook in the far-left column on the first page. As you read across, you will see numbers corresponding to the chapters in your course's casebook. Follow the column up to the top to see where in this Examples and Explanations book the material appears. A blank in a column means that your course's casebook does not cover that material covered in the Examples and Explanations book. The table continues for each of the books on the second page.

Continued on next page

Examples and Explanations Chapters/Sections

Casebook	1.1	1.2	1.3	1.4	1.5	2.1	2.2	3.1	3.2	3.3	4.1	4.2	4.3	5.1	5.2	5.3	5.4	6.1	6.2	6.3	7.1	7.2	7.3	8.1	8.2
Dimino, Smith, & Sollimine, *Voting Rights and Election Law,* 2010						7							8												
Eskridge, Frickey, & Garrett, *Cases and Materials on Legislation,* 4th ed. 2007	1.1, 1.2, 1.3, 1.5	3.3		1.2, 1.3		2.2A	2.2B, 3.3C, 4	3.2	3.1	3.1	5	3.3		6, 7	6, 7	6.7	6, 7	8.1	8.1	8.1	8.2	8.2	8.2	9	9
Foley, Pitts, & Douglas, *Election Law and Litigation,* 2014																									
Gardner & Charles, *Election Law in the American Political System,* 2012						6																			
Issacharoff, Karlan, & Pildes, *The Law of Democracy,* 4th ed. 2012											11	11	11												
Lowenstein, Hasen, & Tokaji, *Election Law,* 5th ed. 2012									11			7	7												
Manning & Stephenson, *Legislation and Regulation,* 3d ed. 2013	1.I													1.II	1.III	i.IV		2	2	2	1.IV	1.IV	1.IV	3, 4, 5	3, 4, 5
Mikva & Lane, *Legislative Process,* 3d ed. 2009	1	1, 9.B, 9.C		3		7.A, 7.B	9.A, 9.D, 9.E	8		7.E	9.F			10, 11	10, 11	10, 11	10, 11		12		4, 5, 11.D	11.D	11.D	10.-D, 12.D	10.D, 12.D
Nelson, *Statutory Interpretation,* 2011														6	6	6	6	2	2	2, 5.C	3	3	3, 4	5.B	5.B
Popkin, *Materials on Legislation,* 5th ed. 2009		17.01, 18.01	18.02, 18.03	17.03		18.05	17.03	16.04	16.04		17.04	17.02, 17.04	17.04	5, 6, 7, 8	2, 3, 4, 5, 6, 7	6, 7, 8	6	5, 6	5, 6	5, 6, 7	6, 9	6, 9	6, 9, 11, 14	10	10
Strauss, *Legislation: Understanding and Using Statutes,* 2005	I	I	I	I	I									III	III	III	III	III, IV	III, IV	III, IV	III, IV	III, IV	III, IV	III, IV	III, IV

continued

Casebook	8.3	9.1	9.2	9.3	9.4	10.1	10.2	10.3	10.4	11.1	11.2	11.3	11.4	12.1	12.2	12.3	13.1	13.2	13.3	14.1	14.2	14.3	15.1	15.2	15.3	16.1	16.2
Dimino, Smith, & Solimine, Voting Rights and Election Law, 2010		1	3	1		6	2	6	6	4	4	5	5	10, 11	10, 11	10, 11	9	9	9	9	9	9	9	9	9	9	9
Eskridge, Frickey, & Garrett, Cases and Materials on Legislation, 4th ed. 2007	9		2.1A				2.1C		2.2C	2.1B	2.1B	2.1B					2.3	2.3	2.3	2.3	2.3	2.3	2.3	2.3	2.3	2.3	2.3
Foley, Pitts, & Douglas, Election Law and Litigation, 2014		IV.A	I.B			II.A, II.E	I.F	II.B, II.C, II.D	II.F, II.G	I.C, I.D	I.C, I.D	I.C, I.D	I.C, I.D, I.E, I.G	IV	IV	IV	III.D	III.D	III.D	III.D	III.D	III.D	III.D	III.D	III.D	III.D	III.D
Gardner & Charles, Election Law in the American Political System, 2012		3, 4	3, 4	3, 4	3, 4	7.A, 7.B	4.B, 4.c	7.C	7.B	5	5	5	5	10	10	10	9	9	9	9	9	9	8.E	8.E	8.E	9.G	9.G
Issacharoff, Karlan, & Pildes, The Law of Democracy, 4th ed. 2012		2	3.A, 3.C	3.B		4.A, 4.C	9	4.A, 4.C	4.D	6, 7	6.7	7, 8	7, 8, 10	12	12	12	5	5	5	5	5	5	5	5	5	5.H	5.H
Lowenstein, Hasen, & Tokaji, Election Law, 5th ed. 2012		2	3	3	3	8	4	8	9	5.I	5.II	5.III	5.IV	6	6	6	12	12	13	14	14	14	16	16	16	15	15
Manning & Stephenson, Legislation and Regulation, 3d ed. 2013	3, 4, 5																										
Mikva & Lane, Legislative Process, 3d ed. 2009	10.D, 12.D	6.A, 6.D							7.C	2.A, 6.D	6.D	6.B, 6.C															
Nelson, Statutory Interpretation, 2011	5.B																										
Popkin, Materials on Legislation, 5th ed. 2009	10	16.01					16.02	16.02	16.02					15, 16.03	16.03		16.04	16.04	16.04	16.04	16.04	16.04					
Strauss, Legislation: Understanding and Using Statutes, 2005	III, IV																										

Table of Books and Articles Cited

Ackerman, Bruce A., & Ian Ayres, Voting With Dollars: A New Paradigm for Campaign Finance (2004), 386

Aldrich, John H., Why Parties?: The Origin and Transformation of Political Parties in America (1995), 243

Alexander, Herbert E., Financing the 1972 Election (1976), 326

Allen, Ronald J., The National Initiative Proposal: A Preliminary Analysis, 58 Neb. L. Rev. 965 (1979), 96

Ansolabehere, Stephen & Nathaniel Persily, Vote Fraud in the Eye of the Beholder: The Role of Public Opinion in the Challenge to Voter Identification Requirements, 121 Harv. L. Rev. 1737 (2008), 309

Aprill, Ellen P., The Law of the Word: Dictionary Shopping in the Supreme Court, 30 Ariz. St. L.J. 275 (1998), 124

_____, Regulating the Political Speech of Noncharitable Exempt Organizations after Citizens United, 10 Election L.J. 363 (2011), 72

Bar-Simian-Tov, Ittai, Legislative Supremacy in the United States? Rethinking the "Enrolled Bill" Doctrine, 97 Geo. L.J. 323 (2009), 9

Bauer, Robert F. & Rebecca H. Gordon, Congressional Ethics: Gifts, Travel, Income, and Post-Employment Restrictions, in The Lobbying Manual (Luneburg), 88

Baumgartner, Frank R., et al., Lobbying and Policy Change: Who Wins, Who Loses, and Why (2009), 60

Bell, Jr., Derrick A., The Referendum: Democracy's Barrier to Racial Equality, 54 Wash. L. Rev. 1 (1978), 93

Bentley, Arthur F., The Process of Government: A Study of Social Pressures (1908), 25

Blatt, William S., Missing the Mark: An Overlooked Statute Redefines the Debate over Statutory Interpretation, 104 Nw. U. L. Rev. Colloquy 147 (2009), 115

Brandenburg, Bert, & Roy A. Schotland, Justice in Peril: The Endangered Balance Between Impartial Courts and Judicial Election Campaigns, 21 Geo. J. Legal Ethics, 1229 (2008), 386

Briffault, Richard, Distrust of Democracy, 63 Tex. L. Rev. 1347 (1985), 93

_____, Public Funding and Democratic Elections, 148 U. Pa. L. Rev. 563 (1999), 385

_____, Super PACs, 96 Minn. L. Rev. 1644 (2012), 364

Broder, David S., Democracy Derailed: Initiative Campaigns and the Power of Money (2000), 93

Brudney, James J., & Corey Ditslear, Canons of Construction and the Elusive Quest for Neutral Reasoning, 58 Vand. L. Rev. 1 (2005), 134–39

Burke, Edmund, Speech to the Electors of Bristol, 1 Burke's Works (1854), 46

Charlow, Robin, Judicial Review, Equal Protection and the Problem with Plebiscites, 79 Cornell L. Rev. 527 (1994), 95

Cain, Bruce E., Garrett's Temptation, 85 Va. L. Rev. 1589 (1999), 244

Charles, Guy-Uriel, Judging the Law of Politics, 103 Mich. L. Rev. 1099 (2005), 245

Chemerinsky, Erwin, Constitutional Law: Principles and Policies (2011), 222

Chomsky, Carol, The Story of Holy Trinity Church v. United States (1892): Spirit and History in Statutory Interpretation, in Statutory Interpretation Stories 2 (William N. Eskridge Jr., Philip P. Frickey, & Elizabeth Garrett eds., 2011), 115

Clark, Kathleen & Beth Nolan, Restrictions on Gifts and Outside Compensation for Executive Branch Employees, in The Lobbying Manual (Luneburg), 88

Cooter, Robert D., & Michael D. Gilbert, A Theory of Direct Democracy and the Single Subject Rule, 110 Colum. L. Rev. 687 (2010), 103

_____, Reply to Hasen and Matsusaka, 110 Colum. L. Rev. Sidebar 59 (2010), 103

Cronin, Thomas, Direct Democracy (1989), 94

Dashev, Elian, Note, Economic Boycotts as Harassment: The Threat to First Amendment Protected Speech in the Aftermath of Doe v. Reed, 45 Loy. L.A. L. Rev. 207 (2011), 378, 380

Davis, Elliott M., Note, The Newer Textualism: Justice Alito's Statutory Interpretation, 30 Harv. J. L. & Pub. Pol'y 983 (2007), 163

Duverger, Maurice, Political Parties (2d English ed. 1959), 260

Elhauge, Einer, Statutory Default Rules: How to Interpret Unclear Legislation (2008), 138

Ellis, Richard J., Democratic Delusions: The Initiative Process in America (2002), 93

Elmendorf, Christopher S., & Edward B. Foley, Gatekeeping vs. Balancing in the Constitutional Law of Elections: Methodological Uncertainty on the High Court, 17 Wm. & Mary Bill of Rts. J. 507 (2008), 310

Epstein, David et al., eds., The Future of the Voting Rights Act (2006), 274

Eskridge, Jr., William N., Dynamic Statutory Interpretation, 135 U. Pa. L. Rev. 1479 (1987), 120

_____, Dynamic Statutory Interpretation (1994), 159

_____, Interpreting Legislative Inaction, 87 Mich. L. Rev. 67 (1988), 174

_____, Federal Lobbying Regulation: History Through 1954, in The Lobbying Manual (Luneburg), 64

_____, The New Textualism, 37 UCLA L. Rev. 621 (1990), 122–24

Eskridge, Jr., William N., & Lauren E. Baer, The Continuum of Deference: Supreme Court Treatment of Agency Statutory Interpretation from Chevron to Hamdan, 96 Geo. L.J. 1083 (2008), 191, 203

Eskridge, Jr., William N,. & John Ferejohn, The Article I, Section 7 Game 80 Geo. L.J. 523 (1992), 26

Eskridge, Jr., William N., & Philip P. Frickey, The Supreme Court, 1993 Term Foreword: Law as Equilibrium, 108 Harv. L. Rev. 26 (1994), 137

_____, Cases and Materials on Legislation: Statutes and the Creation of Public Policy (2d ed. 1995), 137

Eskridge, Jr., William N., Philip P. Frickey, & Elizabeth Garrett, Cases and Materials on Legislation: Statutes and the Creation of Pubic Policy (4th ed. 2007), passim

_____, Legislation and Statutory Interpretation (2d ed. 2006), 142

Eule, Julian N., Judicial Review of Direct Democracy, 99 Yale L.J. 1503 (1990), 95

Fleishman, Joel L., The 1974 Federal Election Campaign Act Amendments: The Shortcomings of Good Intentions, 1975 Duke L.J. 851 (1975), 326

Foley, Edward B., The Future of Bush v. Gore?, 68 Ohio St. L.J. 925 (2007), 304

Frickey, Philip P., & Steven S. Smith, Judicial Review and the Legislative Process: Some Empirical and Normative Aspects of Due Process of Lawmaking, UC Berkeley School of Law, Public Law and Legal Theory Working Paper No. 63 (2001), 54, 55

Friendly, Henry, Benchmarks (1967), 159

Frisina, Laurin, et al., Ballot Formats, Touchscreens, and Undervotes: A Study of the 2006 Midterm Elections in Florida, 7 Election L.J. 25 (2008), 311

Garrett, Elizabeth, Hybrid Democracy, 73 Geo. Wash. L. Rev. 1096 (2005), 95

Garrett, Elizabeth, Ronald M. Levin, & Theodore Ruger, Constitutional Issues Raised by the Lobbying Disclosure Act, in The Lobbying Manual (Luneburg), 70

Gerber, Elisabeth R., The Populist Paradox: Interest Group Influence and the Promise of Direct Legislation (1999), 95

Gerken, Heather K, The Democracy Index (2012), 316

Gilbert, Michael D., Single Subject Rules and the Legislative Process, 67 U. Pitt. L. Rev. 803 (2006), 53

Gluck, Abbe R., The States as Laboratories of Statutory Interpretation: Methodological Consensus and the Modified New Textualism, 119 Yale L.J. 1750 (2010), 122

Gluck, Abbe R., & Lisa Schultz Bressman, Statutory Interpretation from the Inside — An Empirical Study of Congressional Drafting, Delegation, and the Canons: Part I, 65 Stan. L. Rev. 901 (2013), 125

Gora, Joel M., Campaign Finance Reform: Still Searching for a Better Way, 6 J. L. & Pol'y 137 (1997), 327

_____, The Legacy of Buckley v. Valeo, 2 Election L.J. 55 (2003), 327

Hasen, Richard L., The 2012 Voting Wars, Judicial Backstops, and the Resurrection of Bush v. Gore, 81 Geo. Wash. L. Rev. 1865 (2013), 305, 310

_____, Buckley is Dead, Long Live Buckley: The New Campaign Finance Incoherence of McConnell v. Federal Election Commission, 153 U. Pa. L. Rev. 31 (2004), 329

_____, Bush v. Gore and the Future of Equal Protection Law in Elections, 29 Fla. St. U. L. Rev. 377 (2001), 304

_____, The Changing Nature of Campaign Financing for Presidential Primary Candidates, in Nominating the President: Evolution and Revolution in 2008 and Beyond 27 (Jack Citrin & David Karol eds., 2009), 387

_____, Chill Out: A Qualified Defense of Campaign Finance Disclosure Laws in the Internet Age, 27 J. L. & Pol. 557 (2012), 375

_____, Citizens United and the Illusion of Coherence, 109 Mich. L. Rev. 581 (2011), 333

_____, Constitutional Avoidance and Anti-Avoidance by the Roberts Court, 2009 Sup. Ct. Rev. 181 (2010), 158-59

_____, Clipping Coupons for Democracy: An Egalitarian/Public Choice Defense of Campaign Finance Vouchers, 84 Cal. L. Rev. 1 (1996), 25, 386

_____, Congressional Power to Renew the Preclearance Provisions of the Voting Rights Act after Tennessee v. Lane, 66 Ohio St. L.J. 177 (2005), 274

_____, The Constitutionality of a Soft Money Ban After Colorado Republican II, 1 Election L.J. 195 (2002), 350

_____, The Democracy Canon, 62 Stan. L. Rev. 69 (2009), 136, 160-62

_____, End of the Dialogue? Political Polarization, the Supreme Court, and Congress, 86 S. Cal. L. Rev. 205 (2013), 130

_____, Entrenching the Duopoly: Why the Supreme Court Should Not Allow the States to Protect the Democrats and Republicans from Political Competition, 1997 Sup. Ct. Rev. 331 (1998), 242, 263

_____, Lobbying, Rent Seeking, and Democracy, 64 Stan. L. Rev. 191 (2012), 60

_____, The Newer Incoherence: Competition, Social Science, and Balancing in Campaign Finance Law After Randall v. Sorrell, 68 Ohio St. L.J. 849 (2007), 351

_____, The Nine Lives of Buckley v. Valeo, in First Amendment Stories 345 (Richard Garnett & Andrew Koppelman, eds., 2011), 322

_____, Political Dysfunction and Constitutional Change, 61 Drake L. Rev. 989 (2013), 40, 131

_____, The "Political Market" Metaphor and Election Law: A Comment on Issacharoff and Pildes, 50 Stan. L. Rev. 719 (1998), 244

_____, Race or Party? How Courts Should Think About Republican Efforts to Make It Harder to Vote in North Carolina and Elsewhere, 127 Harv. L. Rev. F. 58 (2014), 291, 310

_____, Rethinking the Unconstitutionality of Contribution and Expenditure Limits in Ballot Measure Campaigns, 78 S. Cal. L. Rev. 885 (2005), 347

_____, Shelby County and the Illusion of Minimalism, 22 Wm. & Mary Bill of Rts. J. 713 (2014), 273

_____, The Supreme Court and Election Law (2003), 217, 244, 335

_____, The Surprisingly Complex Case for Disclosure of Contributions and Expenditures Funding Sham Issue Advocacy, 48 UCLA L. Rev. 265 (2000), 367

_____, "Too Plain for Argument?" The Uncertain Congressional Power to Require Parties to Choose Presidential Nominees Through Direct and Equal Primaries, 102 Nw. U. L. Rev. 2009 (2008), 312

_____, The Transformation of the Campaign Financing Regime for U.S. Presidential Elections, in The Funding of Political Parties 225 (Keith D. Ewing, Jacob Rowbottom, & Joo-Cheong Tham eds., 2011), 387

_____, The Untimely Death of Bush v. Gore, 60 Stan. L. Rev. 1 (2007), 305

_____., The Voting Wars (2012), 298, 309

Hasen, Richard L., & John G. Matsusaka, Some Skepticism about the "Separable Preferences" Approach to the Single Subject Rule: A Comment on Cooter & Gilbert, 110 Colum. L. Rev. Sidebar 35 (2010), 103

Hayward, Allison, The Michigan Auto Dealers Prosecution: Exploring the Department of Justice's Mid-Century Posture Toward Campaign Finance Violations, 9 Election L.J. 177 (2010), 323

Hohenstein, Kurt, Coining Corruption: The Making of the American Campaign Finance System (2007), 323, 325

Issacharoff, Samuel, Is Section 5 of the Voting Rights Act a Victim of Its Own Success?, 104 Colum. L. Rev. 1710 (2004), 274

Issacharoff, Samuel & Richard H. Pildes, Politics as Markets: Partisan Lockups of the Democratic Process, 50 Stan. L. Rev. 643 (1998), 244

Jenkins, Timothy W. & A.L. (Lorry) Spitzer, Internal Revenue Code Limitations on Deductibility of Lobbying Expenses by Business and Trade Associations, in The Lobbying Manual (Luneburg), 72

Jenkins, Timothy W. & A.L. (Lorry) Spitzer, Internal Revenue Code Limitations on Lobbying by Tax-Exempt Organizations, in The Lobbying Manual (Luneburg), 72

Key, V.O., Politics, Parties, & Pressure Groups (5th ed. 1964), 241

Keyssar, Alexander, The Right to Vote: The Contested History of Democracy in the United States (2009), 213

Kirchmeier, Jeffrey L., & Samuel A. Thumma, Scaling the Lexicon Fortress: The United States Supreme Court's Use of Dictionaries in the Twenty-First Century, 94 Marq. L. Rev. 77 (2010), 124

Kousser, J. Morgan, Suffrage, in 3 Encyclopedia of American Political History 1236 (Jack P. Greene, ed., 1984), 213

Kousser, Thad, Term Limits and the Dismantling of State Legislative Professionalism (2005), 40

Krishnakumar, Anita S., The Hidden Legacy of Holy Trinity Church: The Unique National Institution Canon, 51 Wm. & Mary L. Rev. 1053 (2009), 115

_____, Toward a Madisonian, Interest-Group Based, Approach to Lobbying Regulation, 58 Ala. L. Rev. 513 (2007), 68

Law, David S., & David Zaring, Law Versus Ideology: The Supreme Court and the Use of Legislative History, 51 Wm. & Mary L. Rev. 1653 (2010), 163

Lawson, Gary, & Stephen Kam, Making Law Out of Nothing at All: The Origins of the Chevron Doctrine, 65 Admin. L. Rev. 1 (2013), 189-90

Lessig, Lawrence, Republic, Lost (2011), 386

Levin, Hillel Y., The Food Stays in the Kitchen: Everything I Needed to Know About Statutory Interpretation I Learned by the Time I Was Nine, 12 Green Bag 2d 337 (2009), 113, 115

Levin, Ronald M., Mead and the Prospective Exercise of Discretion, 54 Admin. L. Rev. 771 (2002), 191

Levinson, Daryl J., & Richard H. Pildes, Separation of Parties, Now Powers, 119 Harv. L. Rev. 2311 (2006), 254

Linde, Hans, Due Process of Lawmaking, 55 Neb. L. Rev. 197 (1976), 55

Lowenstein, Daniel H., California Initiatives and the Single-Subject Rule, 30 UCLA L. Rev. 936 (1983), 101

_____, Campaign Spending and Ballot Propositions: Recent Experience, Public Choice Theory and the First Amendment, 29 UCLA L. Rev. 505 (1982), 95

_____, Initiatives and the New Single Subject Rule, 1 Election L.J. 35 (2002), 102, 104

_____, The Meaning of Bush v. Gore, 68 Ohio St. L.J. 1007 (2007), 304

_____, Political Bribery and the Intermediate Theory of Politics, 32 UCLA L. Rev. 784 (1985), 78

_____, The Supreme Court Has No Theory of Politics — and Be Thankful for Small Favors, in The U.S. Supreme Court and the Electoral Process 283 (David K. Ryden ed., 2002), 244

_____, When is a Campaign Contribution a Bribe?, in Public and Private Corruption 127 (William C. Heffernan & John Kleinig eds., 2004), 79

Lowenstein, Daniel H., Richard L. Hasen, & Daniel P. Tokaji, Election Law — Cases and Materials (5th ed. 2012), *passim*

Lowenstein, Daniel Hays & Robert M. Stern, The First Amendment and Paid Initiative Petition Circulators: A Dissenting View and a Proposal, 17 Hastings Const. L.Q. 175 (1989), 108

Lund, Nelson, The Unbearable Rightness of Bush v. Gore, 23 Cardozo L. Rev. 1219 (2002), 304

Luneburg, William V., et al. eds., The Lobbying Manual (4th ed. 2009), 64

Macey, Jonathan R., Separated Powers and Positive Political Theory: The Tug of War Over Administrative Agencies, 80 Geo. L.J. 671 (1992), 26

Malbin, Michael J., Peter W. Brusoe, & Brendan Galvin, Small Donors, Big Democracy: New York City's Matching Funds as a Model for the Nation and States, 11 Election L.J. 3 (2012), 398

Manning, John F., The Absurdity Doctrine, 116 Harv. L. Rev. 2387 (2003), 129

_____, Federalism and the Generality Problem in Constitutional Interpretation, 122 Harv. L. Rev. 2003(2009), 115

Matsusaka, John G., For the Many or the Few: The Initiative, Public Policy and American Democracy (2004), 93

Matsusaka, John G., & Richard L. Hasen, Aggressive Enforcement of the Single Subject Rule, 9 Election L.J. 399 (2010), 53, 102

Mayer, Kenneth R., Timothy Werner, & Amanda Williams, Do Public Funding Programs Enhance Electoral Competition?, in The Marketplace of Democracy 245 (Michael P. McDonald & John Samples, eds. 2006), 386

Mayer, Lloyd Hitoshi, Disclosures About Disclosure, 44 Ind. L. Rev. 255 (2010), 380

McChesney, Fred S., Money for Nothing: Politicians, Rent Extraction and Political Extortion (1997), 378

_____, Rent Extraction and Rent Creation in the Economic Theory of Regulation, 16 J. Legal Stud. 101 (1987), 378

McCloy, John J., The Great Oil Spill: The Inside Report: Gulf Oil's Bribery and Political Chicanery (1976), 326

McCubbins, Matthew, Roger Noll, & Barry Weingast, Legislative Intent: The Use of Positive Political Theory in Statutory Interpretation, 57 Law & Contemp. Probs. 3 (1994), 26

Table of Books and Articles Cited

McGeveran, William, Mrs. McIntyre's Persona: Bringing Privacy Theory to Election Law, 19 Wm. & Mary Bill Rts. J. 859 (2011), 379

Merrill, Thomas, Justice Stevens and the Chevron Puzzle, 106 Nw. U. L. Rev. 551 (2012), 189

_____, The Story of Chevron: The Making of an Accidental Landmark, in Administrative Law Stories 398 (Peter Strauss ed. 2006), 189

Merrill, Thomas W., & Kristin E. Hickman, Chevron's Domain, 89 Geo. L.J. 833 (2001), 190

Michelman, Frank I., Political Markets and Community Self-Determination: Competing Judicial Models of Local Government Legitimacy, 53 Ind. L.J. 145 (1977-1978), 28

Miller, Michael G., Subsidizing Democracy: How Public Funding Changes Elections and How It Can Work in the Future (2013), 386

Molot, Jonathan T., The Rise and Fall of Textualism, 106 Colum. L. Rev. 1 (2006), 122

Mutch, Robert E., Campaigns, Congress, and the Courts: The Making of Federal Campaign Finance Law (1988), 322–28, 379

_____, The First Federal Campaign Finance Bills, 14 J. Pol'y Hist. 30 (2002), 322

Neuborne, Burt, Campaign Finance Reform & the Constitution: A Critical Look at Buckley v. Valeo (1998), 328

Nownes, Anthony J., Total Lobbying: What Lobbyists Want (and How They Try to Get It) (2006), 60

Olson, Mancur, The Logic of Collective Action: Public Goods and the Theory of Groups (2d ed. 1971), 26

Persily, Nathaniel A., The Law of the Census: How to Count, What to Count, Whom to Count, and Where to Count Them, 32 Cardozo L. Rev. 755 (2011), 230

_____, The Peculiar Geography of Direct Democracy: Why the Initiative, Referendum and Recall Developed in the American West, 2 Mich. L. & Pol'y Rev. 11 (1997), 91

_____, Reply, In Defense of Foxes Guarding Henhouses: The Case for Judicial Acquiescence to Incumbent-Protecting Gerrymanders, 116 Harv. L. Rev. 649 (2002), 244

_____, The Promise and Pitfalls of the New Voting Rights Act, 117 Yale L.J. 174 (2007), 270

Pildes, Richard H., & Richard G. Niemi, Expressive Harms, "Bizarre Districts," and Voting Rights: Evaluating Election-District Appearances After Shaw v. Reno, 92 Mich. L. Rev. 483 (1993), 294

Popkin, William D., Statutes in Court: The History and Theory of Statutory Interpretation (1999), 138

Posner, Richard A., Reflections on Judging (2013), 309

_____, Theories of Economic Regulation, 5 J. Bell Econ. & Mgmt. Sci. 335 (1974), 26

Potter, Trevor & Joseph M. Birkenstock, Political Activity, Lobbying Laws and Gift Rules Guide (3d ed. 2008), 64

Primo, David M., Jeffrey Milyo, & Tim Groseclose, State Campaign Finance Reform, Competitiveness, and Party Advantage in Gubernatorial Elections, in The Marketplace of Democracy 268 (Michael P. McDonald & John Samples, eds. 2006), 386

Rodriguez, Daniel B. & Barry R. Weingast, The Paradox of Expansionist Statutory Interpretation, 101 Nw. U. L. Rev. 1207 (2007), 169

_____, The Positive Political Theory of Legislative History: New Perspectives on the 1964 Civil Rights Act and Its Interpretation, 151 U. Pa. L. Rev. 1417 (2003), 26, 28-29

Rosenkranz, Nicholas Quinn, Federal Rules of Statutory Interpretation, 115 Harv. L. Rev. 2085 (2002), 119

Ross, Stephen F., Where Have You Gone Karl Llewellyn? Should Congress Turn Its Lonely Eyes to You?, 45 Vand. L. Rev. 561 (1992), 139

Rubin, Edward L., Modern Statutes, Loose Canons, and the Limits of Practical Reason: A Response to Farber and Ross, 45 Vand. L. Rev. 579 (1992), 139

Samples, John, The Fallacy of Campaign Finance Reform (2006), 327

Scalia, Antonin, A Matter of Interpretation: Federal Courts and the Law (1997), 123, 137

_____, Assorted Canards of Contemporary Legal Analysis, 40 Case W. Res. L. Rev. 581 (1990), 138

_____, Judicial Deference to Administrative Interpretations of Law, 1989 Duke L.J. 511, 191

Scalia, Antonin, & Bryan A. Garner, Reading Law: the Interpretation of Legal Texts (2012), 134, 138, 144, 150, 179

Schacter, Jane S., Metademocracy: The Changing Structure of Legitimacy in Statutory Interpretation, 108 Harv. L. Rev. 593 (1995), 138

Schauer, Frederick, Ashwander Revisited, 1995 Sup. Ct. Rev. 71 (1996), 159

Schattschneider, E.E., Party Government (1942), 242, 260

Schlozman, Kay Lehman, & John T. Tierney, Organized Interests and American Democracy (1986), 60

Schrag, Peter, Paradise Lost: California's Experience, America's Future (1998), 93

Shapiro, David L., Continuity and Change in Statutory Interpretation, 67 N.Y.U. L. Rev. 921 (1992), 139

Shepsle, Kenneth A, Congress is a "They," Not an "It:" Legislative Intent as Oxymoron, 12 Int'l Rev. L. & Econ. 239 (1992), 114

Sinclair, Barbara, Unorthodox Lawmaking: New Legislative Processes in the U.S. Congress (4th ed. 2011), 30-33, 48

Smith, Bradley A., Some Problems with Taxpayer-Funded Political Campaigns, 148 U. Pa. L. Rev. 591 (1999), 386

Spitzer, Robert J., The Historical Presidency: Growing Executive Power: The Strange Case of the "Protective Return" Pocket Veto, 42:3 Pres. Stud. Q. 637 (2012), 15

Stephenson, Matthew C., & Howell E. Jackson, Lobbyists as Imperfect Agents: Implications for Public Policy in a Pluralist System, 47 Harv. J. on Legis. 1 (2010), 60

Stewart, III, Charles, Voting Technologies, 14 Annual. Rev. of Pol. Sci. 353 (2011), 311

Strauss, Peter L., "Deference" is Too Confusing — Let's Call Them "Chevron Space" and "Skidmore Weight," 112 Colum. L. Rev. 1143 (2012), 189

_____, In Search of Skidmore, Columbia Public Law and Research Paper 13-355 (Jun. 30, 2013), 191

Sunstein, Cass R., Chevron Step Zero, 92 Va. L. Rev. 187 (2006), 190

_____, Interest Groups in American Public Law, 38 Stan. L. Rev. 29 (1985), 28

Susman, Thomas M., The Byrd Amendment, in the Lobbying Manual (Luneburg), 66

Susman, Thomas M., & William V. Luneburg, History of Lobbying Disclosure Reform Proposals Since 1955, in The Lobbying Manual (Luneburg), 65, 69

Task Force on Federal Lobbying Laws, Lobbying Law in the Spotlight: Challenges and Proposed Improvements, American Bar Association (2011), 74

Thurber, James A., Changing the Way Washington Works? Assessing President Obama's Battle with Lobbyists, 41 Presidential Stud. Q. 358 (2011), 74

Tokaji, Daniel P., Leave It to the Lower Courts: On Judicial Intervention in Election Administration, 68 Ohio St. L.J. 1065 (2007), 304

_____, The New Vote Denial: Where Election Reform Meets the Voting Rights Act, 57 S. C. L. Rev. 689 (2006), 290

Torres-Spelliscy, Ciara, Has the Tide Turned in Favor of Disclosure? Revealing Money in Politics After Citizens United and Doe v. Reed, 27 Ga. St. U. L. Rev. 1057 (2011), 374

Truman, David B., The Governmental Process: Political Interests and Public Opinion (1951), 25

Vermeule, Adrian, The Judiciary is a They Not an It: Interpretive Theory and the Fallacy of Division, 14 J. Contemp. Legal Issues 529 (2005), 114

Winger, Richard, The Supreme Court and the Burial of Ballot Access: A Critical Review of Jenness v. Fortson, 1 Election L.J. 235 (2002), 261

Winkler, Adam, "Other People's Money": Corporations, Agency Costs, and Campaign Finance Law, 92 Geo. L.J. 871 (2004), 322

Winter, Ralph K., The History and Theory of Buckley v. Valeo, 6 J. L. Pol'y 93 (1997-1998), 328

Young, Ernest A., Constitutional Avoidance, Resistance Norms, and the Preservation of Judicial Review, 78 Tex. L. Rev. 1549 (2000), 159

Zelizer, Julian E., On Capitol Hill: The Struggle to Reform Congress and Its Consequences, 1948-2000 (2004), 323, 324, 327

_____, Seeds of Cynicism: The Struggle over Campaign Finance, 1956-1974, 14 J. Pol'y Hist. 73 (2002), 323–27

Table of Cases

Allen v. State Board of Elections, 393 U.S. 544 (1969), 268

Almendarez-Torres v. United States, 523 U.S. 224 (1998), 158

Amador Valley Joint Junior High Sch. Dist. v. State Bd. of Equalization, 583 P.2d 1281 (Cal. 1978), 98

American Tradition Partnership v. Bullock, 132 S. Ct. 2490 (2012), 344-45

Anderson v. Celebrezze, 460 U.S. 780 (1983), 261–63, 307

Arizona Free Enterprise Club's Freedom Club PAC v. Bennett, 131 S. Ct. 2806 (2011), 394-99

Arizona v. Inter Tribal Council, 133 S. Ct. 2247 (2013), 305, 314-16

Arkansas Educational Television Commission v. Forbes, 523 U.S. 666 (1998), 261

Armatta v. Kitzhaber, 959 P.2d 49 (Or. 1998), 104

Associated Indus. of Ky. v. Commonwealth, 912 S.W. 3d 947 (Ky. 1995), 75

Auer v. Robbins, 519 U.S. 452 (1997), 204-06

Austin v. Michigan Chamber of Commerce, 494 U.S. 652 (1990), 334-44, 373

Autor v. Blank, 892 F. Supp. 2d 264 (D.D.C. 2012), 74

Avery v. Midland County, 390 U.S. 474 (1968), 228-30, 232-33

Baker v. Carr 369 U.S. 186 (1962), 222 244, 248

Barber v. Thomas, 130 S. Ct. 2499 (2010), 154

Barnhart v. Thomas, 540 U.S. 20 (2003), 150-51

Bartlett v. Strickland, 556 U.S. 1 (2009), 284

Beer v. United States, 425 U.S. 130 (1976), 268-69

Begay v. U.S., 553 U.S. 137 (2008), 154

Bluman v. FEC, 132 S. Ct. 1087 (2012), 345

Bluman v. FEC, 800 F. Supp. 2d 281 (D.D.C. 2011), 345-46

Board of Trustees v. Garrett, 531 US. 356 (2001), 56, 274

Borough of Duryea v. Guarnieri, 131 S. Ct. 2488 (2011), 69

Breedlove v. Suttles, 302 U.S. 277 (1937), 215

Brinkman v. Budish, 692 F. Supp. 2d 855 (S.D. Ohio 2010), 75

Brown v. Socialist Workers '74 Campaign Comm., 459 U.S. 87 (1982), 370, 375-81

Bruesewitz v. Wyeth LLC, 131 S. Ct. 1068 (2011), 141

Buckley v. American Constitutional Law Foundation, 525 U.S. 182 (1999), 106

Buckley v. Valeo, 424 U.S. 1 (1976), 106, 261, 319-90

Burdick v. Takushi, 504 U.S. 428 (1992), 262, 307

Burns v. Fortson, 410 U.S. 686 (1973), 218

Burns v. Richardson, 384 U.S. 73 (1966), 230

Bush v. Gore, 531 U.S. 98 (2000), 297-312

Bush v. Palm Beach Cnty. Canvassing Bd., 531 U.S. 70 (2000), 300

California Democratic Party v. Jones, 530 U.S. 567 (2000), 257-58, 357

California Medical Association v. FEC, 453 U.S. 182 (1981), 330

Cammarano v. United States, 358 U.S. 498 (1959) 72-73

Cane v. Worcester County, 35 F.3d 921 (4th Cir. 1994), 286

Cano v. Davis, 211 F. Supp. 2d 1208 (C.D. Cal. 2002), 287

Carrington v. Rash, 380 U.S. 89 (1965), 218

Carey v. FEC, 791 F. Supp. 2d 121 (D.D.C. 2011), 362

Ctr. for Individual Freedom v. Madigan, 697 F.3d 464 (7th Cir. 2012), 373

Ctr. For Individual Freedom v. Tennant, 706 F.3d 270 (4th Cir. 2013), 373

Chevron v. Nat'l Resources Def. Council, 467 U.S. 837 (1984), 186-98, 200-02

Chisom v. Roemer, 501 U.S. 380 (1991), 175-79

Christopher v. SmithKline Beecham Corp., 132 S. Ct. 2156 (2012), 204

Church of Scientology v. IRS, 484 U.S. 9 (1987), 174

Citizens Against Rent Control v. City of Berkeley, 454 U.S. 290 (1981), 348, 370

Citizens for Tax Reform v. Deters, 518 F.3d 375 (6th Cir. 2008), 109

Citizens United v. FEC, 558 U.S. 310 (2010), 70, 75, 159, 337-45, 374-75, 377

City of Arlington v. FCC, 133 S. Ct. 1863 (2013), 183, 186, 190, 202-03

City of Boerne v. Flores, 521 U.S. 507 (1997), 274

City of Mobile v. Bolden, 446 U.S. 55 (1980), 175, 280-82

City of Rome v. United States, 446 U.S. 156 (1980), 273

Clark v. Martinez, 543 U.S. 371 (2005), 138, 158

Clingman v. Beaver, 544 U.S. 581 (2005), 259

Clinton v. New York, 524 U.S. 417 (1998), 7, 17, 19

Colegrove v. Green, 328 U.S. 549 (1946), 222

Conroy v. Aniskoff, 507 U.S. 511 (1993), 123

Cook v. Gralike, 531 U.S. 510 (2001), 42

Crawford v. Marion County Election Board, 553 U.S. 181 (2008), 305-11

Crawford v. Marion County Election Bd., 472 F.3d 949 (7th Cir. 2007), 306

Daggett v. Commission on Governmental Ethics and Election Practices, 205 F.3d 445 (1st Cir. 2000), 391-94

Davis v. Bandemer, 478 U.S. 109 (1986), 249

Davis v. FEC, 554 U.S. 724 (2008), 356, 395

Doe v. Reed, 130 S. Ct. 2811 (2010), 375-81

Doe v. Reed, 823 F. Supp. 2d 1195 (W.D. Wash. 2011), 376

Dunn v. Blumstein, 405 U.S. 330 (1972), 218

Easley v. Cromartie, 532 U.S. 234 (2001), 295

Evans v. Cornman, 398 U.S. 419 (1970), 218

Evans v. United States, 504 U.S. 255 (1992), 81, 85

Fair Political Practices Comm'n v. Superior Court, 599 P.2d 46 (Cal. 1979), 102

Farrakhan v. Gregoire, 623 F.3d 990 (9th Cir. 2010), 290

Farrakhan v. Washington, 359 F.3d 1116 (9th Cir. 2004), 290

FDA v. Brown & Williamson Tobacco Corp., 529 U.S. 120 (2000), 174

FEC v. Beaumont, 539 U.S. 146 (2003), 335, 350, 360-61

FEC v. Colorado Republican Federal Campaign Committee (Colorado II), 349-50

FEC v. Massachusetts Citizens for Life, 479 U.S. 238 (1986), 334, 336, 339-40, 360, 370

FEC v. Wisconsin Right to Life, 551 U.S. 449 (2007), 338

First National Bank of Boston v. Bellotti, 435 U.S. 765 (1978), 333-34, 370, 373

Fla. League of Prof'l Lobbyists v. Meggs, 87 F.3d 457 (11th Cir. 1996), 75

Flood v. Kuhn, 407 U.S. 248 (1972), 130

Frank v. Walker, ___ F. Supp. 2d ___, 2014 WL 1775431 (E.D. Wis. 2014), 291-92, 309

Fuller v. Bowen, 2013 Cal. App. 4th 1476 (2012), 43

Georgia v. Ashcroft, 539 U.S. 461 (2003), 269-70, 284

Goosby v. Town of Hempstead, 180 F.3d 476 (2d Cir. 1999), 285

Gravel v. United States, 408 U.S. 606 (1972), 49

Gray v. Sanders, 372 U.S. 368 (1963), 223

Green Party of Connecticut v. Garfield, 616 F.3d 189 (2d Cir. 2010), 75

Green v. Bock Laundry Machine Co., 490 U.S. 504 (1989), 126

Green v. New York, 465 F.3d 65 (2d Cir. 2006), 142

Gregory v. Ashcroft, 501 U.S. 452 (1991), 160, 178

Grovey v. Townsend, 295 U.S. 45 (1935), 255

Growe v. Emison, 507 U.S. 25 (1993), 284

Guinn v. United States, 238 U.S. 347 (1915), 211

Hadley v. Junior College District, 397 U.S. 50 (1970), 233

Hamdan v. Rumsfeld, 548 U.S. 557 (2006), 130

Hampton v. Mow Sun Wong, 426 U.S. 88 (1976), 55

Harper v. Virginia State Board of Elections, 383 U.S. 663 (1966), 215-19, 300-02

Hayden v. Pataki, 449 F.3d 305 (2d Cir. 2006), 290

Table of Cases

Hirschey v. F.E.R.C., 777 F.2d 1 (D.C. Cir. 1985), 164

Holder v. Hall, 512 U.S. 874 (1994), 168, 289

Holt Civic Club v. City of Tuscaloosa, 439 U.S. 60 (1978), 219-20

Holy Trinity Church, see Rector, Etc. of Holy Trinity Church v. United States

Hunter v. Underwood, 471 U.S. 222 (1985), 219

Initiative and Referendum Inst. v. Jaeger, 241 F.3d 614 (8th Cir. 2001), 109

In re Advisory Opinion of the Attorney General, 632 So. 2d 1018 (Fla. 1994), 102

In re Kukowski, 356 B.R. 712 (B.A.P. 8th Cir. 2006), 147-49

In re ReadyOne Industries, Inc., 394 S.W. 3d 680 (Tx. App. 2012), 152-53

Inst. of Governmental Advocates v. Fair Political Practices Comm'n, 164 F. Supp. 2d 1183 (E.D. Cal. 2001), 74

Iowa Right to Life v. Tooker, 717 F.3d 576 (8th Cir. 2013), 360

Jarecki v. G.D. Searle & Co., 367 U.S. 303 (1961), 143-47

Jenness v. Fortson, 403 U.S. 471 (1971), 261

Johnson v. DeGrandy, 512 U.S. 997 (1994), 282, 285

Johnson v. Gov. of State of Fla., 405 F.3d 1214 (11th Cir. 2005), 290

Kimbell v. Hooper, 164 A.2d 44 (Vt. 1995), 74

Kobach v. U.S. Elec. Assist. Comm'n, ___ F. Supp. 2d ___, 2014 WL 1094957 (D. Kansas 2014), 315

Koons Buick Pontiac GMC, Inc. v. Nigh, 543 U.S. 50 (2004), 173

Kramer v. Union Free School District No. 15, 395 U.S. 621 (1969), 219-20, 229

Lacy St. Hospitality Service, Inc. v. City of Los Angeles, 22 Cal. Rptr. 3d 805 (Ct. App. 2004), 57

Larios v. Cox, 300 F. Supp. 2d 1320 (N.D. Ga. 2004), 231, 252

Lassiter v. Northampton County Board of Elections, 360 U.S. 45 (1959), 211-12

League of United Latin American Citizens v. Perry, 548 U.S. 399 (2006), 251, 284-85, 295

Ledbetter v. Goodyear Tire & Rubber Company, 550 U.S. 618 (2007), 131

Legislature v. Eu, 816 P.2d 1309 (Cal. 1991), 98

Lehman v. Bradbury, 37 P.3d 989 (Or. 2002), 105

Libertarian Party of Va. v. Judd, 718 F.3d 308 (4th Cir 2013), 106

Lorillard v. Pons, 434 U.S. 575 (1978), 179

Lucas v. 44th General Assembly of Colorado, 377 U.S. 713 (1964), 224-28

Marshall Field & Co. v. Clark, 143 U.S. 649 (1892), 8, 10-12

Marston v. Lewis, 410 U.S. 679 (1973), 218

Md. Right to Life State Political Action Comm. v. Wathersbee, 975 F. Supp. 791 (D. Md. 1997), 75

McConnell v. FEC, 540 U.S. 93 (2003), 336-38, 350, 357-58, 372-73

McCormick v. United States, 500 U.S. 257 (1991), 81

McCutcheon v. FEC, 134 S. Ct. 1434 (2014), 333, 356-61

McDonald v. Smith, 472 U.S. 479 (1985), 69

MCI Communications v. AT&T Corp. 512 U.S. 218 (1994), 192-98

McIntyre v. Ohio Elections Comm'n, 514 U.S. 334 (1995), 70, 370-81

Meyer v. Bradbury, 142 P.3d 1031 (Or. 2006), 105

Meyer v. Grant, 486 U.S. 414 (1988), 107-09

Miller v. Johnson, 515 U.S. 900 (1995), 294

Minnesota Citizens Concerned for Life, Inc. v. Swanson, 692 F.3d 864 (8th Cir. 2012), 374

Minor v. Happersett, 88 U.S. 162 (1874), 214-15

Mont. Auto. Ass'n v. Greely, 632 P.2d 300 (Mont. 1981), 75

Morris v. Gressette 432 U.S. 491 (1977), 268

Munro v. Socialist Workers Party, 479 U.S. 189 (1986), 261-62

National Organization for Marriage v. McKee, 723 F. Supp. 2d 245 (D. Maine 2010), 373

National Association of Manufacturers v. Taylor, 582 F.3d 1 (D.C. Cir. 2009), 70

N.C. Right to Life v. Bartlett, 168 F.3d 705 (4th Cir. 1999), 74

Ne. Ohio Coal. for the Homeless v. Husted, 696 F.3d 580 (6th Cir. 2012), 305

Newberry v. United States, 256 U.S. 232 (1921), 255

New York State Board of Elections v. López Torres, 552 U.S. 196 (2008) 245-46

Nielson v. AT&T Corp., 597 N.W.2d 434 (S.D. 1999), 144

Nixon v. Condon, 286 U.S. 73 (1932), 255

Nixon v. Herndon, 273 U.S. 536 (1927), 255

Nixon v. Shrink Mo. Gov't PAC, 528 U.S. 377 (2000), 348-61

NLRB v. Canning, cert. granted, 133 S. Ct. 2861 (2013), 16

Northwest Austin Municipal Utility District No. One v. Holder, 557 U.S. 193 (2009) ("NAMUDNO"), 159, 274-75

Northwest Austin Municipal Utility District No. One v. Mukasey, 573 F. Supp. 2d 221 (D.D.C. 2008), 274

Obama for Am. v. Husted, 697 F.3d 423 (6th Cir. 2012), 305

Oregon v. Mitchell, 400 U.S. 112 (1970), 212

Owens v. State, 64 Tex. 500 (1885), 161

Palm Beach Cnty. Canvassing Bd. v. Harris, 772 So.2d 1220 (Fla. 2000), 300

People ex rel. Dickinson v. Van de Carr, 84 N.Y.S. 461 (N.Y. App. Div. 1903), 78

Pipefitters Local Union No. 562 v. United States, 407 U.S. 385 (1972), 325

Pittman v. Chicago Board of Education, 64 F.3d 1098 (7th Cir. 1995), 236

Powell v. McCormack, 395 U.S. 486 (1969), 43-45

Presley v. Etowah Cnty. Comm'n, 502 U.S. 491 (1992), 268

Preston v. Leake, 660 F.3d 9 726 (4th Cir. 2011), 74

ProtectMarriage.com v. Bowen, 599 F. Supp. 2d 11197 (E.D. Cal. 2009), 378

Public Citizen v. United States District Court, 486 F.3d 1342 (D.C. Cir. 2007), 7, 10, 11-12

Purcell v. Gonzalez, 549 U.S. 1 (2006), 309

Randall v. Sorrell, 548 U.S. 230 (2006), 245, 351-61

Raven v. Deukmejian, 801 P.2d 1077 (Cal. 1990), 98

The Real Truth About Abortion, Inc. v. FEC, 681 F.3d 544 (4th Cir. 202), 373

Rector, Etc. of Holy Trinity Church v. United States, 143 U.S. 457 (1892), 115-19, 134, 164

Reform Party of Allegheny County v. Department of Elections, 174 F.3d 305 (3d Cir. 1999), 263

Regan v. Taxation with Representation of Washington, 461 U.S. 540 (1983), 73

Reno v. Bossier Parish School Bd., 520 U.S. 471 (1997) (Bossier Parish I), 271

Reno v. Bossier Parish School Bd., 528 U.S. 320 (2000) (Bossier Parish II), 271

Republican Party of Texas v. Dietz, 940 S.W.2d 86 (Tx. 1997), 256

Reynolds v. Sims, 377 U.S. 533 (1964), 223-24, 300

Richardson v. Ramirez, 418 U.S. 24 (1974), 219

Rust v. Sullivan, 500 U.S. 173 (1991), 158

Salyer Land Co. v. Tulare Lake Basin Water Storage District, 410 U.S. 719 (1973), 232-36

Sandusky Cnty. Dem. Party v. Blackwell, 387 F.3d 565 (6th Cir. 2004), 313

Schaefer v. Townsend, 215 F.3d 1031 (9th Cir. 2000), 37

Senate of the State of California v. Jones, 988 P.2d 1089 (Cal. 1999), 102

Shaw v. Reno, 509 U.S. 630 (1993), 293-94

Shelby County v. Holder, 133 S. Ct. 2612 (2013), 266, 273-80

Shelby County v. Holder, 679 F.3d 848 (D.C. Cir. 2012), 275

Shelby County v. Holder, 811 F. Supp. 2d 44 (D.D.C. 2011), 275

Simmons v. Galvin, 575 F.3d 24 (1st Cir. 2009), 290

Sissel v. U.S. Dep't of Health & Human Services, 951 F. Supp. 2d 159 (D.D.C. 2013), 13

Skafte v. Rorex, 553 P.2d 830 (Colo. 1976), 219

Skidmore v. Swift & Co., 323 U.S. 134 (1944), 200-206

Skilling v. United States, 561 U.S. 358 (2010), 87

Smith v. Allwright, 321 U.S. 649 (1944), 255

South Carolina v. Katzenbach, 383 U.S. 301 (1966), 273, 276, 278

SpeechNow.Org. v. FEC, 599 F.3d 686 (D.C. Cir. 2010), 362

State v. Alaska Civil Liberties Union, 978 P.2d 697 (Alaska 1999), 74

Strauss v. Horton, 207 P.3d 48 (Cal. 2009), 99

Symm v. United States, 439 U.S. 1104 (1979), 219

Tashjian v. Republican Party of Connecticut, 479 U.S. 208 (1986), 256-57, 357

Terry v. Adams, 345 U.S. 461 (1953), 255

Texas v. Holder, 888 F. Supp. 2d 113 (D.D.C. 2012), 270

Textile Mills Securities Corporation v. Commissioner of Internal Revenue, 314 U.S. 326 (1941), 72

Thalheimer v. City of San Diego, 645 F.3d 1109 (9th Cir. 2011), 359

Thalheimer v. City of San Diego, 2012 WL 177414 (S.D. Cal. 2012), 359

Timmons v. Twin Cities Area New Party, 520 U.S. 351 (1997), 261-63, 307

Thornburg v. Gingles, 478 U.S. 30 (1986), 166, 282-88, 295-96

United States v. Alvarez, 132 S. Ct. 2537 (2012), 129

United States v. Brewster, 408 U.S. 501 (1972), 48

United States v. Brewster, 506, F.2d 62 (D.C. Cir. 1974), 80-81

United States v. Classic, 313 U.S. 299 (1941), 255

United States v. Danielczyk, 683 F.3d 611 (4th Cir. 2012), 360

United States v. Johnson, 383 U.S. 169 (1966), 47, 49

United States v. Mead, 533 U.S. 218 (2001), 198-202

United States v. McGregor, 879 F. Supp. 2d 1308 (M.D. Ala. 2012), 82

United States v. Munoz-Flores, 495 U.S. 385 (1990), 11, 12

United States v. Nasser, 476 F.2d 1111 (7th Cir. 1973), 75

United States v. Pipefitters Local Union No. 562, 434 F.2d 1116 (8th Cir. 1970), 324-25

United States v. Rayburn House Office Bldg., 497 F.3d 654 (D.C. Cir. 2007), 50

United States v. Renzi, 651 F.3d 1012 (2011), 50-52

United States v. Siegelman, 640 F.3d 1159 (11th Cir. 2011), 82-85

United States v. Sun-Diamond Growers of California, 526 U.S. 398 (1999), 86

United States v. Village of Port Chester, 704 F. Supp. 2d 411 (S.D.N.Y. 2010), 286

United States v. Windsor, 133 S. Ct. 2675 (2013), 170-73

U.S. Nat. Bank of Oregon v. Indep. Ins. Agents of Am., Inc., 508 U.S. 439 (1993), 9

U.S. Term Limits v. Thornton, 514 U.S. 779 (1995), 40, 41

Vieth v. Jubelirer, 541 U.S. 267 (2004), 249-52

Vieth v. Pennsylvania, 195 F. Supp. 2d 672 (M.d. Pa. 2002), 231

Wachovia Bank v. Schmidt, 546 U.S. 303 (2006), 180-82

Washington State Grange v. Washington State Republican Party, 552 U.S. 442 (2008), 258

Wesberry v. Sanders, 376 U.S. 1 (1964) 223

Western Tradition Partnership v. Attorney General, 271 P.3d 1 (Mont. 2011), 344

Wexler v. Anderson, 452 F.3d 1226 (11th Cir. 2006), 311

Whitcomb v. Chavis, 403 U.S. 124 (1971), 280

White v. Regester, 412 U.S. 755 (1973), 280

Williams v. Rhodes, 393 U.S. 23 (1968), 261

Wisconsin Right to Life v. Federal Election Commission, 546 U.S. 410 (2006), 338

Yick Wo v. Hopkins, 118 U.S. 356 (1886), 218

Zimmer v. McKeithen, 485 F.2d 1297 (5th Cir. 1973), 280, 283

Zuber v. Allen, 396 U.S. 168 (1969), 167-69

Index

Affordable Care Act, 13-14, 32-33, 63
Anderson-Burdick balancing test, 262-63, 307-11

Ballot access, *see* Political parties; Minor parties
 and independent candidates
Bicameralism, *see* Legislative process; Formal
 requirements for federal legislation;
 Bicameralism and presentment
Bills becoming law, *see* Legislative process;
 Legislative bill process
Bribery, 76-90
 Elements of bribery, 76-86
  Campaign contributions as bribes, 79-85
 Ethics and gift rules, relation to,
  88-90
 Hobbs Act, relation to, 81-82, 87
 Illegal gratuities statute, relation to, 86-87

Campaign Finance, 319-99
 Bipartisan Campaign Reform Act
  (McCain-Feingold), 331, 335-36, 350,
  356, 369, 372-73
 Contribution limitations, 329-33
  Aggregate contribution limitations,
   331-33, 356-61
  Low contribution limits, 348-61
  Soft money, 350, 357-61
  Super PACs, 361-65
   Contrast with 501(c) organizations,
   381-85
 Disclosure, 367-85
  501(c) organizations, 381-85
  Government interests v. right
   to anonymity, 367-81
 Expenditure limitations, *see* Spending limitations
 Federal Election Campaign Act, 324-32,
  335-36, 368-69
 First Amendment issue, Introduction to,
  320-22
 Introduction, 319-28
 Public financing, 385-99
  Constitutional issues, 388-99
   Discrimination against minor parties,
   388-90

   Impermissibility of certain
    matching funds, 394-99
   Voluntariness, 390-94
  Pro and con, 88
 Spending limitations, 329-46
  Foreign spending ban, 345-46
Canons of construction; *see* Statutory
 interpretation; Canons of construction
Chevron deference, *see* Statutory interpretation;
 Agency interpretation; *Chevron* deference

Deliberation, 28, 55-58
Direct democracy, 91-109
 Content restrictions, 97-105
 Contribution and expenditure limitations in,
  ban on, 333-34, 348
 Financing qualification drives, 105-109
 Petitioning rules, 105-109
 Pro and Con, 91-97
 Single subject rule, 97-105
Due process of lawmaking, *see* Regulating
 legislators; Due process of lawmaking
Duverger's Law, *see* Political parties; Minor
 parties and independent candidates
Dynamic statutory interpretation,
 see Statutory interpretation; Theories of
 interpretation

Election administration, 297-316
 Federal law governing
  election administration, 312-16
  Elections Clause and, 312, 314-16
  Help America Vote Act, 313
  National Voter Registration Act, 313
  Uniform Overseas Citizen Absentee
   Voting Act, 314
  United States Election
   Assistance Commission, 303-04
 Florida 2000 controversy, 297-303
 Voter identification and
  related controversies, 303-311
Enrolled bill rule, *see* Legislative process; Formal
 requirements for federal legislation;
 Enrolled bill rule

419

Equal protection claims, *see* Election
    administration, Right to Vote, Political
    parties; Minor parties and independent
    candidates, Political parties; partisan
    gerrymandering, Voting Rights Act;
    racial gerrymandering

Filibuster, *see* Legislative process; Formal
    requirements for federal legislation;
    Senate rules (including filibusters)
First Amendment, *see* Campaign Finance,
    Lobbying, Political parties; Minor
    parties and independent candidates
    Petition clause, 60, 69

Gerrymandering, *see* Political parties; Political
    gerrymandering; *see also* Voting Rights
    Act, Racial gerrymandering
Gifts to legislators, *see* Bribery; Ethics and gift
    rules, relation to

Hobbs Act, *see* Bribery; Hobbs Act, relation to
Hybrid democracy, *see* Direct democracy

Initiative, *see* Direct democracy
Intentionalism, *see* Statutory interpretation;
    Theories of interpretation

Legislative history; *see* Statutory interpretation;
    Legislative history; *see also* Statutory
    interpretation; Debate between
    legislative history and New
    Textualism
Legislative process, 1-109
    Formal requirements for federal legislation,
        3-19
        Bicameralism and presentment, 6-14
        Enrolled bill rule, 8-11, 12-13
        House of Representatives rules, 19-22
        Origination clause, 11-14
        Senate rules (including filibusters),
            22-25, 30-33
        Veto power, 14-19
    Legislative bill process, 3-33
    Theories of legislative process, 25-29
        Normative theories, 27-29
        Positive theories, 25-27
            Pluralism, 25-26
            Proceduralism, 26-27
            Positive political theory, 26-27
            Public choice theory, 25-26
    Unorthodox lawmaking, 29-33

Line item veto, *see* Legislative process; Formal
    requirements for federal legislation;
    Veto power
Literacy tests, *see* Right to vote; Literacy tests
Lobbying, 59-76
    Constitutional questions about novel
        lobbying laws, 74-76
    Disclosure, 64-71
    Honest Leadership and Open
        Government Act, 69-71, 88-90
    How lobbying works, 59-64
    Lobbying Disclosure Act, 65-71
    Obama administration rules, 74
    State laws, 73
    Tax law and lobbying, 71-73
Logrolling, *see* Regulating legislators; Single
    subject rule

One person, one vote rule, *see* Right to vote; Vote
    dilution (one person, one vote rule)
Origination clause, *see* Legislative process;
    Formal requirements for federal
    legislation; Origination clause

Qualifications for Office, *see* Regulating
    Legislators; Qualifications for office

Pluralism, *see* Legislative process; Theories of
    legislative process; Positive theories;
    Pluralism
Pocket veto, *see* Legislative process; Formal
    requirements for federal legislation;
    Veto power
Political question doctrine, 44-45, 222, 249
Political parties, 241-63
    Minor parties and independent candidates,
        260-63, 388-90
    Obligations and associational rights of
        political parties, 254-60
    Partisan gerrymandering, 247-53
    Political competition in political science
        and law, 241-47
    Political markets approach, 244-47
Positive political theory, *see* Legislative process;
    Theories of legislative process; Positive
    theories, Positive political theory
Proceduralism, *see* Legislative process; Theories
    of Legislative process; Positive theories,
    Proceduralism
Public choice theory, *see* Legislative process;
    Theories of legislative process; Positive
    theories, Public choice theory

Purposivism, *see* Statutory interpretation; Theories of interpretation

Presentment, *see* Legislative process; Formal requirements for federal legislation; Bicameralism and presentment

Recall, *see* Direct democracy

Redistricting, 237-39; *see also* Right to vote; Vote dilution (one person, one vote rule), Political parties; Partisan gerrymandering, Voting Rights Act; Racial gerrymandering
   Introduction to redistricting, 237-39

Referendum, *see* Direct democracy

Regulating legislators, 35-58; *see also* Lobbying, Bribery
  Due process of lawmaking, 55-58
  Qualifications for office, 35-46
  Single subject rule, 52-54
  Speech or debate clause, 46-52, 77, 80
  Term limits, 39-43

Rent-seeking, 27

Residency requirements for legislators, *see* Regulating legislators; Qualifications for office

Right to vote, 209-36, *see also* Voting Rights Act
  African-American suffrage, 213-15; *see also* Voting Rights Act
  Fundamental right status, 213-19
    Exceptions for felons, minors, non-citizens and non-residents, 219-20
  Literacy tests, 209-19
  Poll taxes, 215-19
  Redistricting, *see* Redistricting
  Vote dilution (one person, one vote rule), 220-32
    Extensions of one person, one-vote rule to local areas, 228-32
    Exception for special purpose election districts, 232-36
  Women's suffrage, 214-15

Same-sex marriage and legislative animus, 170-73

Single subject rule, *see* Regulating legislators; Single subject rule; *see also* Direct democracy; Single subject rule

Speech or debate clause; *see* Regulating legislators; Speech or debate clause

Statutory interpretation
  Agency interpretation, 183-206
    Auer deference, 204-06
    Chevron deference, 183-98
    Skidmore Deference, 198-206
  Canons of construction, 124, 133-62
    Substantive canons, 136-39, 153-62
      Avoidance canon, 158-59
      Democracy canon, 161-62
      Federalism canons, 160-61
      Rule of lenity, 154-57
    Textual canons, 134,
      Ejusdem generis, 144, 152
      Expressio unius, 134, 140-42
      Grammar and punctuation, 147-53
        Last antecedent rule, 149-50, 152
      In pari materia, 179-80
      Noscitur a sociis, 142-44, 146, 152
      Whole act rule, 179
  Debate over legislative history and New Textualism, 122-29
  Legislative history, 163-82
    Legislative silence, 173-79
    Other statutes, 179-82
    Types of legislative history, 163-73
  Stare decisis and, 129-31
  Theories of interpretation, 119-21
  Theory and practice, 113-31

Term limits, *see* Regulating legislators; Term limits

Textualism, *see* Statutory interpretation; Debate over legislative history and New textualism

Veto power, *see* Legislative process; Formal requirements for federal legislation; Veto power

Voting rights; *see* Right to vote; *see also* Voting Rights Act

Voting Rights Act, 166-68, 175-79, 265-96
  Dole compromise, 166, 282
  Judicial elections and, 175-79
  Origins, 265-73
  Racial gerrymandering, 292-96

Voting Rights Act (*continued*)
  Section 2
    Felon disenfranchisement claims,
      288-90
    History, 175-79
    Racial gerrymandering cases, relation to,
      292-96
    Redistricting standards (*Gingles* test), 280-88
    Vote denial standards, 288-92

Section 5
  Constitutionality, 273-80
  Preclearance rules, 265-73
  Voting Rights Amendments Act,
    279-80

White Primary Cases, *see* Political parties;
    Obligations and associational rights of
    political parties